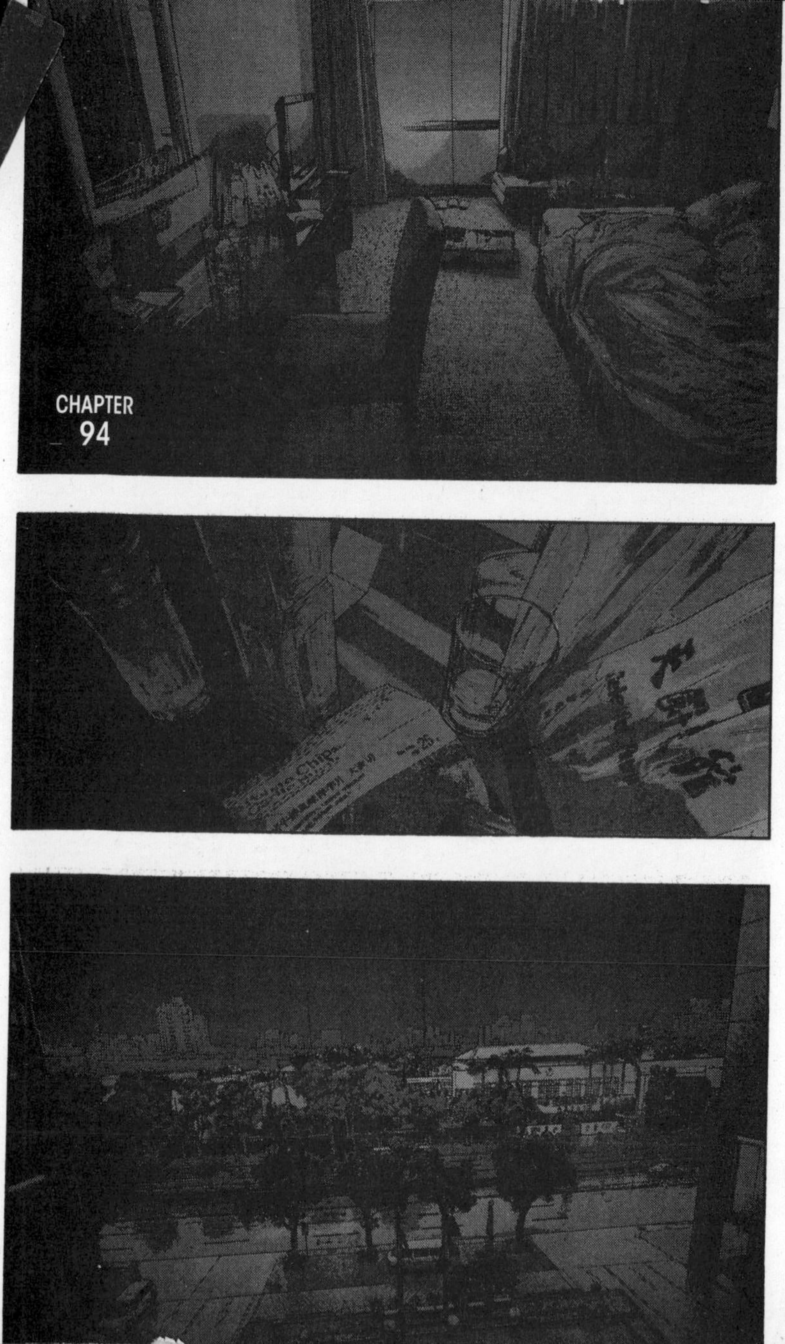
CHAPTER
94

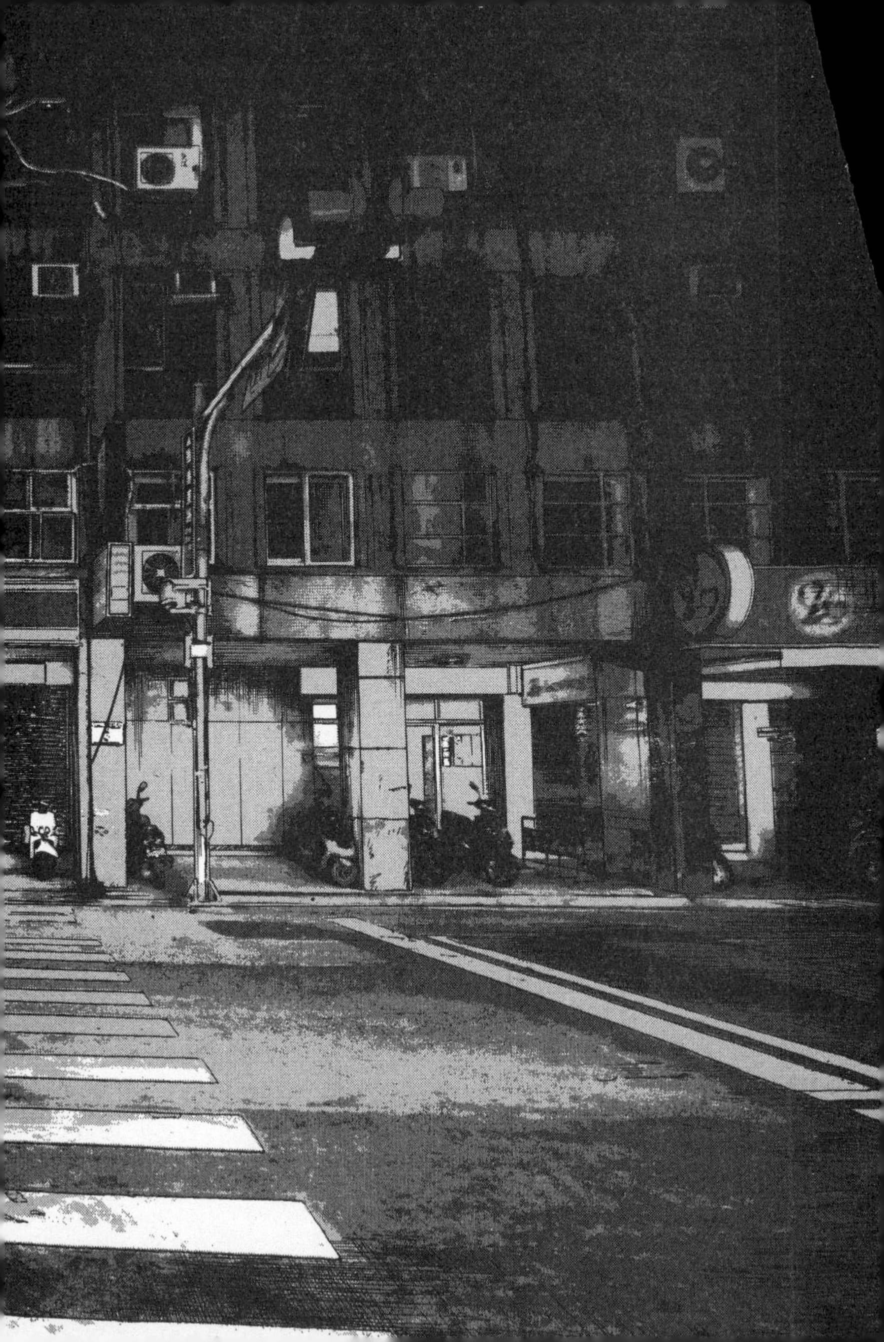

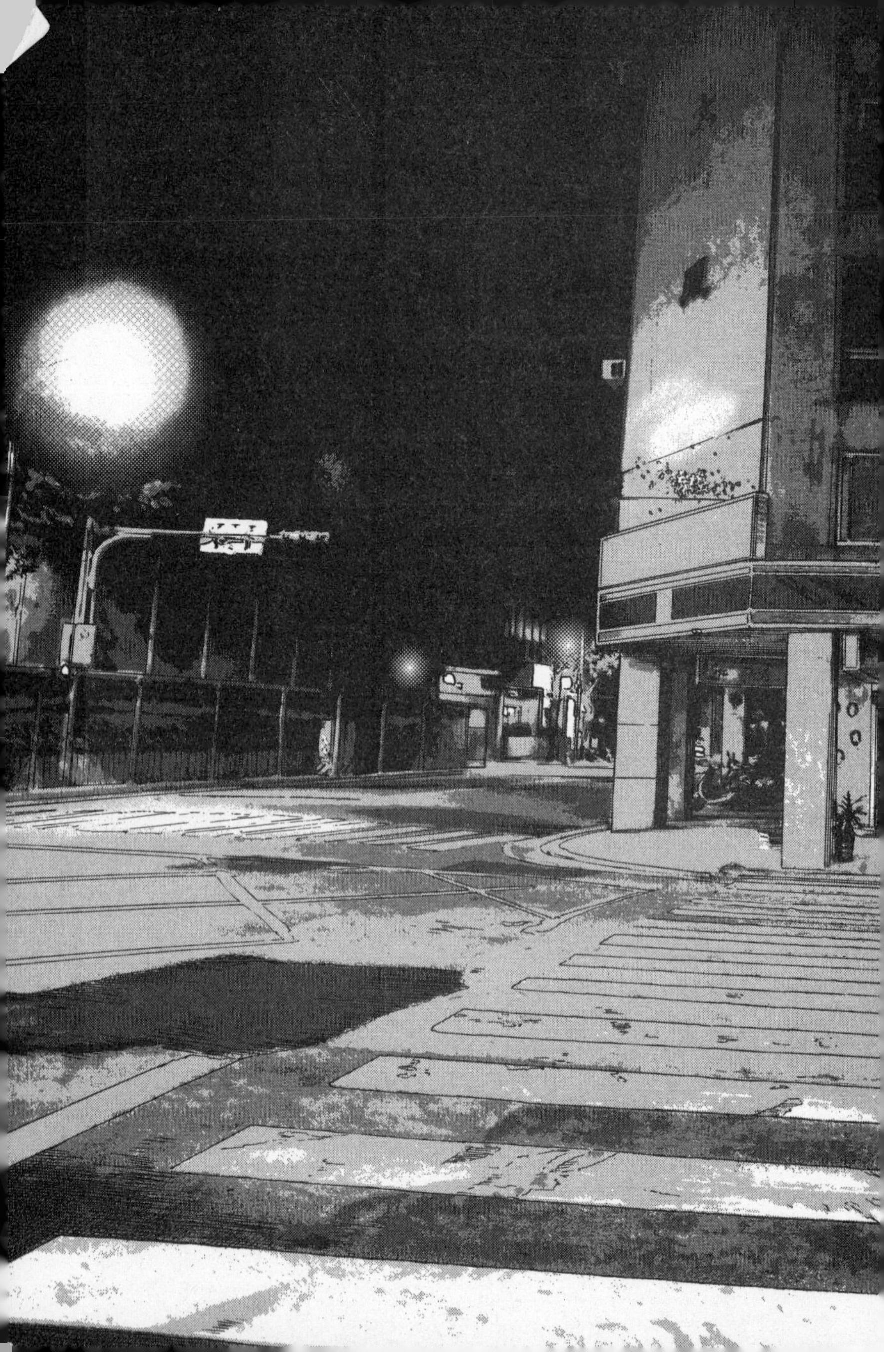

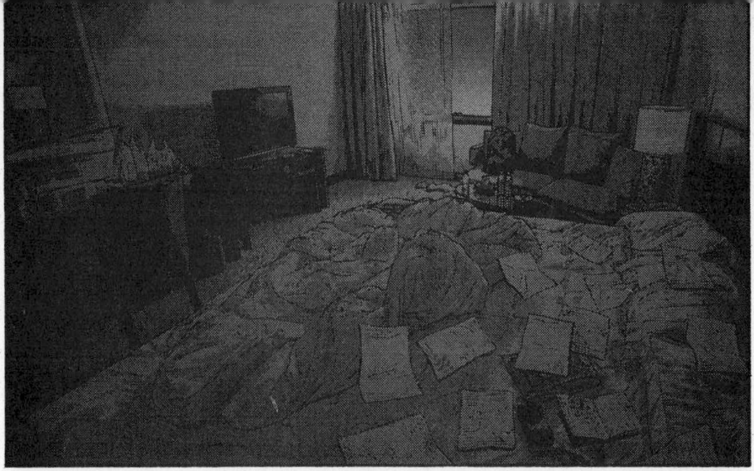

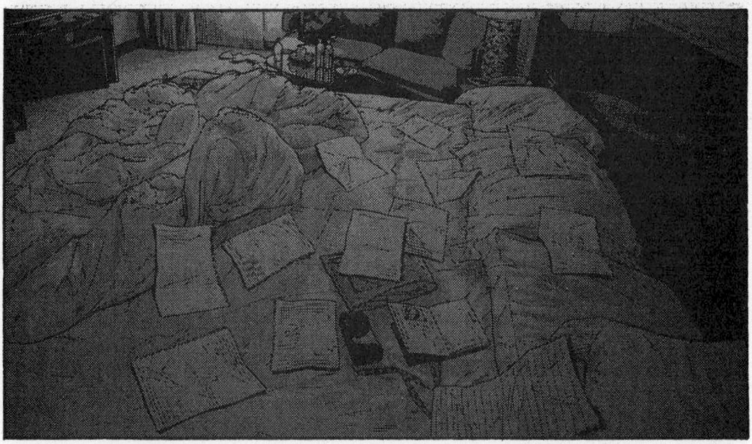

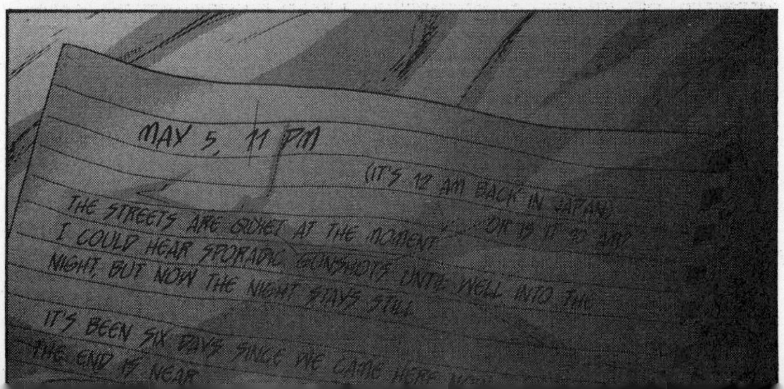
MAY 5, 11 PM
(IT'S 12 AM BACK IN JAPAN)
THE STREETS ARE QUIET AT THE MOMENT ...OR IS IT
I COULD HEAR SPORADIC GUNSHOTS UNTIL WELL INTO THE
NIGHT, BUT NOW THE NIGHT STAYS STILL
IT'S BEEN SIX DAYS SINCE WE CAME HERE
THE END IS NEAR

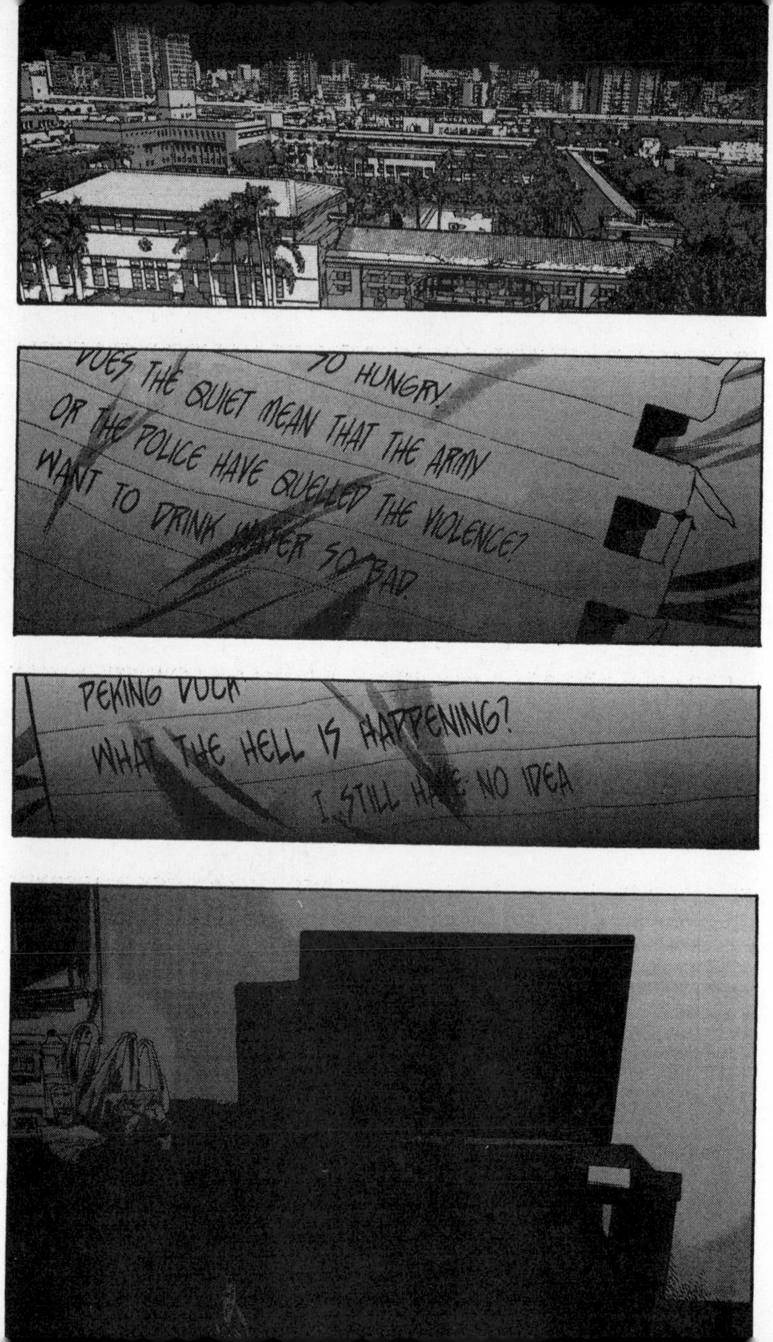
SO HUNGRY.
DOES THE QUIET MEAN THAT THE ARMY
OR THE POLICE HAVE QUELLED THE VIOLENCE?
WANT TO DRINK WATER SO BAD.
PEKING DUCK
WHAT THE HELL IS HAPPENING?
I STILL HAVE NO IDEA

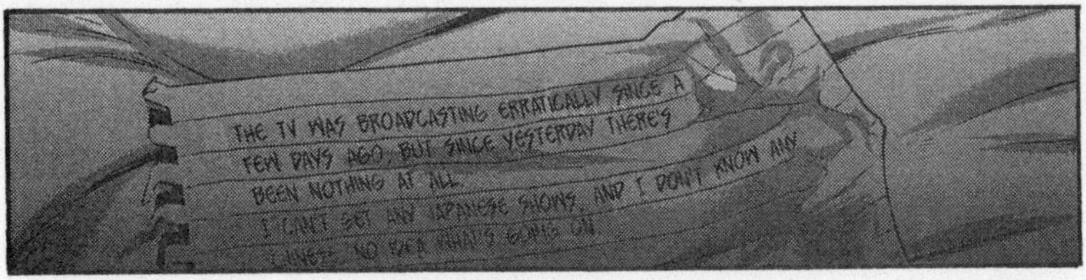
THE TV WAS BROADCASTING ERRATICALLY SINCE A FEW DAYS AGO, BUT SINCE YESTERDAY THERE'S BEEN NOTHING AT ALL.
I CAN'T GET ANY JAPANESE SHOWS, AND I DON'T KNOW ANY

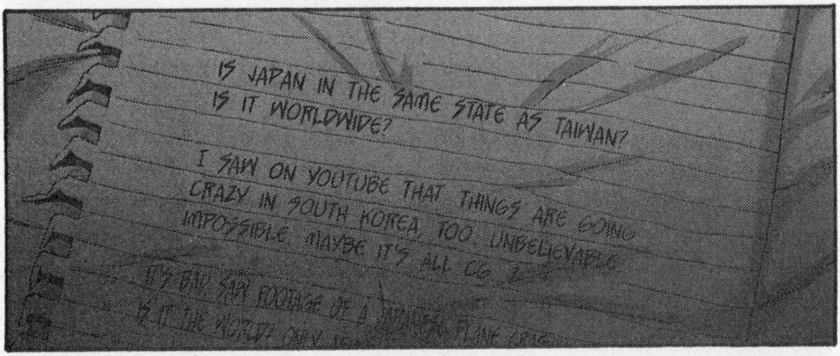
IS JAPAN IN THE SAME STATE AS TAIWAN?
IS IT WORLDWIDE?
I SAW ON YOUTUBE THAT THINGS ARE GOING CRAZY IN SOUTH KOREA, TOO. UNBELIEVABLE. IMPOSSIBLE. MAYBE IT'S ALL CG...

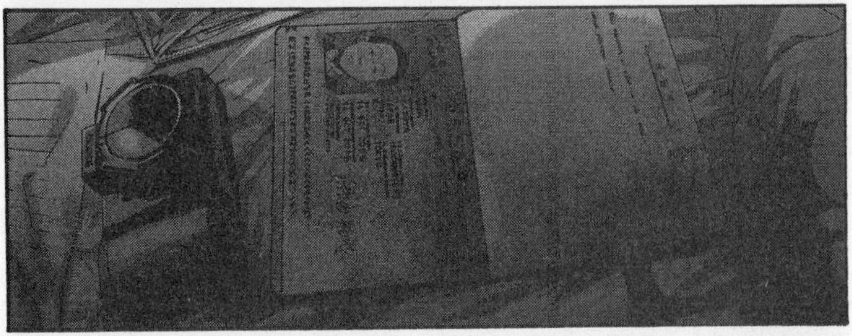

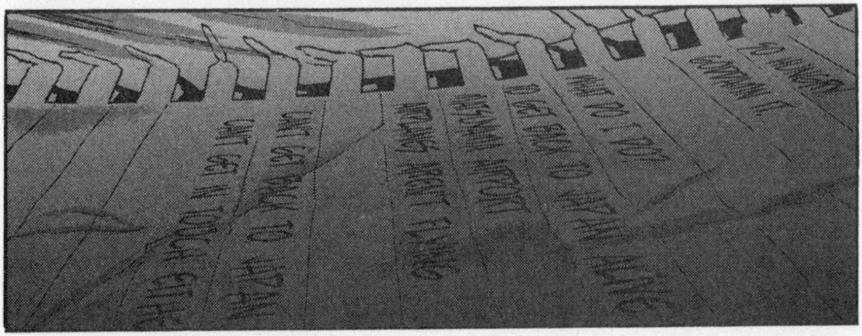
SO HUNGRY
CONTAIN IT.
WHAT DO I DO?
TO GET BACK TO JAPAN ALIVE
MATSUYAMA AIRPORT
AIRPLANES AREN'T FLYING
CAN'T GET BACK TO JAPAN
CAN'T GET IN TOUCH EITHE

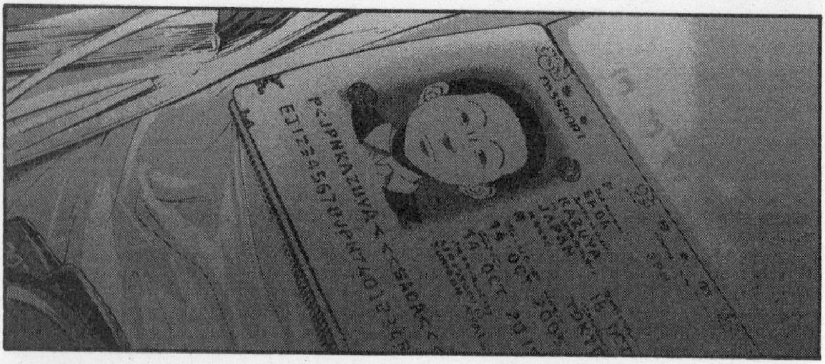

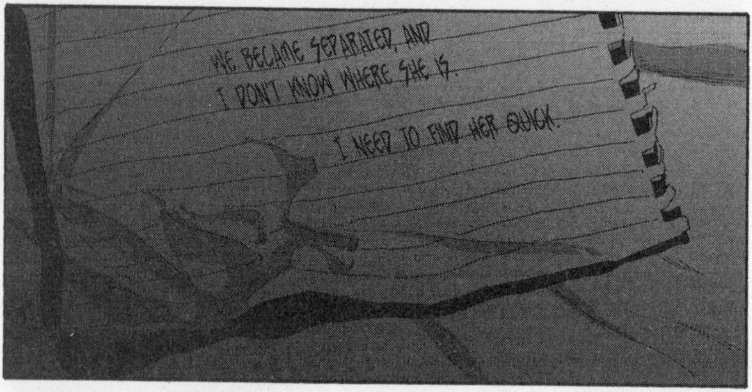
WE BECAME SEPARATED, AND
I DON'T KNOW WHERE SHE IS.
I NEED TO FIND HER QUICK.

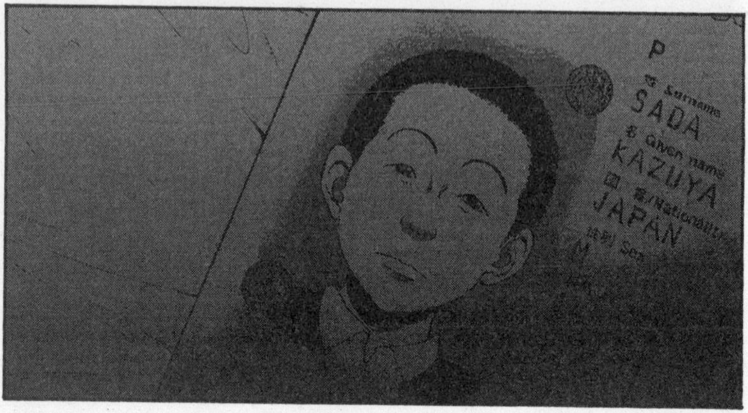
P
Surname
SADA
Given name
KAZUYA
Nationality
JAPAN
Sex
M

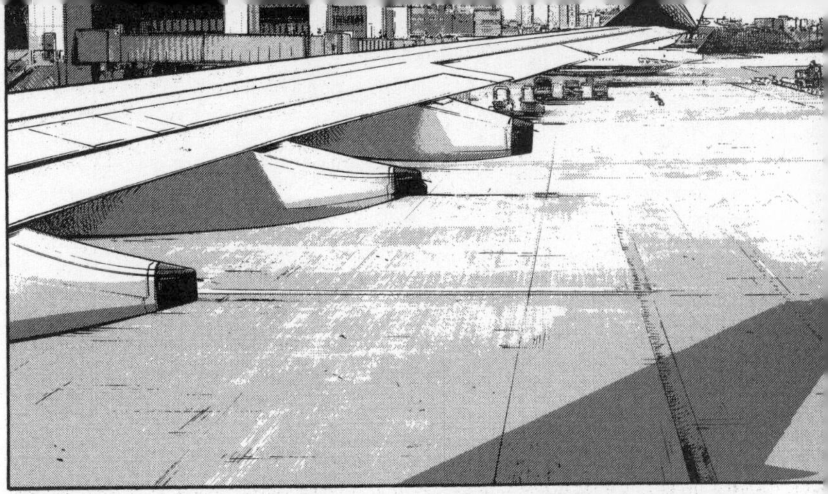

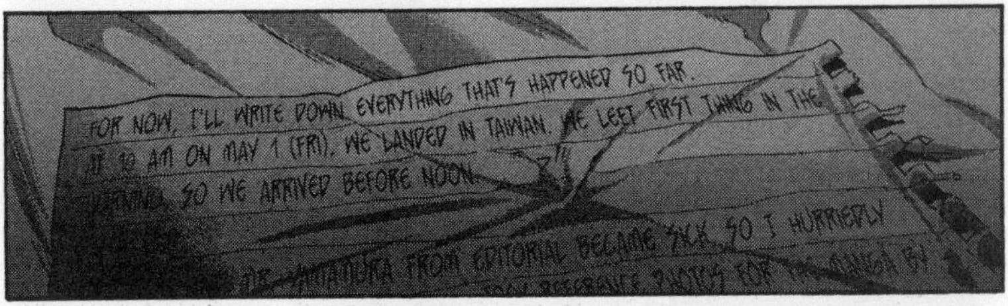
FOR NOW, I'LL WRITE DOWN EVERYTHING THAT'S HAPPENED SO FAR.
AT 10 AM ON MAY 1 (FRI), WE LANDED IN TAIWAN. WE LEFT FIRST THING IN THE
SO WE ARRIVED BEFORE NOON.

NOTE: SPOKEN MANDARIN CHINESE WILL FALL WITHIN POINTED BRACKETS, <LIKE THIS>.

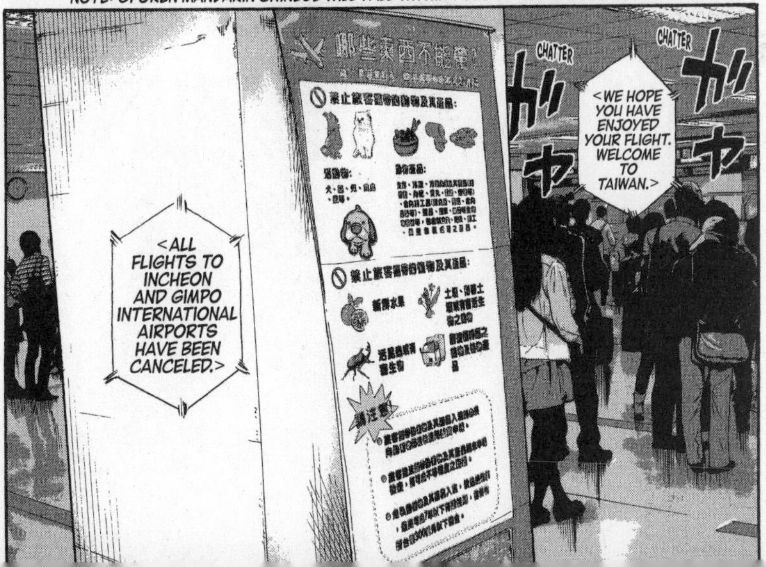
CHATTER
ガヤ
CHATTER
ガヤ
<WE HOPE YOU HAVE ENJOYED YOUR FLIGHT. WELCOME TO TAIWAN.>
<ALL FLIGHTS TO INCHEON AND GIMPO INTERNATIONAL AIRPORTS HAVE BEEN CANCELED.>

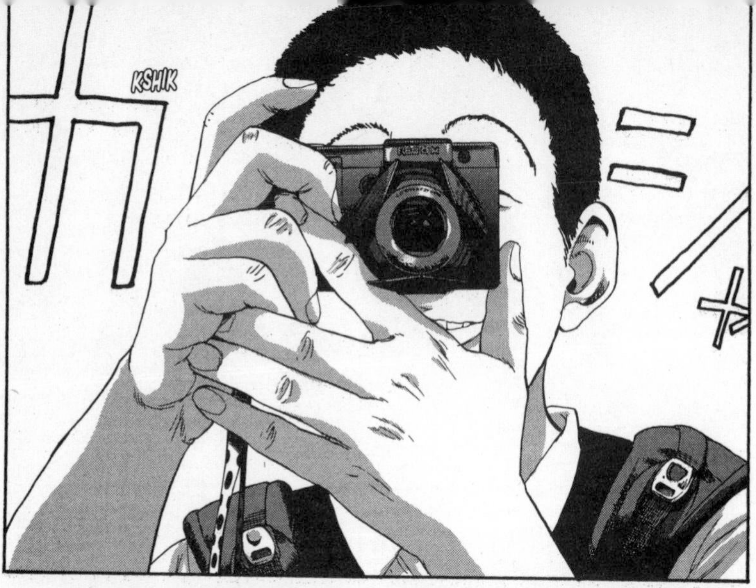
KSHIK

NOTE: SPOKEN ENGLISH WILL FALL WITHIN SQUARE BRACKETS, [LIKE THIS].

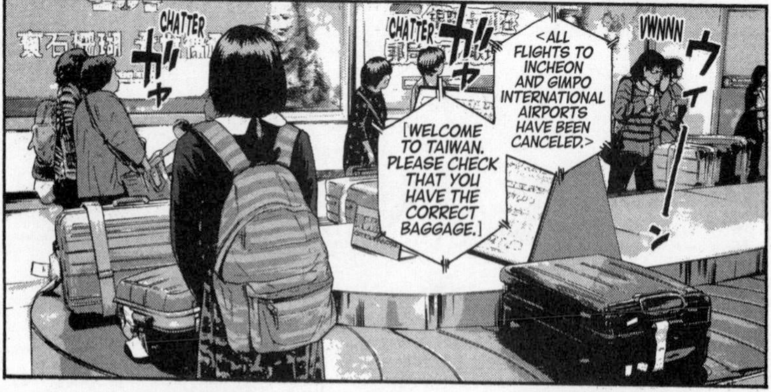
VWNNN
<ALL FLIGHTS TO INCHEON AND GIMPO INTERNATIONAL AIRPORTS HAVE BEEN CANCELED.>
[WELCOME TO TAIWAN. PLEASE CHECK THAT YOU HAVE THE CORRECT BAGGAGE.]
CHATTER
CHATTER

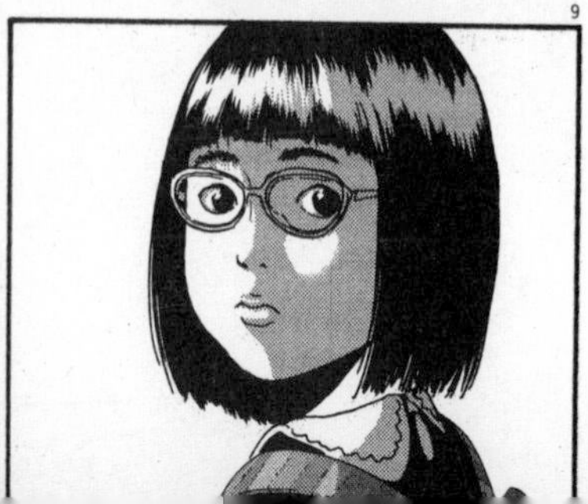

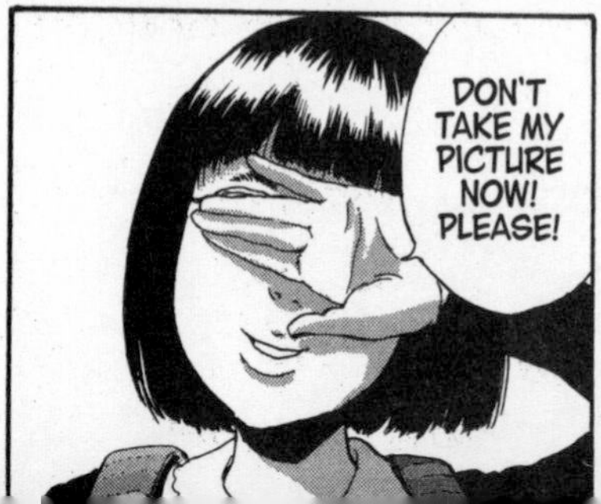
DON'T TAKE MY PICTURE NOW! PLEASE!

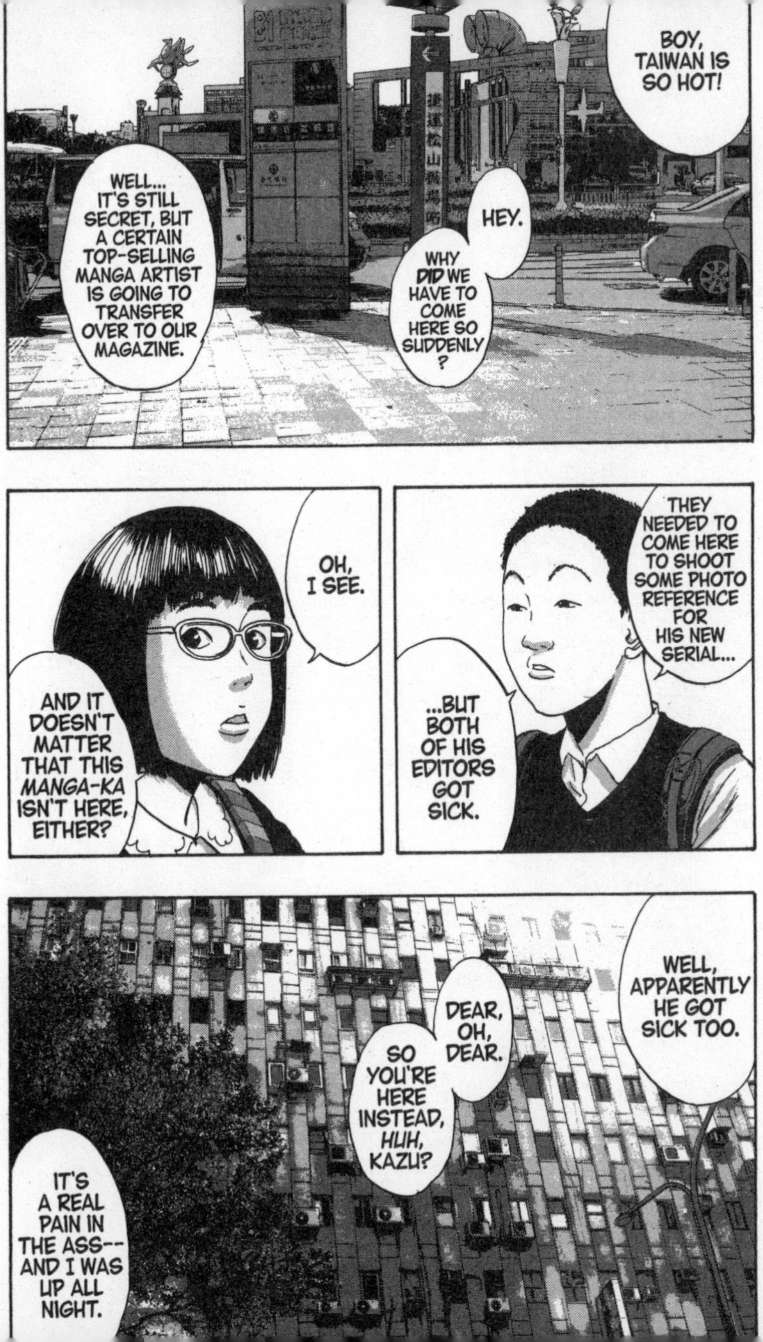
BOY, TAIWAN IS SO HOT!
HEY.
WHY DID WE HAVE TO COME HERE SO SUDDENLY?
WELL... IT'S STILL SECRET, BUT A CERTAIN TOP-SELLING MANGA ARTIST IS GOING TO TRANSFER OVER TO OUR MAGAZINE.
THEY NEEDED TO COME HERE TO SHOOT SOME PHOTO REFERENCE FOR HIS NEW SERIAL...
...BUT BOTH OF HIS EDITORS GOT SICK.
OH, I SEE.
AND IT DOESN'T MATTER THAT THIS MANGA-KA ISN'T HERE, EITHER?
WELL, APPARENTLY HE GOT SICK TOO.
DEAR, OH, DEAR.
SO YOU'RE HERE INSTEAD, HUH, KAZU?
IT'S A REAL PAIN IN THE ASS-- AND I WAS UP ALL NIGHT.

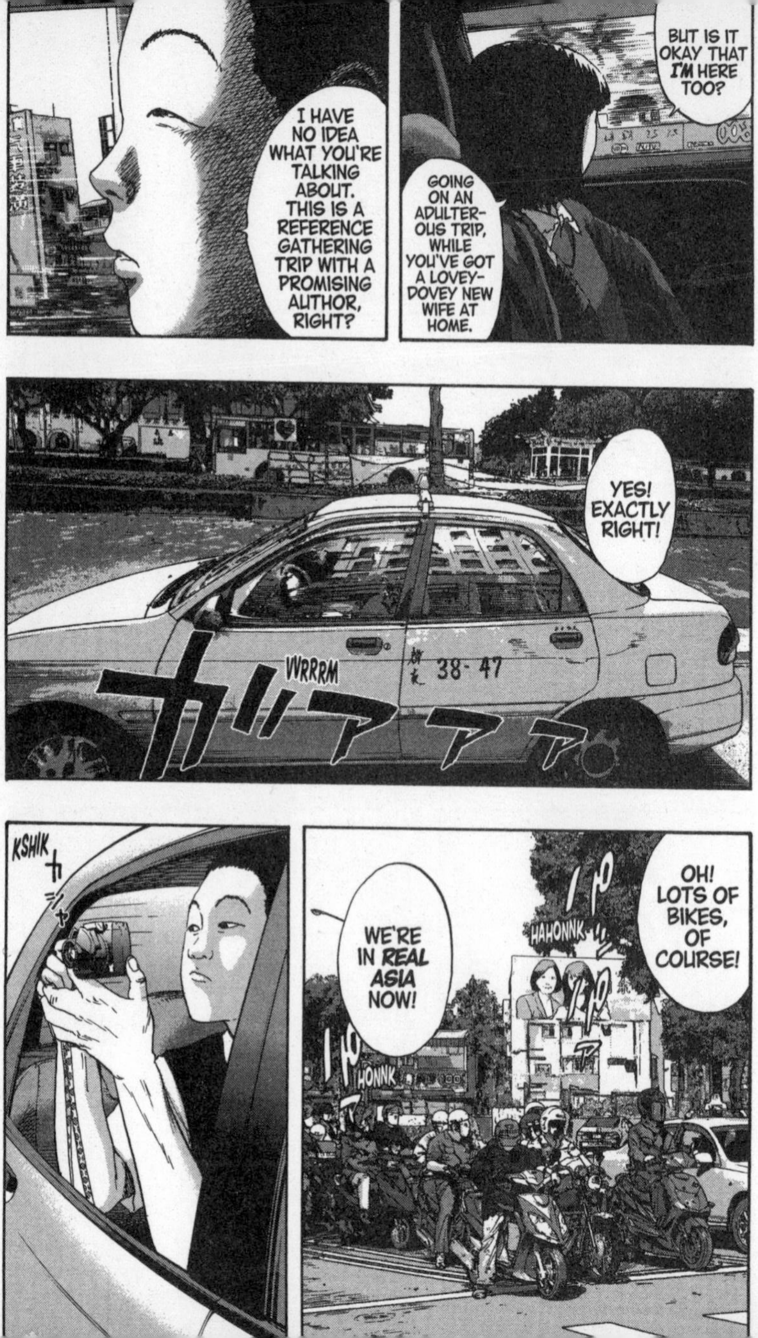
BUT IS IT OKAY THAT I'M HERE TOO?
GOING ON AN ADULTEROUS TRIP, WHILE YOU'VE GOT A LOVEY-DOVEY NEW WIFE AT HOME.
I HAVE NO IDEA WHAT YOU'RE TALKING ABOUT. THIS IS A REFERENCE GATHERING TRIP WITH A PROMISING AUTHOR, RIGHT?
YES! EXACTLY RIGHT!
VVRRRM
38-47
OH! LOTS OF BIKES, OF COURSE!
HAHONNK
WE'RE IN REAL ASIA NOW!
HONNK
KSHIK

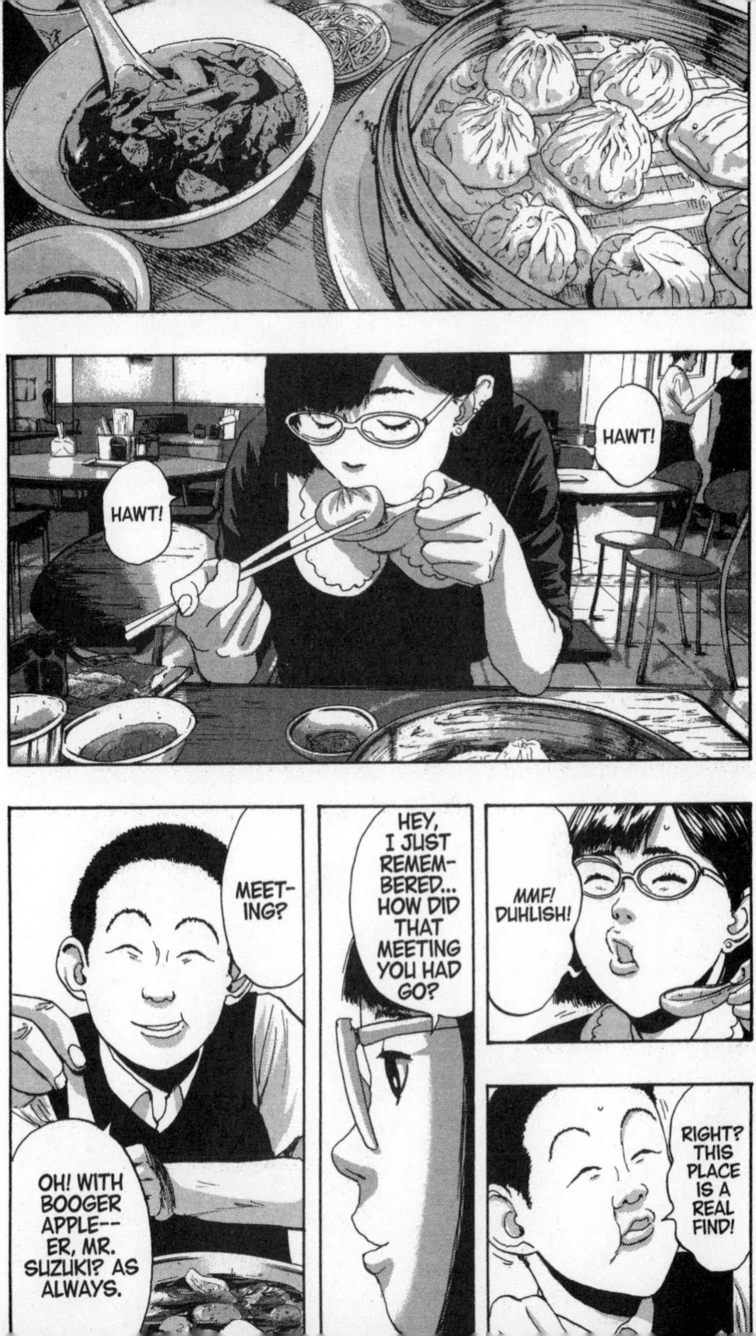
HAWT!
HAWT!
MMF! DUHLISH!
RIGHT? THIS PLACE IS A REAL FIND!
HEY, I JUST REMEMBERED... HOW DID THAT MEETING YOU HAD GO?
MEET-ING?
OH! WITH BOOGER APPLER-- ER, MR. SUZUKI? AS ALWAYS.

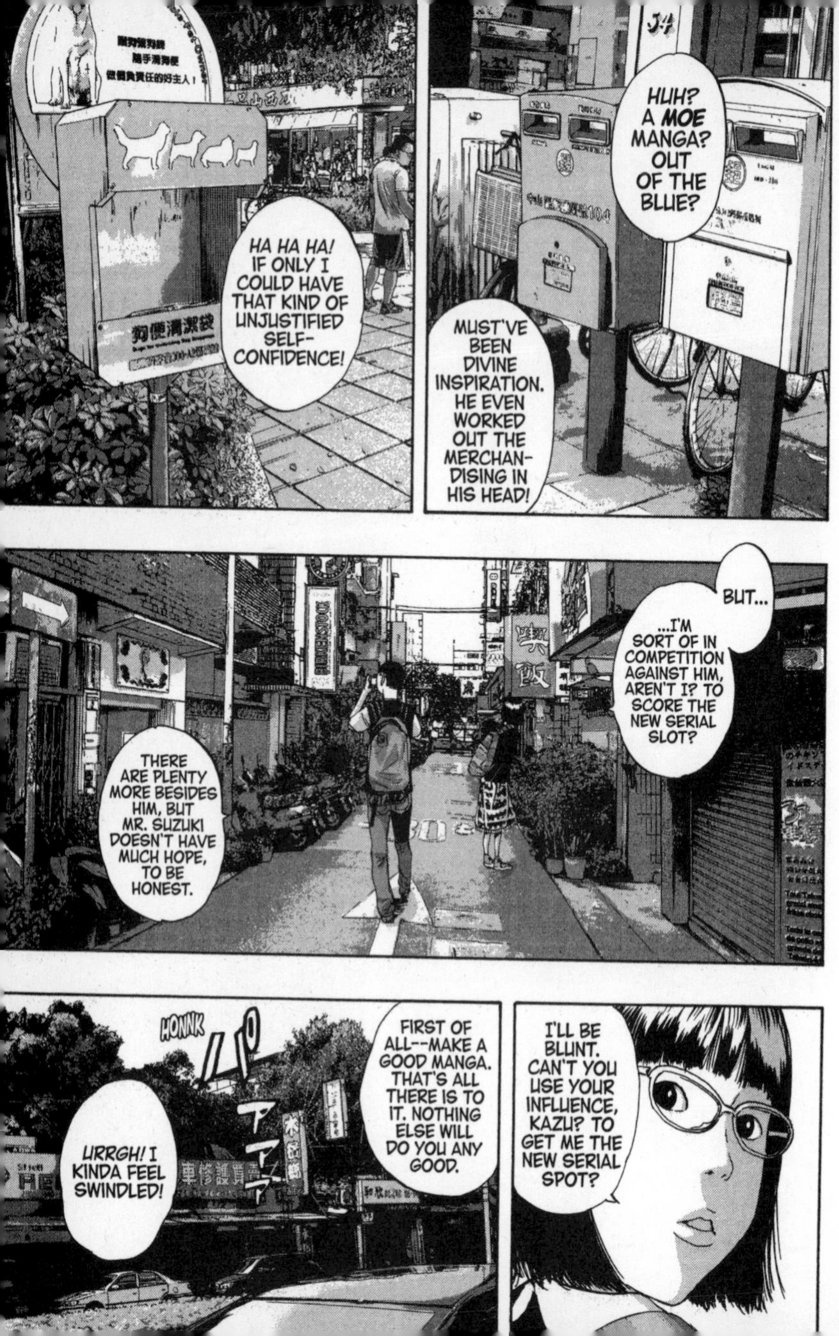
HUH? A MOE MANGA? OUT OF THE BLUE?
MUST'VE BEEN DIVINE INSPIRATION. HE EVEN WORKED OUT THE MERCHANDISING IN HIS HEAD!
HA HA HA! IF ONLY I COULD HAVE THAT KIND OF UNJUSTIFIED SELF-CONFIDENCE!
BUT...
...I'M SORT OF IN COMPETITION AGAINST HIM, AREN'T I? TO SCORE THE NEW SERIAL SLOT?
THERE ARE PLENTY MORE BESIDES HIM, BUT MR. SUZUKI DOESN'T HAVE MUCH HOPE, TO BE HONEST.
I'LL BE BLUNT. CAN'T YOU USE YOUR INFLUENCE, KAZU? TO GET ME THE NEW SERIAL SPOT?
FIRST OF ALL--MAKE A GOOD MANGA. THAT'S ALL THERE IS TO IT. NOTHING ELSE WILL DO YOU ANY GOOD.
HONNK
URRGH! I KINDA FEEL SWINDLED!

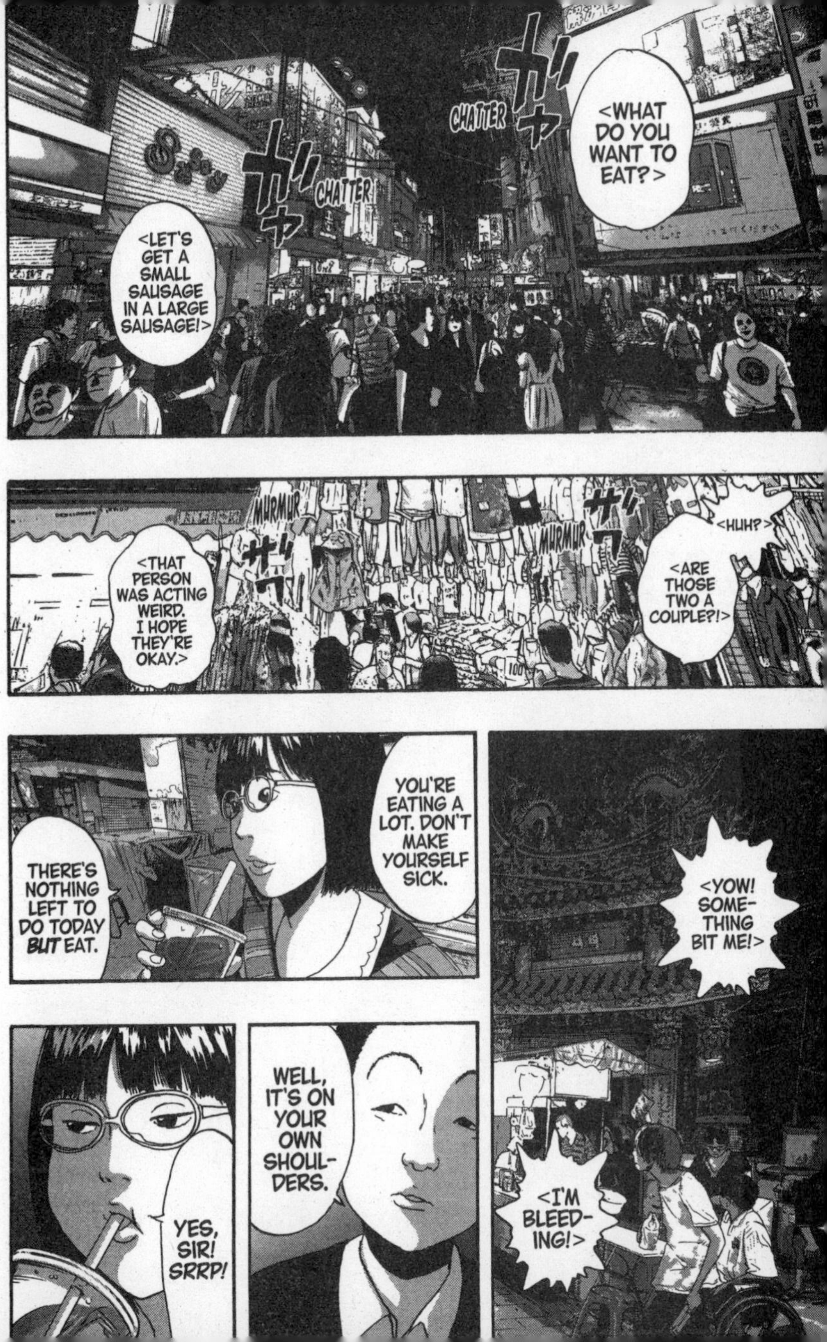
CHATTER
<WHAT DO YOU WANT TO EAT?>
CHATTER
<LET'S GET A SMALL SAUSAGE IN A LARGE SAUSAGE!>
<HUH?>
<ARE THOSE TWO A COUPLE?!>
MURMUR
MURMUR
<THAT PERSON WAS ACTING WEIRD. I HOPE THEY'RE OKAY.>
<YOW! SOMETHING BIT ME!>
<I'M BLEEDING!>
YOU'RE EATING A LOT. DON'T MAKE YOURSELF SICK.
THERE'S NOTHING LEFT TO DO TODAY *BUT* EAT.
WELL, IT'S ON YOUR OWN SHOULDERS.
YES, SIR! SRRP!

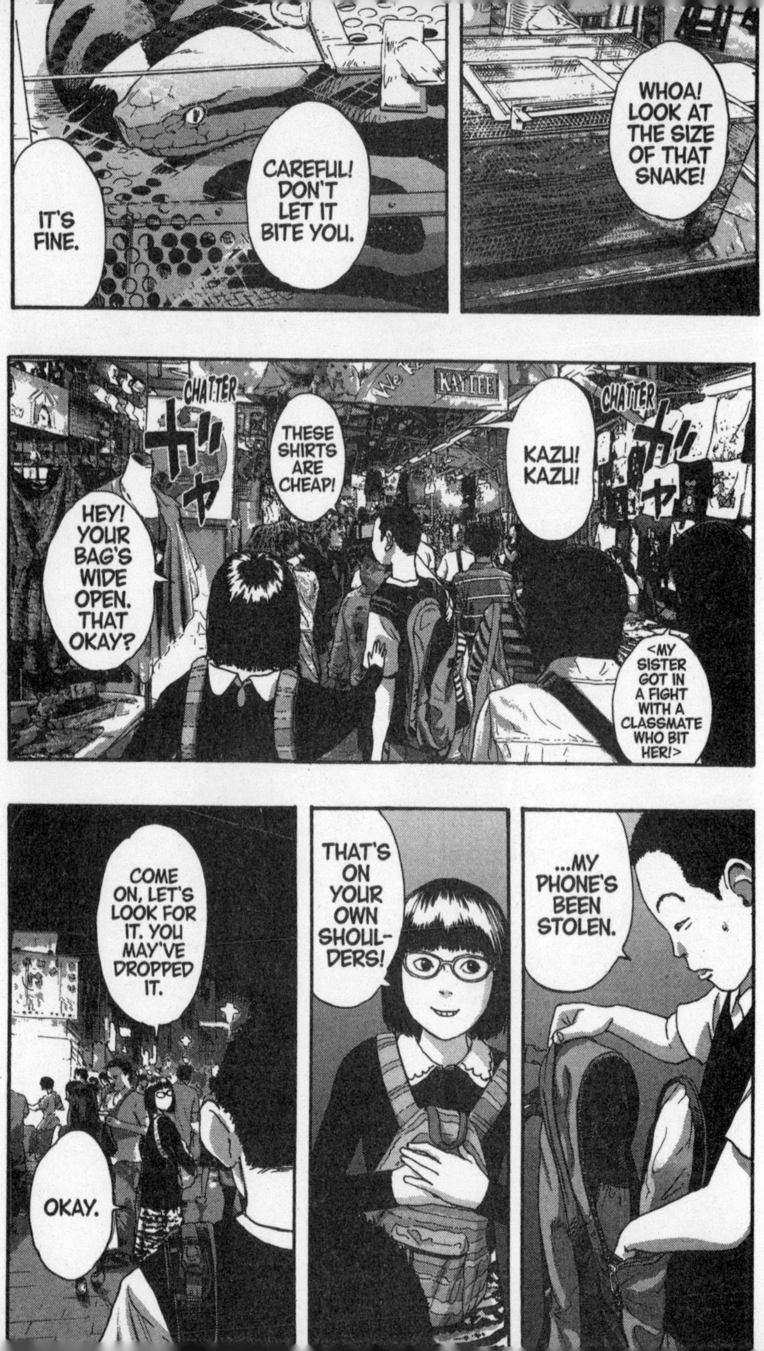
WHOA! LOOK AT THE SIZE OF THAT SNAKE!
CAREFUL! DON'T LET IT BITE YOU.
IT'S FINE.
KAYTEE
CHATTER
ガヤ
KAZU! KAZU!
<MY SISTER GOT IN A FIGHT WITH A CLASSMATE WHO BIT HER!>
THESE SHIRTS ARE CHEAP!
CHATTER
ガヤ
HEY! YOUR BAG'S WIDE OPEN. THAT OKAY?
...MY PHONE'S BEEN STOLEN.
THAT'S ON YOUR OWN SHOULDERS!
COME ON, LET'S LOOK FOR IT. YOU MAY'VE DROPPED IT.
OKAY.

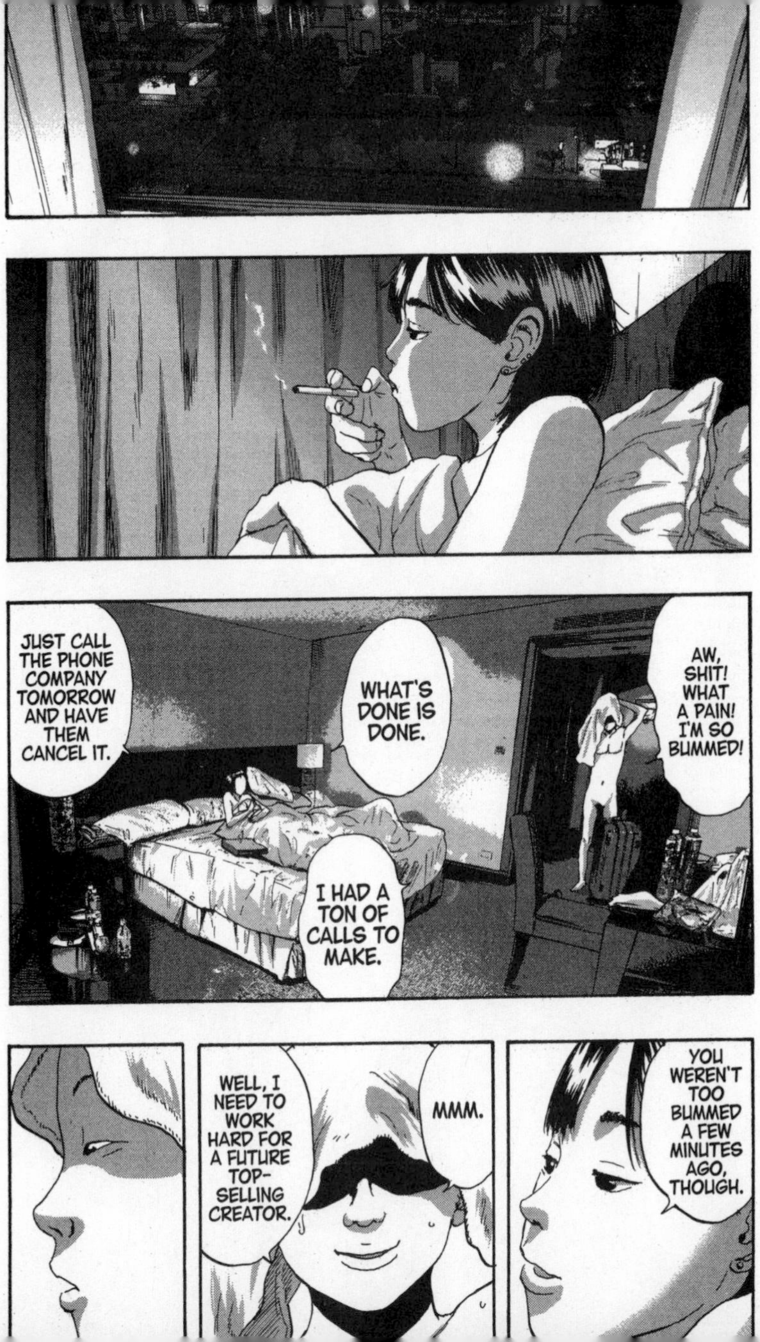
AW, SHIT! WHAT A PAIN! I'M SO BUMMED!
WHAT'S DONE IS DONE.
I HAD A TON OF CALLS TO MAKE.
JUST CALL THE PHONE COMPANY TOMORROW AND HAVE THEM CANCEL IT.
YOU WEREN'T TOO BUMMED A FEW MINUTES AGO, THOUGH.
MMM.
WELL, I NEED TO WORK HARD FOR A FUTURE TOP-SELLING CREATOR.

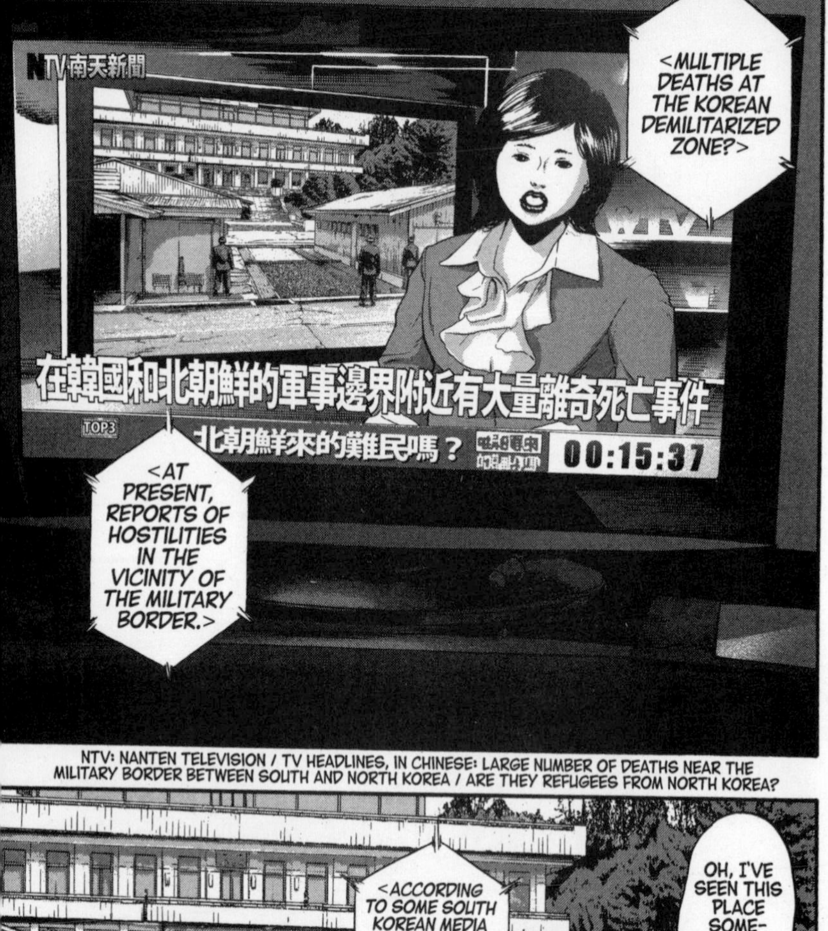
NTV南天新聞
<MULTIPLE DEATHS AT THE KOREAN DEMILITARIZED ZONE?>
在韓國和北朝鮮的軍事邊界附近有大量離奇死亡事件
TOP3
北朝鮮來的難民嗎？
00:15:37
<AT PRESENT, REPORTS OF HOSTILITIES IN THE VICINITY OF THE MILITARY BORDER.>

NTV: NANTEN TELEVISION / TV HEADLINES, IN CHINESE: LARGE NUMBER OF DEATHS NEAR THE MILITARY BORDER BETWEEN SOUTH AND NORTH KOREA / ARE THEY REFUGEES FROM NORTH KOREA?

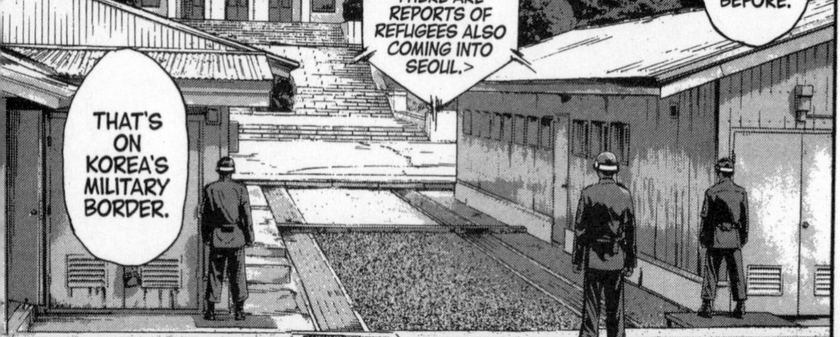
OH, I'VE SEEN THIS PLACE SOME-WHERE BEFORE.
<ACCORDING TO SOME SOUTH KOREAN MEDIA SOURCES, THERE ARE REPORTS OF REFUGEES ALSO COMING INTO SEOUL.>
THAT'S ON KOREA'S MILITARY BORDER.

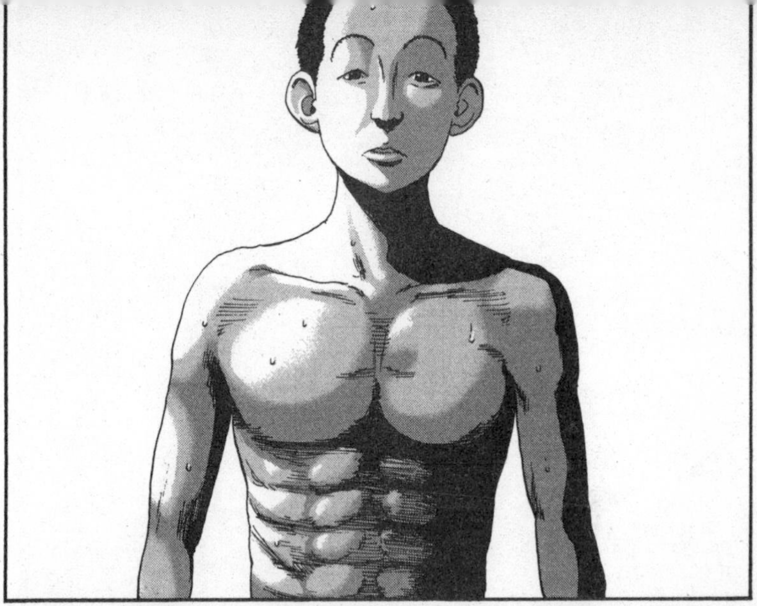

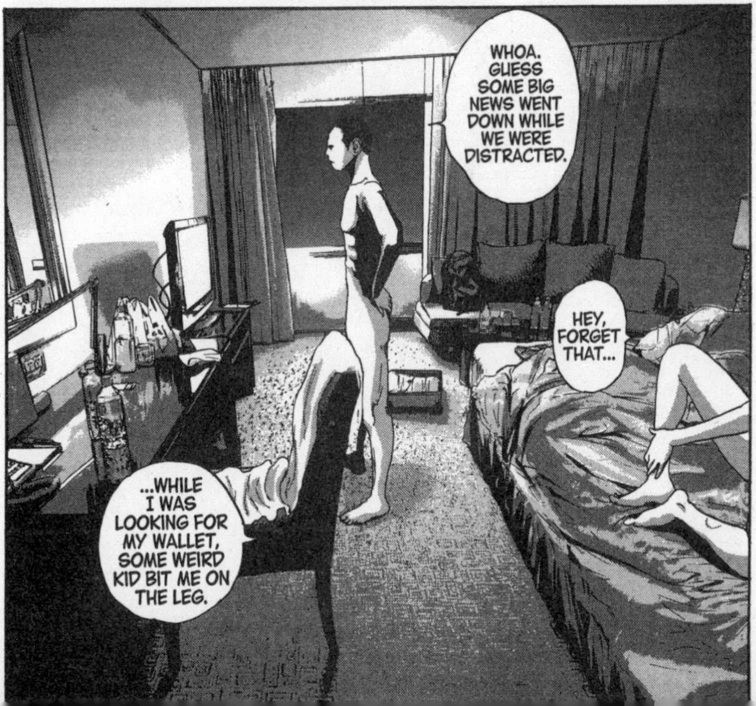
WHOA. GUESS SOME BIG NEWS WENT DOWN WHILE WE WERE DISTRACTED.
HEY, FORGET THAT...
...WHILE I WAS LOOKING FOR MY WALLET, SOME WEIRD KID BIT ME ON THE LEG.

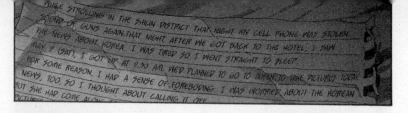

WHILE STROLLING IN THE SHILIN DISTRICT THAT NIGHT MY CELL PHONE WAS STOLEN. I HEARD THE SOUND OF GUNS AGAIN. THAT NIGHT AFTER WE GOT BACK TO THE HOTEL, I SAW THE NEWS ABOUT KOREA. I WAS TIRED SO I WENT STRAIGHT TO SLEEP.

MAY 2 (SAT) I GOT UP AT 9:30 AM. WE'D PLANNED TO GO TO JIUFEN TO TAKE PICTURES TODAY. FOR SOME REASON, I HAD A SENSE OF FOREBODING. I WAS WORRIED ABOUT THE KOREAN NEWS, TOO, SO I THOUGHT ABOUT CALLING IT OFF. BUT SHE HAD COME ALONG...

CLATTER カチャ

CLATTER カチャ

MURMUR ザワ

MURMUR ザワ

CHAPTER
95

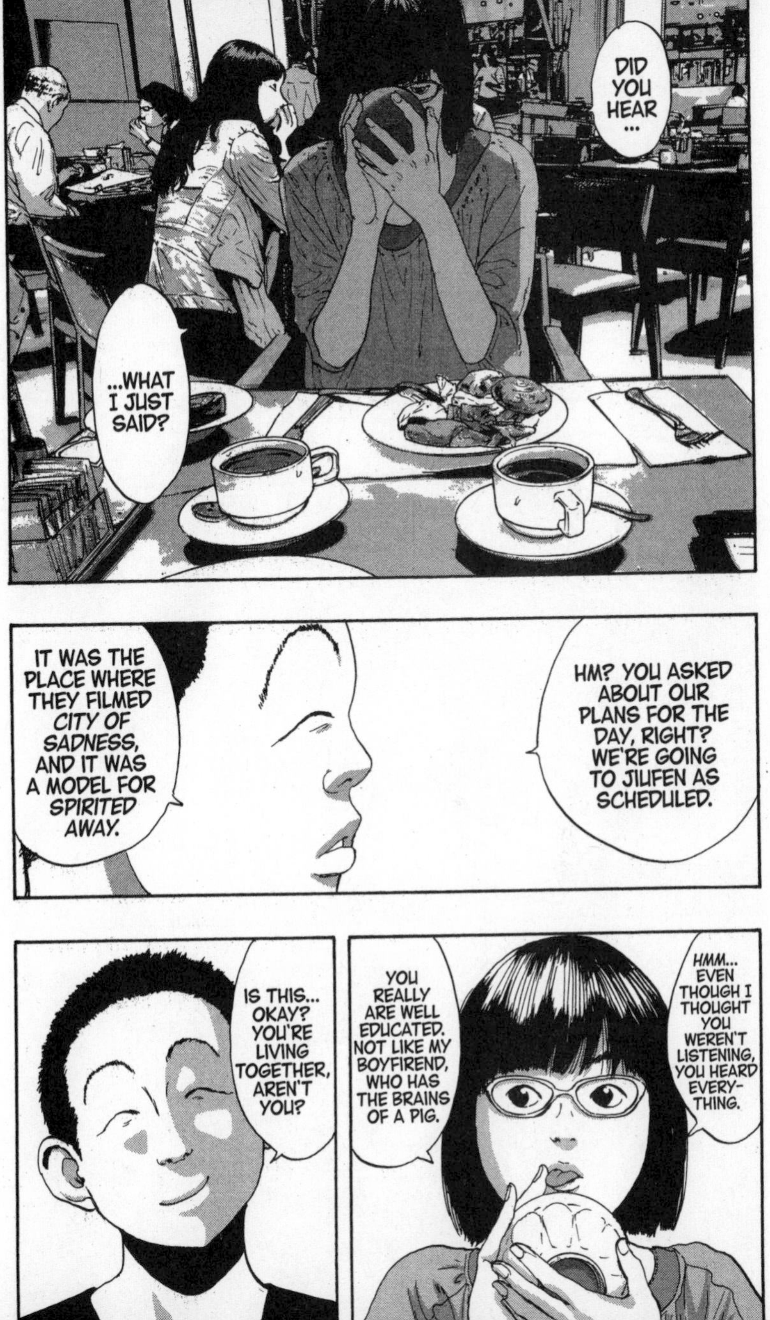
DID YOU HEAR ...
...WHAT I JUST SAID?
HM? YOU ASKED ABOUT OUR PLANS FOR THE DAY, RIGHT? WE'RE GOING TO JIUFEN AS SCHEDULED.
IT WAS THE PLACE WHERE THEY FILMED *CITY OF SADNESS*, AND IT WAS A MODEL FOR *SPIRITED AWAY*.
HMM... EVEN THOUGH I THOUGHT YOU WEREN'T LISTENING, YOU HEARD EVERY-THING.
YOU REALLY ARE WELL EDUCATED. NOT LIKE MY BOYFIREND, WHO HAS THE BRAINS OF A PIG.
IS THIS... OKAY? YOU'RE LIVING TOGETHER, AREN'T YOU?

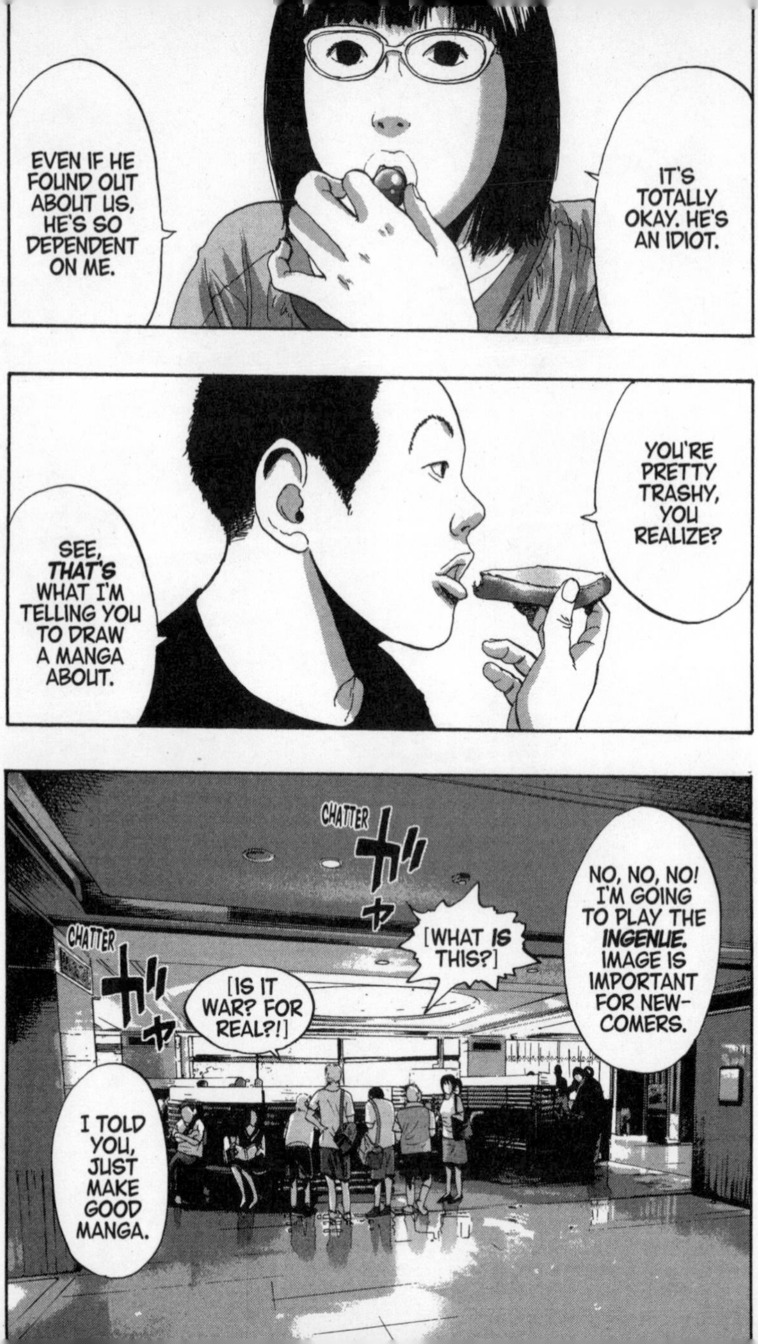
IT'S TOTALLY OKAY. HE'S AN IDIOT.
EVEN IF HE FOUND OUT ABOUT US, HE'S SO DEPENDENT ON ME.
YOU'RE PRETTY TRASHY, YOU REALIZE?
SEE, ***THAT'S*** WHAT I'M TELLING YOU TO DRAW A MANGA ABOUT.
NO, NO, NO! I'M GOING TO PLAY THE ***INGENUE.*** IMAGE IS IMPORTANT FOR NEW-COMERS.
CHATTER
ガヤ
[WHAT ***IS*** THIS?]
CHATTER
ガヤ
[IS IT WAR? FOR REAL?!]
I TOLD YOU, JUST MAKE GOOD MANGA.

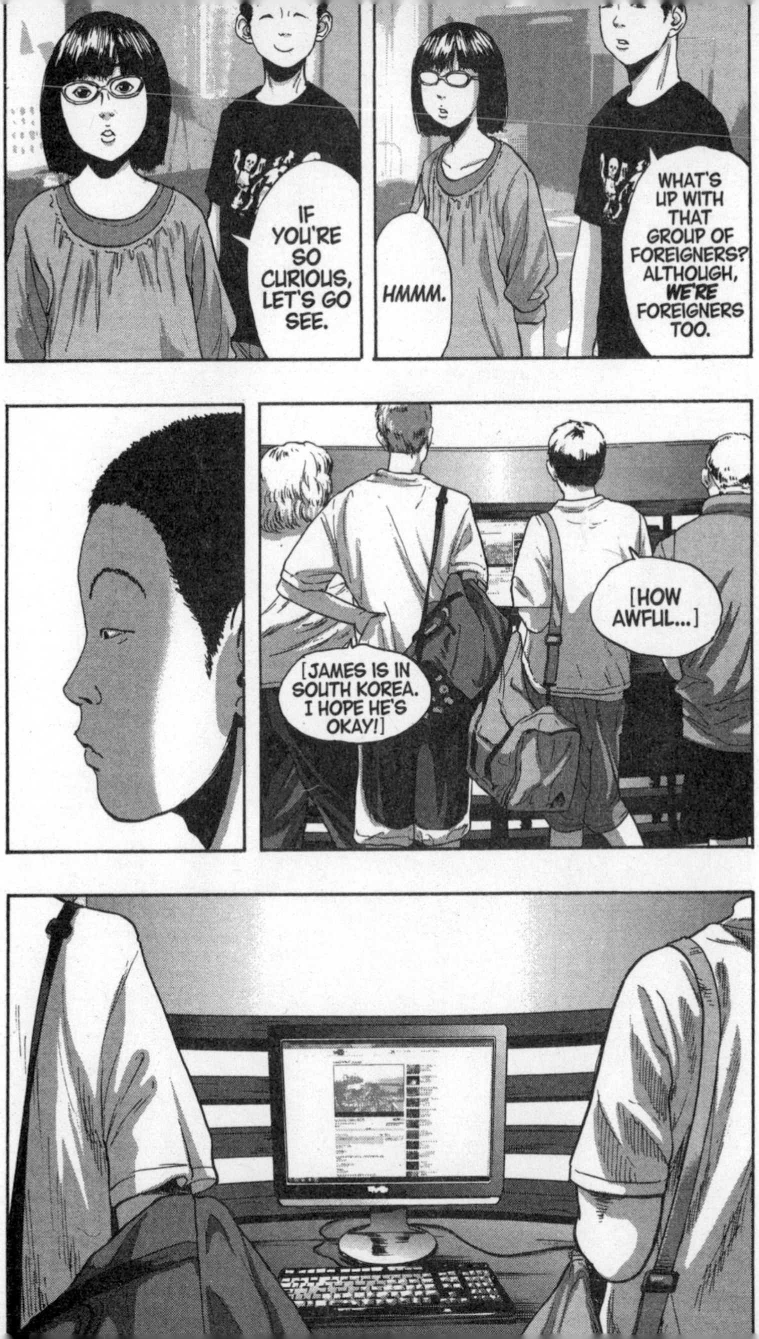
WHAT'S UP WITH THAT GROUP OF FOREIGNERS? ALTHOUGH, *WE'RE* FOREIGNERS TOO.
HMMM.
IF YOU'RE SO CURIOUS, LET'S GO SEE.
[HOW AWFUL...]
[JAMES IS IN SOUTH KOREA. I HOPE HE'S OKAY!]

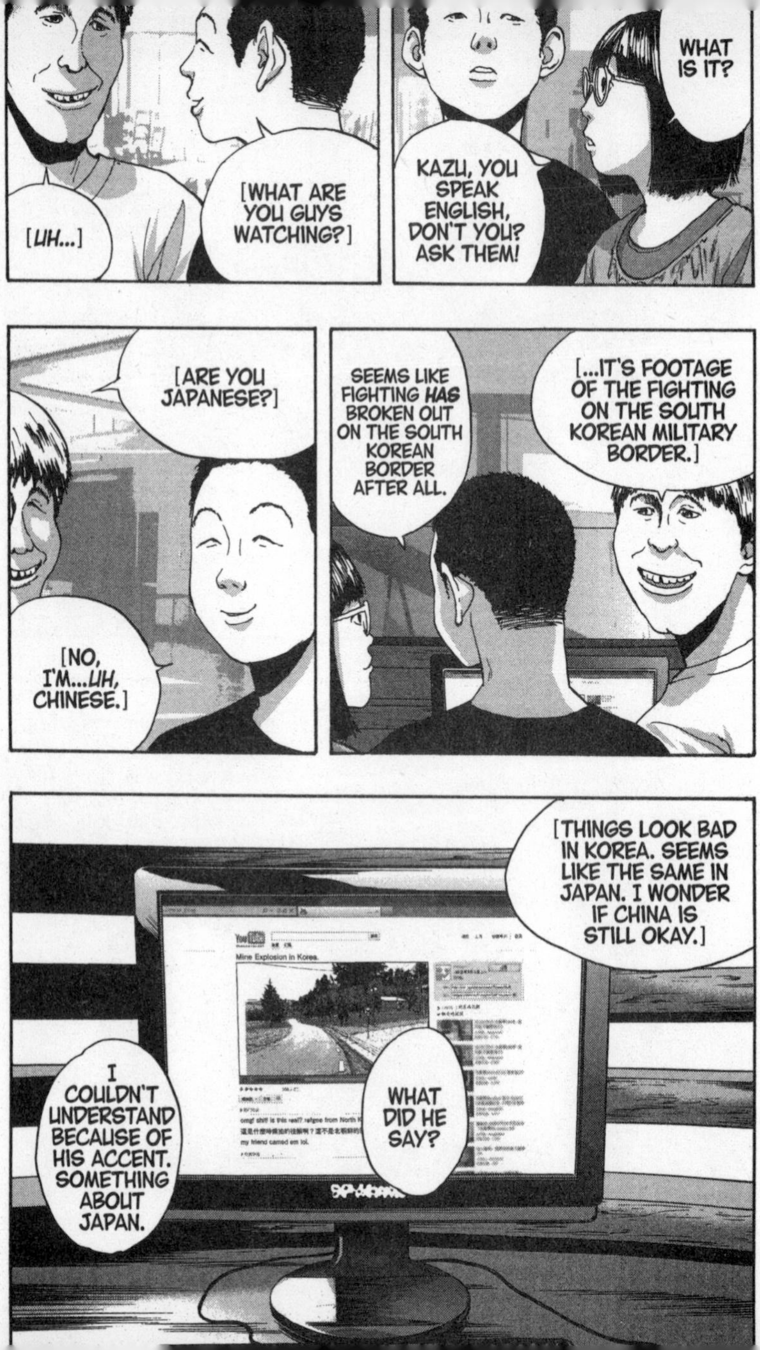
WHAT IS IT?
KAZU, YOU SPEAK ENGLISH, DON'T YOU? ASK THEM!
[WHAT ARE YOU GUYS WATCHING?]
[UH...]
[...IT'S FOOTAGE OF THE FIGHTING ON THE SOUTH KOREAN MILITARY BORDER.]
SEEMS LIKE FIGHTING ***HAS*** BROKEN OUT ON THE SOUTH KOREAN BORDER AFTER ALL.
[ARE YOU JAPANESE?]
[NO, I'M...UH, CHINESE.]
[THINGS LOOK BAD IN KOREA. SEEMS LIKE THE SAME IN JAPAN. I WONDER IF CHINA IS STILL OKAY.]
Mine Explosion in Korea.
WHAT DID HE SAY?
I COULDN'T UNDERSTAND BECAUSE OF HIS ACCENT. SOMETHING ABOUT JAPAN.

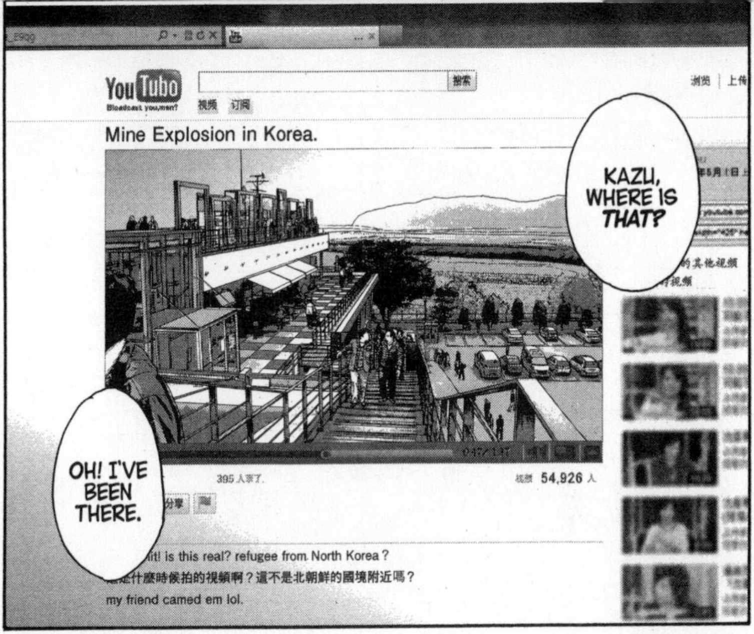
KAZU, WHERE IS THAT?
OH! I'VE BEEN THERE.
YouTubo
Bloadcast you,men?
Mine Explosion in Korea.
395 人看了.
54,926 人
shit! is this real? refugee from North Korea?
什麼時候拍的視頻啊？這不是北朝鮮的國境附近嗎？
my friend camed em lol.

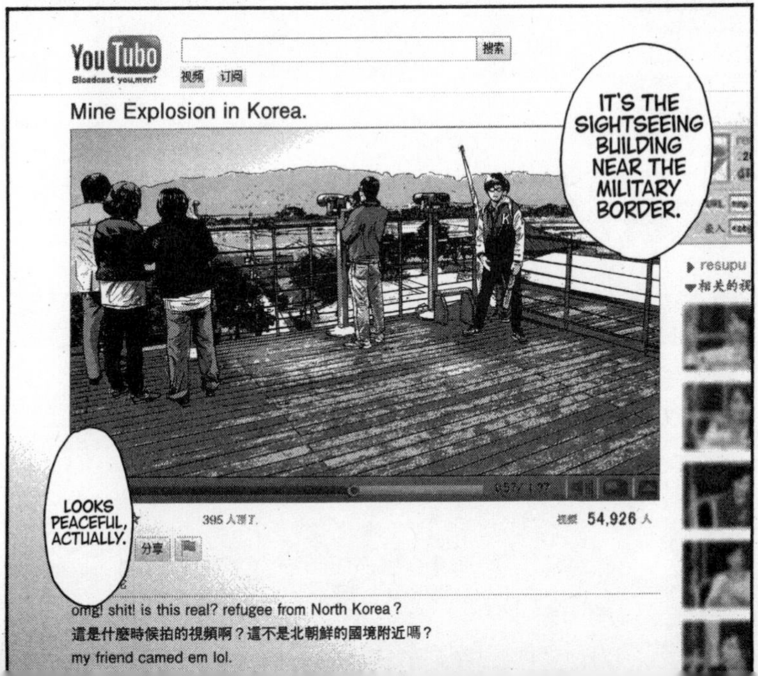
IT'S THE SIGHTSEEING BUILDING NEAR THE MILITARY BORDER.
LOOKS PEACEFUL, ACTUALLY.
YouTubo
Bloadcast you,men?
搜索
视频 订阅
Mine Explosion in Korea.
resupu
395 人看了.
54,926 人
分享
omg! shit! is this real? refugee from North Korea?
這是什麼時候拍的視頻啊？這不是北朝鮮的國境附近嗎？
my friend camed em lol.

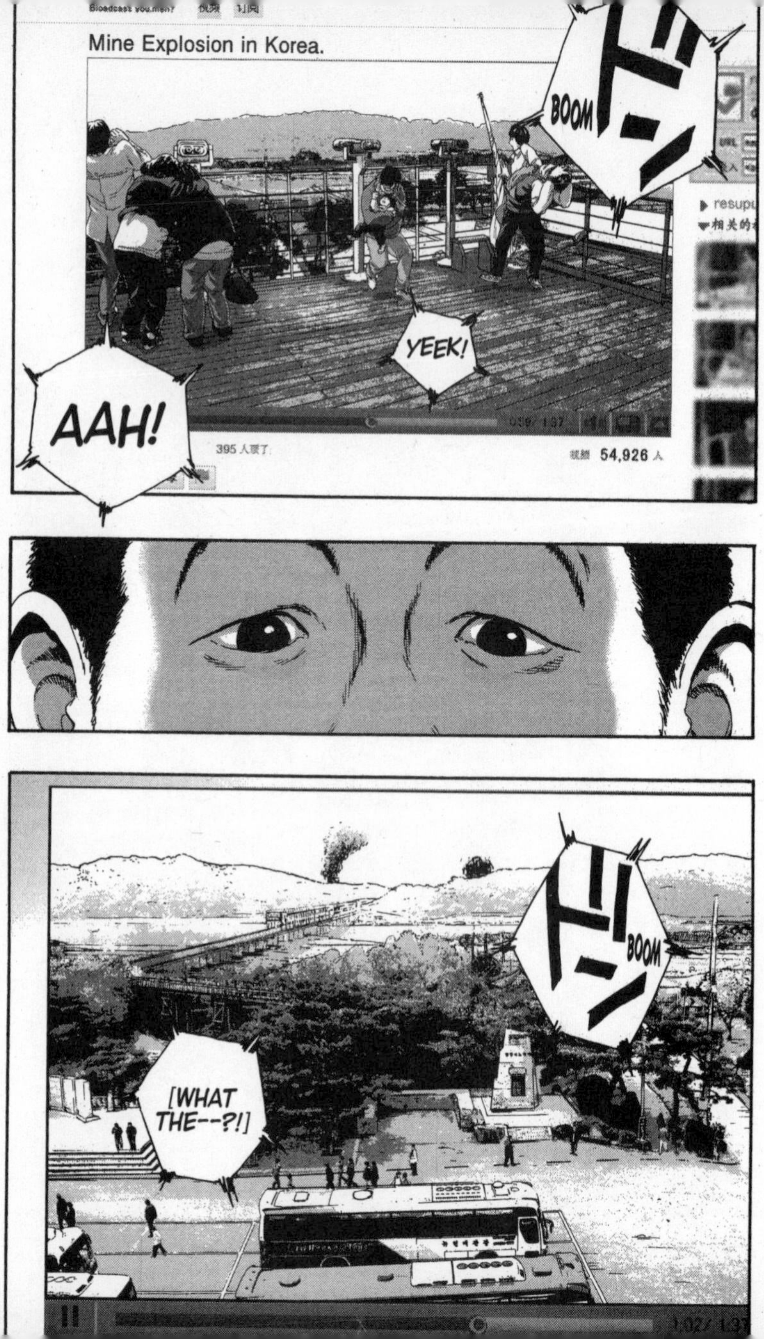
Mine Explosion in Korea.
BOOM
YEEK!
AAH!
54,926 人
BOOM
[WHAT THE--?!]

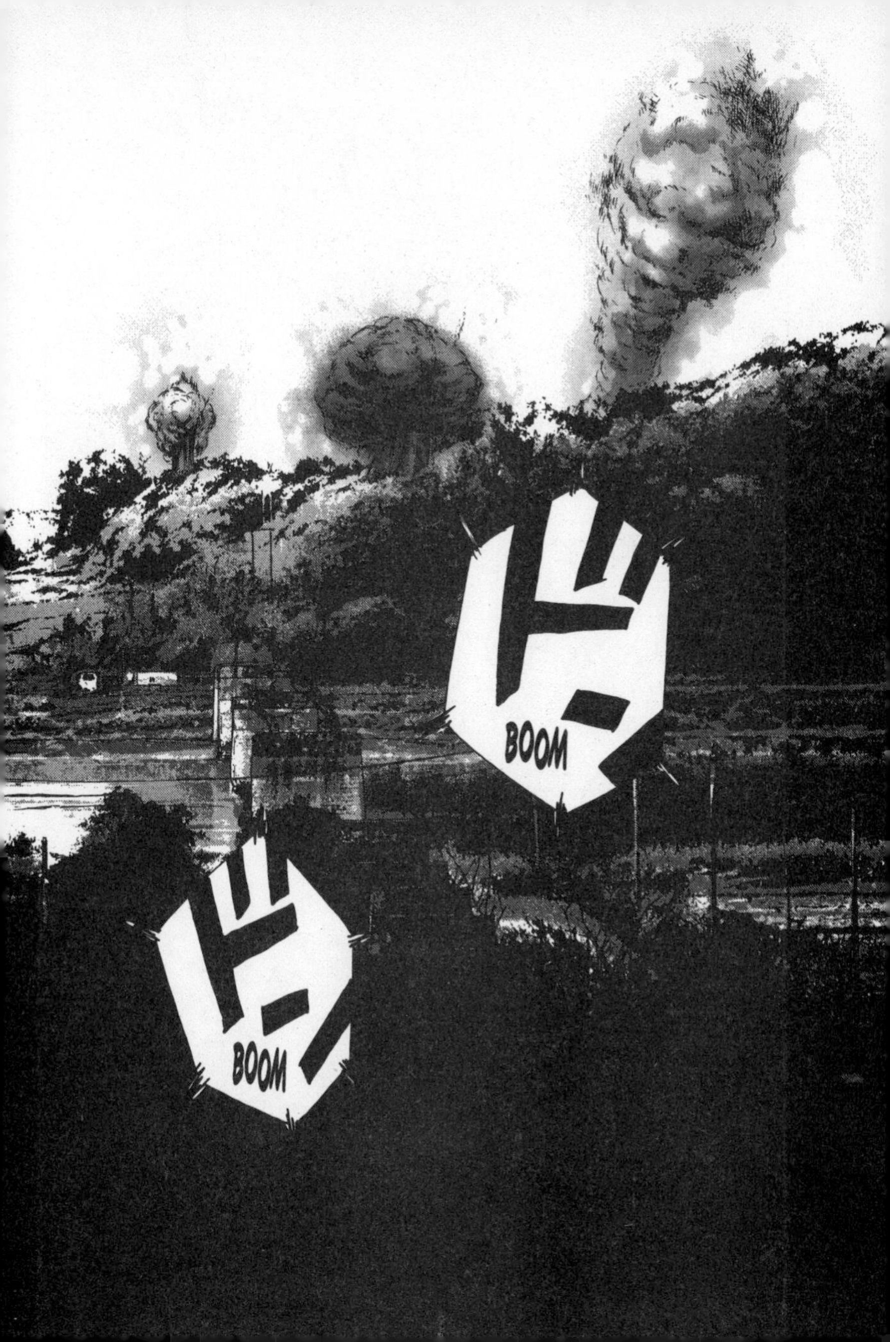
ドン
BOOM
ドン
BOOM

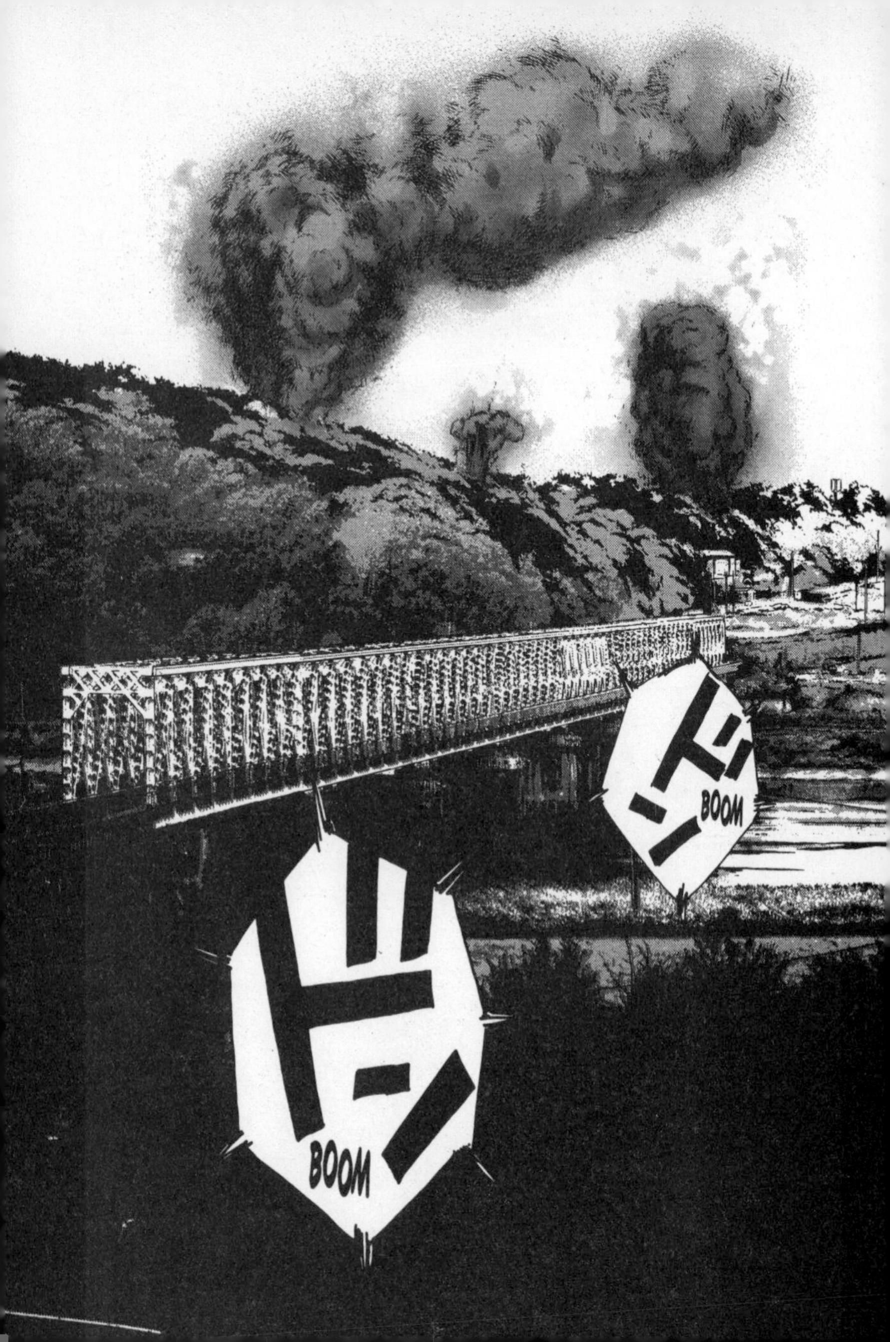
ドーン
BOOM
ドーン
BOOM

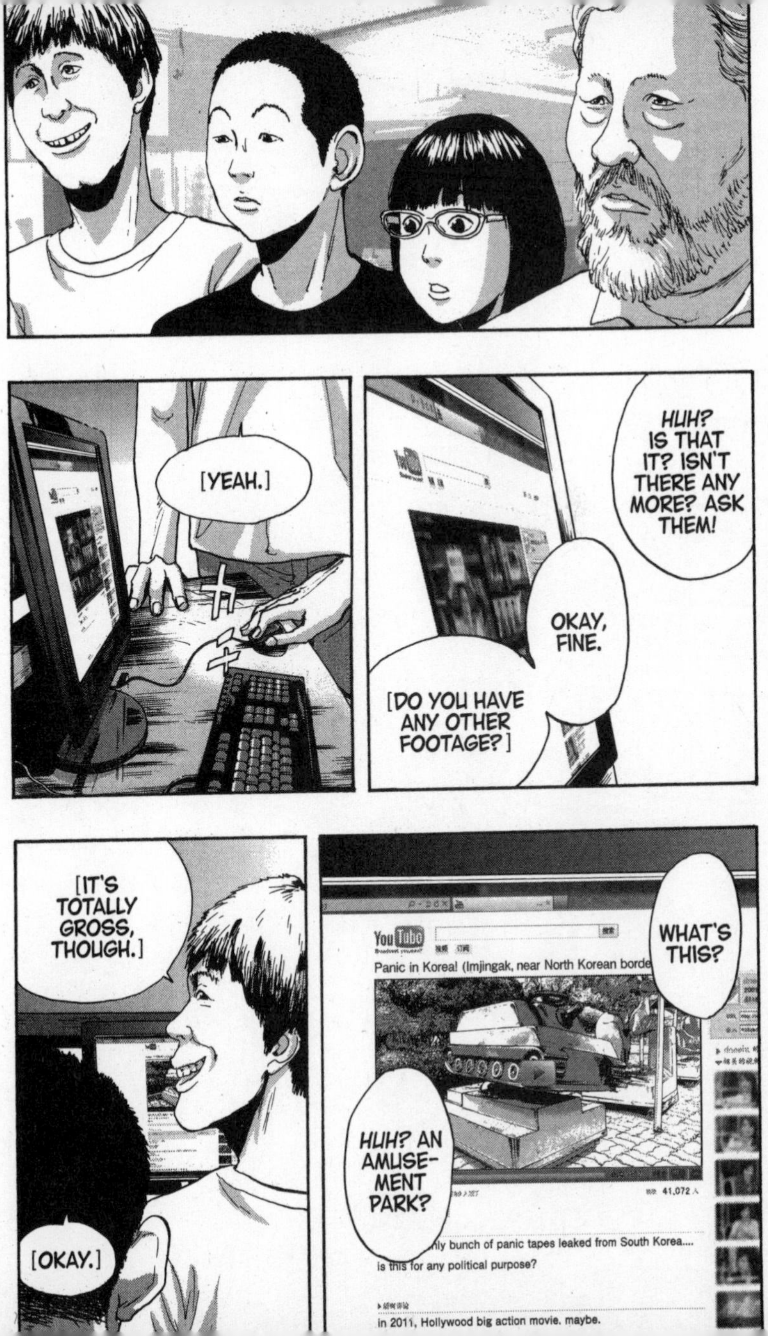
HUH? IS THAT IT? ISN'T THERE ANY MORE? ASK THEM!
OKAY, FINE.
[DO YOU HAVE ANY OTHER FOOTAGE?]
[YEAH.]
WHAT'S THIS?
Panic in Korea! (Imjingak, near North Korean borde
41,072
nly bunch of panic tapes leaked from South Korea....
is this for any political purpose?
in 2011, Hollywood big action movie. maybe.
HUH? AN AMUSE-MENT PARK?
[IT'S TOTALLY GROSS, THOUGH.]
[OKAY.]

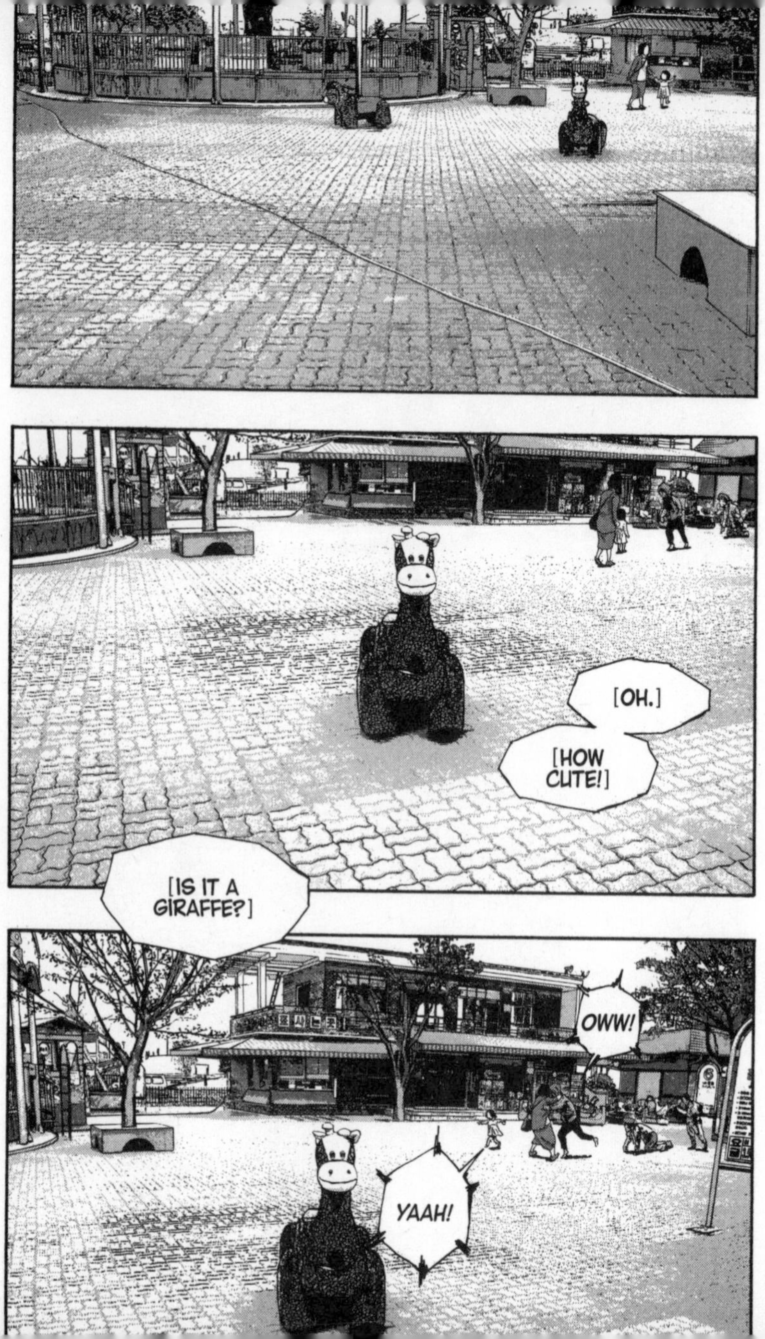
[OH.]
[HOW CUTE!]
[IS IT A GIRAFFE?]
OWW!
YAAH!

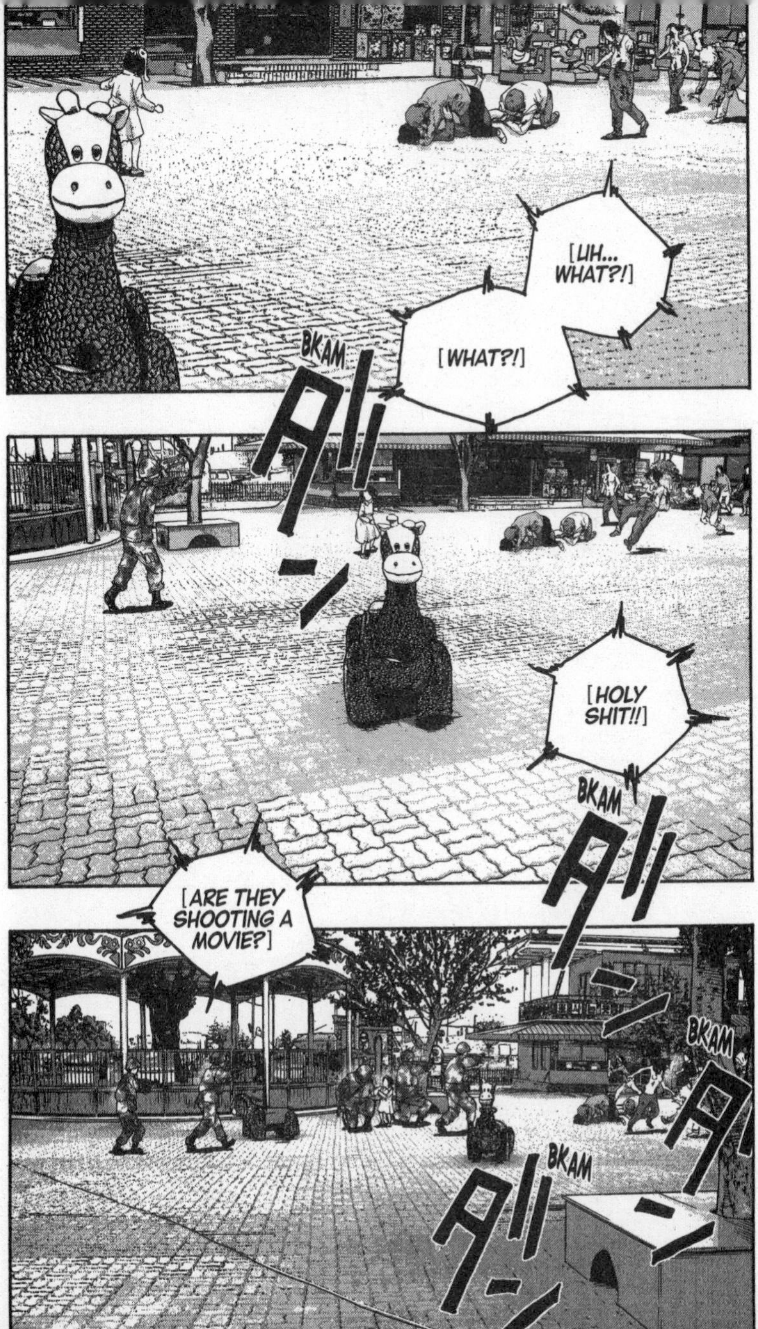
[UH...
WHAT?!]
[WHAT?!]
BKAM
ダーン
[HOLY
SHIT!!]
BKAM
ダーン
[ARE THEY
SHOOTING A
MOVIE?]
BKAM
ダーン
BKAM
ダーン

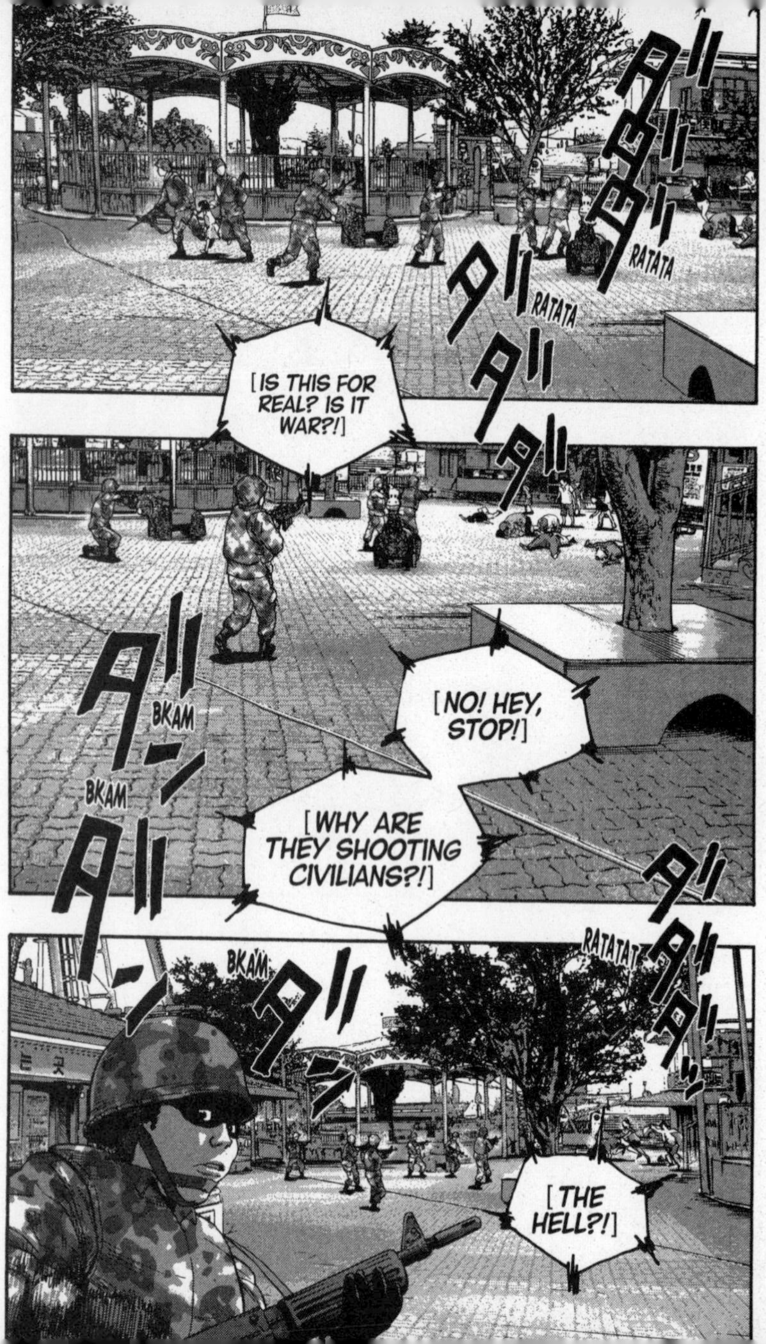
RATATA
RATATA
[IS THIS FOR REAL? IS IT WAR?!]
[NO! HEY, STOP!]
BKAM
BKAM
[WHY ARE THEY SHOOTING CIVILIANS?!]
RATATAT
BKAM
[THE HELL?!]

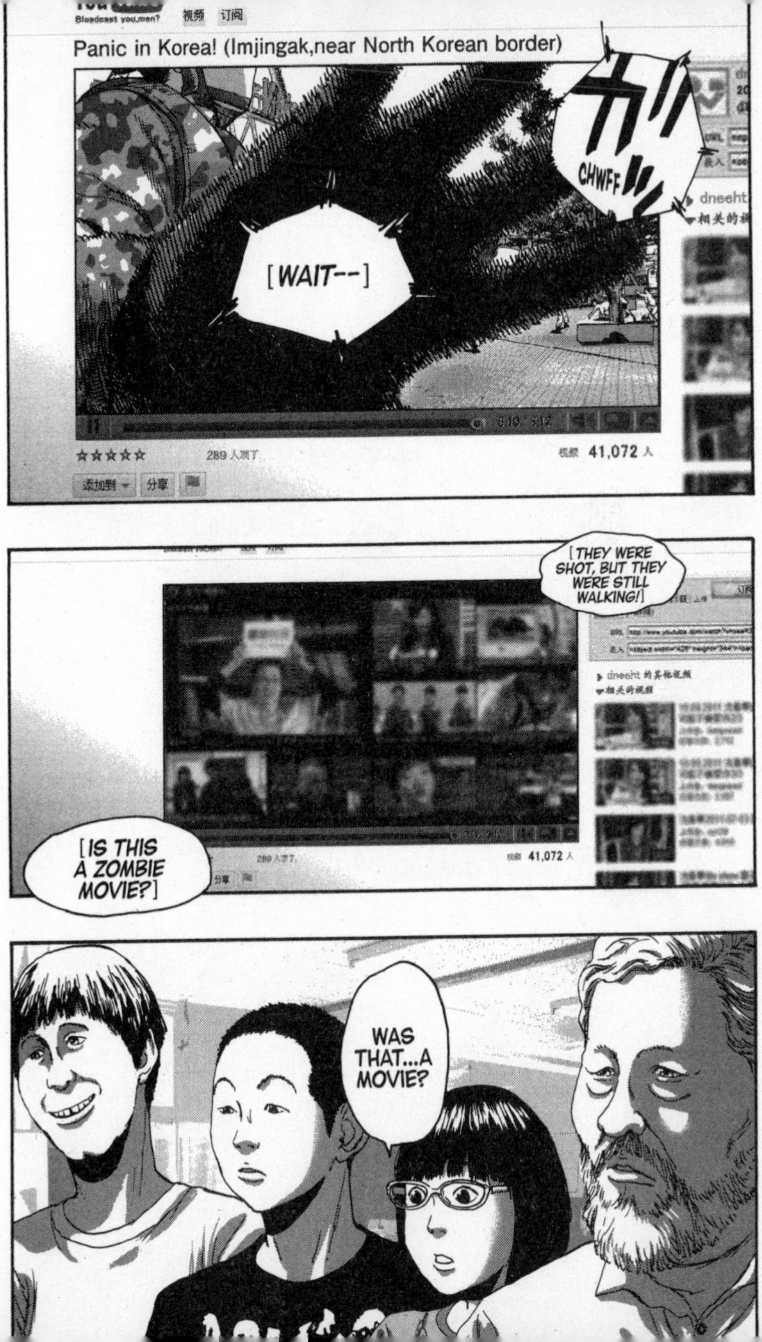
Bloadcast you,men?
视频
订阅
Panic in Korea! (Imjingak,near North Korean border)
CHWFF
dneeht
[WAIT--]
289 人评了
视频 41,072 人
添加到
分享
[THEY WERE SHOT, BUT THEY WERE STILL WALKING!]
dneeht 的其他视频
相关的视频
41,072 人
[IS THIS A ZOMBIE MOVIE?]
分享
WAS THAT...A MOVIE?

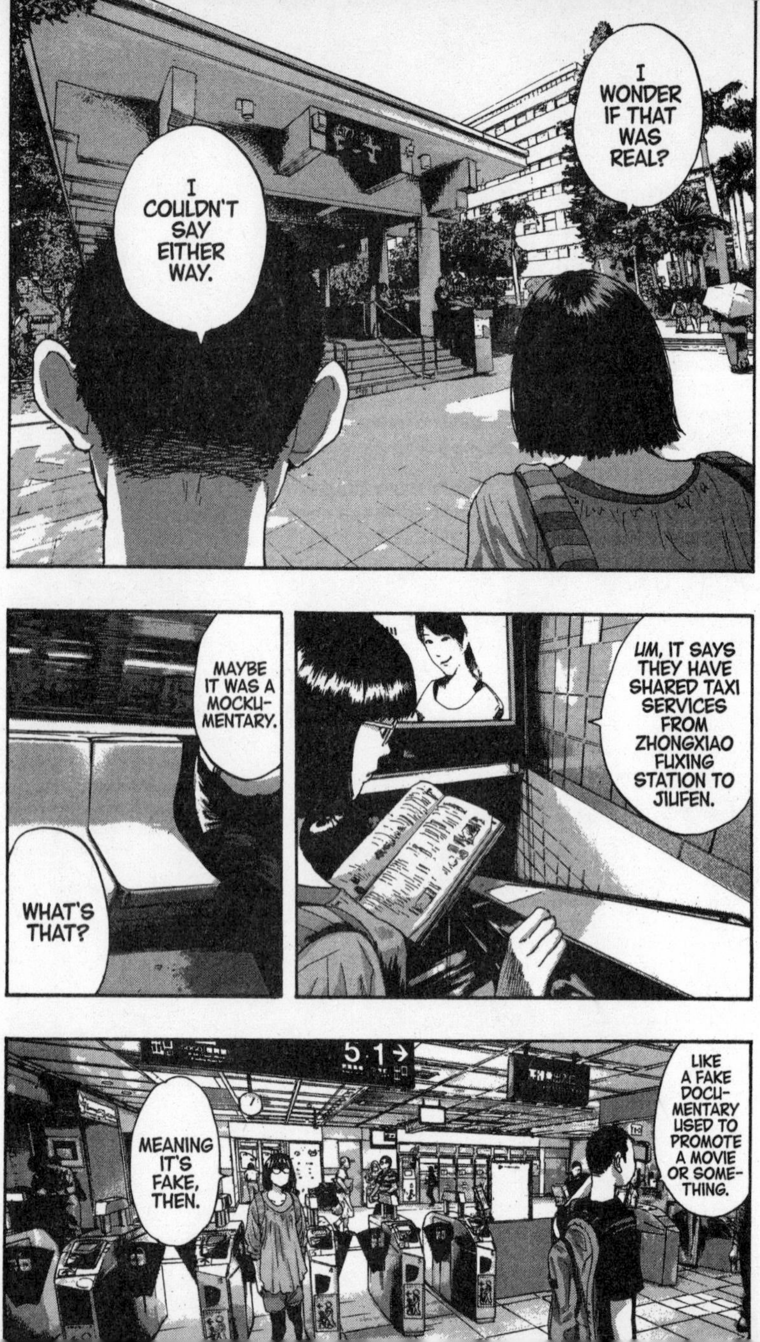
I WONDER IF THAT WAS REAL?
I COULDN'T SAY EITHER WAY.
UM, IT SAYS THEY HAVE SHARED TAXI SERVICES FROM ZHONGXIAO FUXING STATION TO JIUFEN.
MAYBE IT WAS A MOCKU-MENTARY.
WHAT'S THAT?
LIKE A FAKE DOCU-MENTARY USED TO PROMOTE A MOVIE OR SOME-THING.
MEANING IT'S FAKE, THEN.

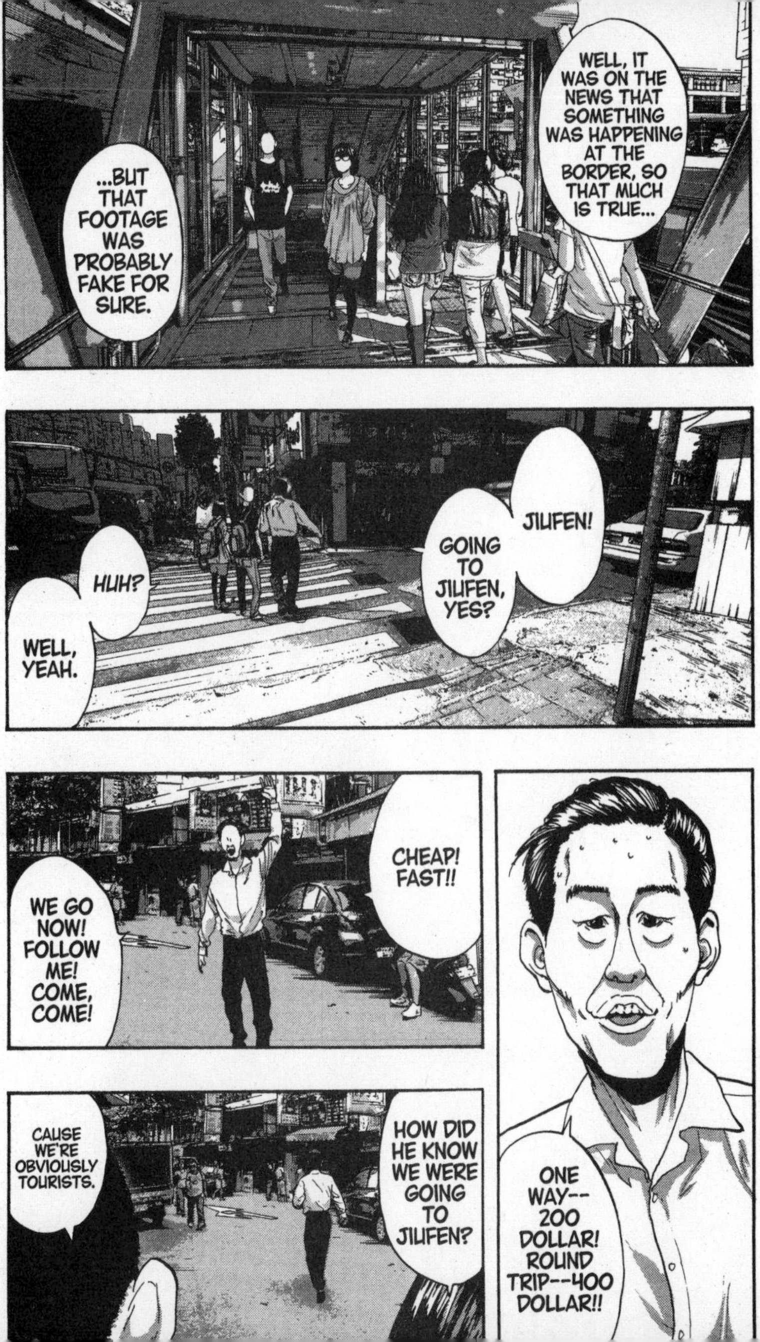
WELL, IT WAS ON THE NEWS THAT SOMETHING WAS HAPPENING AT THE BORDER, SO THAT MUCH IS TRUE...
...BUT THAT FOOTAGE WAS PROBABLY FAKE FOR SURE.
JIUFEN!
GOING TO JIUFEN, YES?
HUH?
WELL, YEAH.
ONE WAY--200 DOLLAR! ROUND TRIP--400 DOLLAR!!
CHEAP! FAST!!
WE GO NOW! FOLLOW ME! COME, COME!
HOW DID HE KNOW WE WERE GOING TO JIUFEN?
CAUSE WE'RE OBVIOUSLY TOURISTS.

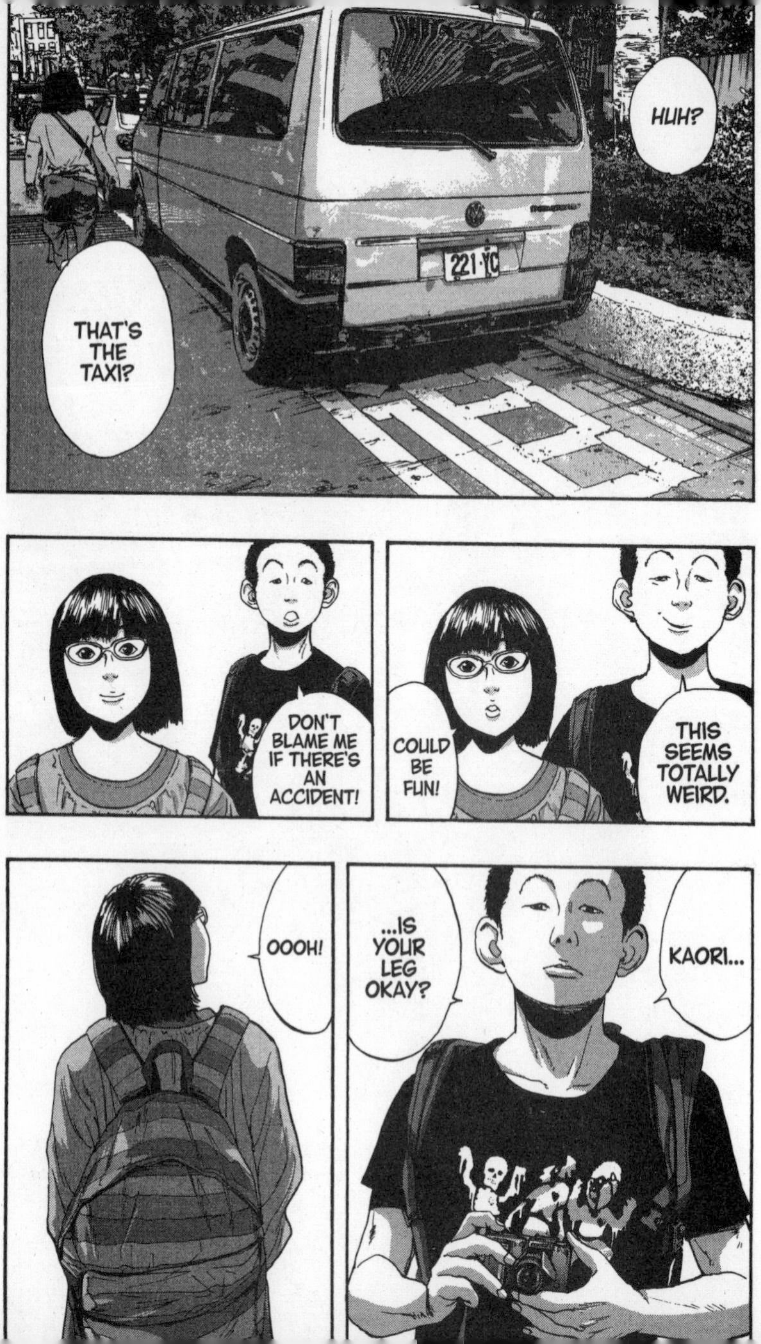
HUH?
THAT'S THE TAXI?
THIS SEEMS TOTALLY WEIRD.
COULD BE FUN!
DON'T BLAME ME IF THERE'S AN ACCIDENT!
KAORI...
...IS YOUR LEG OKAY?
OOOH!

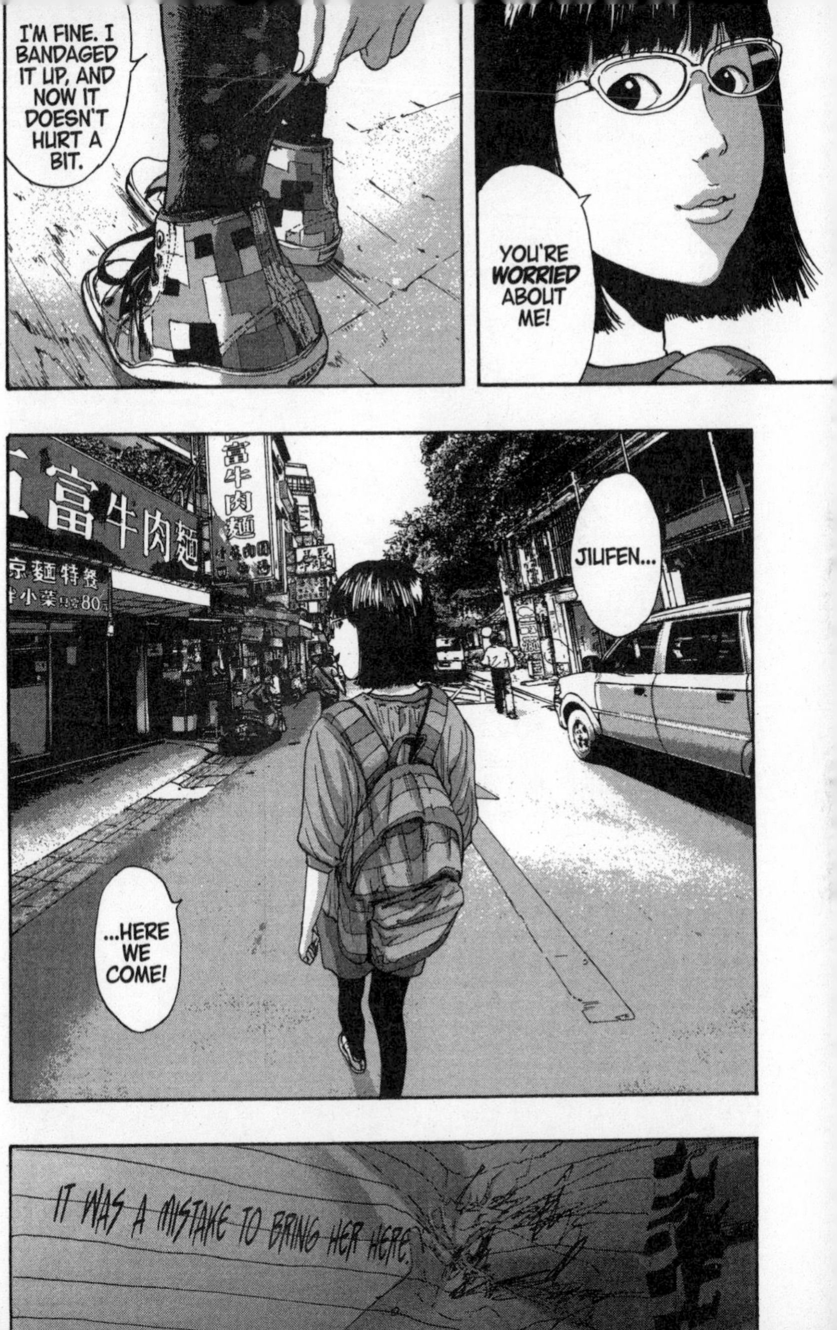
YOU'RE WORRIED ABOUT ME!
I'M FINE. I BANDAGED IT UP, AND NOW IT DOESN'T HURT A BIT.
JIUFEN...
富牛肉麵
富牛肉麵
京麵特餐
...HERE WE COME!
IT WAS A MISTAKE TO BRING HER HERE.

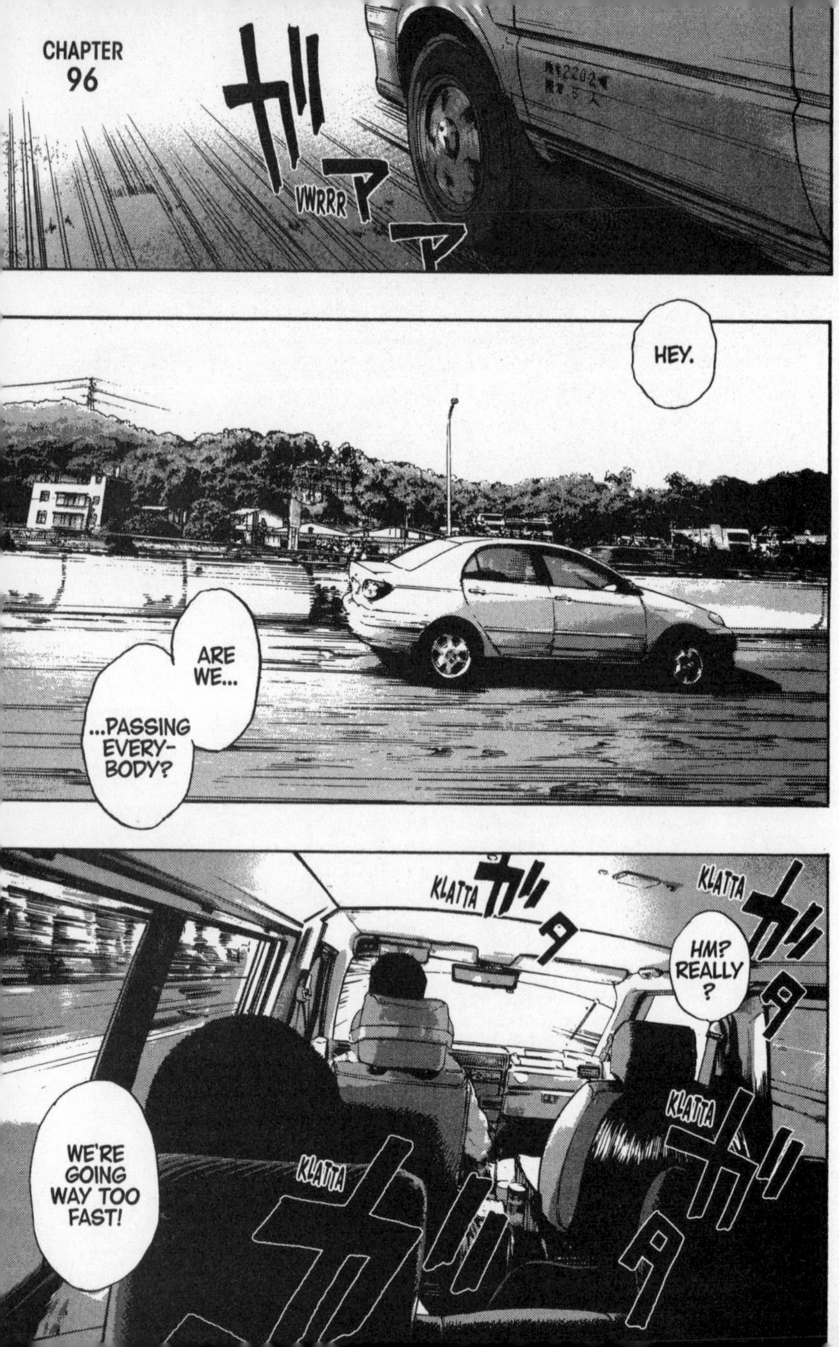
CHAPTER 96
VWRRR
HEY.
ARE WE...
...PASSING EVERYBODY?
KLATTA
HM? REALLY?
KLATTA
KLATTA
WE'RE GOING WAY TOO FAST!
KLATTA

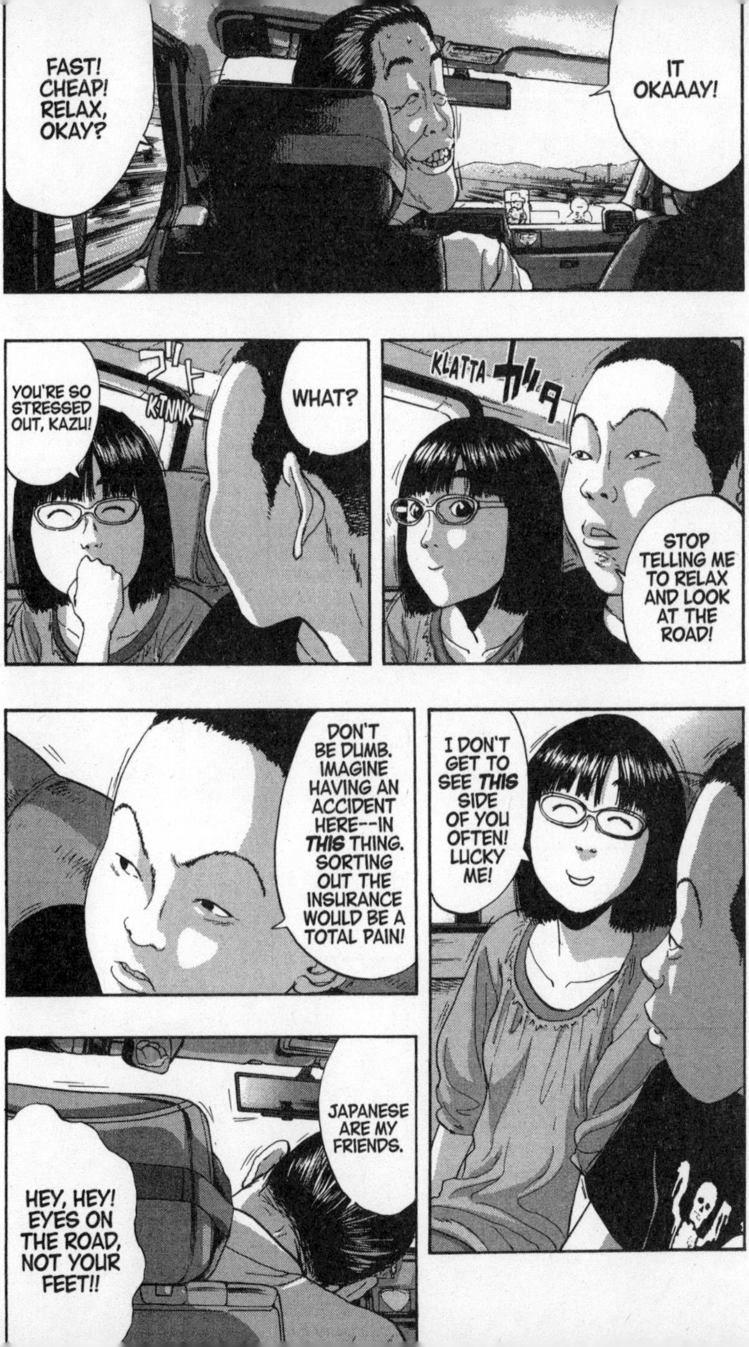
FAST! CHEAP! RELAX, OKAY?
IT OKAAAY!
YOU'RE SO STRESSED OUT, KAZU!
KINNK
WHAT?
KLATTA
STOP TELLING ME TO RELAX AND LOOK AT THE ROAD!
DON'T BE DUMB. IMAGINE HAVING AN ACCIDENT HERE--IN **THIS** THING. SORTING OUT THE INSURANCE WOULD BE A TOTAL PAIN!
I DON'T GET TO SEE **THIS** SIDE OF YOU OFTEN! LUCKY ME!
JAPANESE ARE MY FRIENDS.
HEY, HEY! EYES ON THE ROAD, NOT YOUR FEET!!

JAPANESE ARE MY FRIENDS. THEY ALWAYS SO PLEASED!

WATCH THE ROAD, I SAID!!

HUH? WHAT?

OH! THESE ARE COMMENTS FROM PASSENGERS.

A DIARY?

DIARY! DIARY!

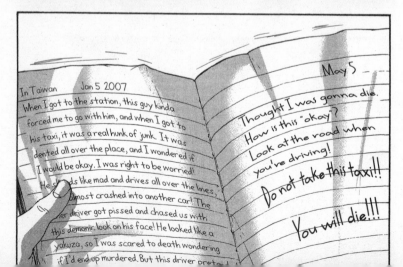

In Taiwan   Jan 5 2007
When I got to the station, this guy kinda forced me to go with him, and when I got to his taxi, it was a real hunk of junk. It was dented all over the place, and I wondered if I would be okay. I was right to be worried! He speeds like mad and drives all over the lines. ...lmost crashed into another car! The ...er driver got pissed and chased us with this demonic look on his face! He looked like a yakuza, so I was scared to death wondering if I'd end up murdered. But this driver prot...

May 5
Thought I was gonna die. How is this "okay"? Look at the road when you're driving! Do not take this taxi!! You will die!!!

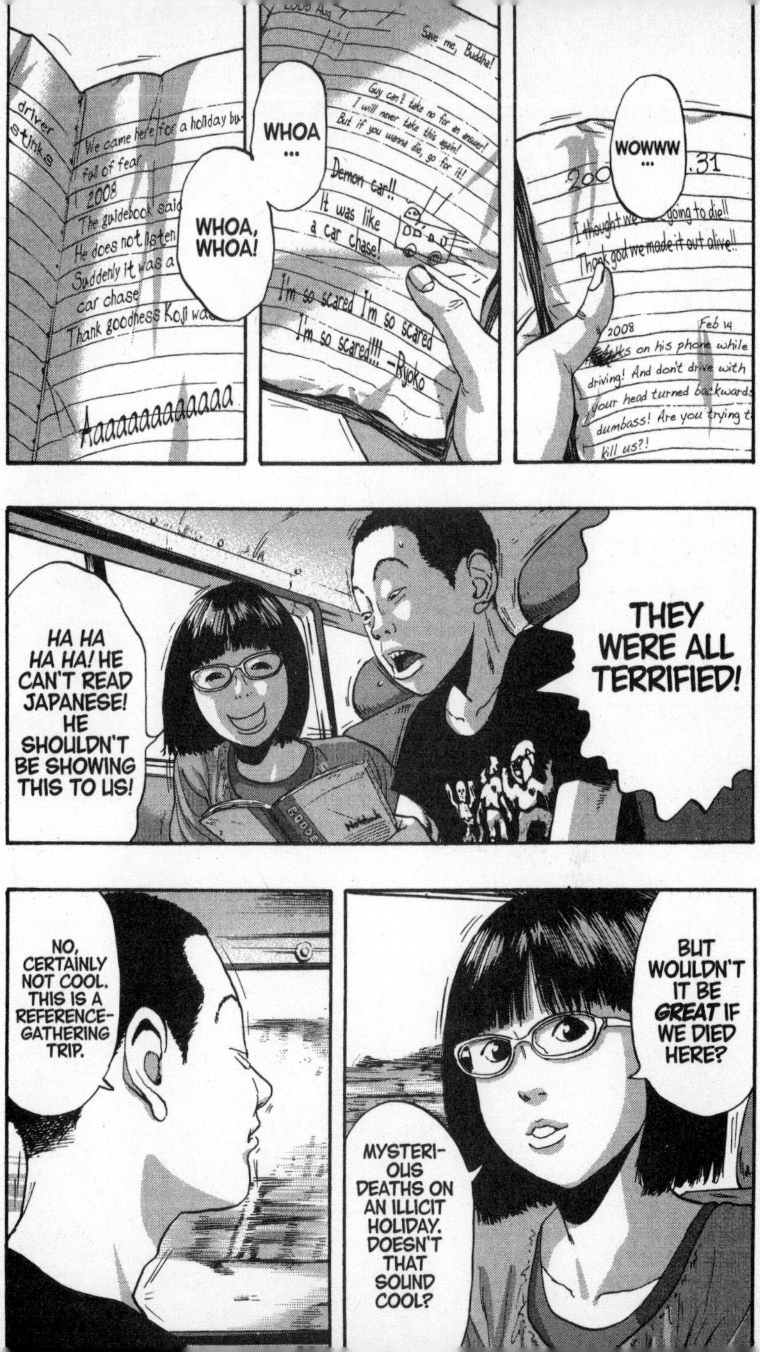
WOWWW…
Thank god we made it out alive!!
2008 Feb 14
driving! And don't drive with
dumbass! Are you trying
kill us?!
Save me, Buddha!
Guy can't take no for an answer!
I will never take this again!
But if you wanna die, go for it!
WHOA…
Demon car!!
It was like a car chase!
WHOA, WHOA!
I'm so scared I'm so scared I'm so scared!!! –Ryoko
driver stinks
We came here for a holiday bu
full of fear
2008
The guidebook said
He does not listen
Suddenly it was a
car chase
Thank goodness Koji wa
Aaaaaaaaaaaa
THEY WERE ALL TERRIFIED!
HA HA HA HA! HE CAN'T READ JAPANESE! HE SHOULDN'T BE SHOWING THIS TO US!
BUT WOULDN'T IT BE GREAT IF WE DIED HERE?
MYSTERIOUS DEATHS ON AN ILLICIT HOLIDAY. DOESN'T THAT SOUND COOL?
NO, CERTAINLY NOT COOL. THIS IS A REFERENCE-GATHERING TRIP.

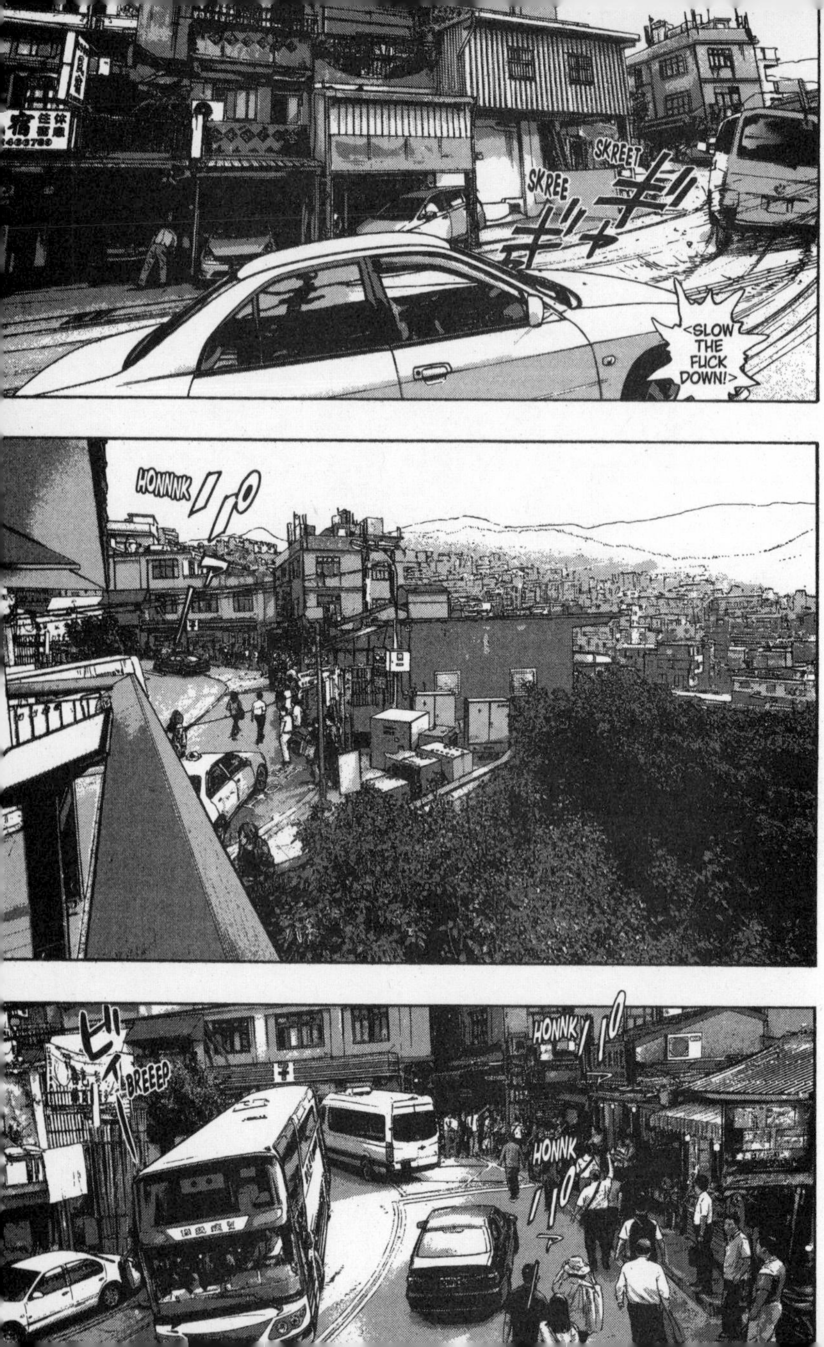
SKREET
SKREE
<SLOW THE FUCK DOWN!>
HONNNK
HONNK
HONNK
BREEEP

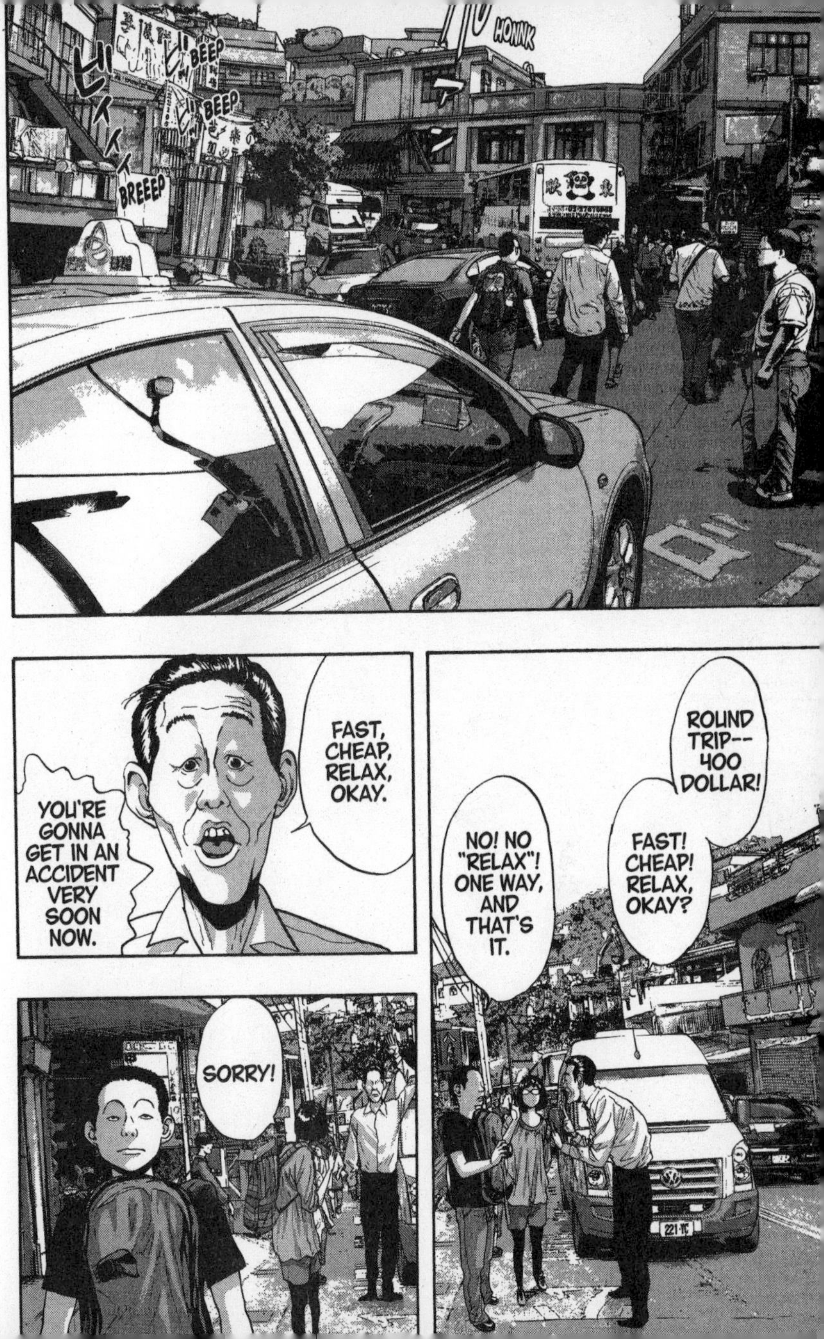
HONNK
BEEP
BEEP
BREEEP
ROUND TRIP-- 400 DOLLAR!
FAST! CHEAP! RELAX, OKAY?
NO! NO "RELAX"! ONE WAY, AND THAT'S IT.
FAST, CHEAP, RELAX, OKAY.
YOU'RE GONNA GET IN AN ACCIDENT VERY SOON NOW.
SORRY!

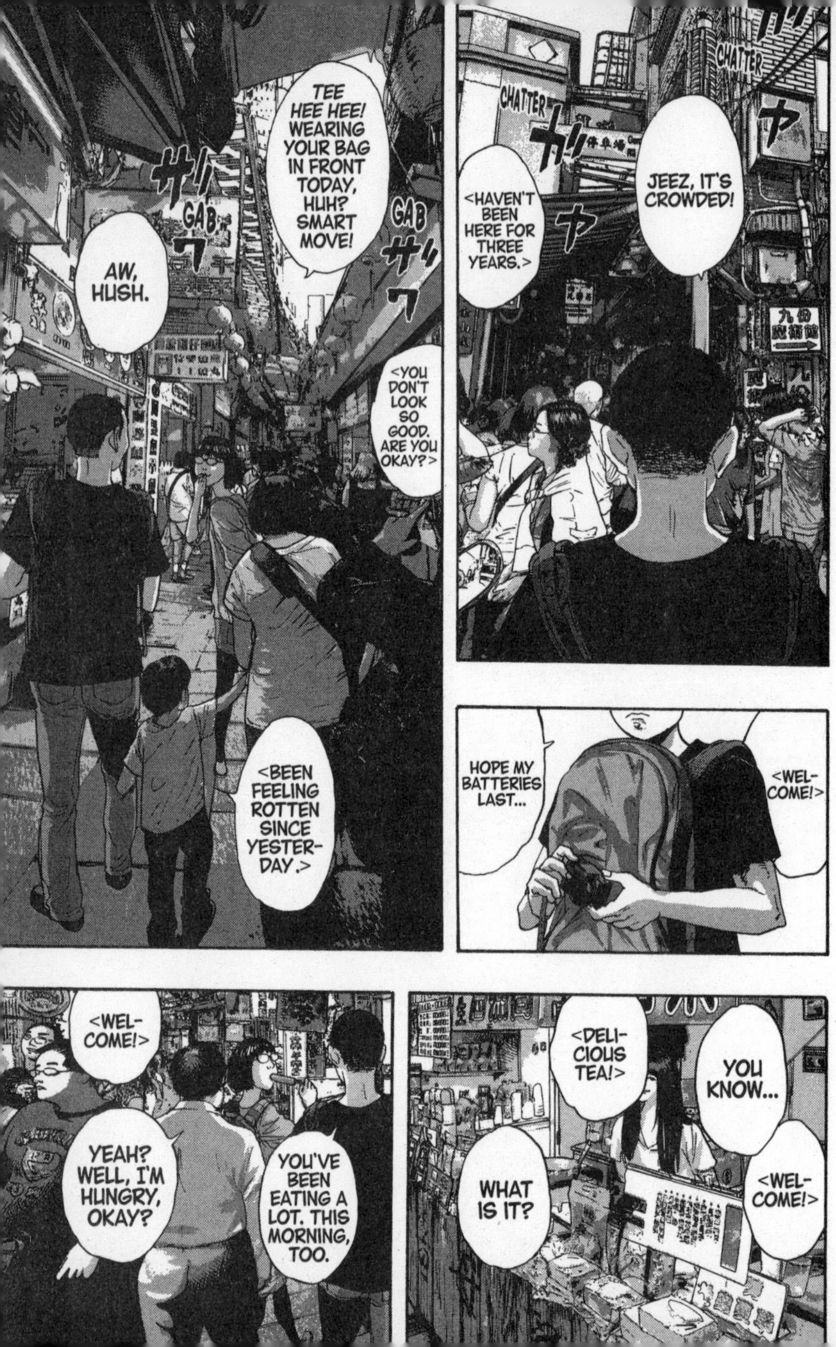
CHATTER
CHATTER
JEEZ, IT'S CROWDED!
<HAVEN'T BEEN HERE FOR THREE YEARS.>
<WEL-COME!>
HOPE MY BATTERIES LAST...
TEE HEE HEE! WEARING YOUR BAG IN FRONT TODAY, HUH? SMART MOVE!
GAB
<YOU DON'T LOOK SO GOOD. ARE YOU OKAY?>
GAB
AW, HUSH.
<BEEN FEELING ROTTEN SINCE YESTER-DAY.>
YOU KNOW...
<DELI-CIOUS TEA!>
<WEL-COME!>
WHAT IS IT?
<WEL-COME!>
YOU'VE BEEN EATING A LOT. THIS MORNING, TOO.
YEAH? WELL, I'M HUNGRY, OKAY?

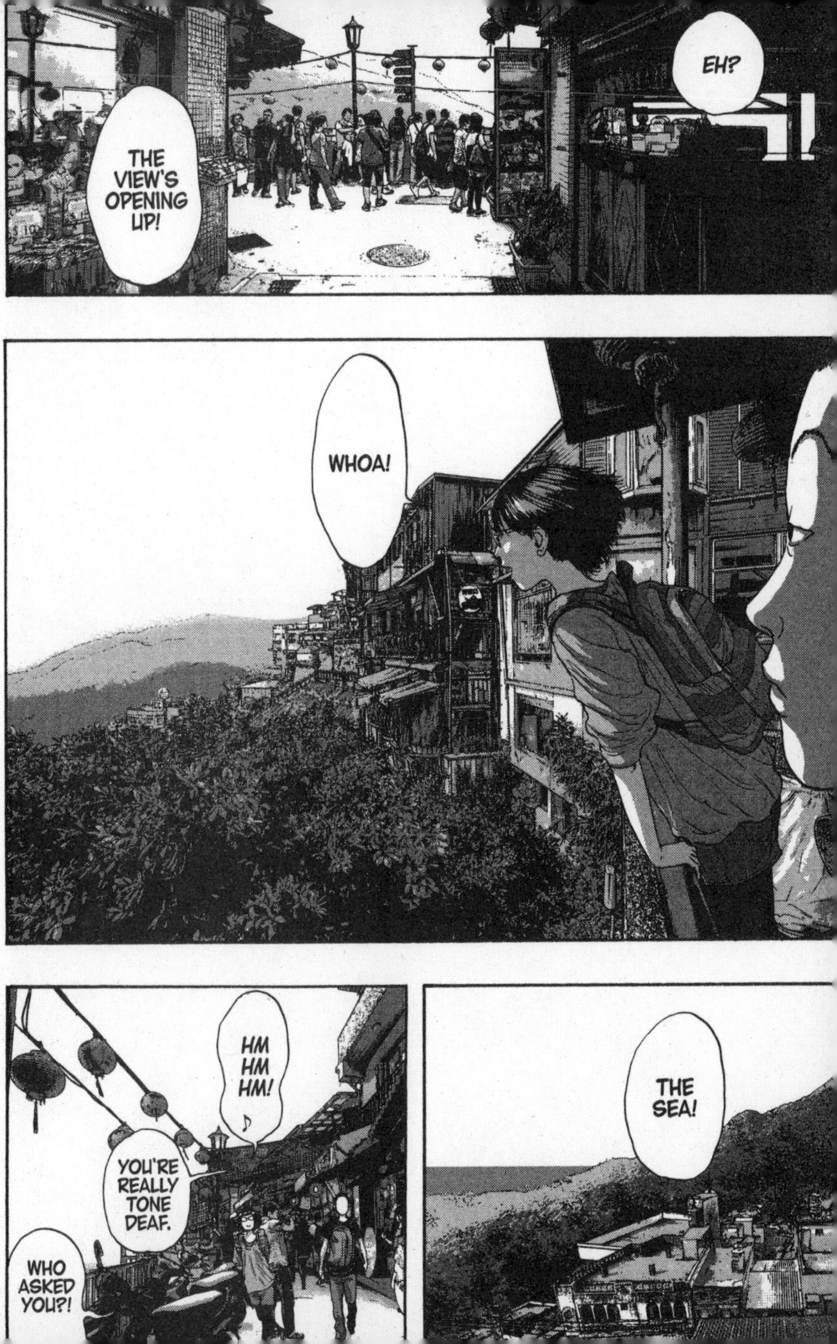
EH?
THE VIEW'S OPENING UP!
WHOA!
THE SEA!
HM HM HM! ♪
YOU'RE REALLY TONE DEAF.
WHO ASKED YOU?!

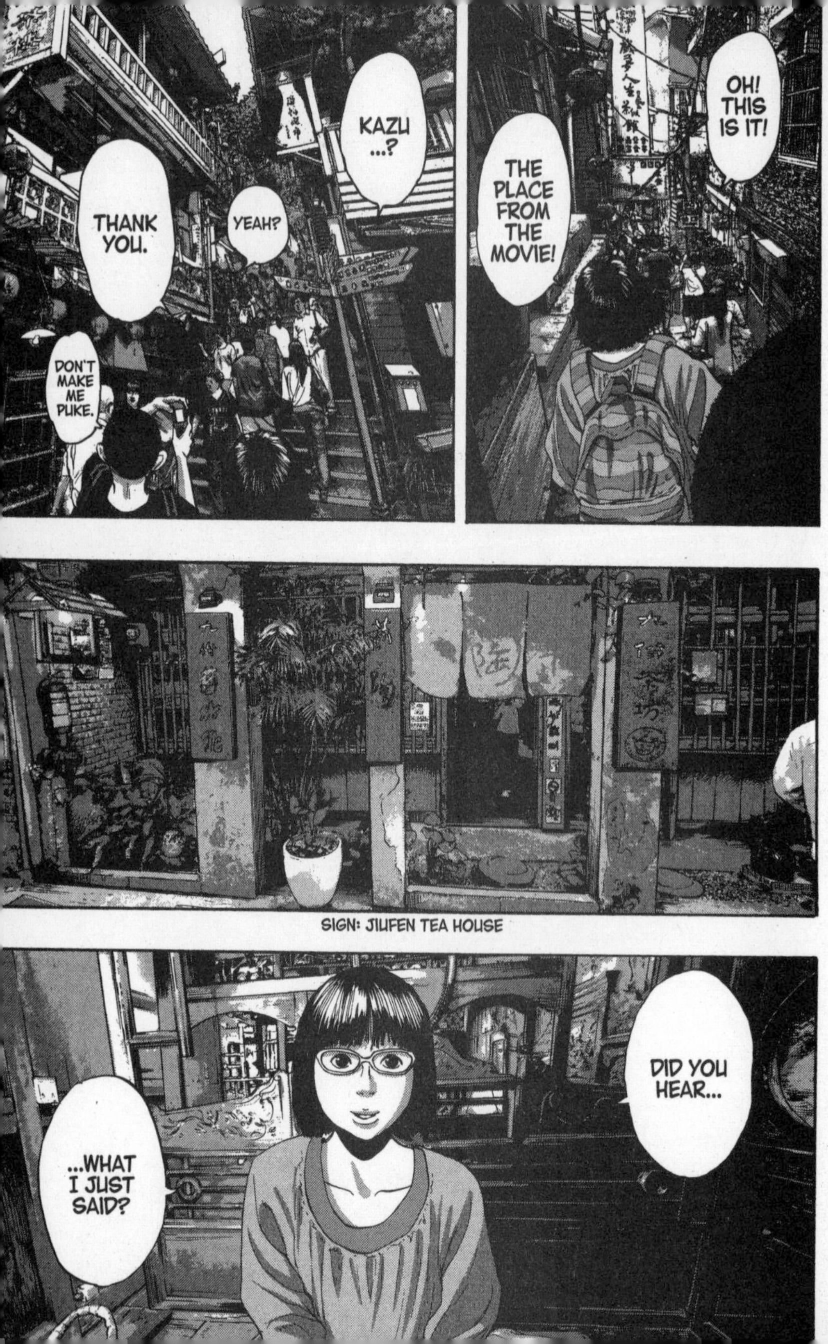
OH! THIS IS IT!
THE PLACE FROM THE MOVIE!
KAZU ...?
YEAH?
THANK YOU.
DON'T MAKE ME PUKE.
SIGN: JIUFEN TEA HOUSE
DID YOU HEAR...
...WHAT I JUST SAID?

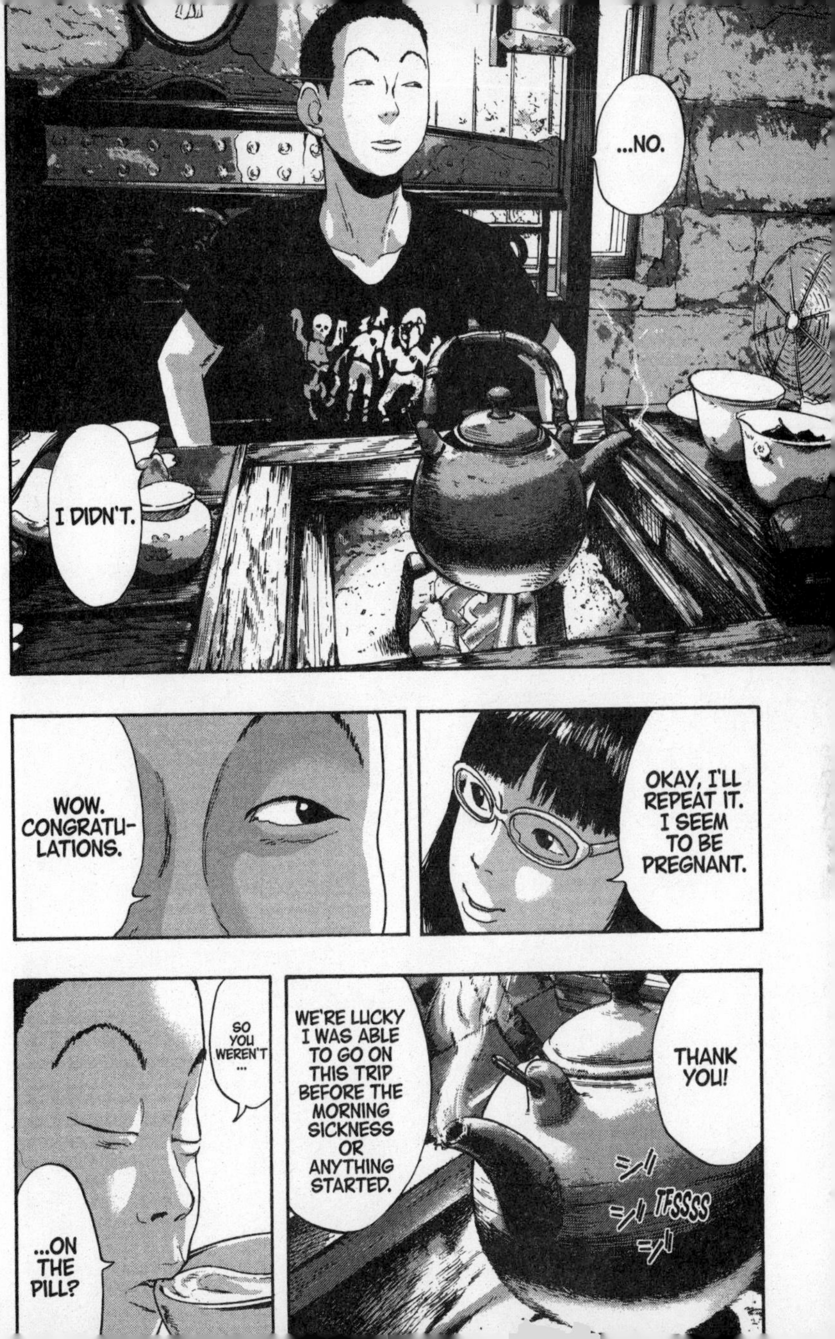
...NO.
I DIDN'T.
OKAY, I'LL REPEAT IT. I SEEM TO BE PREGNANT.
WOW. CONGRATULATIONS.
THANK YOU!
TFSSSS
WE'RE LUCKY I WAS ABLE TO GO ON THIS TRIP BEFORE THE MORNING SICKNESS OR ANYTHING STARTED.
SO YOU WEREN'T ...
...ON THE PILL?

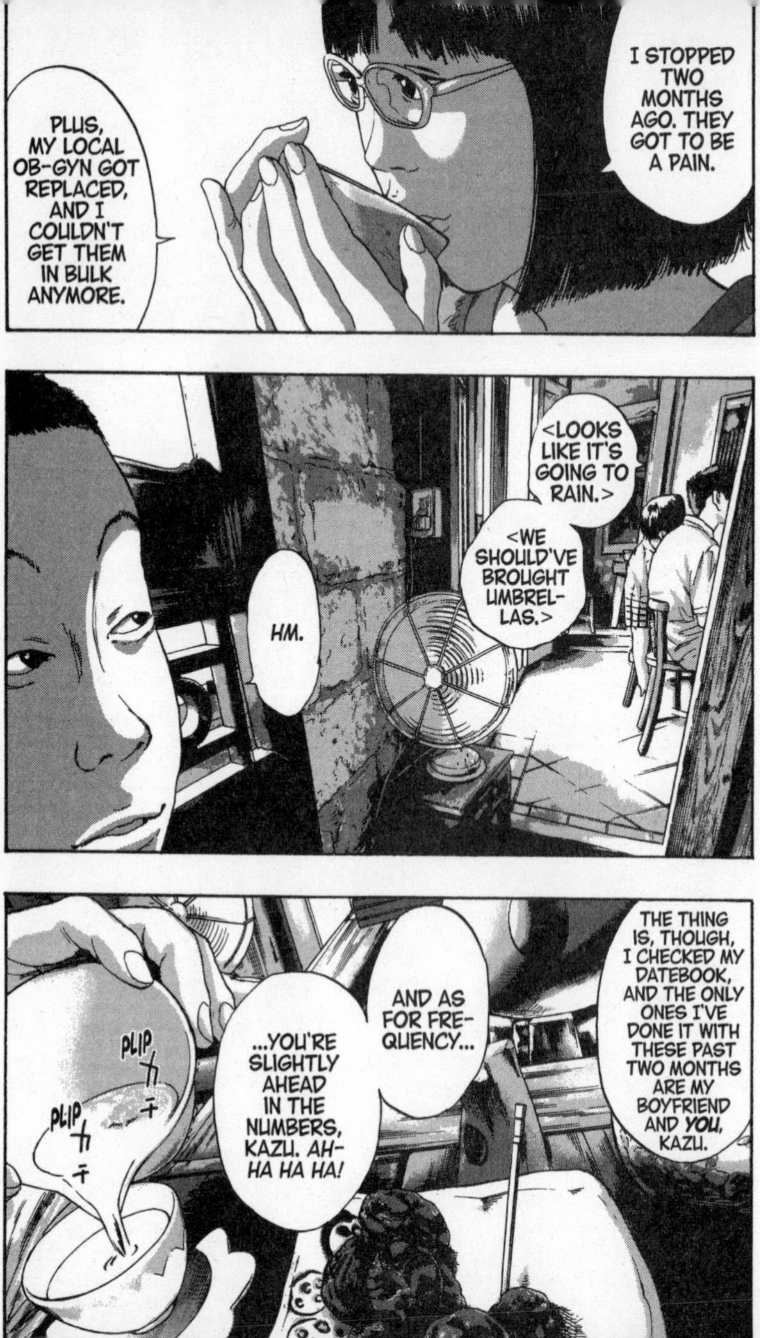
I STOPPED TWO MONTHS AGO. THEY GOT TO BE A PAIN.
PLUS, MY LOCAL OB-GYN GOT REPLACED, AND I COULDN'T GET THEM IN BULK ANYMORE.
<LOOKS LIKE IT'S GOING TO RAIN.>
<WE SHOULD'VE BROUGHT UMBREL-LAS.>
HM.
THE THING IS, THOUGH, I CHECKED MY DATEBOOK, AND THE ONLY ONES I'VE DONE IT WITH THESE PAST TWO MONTHS ARE MY BOYFRIEND AND *YOU*, KAZU.
AND AS FOR FRE-QUENCY...
...YOU'RE SLIGHTLY AHEAD IN THE NUMBERS, KAZU. AH-HA HA HA!
PLIP
PLIP

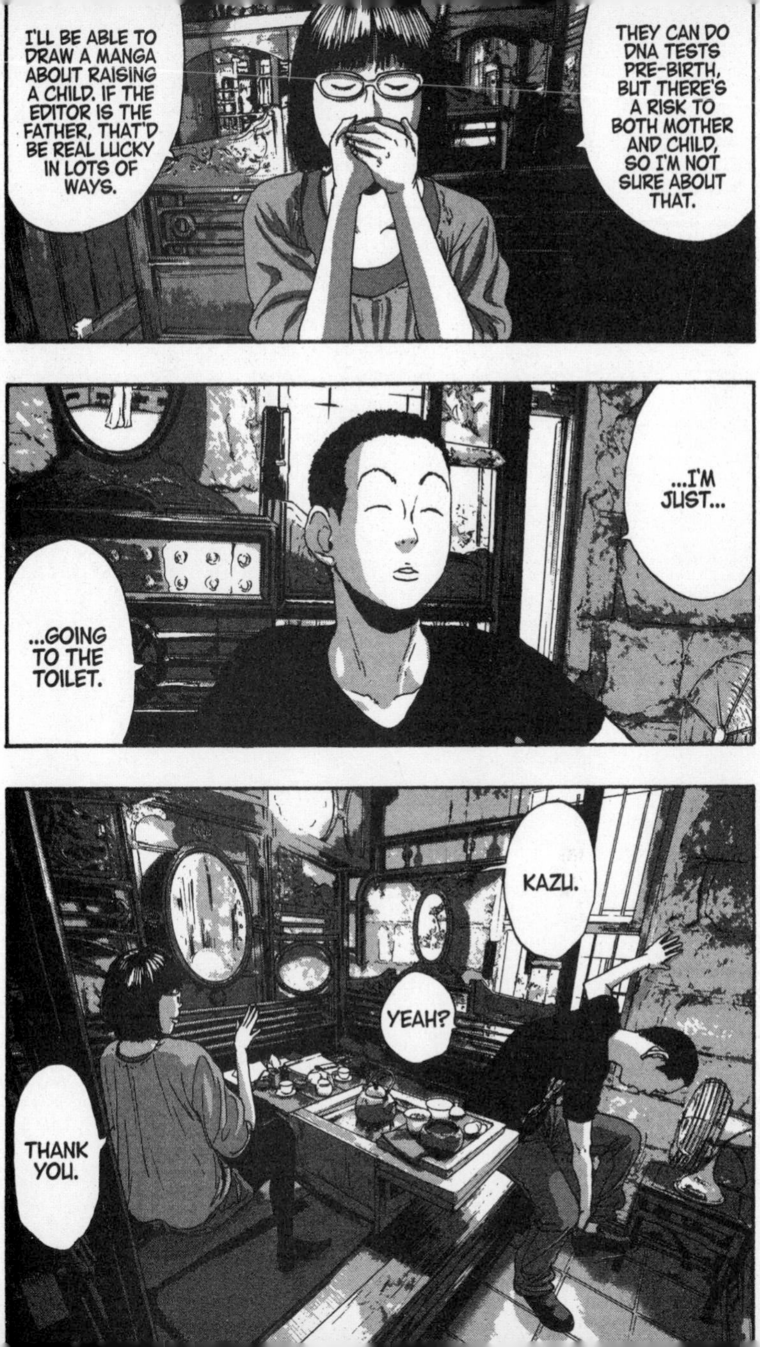

THEY CAN DO DNA TESTS PRE-BIRTH, BUT THERE'S A RISK TO BOTH MOTHER AND CHILD, SO I'M NOT SURE ABOUT THAT.
I'LL BE ABLE TO DRAW A MANGA ABOUT RAISING A CHILD. IF THE EDITOR IS THE FATHER, THAT'D BE REAL LUCKY IN LOTS OF WAYS.
...I'M JUST...
...GOING TO THE TOILET.
KAZU.
YEAH?
THANK YOU.

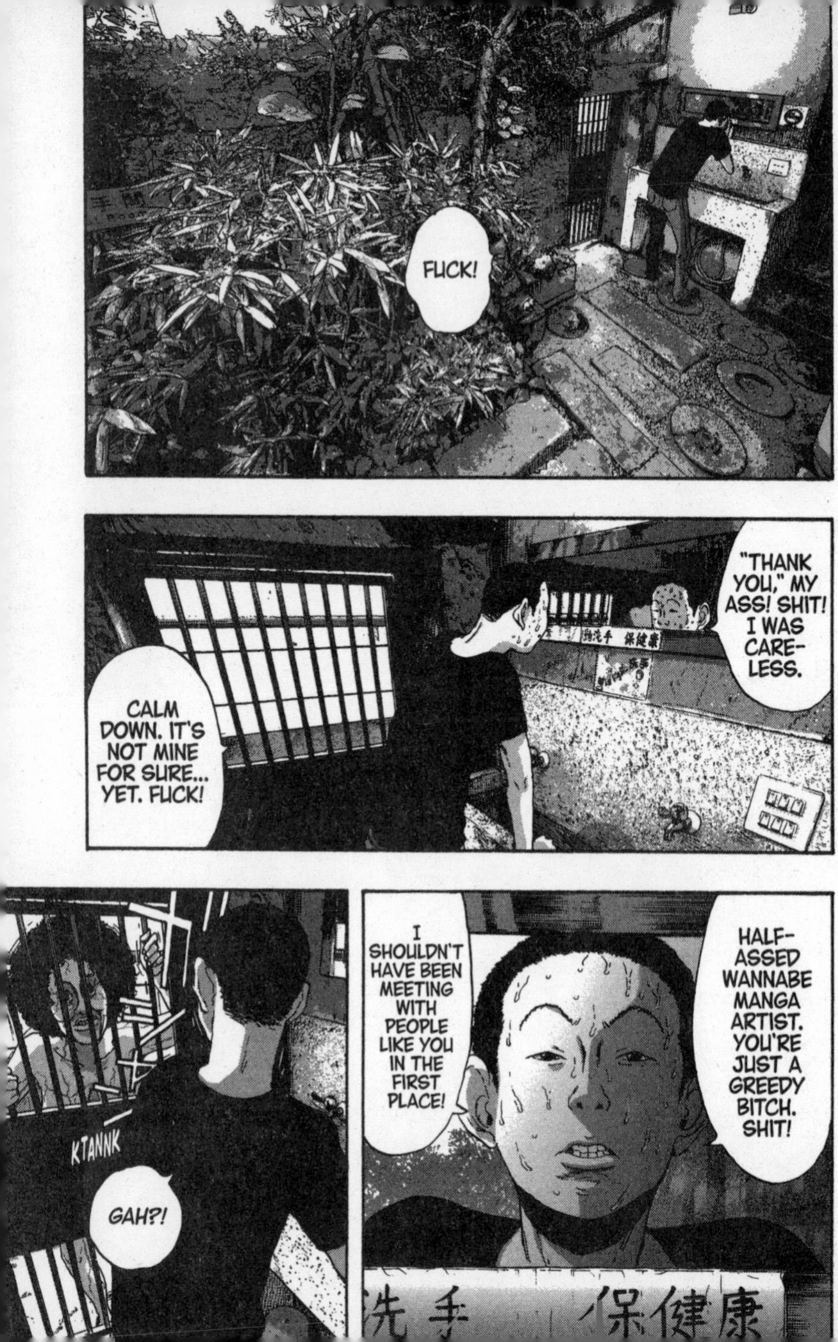
FUCK!
"THANK YOU," MY ASS! SHIT! I WAS CARE-LESS.
CALM DOWN. IT'S NOT MINE FOR SURE... YET. FUCK!
HALF-ASSED WANNABE MANGA ARTIST. YOU'RE JUST A GREEDY BITCH. SHIT!
I SHOULDN'T HAVE BEEN MEETING WITH PEOPLE LIKE YOU IN THE FIRST PLACE!
洗手 保健康
KTANNK
GAH?!

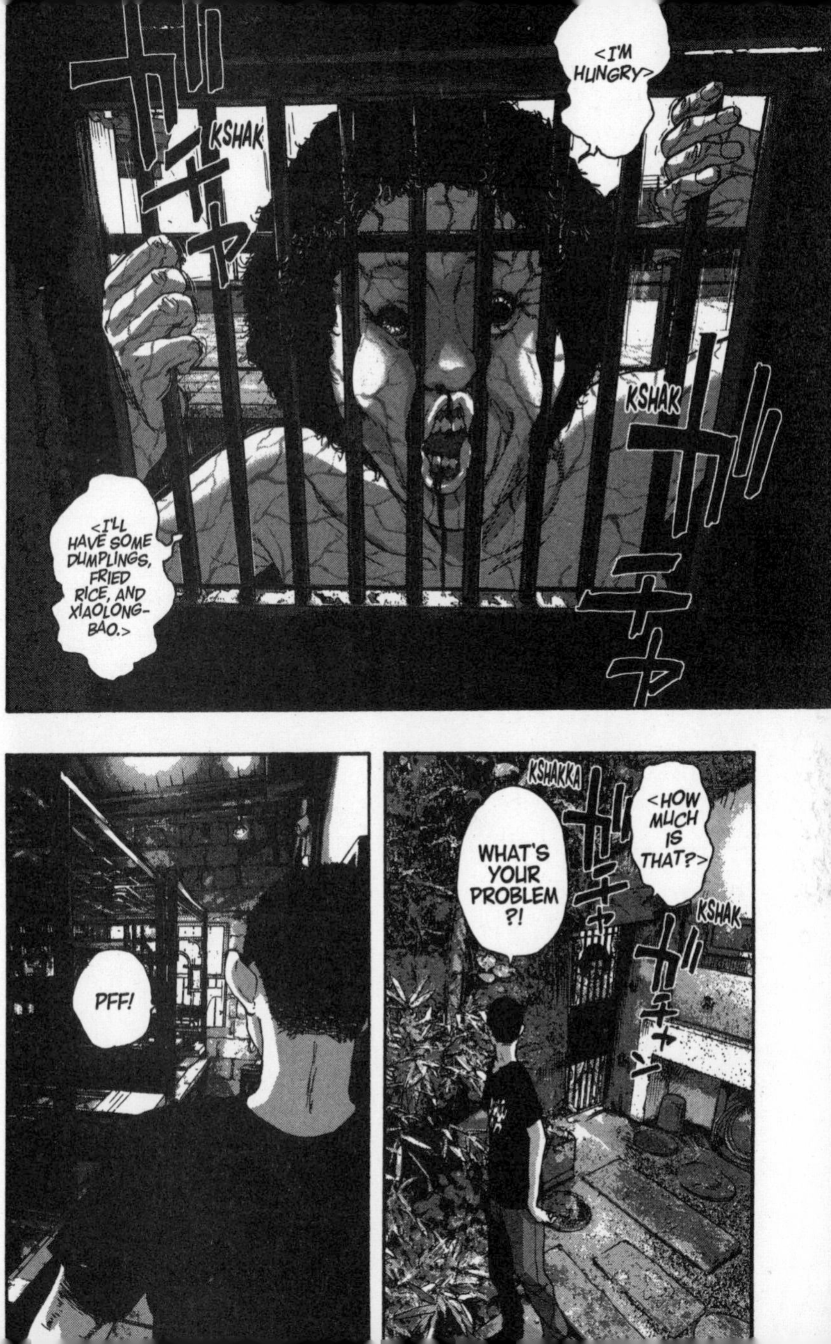
<I'M HUNGRY>
KSHAK
KSHAK
<I'LL HAVE SOME DUMPLINGS, FRIED RICE, AND XIAOLONG-BAO.>
<HOW MUCH IS THAT?>
KSHAKKA
WHAT'S YOUR PROBLEM ?!
KSHAK
PFF!

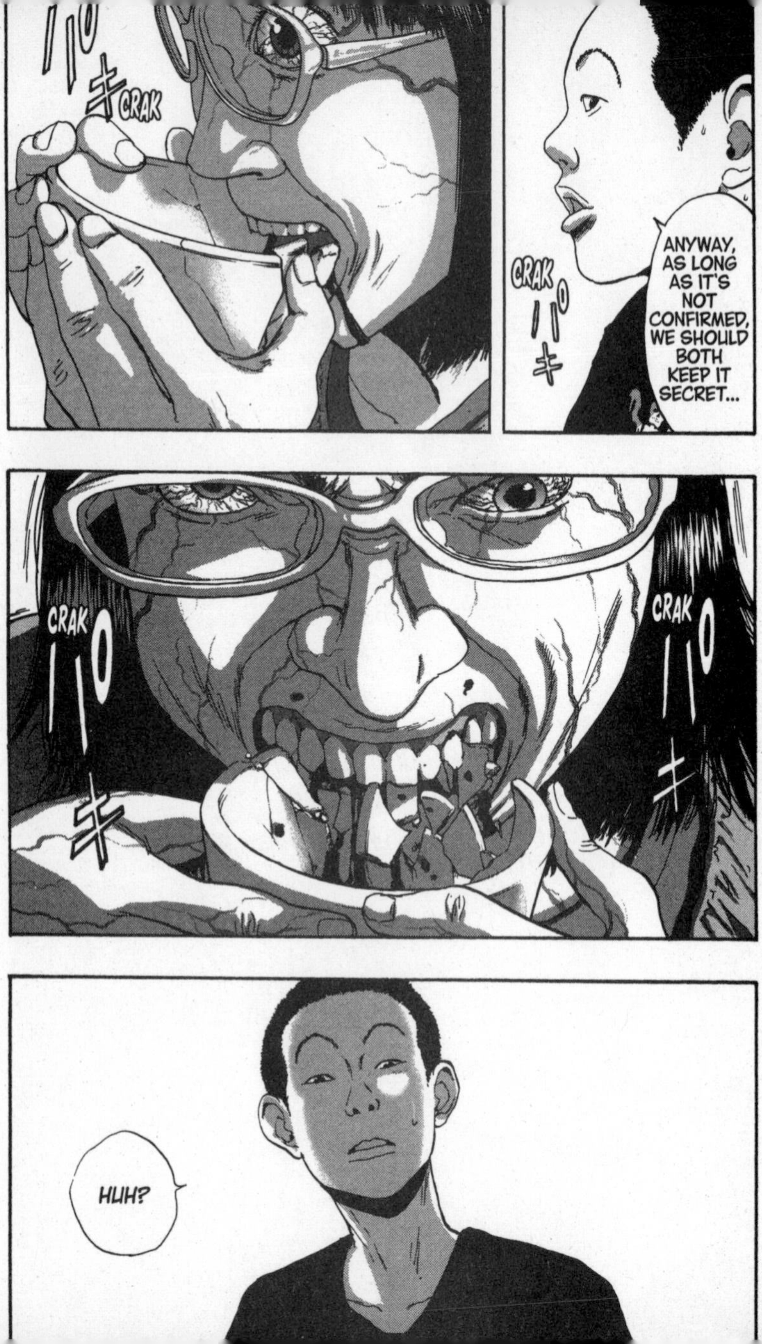
CRAK
ANYWAY, AS LONG AS IT'S NOT CONFIRMED, WE SHOULD BOTH KEEP IT SECRET...
CRAK
CRAK
CRAK
HUH?

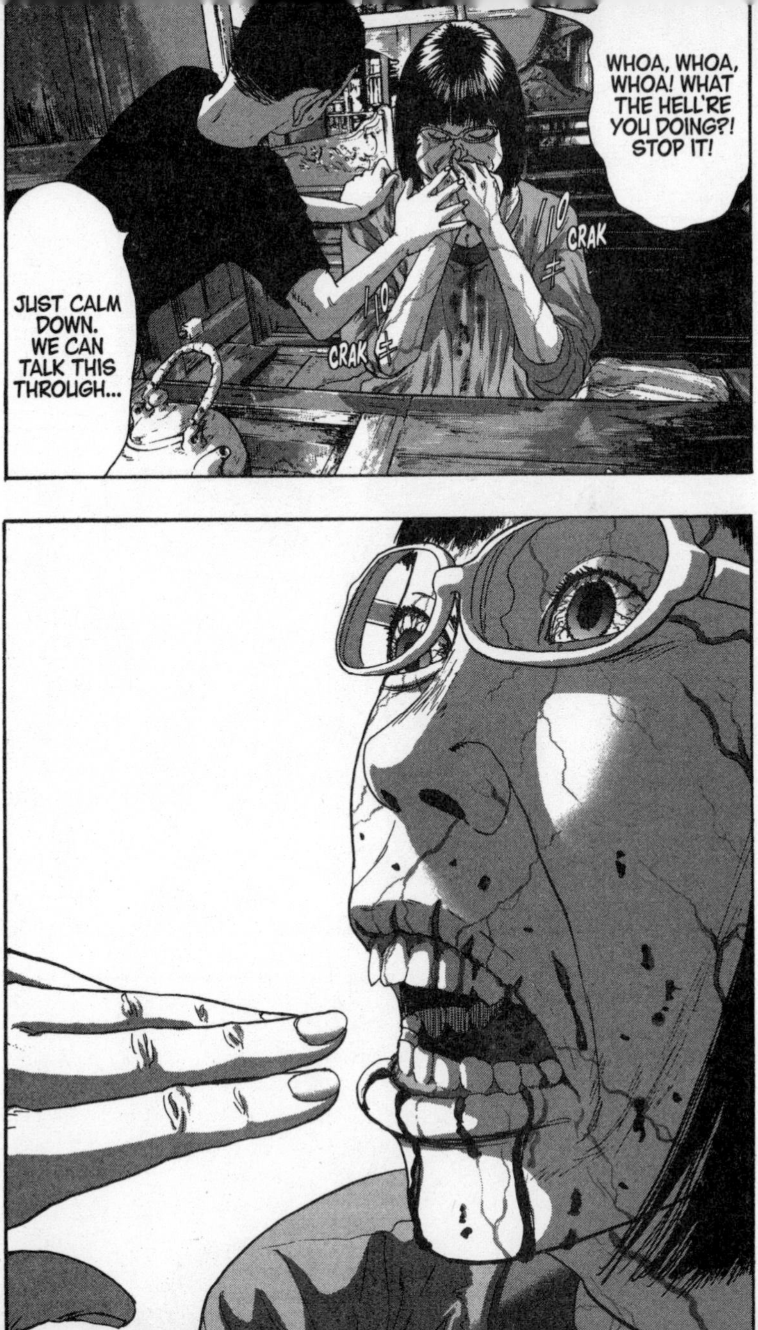
WHOA, WHOA, WHOA! WHAT THE HELL'RE YOU DOING?! STOP IT!
CRAK
CRAK
JUST CALM DOWN. WE CAN TALK THIS THROUGH...

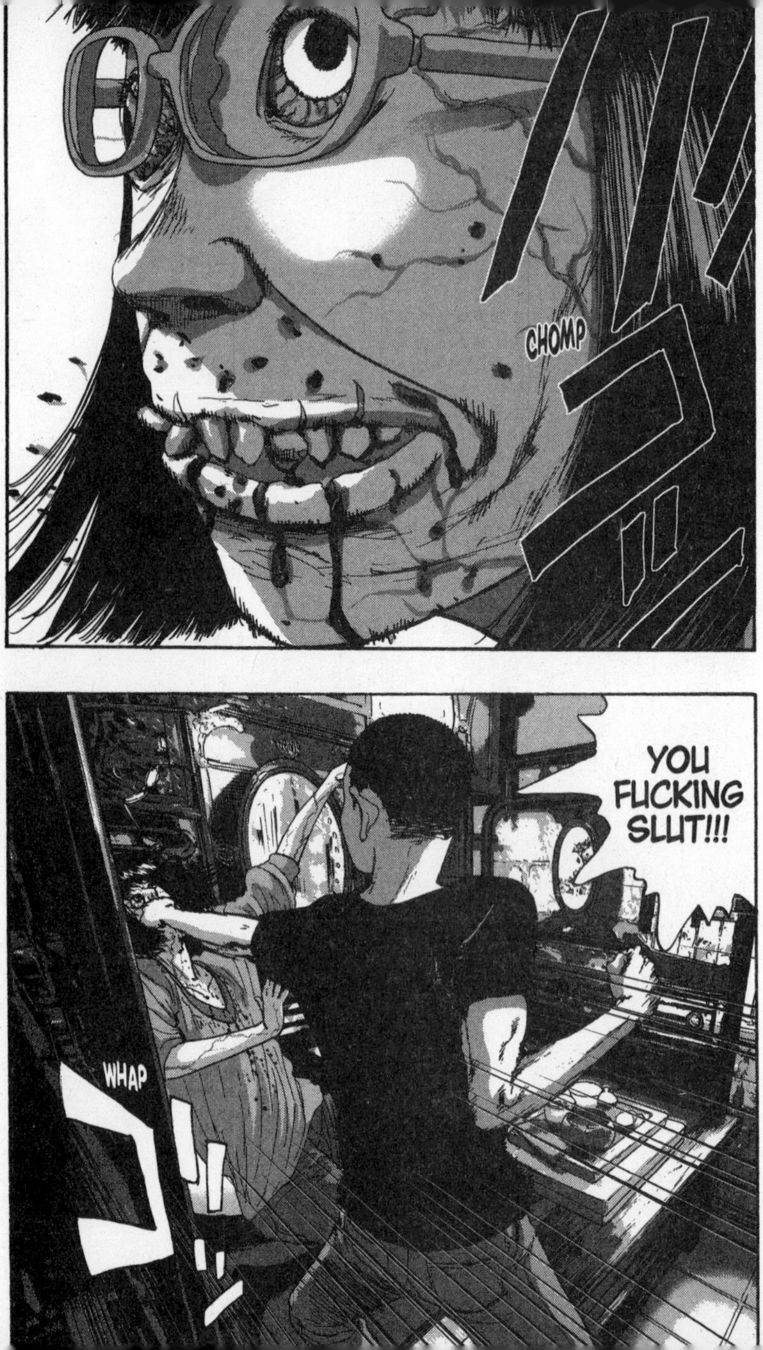
CHOMP
YOU FUCKING SLUT!!!
WHAP

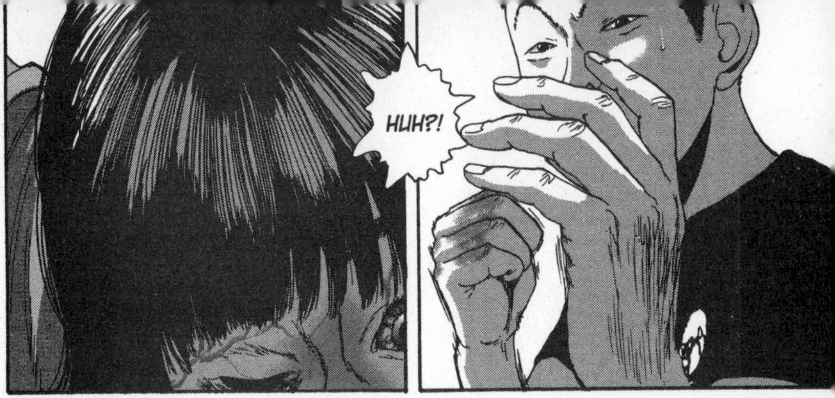
HUH?!

18

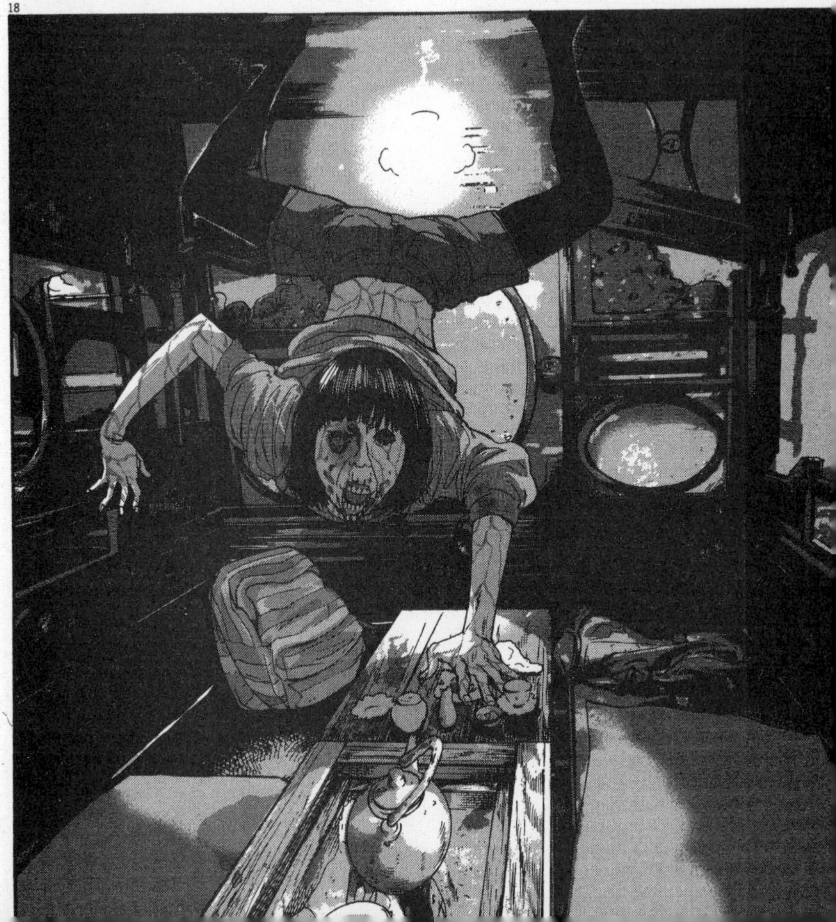

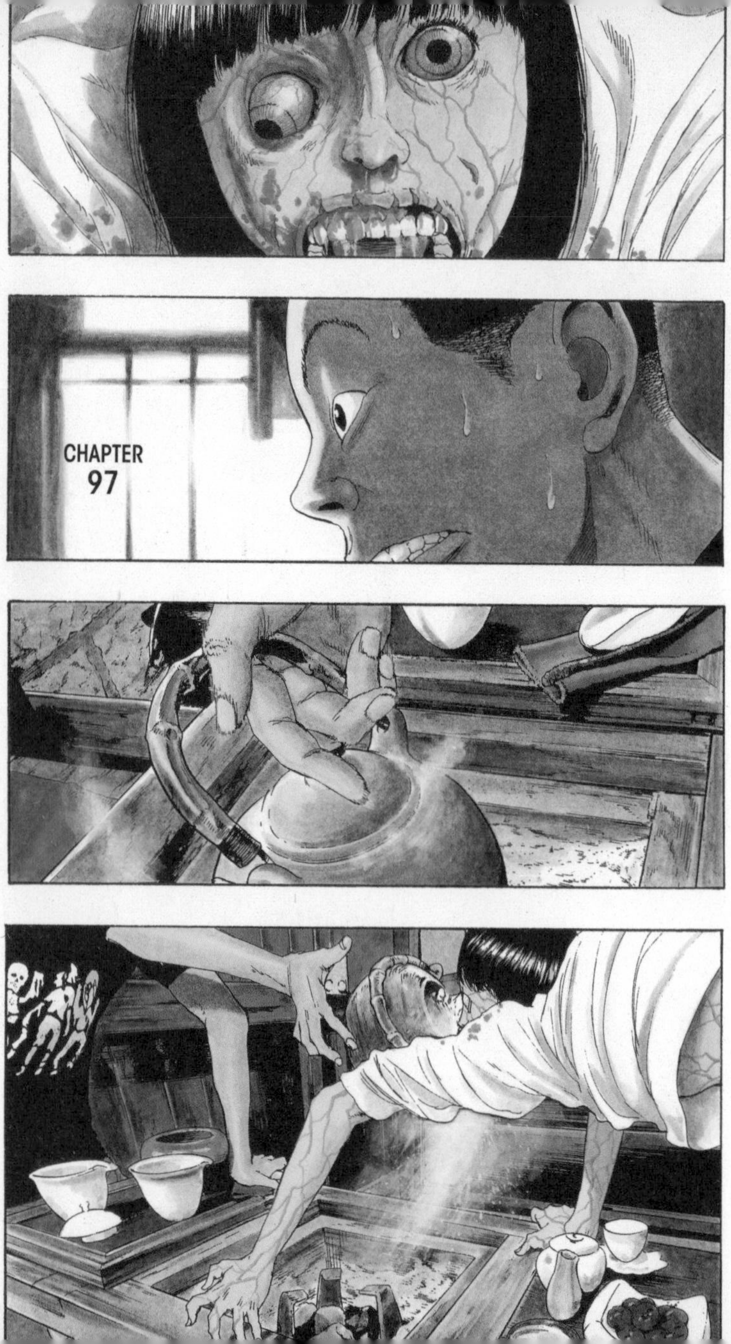
CHAPTER
97

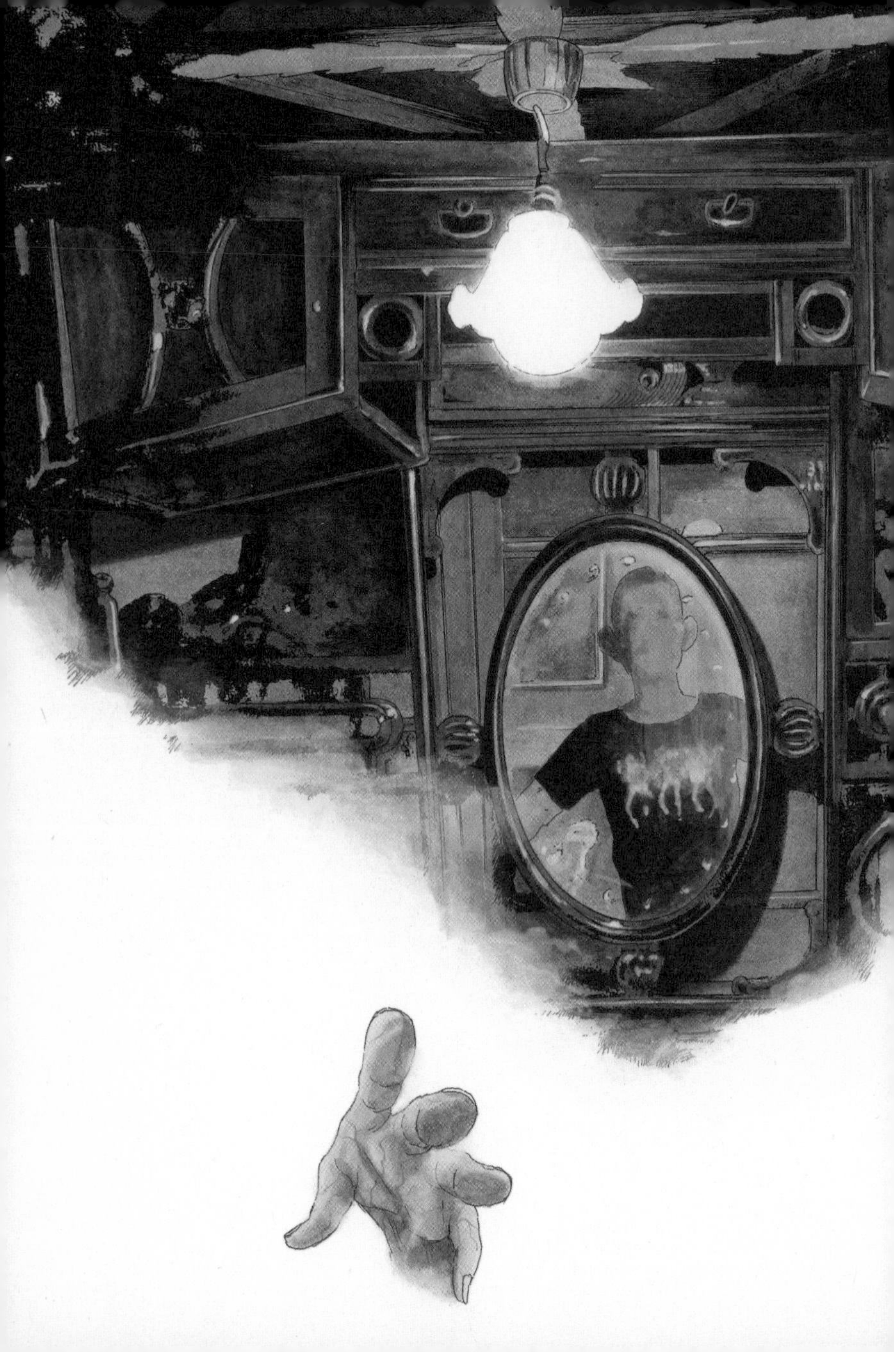

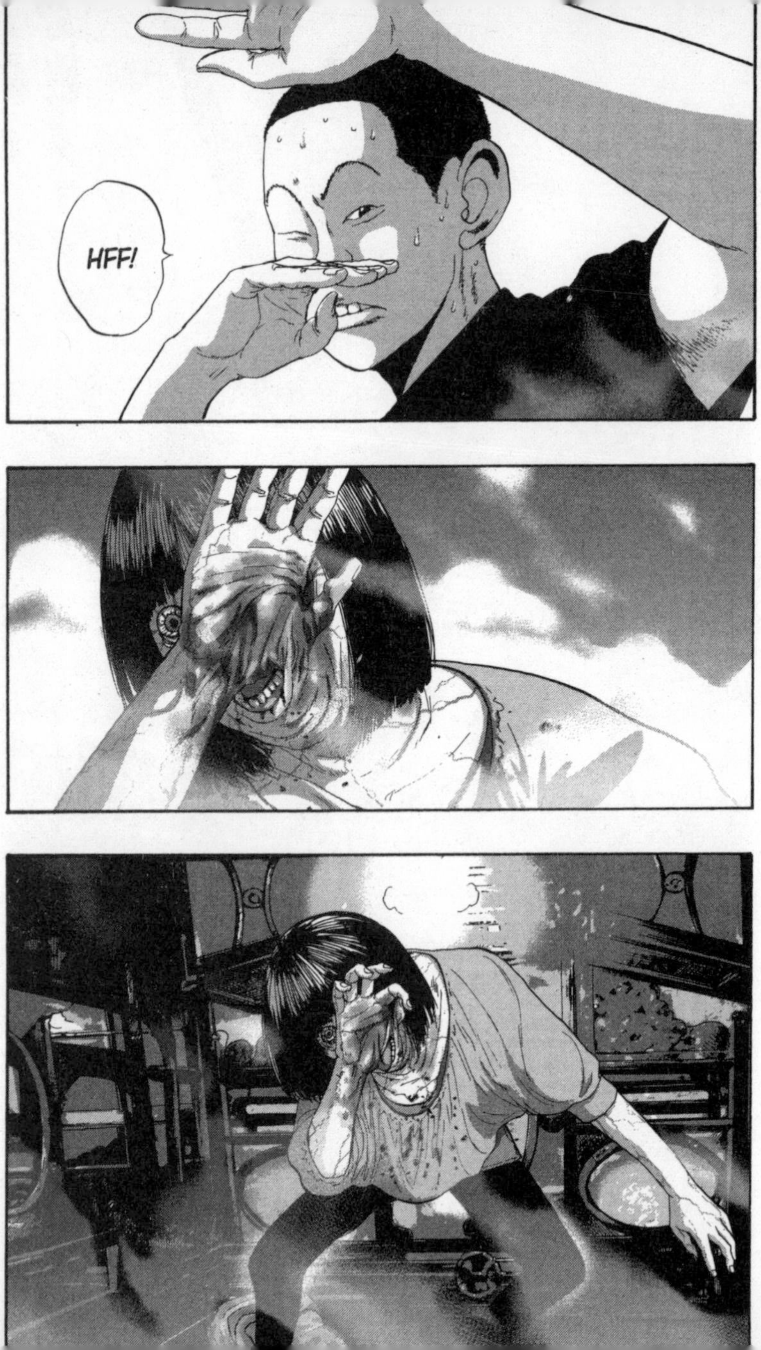
HFF!

FWSH

GRAB

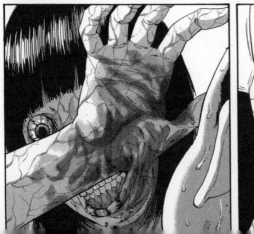

UAAH!

SQUEEZE

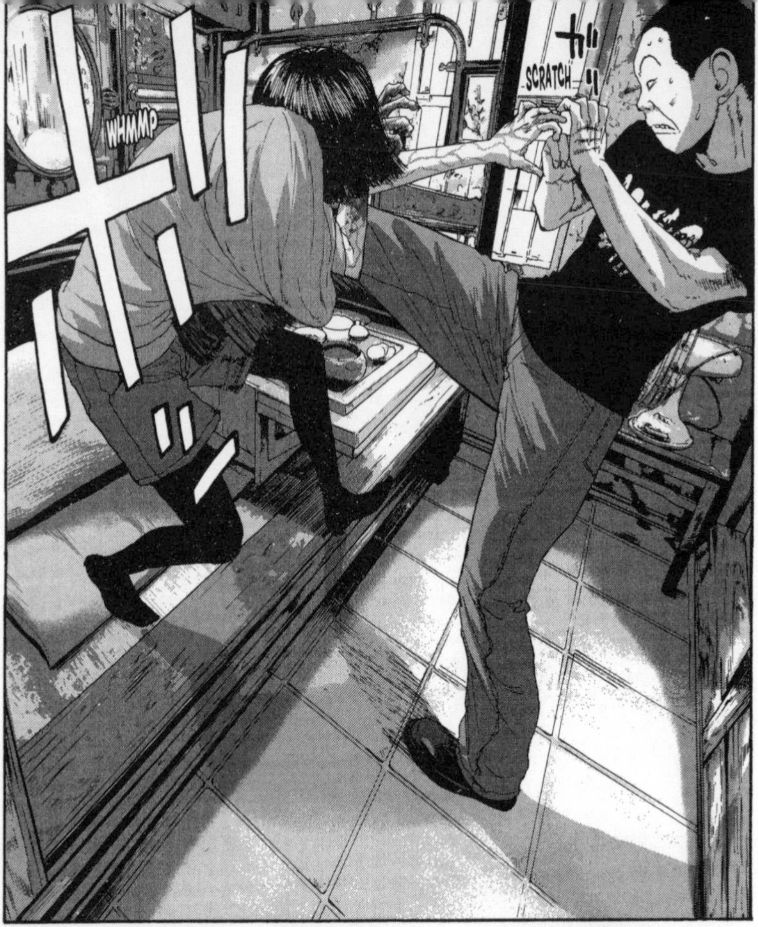
SCRATCH
WHMMP
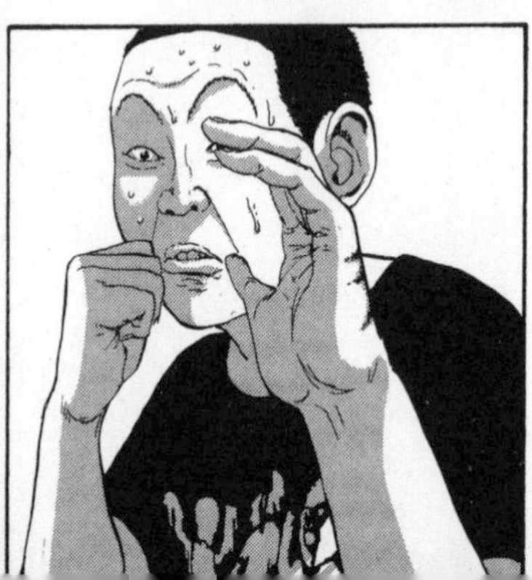
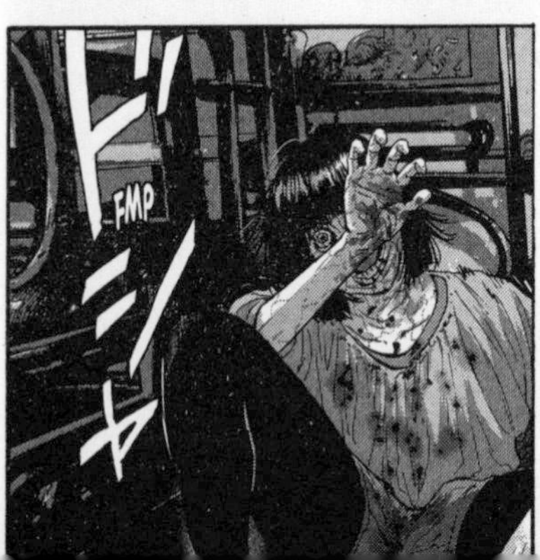
FMP

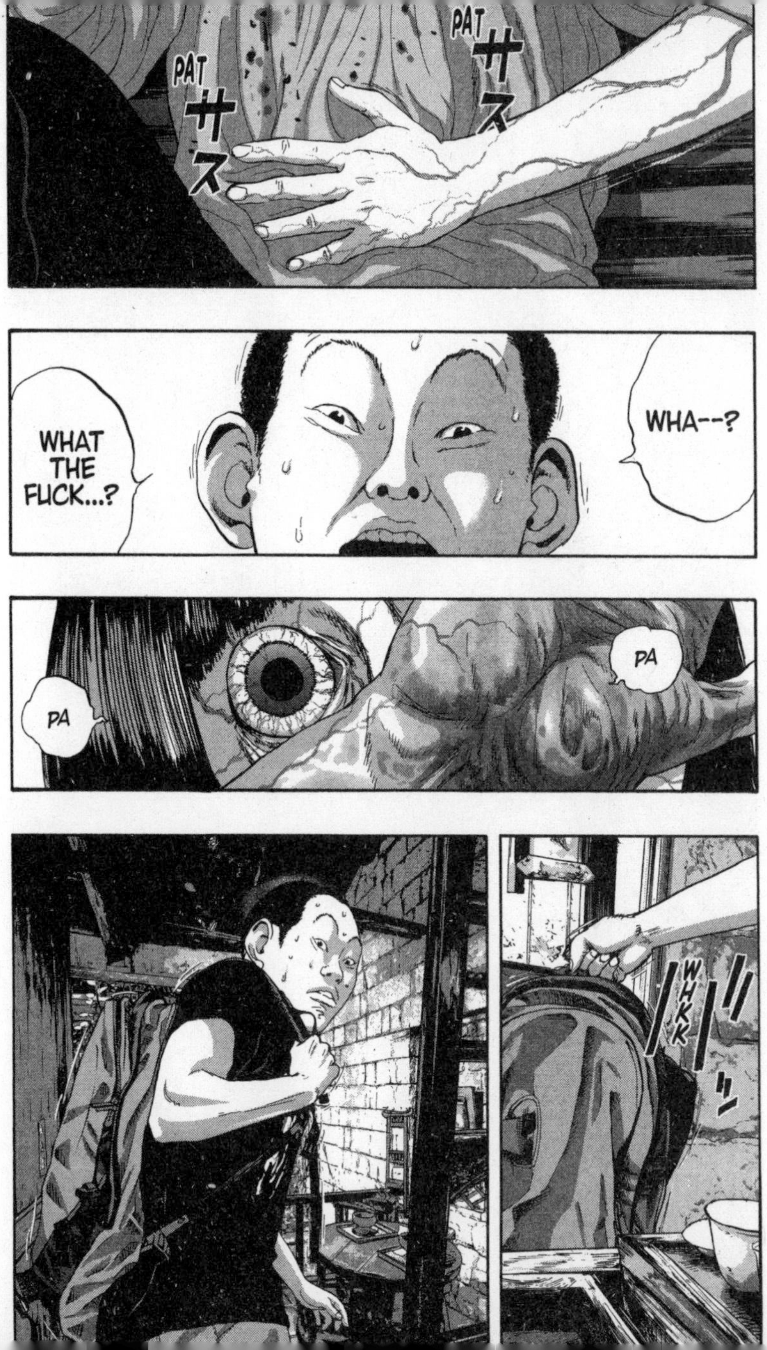
PAT
サス
PAT
サス
WHA--?
WHAT THE FUCK...?
PA
PA
WHKK
ッ

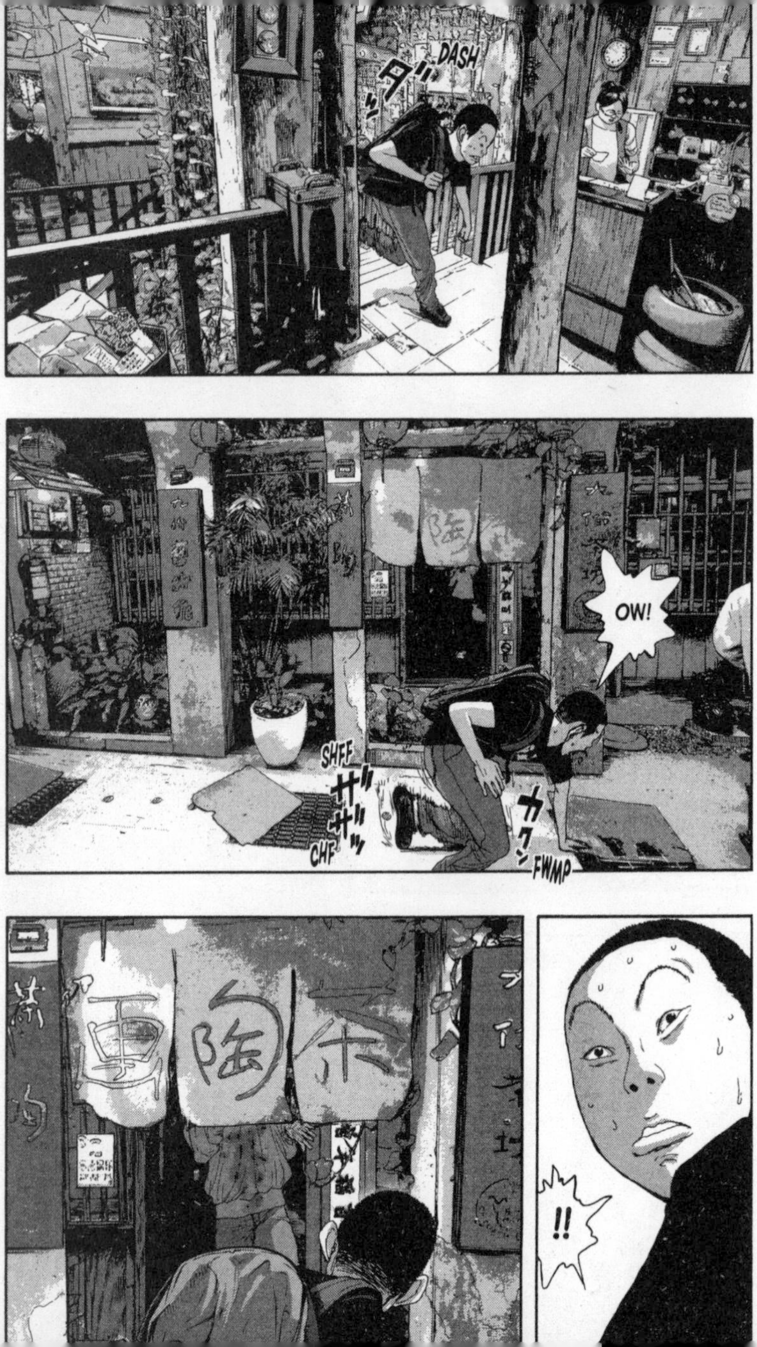
DASH
ダッ
OW!
カクン
FWMP
SHFF
ザザッ
CHF
!!

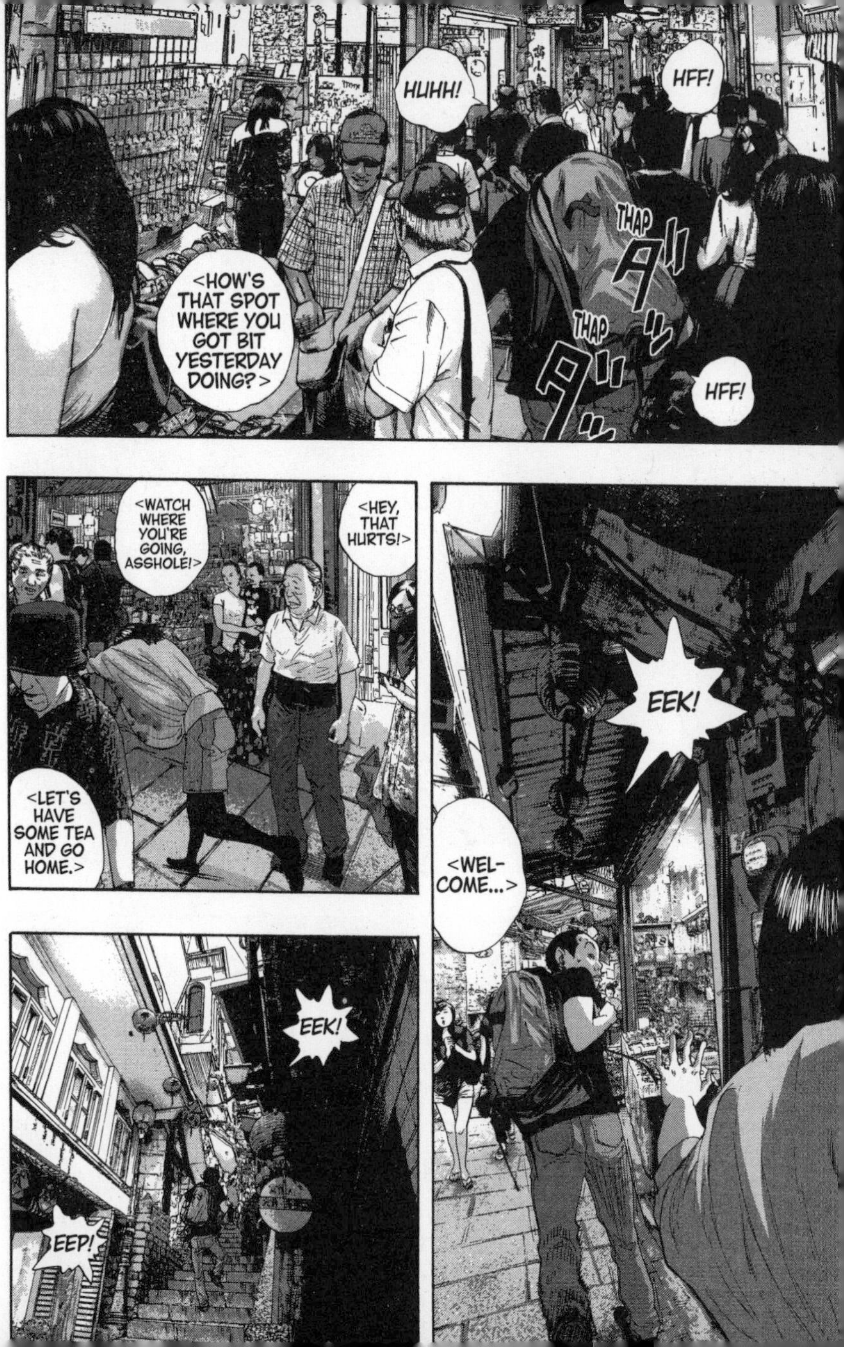
HFF!
HUHH!
THAP
THAP
HFF!
<HOW'S THAT SPOT WHERE YOU GOT BIT YESTERDAY DOING?>
EEK!
<WEL-COME...>
<HEY, THAT HURTS!>
<WATCH WHERE YOU'RE GOING, ASSHOLE!>
<LET'S HAVE SOME TEA AND GO HOME.>
EEK!
EEP!

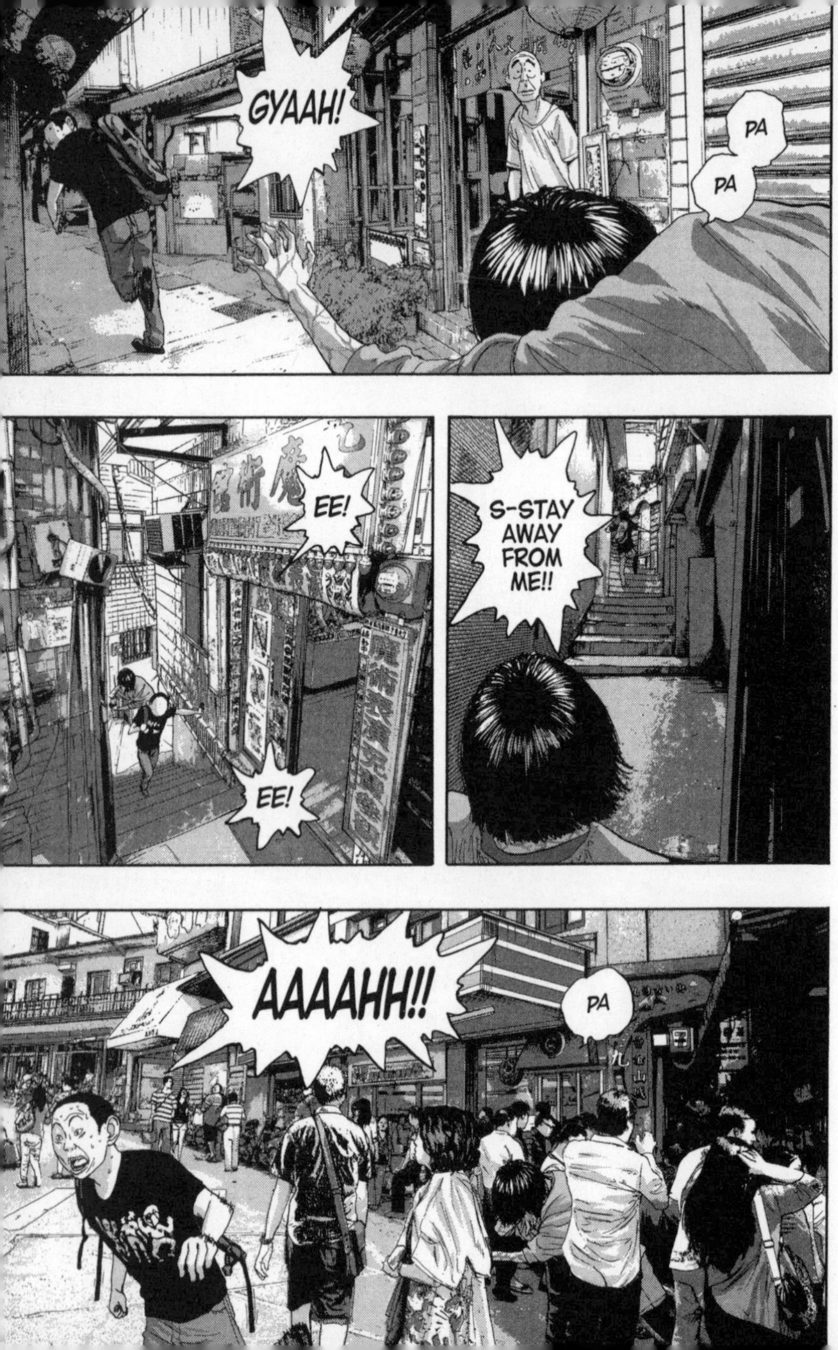
PA
PA
GYAAH!
S-STAY AWAY FROM ME!!
EE!
EE!
PA
AAAAHH!!

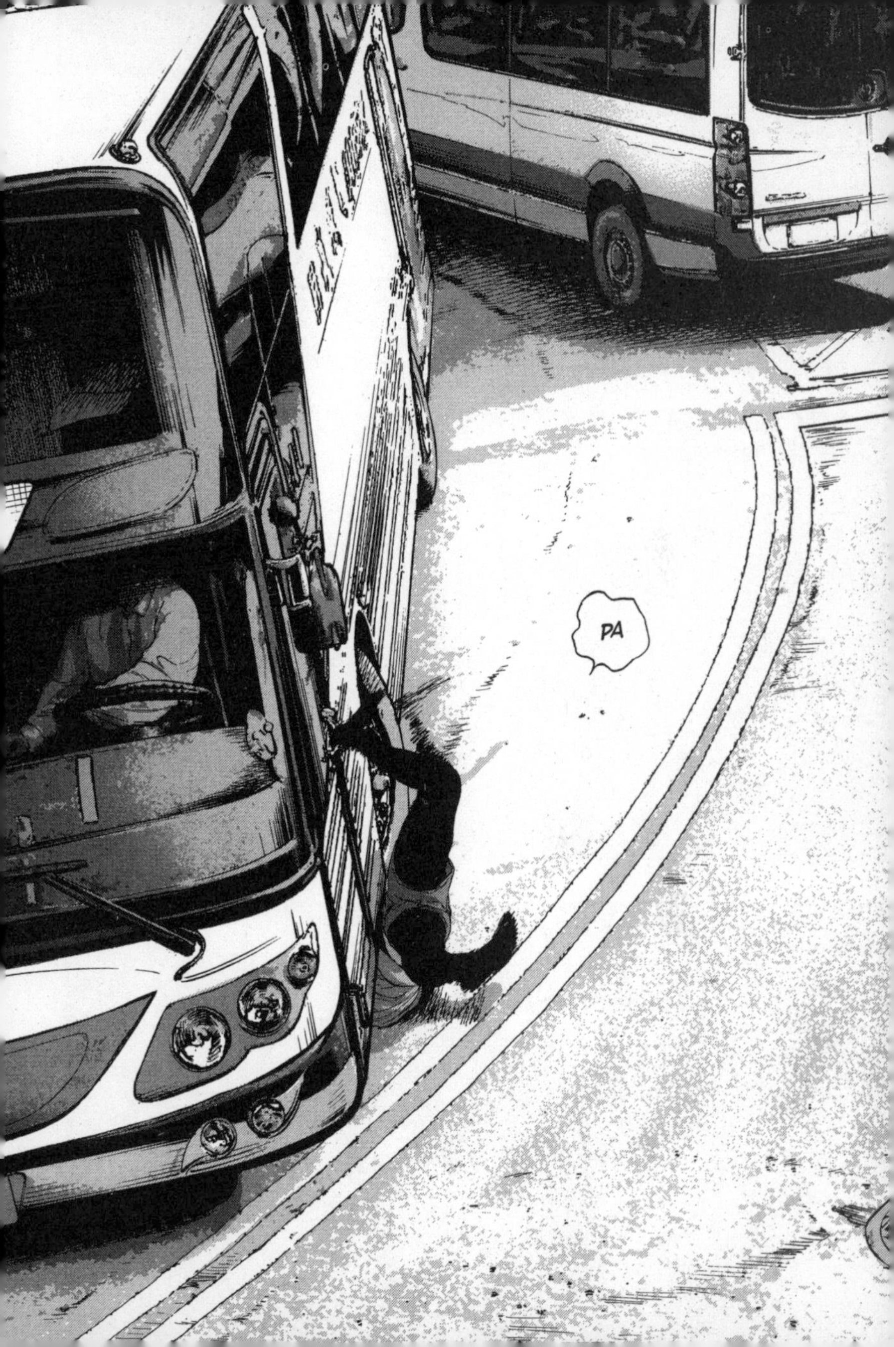
PA

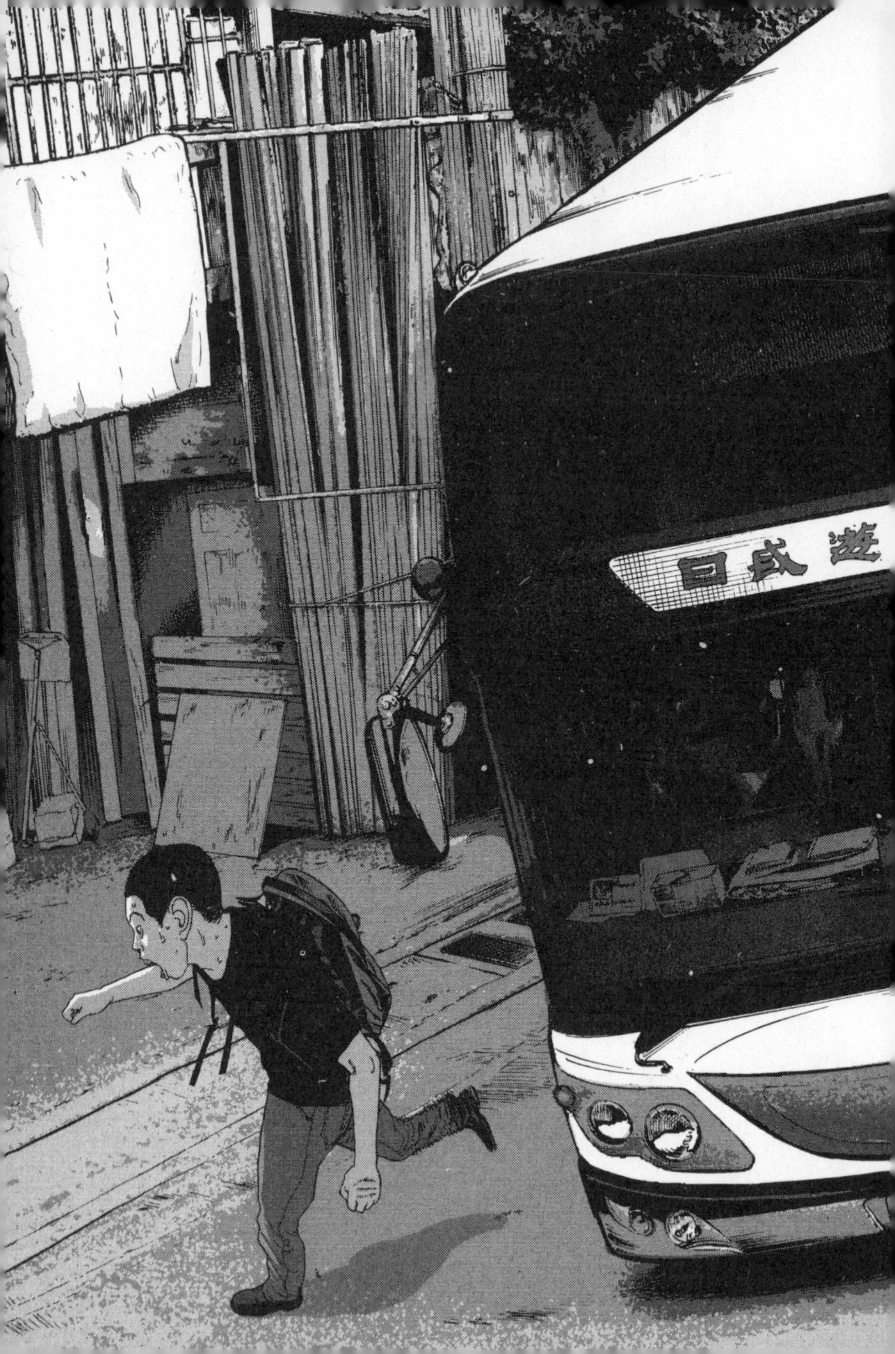

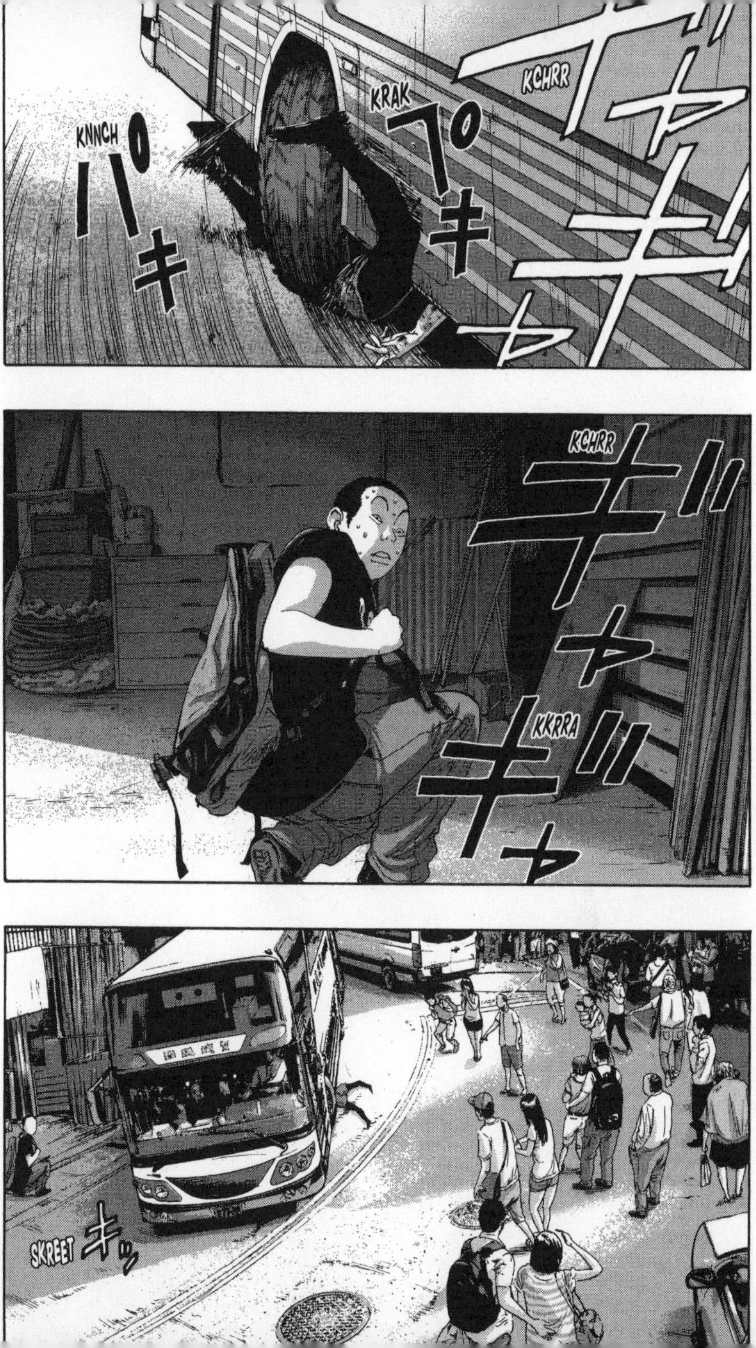
KCHRR
KRAK
ペキ
KNNCH
パキ
KCHRR
KKRRA
SKREET
キッ

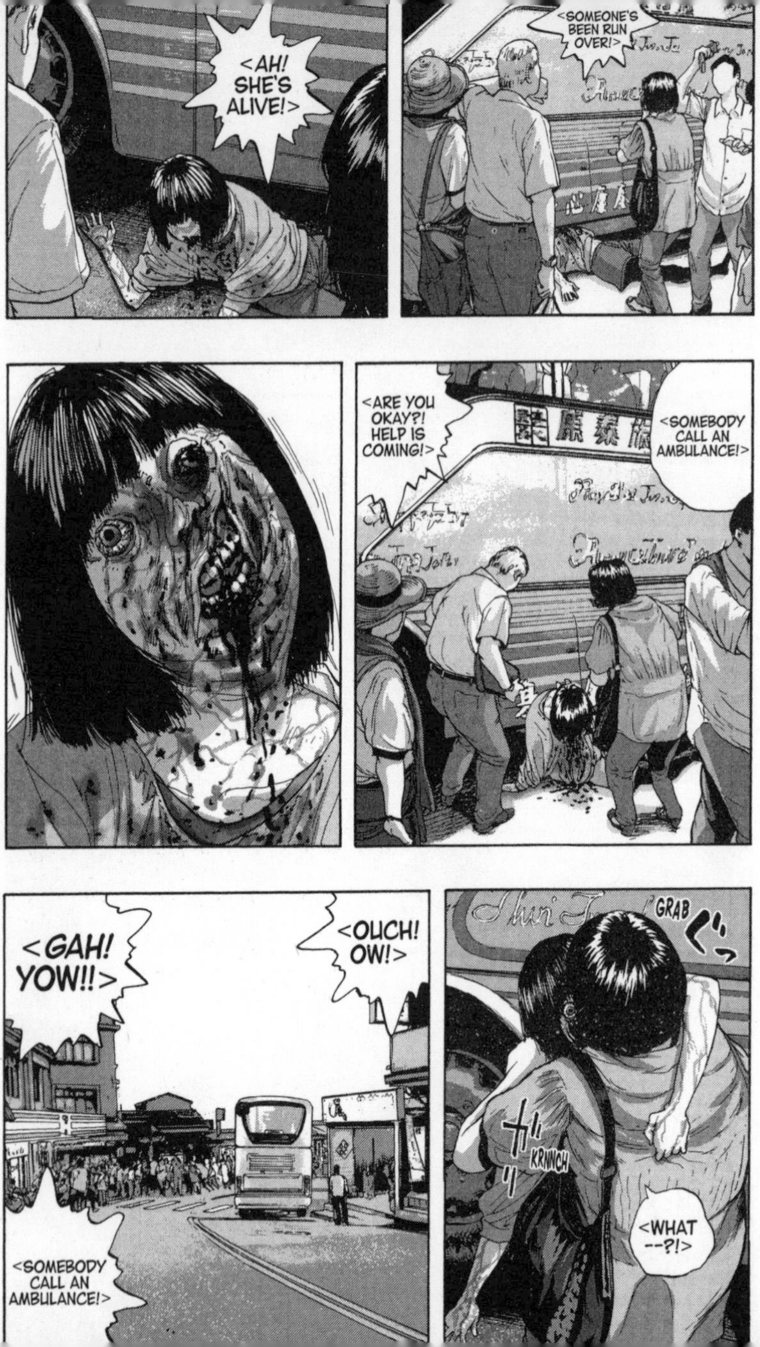

<SOMEONE'S BEEN RUN OVER!>
<AH! SHE'S ALIVE!>
<SOMEBODY CALL AN AMBULANCE!>
<ARE YOU OKAY?! HELP IS COMING!>
GRAB
<WHAT --?!>
KRNNCH
<OUCH! OW!>
<GAH! YOW!!>
<SOMEBODY CALL AN AMBULANCE!>

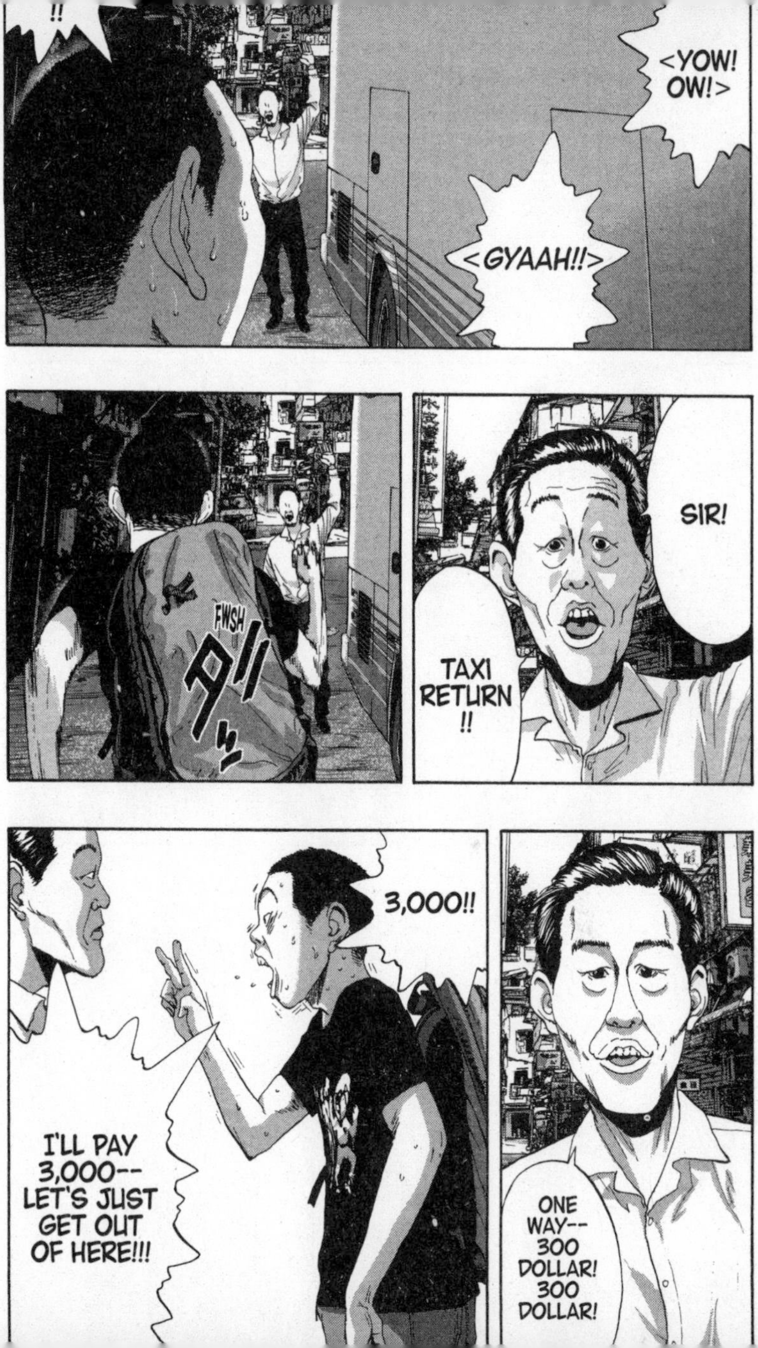
<YOW! OW!>
<GYAAH!!>
!!
SIR!
TAXI RETURN !!
FWSH
ダッ
ONE WAY-- 300 DOLLAR! 300 DOLLAR!
3,000!!
I'LL PAY 3,000-- LET'S JUST GET OUT OF HERE!!!

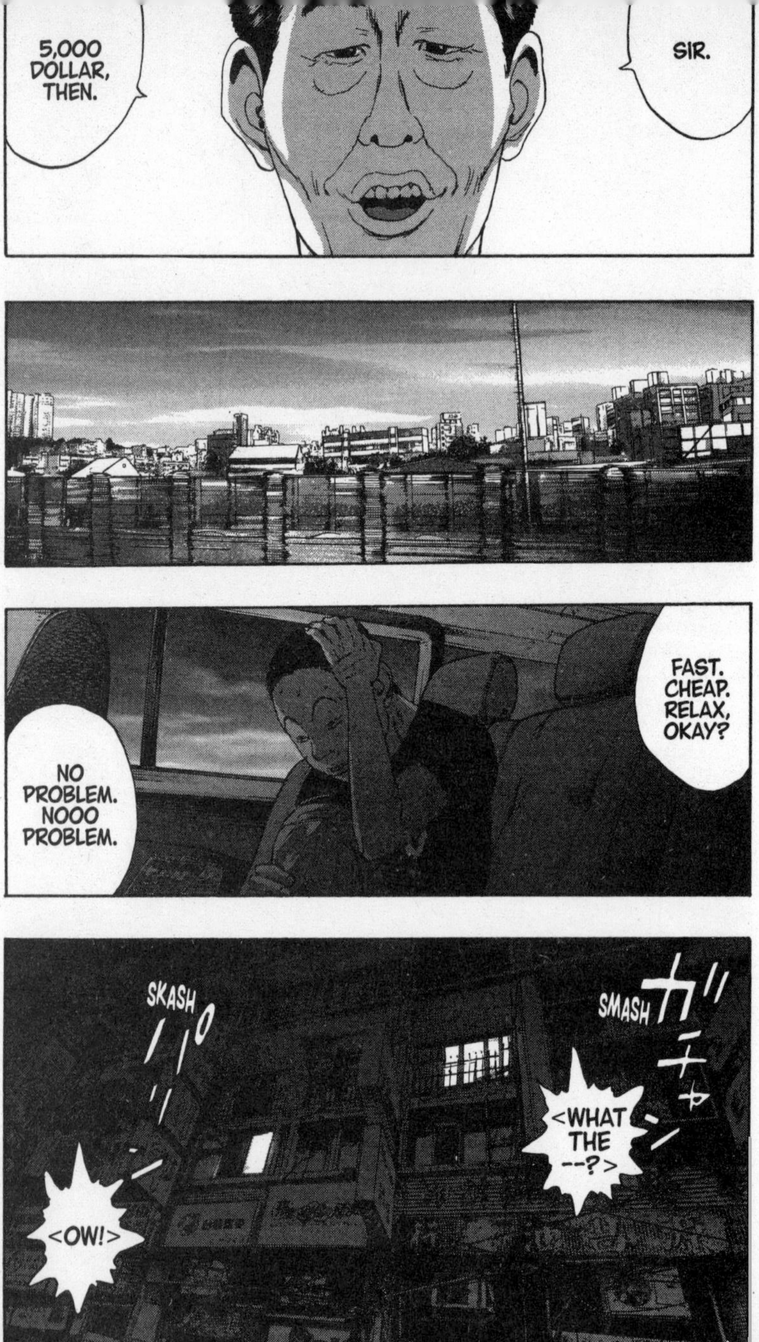
SIR.
5,000 DOLLAR, THEN.
FAST. CHEAP. RELAX, OKAY?
NO PROBLEM. NOOO PROBLEM.
SMASH
<WHAT THE --?>
SKASH
<OW!>

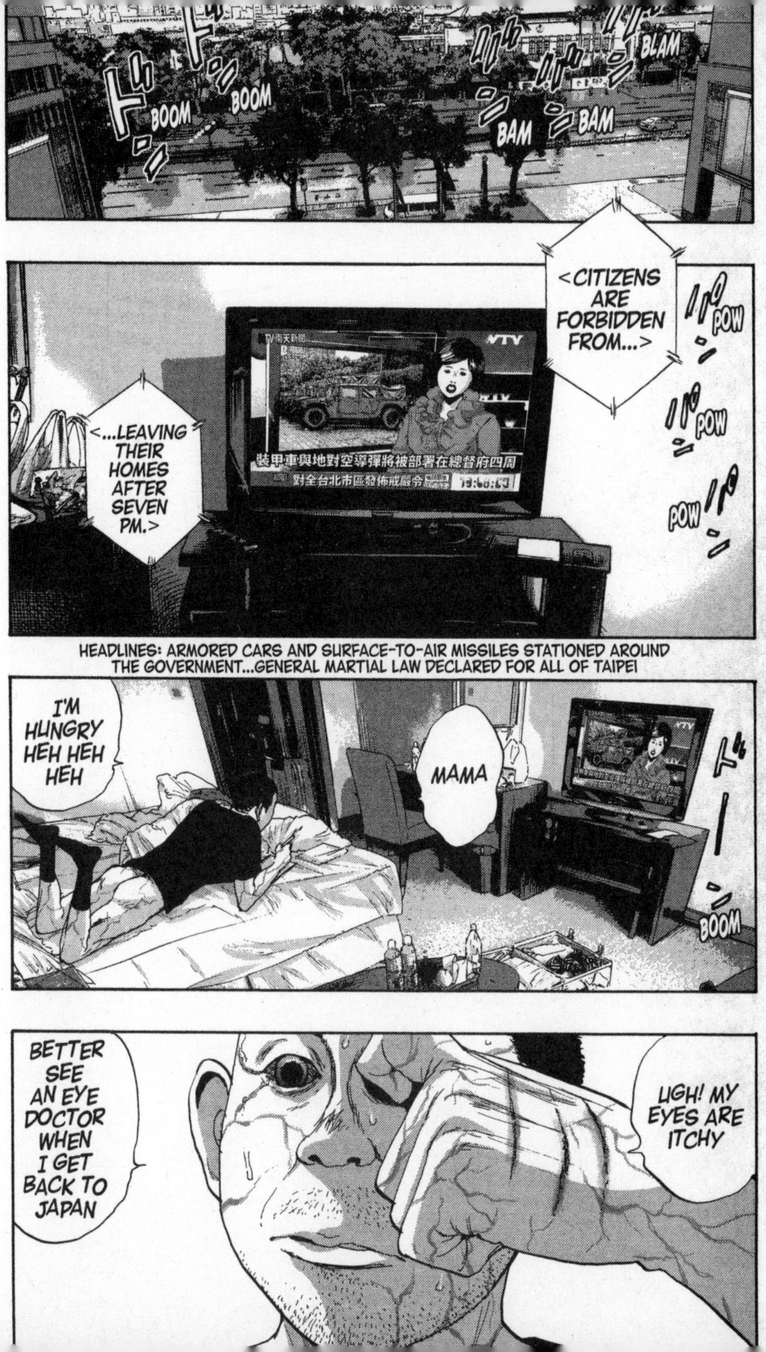
BLAM
BAM
BAM
BOOM
BOOM
<CITIZENS ARE FORBIDDEN FROM...>
POW
POW
POW
裝甲車與地對空導彈將被部署在總督府四周
對全台北市區發佈戒嚴令
<...LEAVING THEIR HOMES AFTER SEVEN PM.>
HEADLINES: ARMORED CARS AND SURFACE-TO-AIR MISSILES STATIONED AROUND THE GOVERNMENT...GENERAL MARTIAL LAW DECLARED FOR ALL OF TAIPEI
BOOM
MAMA
I'M HUNGRY HEH HEH HEH
UGH! MY EYES ARE ITCHY
BETTER SEE AN EYE DOCTOR WHEN I GET BACK TO JAPAN

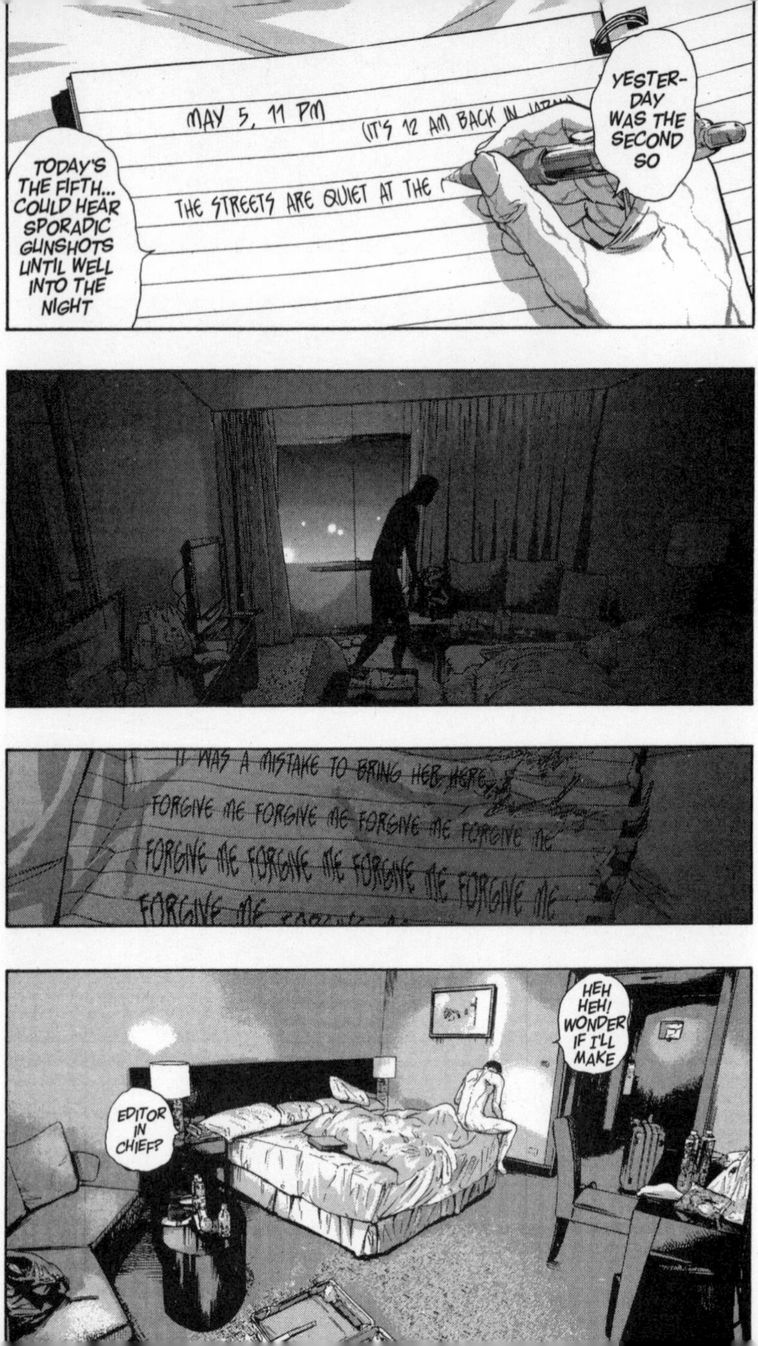
YESTER-DAY WAS THE SECOND SO
MAY 5, 11 PM
(IT'S 12 AM BACK IN
THE STREETS ARE QUIET AT THE
TODAY'S THE FIFTH... COULD HEAR SPORADIC GUNSHOTS UNTIL WELL INTO THE NIGHT
IT WAS A MISTAKE TO BRING HER HERE.
FORGIVE ME FORGIVE ME FORGIVE ME FORGIVE ME
FORGIVE ME FORGIVE ME FORGIVE ME FORGIVE ME
FORGIVE ME
HEH HEH! WONDER IF I'LL MAKE
EDITOR IN CHIEF?

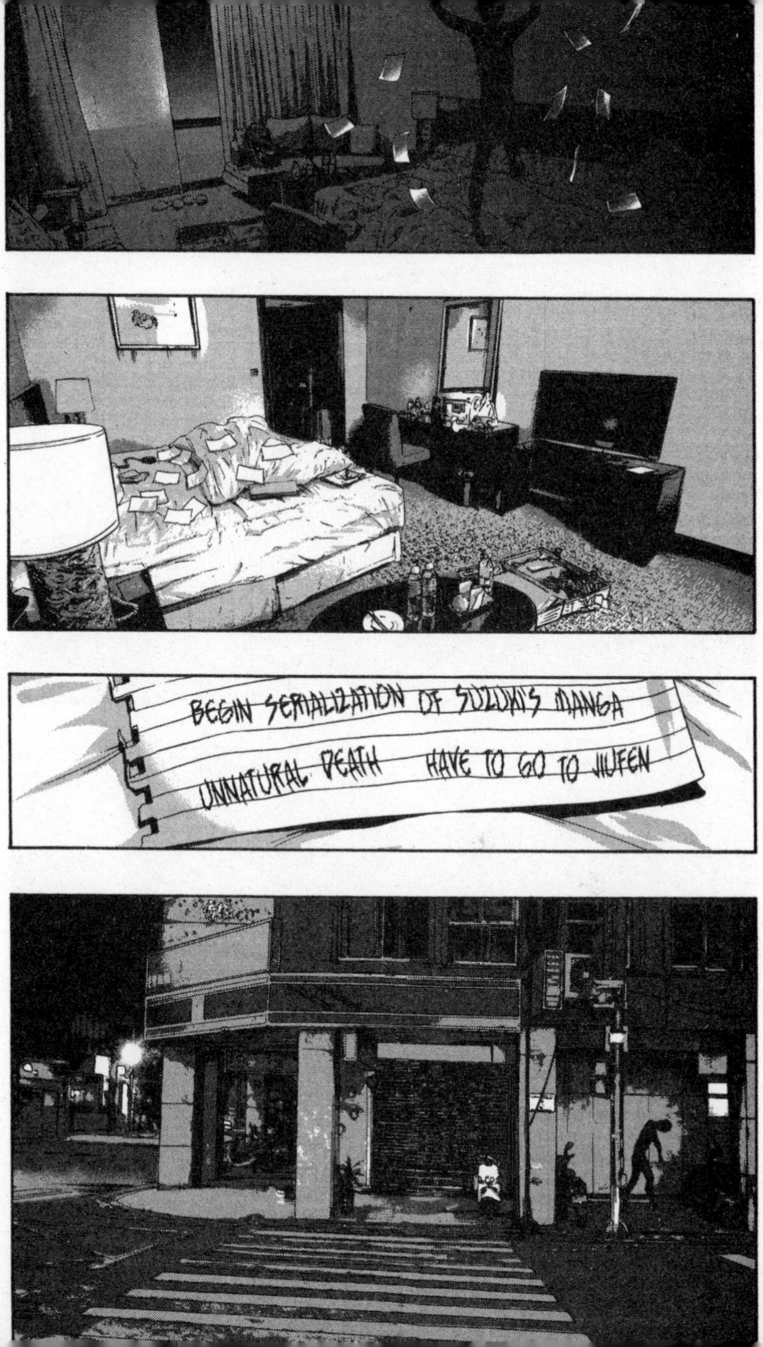
BEGIN SERIALIZATION OF SUZUKI'S MANGA
UNNATURAL DEATH
HAVE TO GO TO JIUFEN

I AM
A HERO

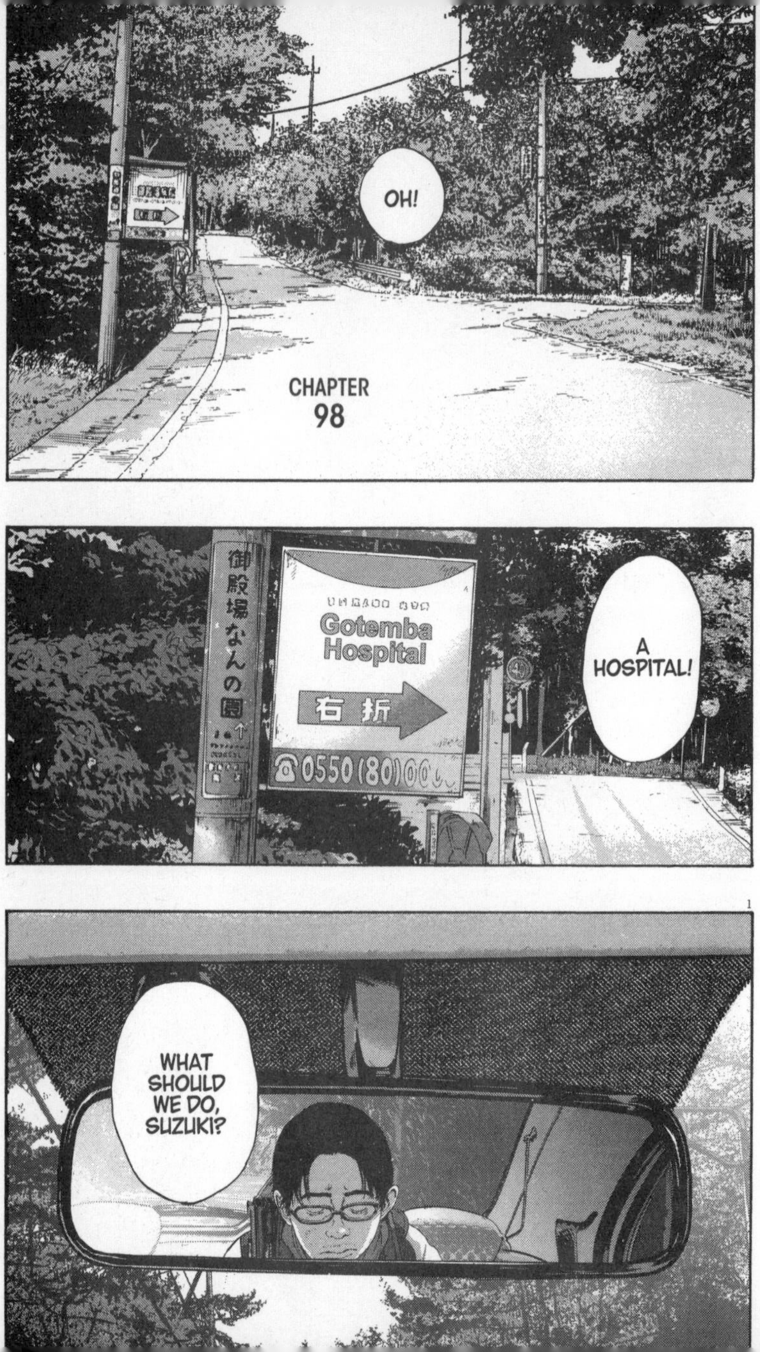
OH!
CHAPTER 98
御殿場なんの園
Gotemba Hospital
右折
A HOSPITAL!
WHAT SHOULD WE DO, SUZUKI?

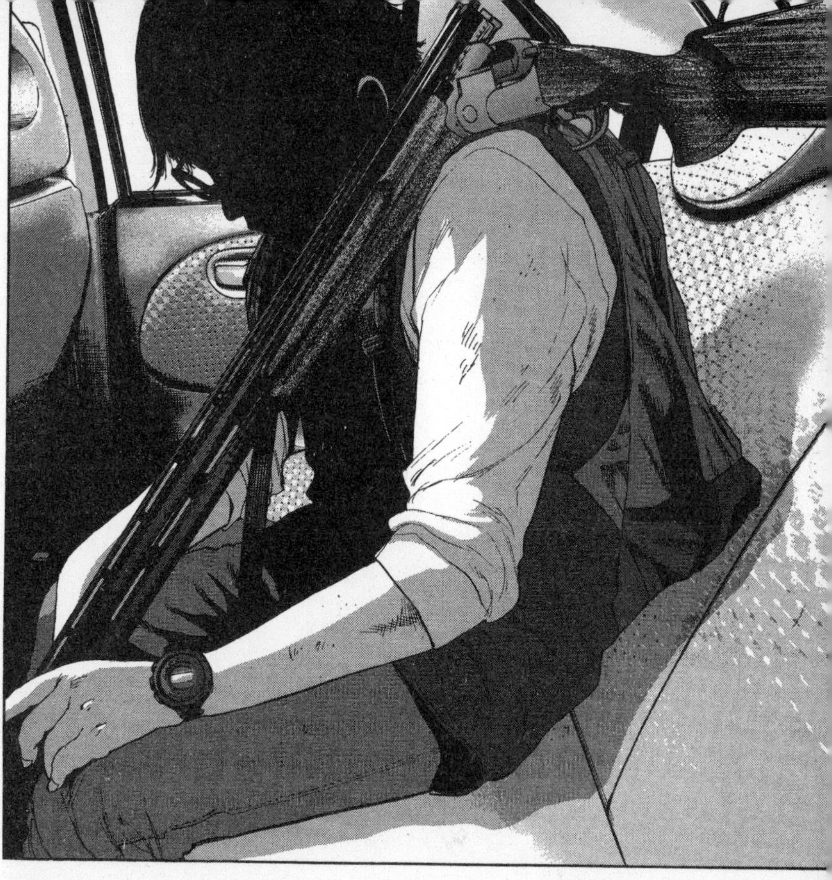
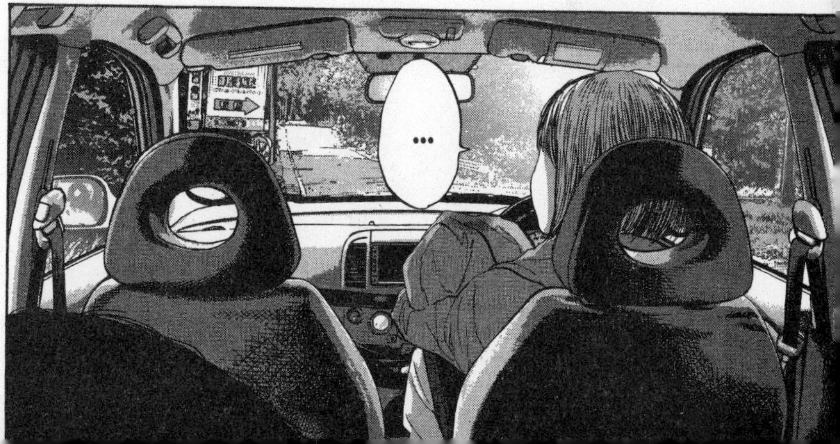
...

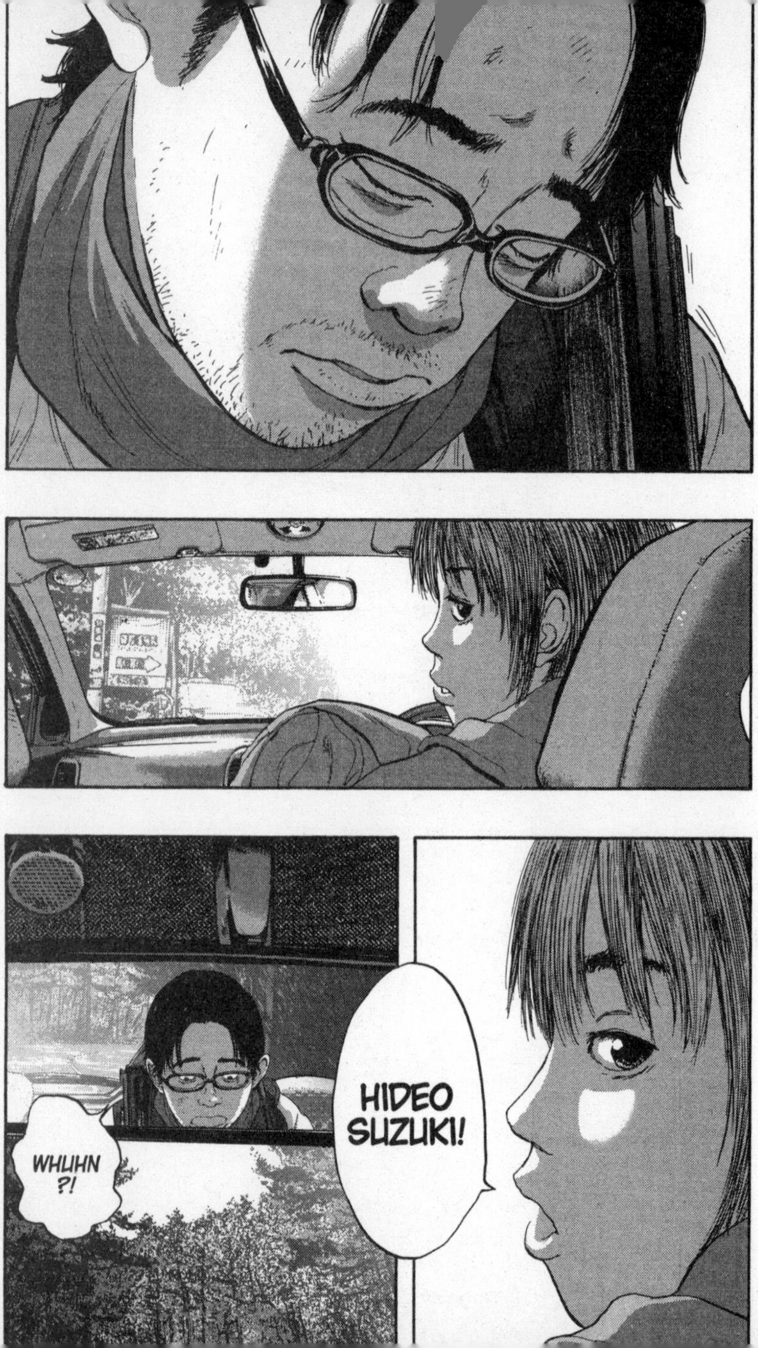
HIDEO SUZUKI!
WHUHN ?!

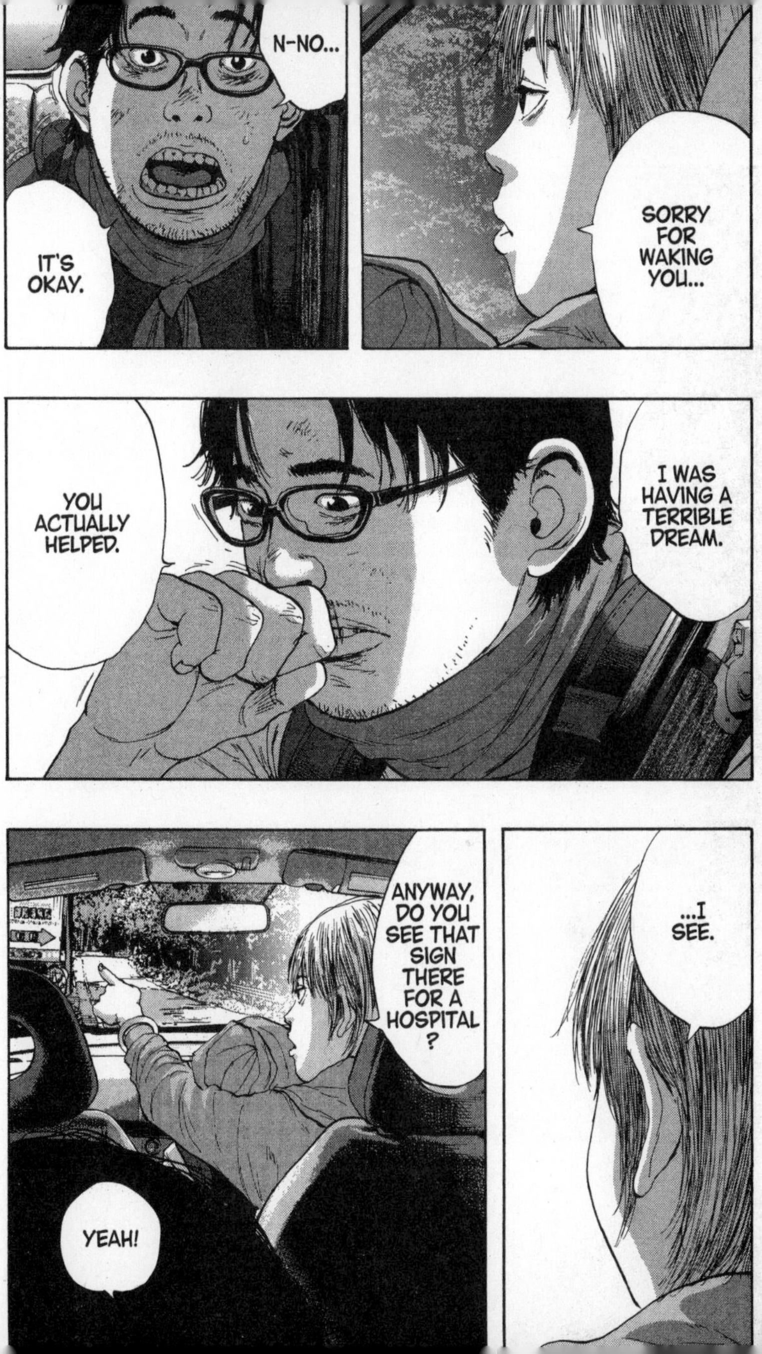
SORRY FOR WAKING YOU...
N-NO...
IT'S OKAY.
I WAS HAVING A TERRIBLE DREAM.
YOU ACTUALLY HELPED.
...I SEE.
ANYWAY, DO YOU SEE THAT SIGN THERE FOR A HOSPITAL?
YEAH!

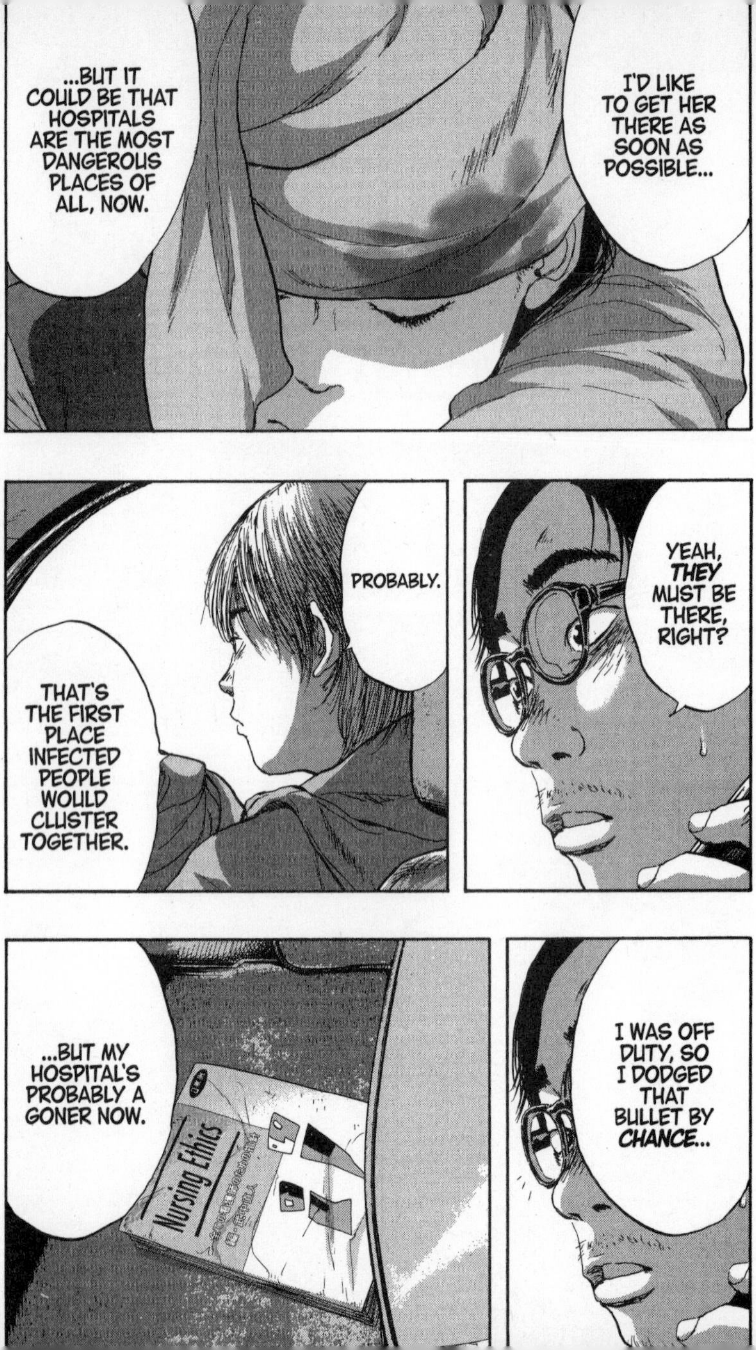
I'D LIKE TO GET HER THERE AS SOON AS POSSIBLE...
...BUT IT COULD BE THAT HOSPITALS ARE THE MOST DANGEROUS PLACES OF ALL, NOW.
YEAH, *THEY* MUST BE THERE, RIGHT?
PROBABLY.
THAT'S THE FIRST PLACE INFECTED PEOPLE WOULD CLUSTER TOGETHER.
I WAS OFF DUTY, SO I DODGED THAT BULLET BY *CHANCE*...
...BUT MY HOSPITAL'S PROBABLY A GONER NOW.
Nursing Ethics

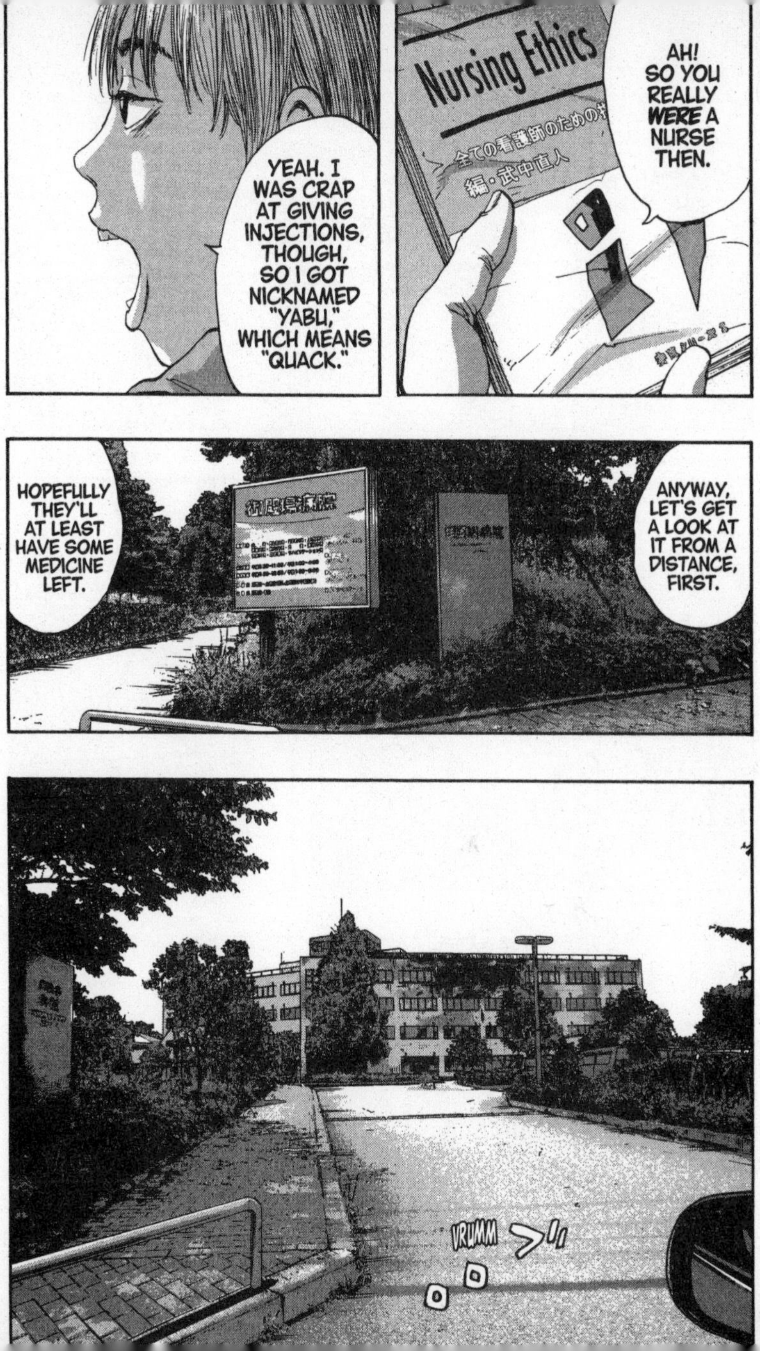
Nursing Ethics
編・武中直人
AH! SO YOU REALLY WERE A NURSE THEN.
YEAH. I WAS CRAP AT GIVING INJECTIONS, THOUGH, SO I GOT NICKNAMED "YABU," WHICH MEANS "QUACK."
ANYWAY, LET'S GET A LOOK AT IT FROM A DISTANCE, FIRST.
HOPEFULLY THEY'LL AT LEAST HAVE SOME MEDICINE LEFT.
VRUMM

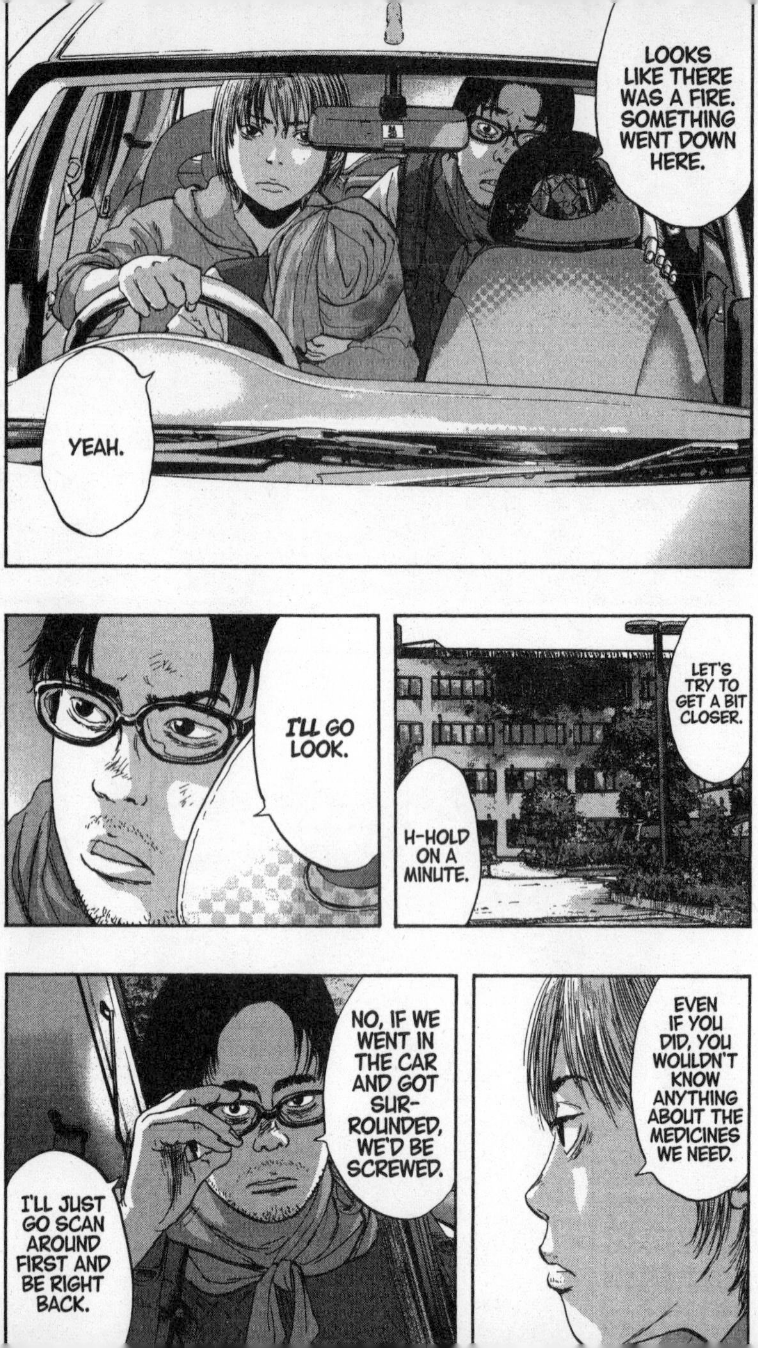
LOOKS LIKE THERE WAS A FIRE. SOMETHING WENT DOWN HERE.
YEAH.
LET'S TRY TO GET A BIT CLOSER.
H-HOLD ON A MINUTE.
I'LL GO LOOK.
EVEN IF YOU DID, YOU WOULDN'T KNOW ANYTHING ABOUT THE MEDICINES WE NEED.
NO, IF WE WENT IN THE CAR AND GOT SURROUNDED, WE'D BE SCREWED.
I'LL JUST GO SCAN AROUND FIRST AND BE RIGHT BACK.

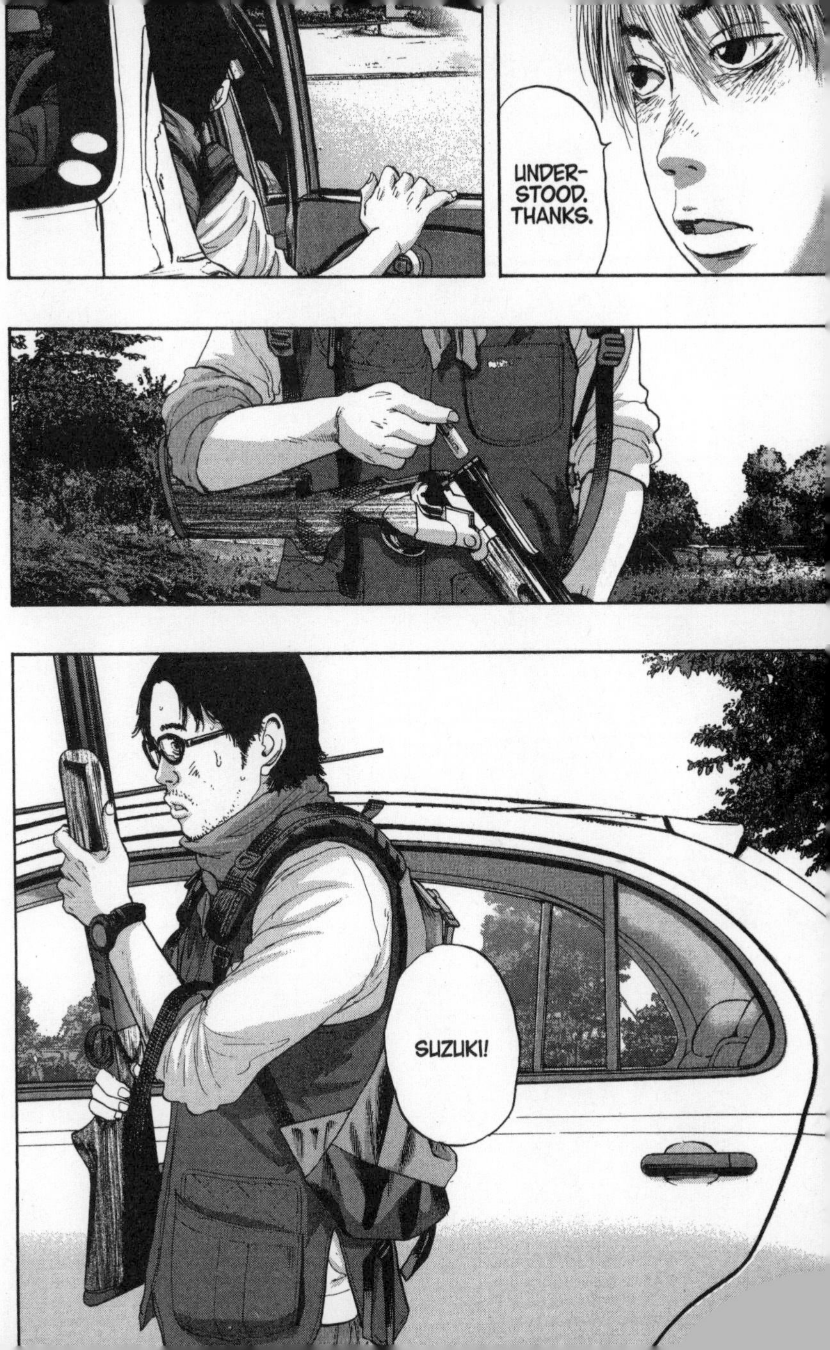
UNDER-STOOD. THANKS.
SUZUKI!

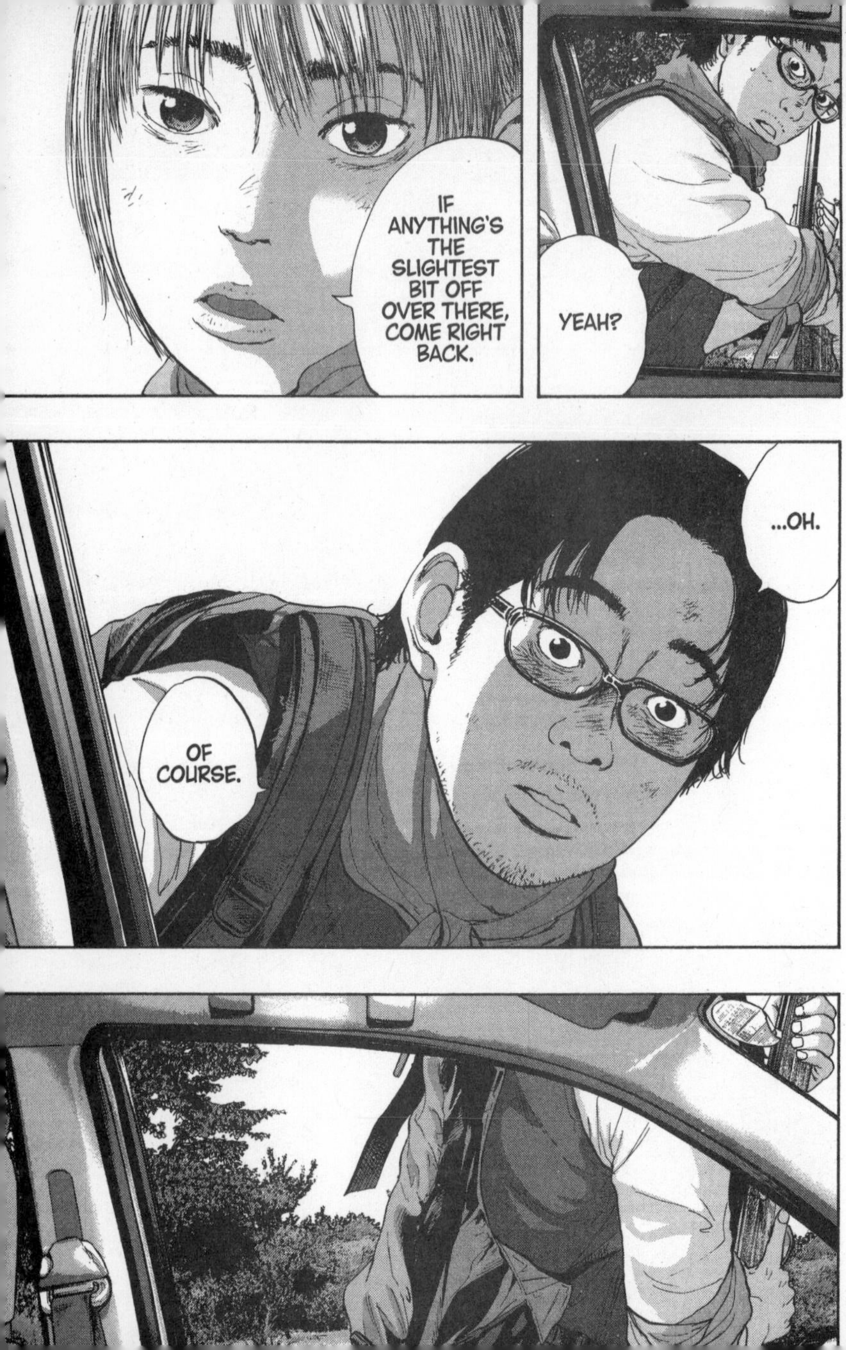
YEAH?
IF ANYTHING'S THE SLIGHTEST BIT OFF OVER THERE, COME RIGHT BACK.
...OH.
OF COURSE.

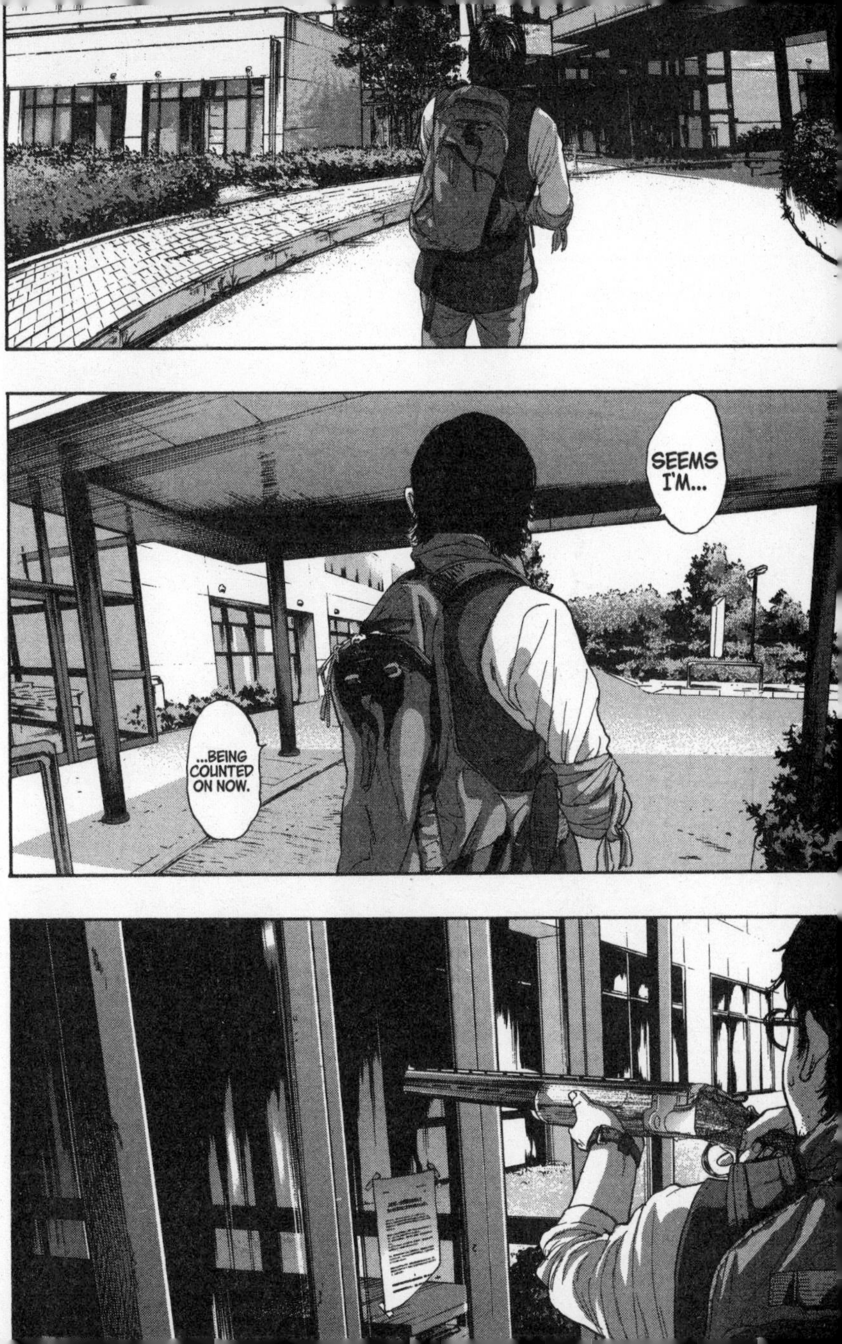
SEEMS I'M...
...BEING COUNTED ON NOW.

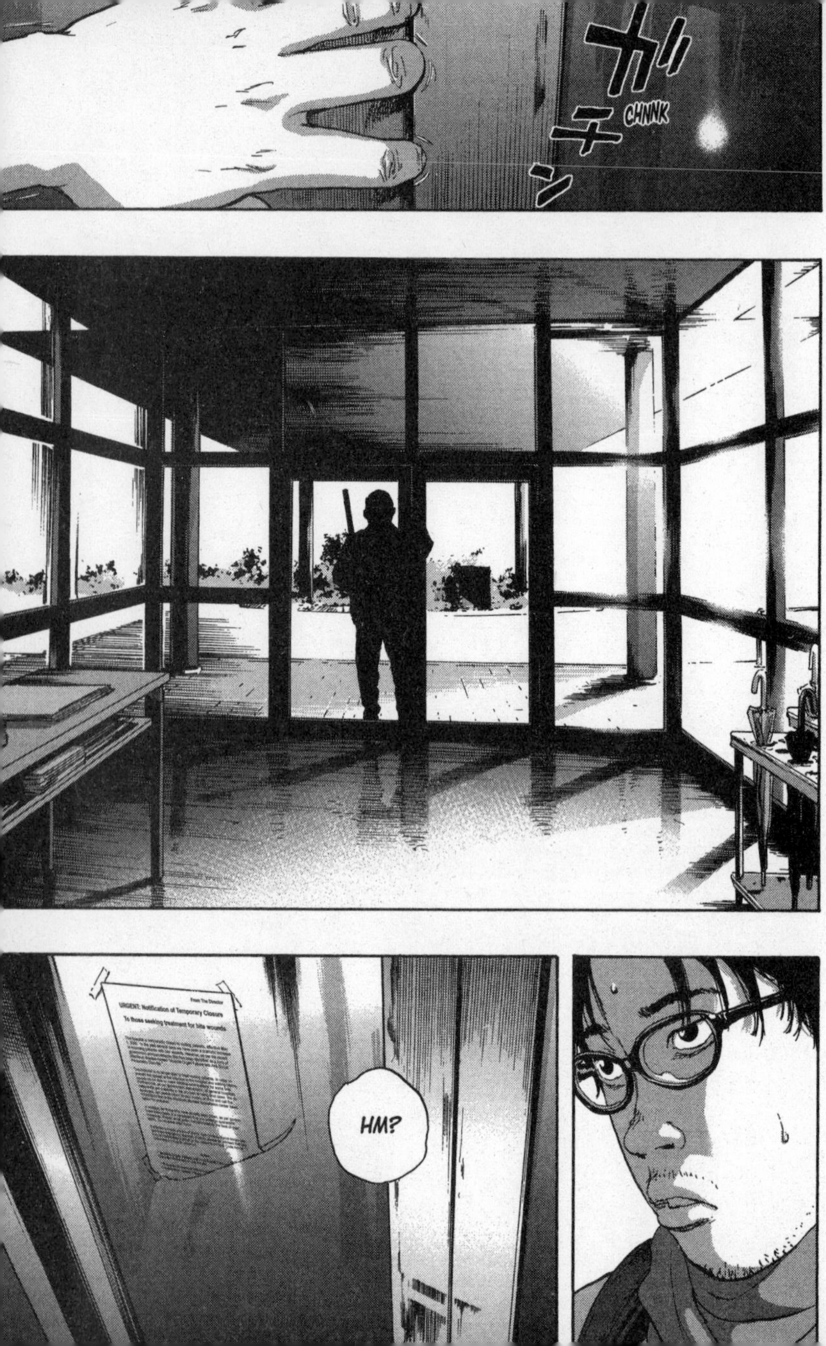
ガチン
CHNNK
From The Director
URGENT: Notification of Temporary Closure
To those seeking treatment for bite wounds
HM?

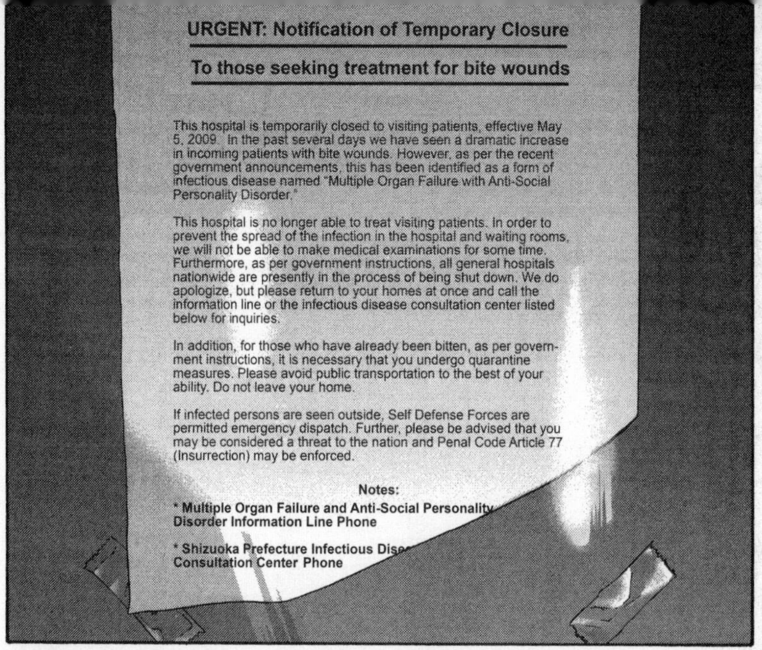
URGENT: Notification of Temporary Closure
To those seeking treatment for bite wounds
This hospital is temporarily closed to visiting patients, effective May 5, 2009. In the past several days we have seen a dramatic increase in incoming patients with bite wounds. However, as per the recent government announcements, this has been identified as a form of infectious disease named "Multiple Organ Failure with Anti-Social Personality Disorder."
This hospital is no longer able to treat visiting patients. In order to prevent the spread of the infection in the hospital and waiting rooms, we will not be able to make medical examinations for some time. Furthermore, as per government instructions, all general hospitals nationwide are presently in the process of being shut down. We do apologize, but please return to your homes at once and call the information line or the infectious disease consultation center listed below for inquiries.
In addition, for those who have already been bitten, as per government instructions, it is necessary that you undergo quarantine measures. Please avoid public transportation to the best of your ability. Do not leave your home.
If infected persons are seen outside, Self Defense Forces are permitted emergency dispatch. Further, please be advised that you may be considered a threat to the nation and Penal Code Article 77 (Insurrection) may be enforced.
Notes:
* Multiple Organ Failure and Anti-Social Personality
Disorder Information Line Phone
* Shizuoka Prefecture Infectious Dis
Consultation Center Phone

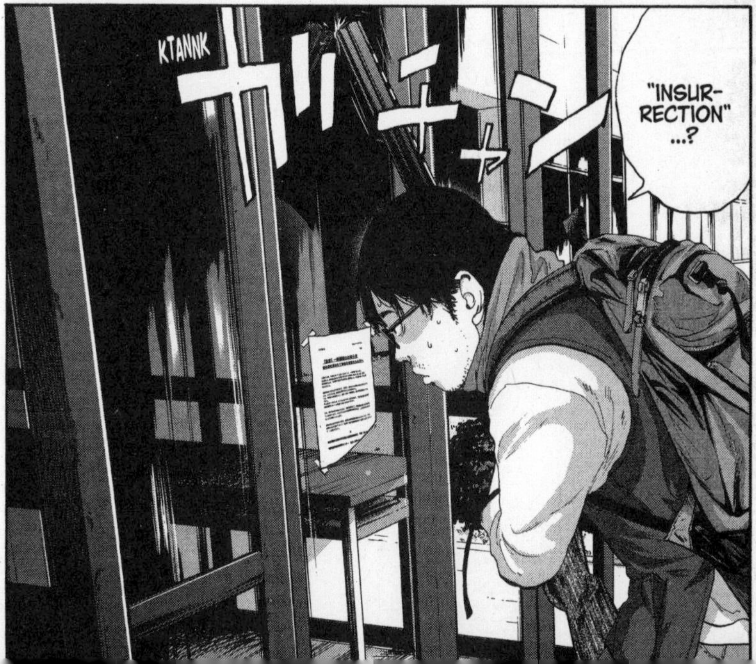
"INSURRECTION" ...?
KTANNK

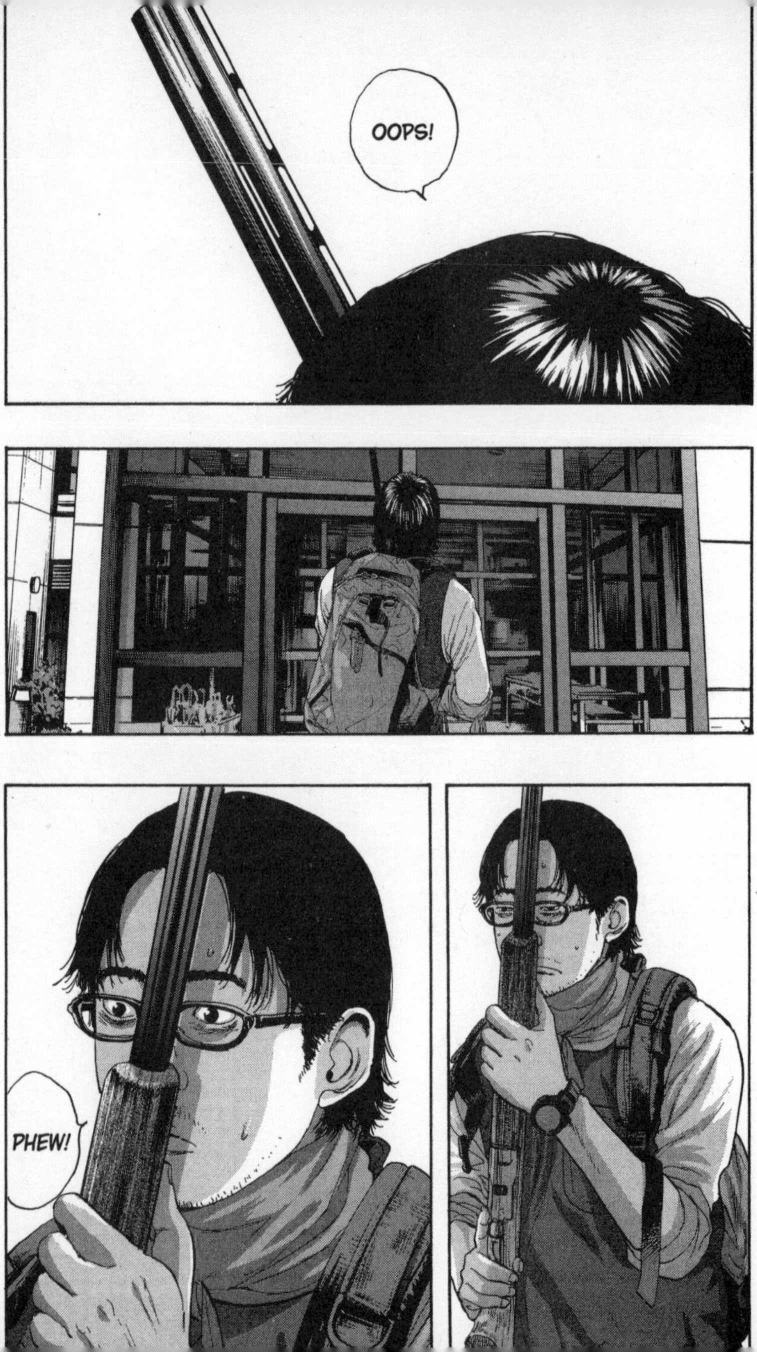
OOPS!
PHEW!

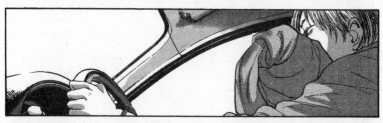

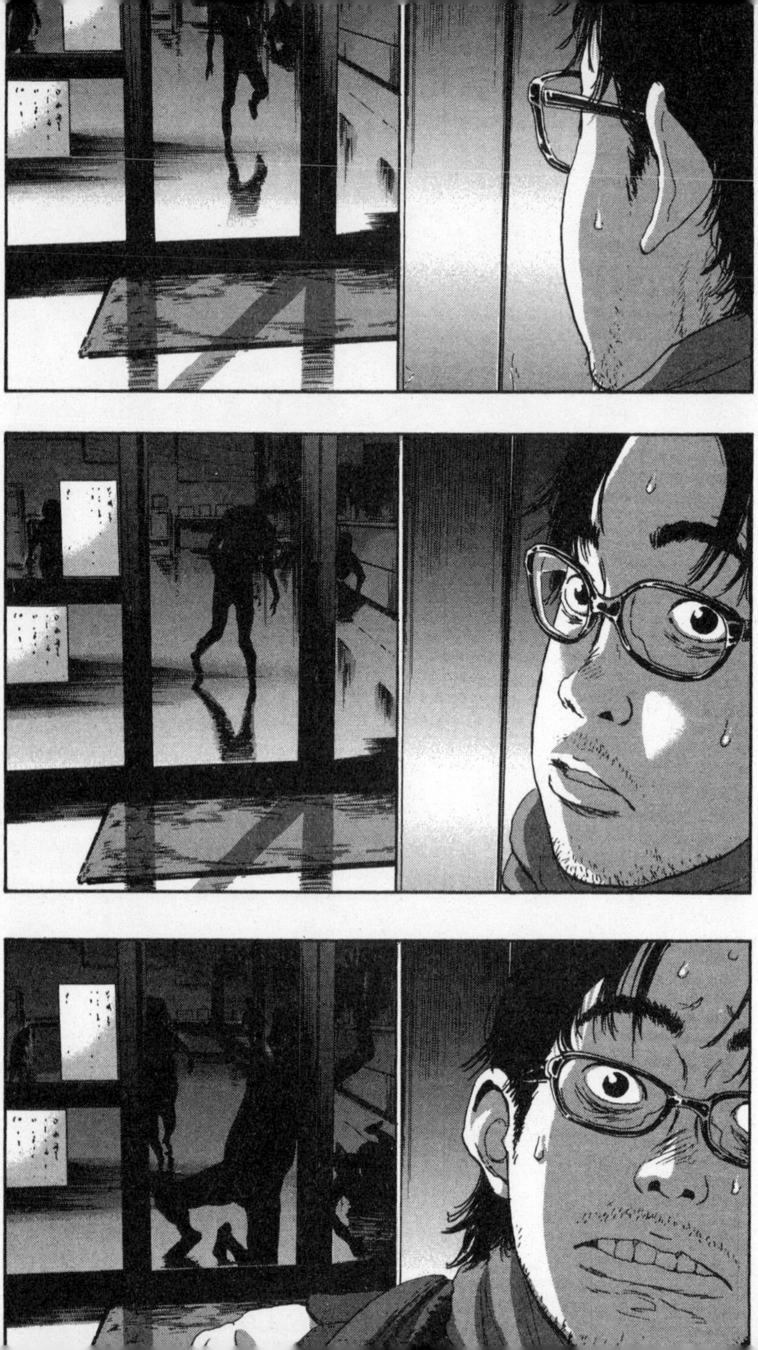

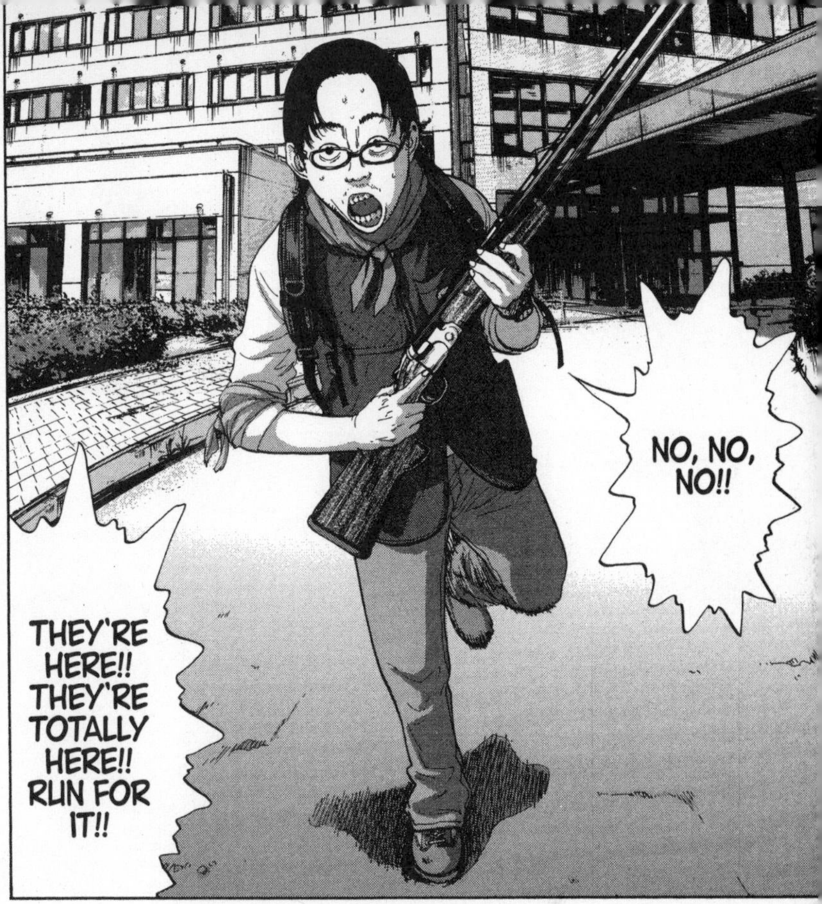
NO, NO, NO!!
THEY'RE HERE!! THEY'RE TOTALLY HERE!! RUN FOR IT!!
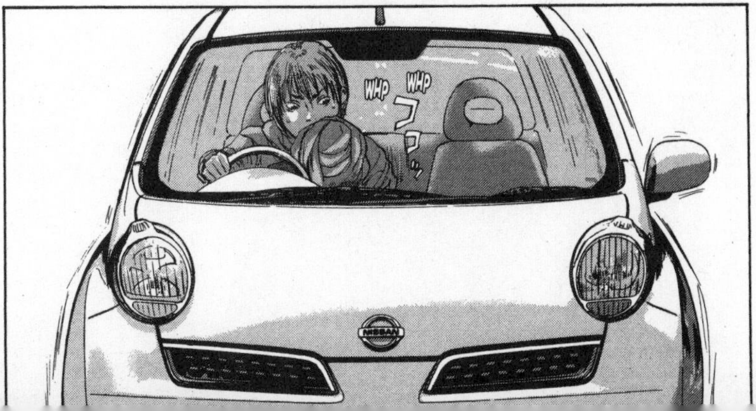
WHP
WHP

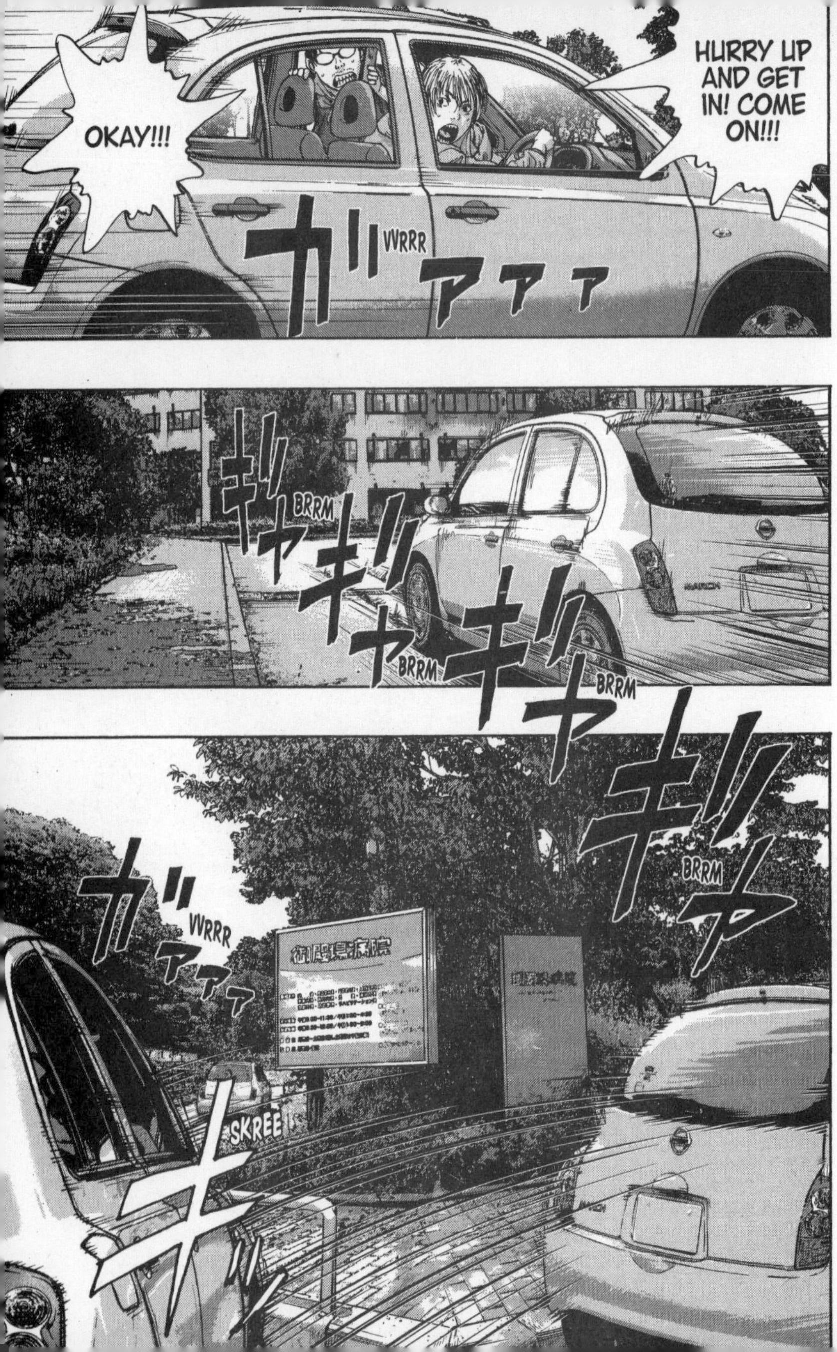
HURRY UP AND GET IN! COME ON!!!
OKAY!!!
VVRRR
BRRM
BRRM
BRRM
BRRM
VVRRR
SKREE

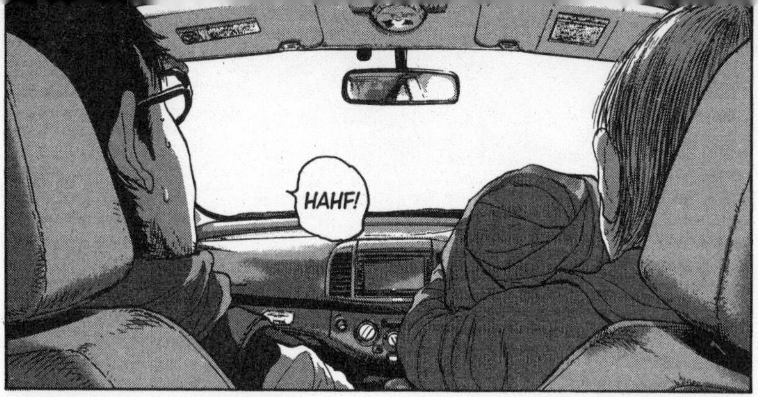
HAHF!

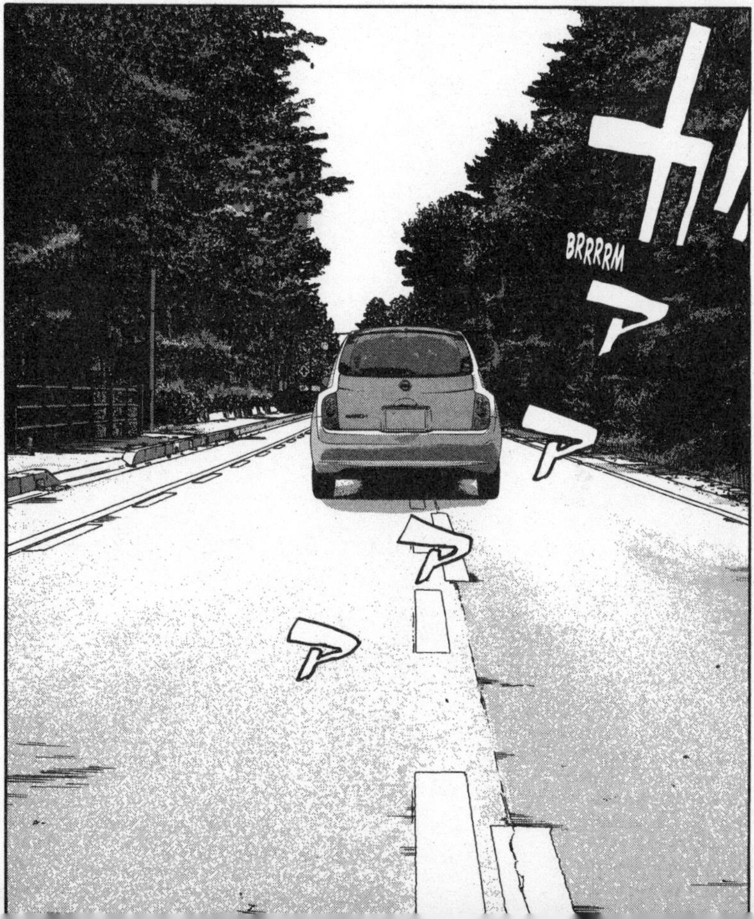
BRRRRM

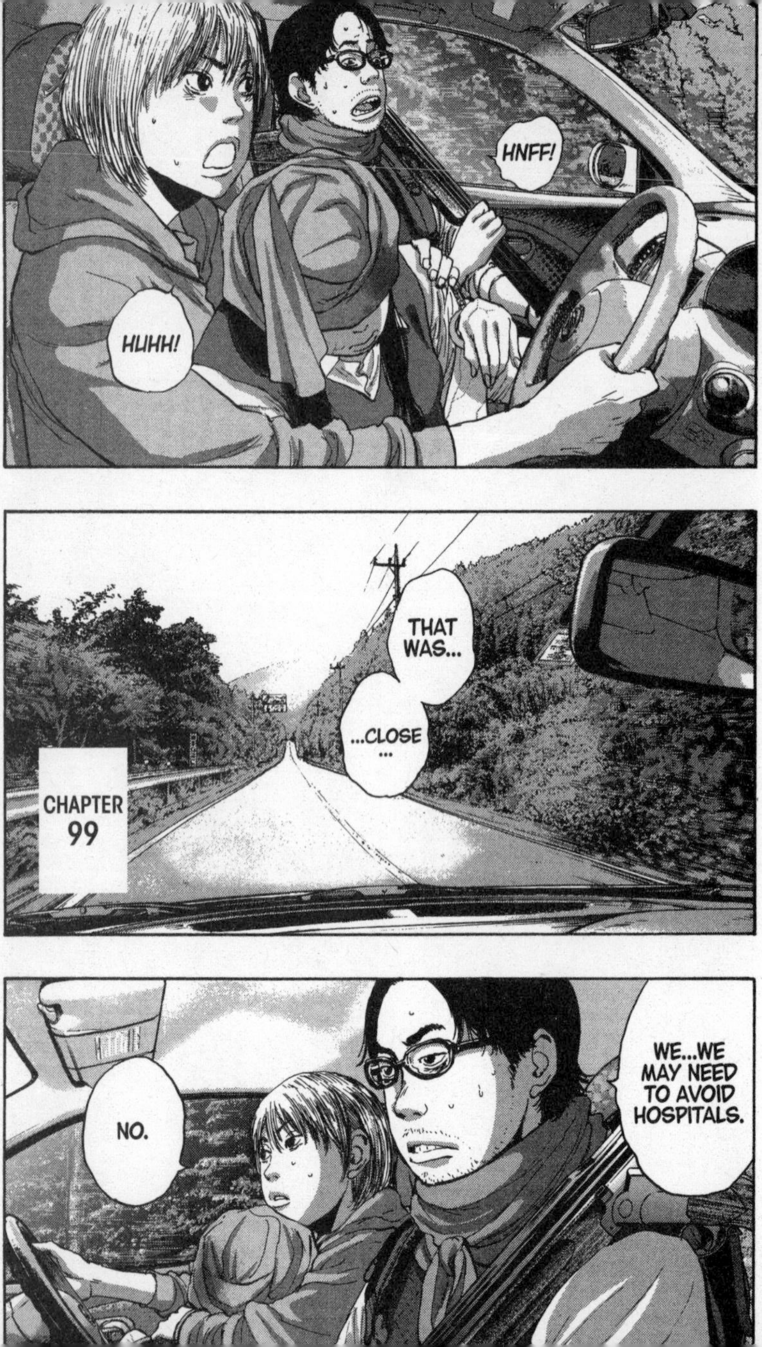
HNFF!
HUHH!
THAT WAS...
...CLOSE ...
CHAPTER 99
WE...WE MAY NEED TO AVOID HOSPITALS.
NO.

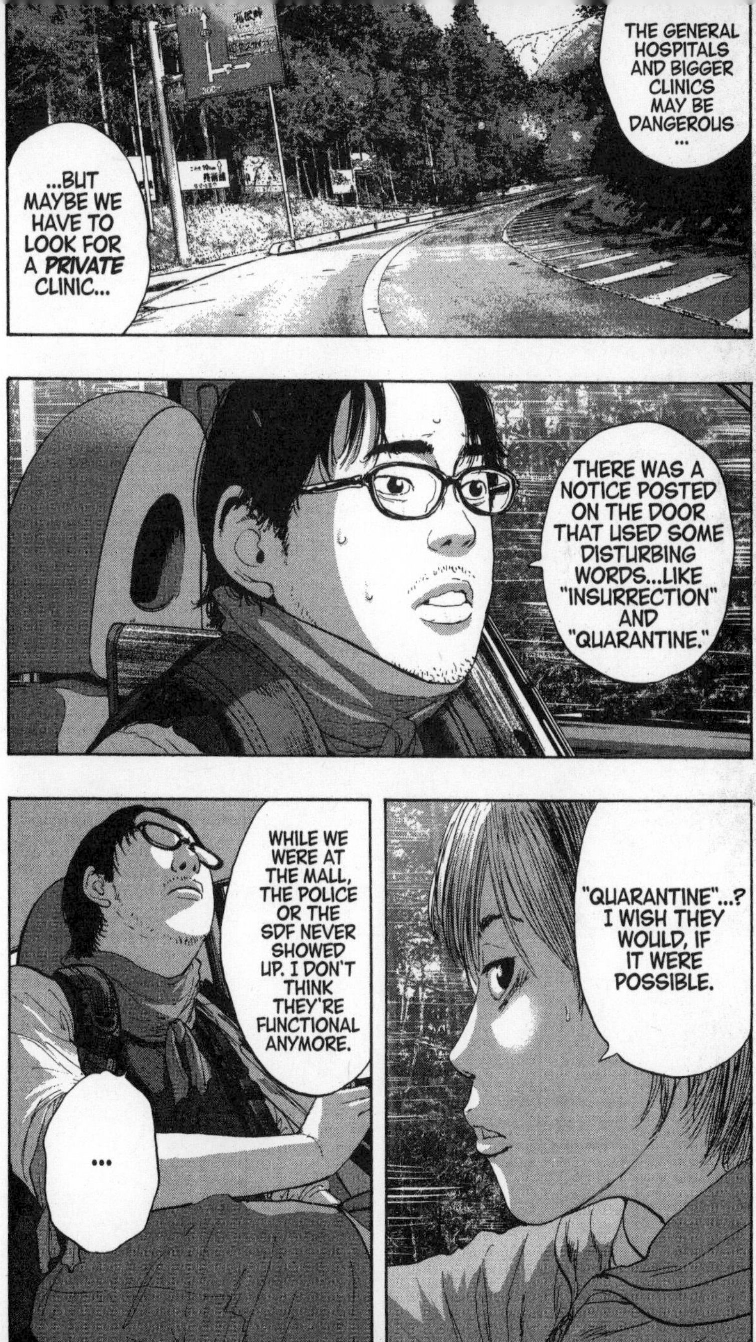
THE GENERAL HOSPITALS AND BIGGER CLINICS MAY BE DANGEROUS ...
...BUT MAYBE WE HAVE TO LOOK FOR A *PRIVATE* CLINIC...
THERE WAS A NOTICE POSTED ON THE DOOR THAT USED SOME DISTURBING WORDS...LIKE "INSURRECTION" AND "QUARANTINE."
"QUARANTINE"...? I WISH THEY WOULD, IF IT WERE POSSIBLE.
WHILE WE WERE AT THE MALL, THE POLICE OR THE SDF NEVER SHOWED UP. I DON'T THINK THEY'RE FUNCTIONAL ANYMORE.
...

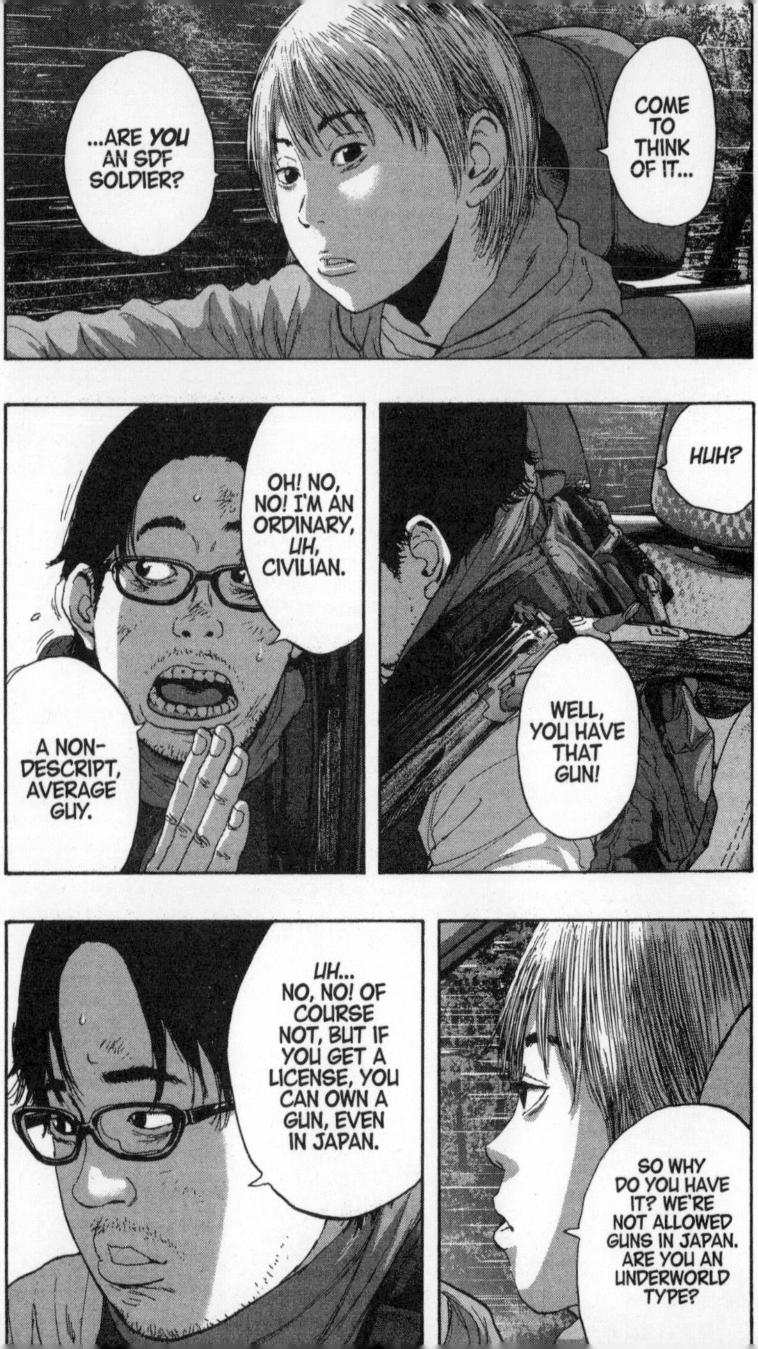
COME TO THINK OF IT...
...ARE *YOU* AN SDF SOLDIER?
HUH?
WELL, YOU HAVE THAT GUN!
OH! NO, NO! I'M AN ORDINARY, UH, CIVILIAN.
A NON-DESCRIPT, AVERAGE GUY.
SO WHY DO YOU HAVE IT? WE'RE NOT ALLOWED GUNS IN JAPAN. ARE YOU AN UNDERWORLD TYPE?
UH... NO, NO! OF COURSE NOT, BUT IF YOU GET A LICENSE, YOU CAN OWN A GUN, EVEN IN JAPAN.

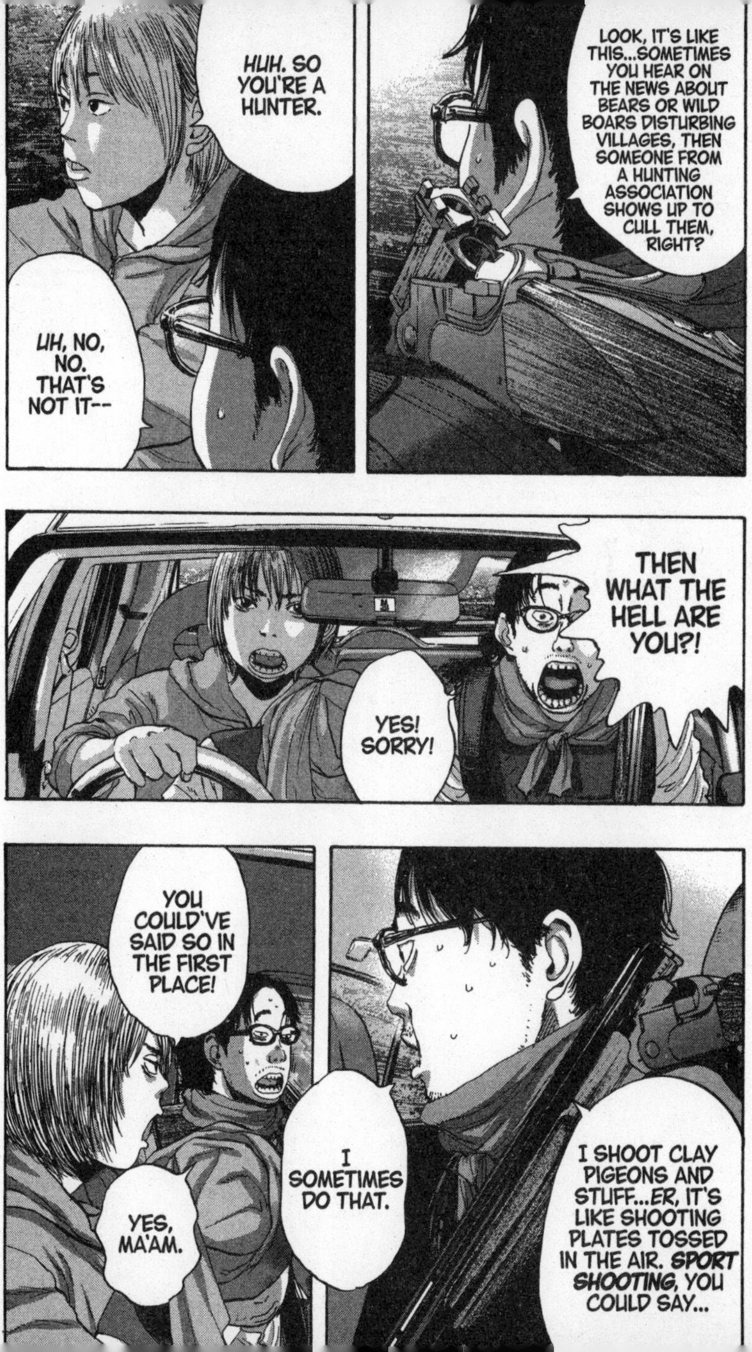
LOOK, IT'S LIKE THIS...SOMETIMES YOU HEAR ON THE NEWS ABOUT BEARS OR WILD BOARS DISTURBING VILLAGES, THEN SOMEONE FROM A HUNTING ASSOCIATION SHOWS UP TO CULL THEM, RIGHT?
HUH. SO YOU'RE A HUNTER.
UH, NO, NO. THAT'S NOT IT--
THEN WHAT THE HELL ARE YOU?!
YES! SORRY!
I SHOOT CLAY PIGEONS AND STUFF...ER, IT'S LIKE SHOOTING PLATES TOSSED IN THE AIR. SPORT SHOOTING, YOU COULD SAY...
I SOMETIMES DO THAT.
YOU COULD'VE SAID SO IN THE FIRST PLACE!
YES, MA'AM.

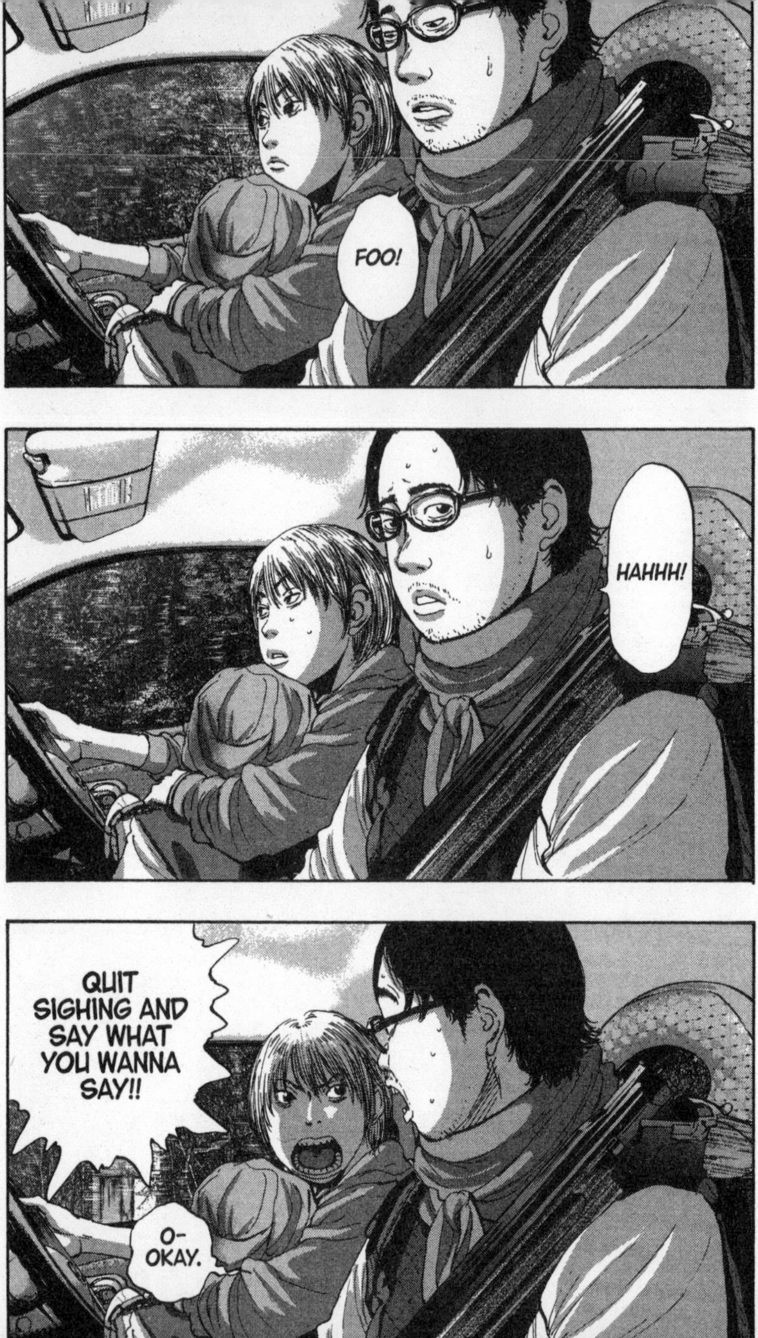
FOO!
HAHHH!
QUIT SIGHING AND SAY WHAT YOU WANNA SAY!!
O- OKAY.

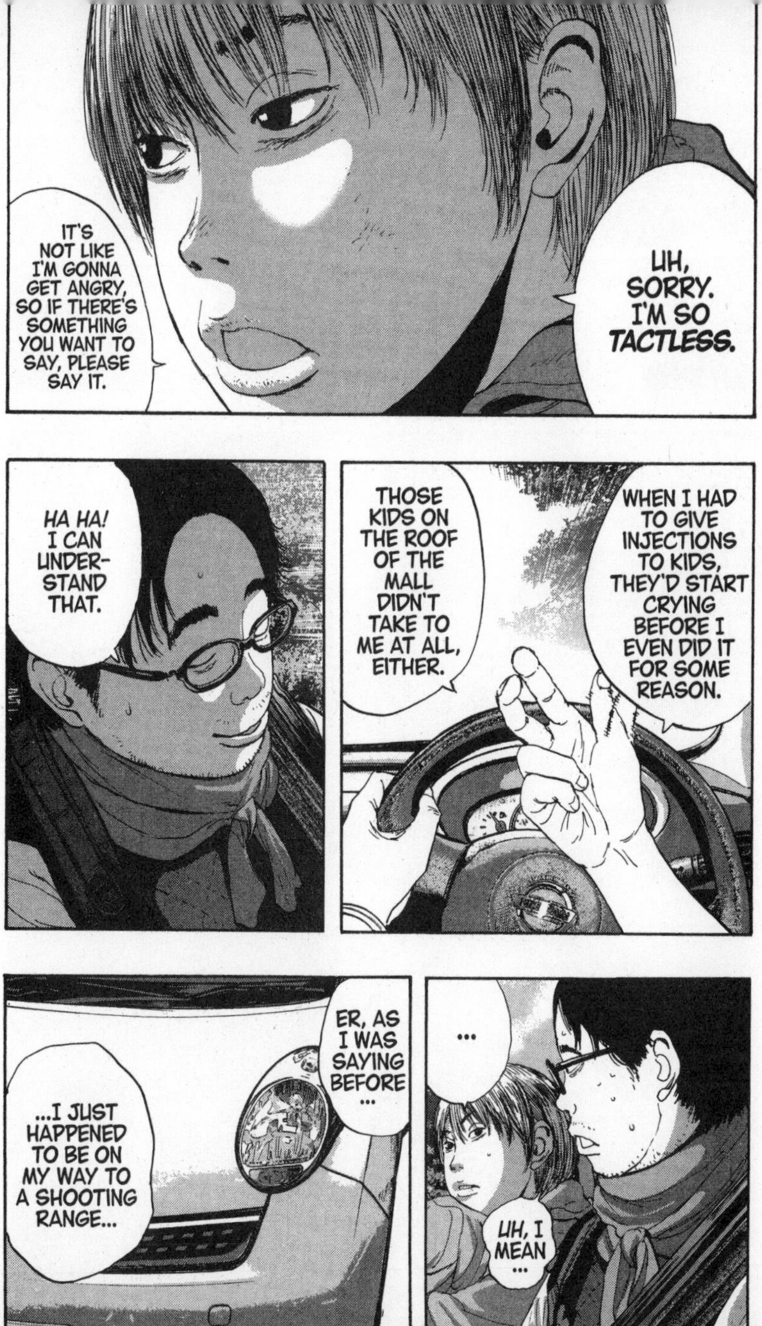
UH, SORRY. I'M SO *TACTLESS.*
IT'S NOT LIKE I'M GONNA GET ANGRY, SO IF THERE'S SOMETHING YOU WANT TO SAY, PLEASE SAY IT.
WHEN I HAD TO GIVE INJECTIONS TO KIDS, THEY'D START CRYING BEFORE I EVEN DID IT FOR SOME REASON.
THOSE KIDS ON THE ROOF OF THE MALL DIDN'T TAKE TO ME AT ALL, EITHER.
HA HA! I CAN UNDER-STAND THAT.
...
UH, I MEAN ...
ER, AS I WAS SAYING BEFORE ...
...I JUST HAPPENED TO BE ON MY WAY TO A SHOOTING RANGE...

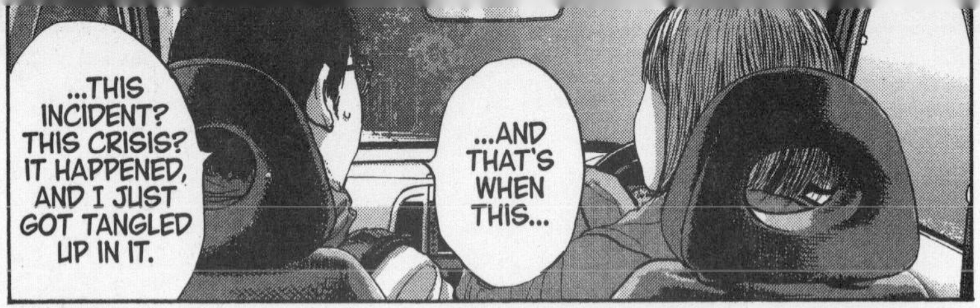
...AND THAT'S WHEN THIS...
...THIS INCIDENT? THIS CRISIS? IT HAPPENED, AND I JUST GOT TANGLED UP IN IT.

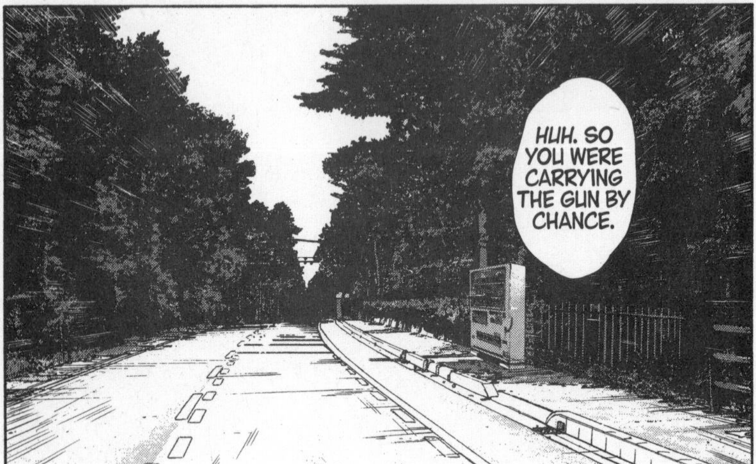
HUH. SO YOU WERE CARRYING THE GUN BY CHANCE.

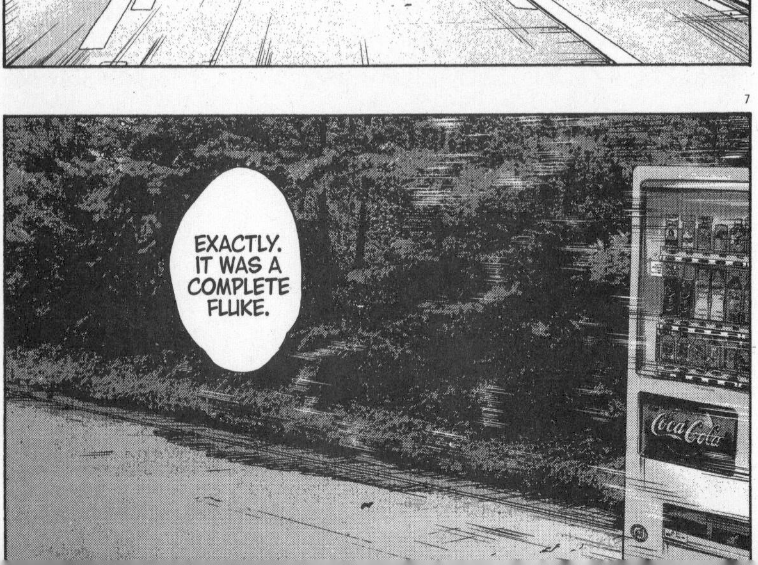
EXACTLY. IT WAS A COMPLETE FLUKE.
Coca-Cola

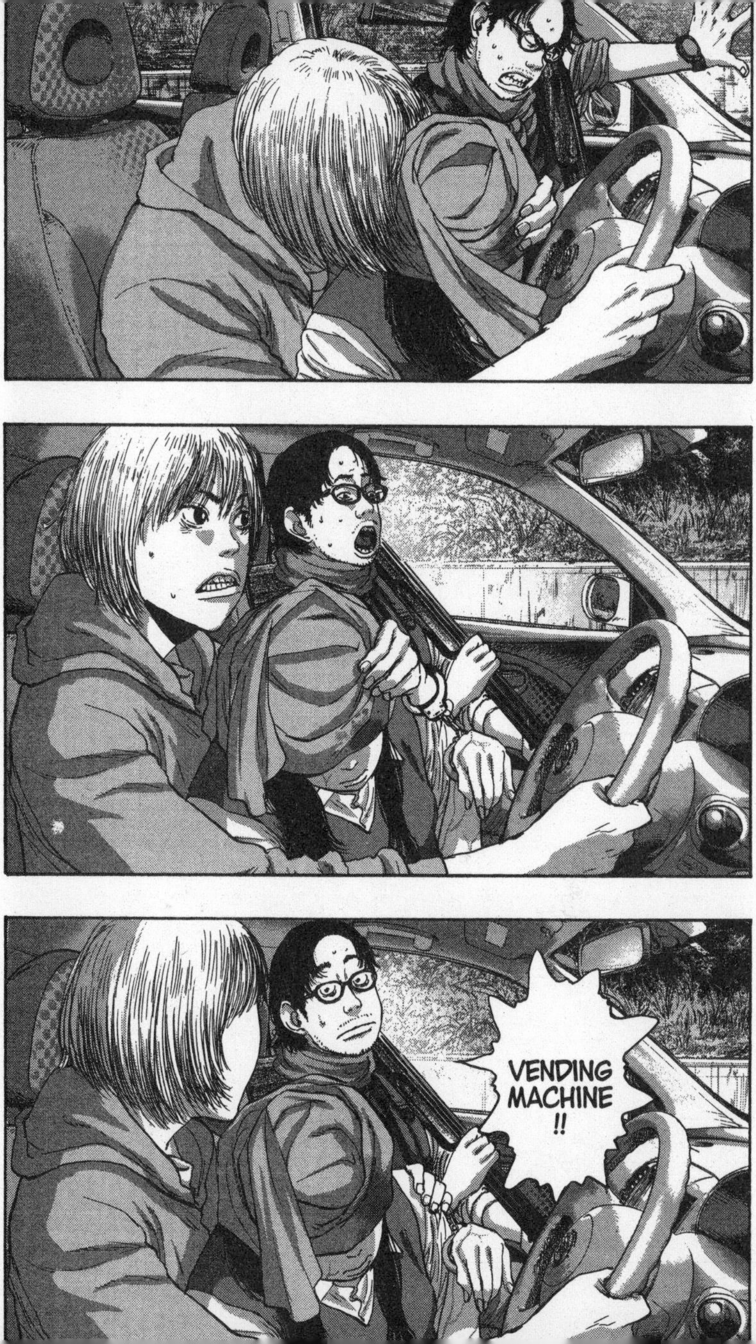
VENDING MACHINE !!

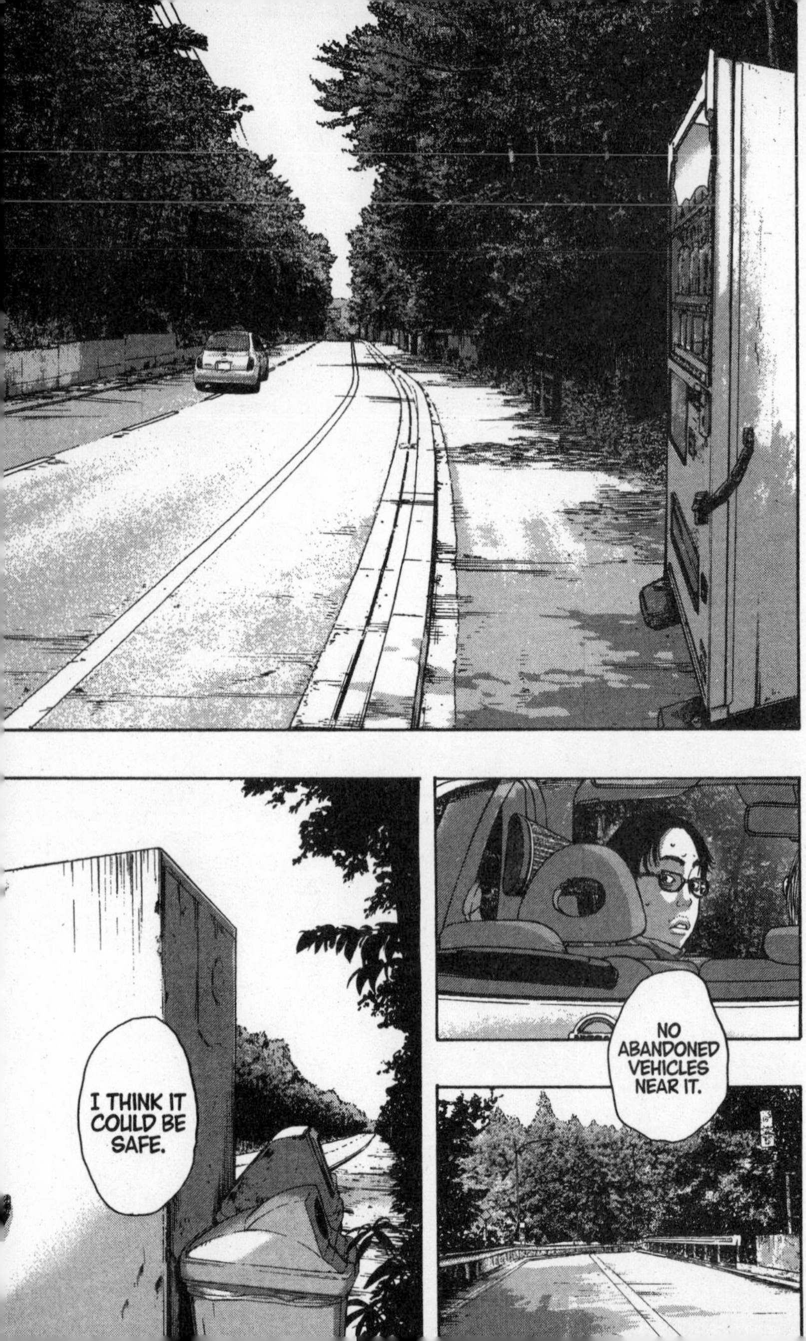
NO ABANDONED VEHICLES NEAR IT.
I THINK IT COULD BE SAFE.

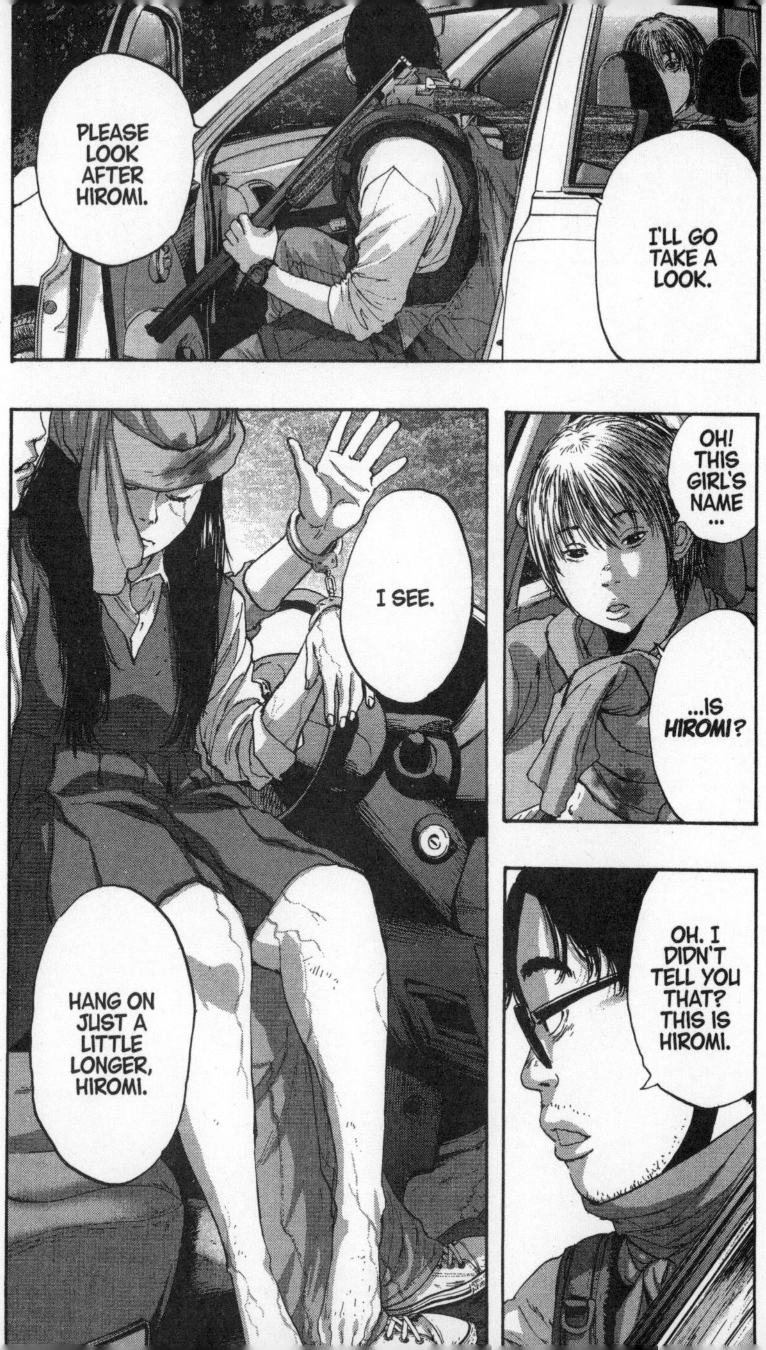
I'LL GO TAKE A LOOK.
PLEASE LOOK AFTER HIROMI.
OH! THIS GIRL'S NAME...
...IS *HIROMI*?
OH. I DIDN'T TELL YOU THAT? THIS IS HIROMI.
I SEE.
HANG ON JUST A LITTLE LONGER, HIROMI.

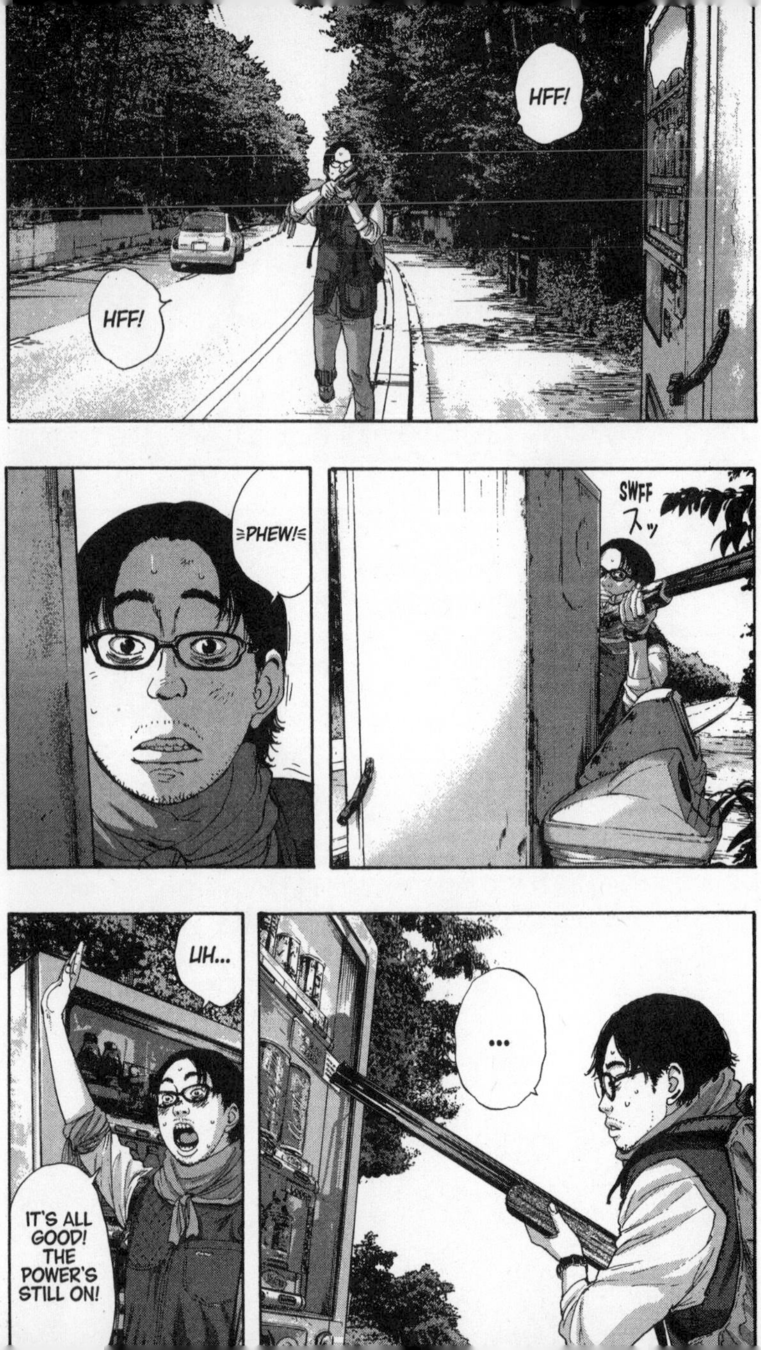
HFF!
HFF!
SWFF
スッ
PHEW!
...
UH...
IT'S ALL GOOD! THE POWER'S STILL ON!

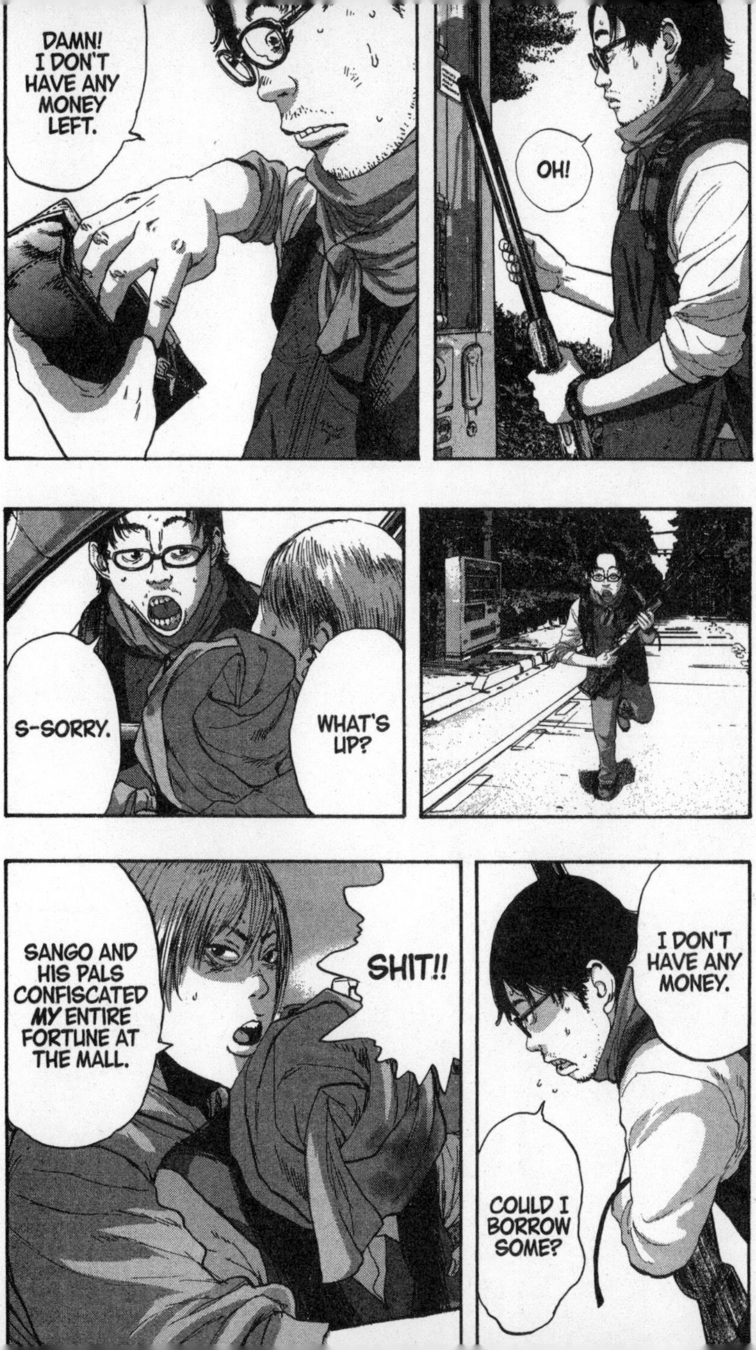
OH!
DAMN! I DON'T HAVE ANY MONEY LEFT.
WHAT'S UP?
S-SORRY.
I DON'T HAVE ANY MONEY.
COULD I BORROW SOME?
SHIT!!
SANGO AND HIS PALS CONFISCATED MY ENTIRE FORTUNE AT THE MALL.

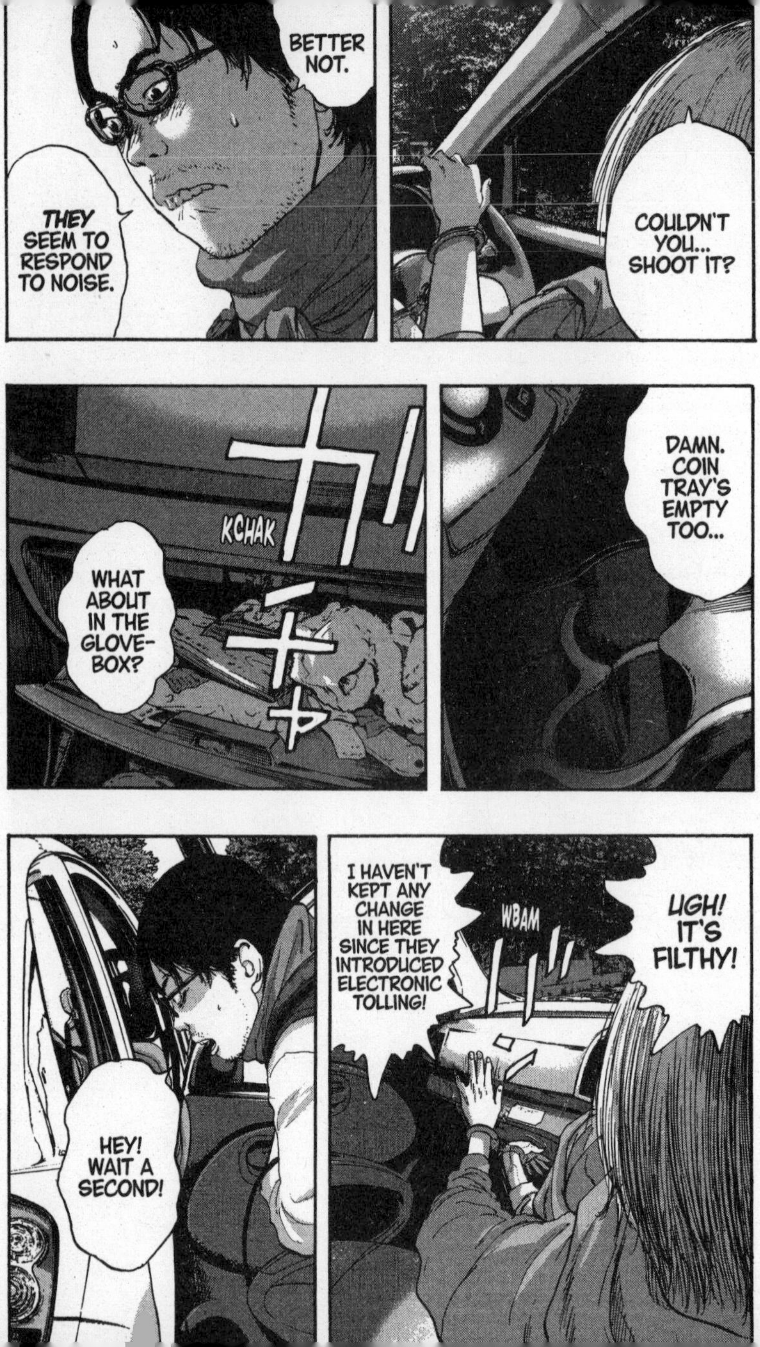

COULDN'T YOU... SHOOT IT?
BETTER NOT.
THEY SEEM TO RESPOND TO NOISE.
DAMN. COIN TRAY'S EMPTY TOO...
KCHAK
WHAT ABOUT IN THE GLOVE-BOX?
UGH! IT'S FILTHY!
WBAM
I HAVEN'T KEPT ANY CHANGE IN HERE SINCE THEY INTRODUCED ELECTRONIC TOLLING!
HEY! WAIT A SECOND!

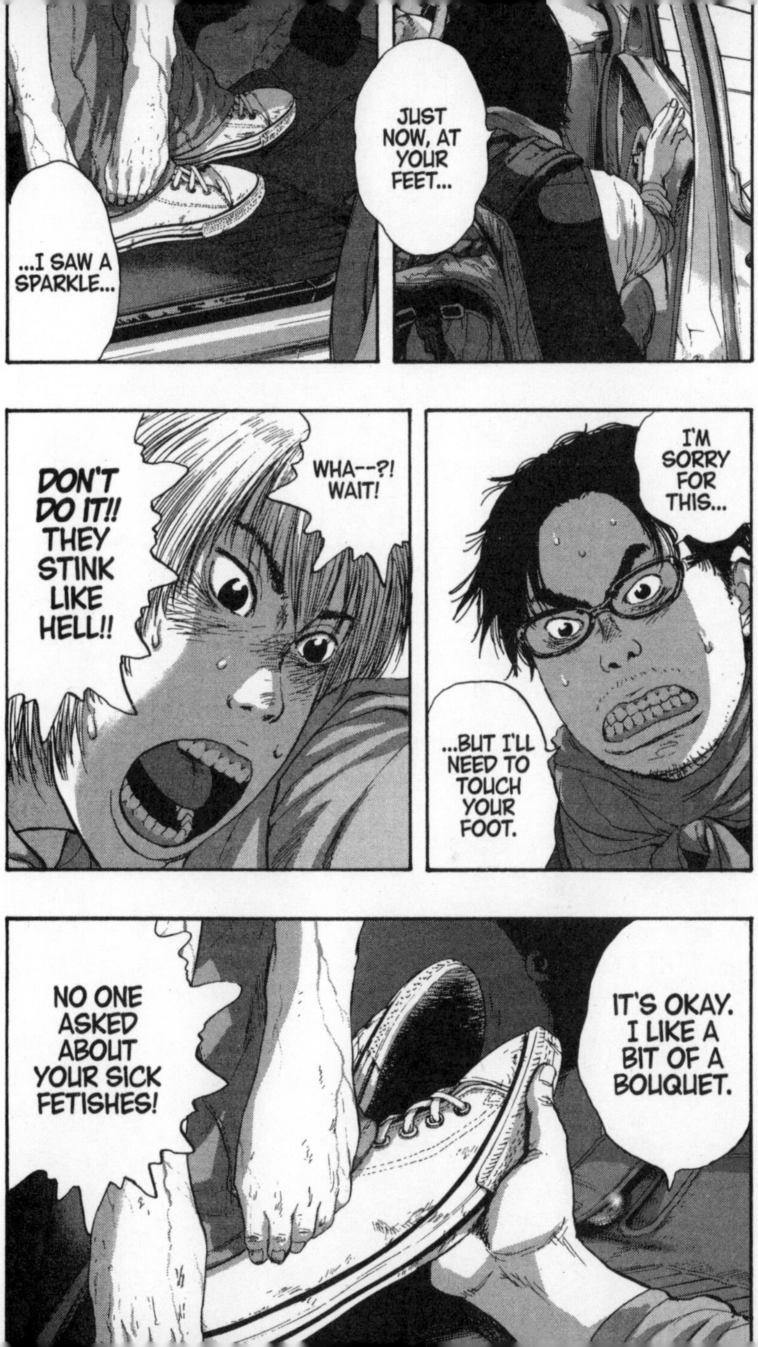
JUST NOW, AT YOUR FEET...
...I SAW A SPARKLE...
I'M SORRY FOR THIS...
...BUT I'LL NEED TO TOUCH YOUR FOOT.
WHA--?! WAIT!
DON'T DO IT!! THEY STINK LIKE HELL!!
IT'S OKAY. I LIKE A BIT OF A BOUQUET.
NO ONE ASKED ABOUT YOUR SICK FETISHES!

STOP
RIGHT
THERE
!!!

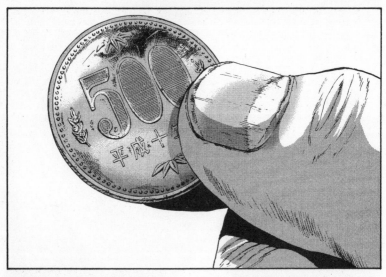

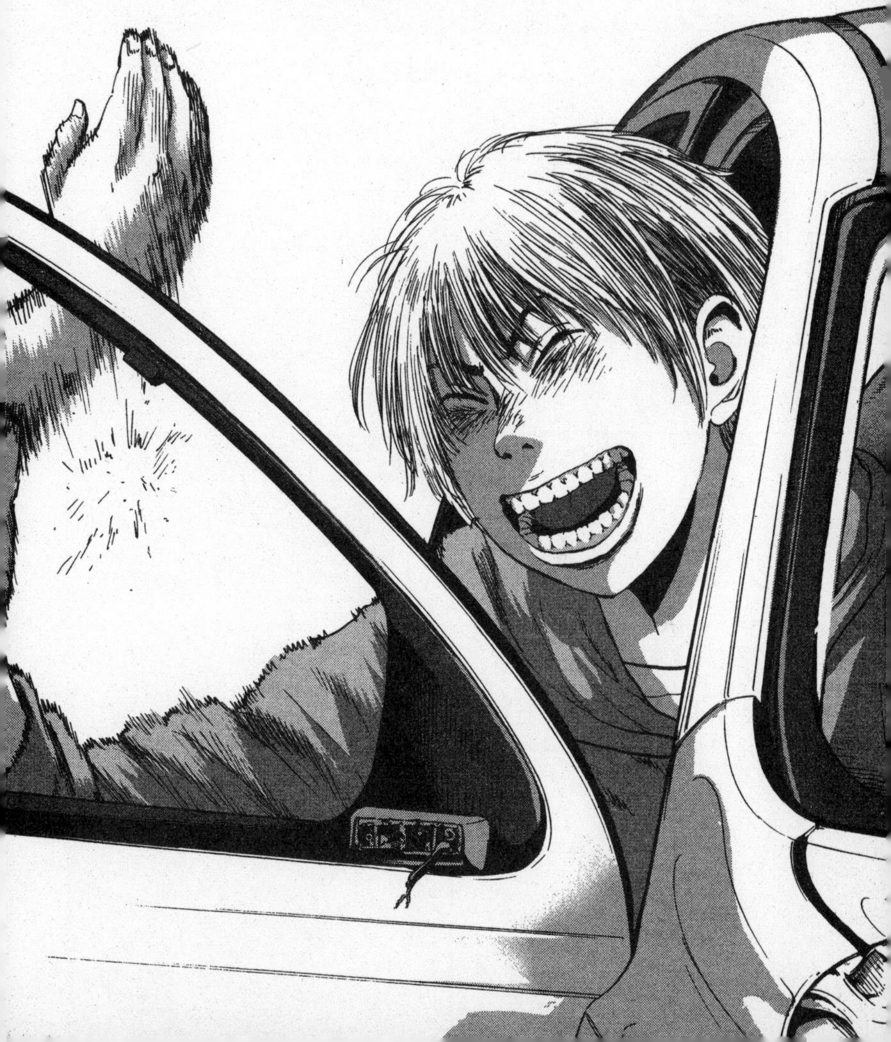

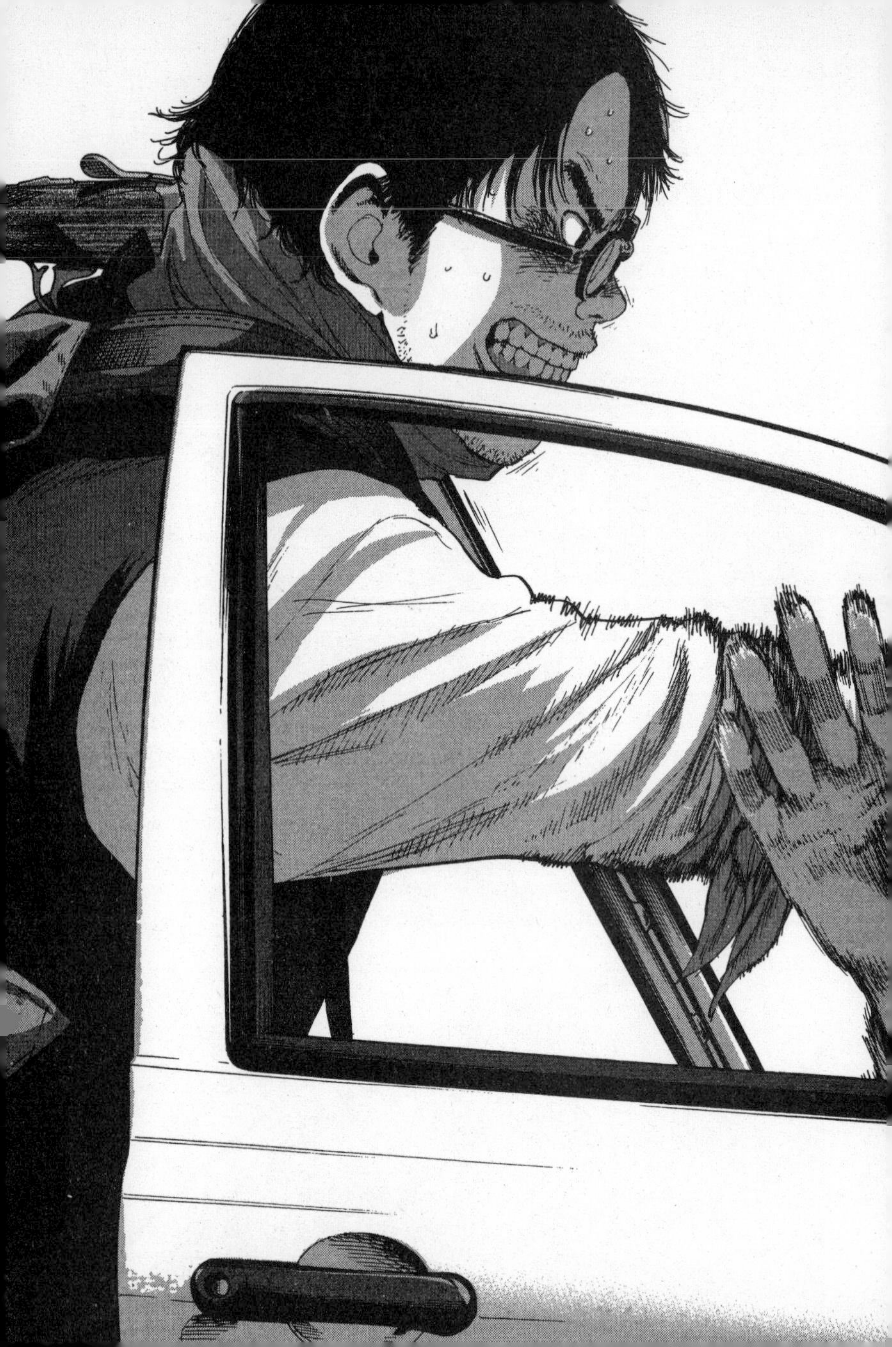

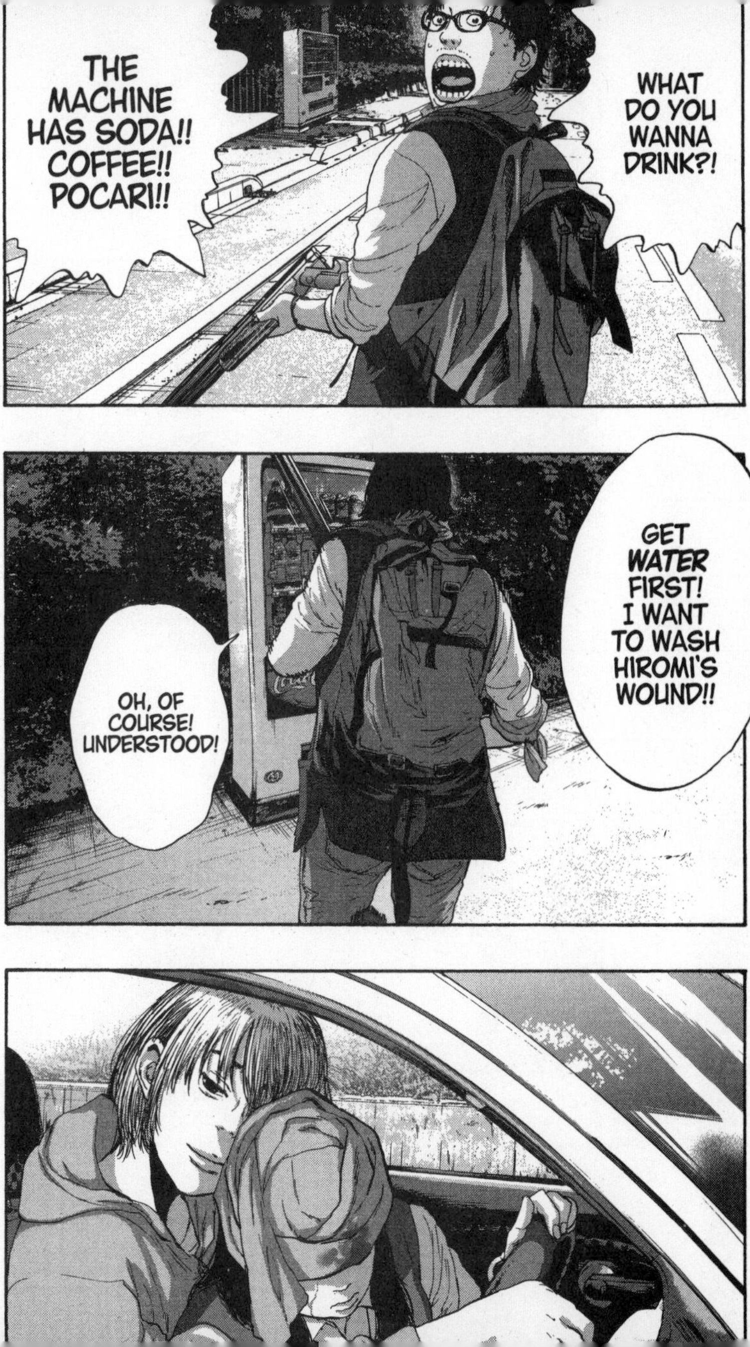
WHAT DO YOU WANNA DRINK?!
THE MACHINE HAS SODA!! COFFEE!! POCARI!!
GET WATER FIRST! I WANT TO WASH HIROMI'S WOUND!!
OH, OF COURSE! UNDERSTOOD!

CHAPTER 100

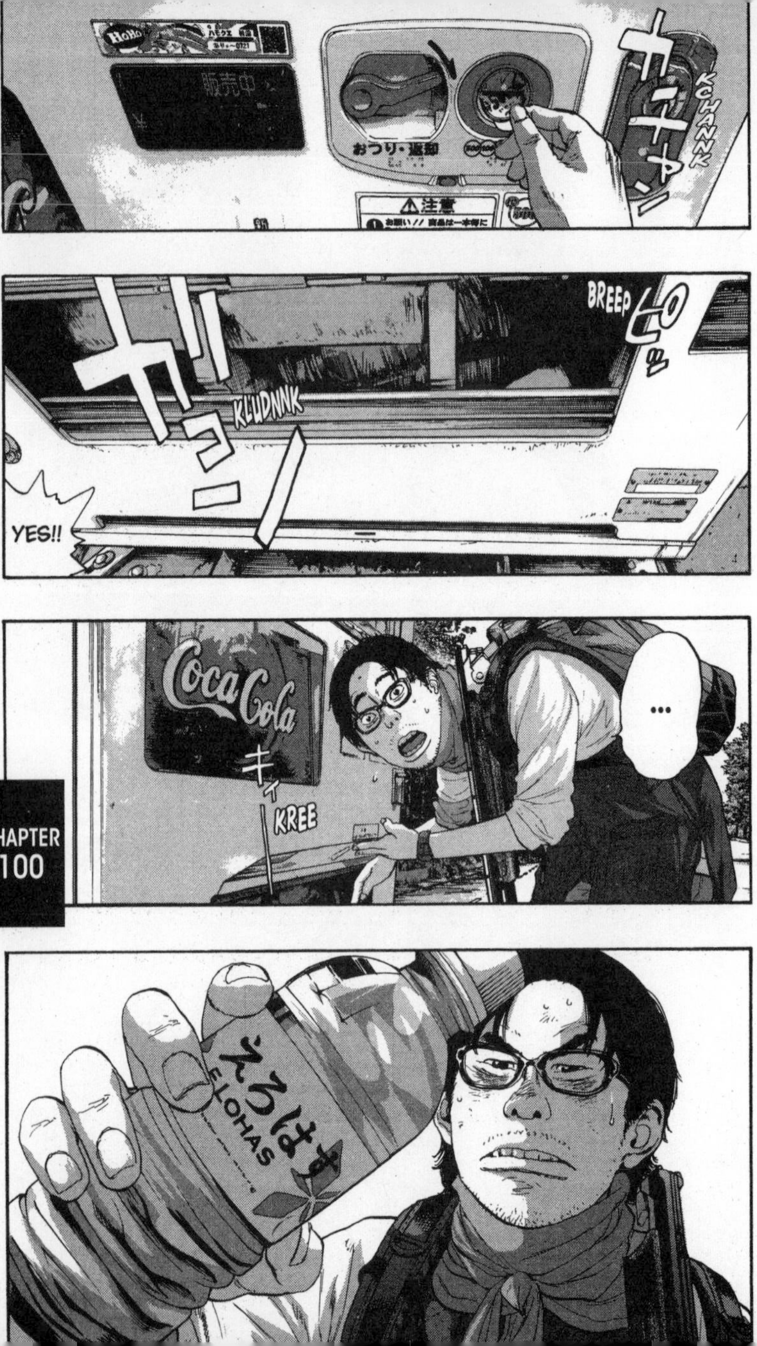
KCHANNK
BREEP
KLUDNNK
YES!!
...
KREE

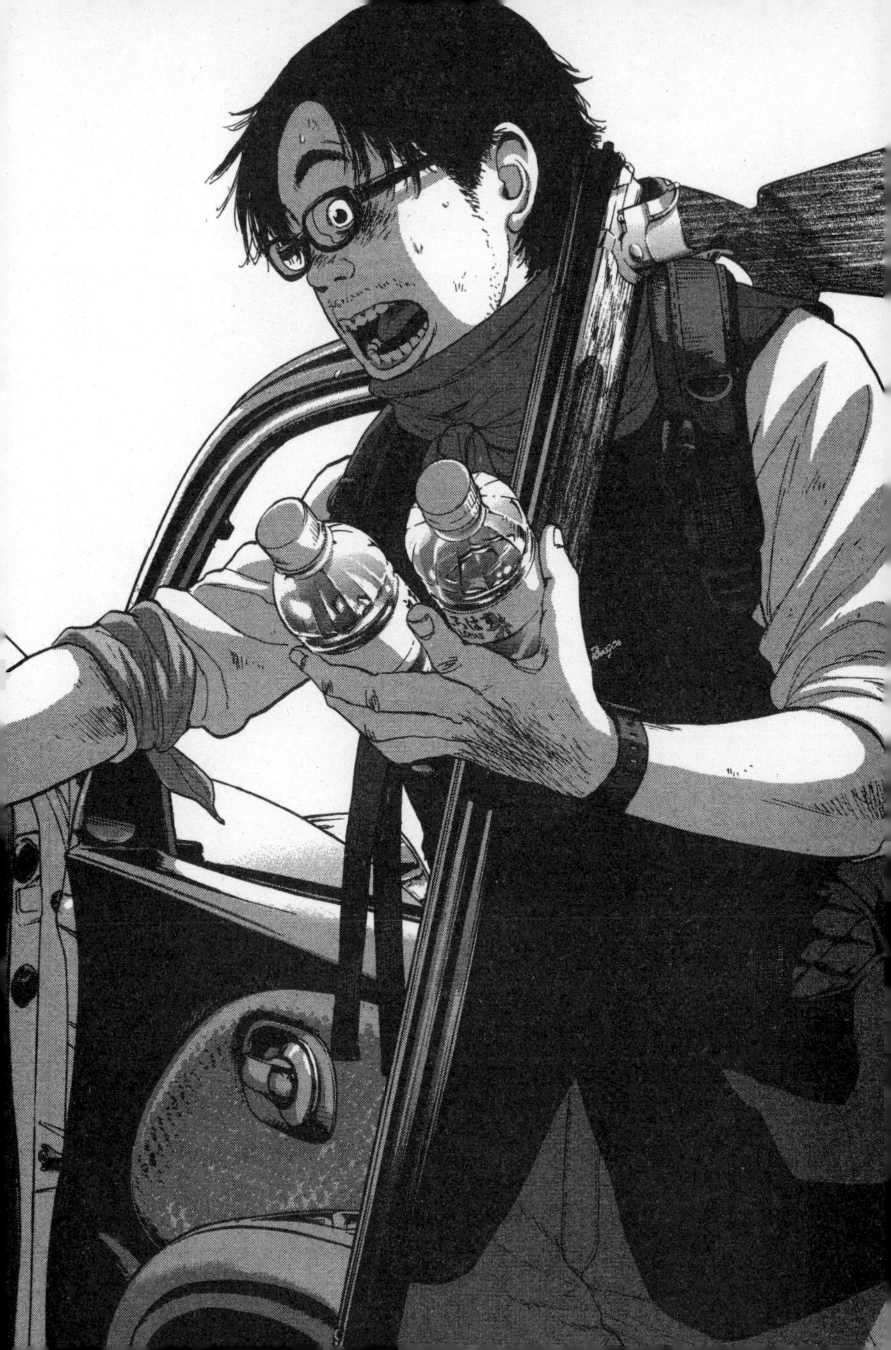

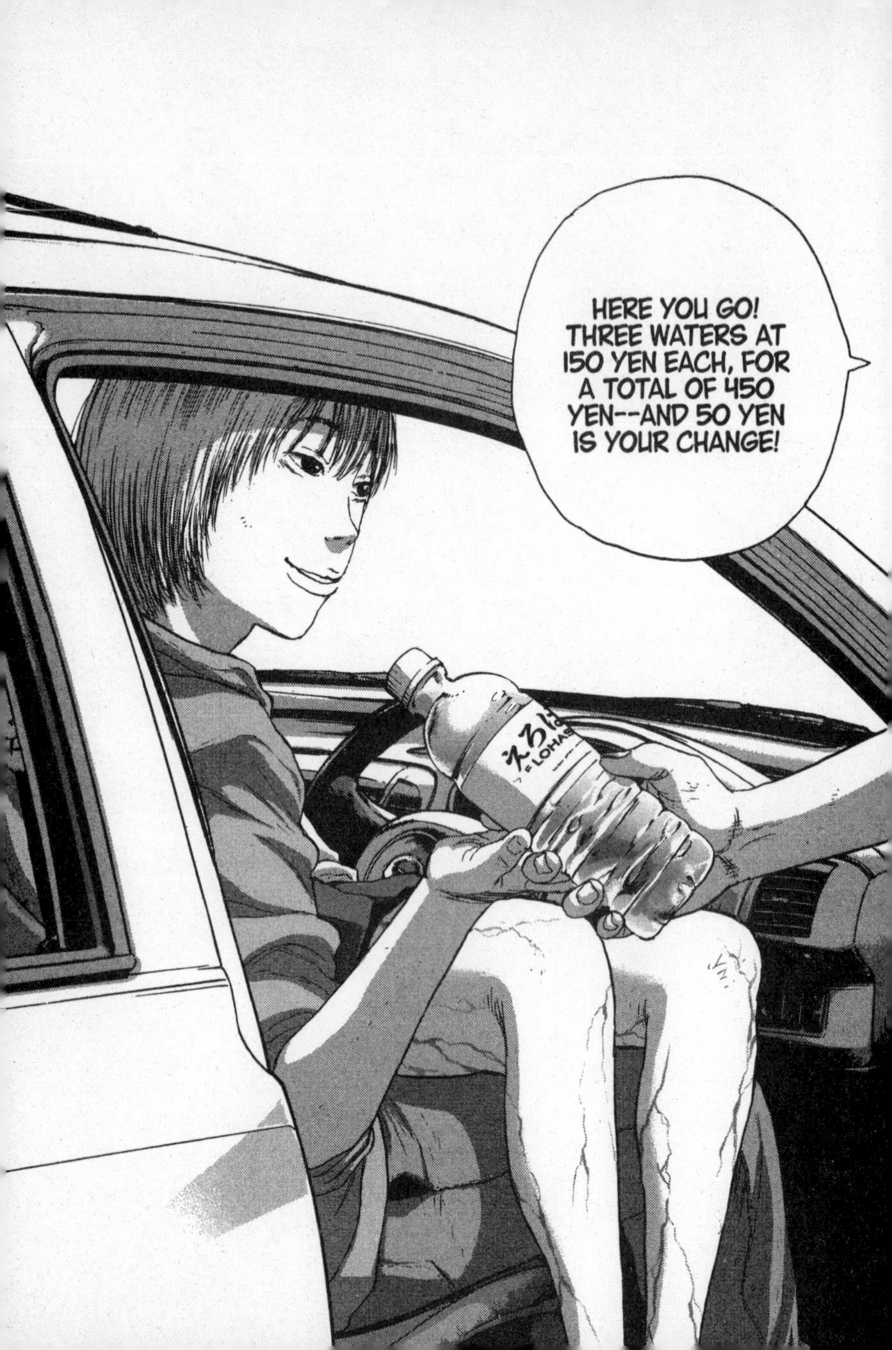
HERE YOU GO! THREE WATERS AT 150 YEN EACH, FOR A TOTAL OF 450 YEN--AND 50 YEN IS YOUR CHANGE!

THE BLEEDING'S STOPPED FOR NOW, BUT WITH THE BLOOD CAKED ON THERE, IT'S A HOTBED FOR BACTERIA. I'LL JUST WIPE IT CLEAN, OKAY?

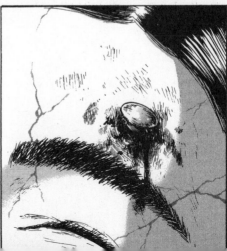

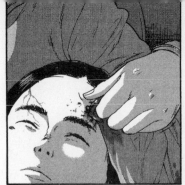
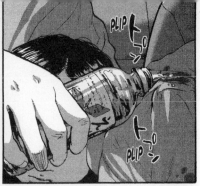

SORRY 'BOUT THIS.

WE'LL FIND A HOSPITAL AND GET THAT TREATED AS SOON AS WE CAN.

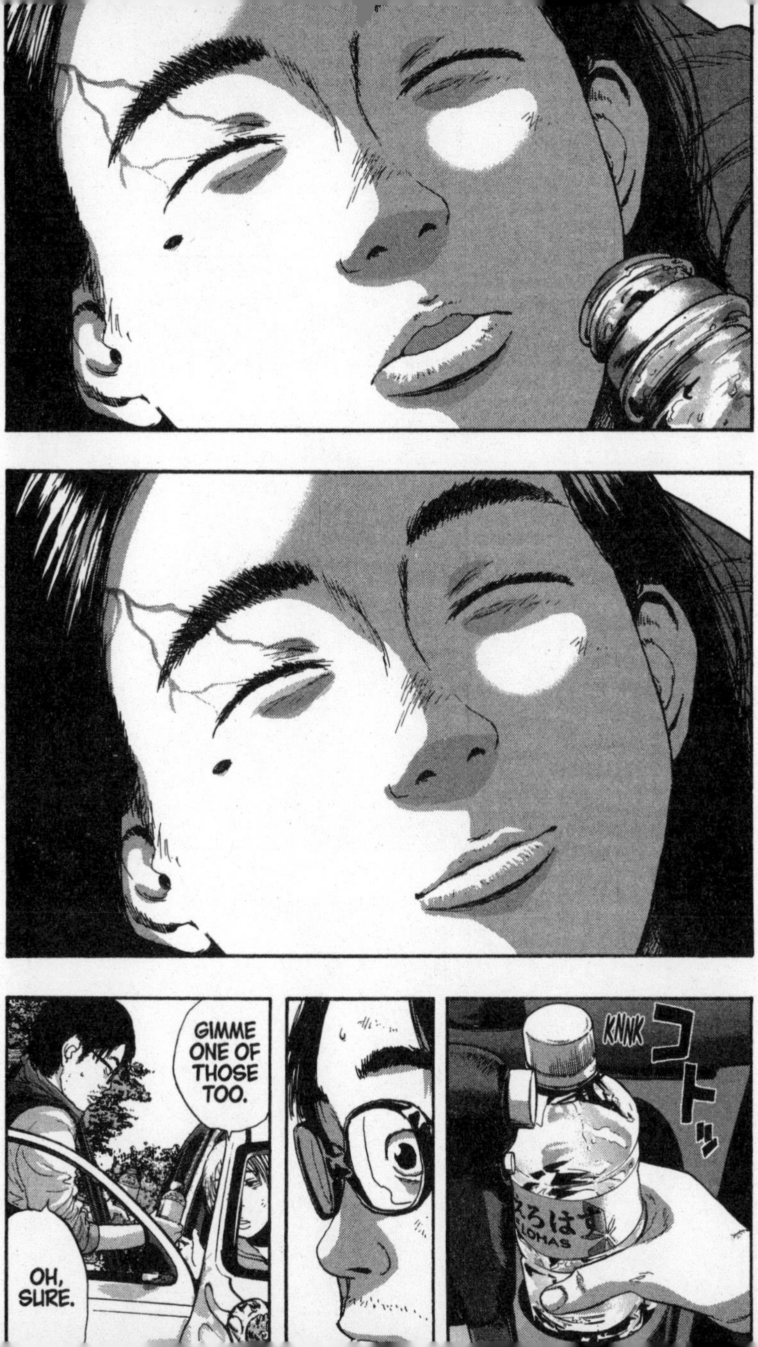
KNNK
コトッ
LOHAS
GIMME ONE OF THOSE TOO.
OH, SURE.

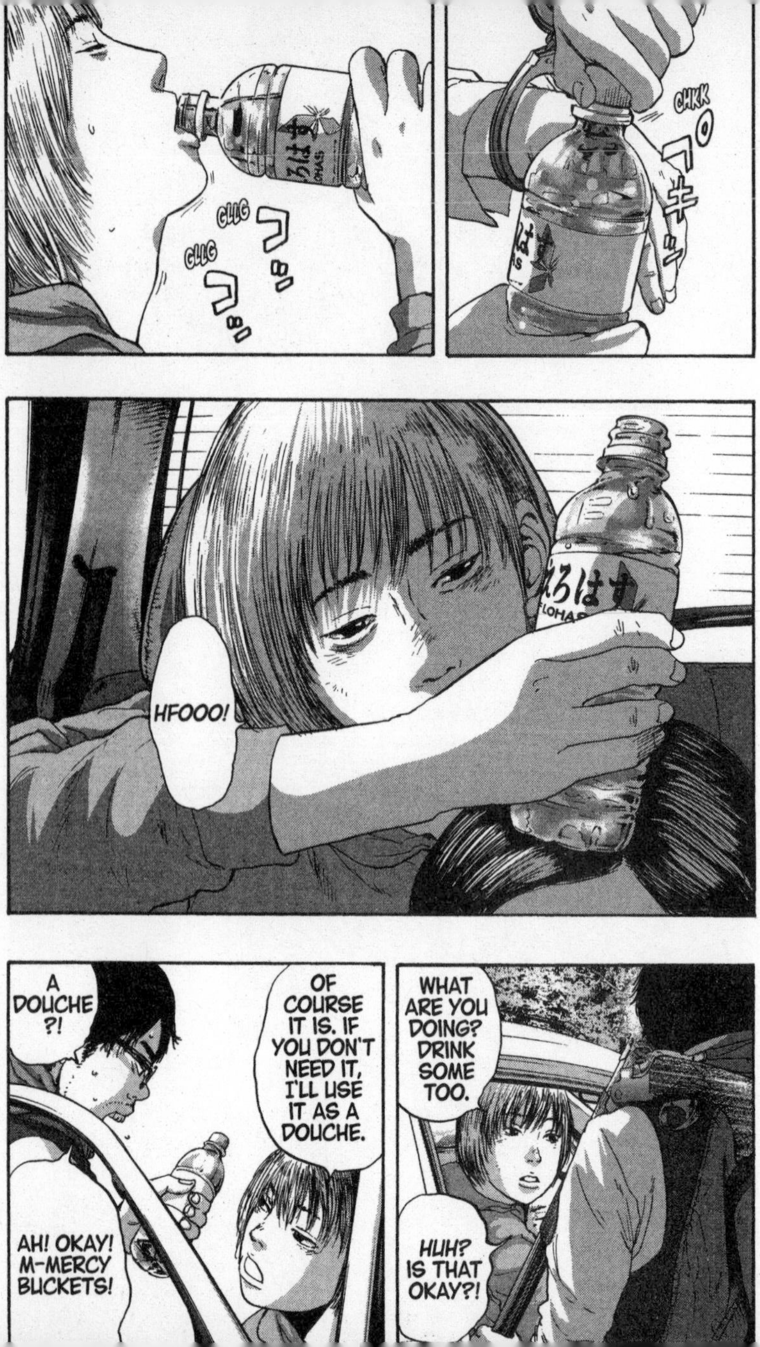
CHKK
GLLG
GLLG
HFOOO!
WHAT ARE YOU DOING? DRINK SOME TOO.
HUH? IS THAT OKAY?!
OF COURSE IT IS. IF YOU DON'T NEED IT, I'LL USE IT AS A DOUCHE.
A DOUCHE?!
AH! OKAY! M-MERCY BUCKETS!

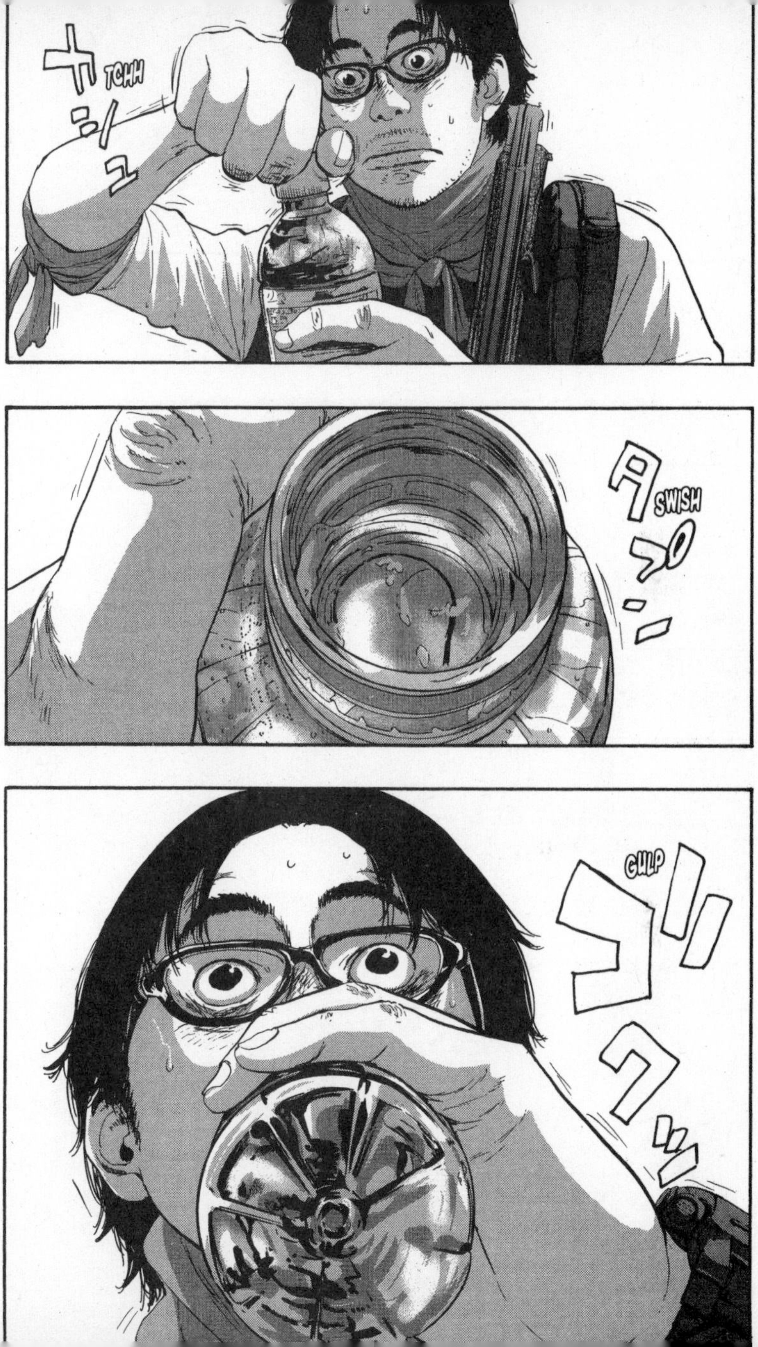

カシュ TCHH
タプ SWISH
ゴクッ GULP

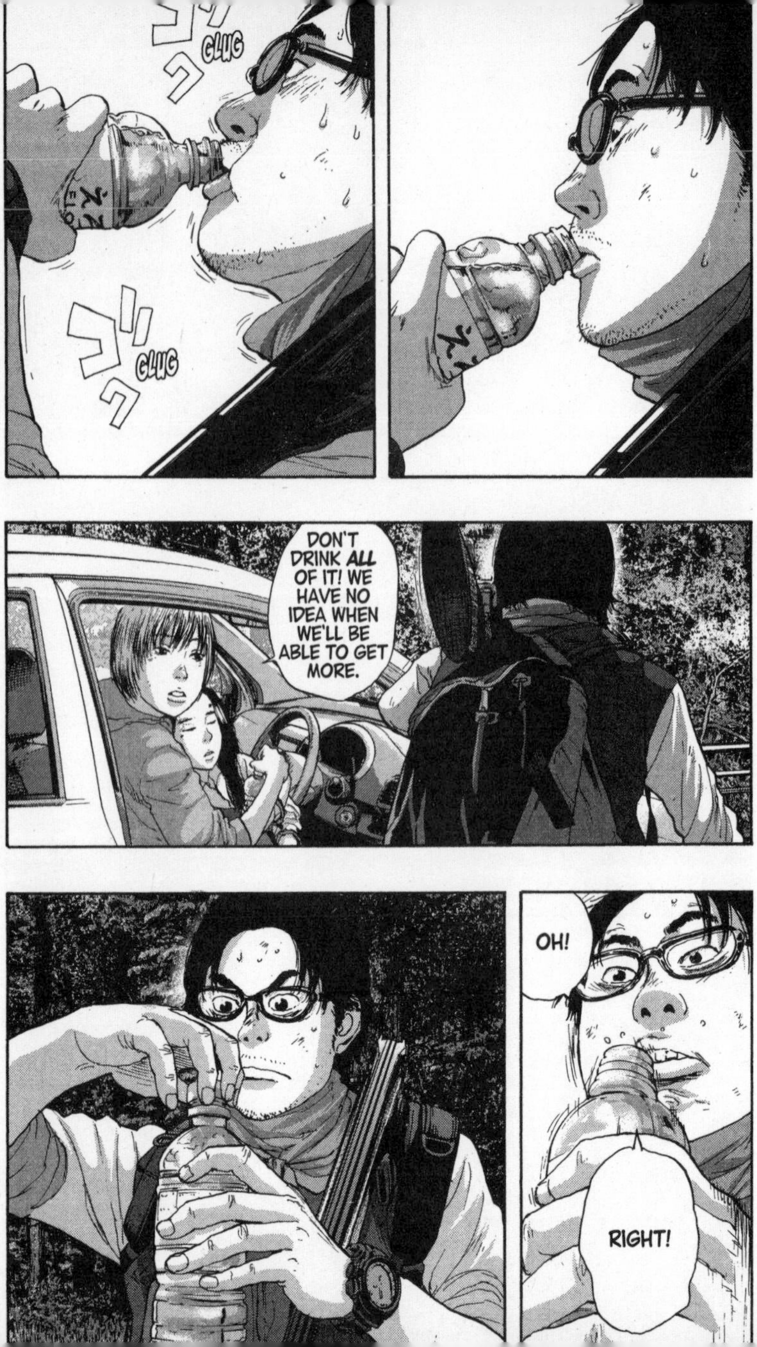
GLUG
GLUG
DON'T DRINK ALL OF IT! WE HAVE NO IDEA WHEN WE'LL BE ABLE TO GET MORE.
OH!
RIGHT!

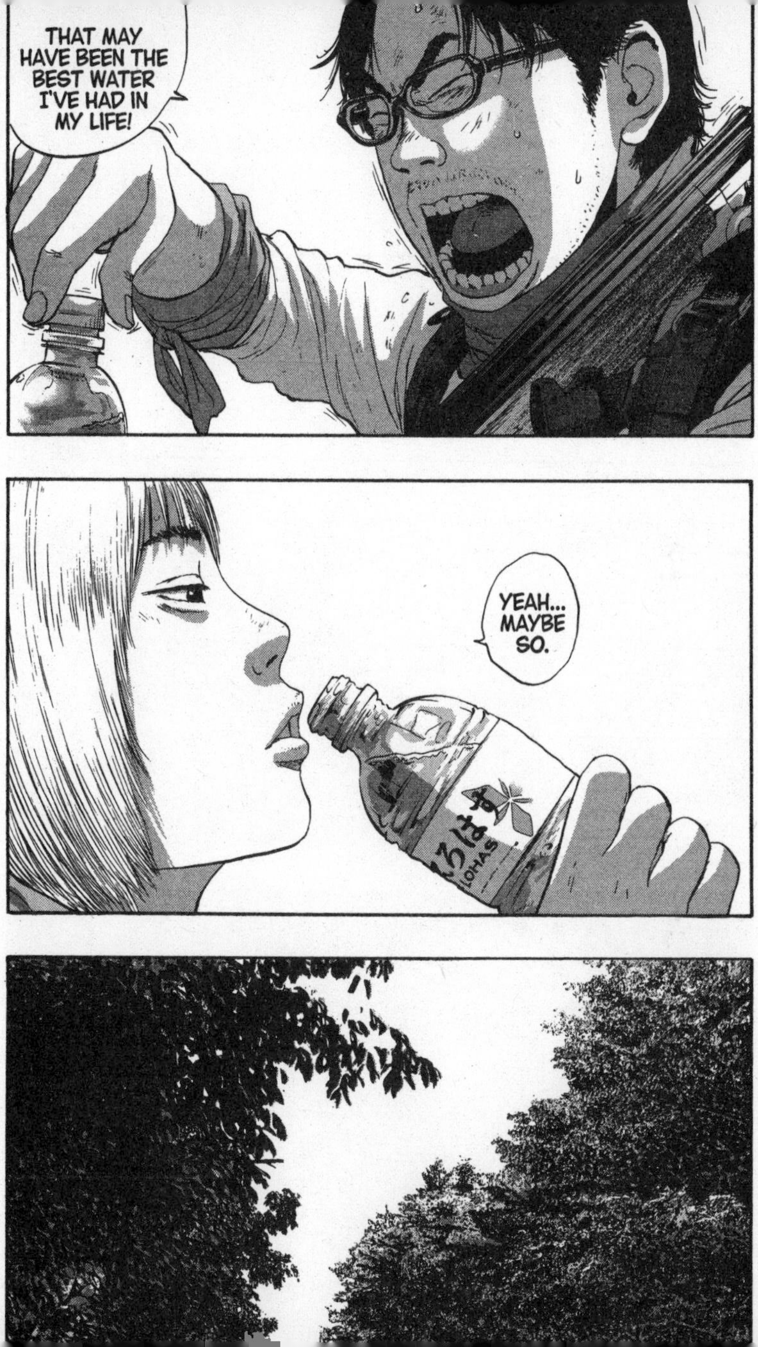
THAT MAY HAVE BEEN THE BEST WATER I'VE HAD IN MY LIFE!
YEAH... MAYBE SO.

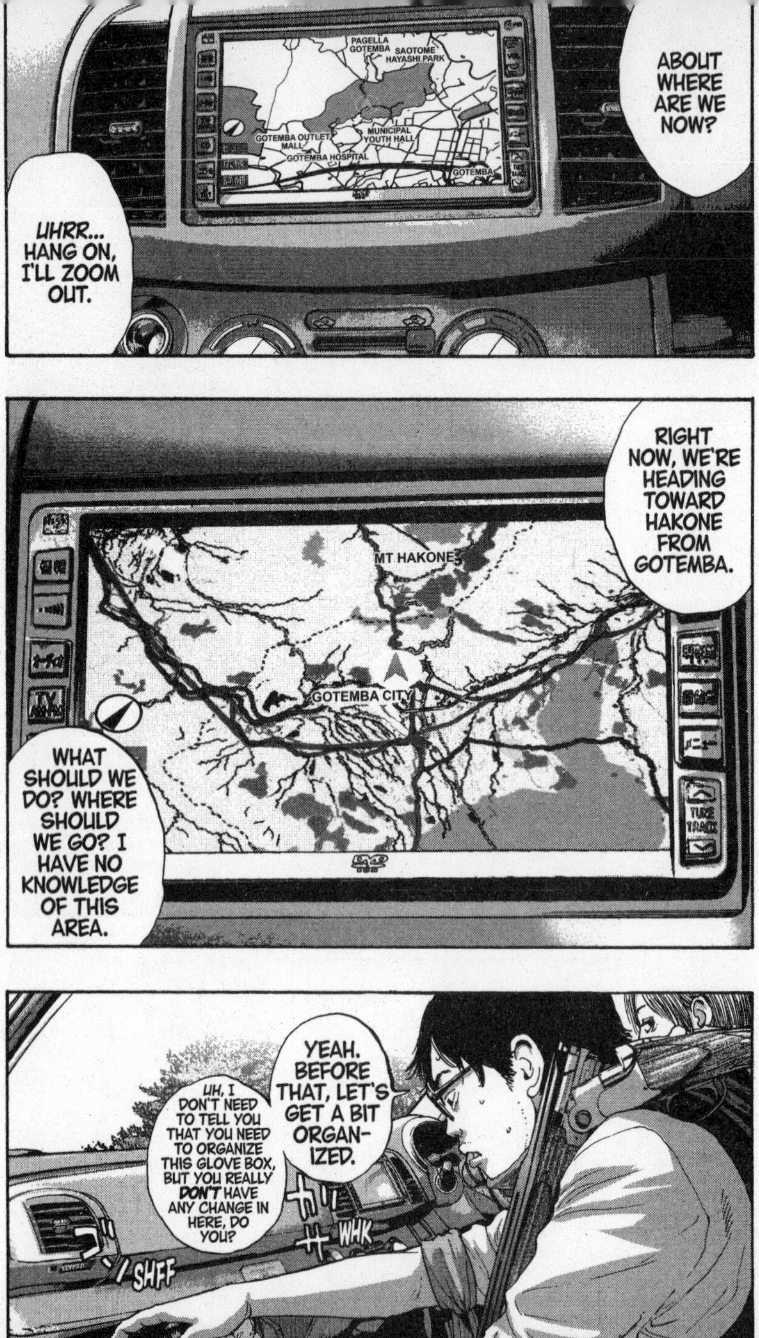
ABOUT WHERE ARE WE NOW?
PAGELLA GOTEMBA
SAOTOME HAYASHI PARK
MUNICIPAL YOUTH HALL
GOTEMBA OUTLET MALL
GOTEMBA HOSPITAL
GOTEMBA
UHRR... HANG ON, I'LL ZOOM OUT.
RIGHT NOW, WE'RE HEADING TOWARD HAKONE FROM GOTEMBA.
MT HAKONE
GOTEMBA CITY
WHAT SHOULD WE DO? WHERE SHOULD WE GO? I HAVE NO KNOWLEDGE OF THIS AREA.
YEAH. BEFORE THAT, LET'S GET A BIT ORGAN-IZED.
UH, I DON'T NEED TO TELL YOU THAT YOU NEED TO ORGANIZE THIS GLOVE BOX, BUT YOU REALLY ***DON'T*** HAVE ANY CHANGE IN HERE, DO YOU?
WHK
SHFF

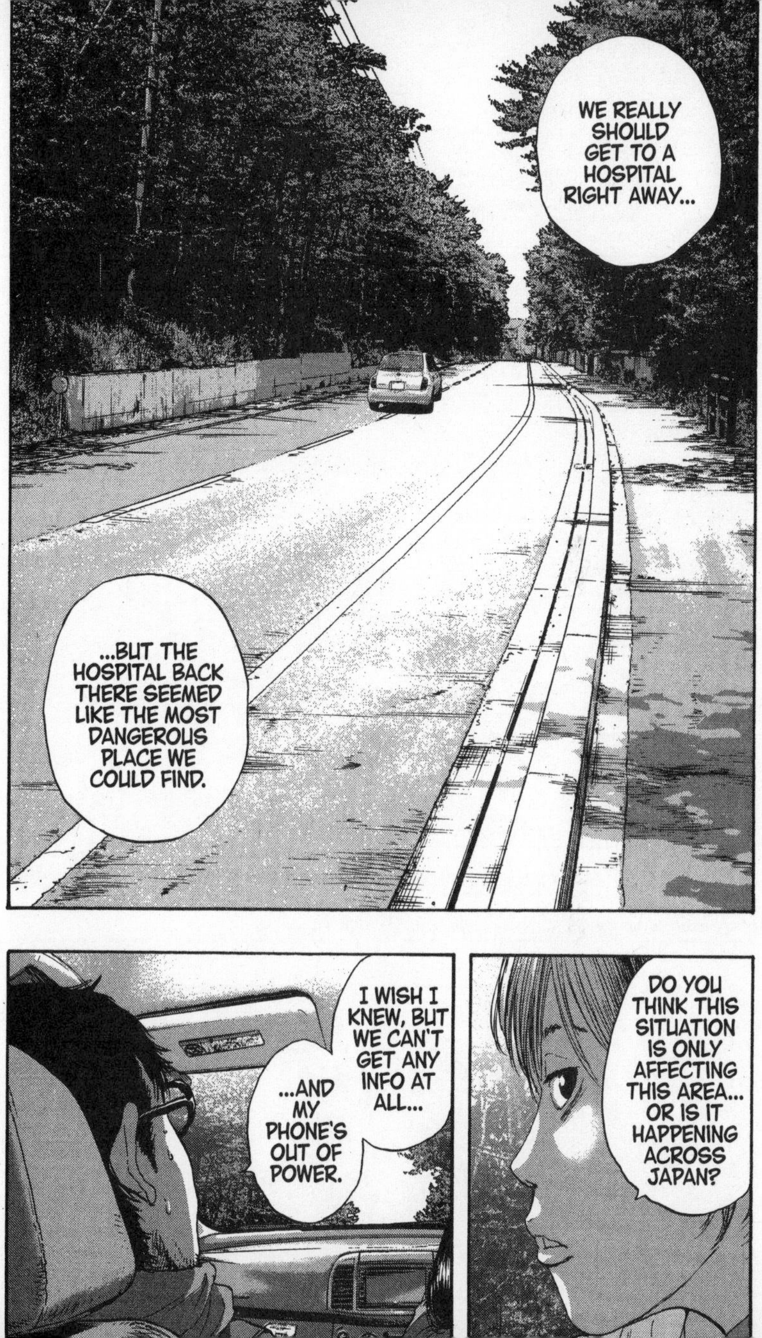
WE REALLY SHOULD GET TO A HOSPITAL RIGHT AWAY...
...BUT THE HOSPITAL BACK THERE SEEMED LIKE THE MOST DANGEROUS PLACE WE COULD FIND.
DO YOU THINK THIS SITUATION IS ONLY AFFECTING THIS AREA... OR IS IT HAPPENING ACROSS JAPAN?
I WISH I KNEW, BUT WE CAN'T GET ANY INFO AT ALL...
...AND MY PHONE'S OUT OF POWER.

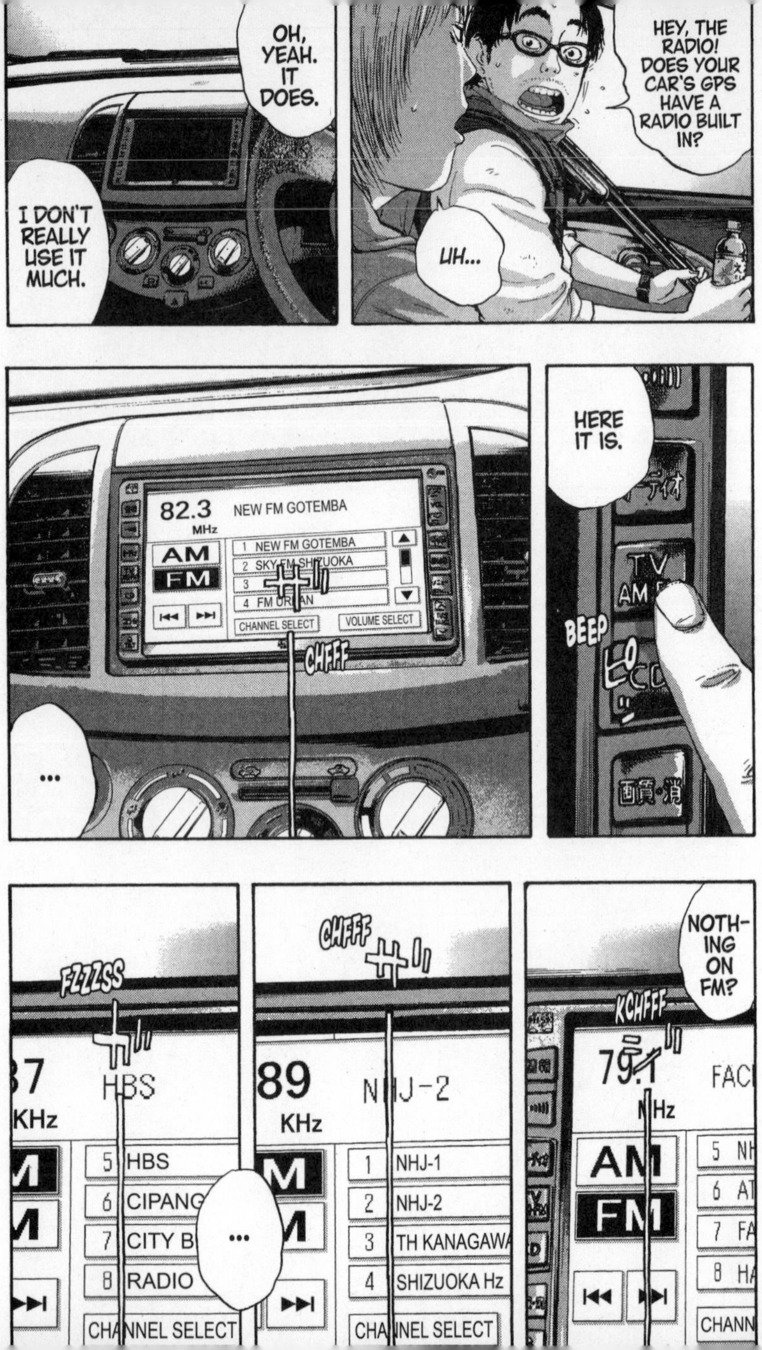
HEY, THE RADIO! DOES YOUR CAR'S GPS HAVE A RADIO BUILT IN?
UH...
OH, YEAH. IT DOES.
I DON'T REALLY USE IT MUCH.
HERE IT IS.
BEEP
82.3 NEW FM GOTEMBA
MHz
AM
FM
1 NEW FM GOTEMBA
2 SKY FM SHIZUOKA
4 FM URBAN
CHANNEL SELECT
VOLUME SELECT
CHFFF
...
NOTHING ON FM?
KCHFFF
79.1
MHz
AM
FM
CHFFF
89 NHJ-2
KHz
1 NHJ-1
2 NHJ-2
3 TH KANAGAWA
4 SHIZUOKA Hz
CHANNEL SELECT
FZZZSS
HBS
KHz
5 HBS
6 CIPANG
8 RADIO
CHANNEL SELECT
...

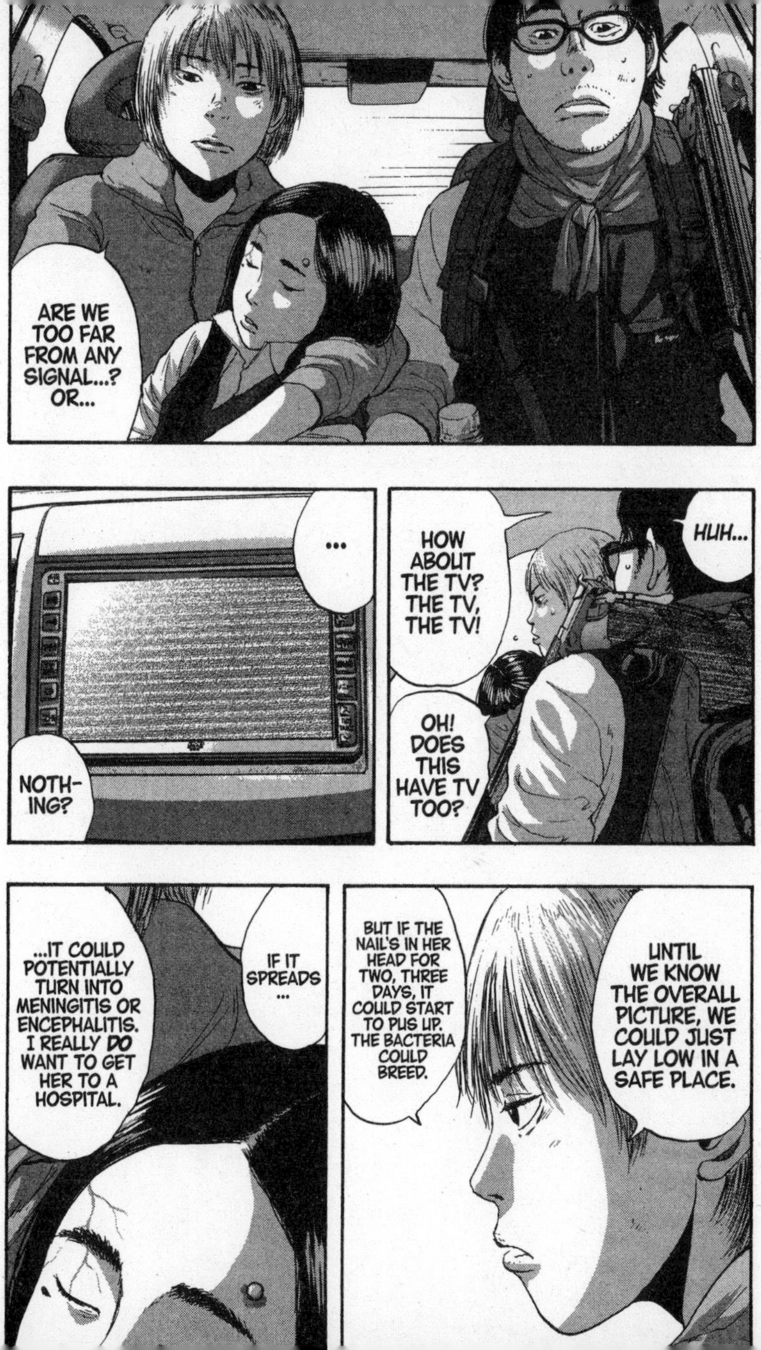
ARE WE TOO FAR FROM ANY SIGNAL...? OR...
HUH...
HOW ABOUT THE TV? THE TV, THE TV!
OH! DOES THIS HAVE TV TOO?
...
NOTH-ING?
UNTIL WE KNOW THE OVERALL PICTURE, WE COULD JUST LAY LOW IN A SAFE PLACE.
BUT IF THE NAIL'S IN HER HEAD FOR TWO, THREE DAYS, IT COULD START TO PUS UP. THE BACTERIA COULD BREED.
IF IT SPREADS ...
...IT COULD POTENTIALLY TURN INTO MENINGITIS OR ENCEPHALITIS. I REALLY **DO** WANT TO GET HER TO A HOSPITAL.

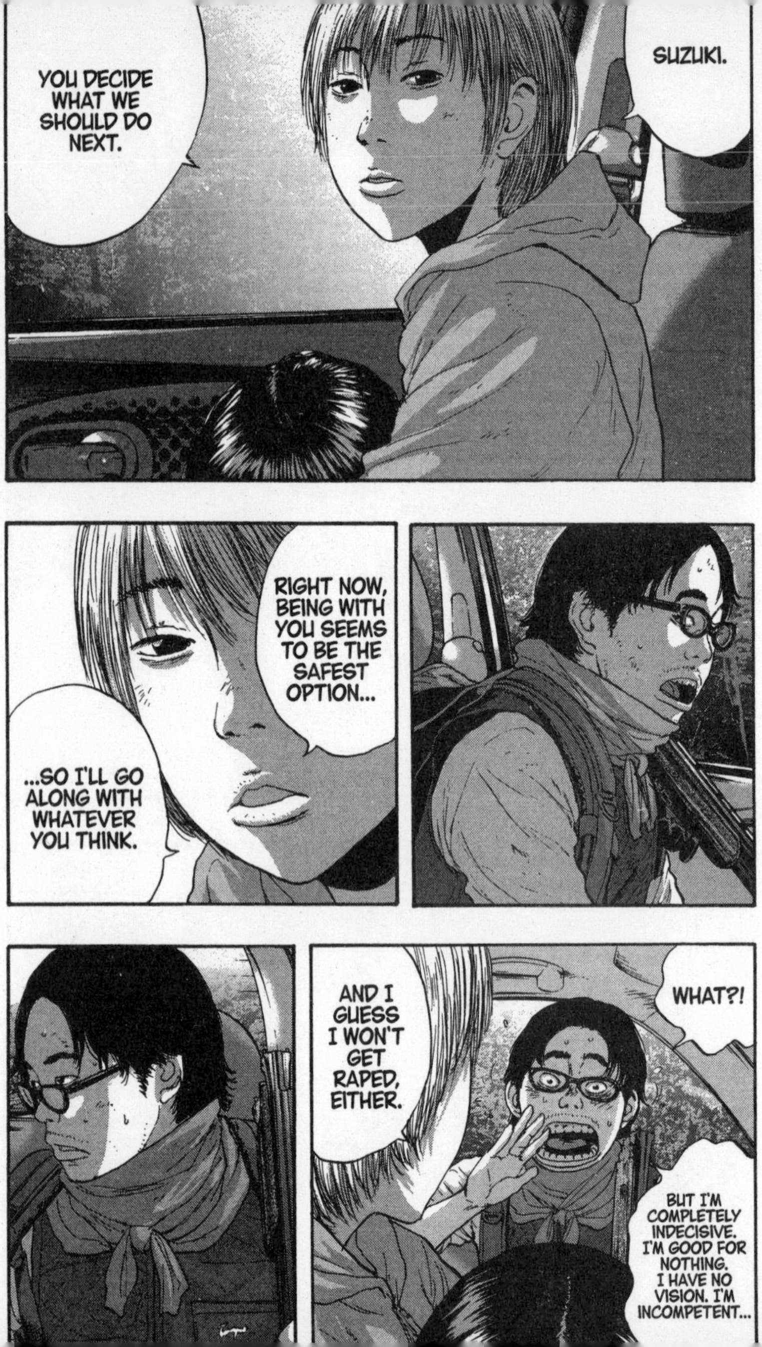
SUZUKI.
YOU DECIDE WHAT WE SHOULD DO NEXT.
RIGHT NOW, BEING WITH YOU SEEMS TO BE THE SAFEST OPTION...
...SO I'LL GO ALONG WITH WHATEVER YOU THINK.
AND I GUESS I WON'T GET RAPED, EITHER.
WHAT?!
BUT I'M COMPLETELY INDECISIVE. I'M GOOD FOR NOTHING. I HAVE NO VISION. I'M INCOMPETENT...

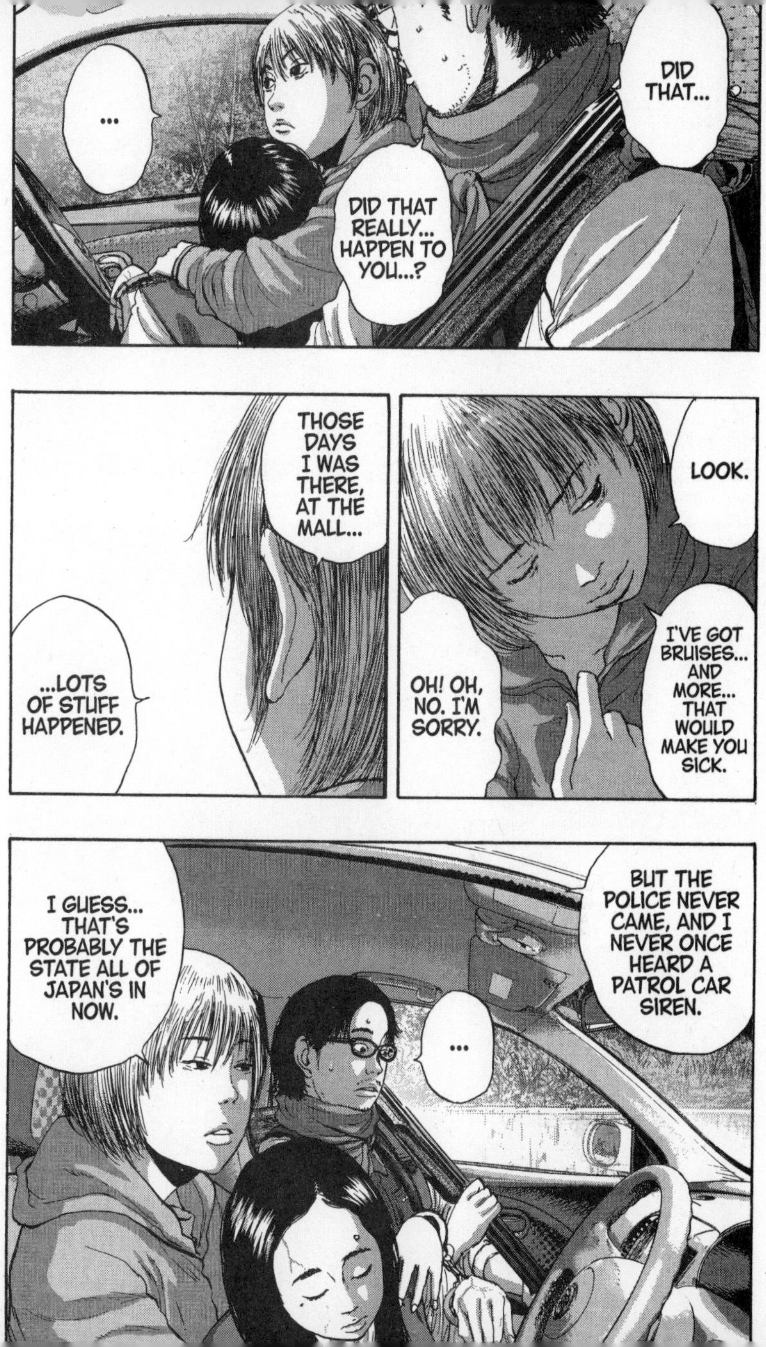
DID THAT...
DID THAT REALLY... HAPPEN TO YOU...?
...
LOOK.
I'VE GOT BRUISES... AND MORE... THAT WOULD MAKE YOU SICK.
OH! OH, NO. I'M SORRY.
THOSE DAYS I WAS THERE, AT THE MALL...
...LOTS OF STUFF HAPPENED.
BUT THE POLICE NEVER CAME, AND I NEVER ONCE HEARD A PATROL CAR SIREN.
...
I GUESS... THAT'S PROBABLY THE STATE ALL OF JAPAN'S IN NOW.

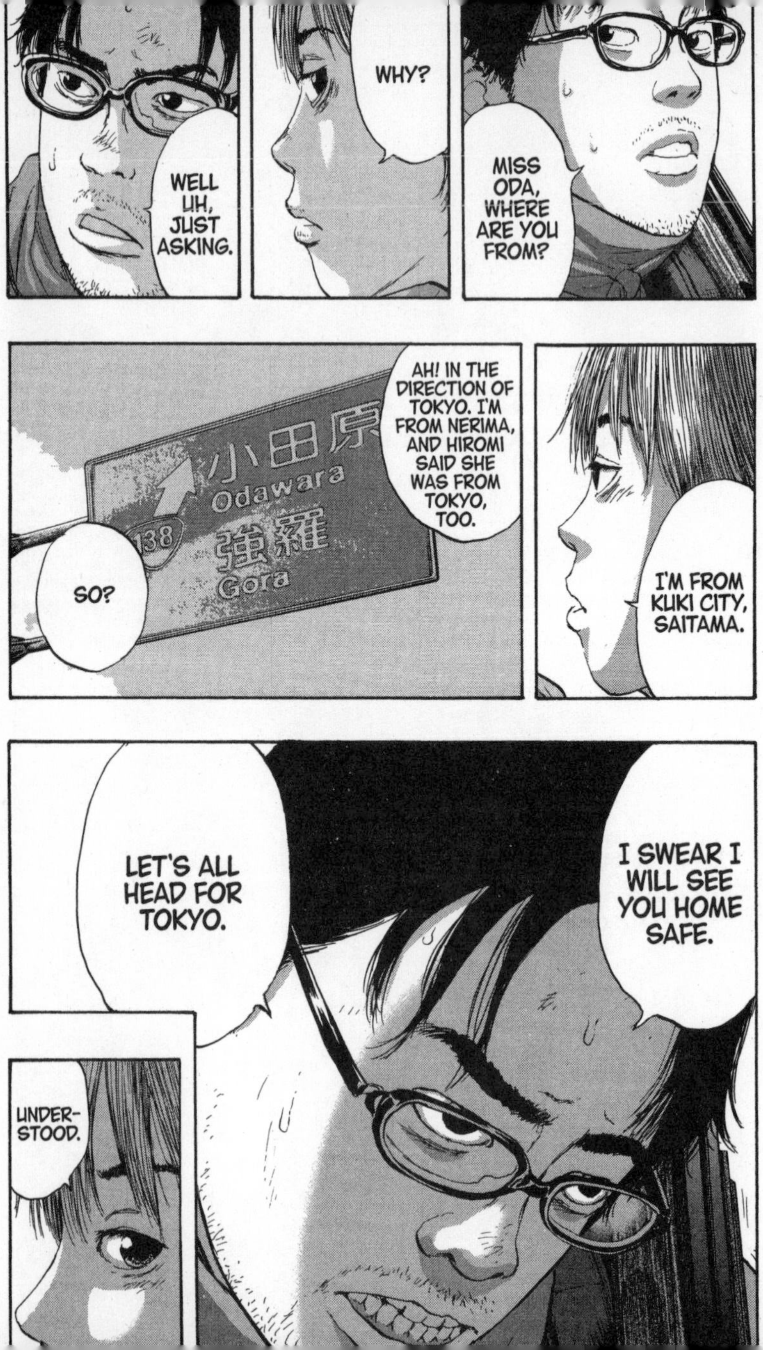
MISS ODA, WHERE ARE YOU FROM?
WHY?
WELL UH, JUST ASKING.
I'M FROM KUKI CITY, SAITAMA.
AH! IN THE DIRECTION OF TOKYO. I'M FROM NERIMA, AND HIROMI SAID SHE WAS FROM TOKYO, TOO.
小田原
Odawara
138
強羅
Gora
SO?
I SWEAR I WILL SEE YOU HOME SAFE.
LET'S ALL HEAD FOR TOKYO.
UNDER-STOOD.

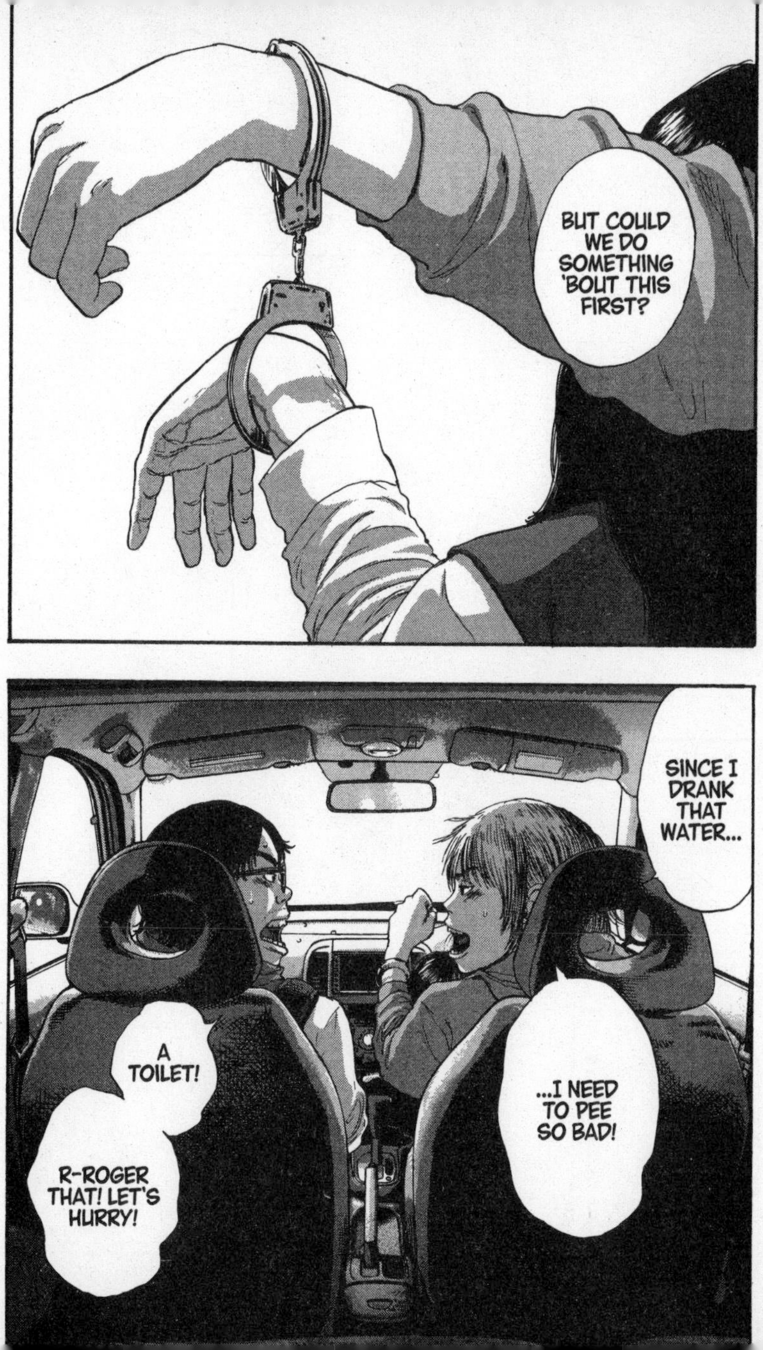
BUT COULD WE DO SOMETHING 'BOUT THIS FIRST?
SINCE I DRANK THAT WATER...
...I NEED TO PEE SO BAD!
A TOILET!
R-ROGER THAT! LET'S HURRY!

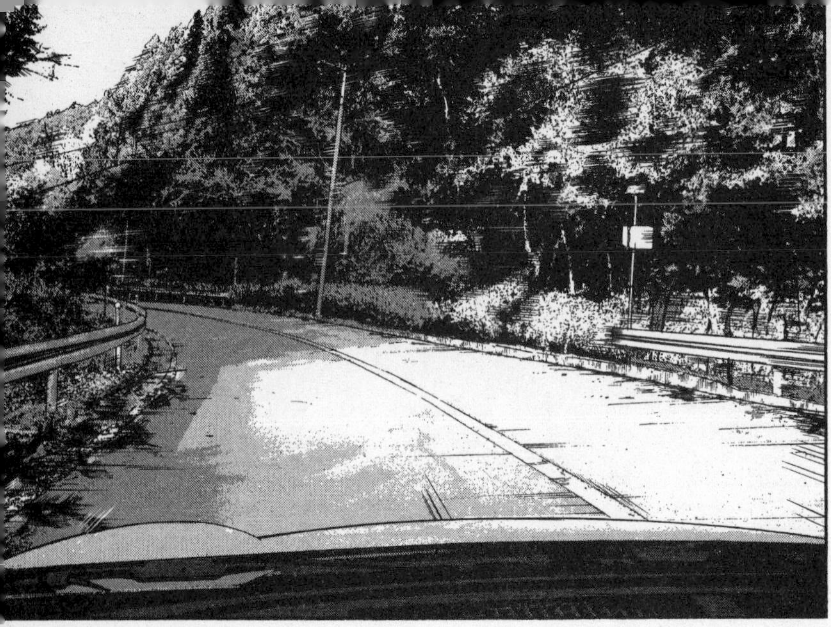

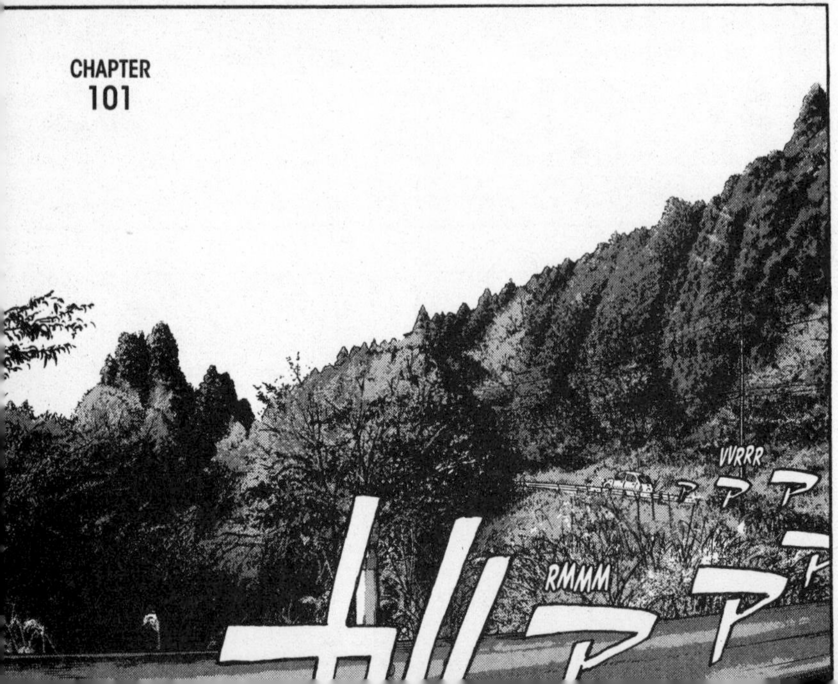
CHAPTER
101
VVRRR
RMMM

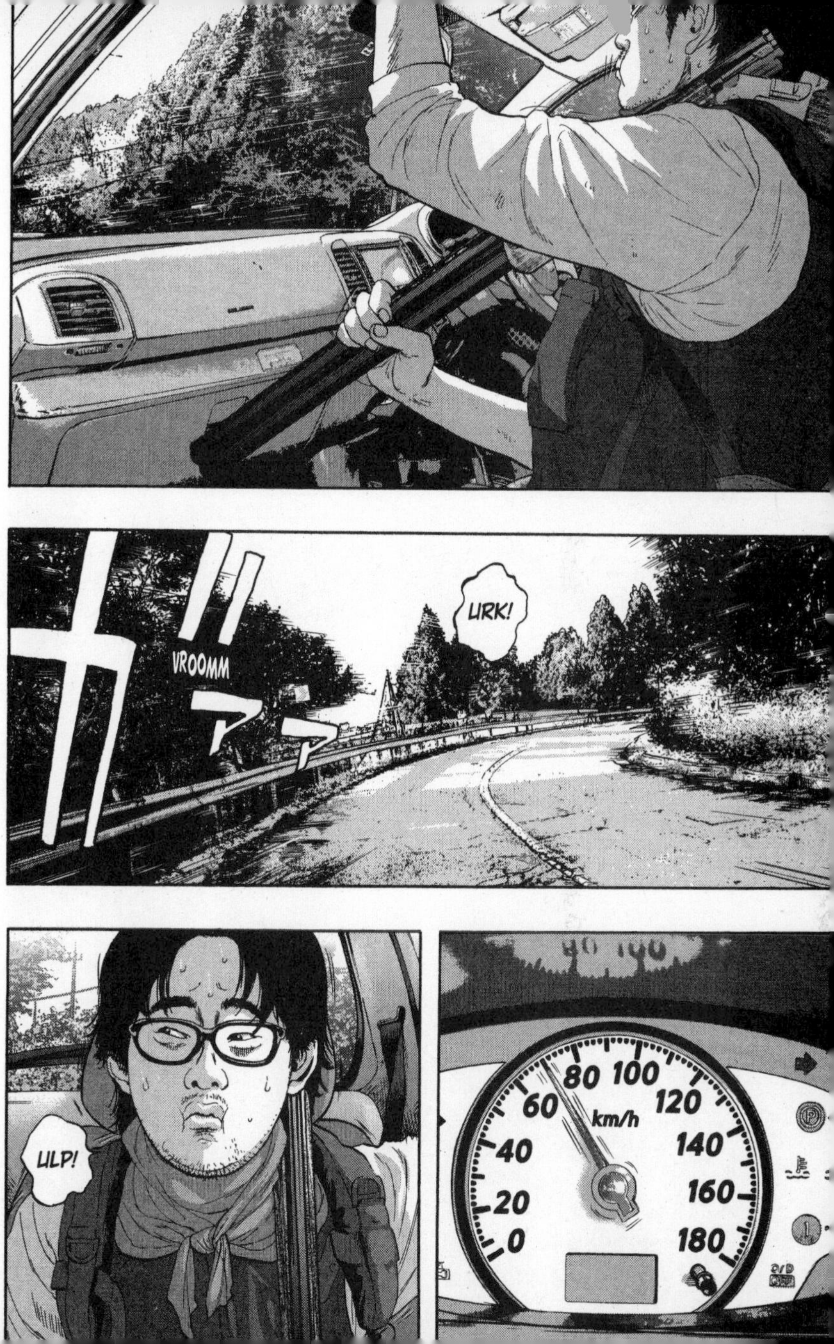

URK!
VROOMM
0 20 40 60 80 100 120 140 160 180 km/h
ULP!

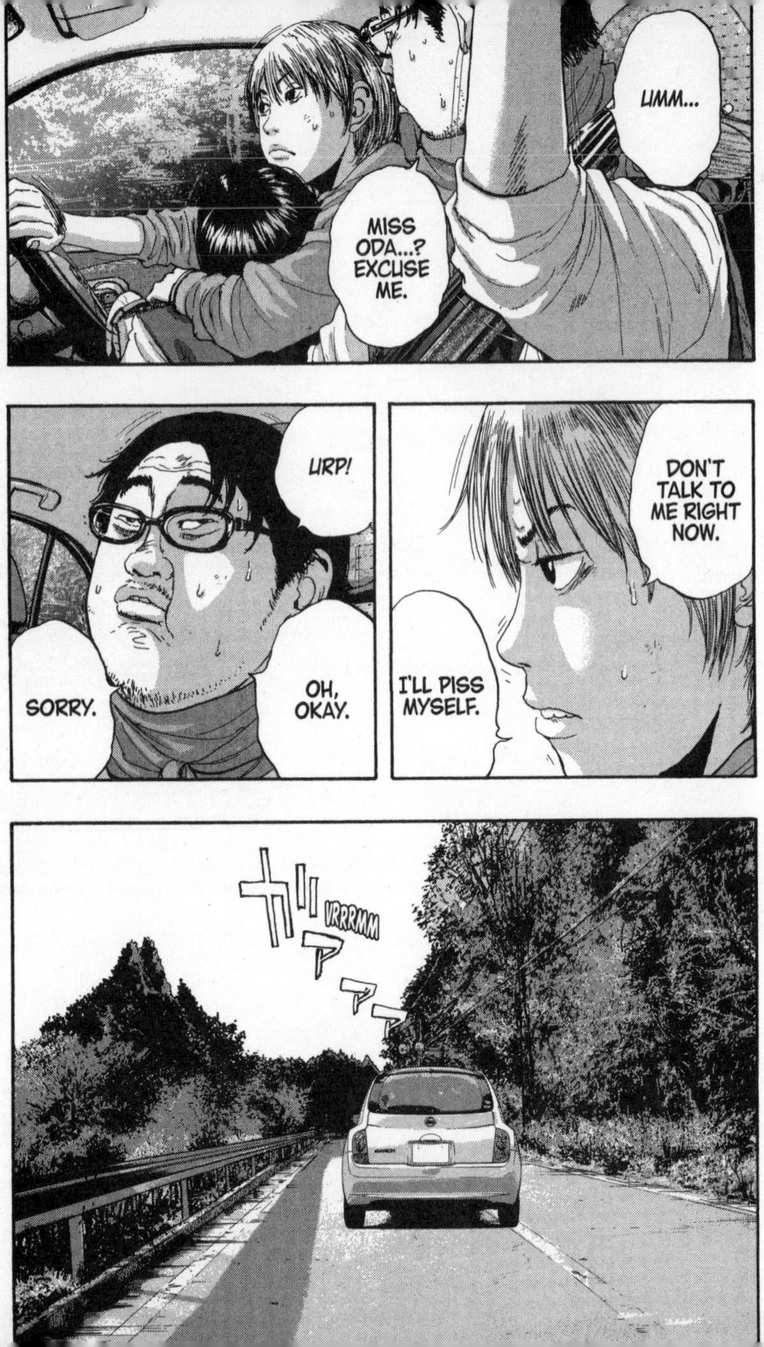
UMM...
MISS ODA...? EXCUSE ME.
DON'T TALK TO ME RIGHT NOW.
I'LL PISS MYSELF.
URP!
OH, OKAY.
SORRY.
VRRRMM

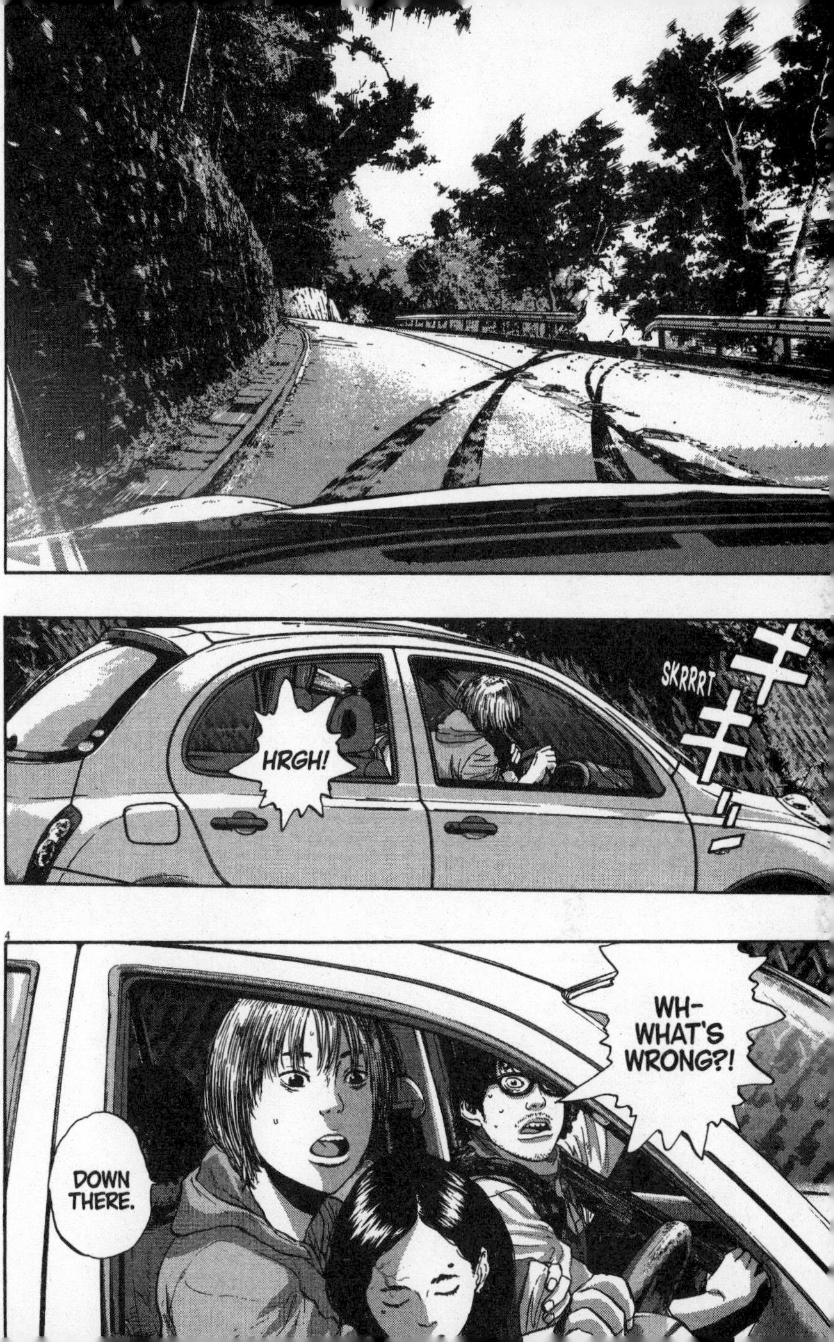
SKRRRT
HRGH!
WH- WHAT'S WRONG?!
DOWN THERE.

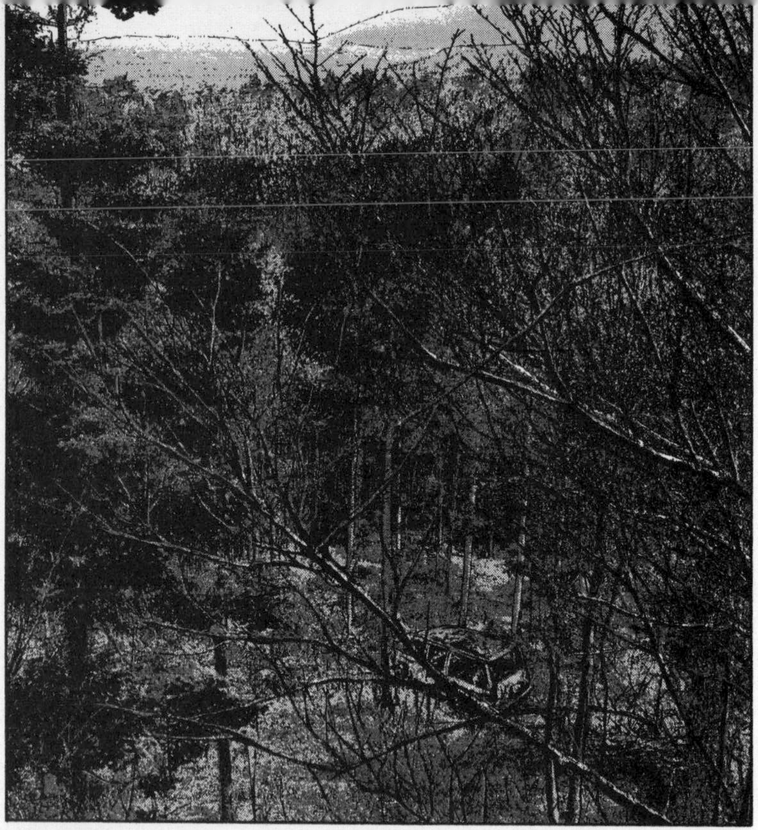
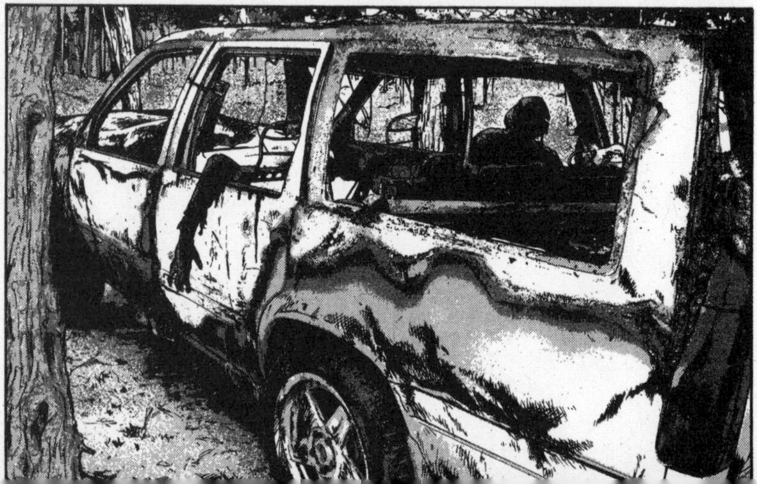

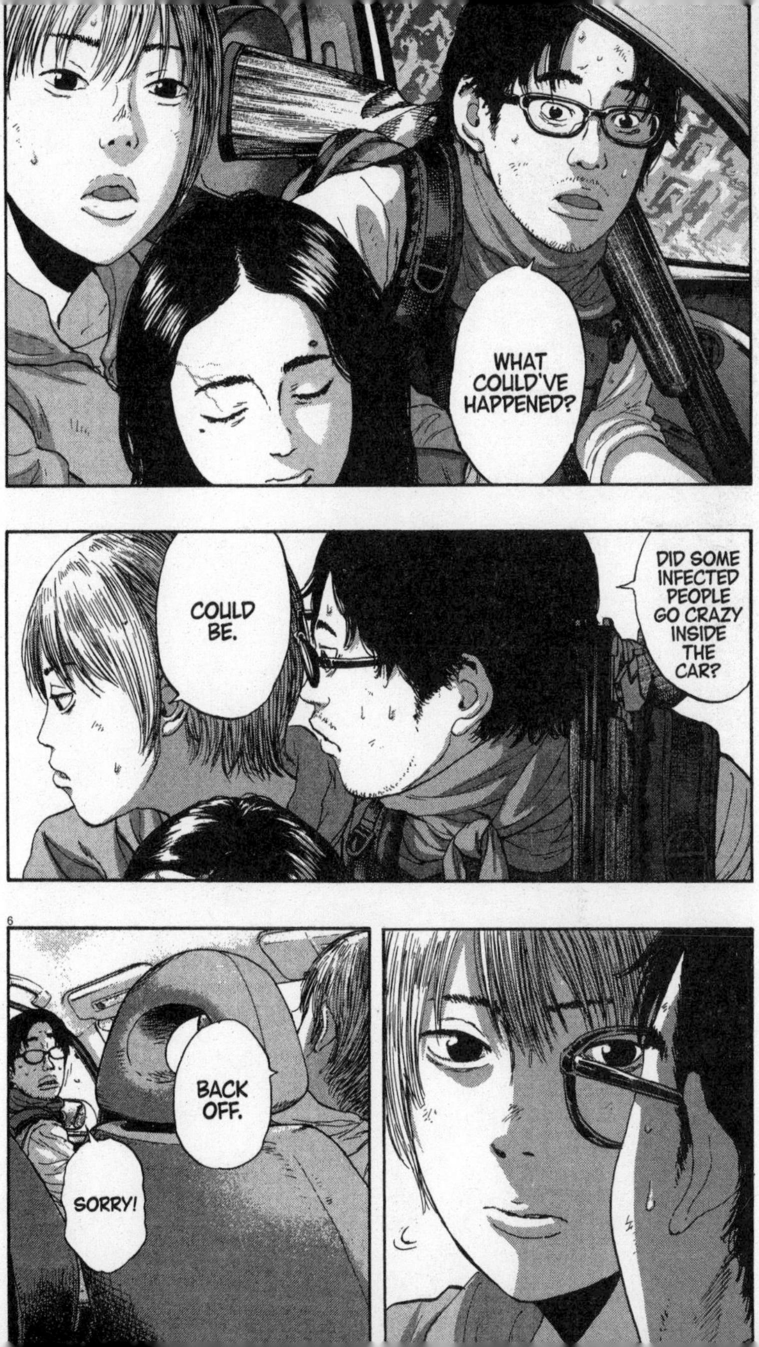
WHAT COULD'VE HAPPENED?
DID SOME INFECTED PEOPLE GO CRAZY INSIDE THE CAR?
COULD BE.
BACK OFF.
SORRY!

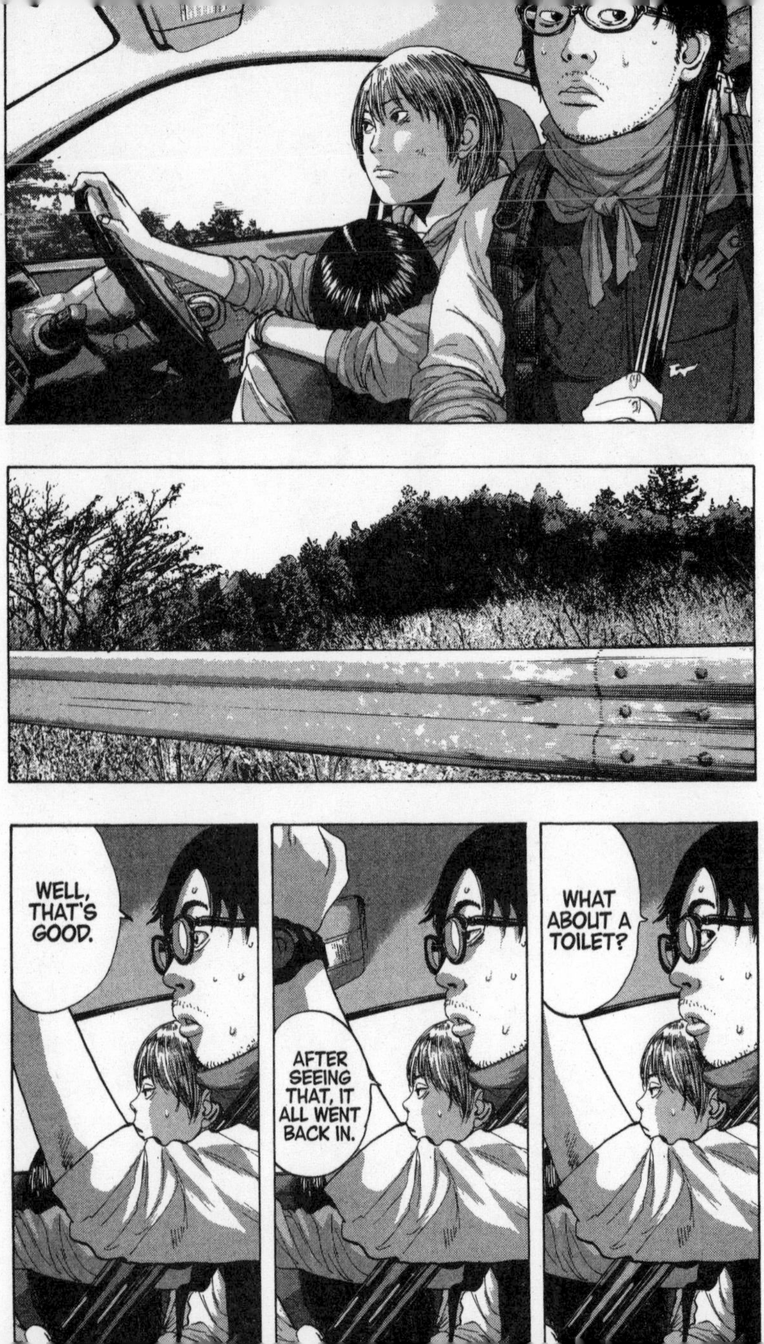
WHAT ABOUT A TOILET?
AFTER SEEING THAT, IT ALL WENT BACK IN.
WELL, THAT'S GOOD.

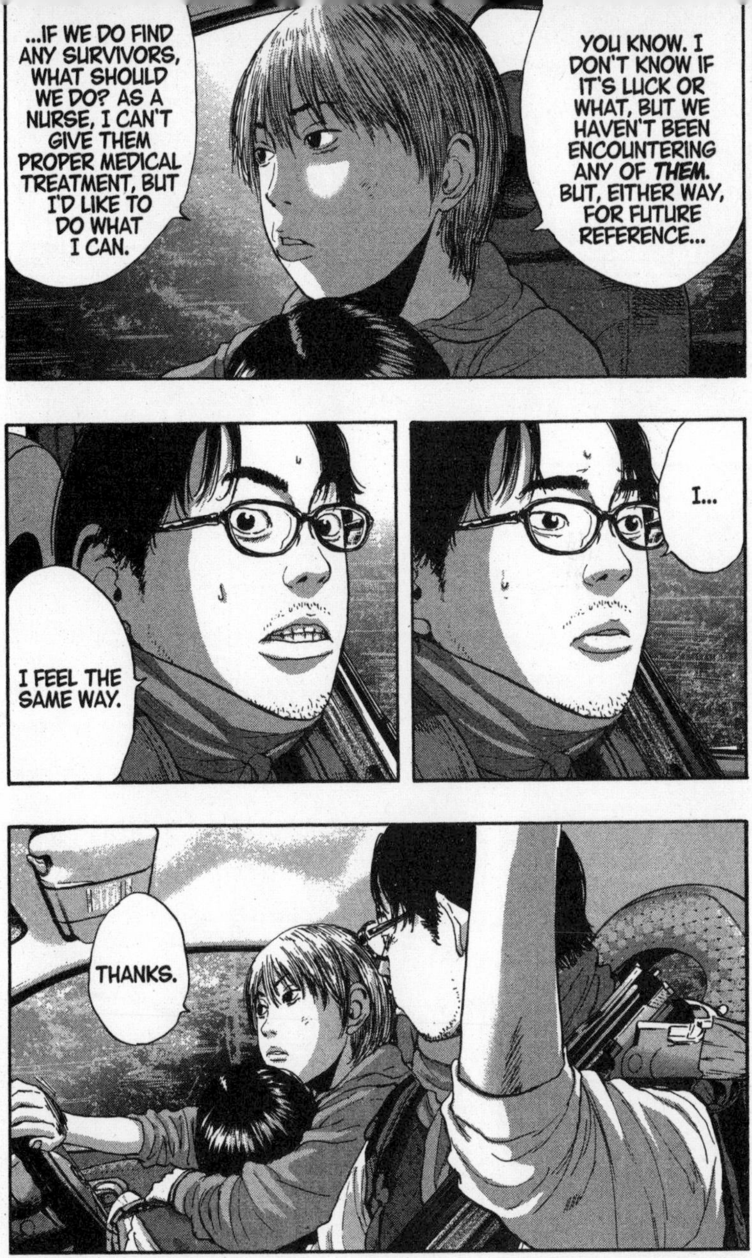
YOU KNOW. I DON'T KNOW IF IT'S LUCK OR WHAT, BUT WE HAVEN'T BEEN ENCOUNTERING ANY OF *THEM*. BUT, EITHER WAY, FOR FUTURE REFERENCE...
...IF WE DO FIND ANY SURVIVORS, WHAT SHOULD WE DO? AS A NURSE, I CAN'T GIVE THEM PROPER MEDICAL TREATMENT, BUT I'D LIKE TO DO WHAT I CAN.
I...
I FEEL THE SAME WAY.
THANKS.

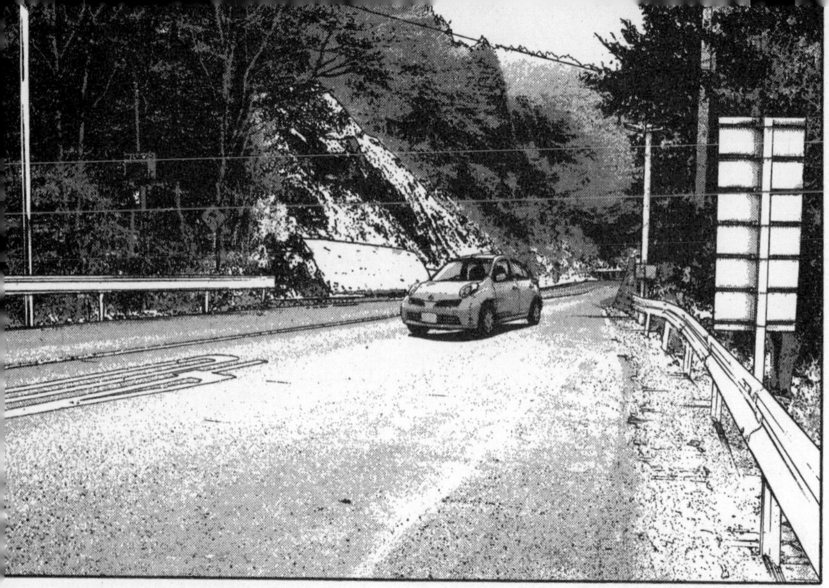

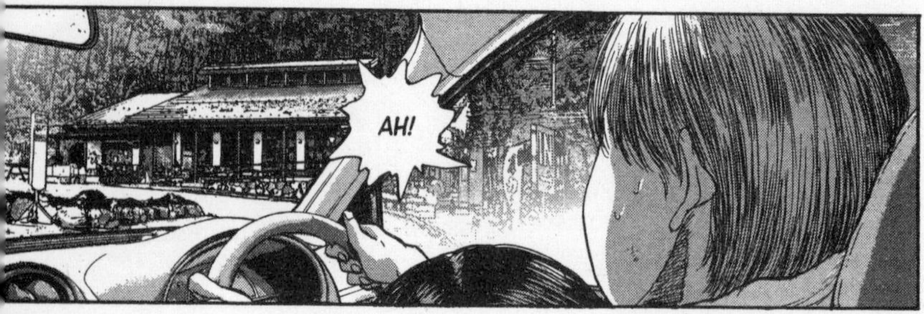
AH!

SIGN: OTOME PASS / FUJISAN-YA / SOUVENIRS, DINING, SOBA

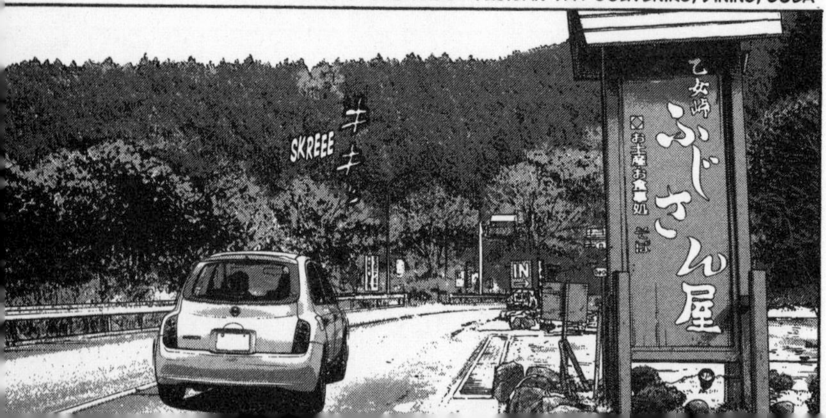
SKREEE
乙女峠
ふじさん屋
IN

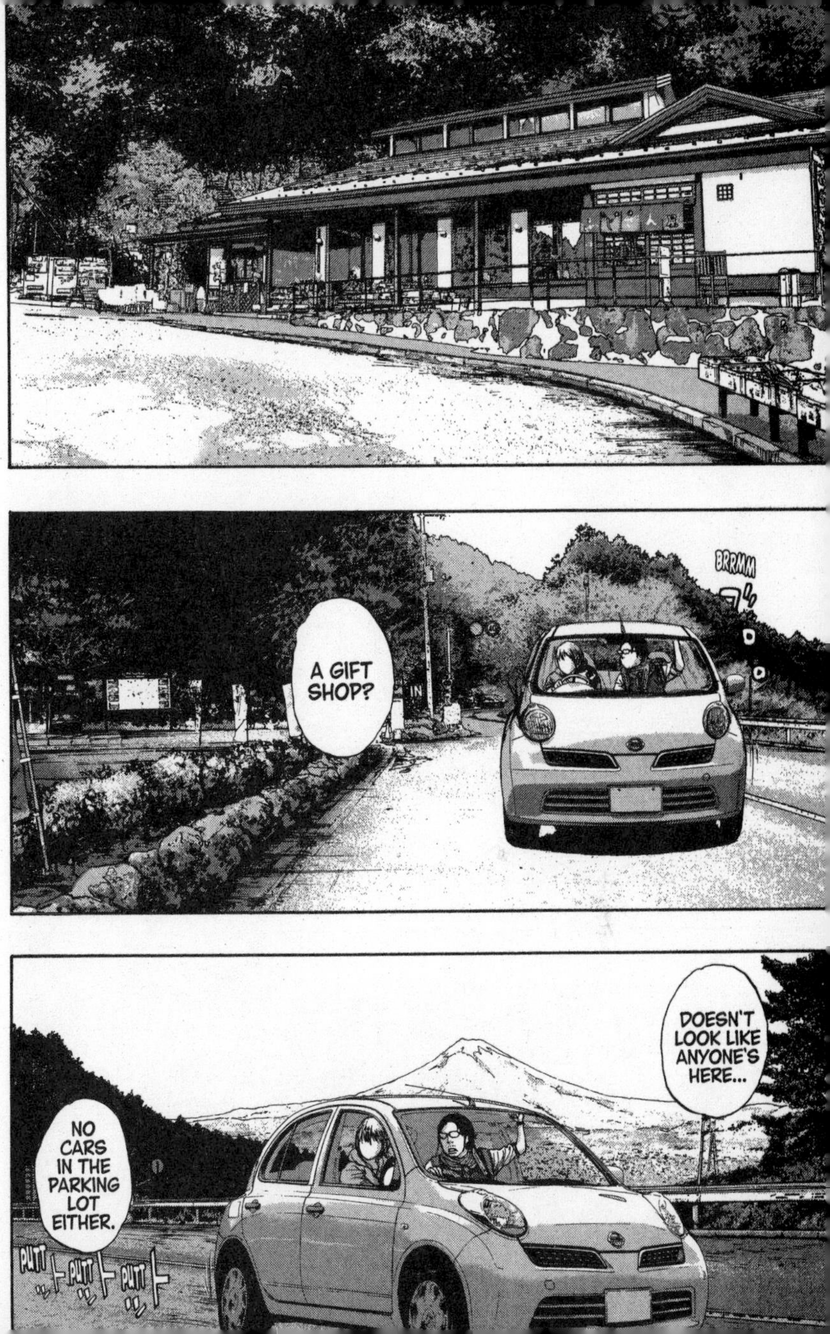
BRRMM
A GIFT SHOP?
DOESN'T LOOK LIKE ANYONE'S HERE...
NO CARS IN THE PARKING LOT EITHER.
PUTT PUTT PUTT

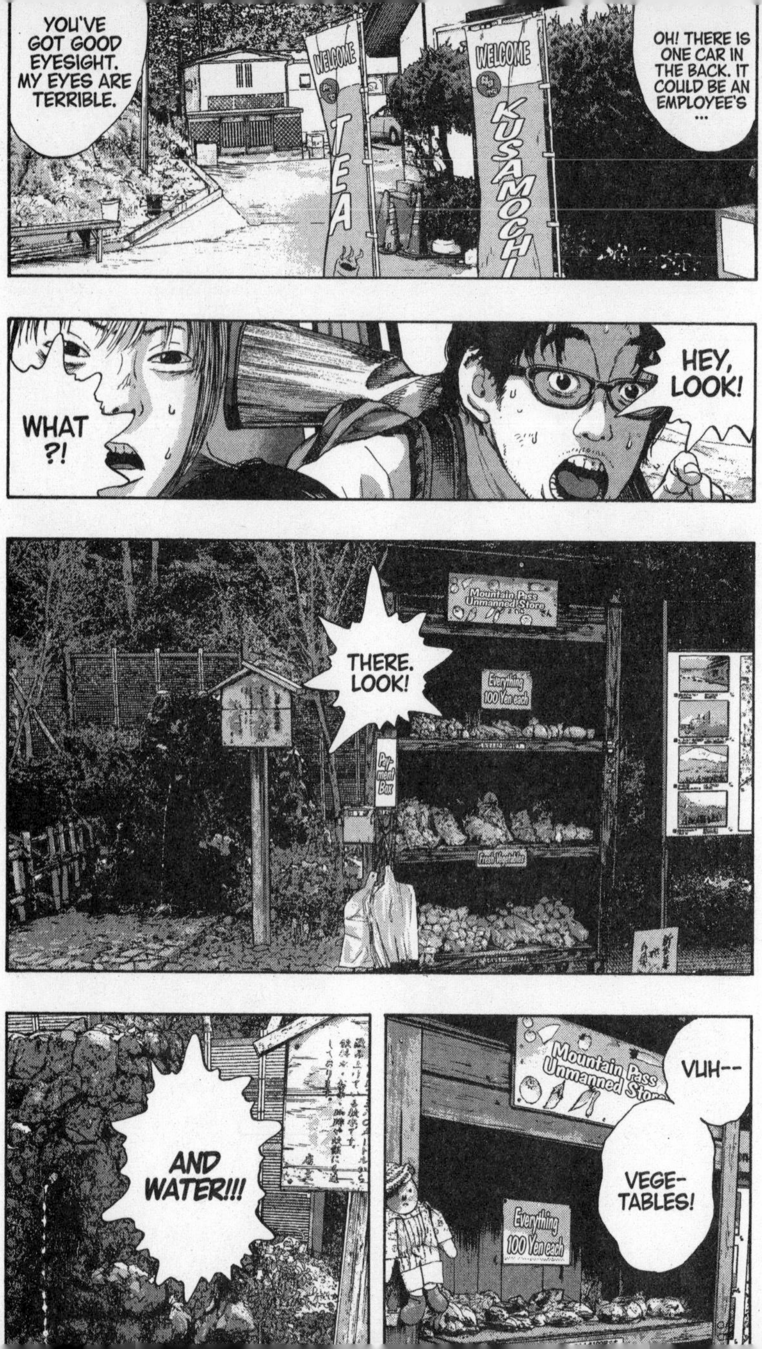
OH! THERE IS ONE CAR IN THE BACK. IT COULD BE AN EMPLOYEE'S ...
WELCOME KUSAMOCHI
WELCOME TEA
YOU'VE GOT GOOD EYESIGHT. MY EYES ARE TERRIBLE.
HEY, LOOK!
WHAT ?!
Mountain Pass Unmanned Store
THERE. LOOK!
Everything 100 Yen each
Payment Box
Fresh Vegetables
Mountain Pass Unmanned Store
VUH--
VEGE-TABLES!
Everything 100 Yen each
AND WATER!!!

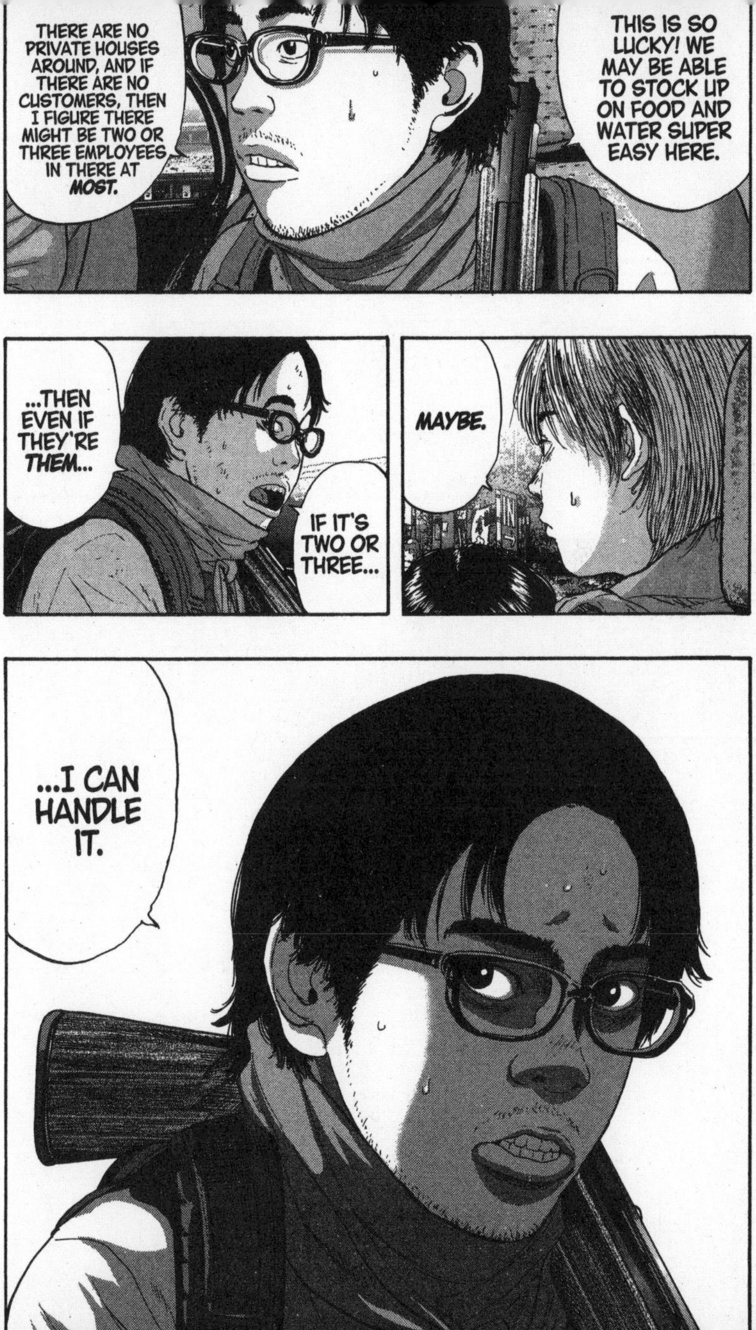
THIS IS SO LUCKY! WE MAY BE ABLE TO STOCK UP ON FOOD AND WATER SUPER EASY HERE.
THERE ARE NO PRIVATE HOUSES AROUND, AND IF THERE ARE NO CUSTOMERS, THEN I FIGURE THERE MIGHT BE TWO OR THREE EMPLOYEES IN THERE AT MOST.
MAYBE.
IF IT'S TWO OR THREE...
...THEN EVEN IF THEY'RE THEM...
...I CAN HANDLE IT.

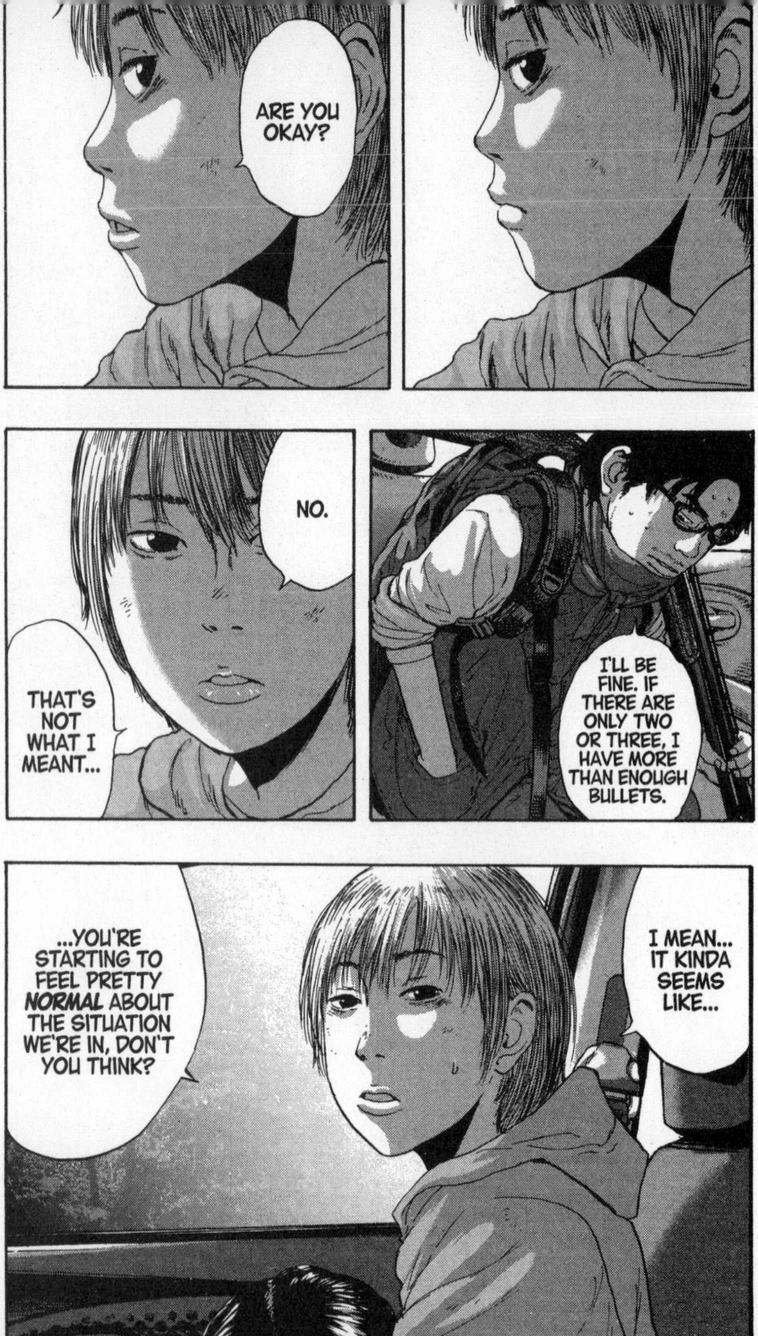
ARE YOU OKAY?
I'LL BE FINE. IF THERE ARE ONLY TWO OR THREE, I HAVE MORE THAN ENOUGH BULLETS.
NO.
THAT'S NOT WHAT I MEANT...
I MEAN... IT KINDA SEEMS LIKE...
...YOU'RE STARTING TO FEEL PRETTY **NORMAL** ABOUT THE SITUATION WE'RE IN, DON'T YOU THINK?

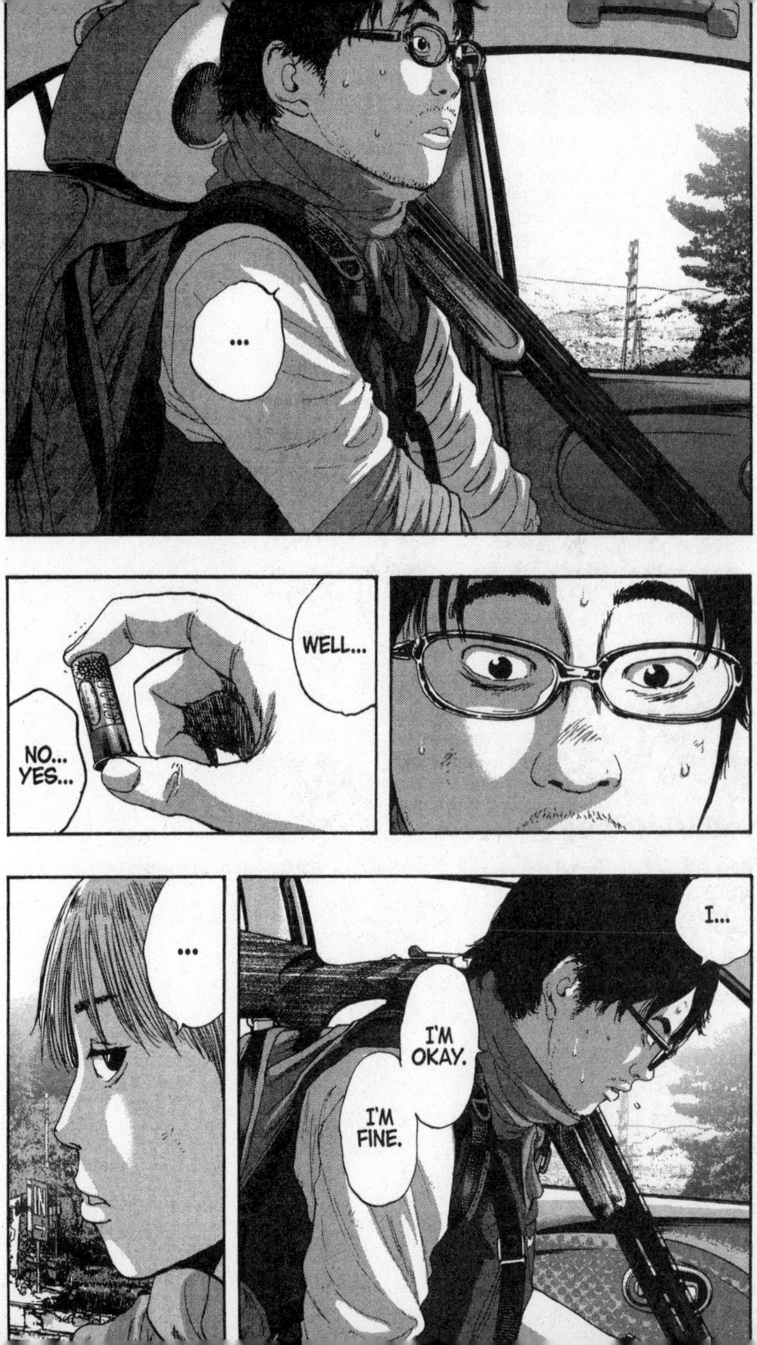
...
WELL...
NO... YES...
I...
I'M OKAY.
I'M FINE.
...

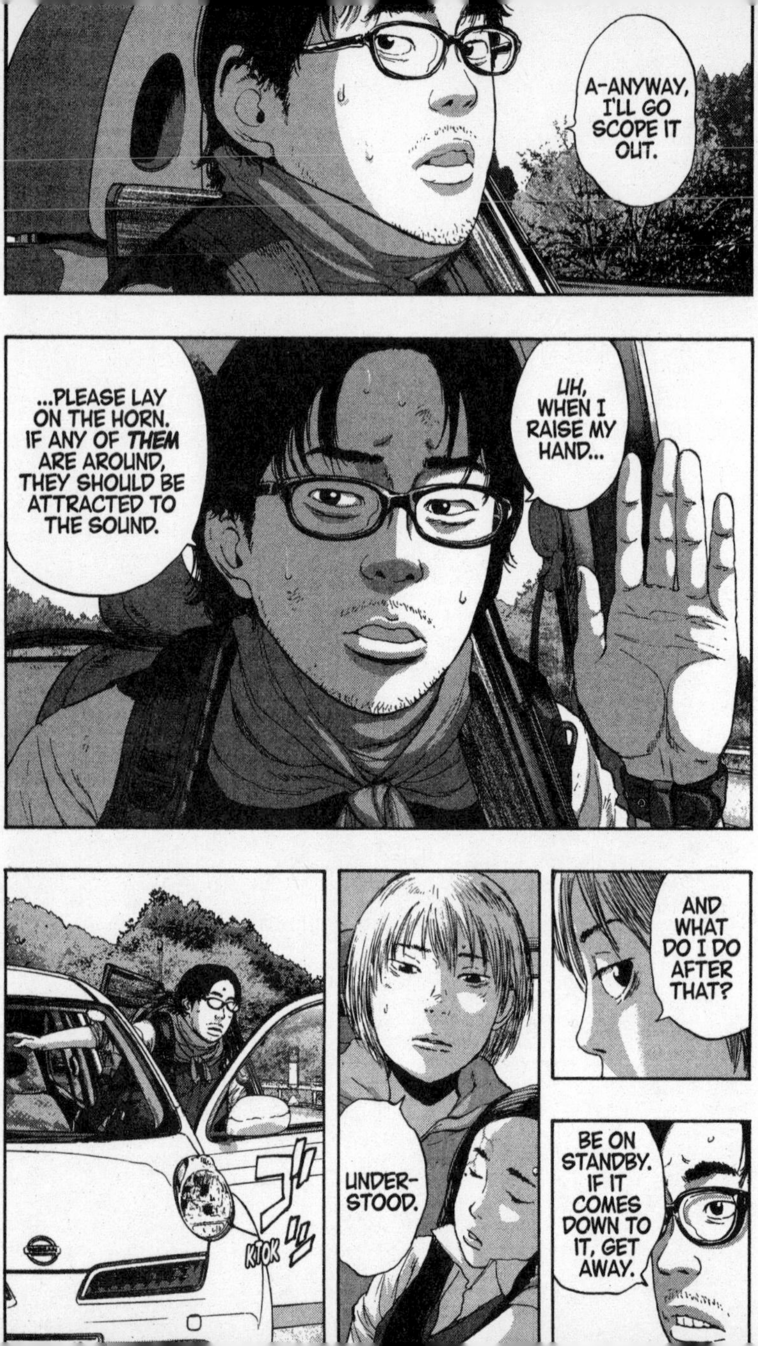
A-ANYWAY, I'LL GO SCOPE IT OUT.
UH, WHEN I RAISE MY HAND...
...PLEASE LAY ON THE HORN. IF ANY OF *THEM* ARE AROUND, THEY SHOULD BE ATTRACTED TO THE SOUND.
AND WHAT DO I DO AFTER THAT?
BE ON STANDBY. IF IT COMES DOWN TO IT, GET AWAY.
UNDER-STOOD.
KTOK

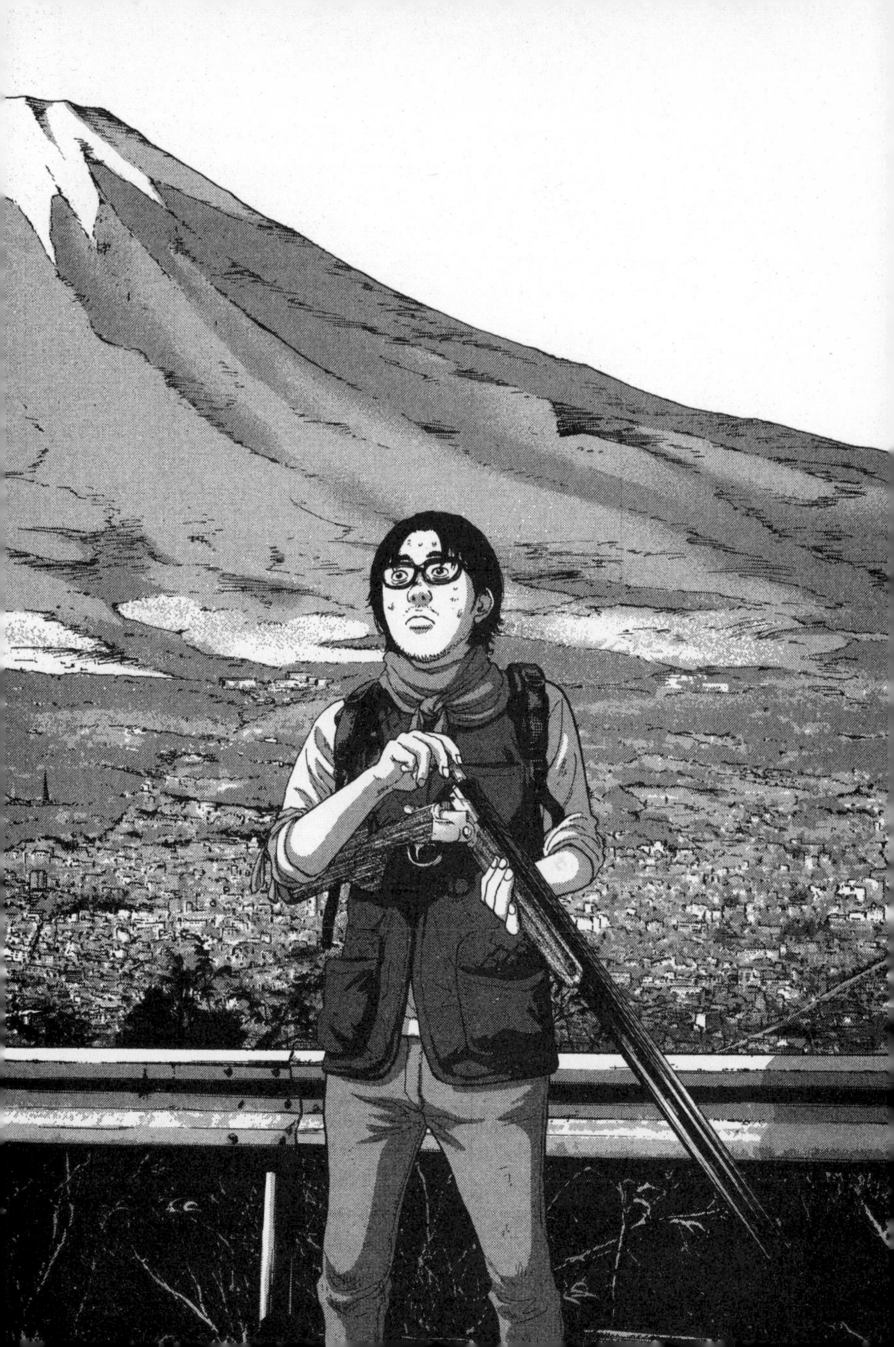

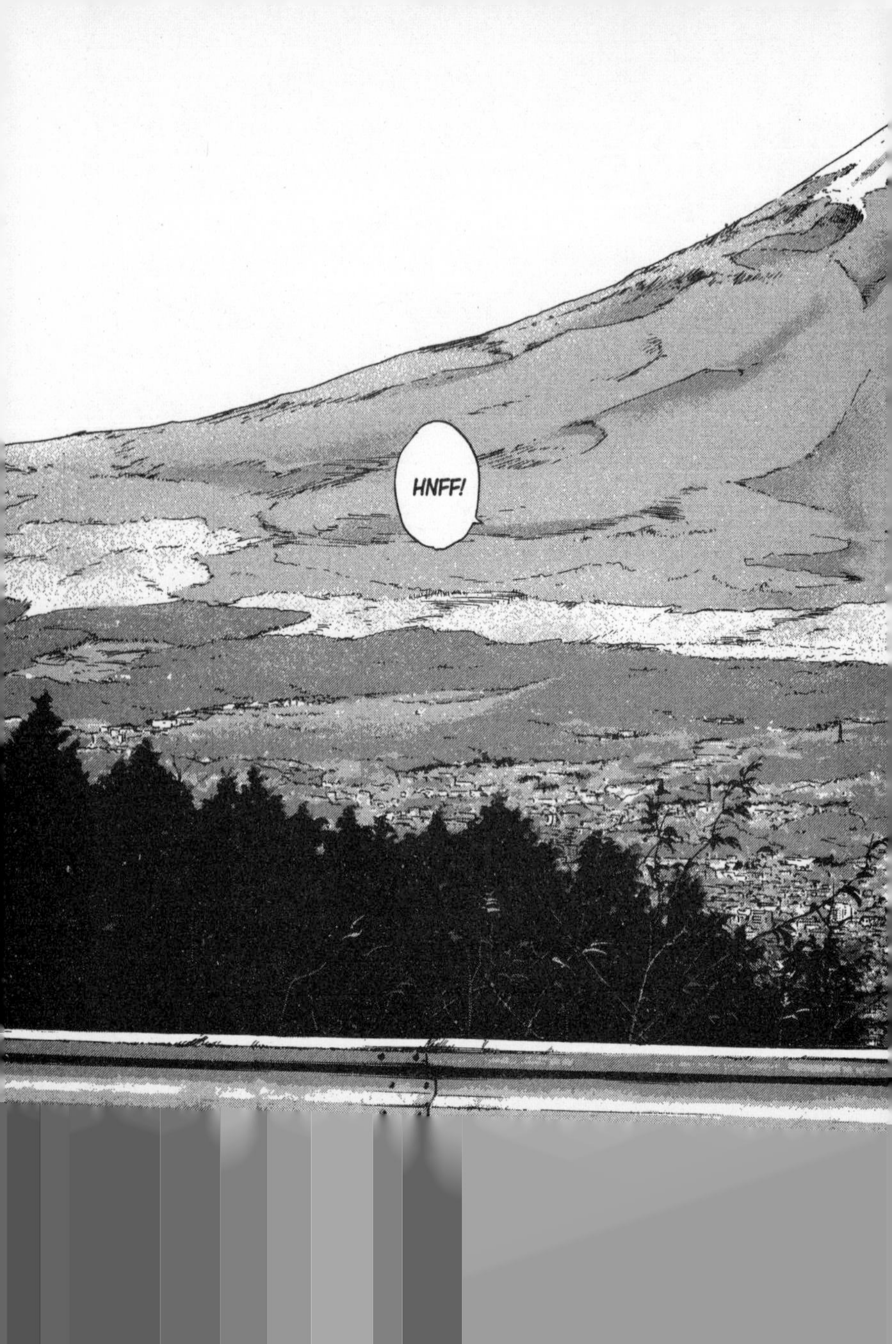
HNFF!

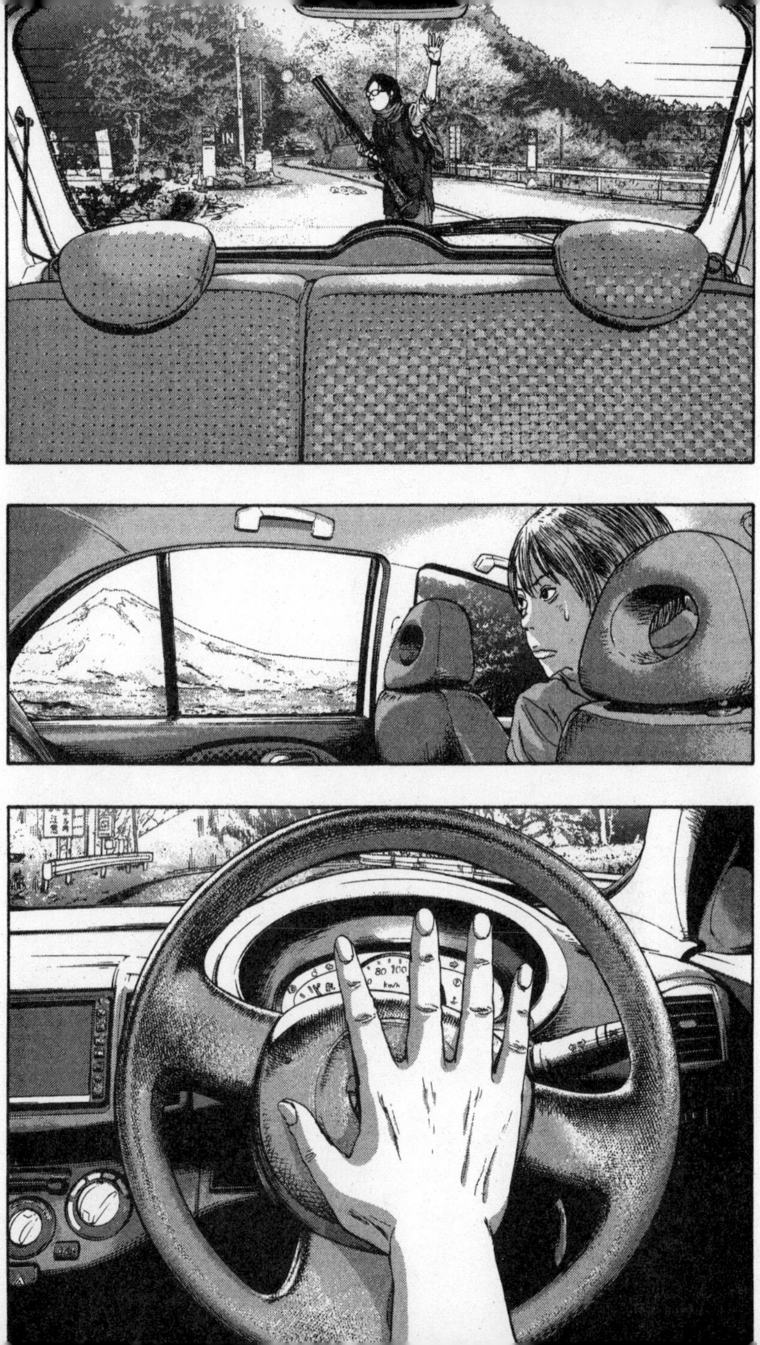
IN

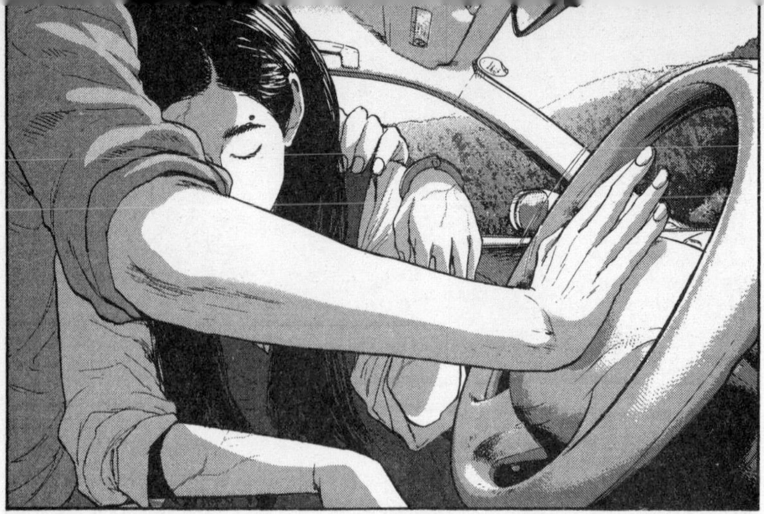

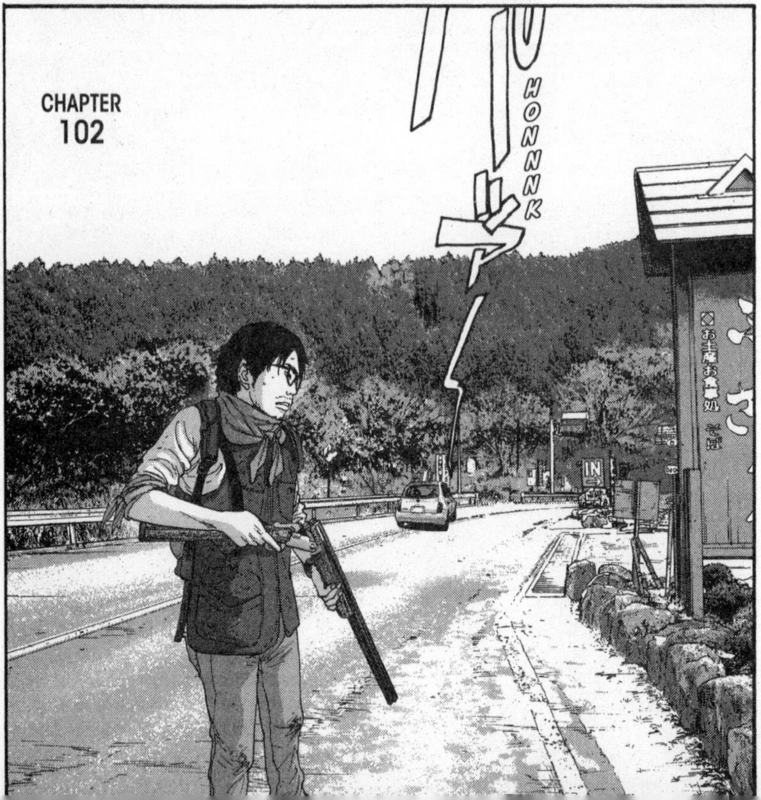
CHAPTER 102
HONNNNK
お土産お食事処
IN

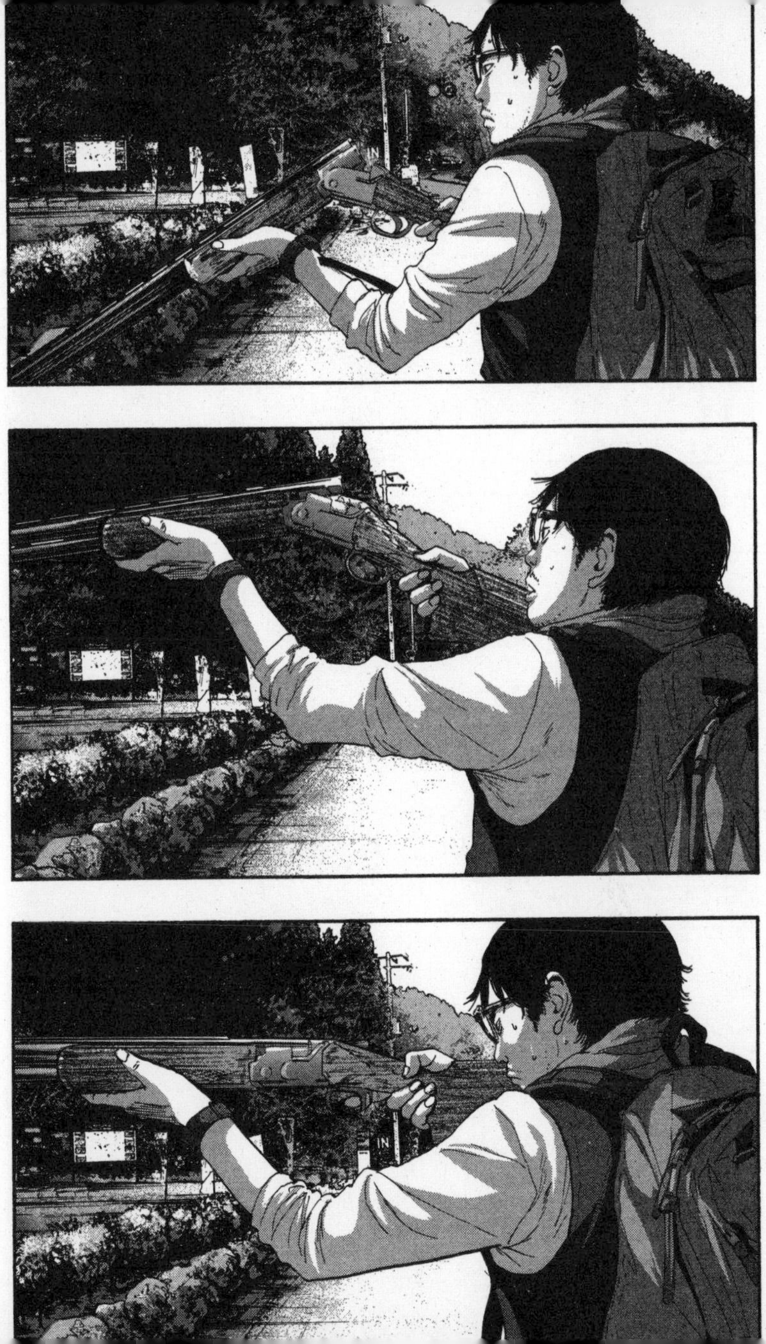

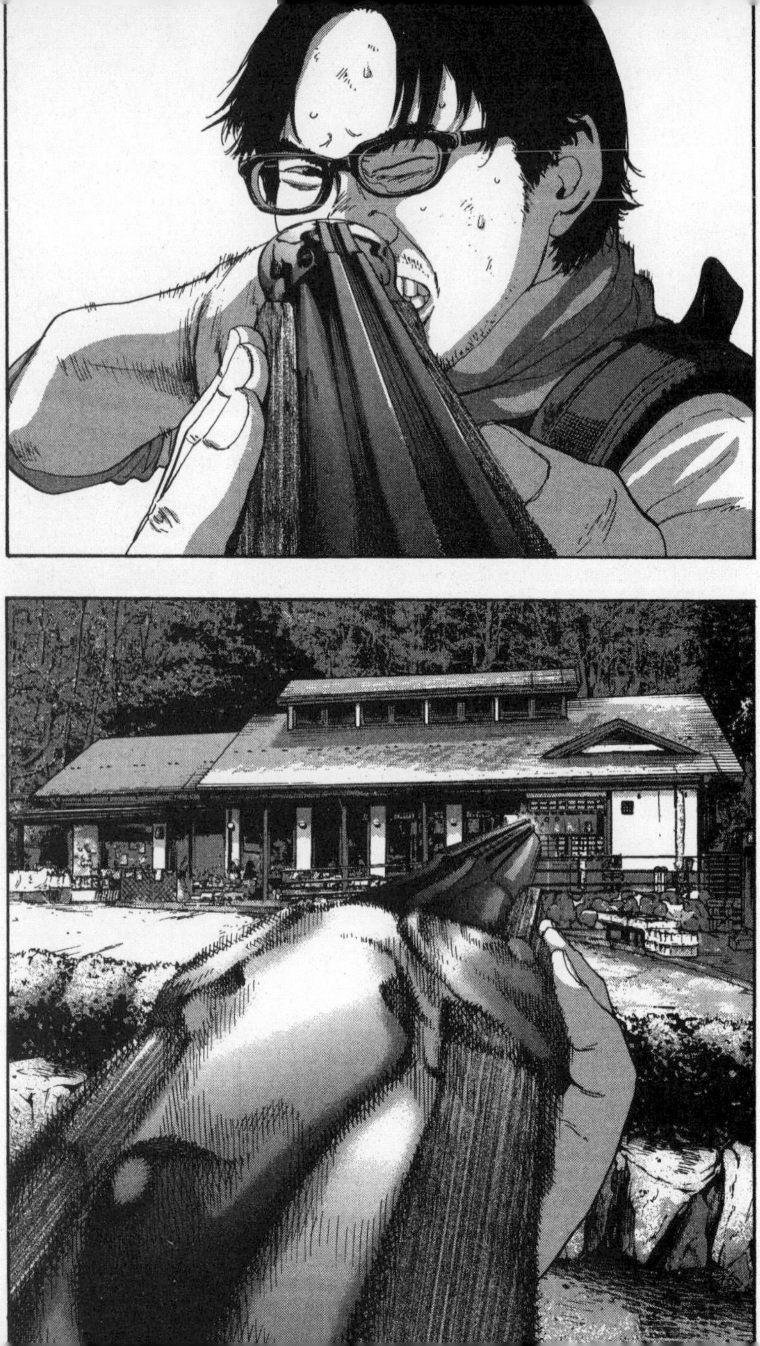

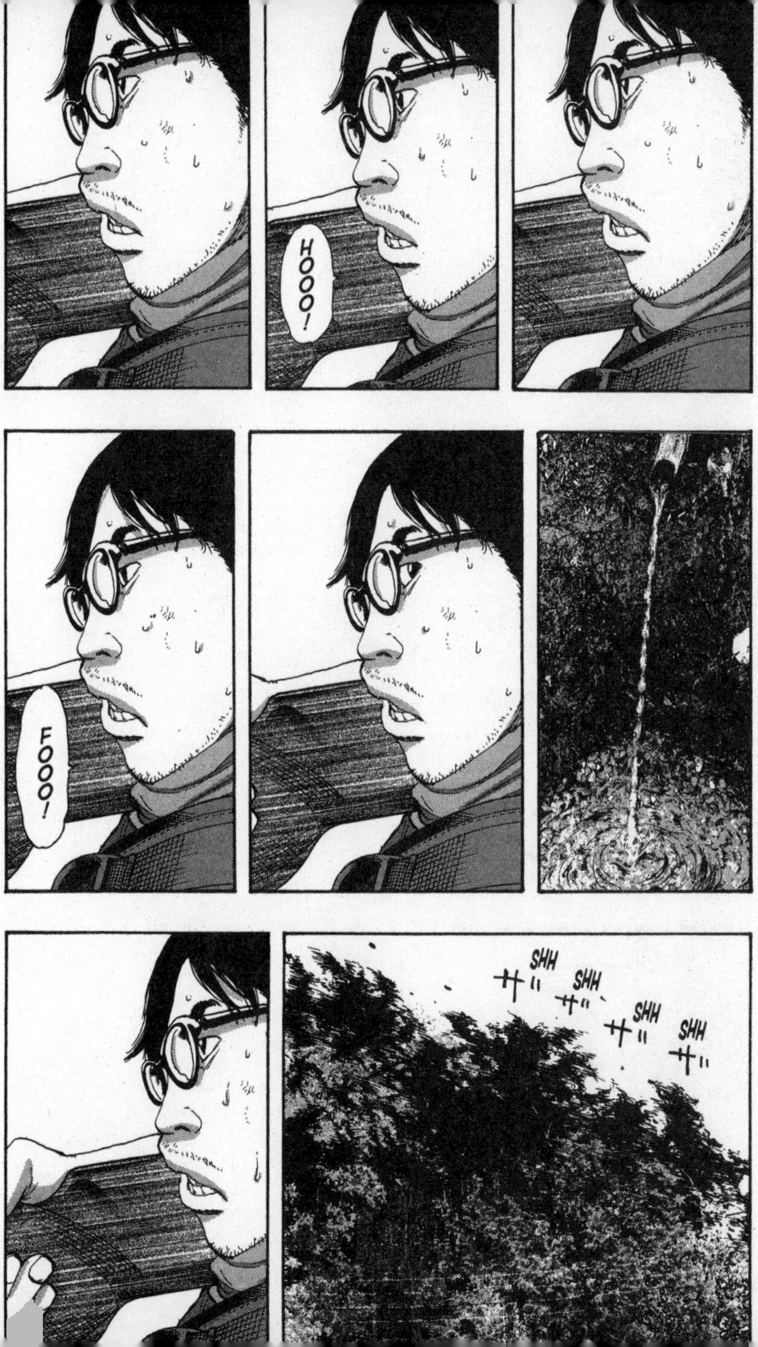
HOOO!
FOOO!
SHH
SHH
SHH
SHH

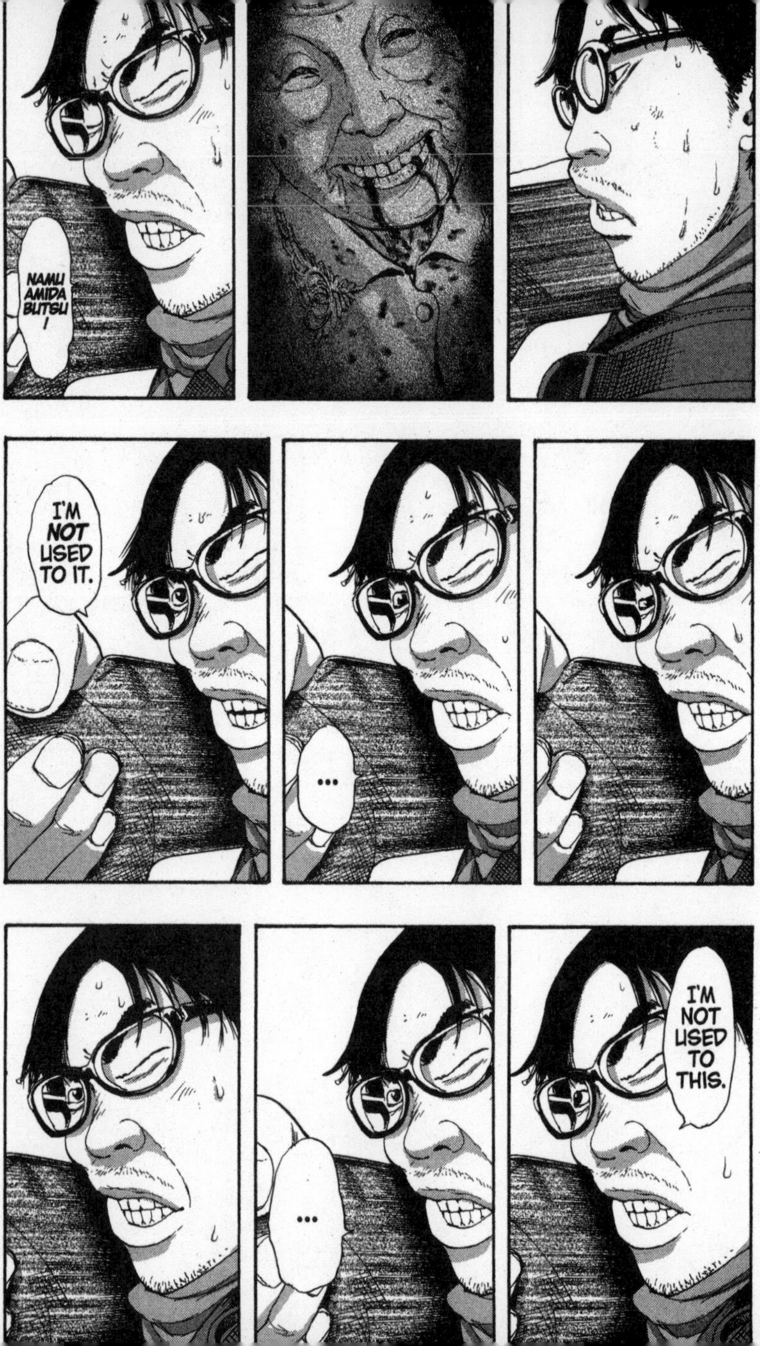
NAMU AMIDA BUTSU!
...
I'M NOT USED TO IT.
I'M NOT USED TO THIS.
...

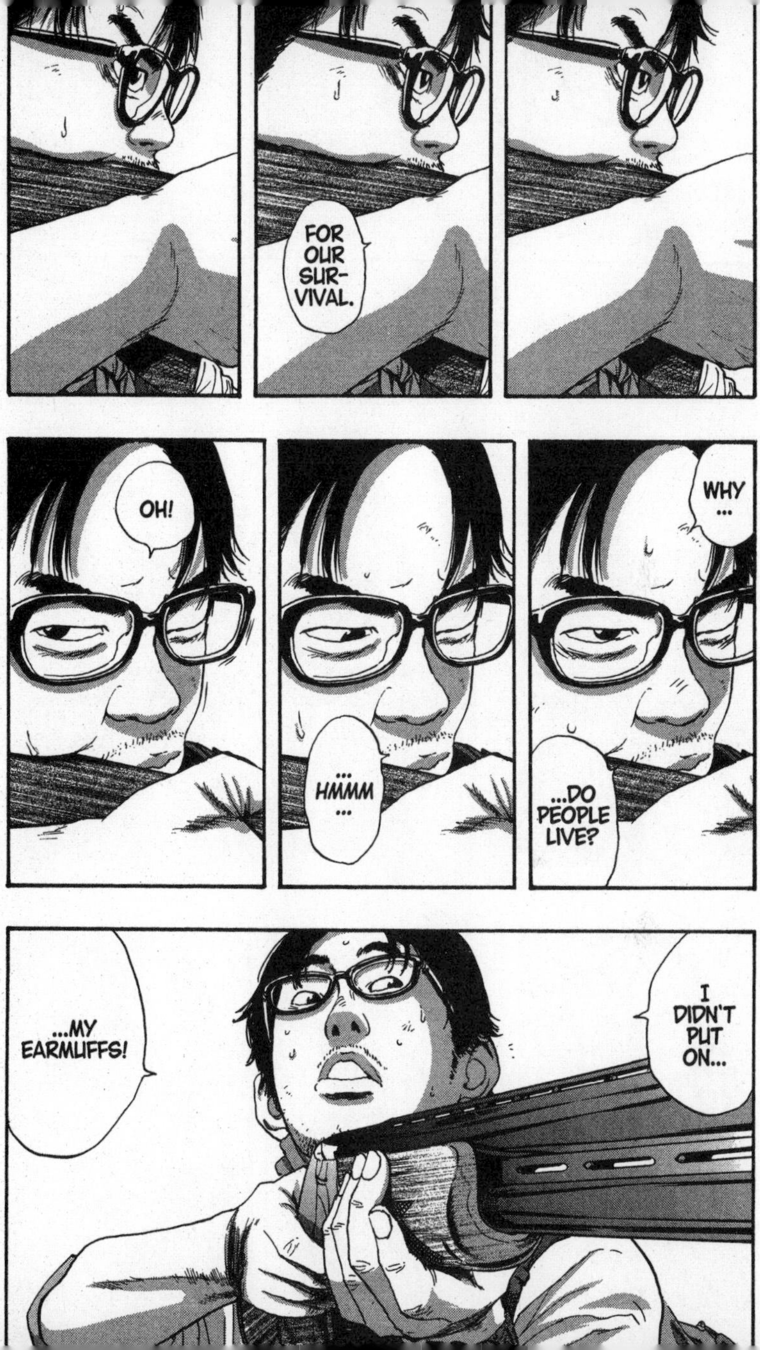
FOR OUR SURVIVAL.
WHY ...
...DO PEOPLE LIVE?
... HMMM ...
OH!
I DIDN'T PUT ON...
...MY EARMUFFS!

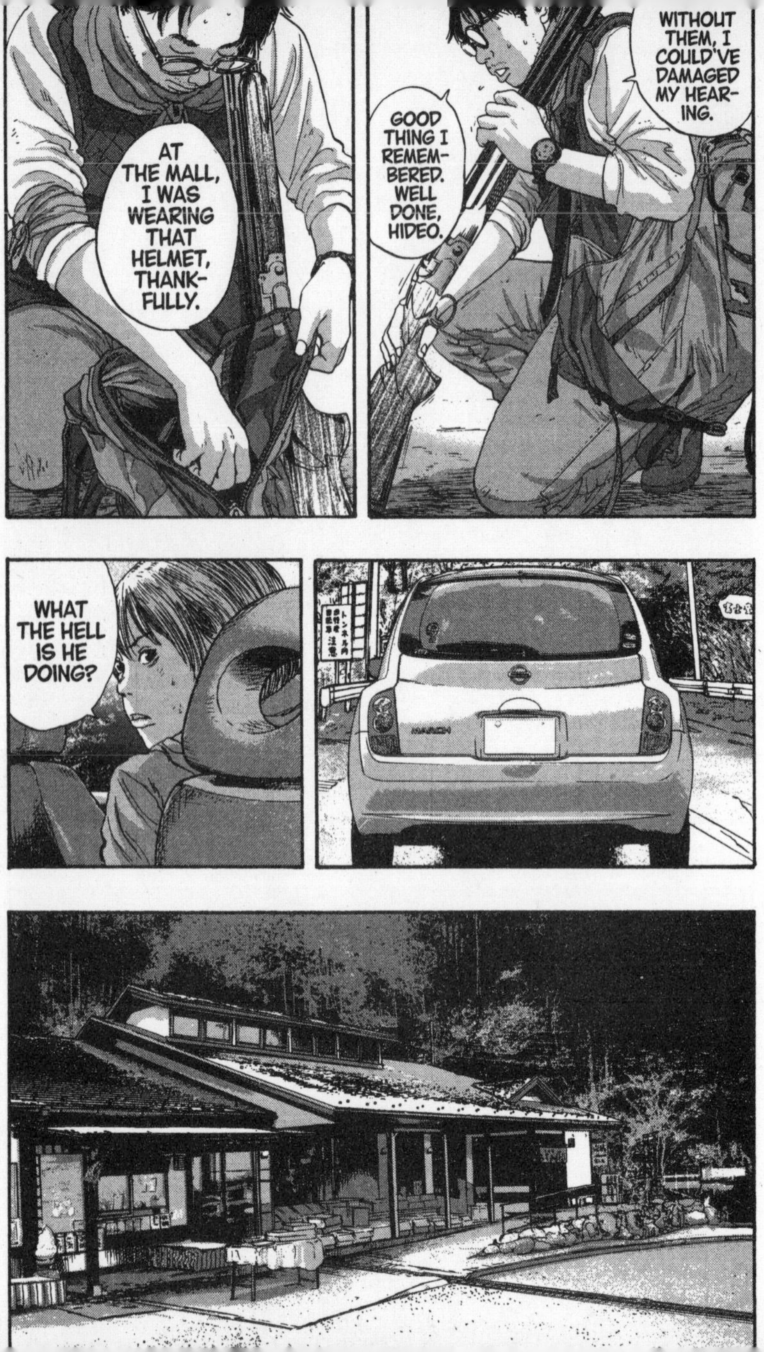
WITHOUT THEM, I COULD'VE DAMAGED MY HEAR-ING.
GOOD THING I REMEM-BERED. WELL DONE, HIDEO.
AT THE MALL, I WAS WEARING THAT HELMET, THANK-FULLY.
WHAT THE HELL IS HE DOING?

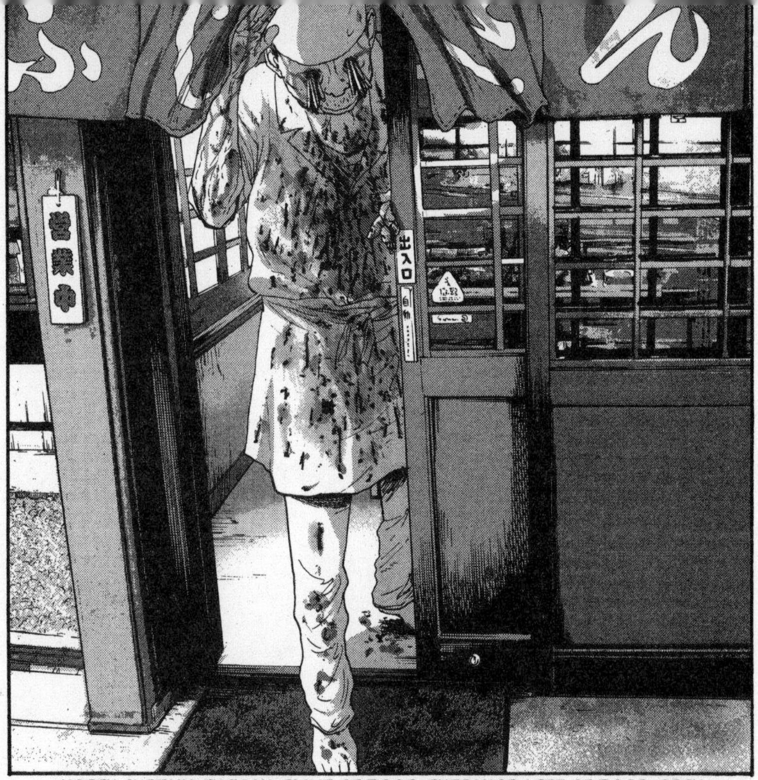
営業中
出入口

NOREN CURTAIN: FUJISAN. RIGHT OF DOOR: ENTRANCE. LEFT OF DOOR: OPEN.

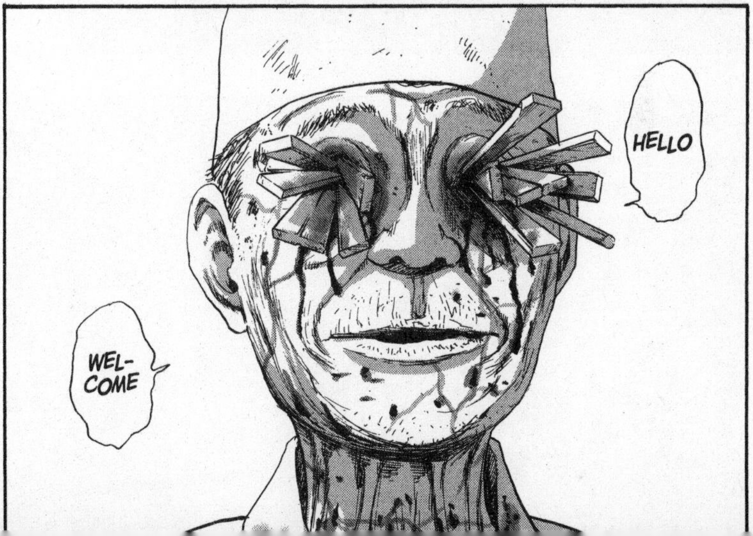
HELLO
WEL-
COME

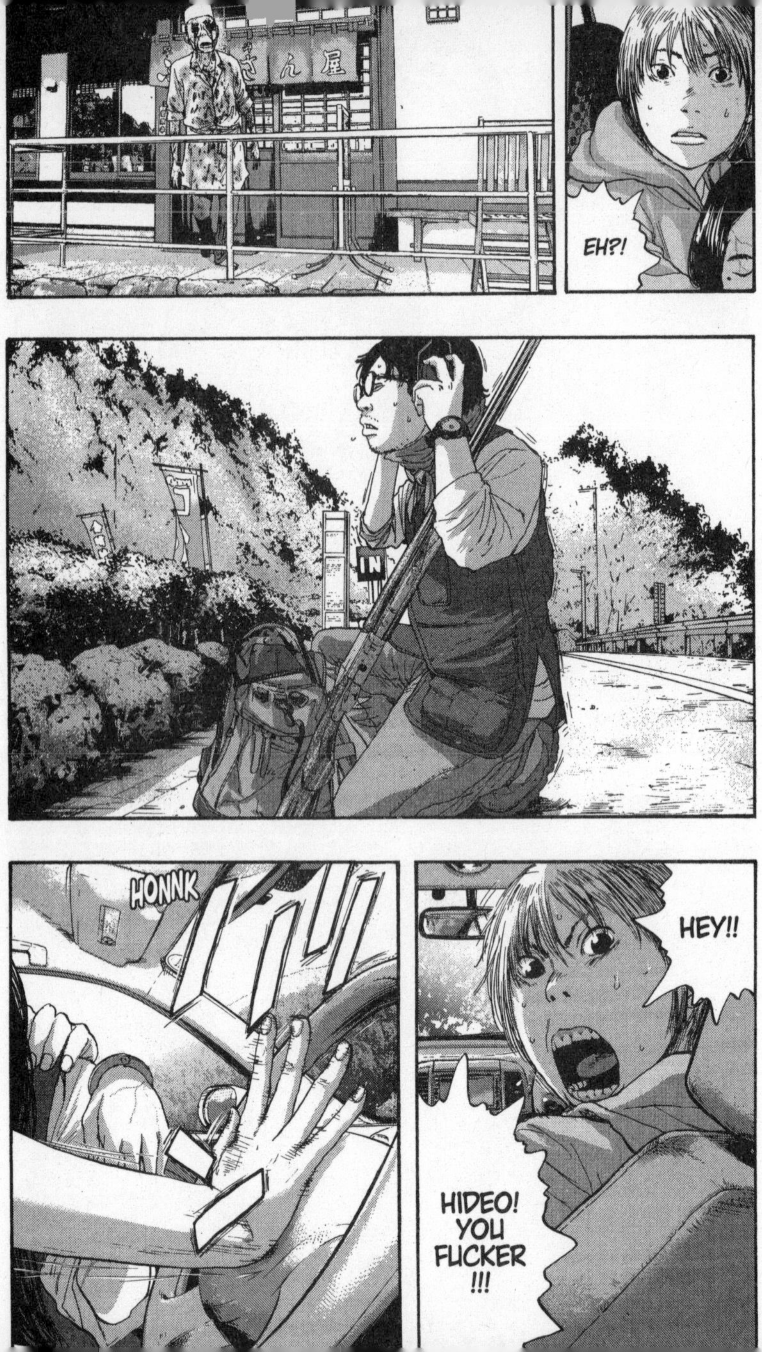
EH?!
HEY!!
HIDEO! YOU FUCKER !!!
HONNK

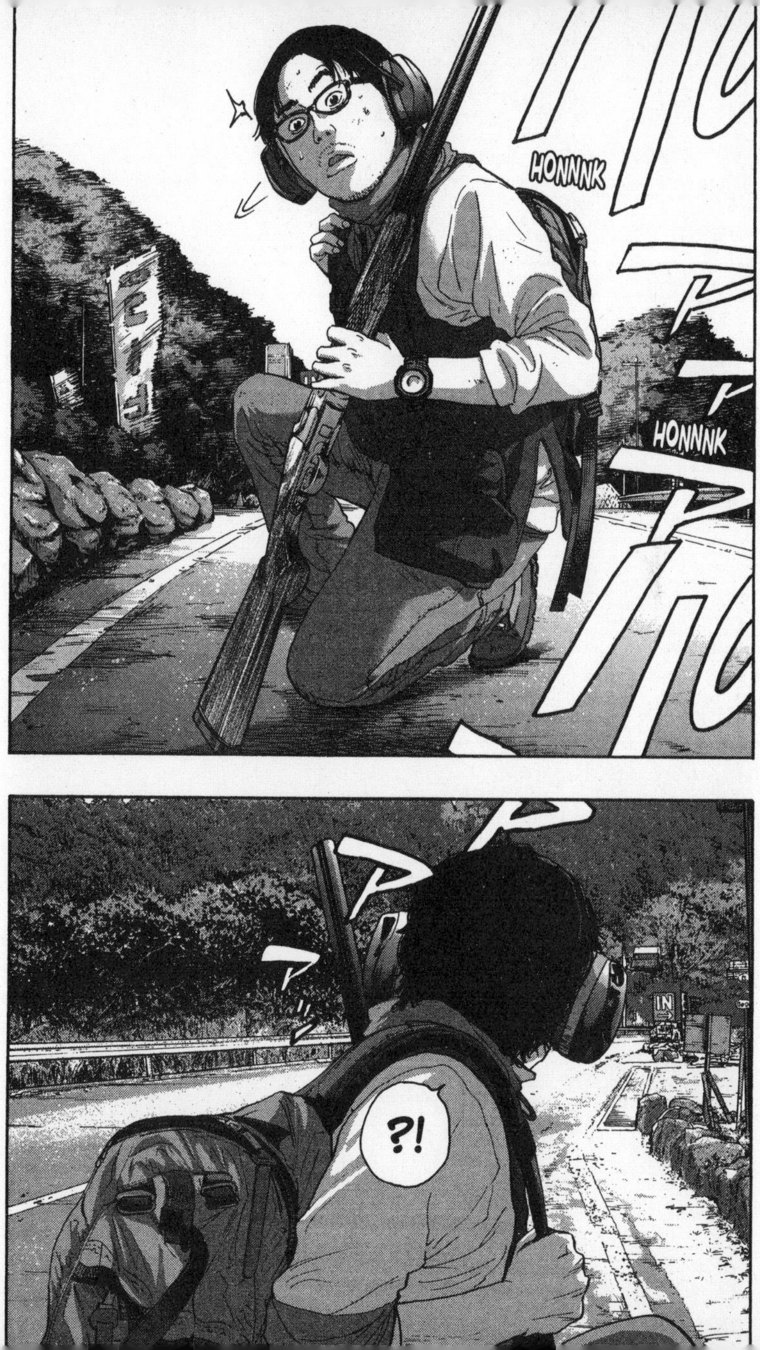
HONNNK
HONNNK
?!

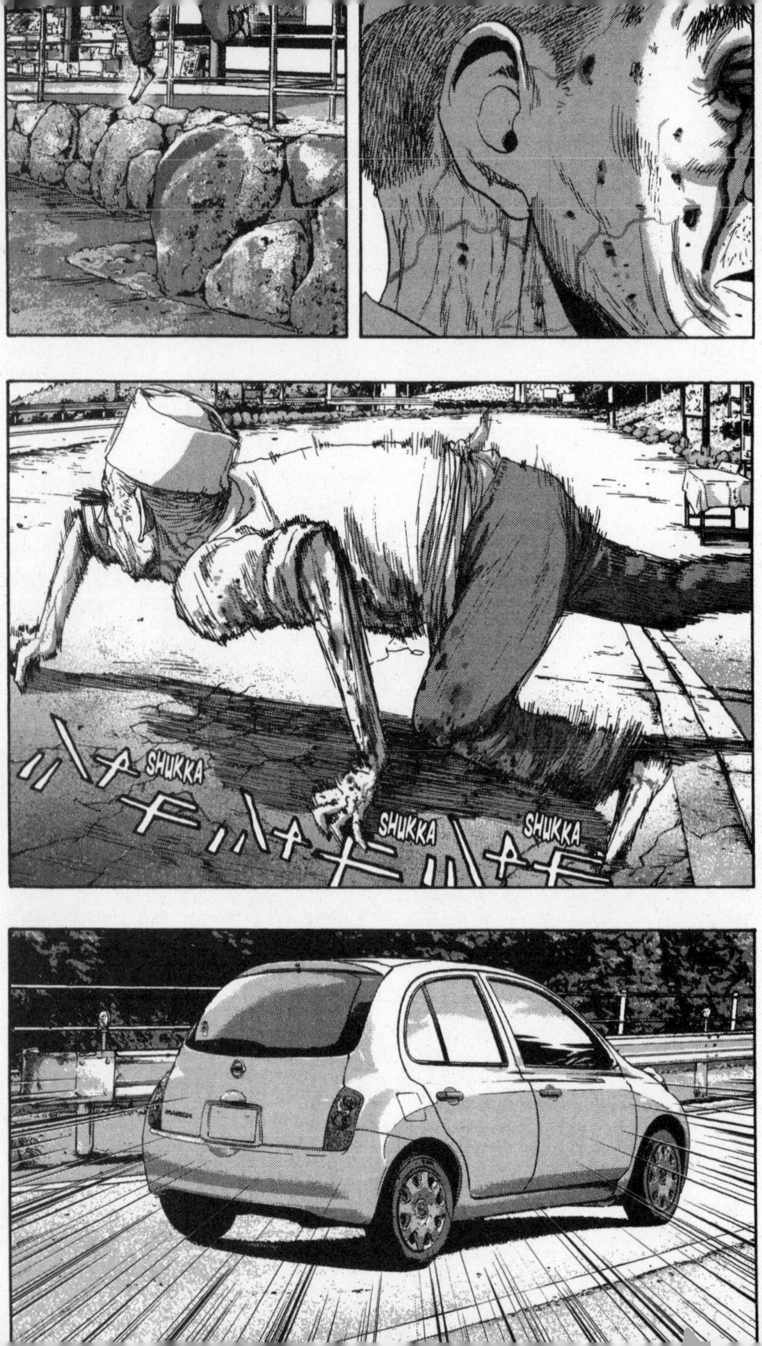
SHUKKA
SHUKKA
SHUKKA

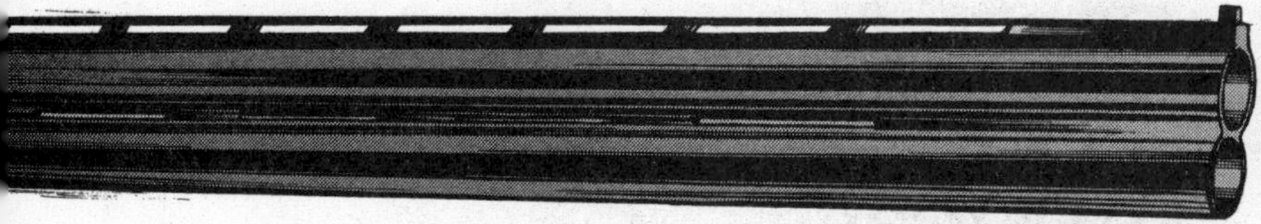

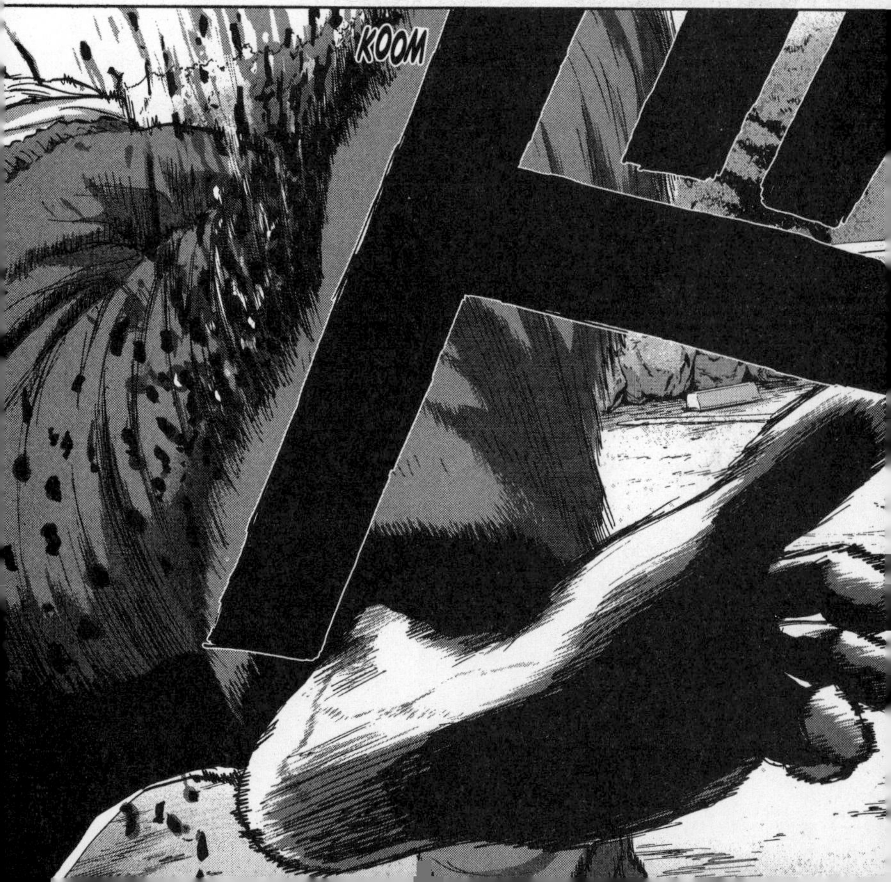
KOOM

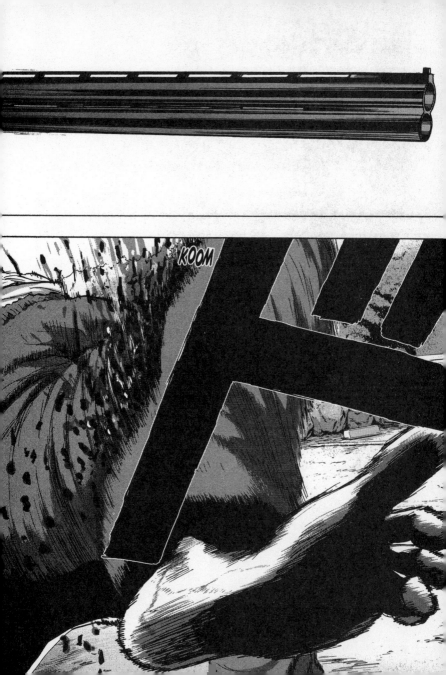

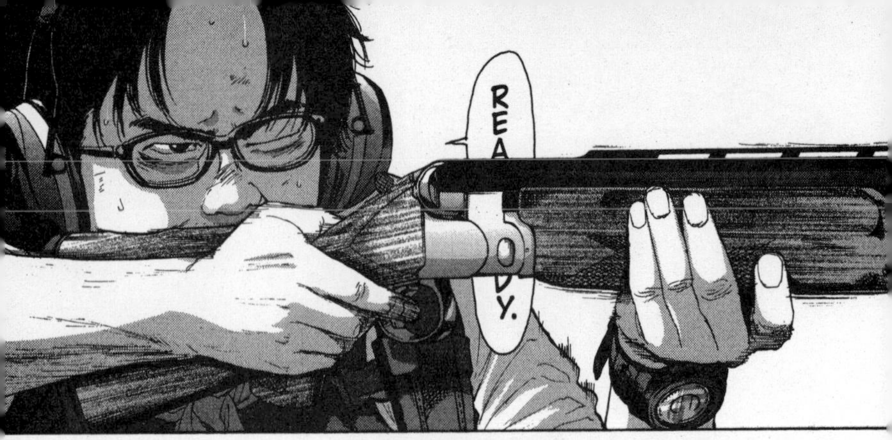
READY.
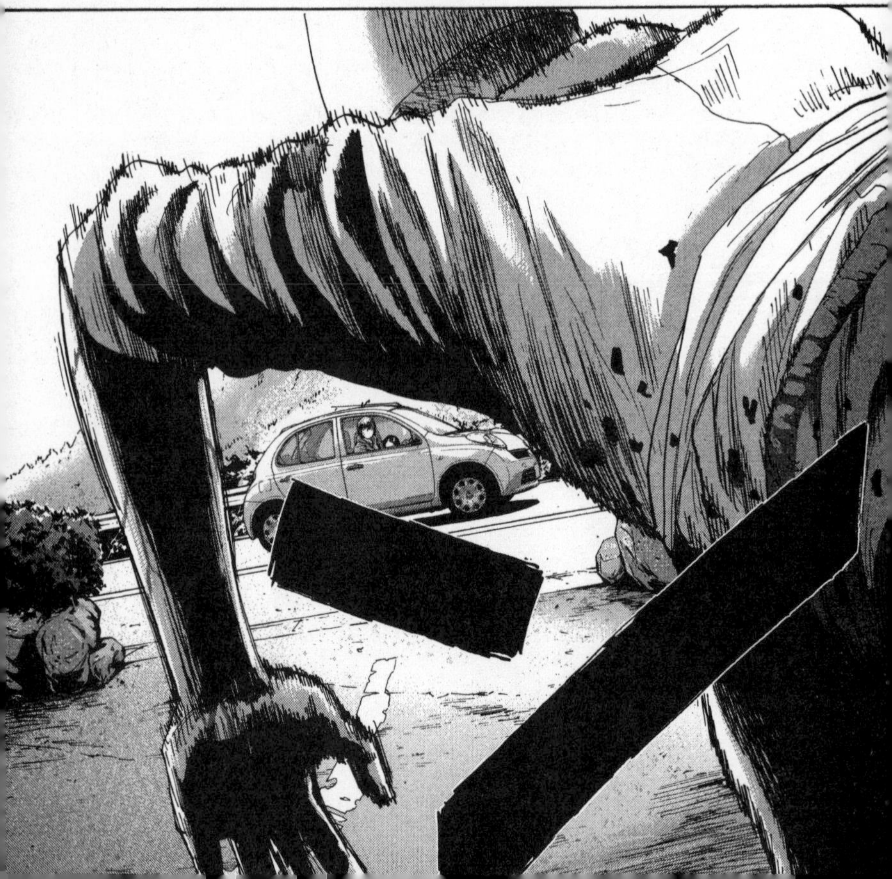

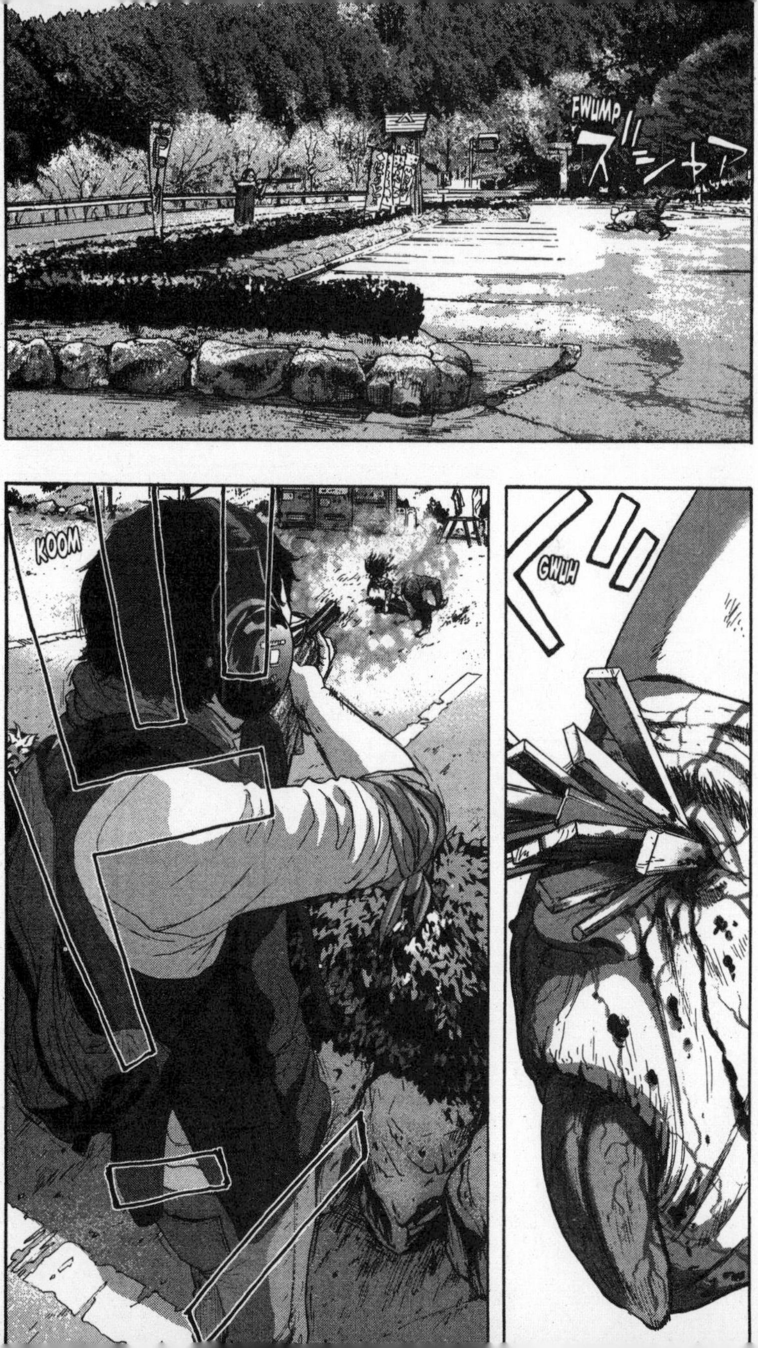
FWUMP
ズシャア
GWUH
KOOM

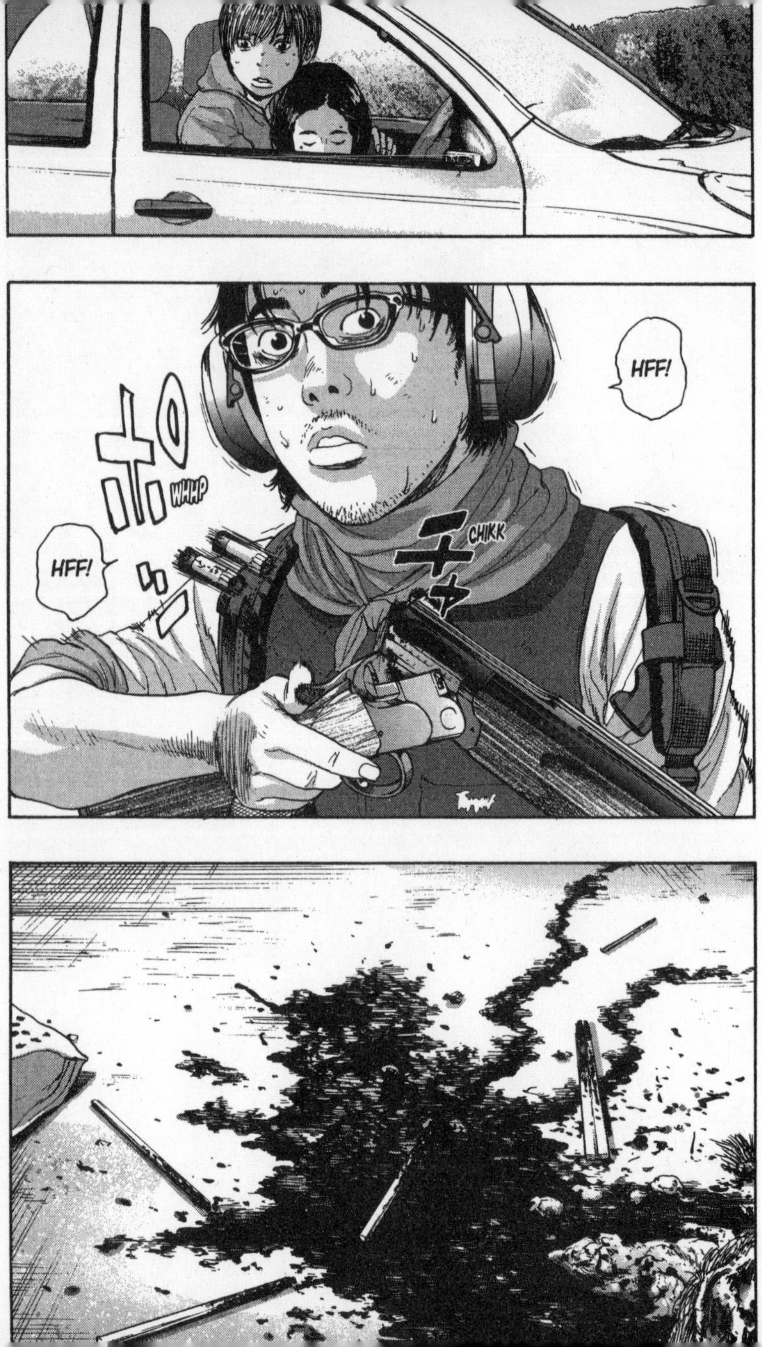
HFF!
WHHP
CHIKK
HFF!

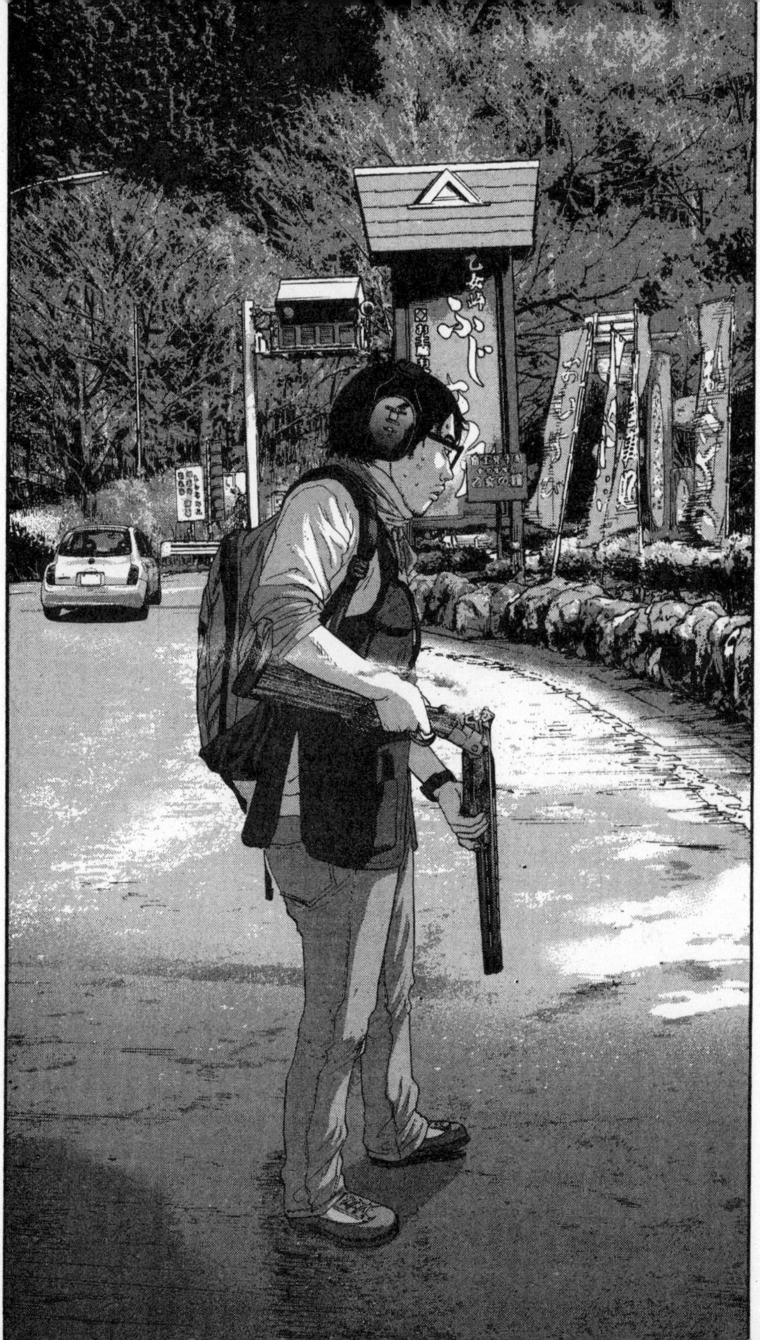
乙女峠

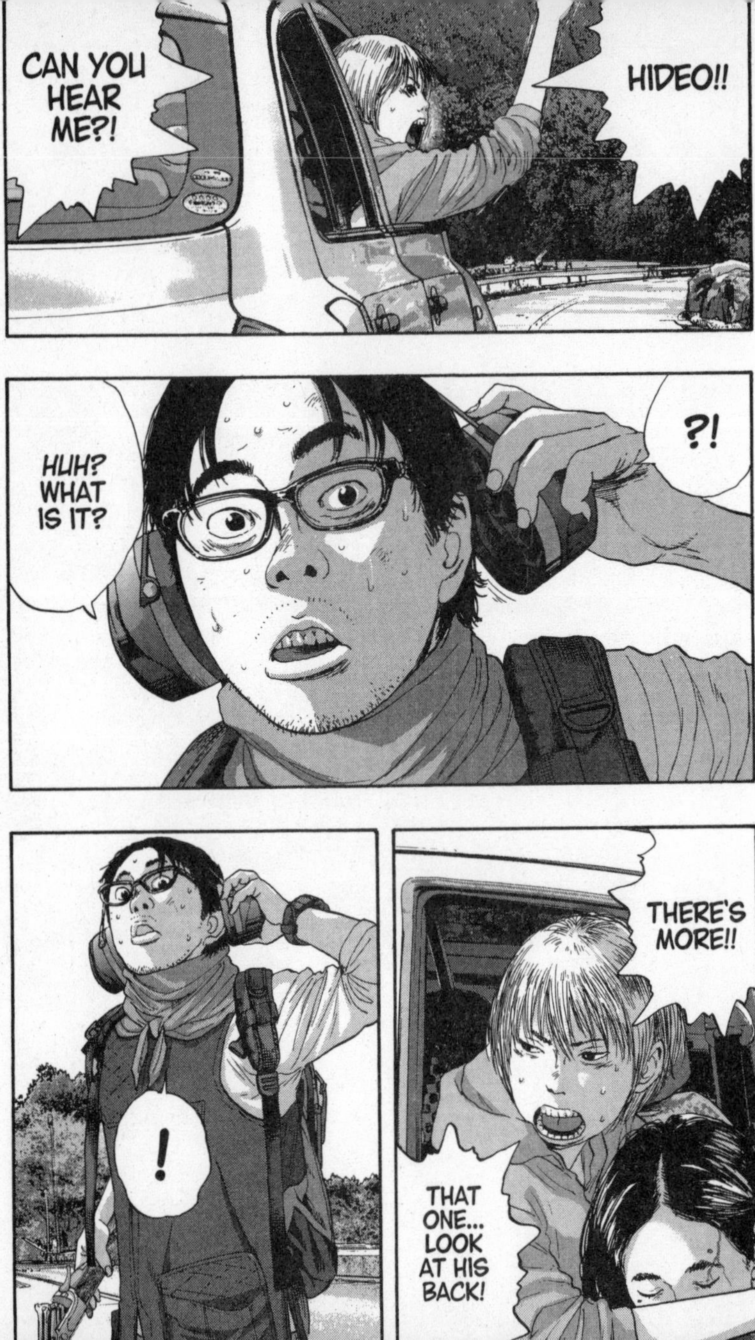
HIDEO!!
CAN YOU HEAR ME?!
?!
HUH? WHAT IS IT?
THERE'S MORE!!
THAT ONE... LOOK AT HIS BACK!
!

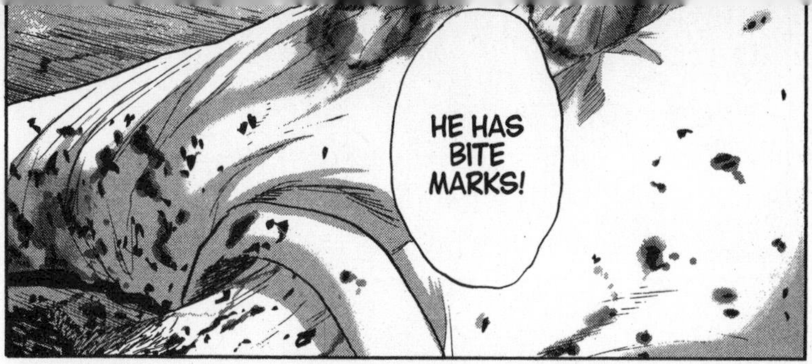
HE HAS BITE MARKS!
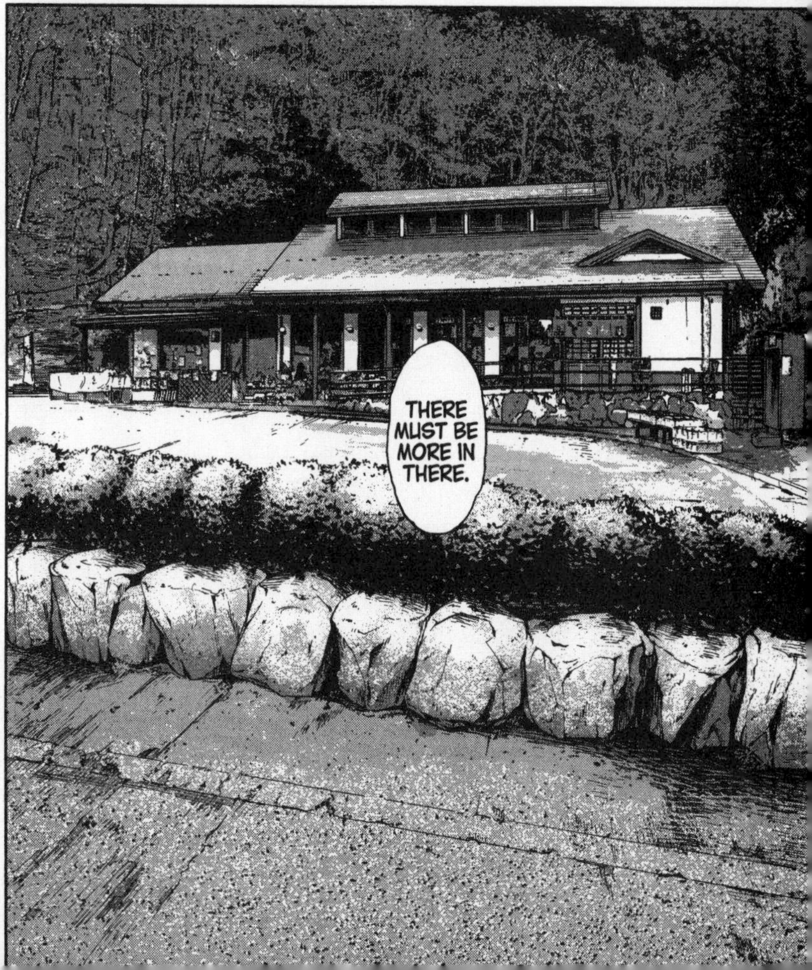
THERE MUST BE MORE IN THERE.

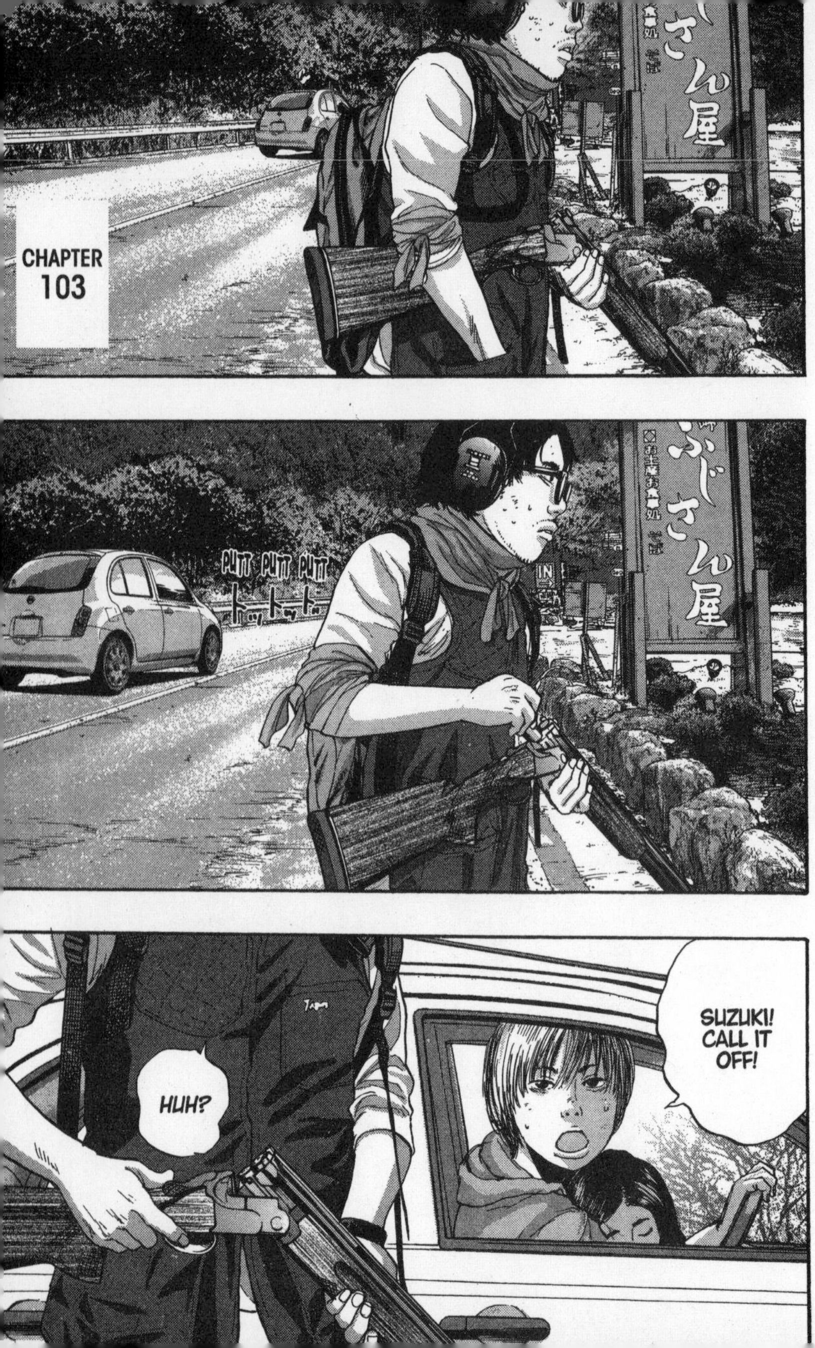
CHAPTER
103
ふじさん屋
PUTT PUTT PUTT
トットットッ
SUZUKI! CALL IT OFF!
HUH?

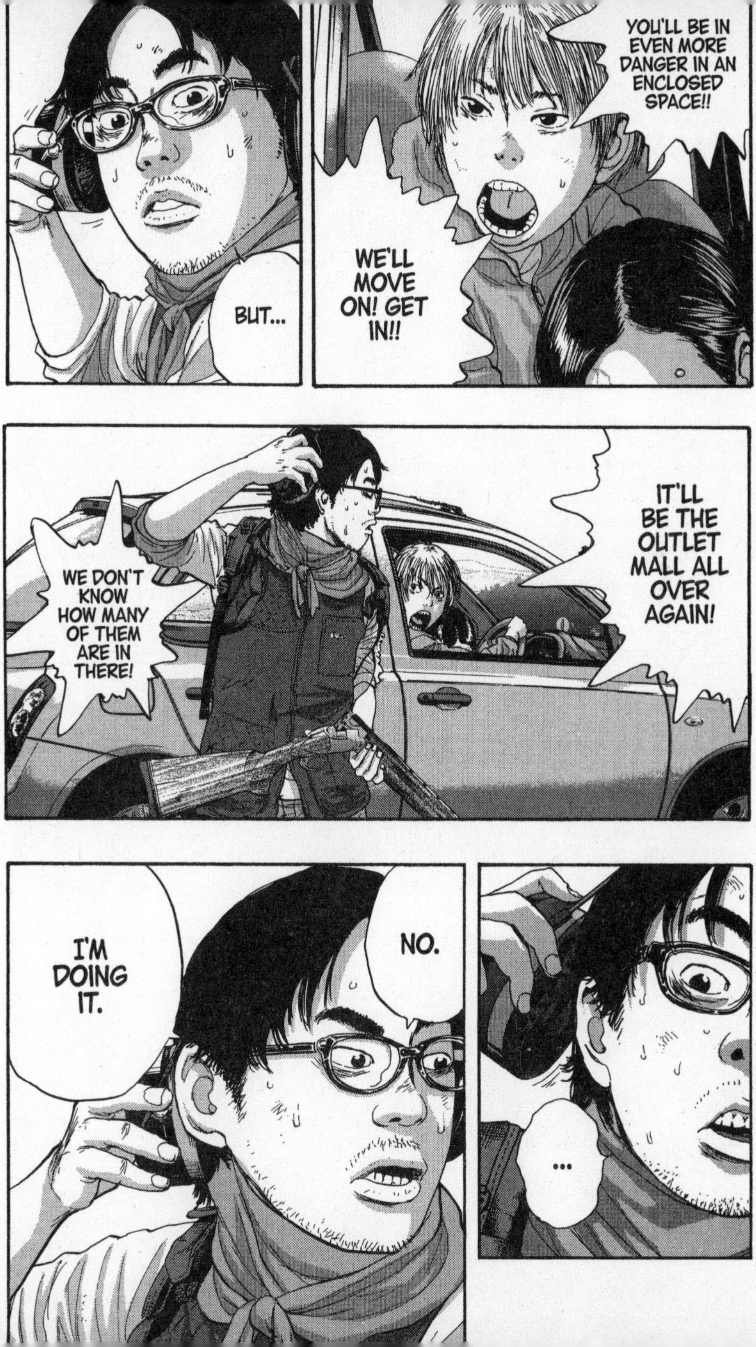
YOU'LL BE IN EVEN MORE DANGER IN AN ENCLOSED SPACE!!
WE'LL MOVE ON! GET IN!!
BUT...
IT'LL BE THE OUTLET MALL ALL OVER AGAIN!
WE DON'T KNOW HOW MANY OF THEM ARE IN THERE!
...
NO.
I'M DOING IT.

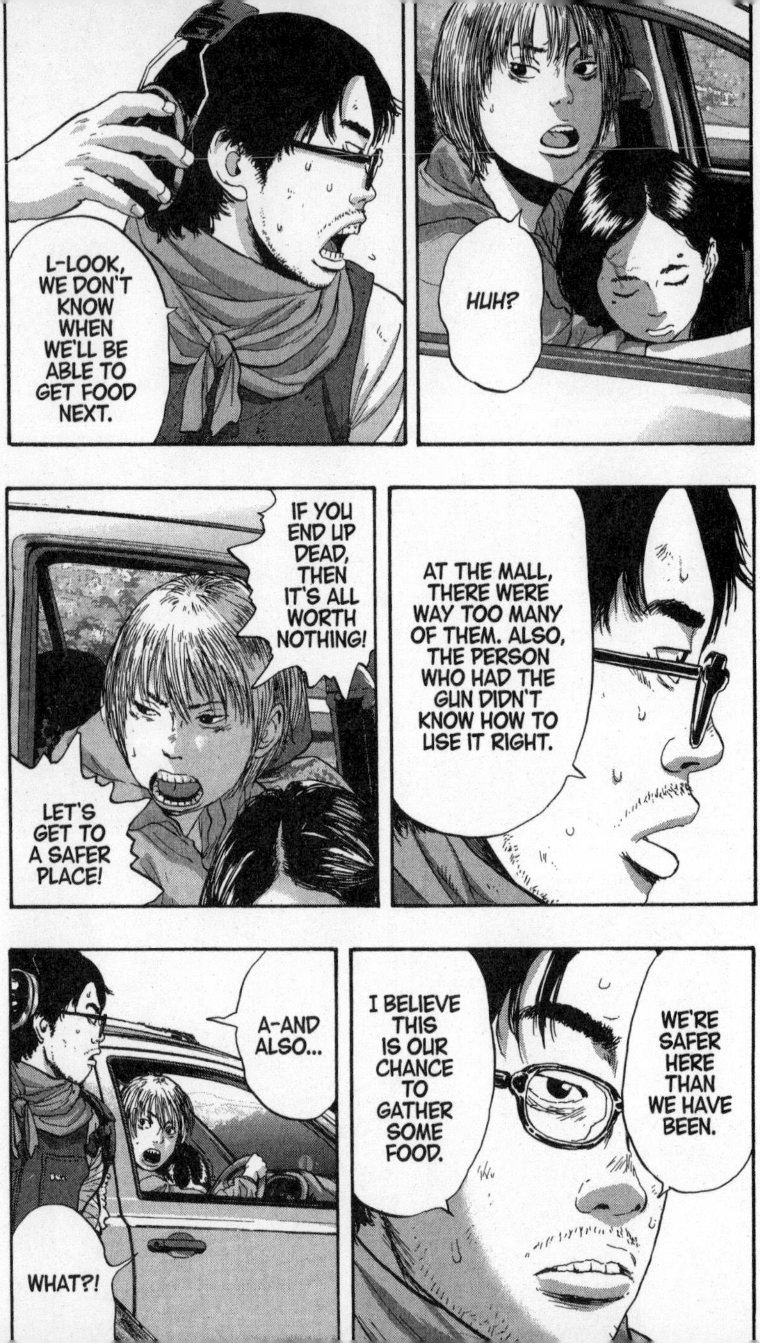
HUH?
L-LOOK, WE DON'T KNOW WHEN WE'LL BE ABLE TO GET FOOD NEXT.
AT THE MALL, THERE WERE WAY TOO MANY OF THEM. ALSO, THE PERSON WHO HAD THE GUN DIDN'T KNOW HOW TO USE IT RIGHT.
IF YOU END UP DEAD, THEN IT'S ALL WORTH NOTHING!
LET'S GET TO A SAFER PLACE!
WE'RE SAFER HERE THAN WE HAVE BEEN.
I BELIEVE THIS IS OUR CHANCE TO GATHER SOME FOOD.
A-AND ALSO...
WHAT?!

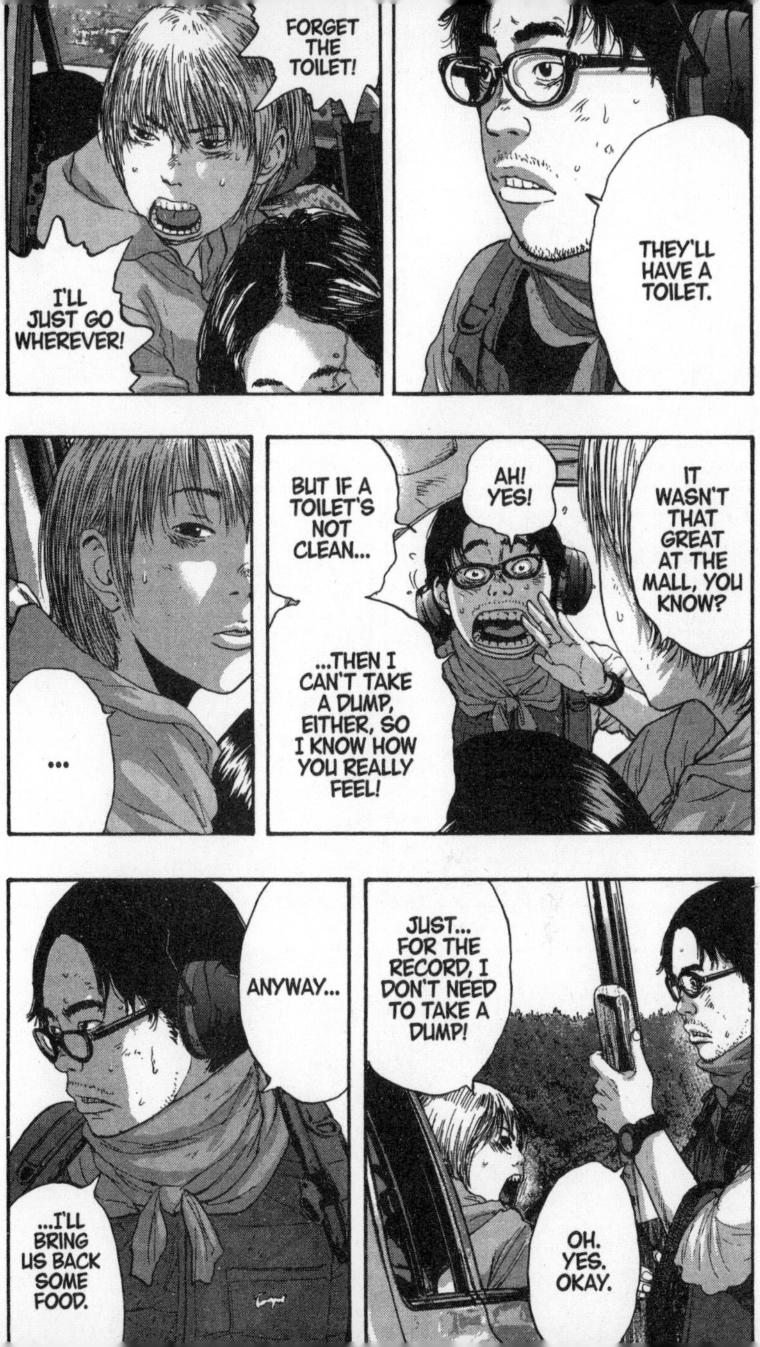
THEY'LL HAVE A TOILET.
FORGET THE TOILET!
I'LL JUST GO WHEREVER!
IT WASN'T THAT GREAT AT THE MALL, YOU KNOW?
AH! YES!
BUT IF A TOILET'S NOT CLEAN...
...THEN I CAN'T TAKE A DUMP, EITHER, SO I KNOW HOW YOU REALLY FEEL!
...
JUST... FOR THE RECORD, I DON'T NEED TO TAKE A DUMP!
OH. YES. OKAY.
ANYWAY...
...I'LL BRING US BACK SOME FOOD.

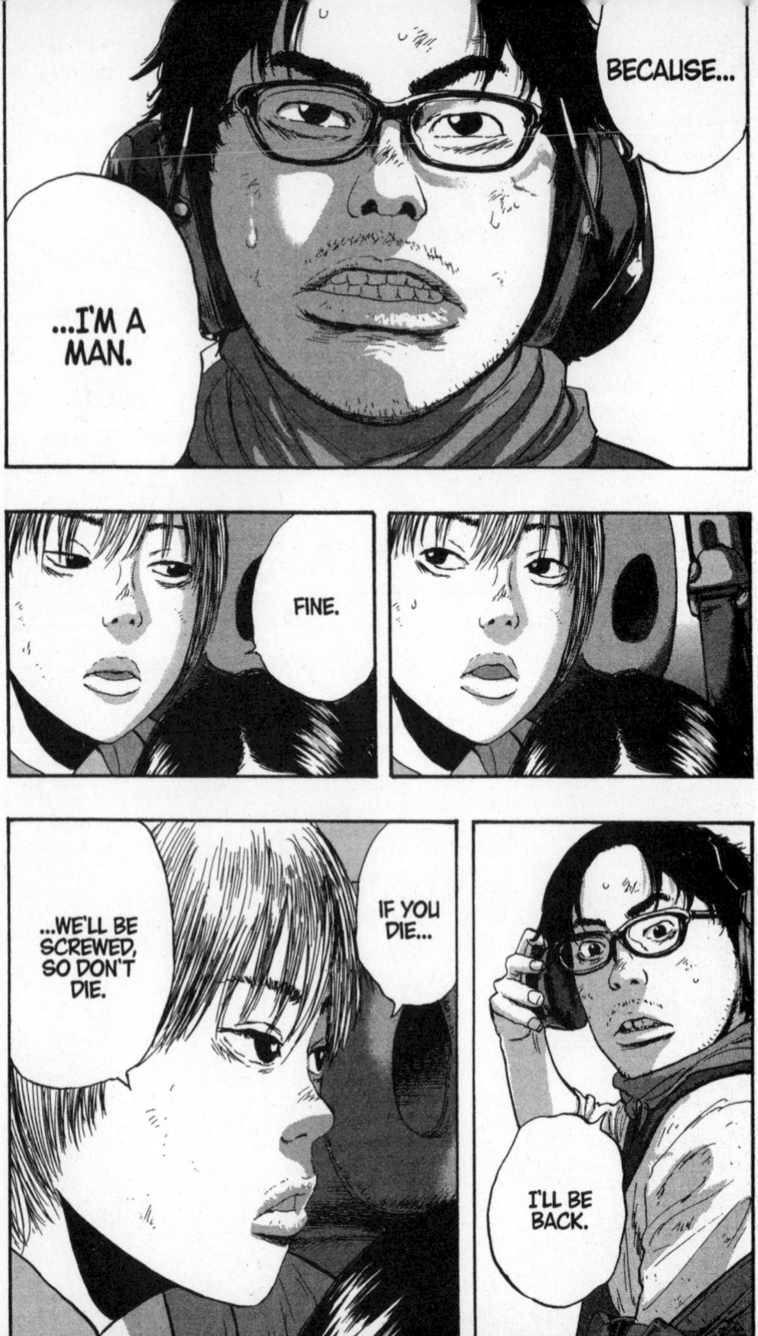
BECAUSE...
...I'M A MAN.
FINE.
I'LL BE BACK.
IF YOU DIE...
...WE'LL BE SCREWED, SO DON'T DIE.

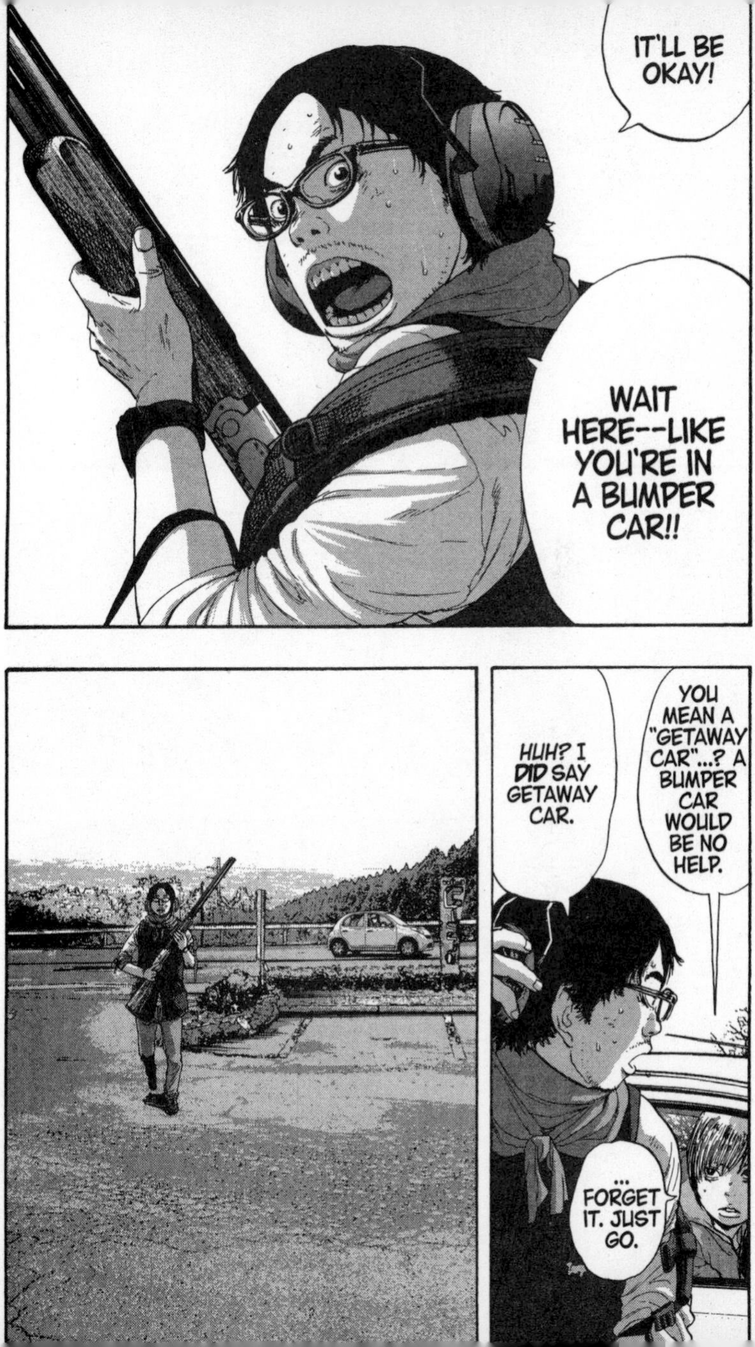
IT'LL BE OKAY!
WAIT HERE--LIKE YOU'RE IN A BUMPER CAR!!
YOU MEAN A "GETAWAY CAR"...? A BUMPER CAR WOULD BE NO HELP.
HUH? I **DID** SAY GETAWAY CAR.
... FORGET IT. JUST GO.

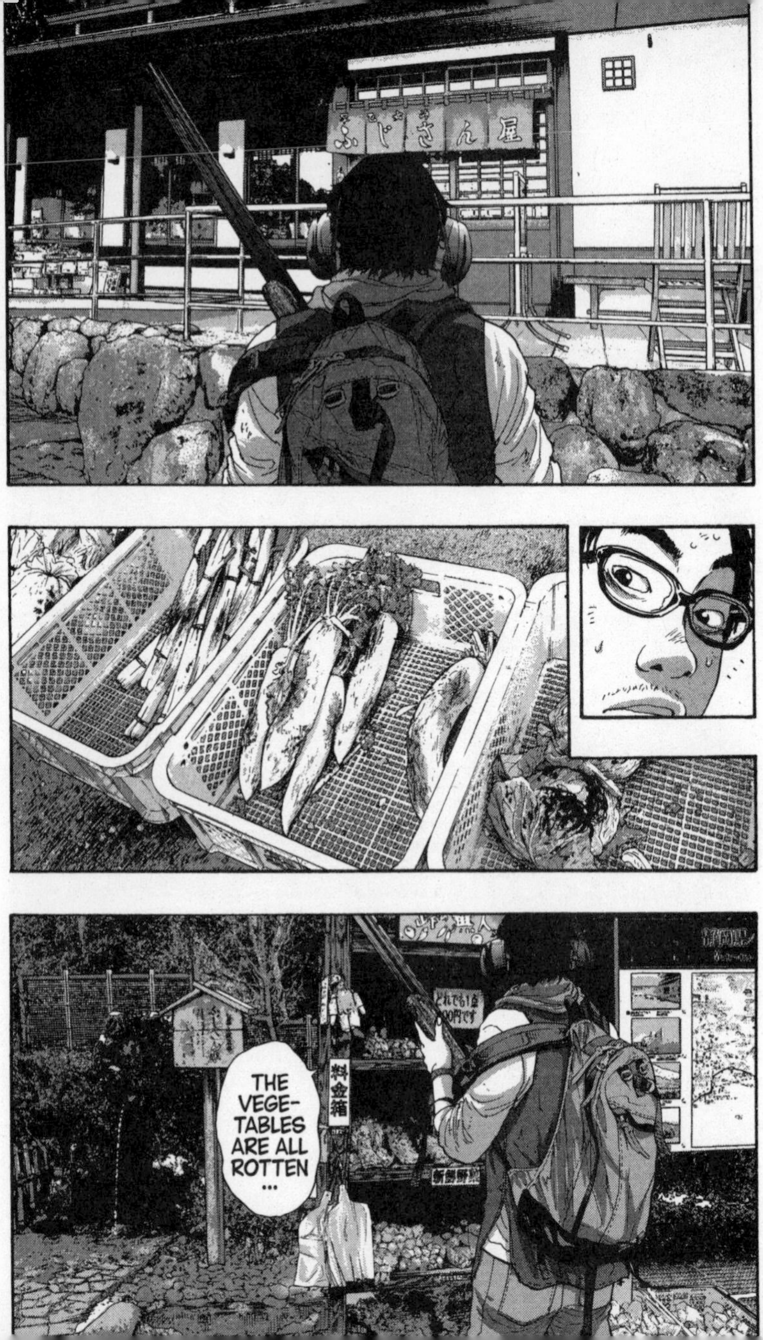
ふじさん屋
料金箱
THE VEGE- TABLES ARE ALL ROTTEN ...

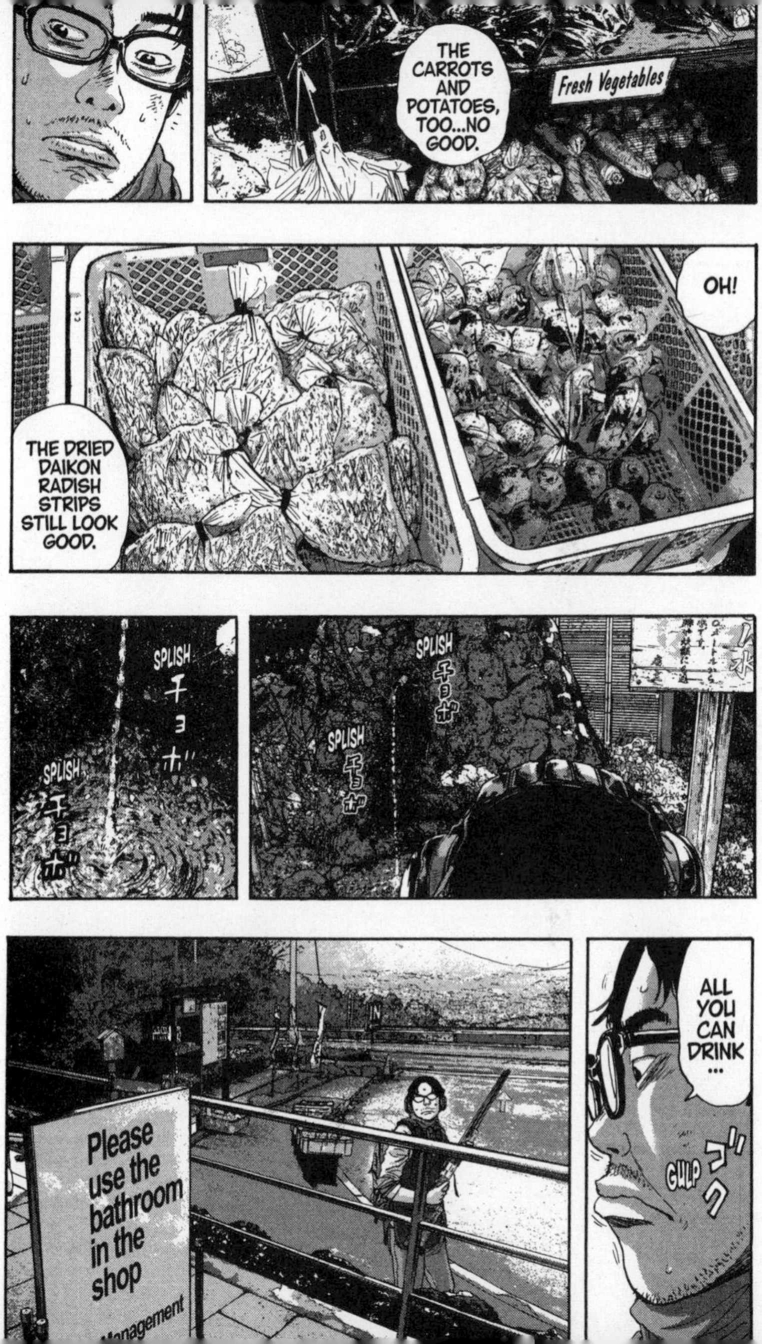

Fresh Vegetables
THE CARROTS AND POTATOES, TOO...NO GOOD.
OH!
THE DRIED DAIKON RADISH STRIPS STILL LOOK GOOD.
SPLISH
チョボ
SPLISH
チョボ
SPLISH
チョボ
SPLISH
チョボ
ALL YOU CAN DRINK...
GULP
ゴク
Please use the bathroom in the shop
Management

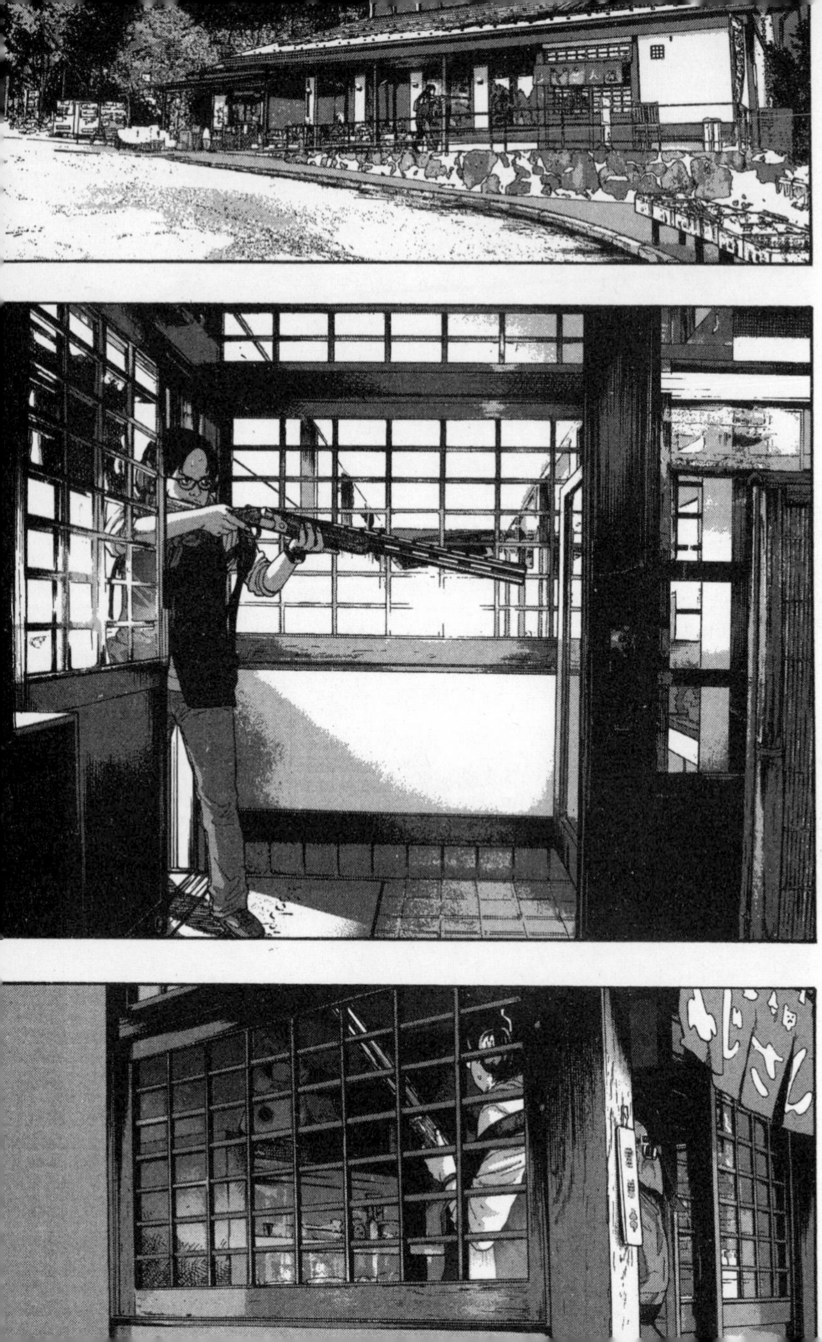

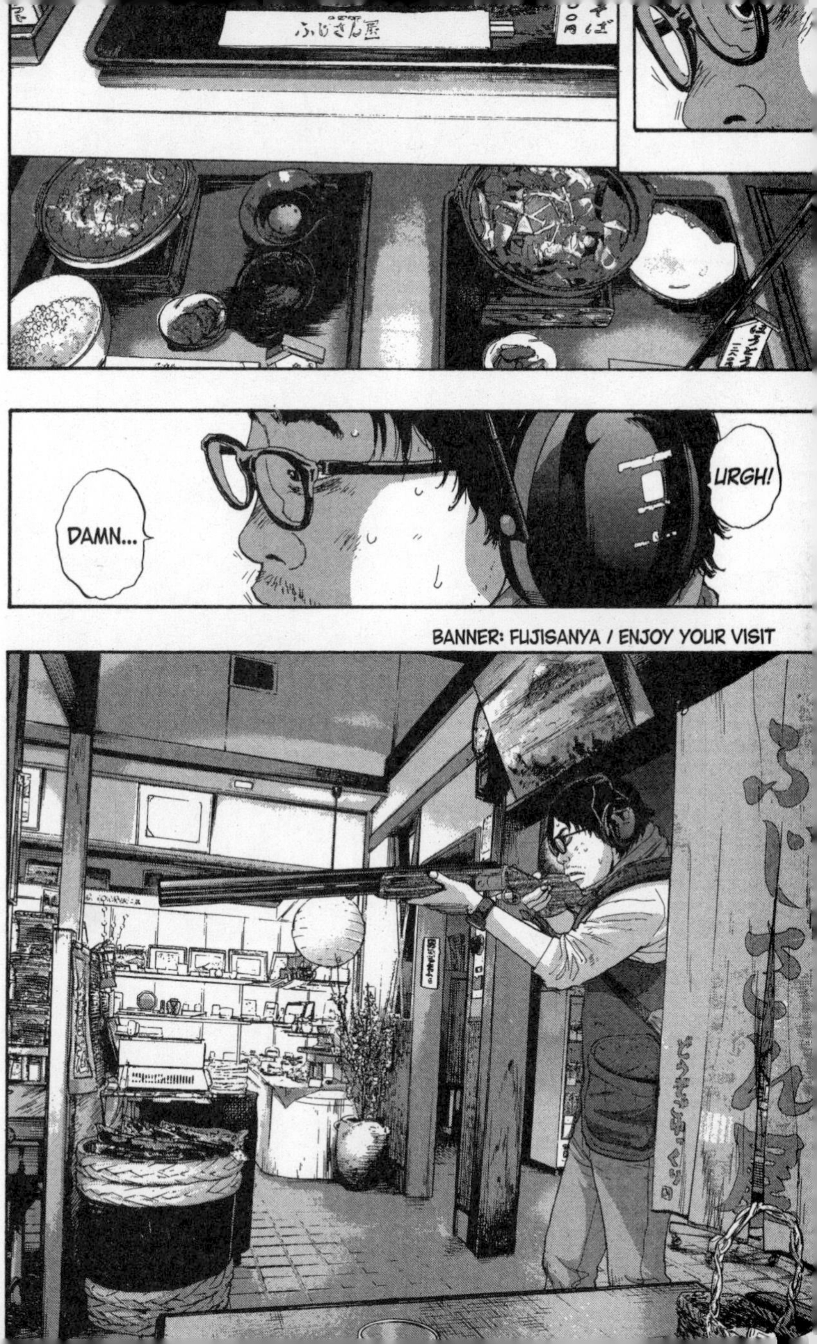
ふじさん屋
URGH!
DAMN...
BANNER: FUJISANYA / ENJOY YOUR VISIT

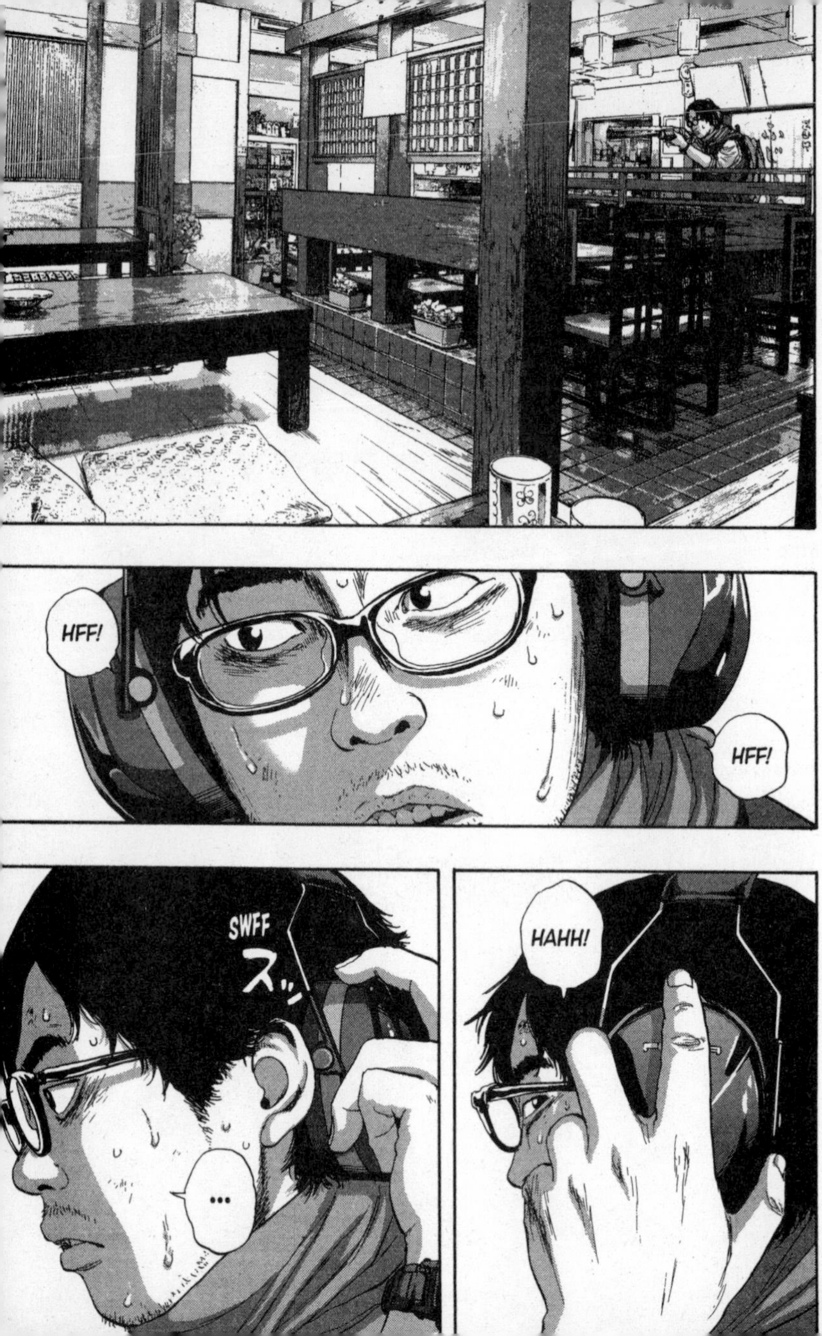

HFF!
HFF!
HAHH!
SWFF
スッ
...

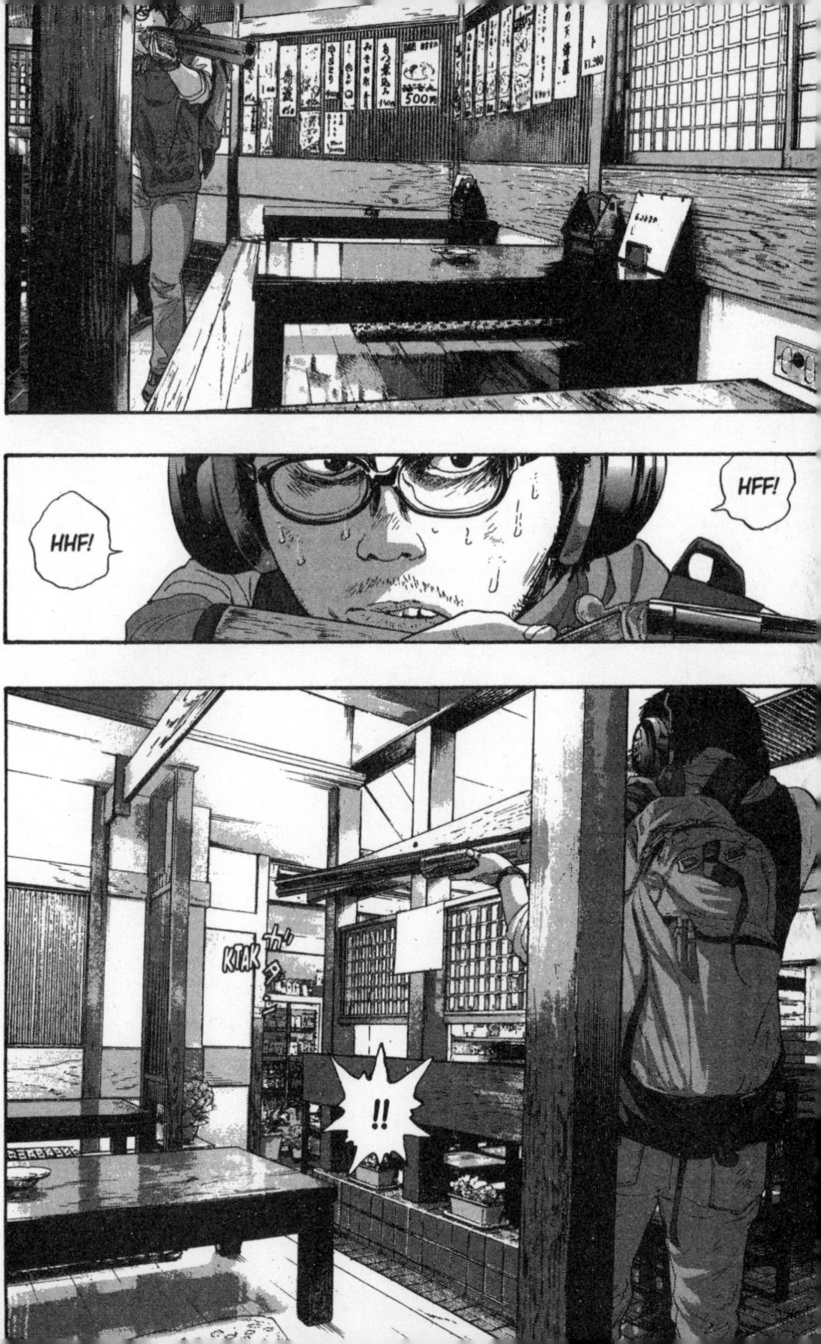
HFF!
HHF!
KTAK
!!

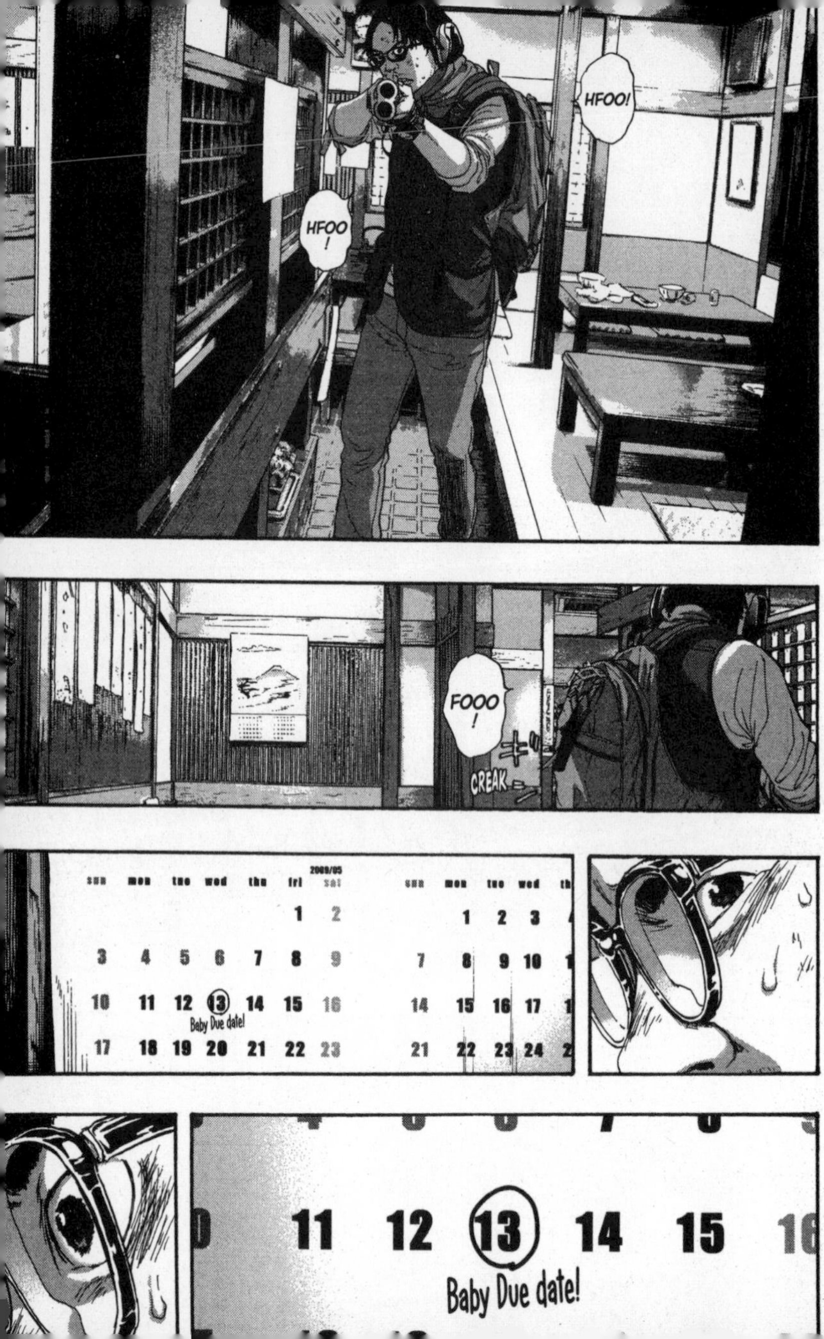
HFOO!
HFOO!
FOOO!
CREAK
sun mon tue wed thu fri sat
1 2
3 4 5 6 7 8 9
10 11 12 13 14 15 16
Baby Due date!
17 18 19 20 21 22 23
11 12 13 14 15 16
Baby Due date!

I WILL KILL...

...IN ORDER...

...TO LIVE...

HFF!

HAHH!

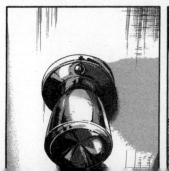

KTAK

CREAK

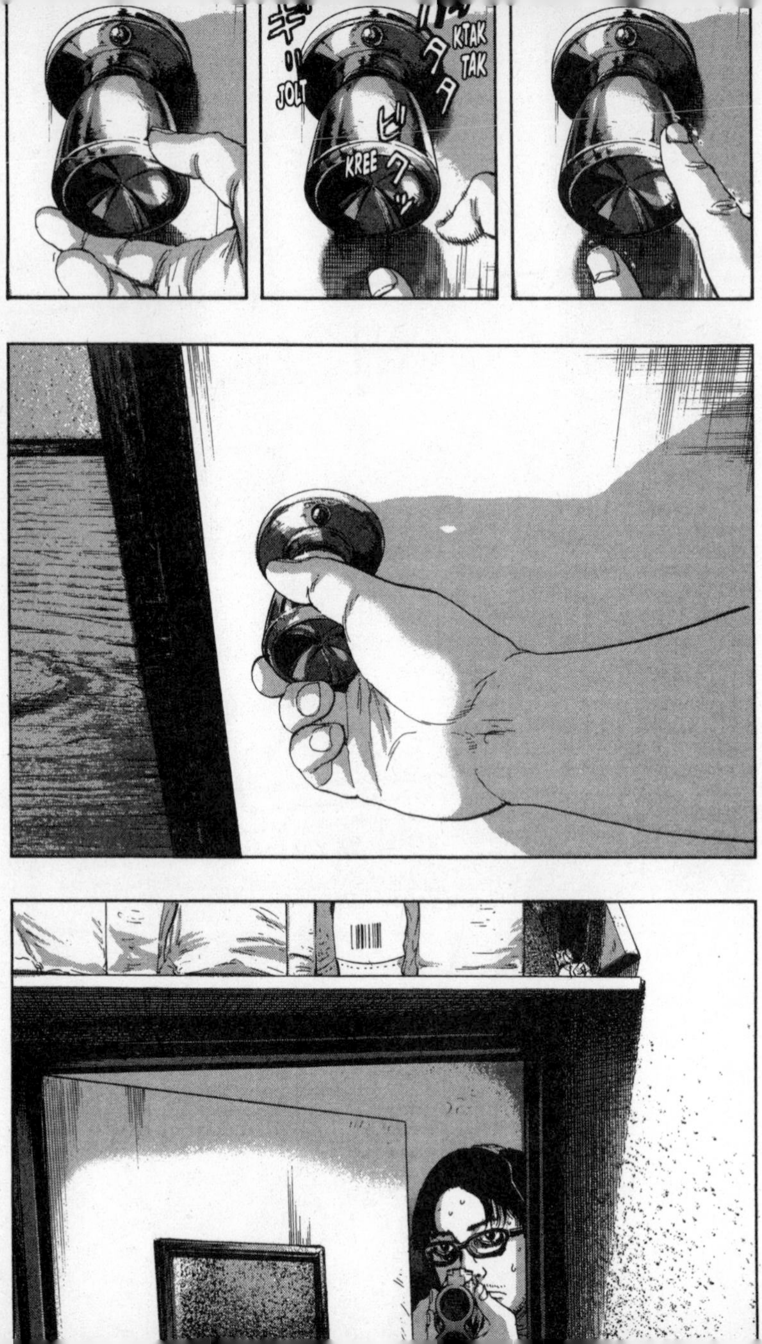
KTAK TAK
KREE
JOLT

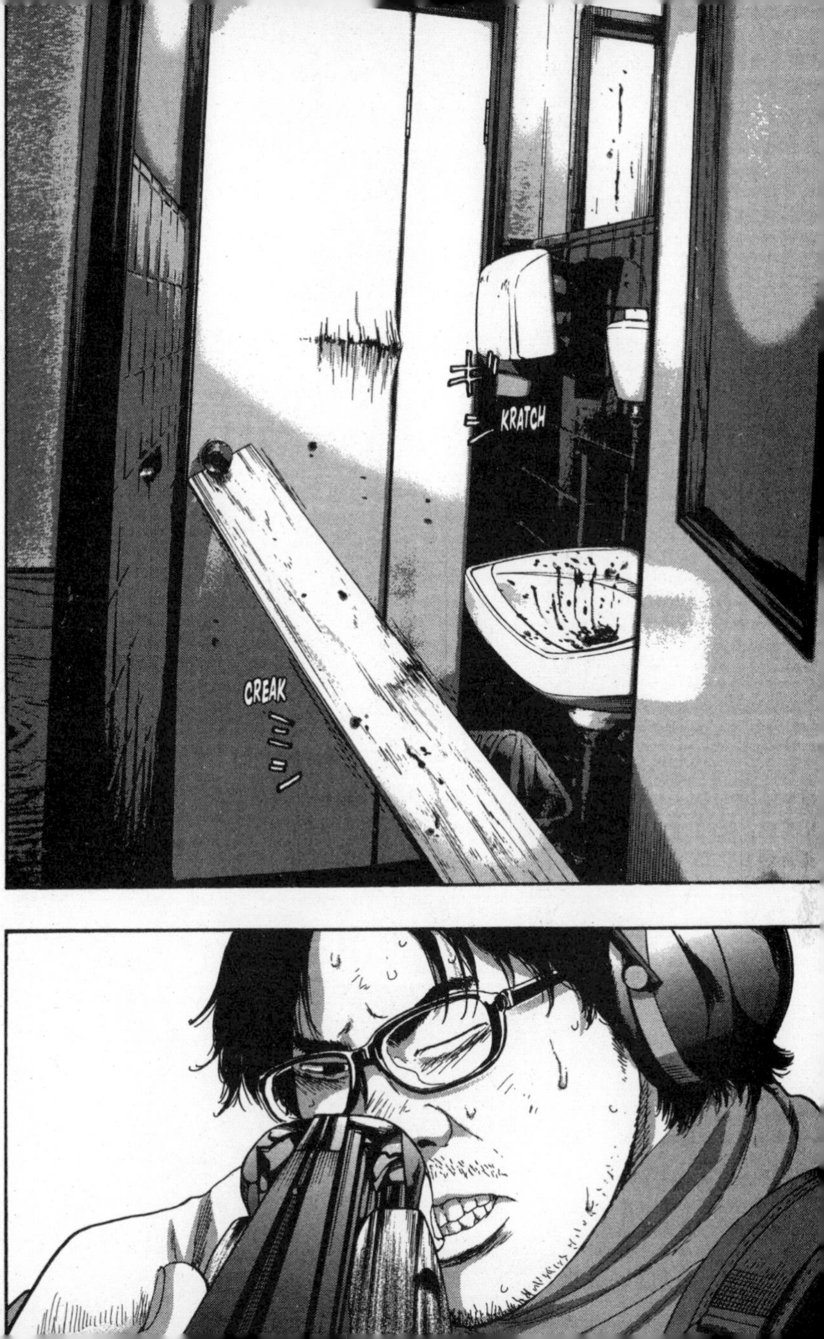
KRATCH
CREAK

HNFF!

HRR!

HAHH!

HFF!

THE...

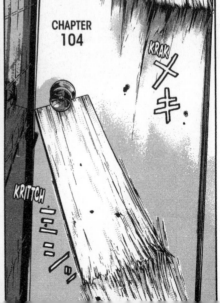

CHAPTER
104

KRAK

KRITTCH

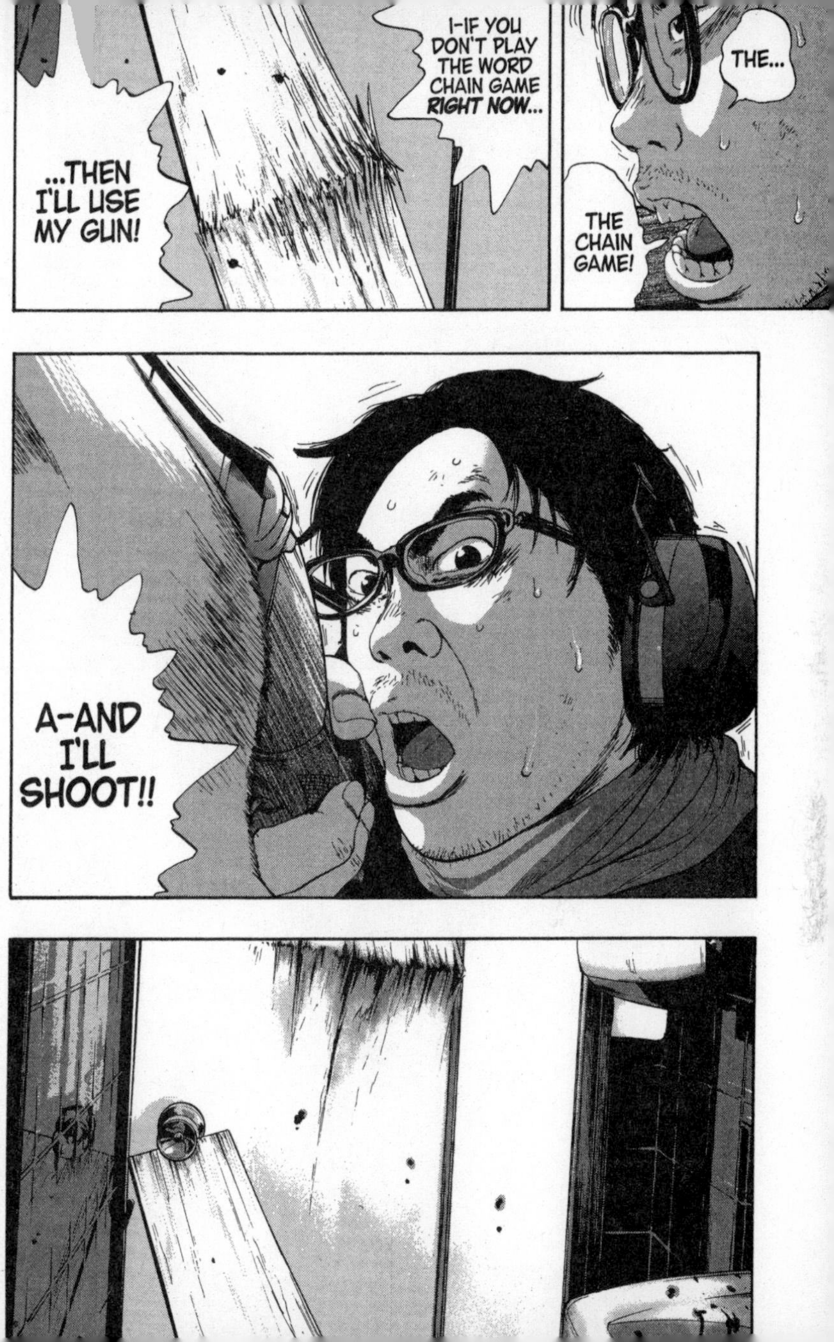
THE...
THE CHAIN GAME!
I-IF YOU DON'T PLAY THE WORD CHAIN GAME RIGHT NOW...
...THEN I'LL USE MY GUN!
A-AND I'LL SHOOT!!

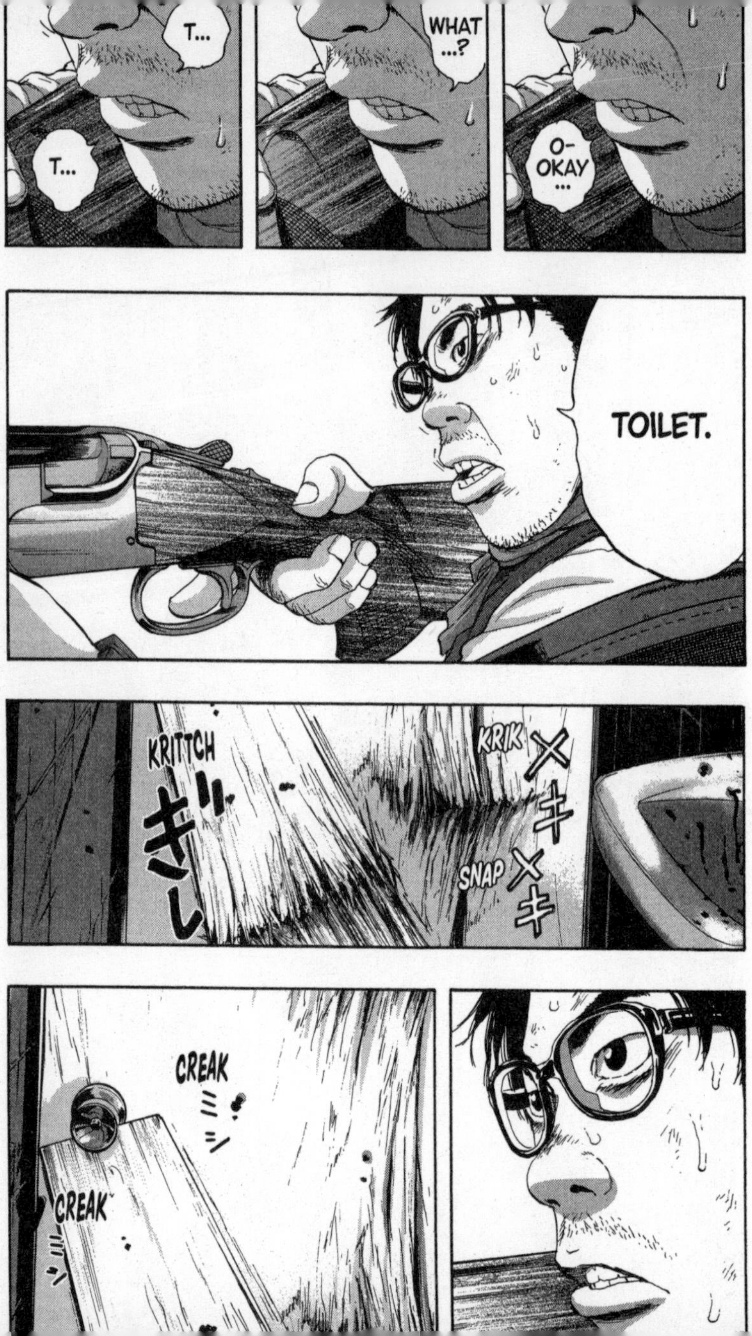
O-
OKAY
...
WHAT
...?
T...
T...
TOILET.
KRIK
SNAP
KRITTCH
CREAK
CREAK

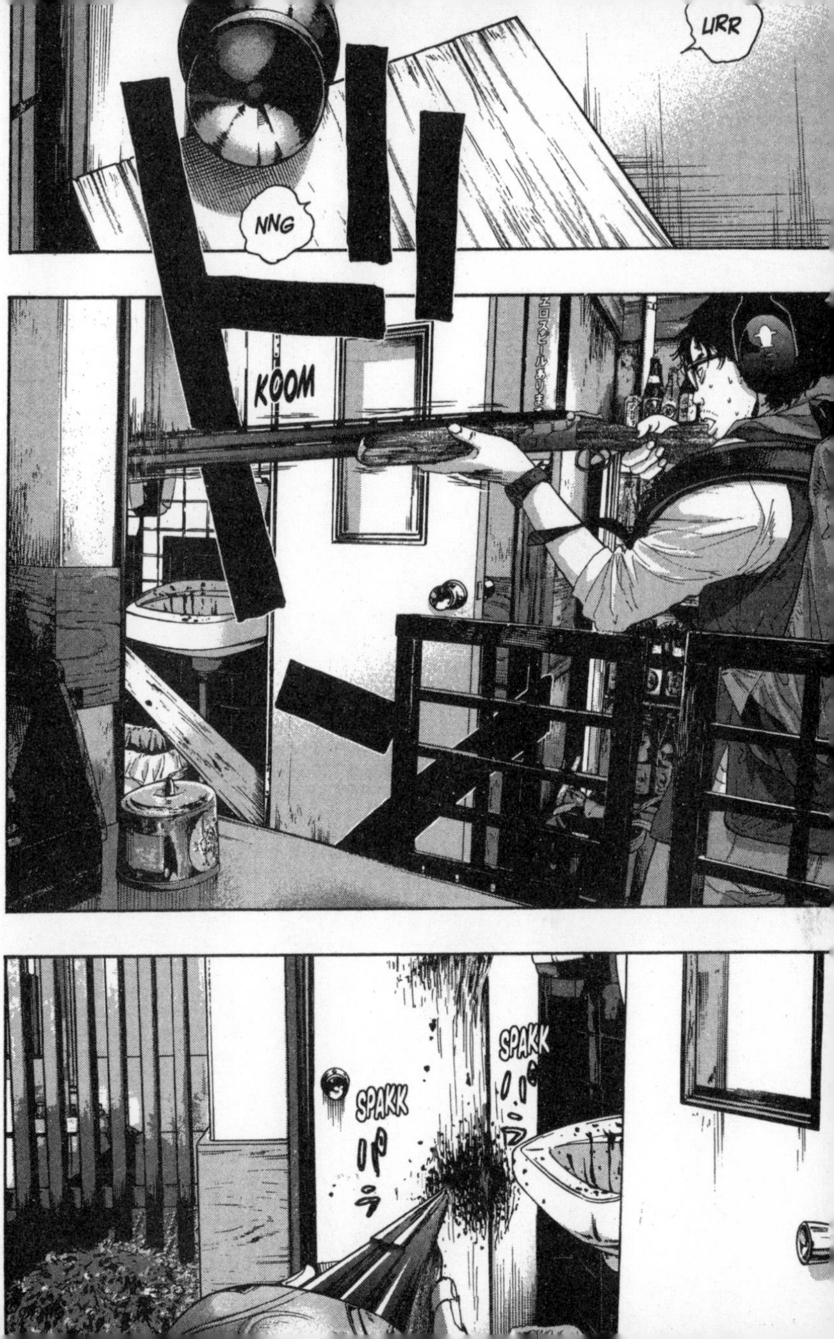
URR
NNG
エロスビールありま
KOOM
SPAKK
SPAKK

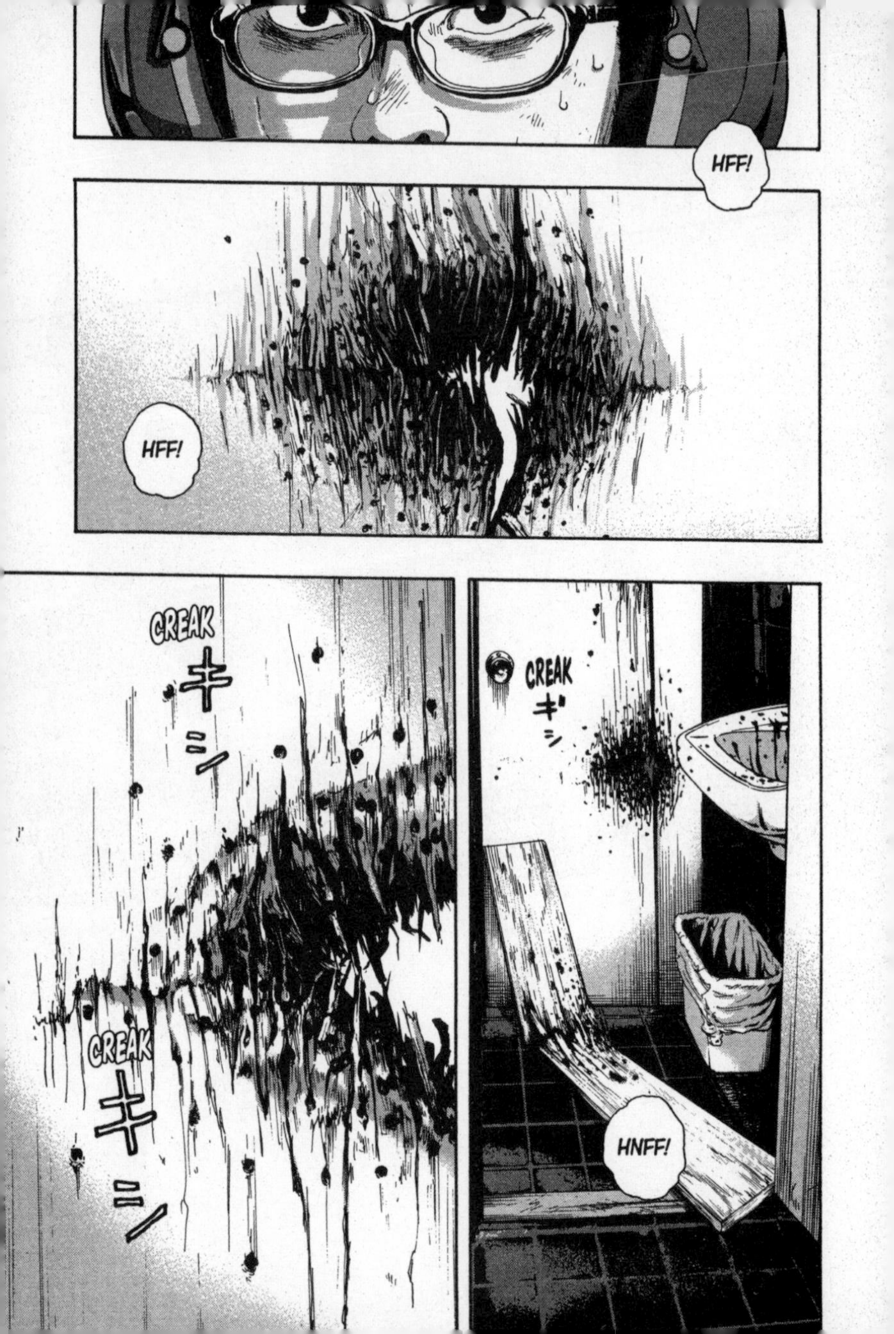
HFF!
HFF!
CREAK
ギシ
HNFF!
CREAK
キシ
CREAK
キシ

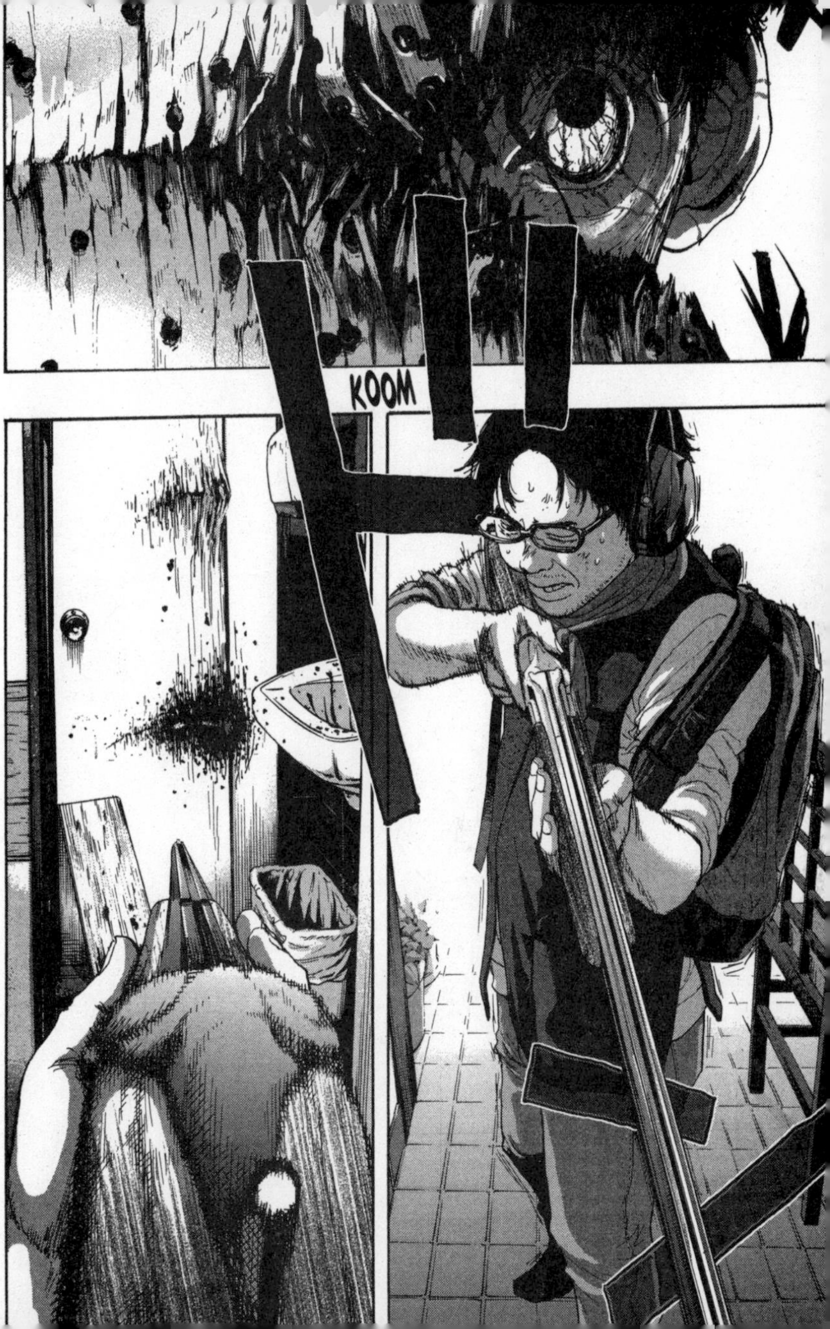
KOOM

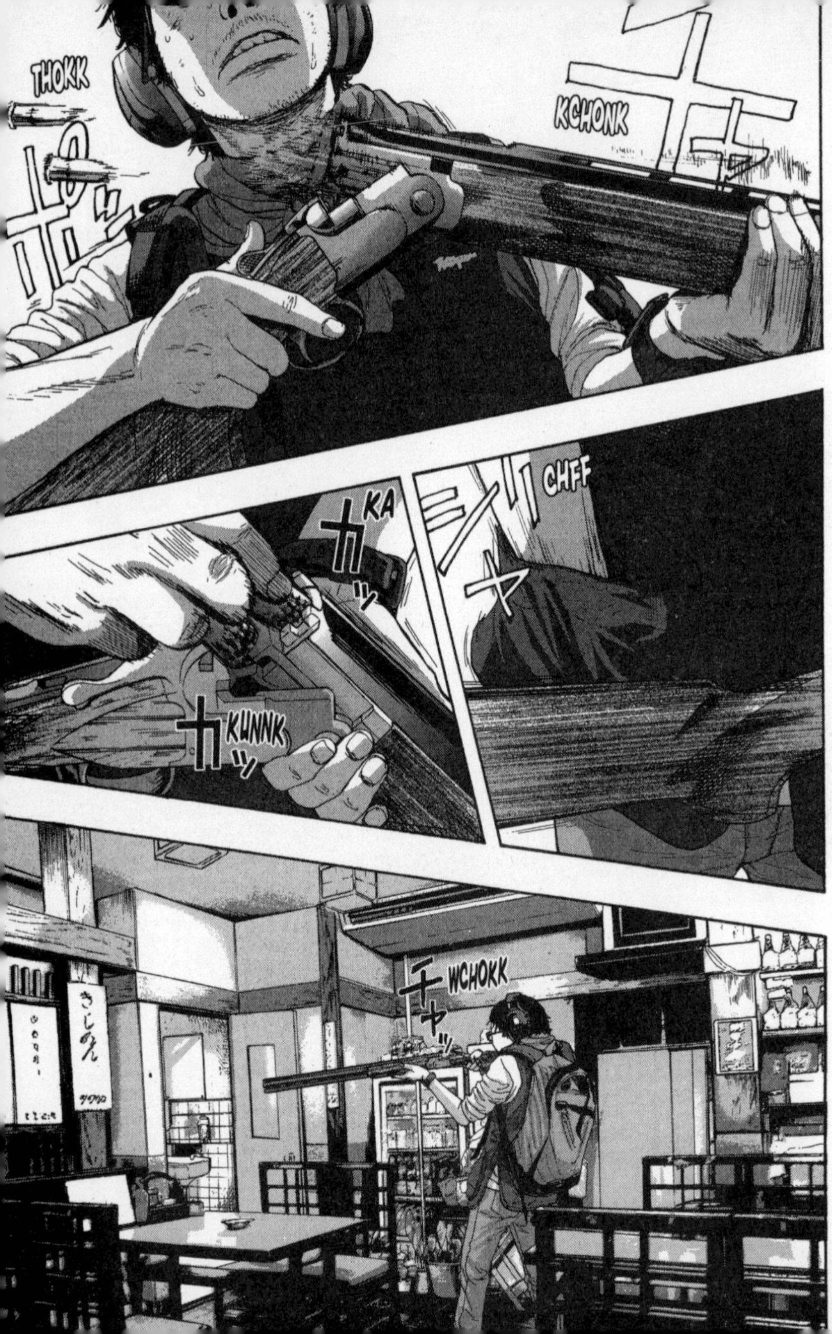
KCHONK
THOKK
CHFF
KA
KUNNK
WCHOKK

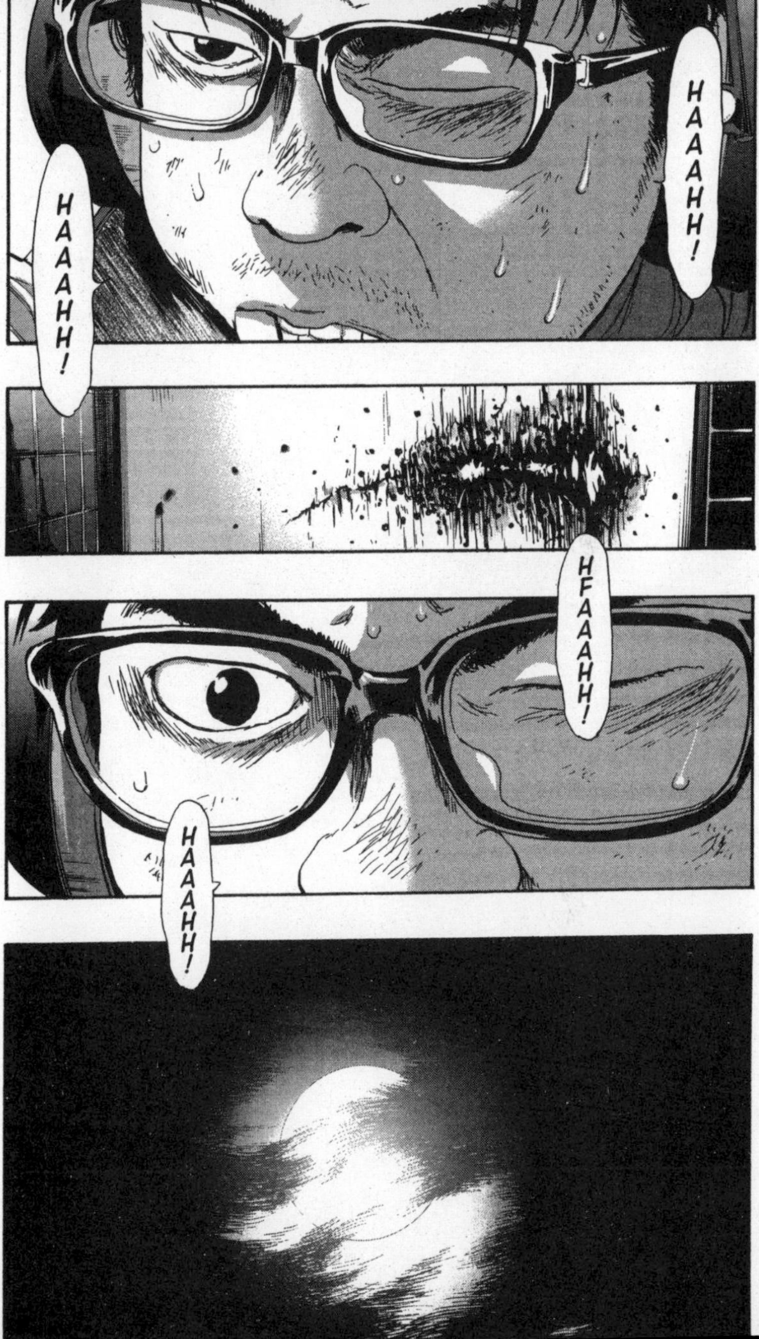
HAAAAHH!
HAAAAHH!
HFAAAAHH!
HAAAAHH!

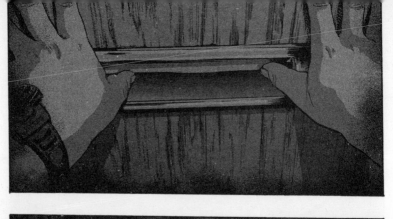

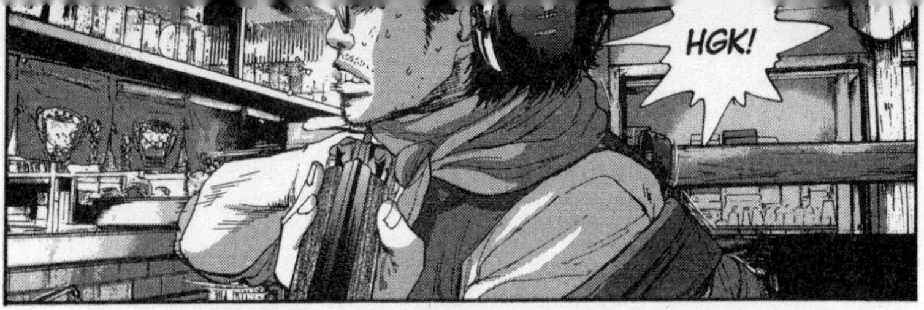
HGK!
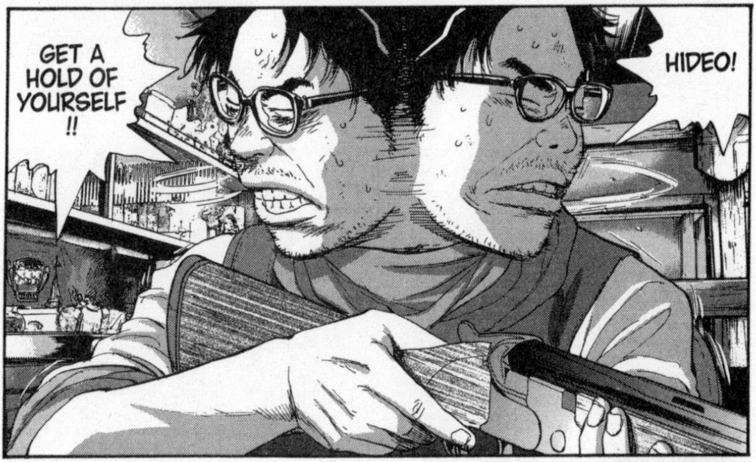
HIDEO!
GET A HOLD OF YOURSELF !!
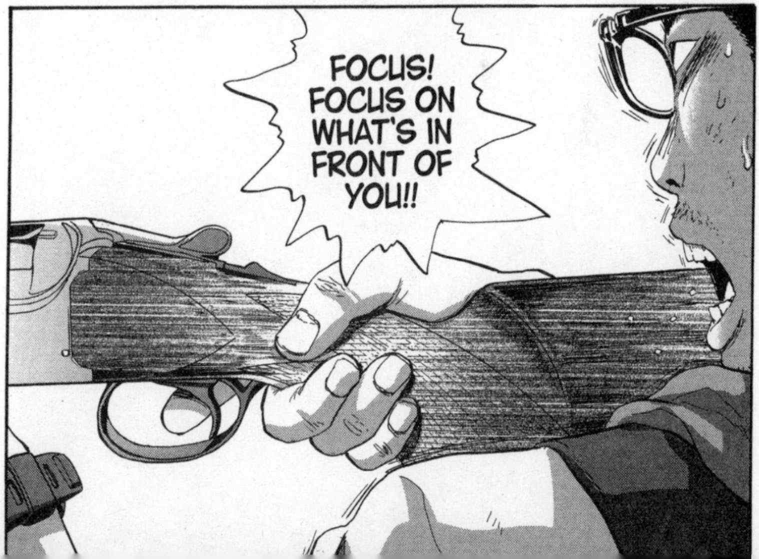
FOCUS! FOCUS ON WHAT'S IN FRONT OF YOU!!

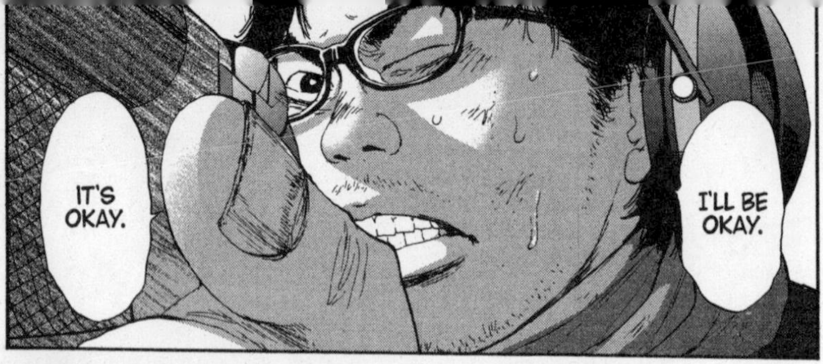
I'LL BE OKAY.
IT'S OKAY.
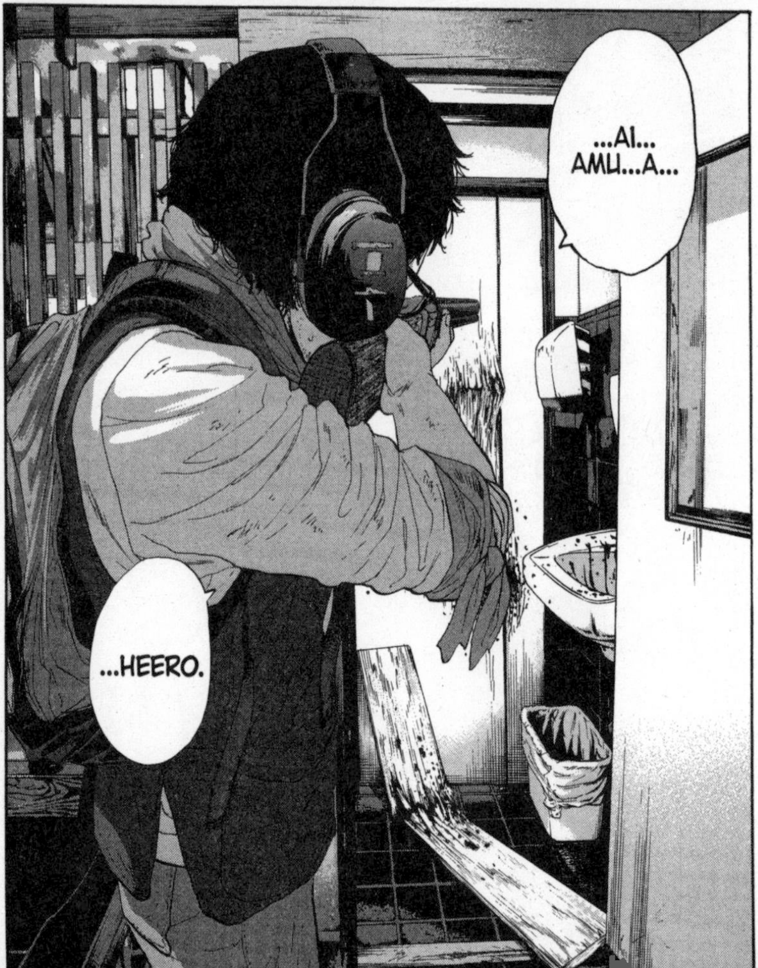
...AI... AMU...A...
...HEERO.

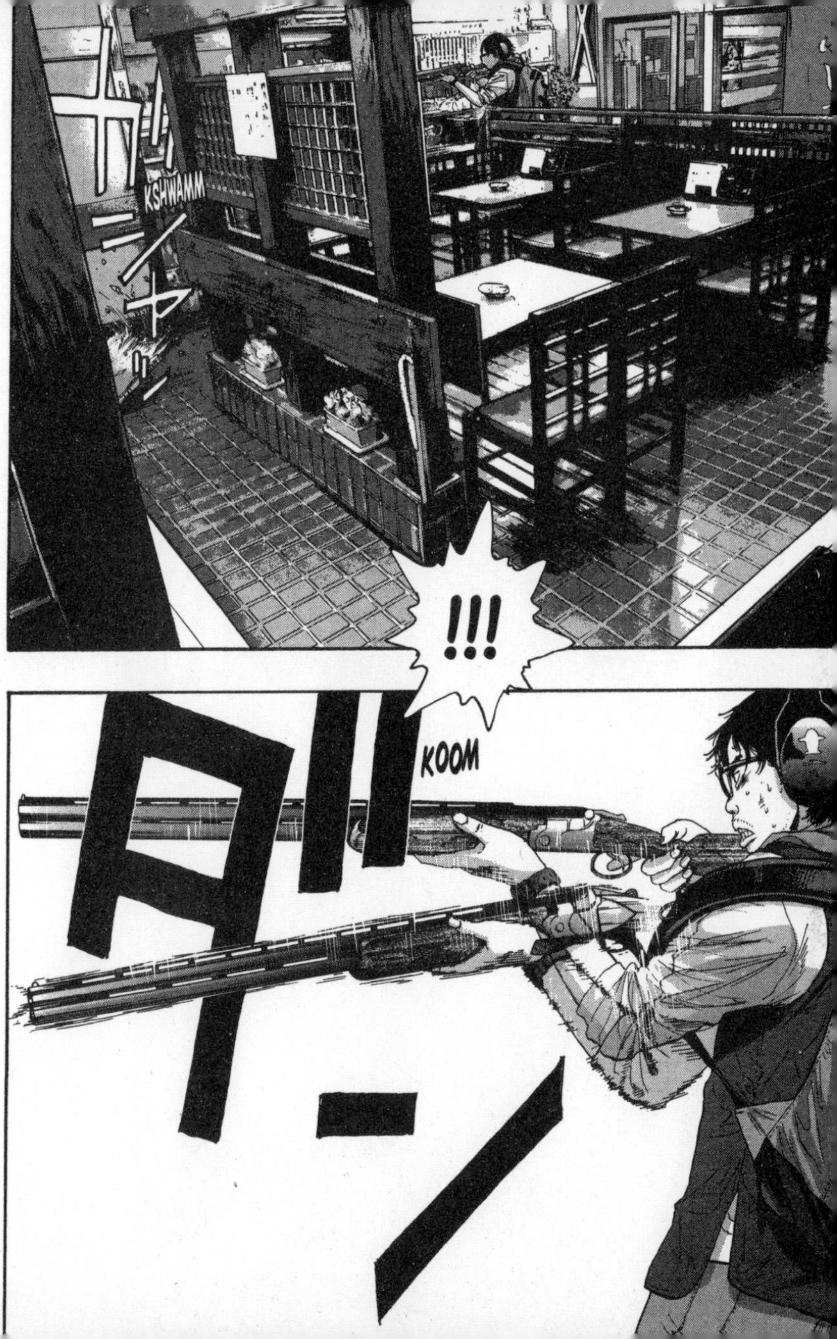
KSHWAMM
!!!
KOOM

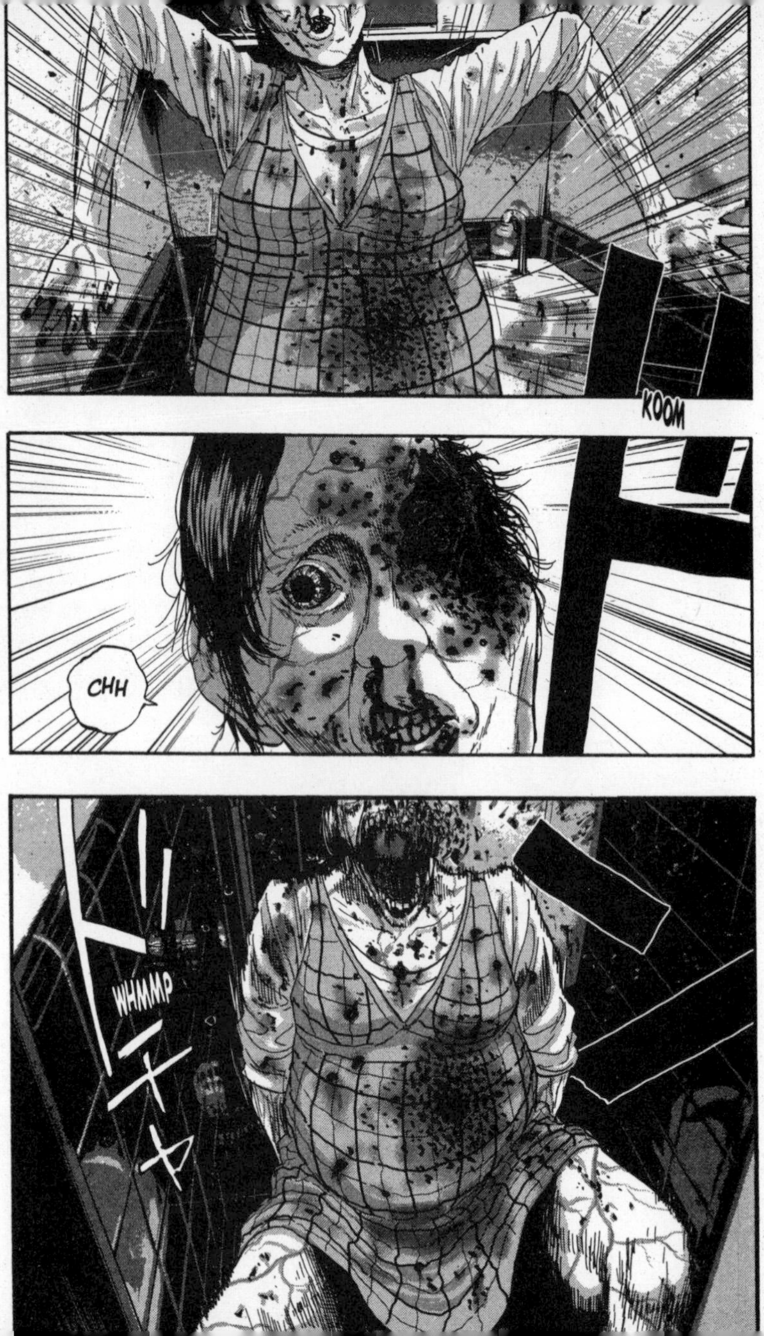
KOOM
CHH
WHMMP

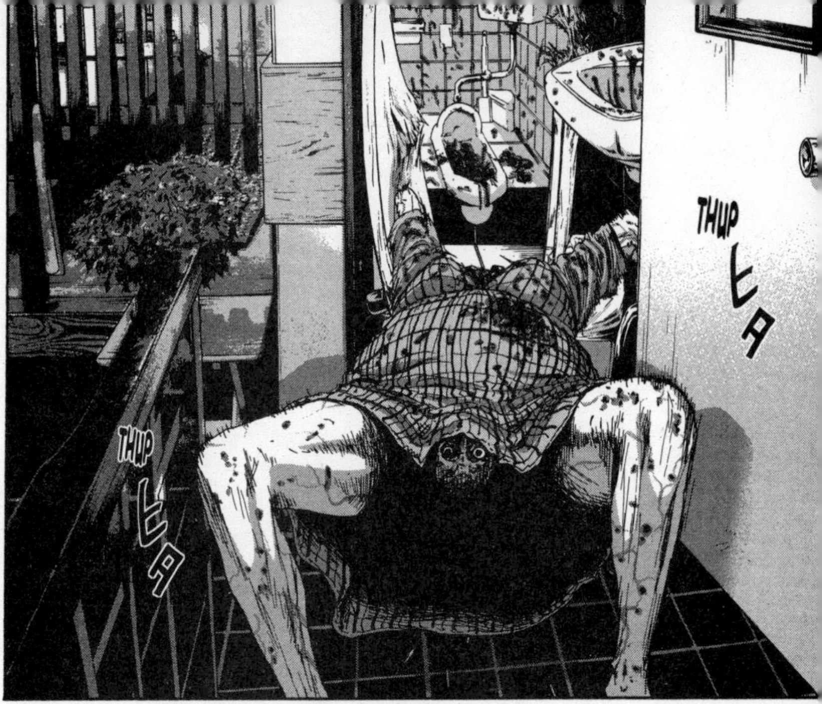
THUP ヒタ
THUP ヒタ
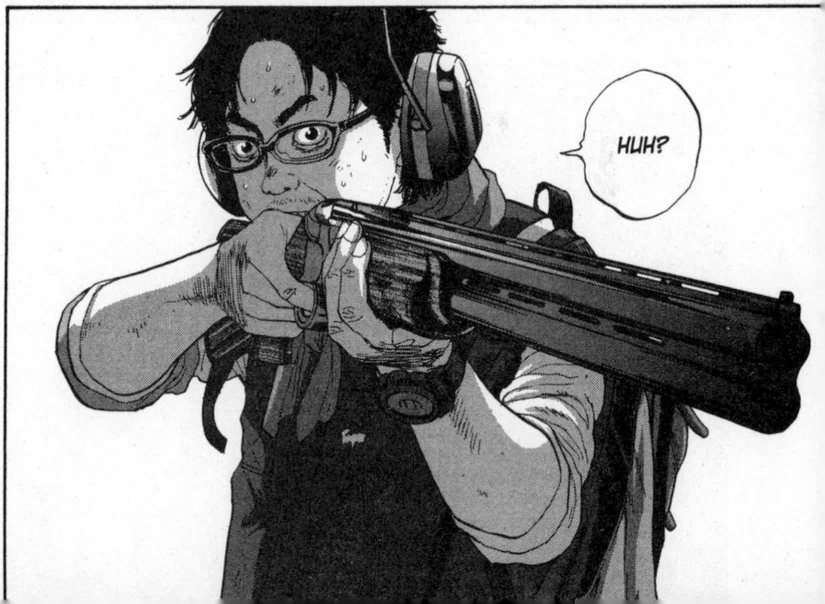
HUH?

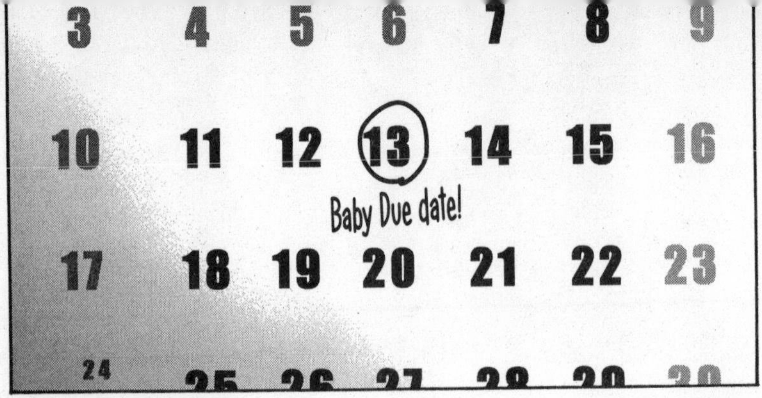
3 4 5 6 7 8 9
10 11 12 13 14 15 16
Baby Due date!
17 18 19 20 21 22 23
24

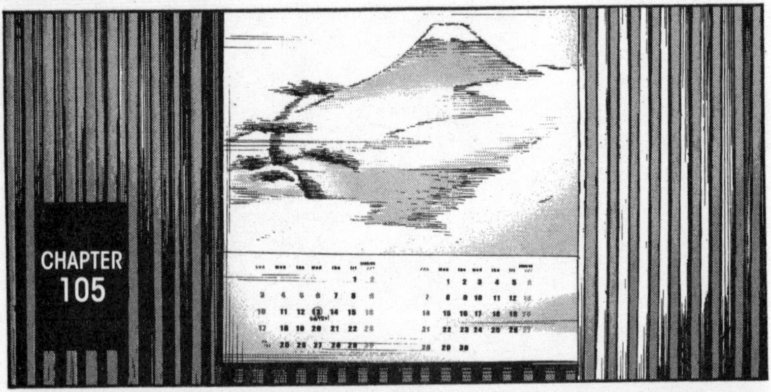
CHAPTER 105

PACKETS: BORRAGINOL B HEMORRHOID CREAM

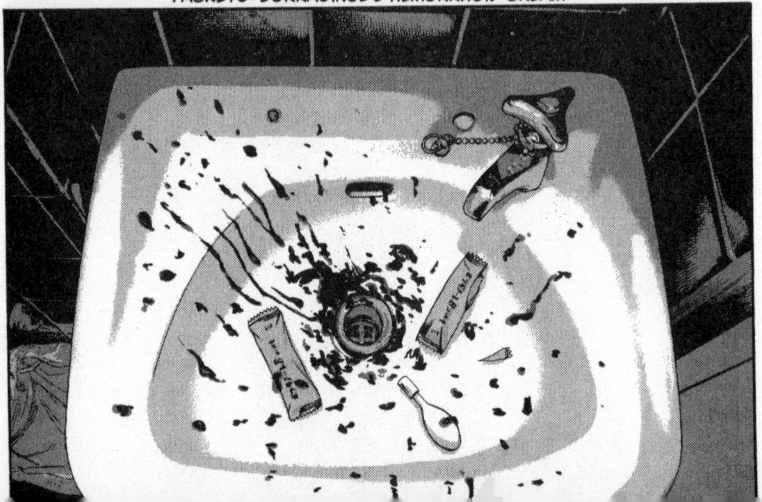

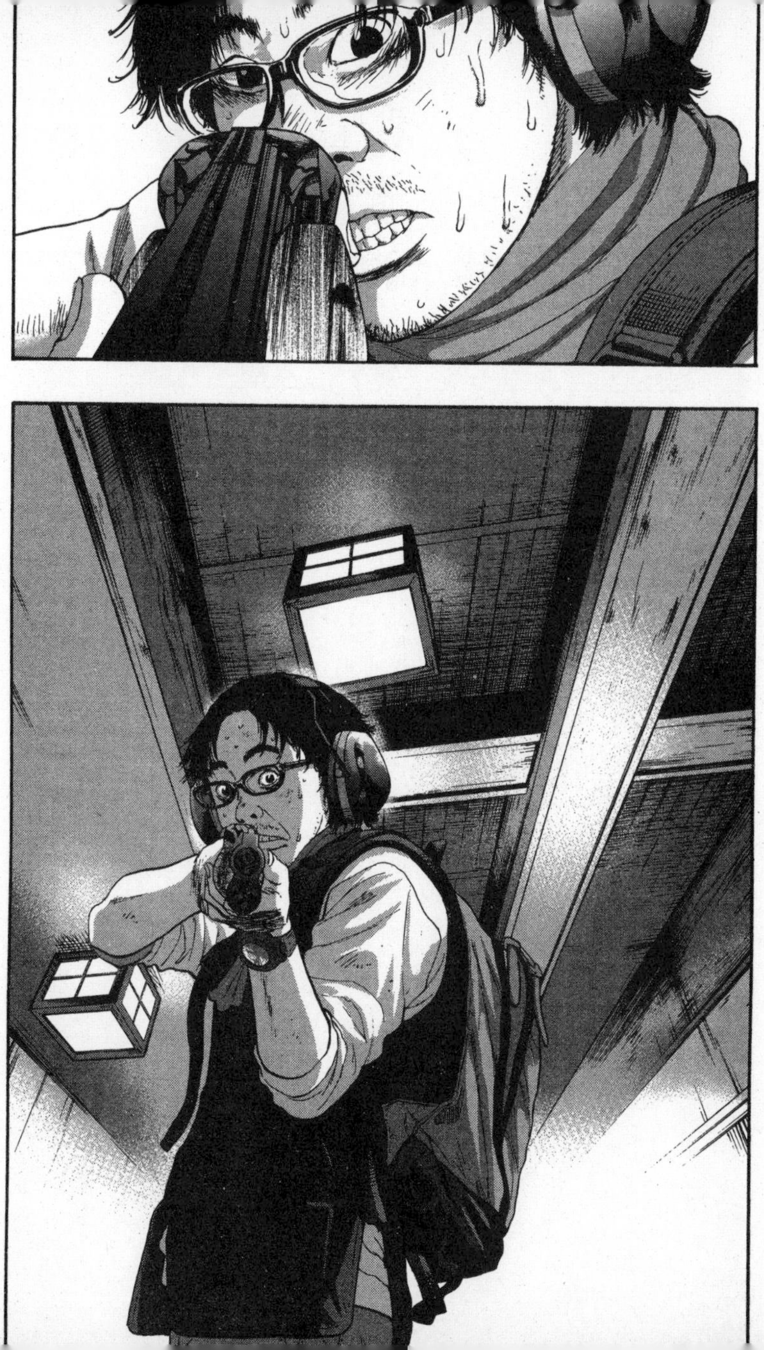

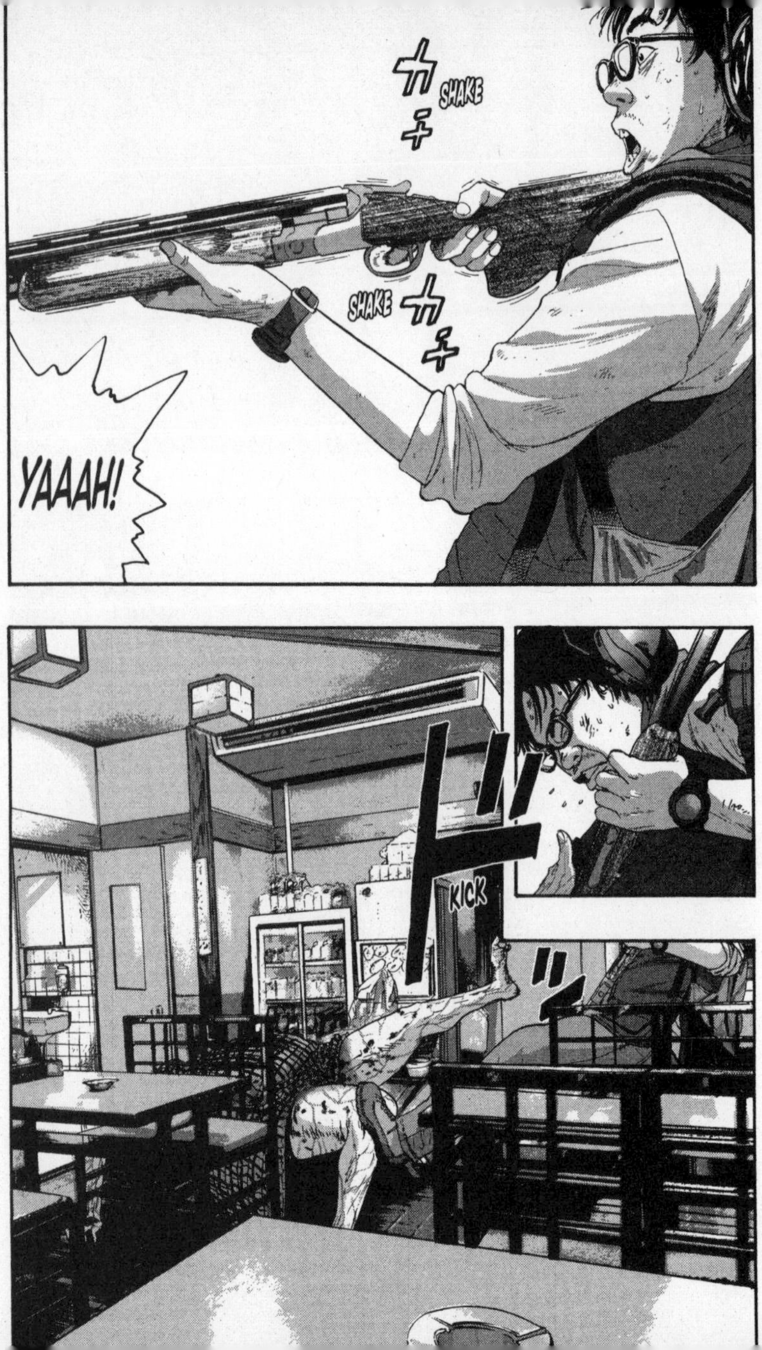

SHAKE
SHAKE
YAAAH!
KICK

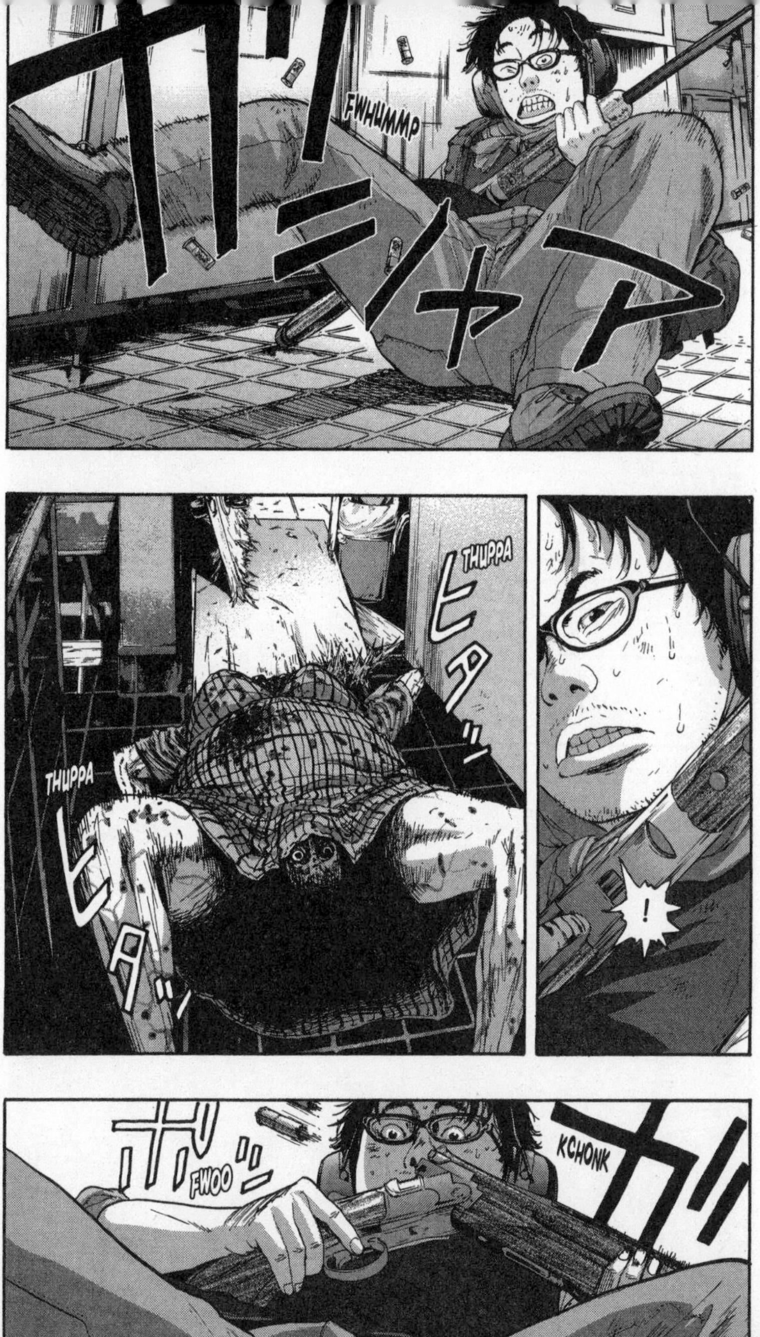
FWHUMMP
!
THUPPA
THUPPA
KCHONK
FWOO

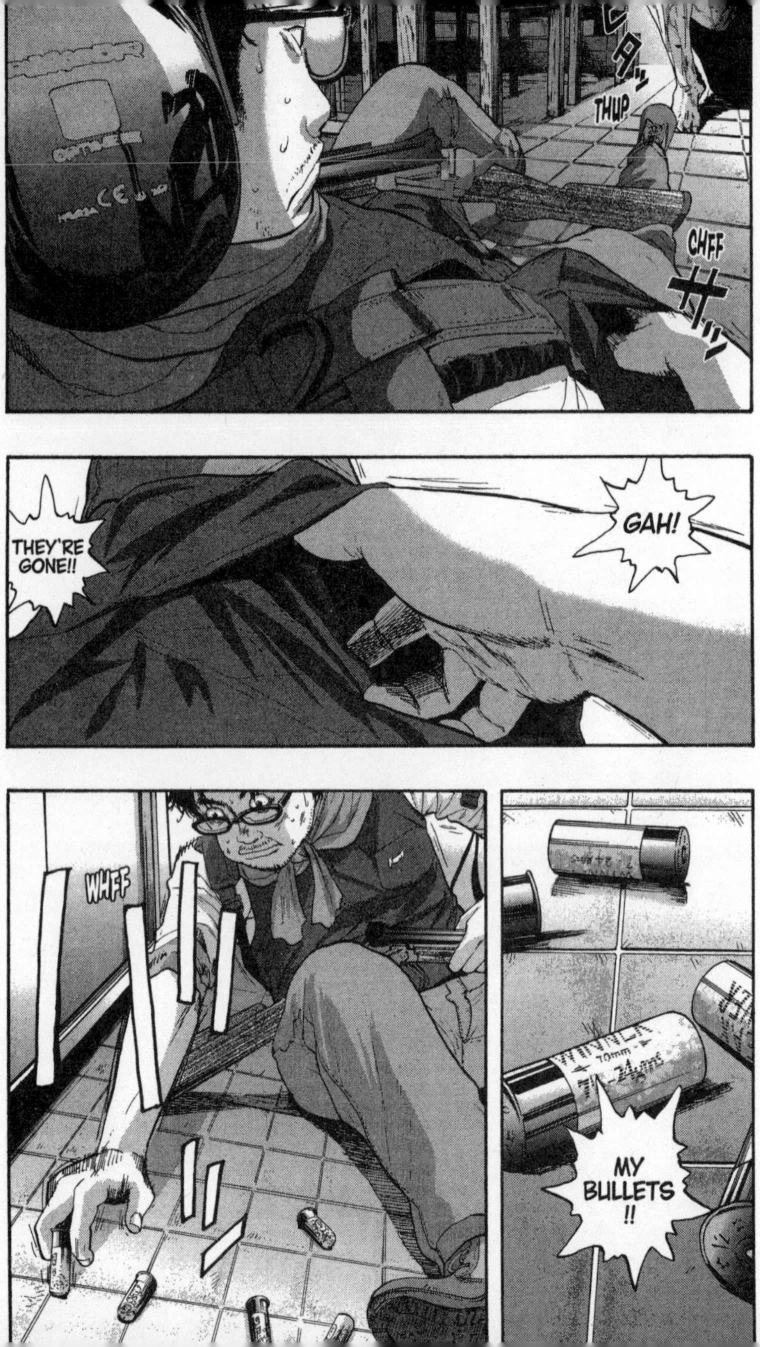
THUP
CHFF
GAH!
THEY'RE GONE!!
MY BULLETS !!
WHFF

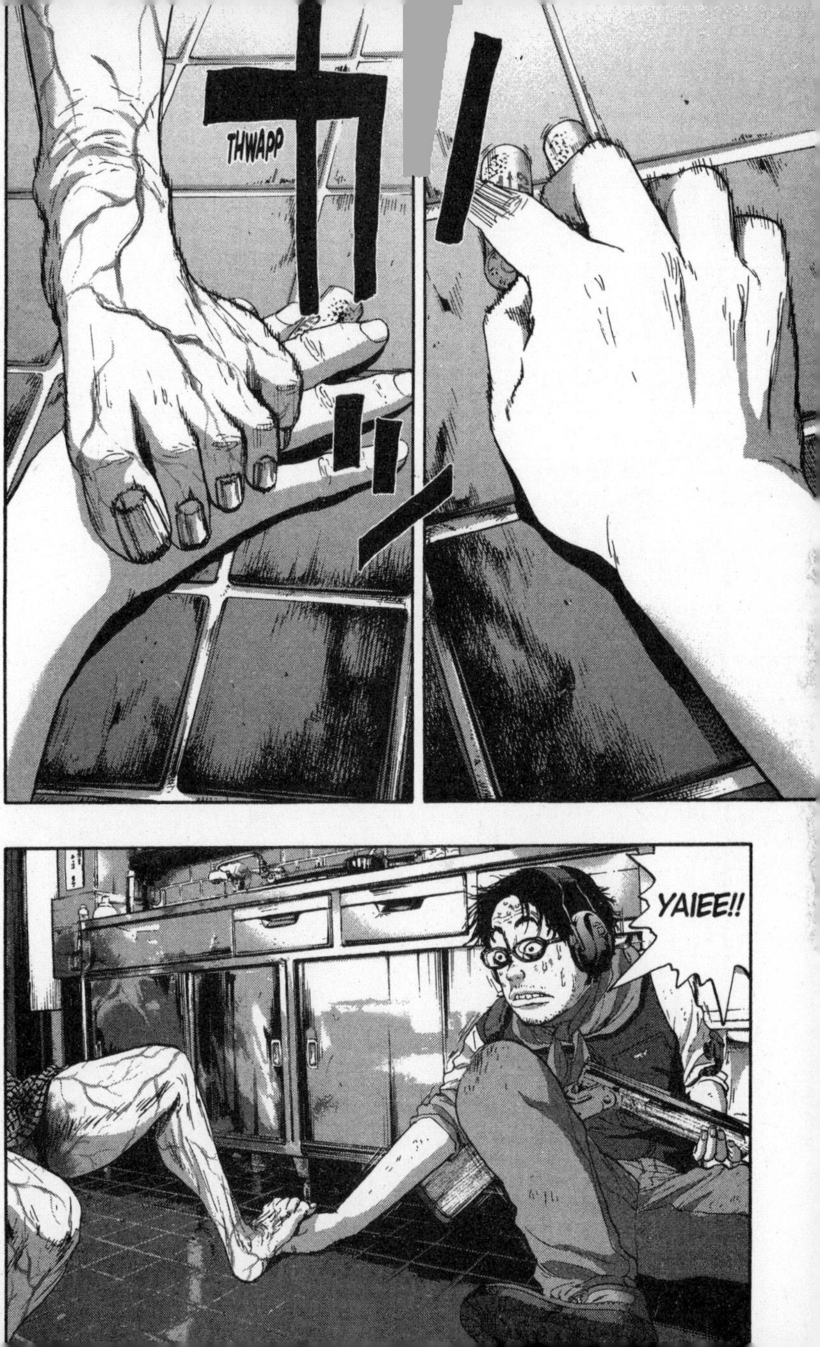
THWAPP
YAIEE!!

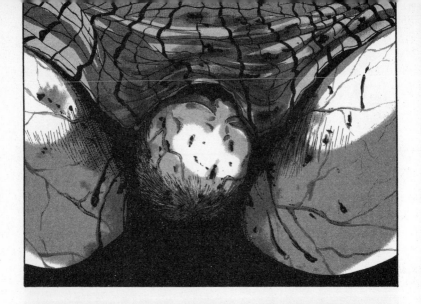

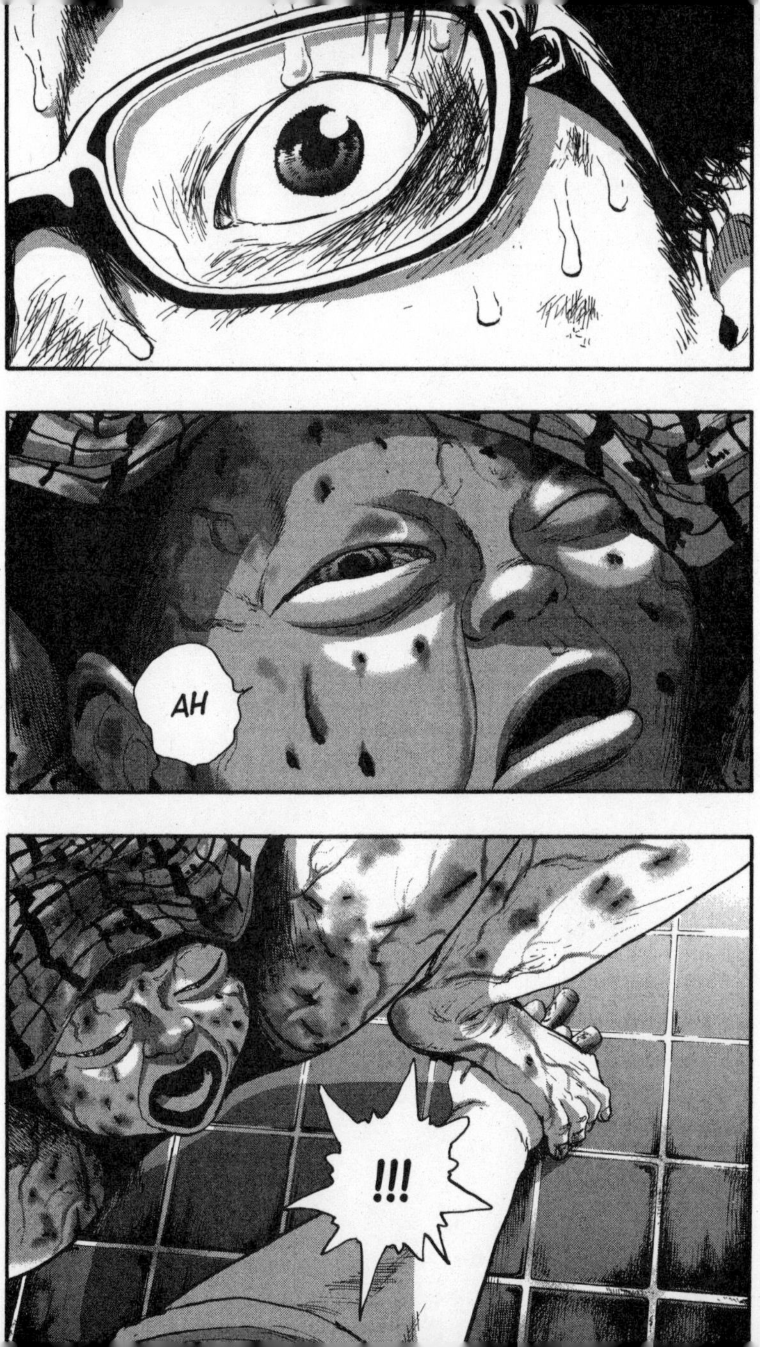
AH
!!!

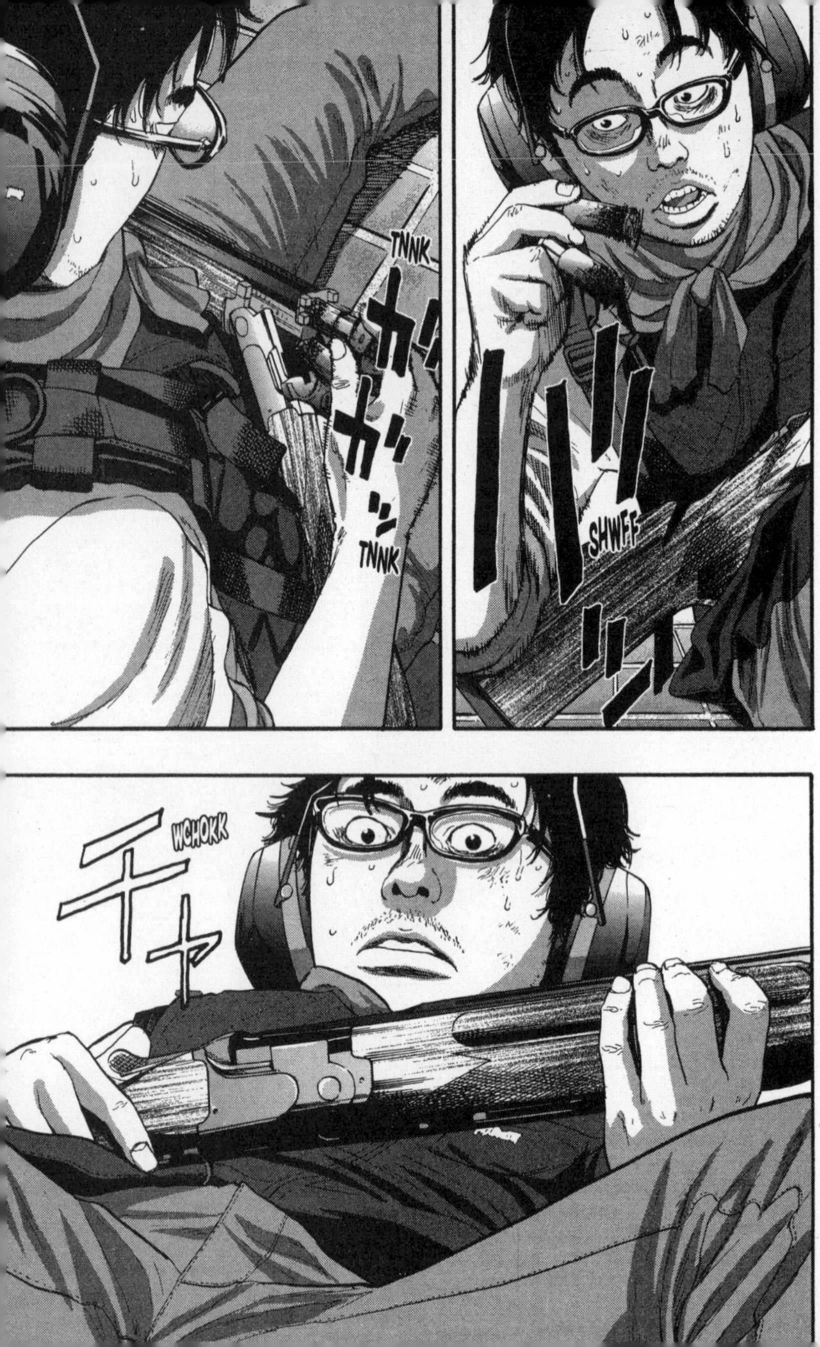
SHWFF
TNNK
TNNK
WCHOKK

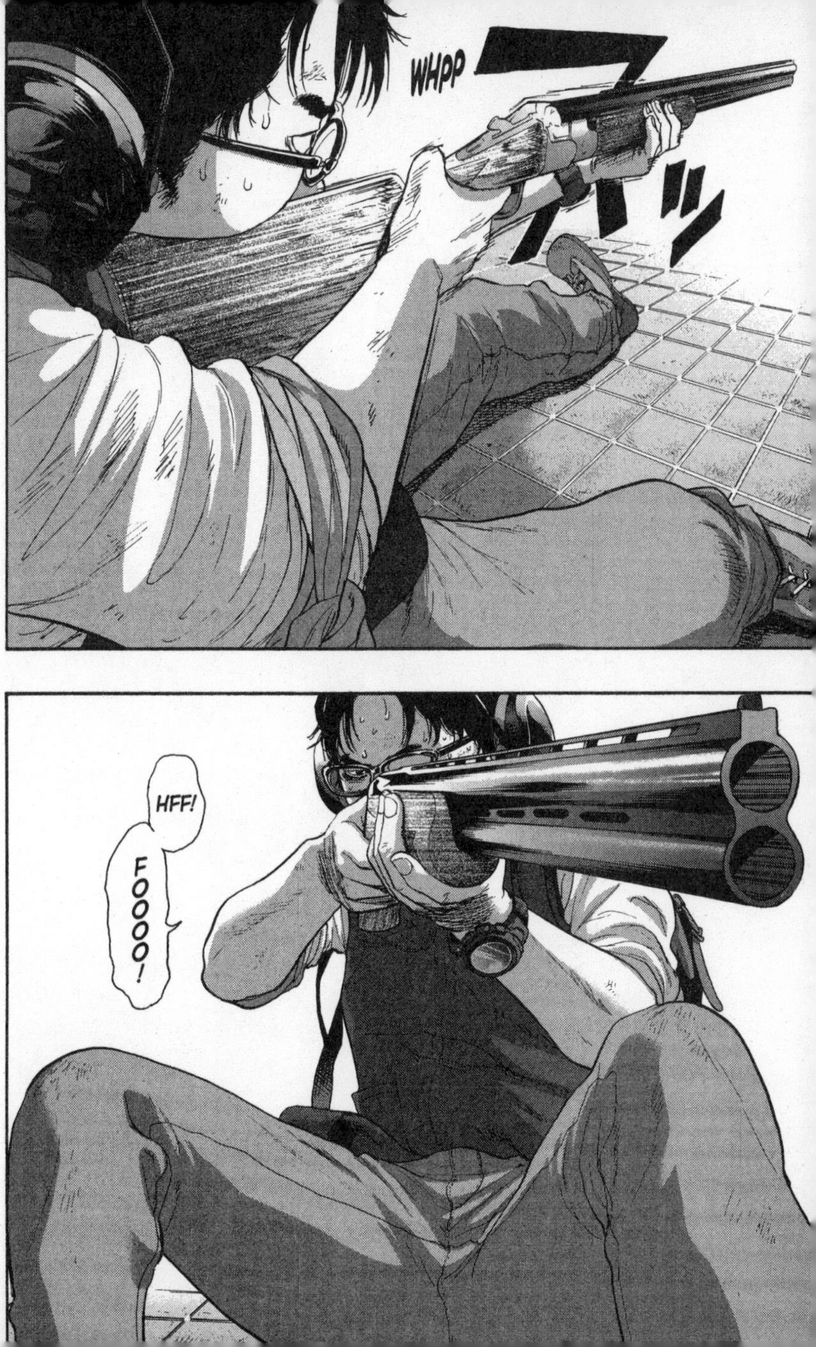
WHPP
HFF!
FOOOOO!

KOOM
THCH
I...
...MISSED ?!

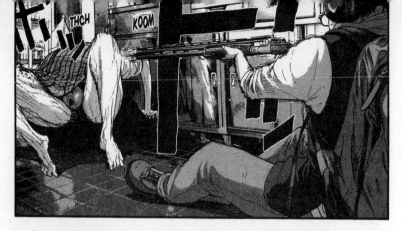

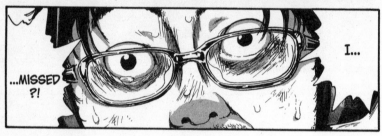

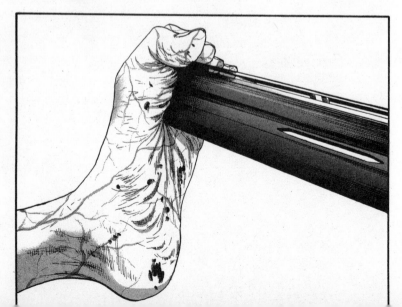

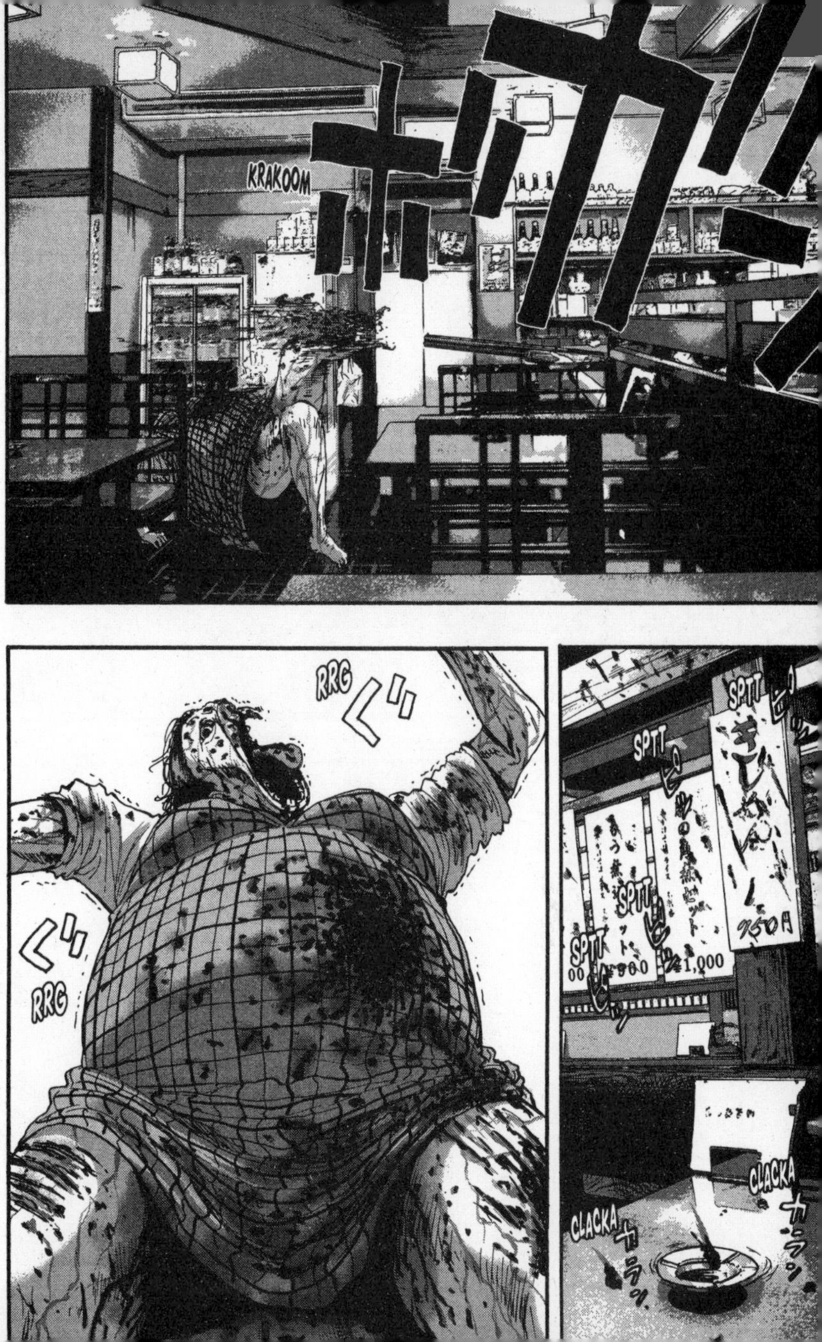
KRAKOOM
SPTT
SPTT
SPTT
SPTT
950円
¥1,000
CLACKA
CLACKA
RRG
RRG

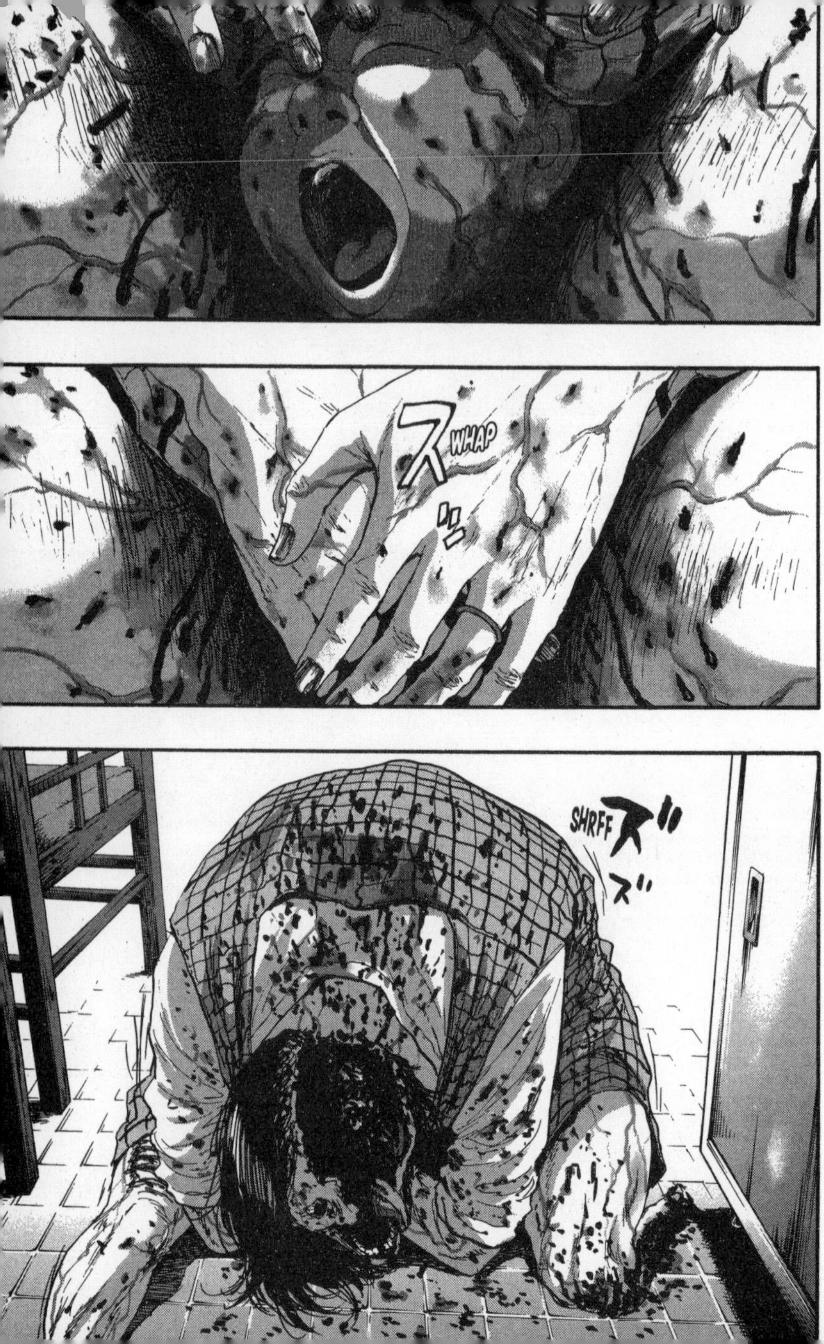

ス
WHAP
SHRFF
ズ
ズ

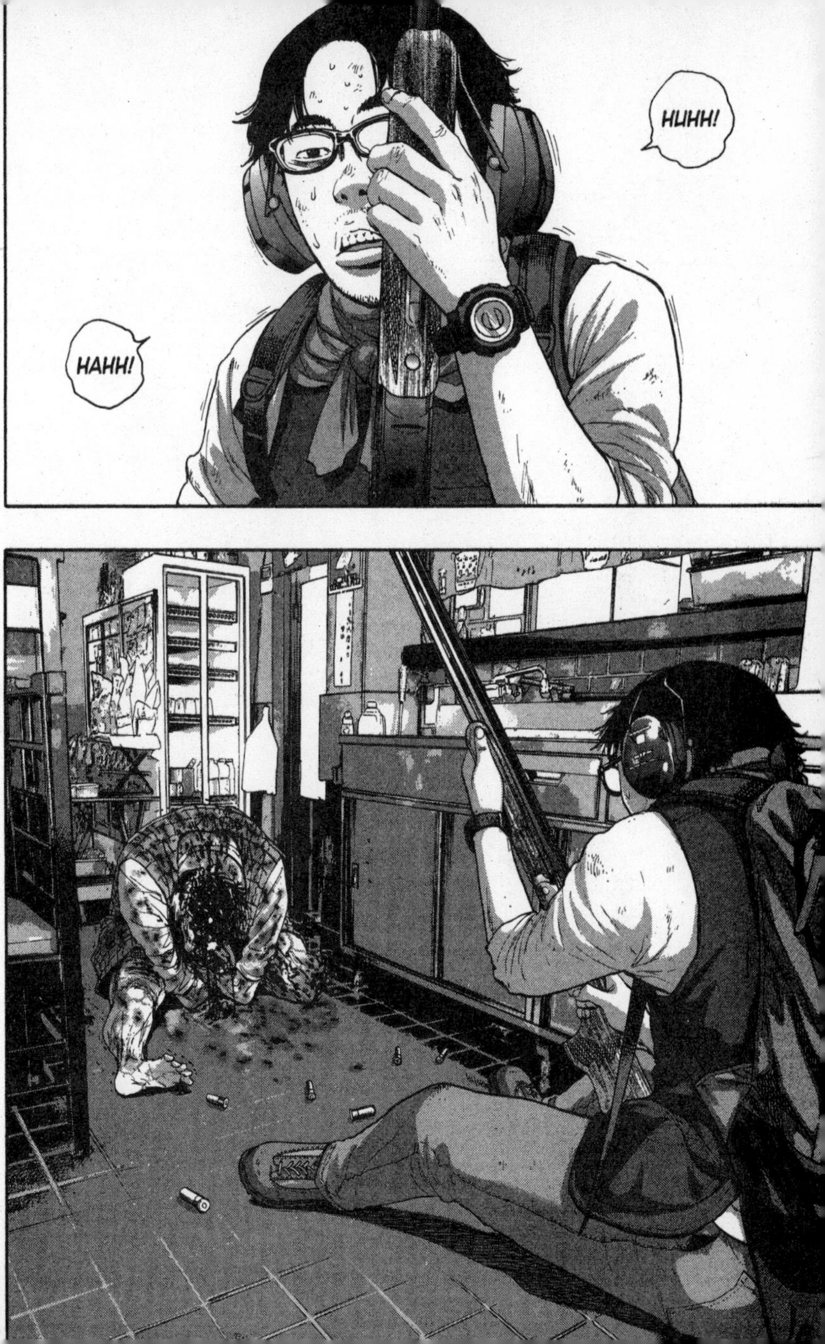
HUHH!
HAHH!

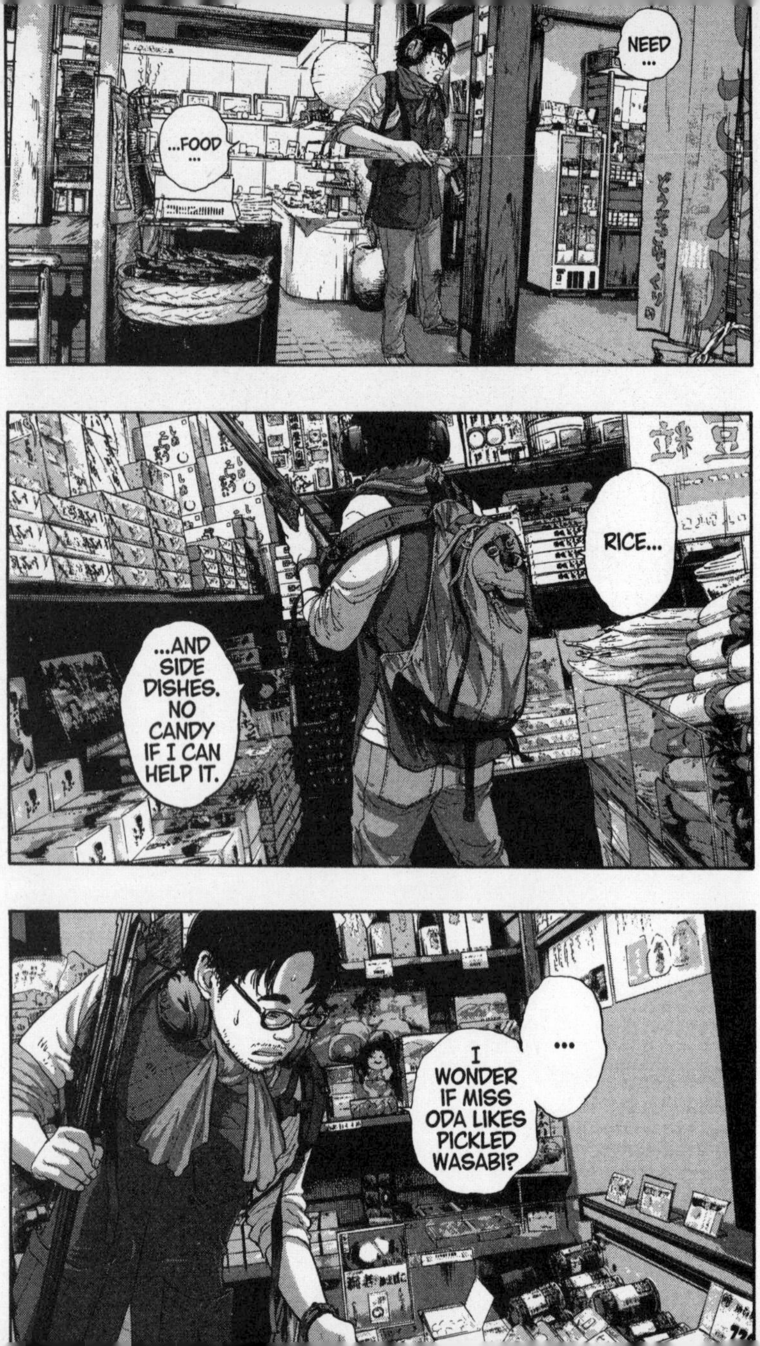
NEED ...
...FOOD ...
RICE...
...AND SIDE DISHES. NO CANDY IF I CAN HELP IT.
...
I WONDER IF MISS ODA LIKES PICKLED WASABI?

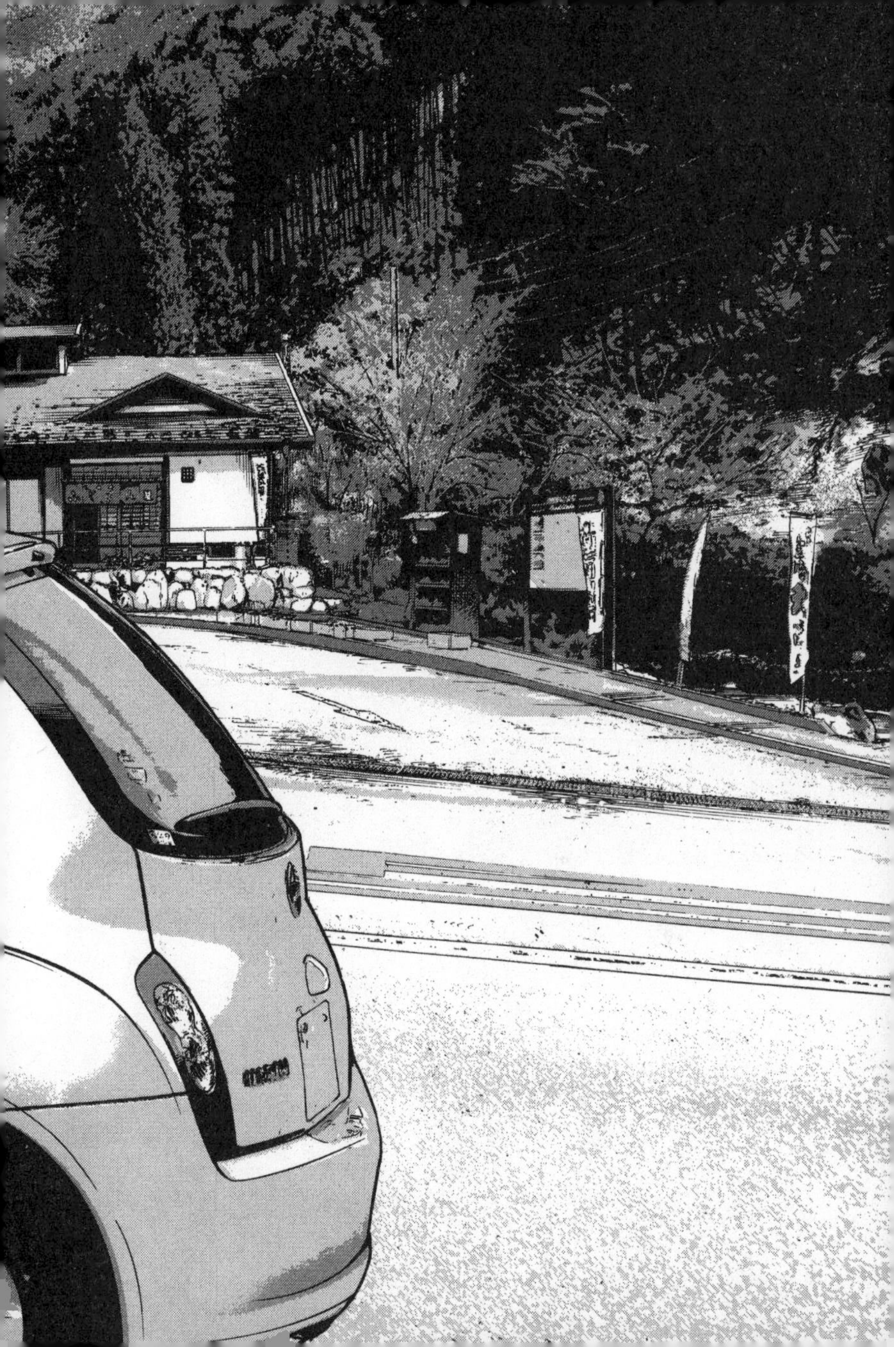

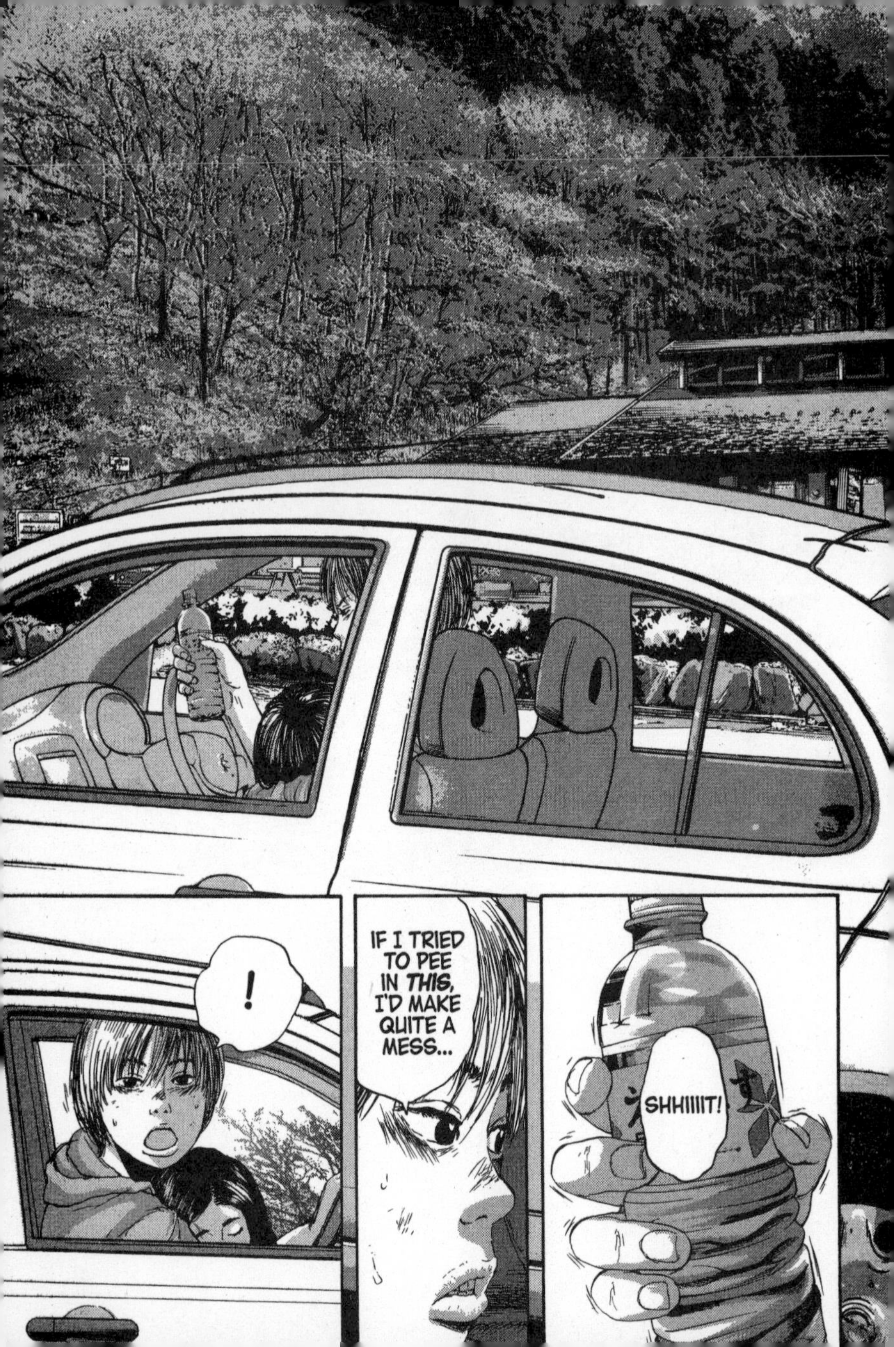
SHHIIIIT!
IF I TRIED TO PEE IN THIS, I'D MAKE QUITE A MESS...
!

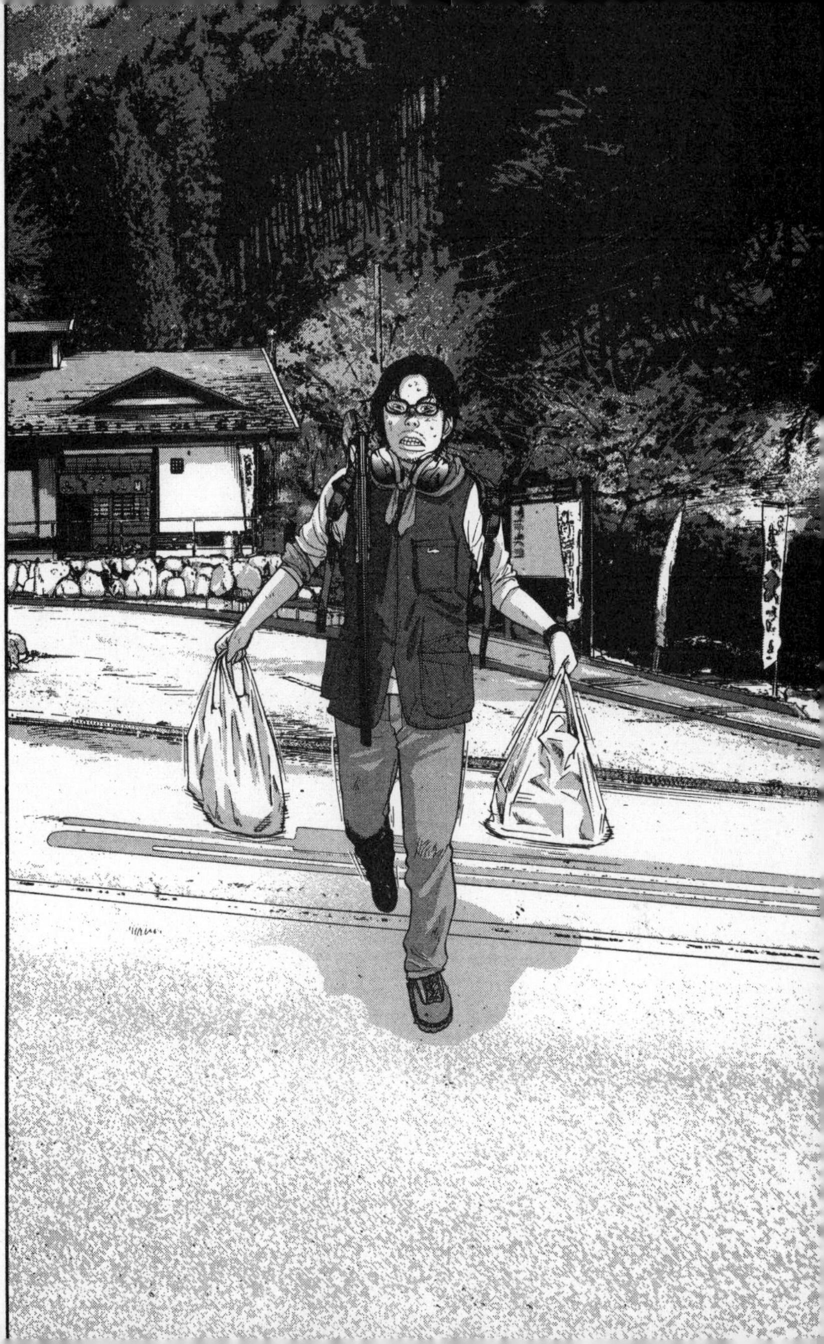

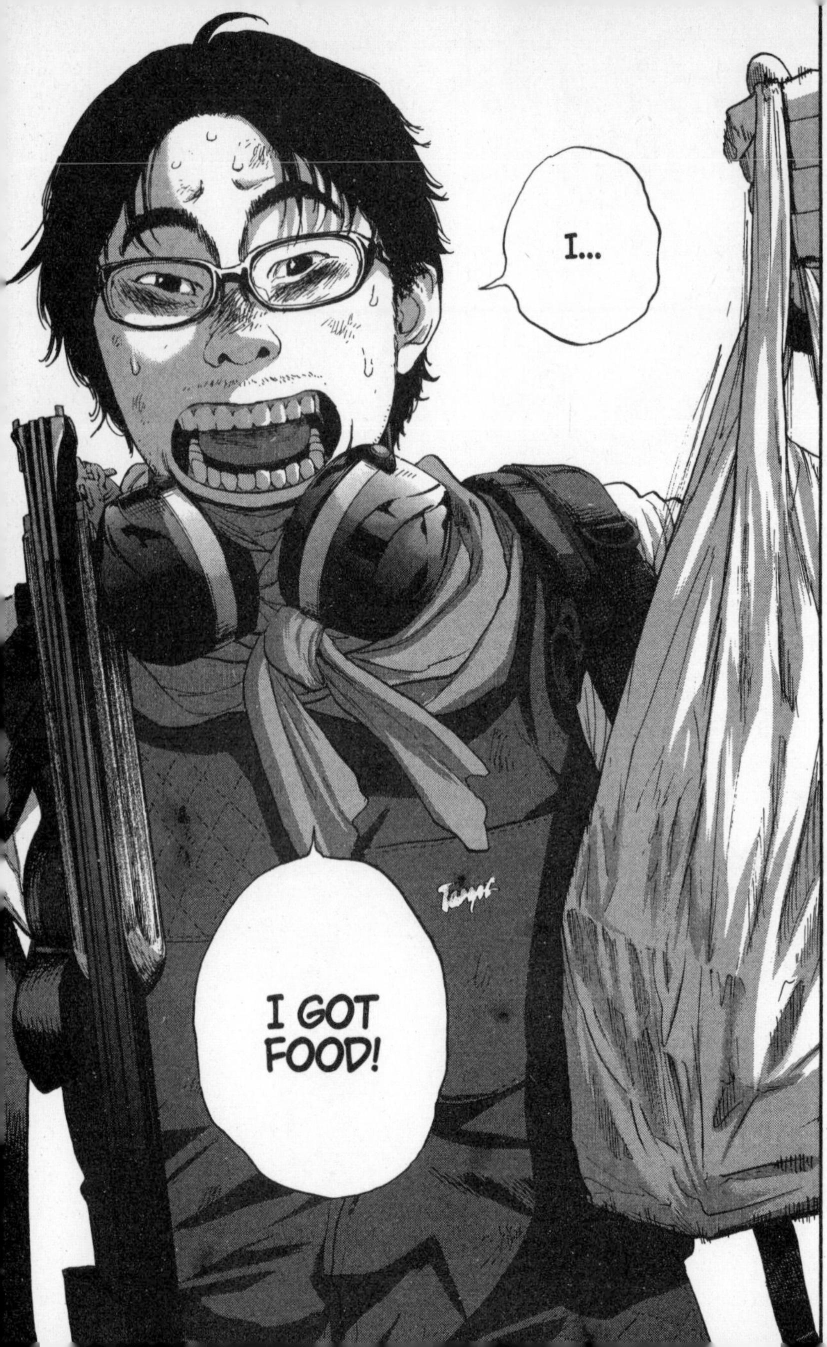
I...
I GOT FOOD!

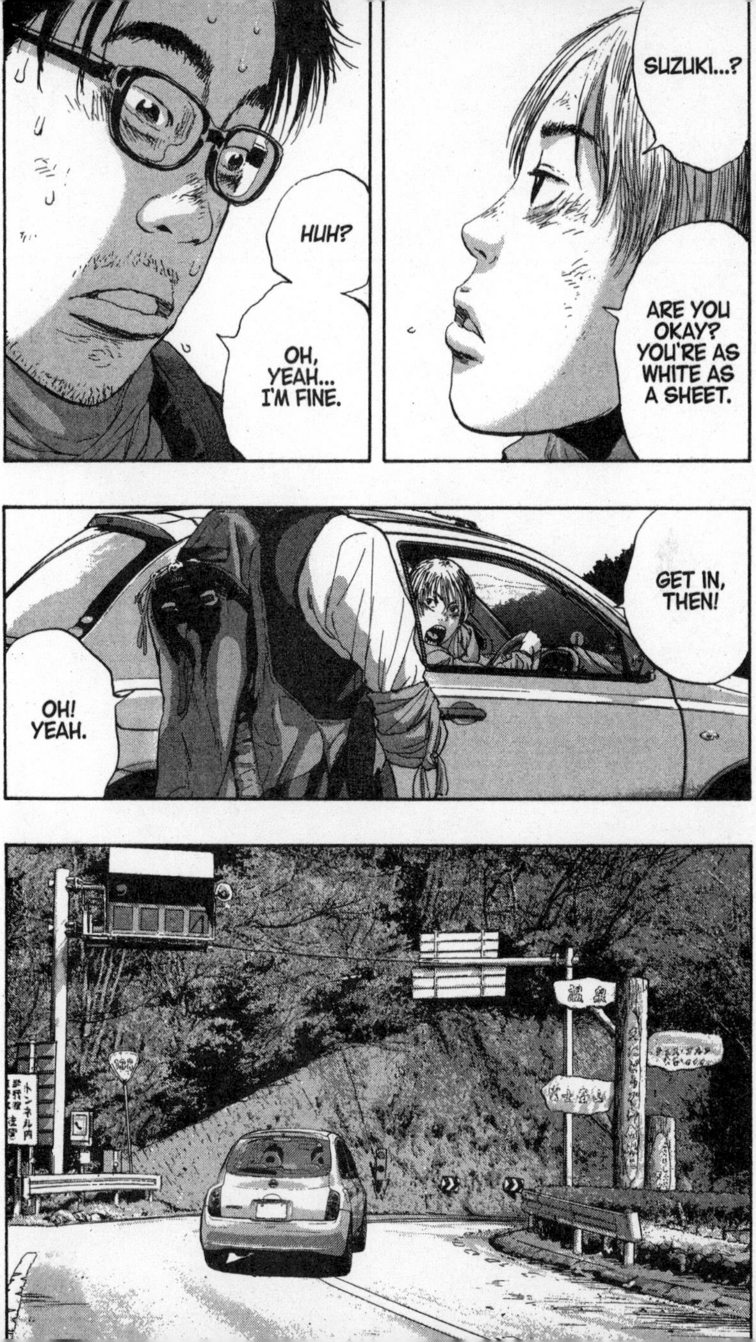
SUZUKI...?
ARE YOU OKAY? YOU'RE AS WHITE AS A SHEET.
HUH?
OH, YEAH... I'M FINE.
GET IN, THEN!
OH! YEAH.

I AM
A HERO

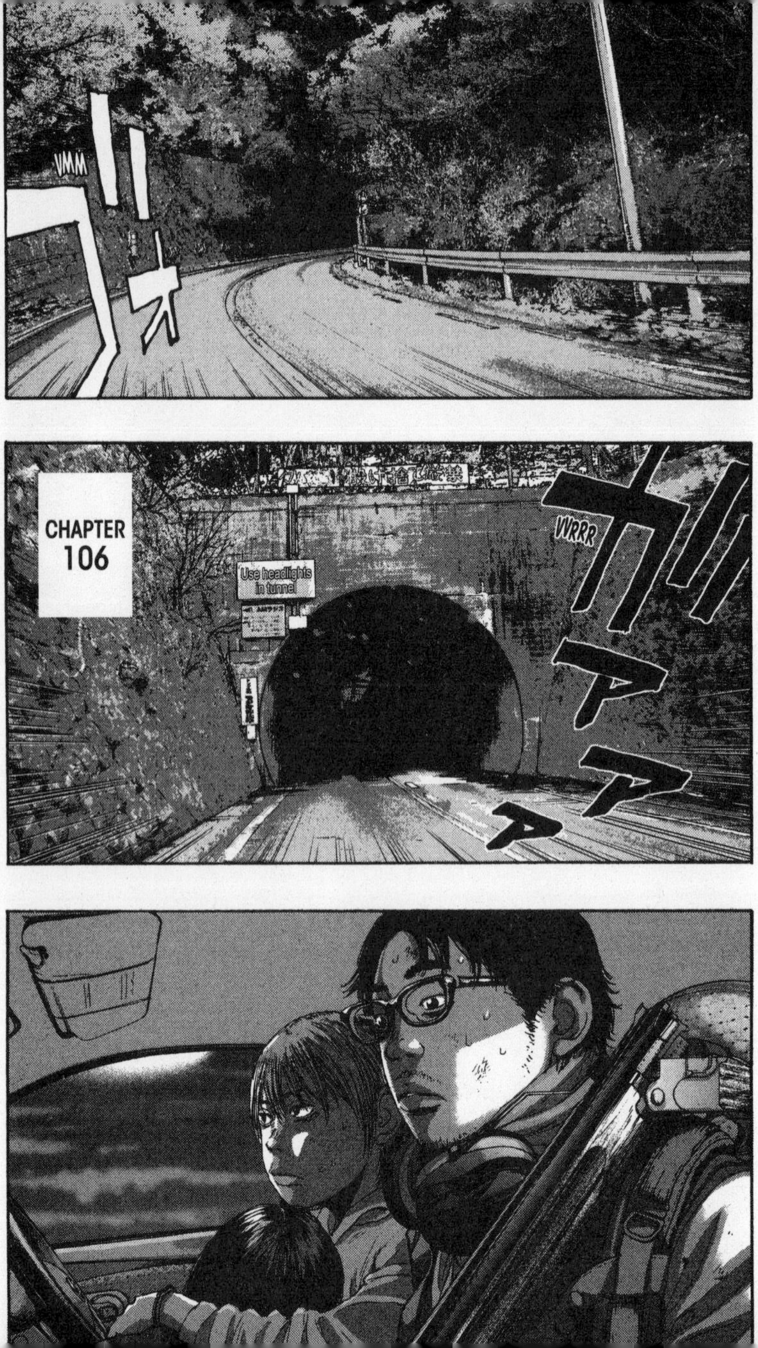
VMM
VVRRR
CHAPTER 106
Use headlights in tunnel

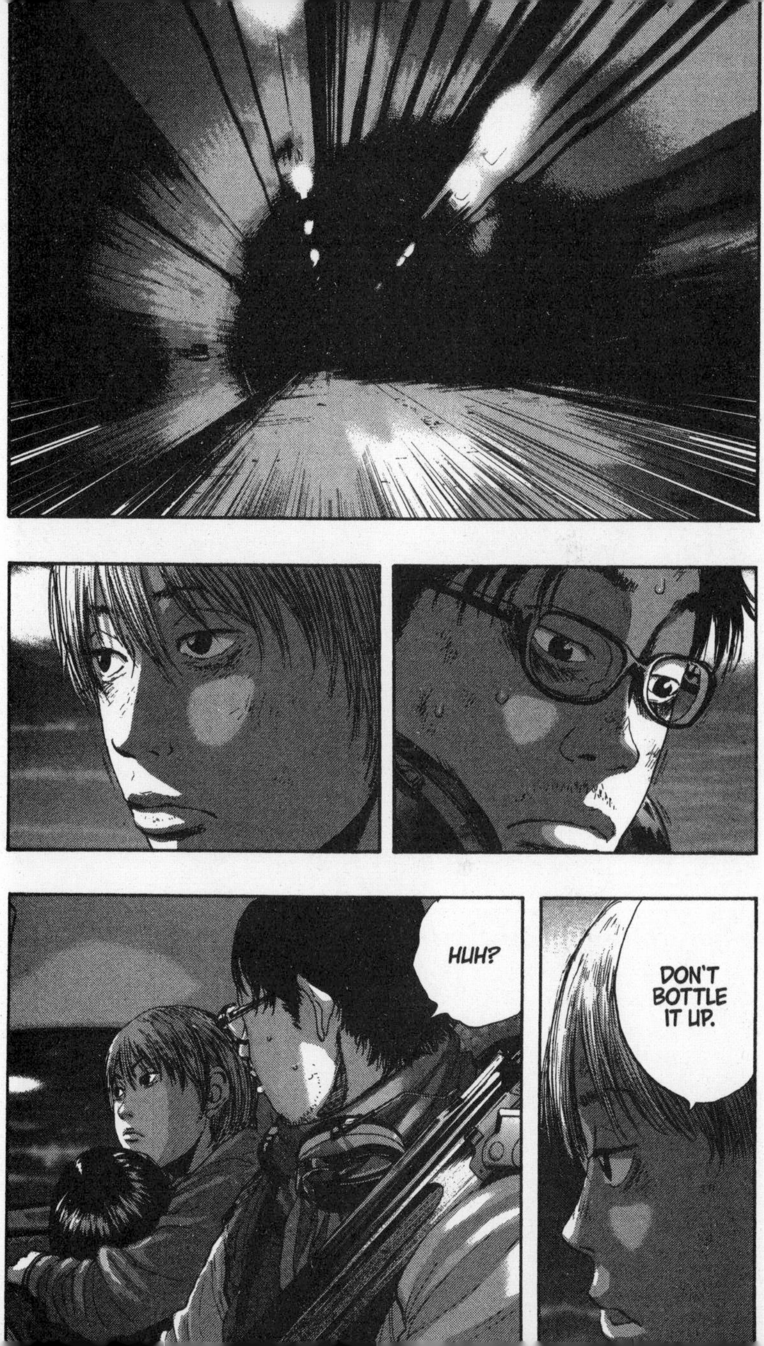
DON'T BOTTLE IT UP.
HUH?

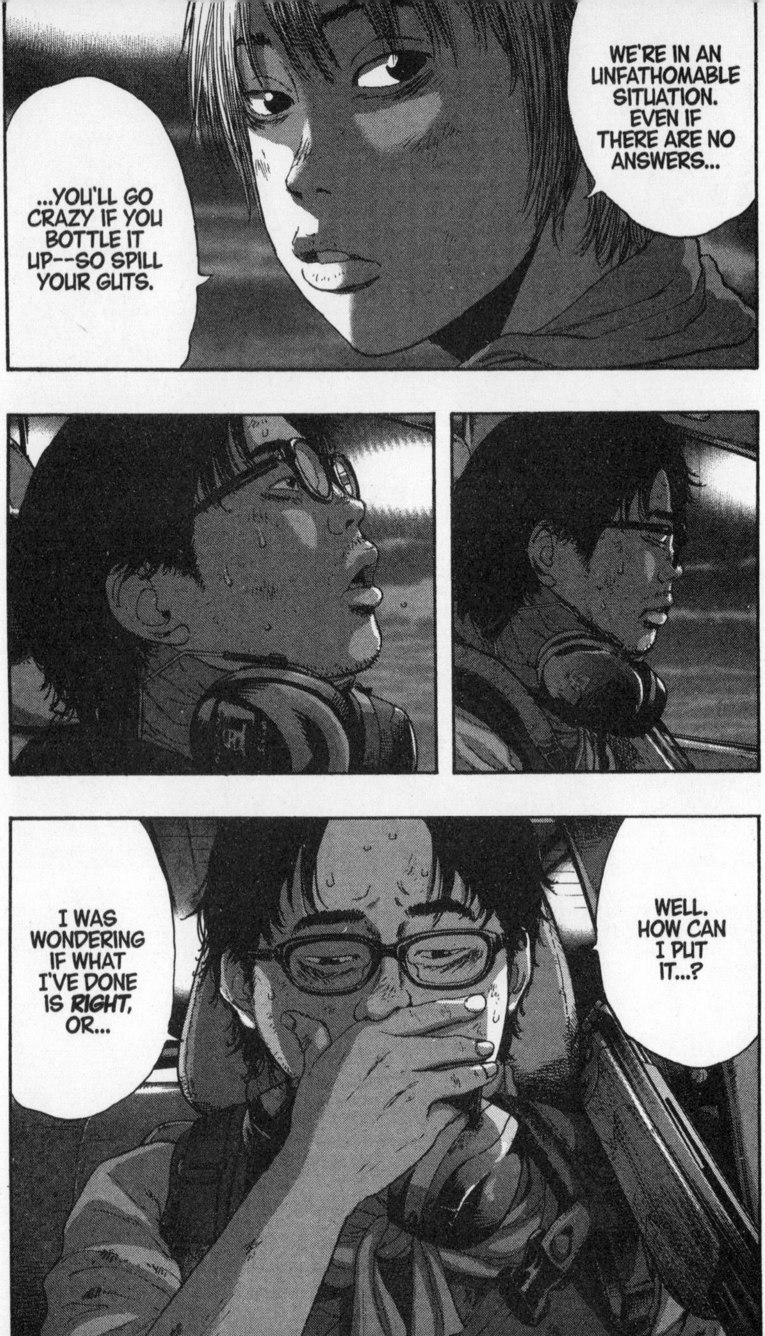
WE'RE IN AN UNFATHOMABLE SITUATION. EVEN IF THERE ARE NO ANSWERS...
...YOU'LL GO CRAZY IF YOU BOTTLE IT UP--SO SPILL YOUR GUTS.
WELL. HOW CAN I PUT IT...?
I WAS WONDERING IF WHAT I'VE DONE IS RIGHT, OR...

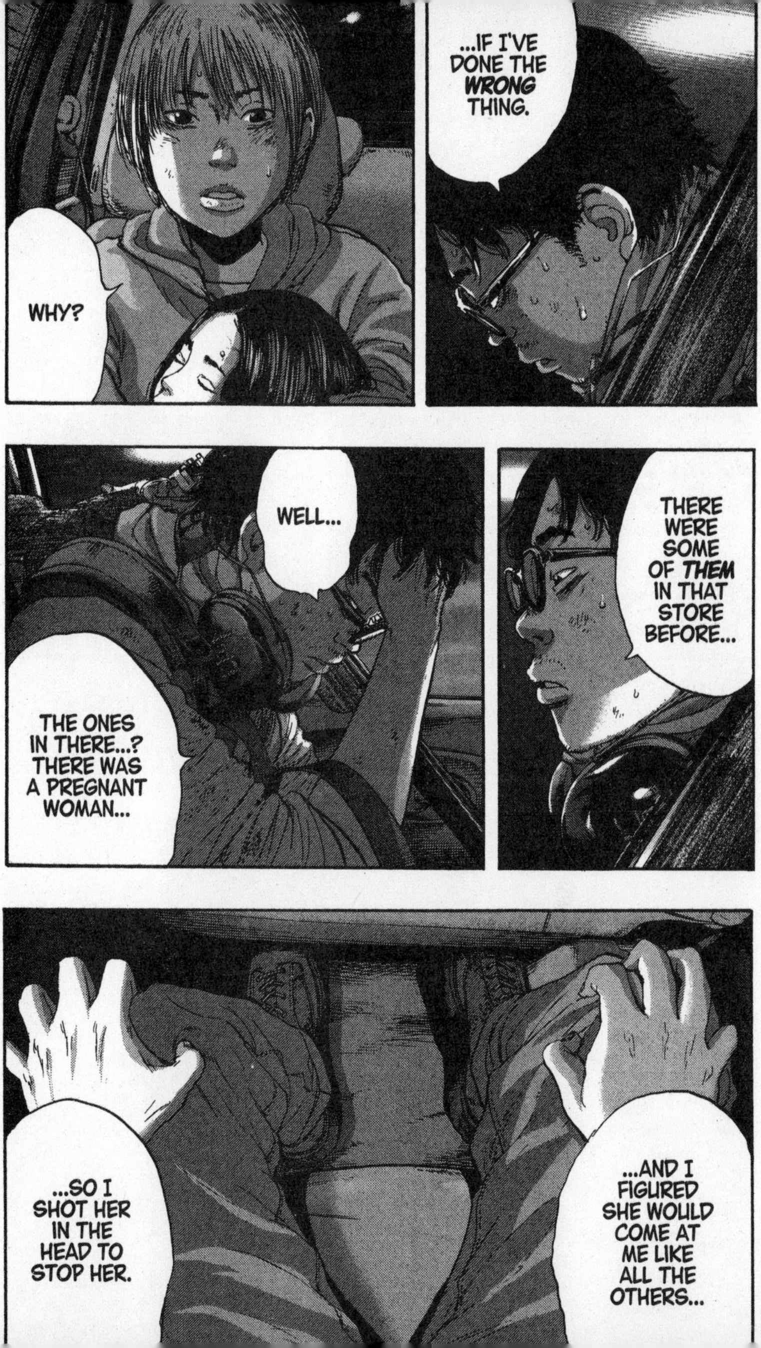
...IF I'VE DONE THE *WRONG* THING.
WHY?
THERE WERE SOME OF *THEM* IN THAT STORE BEFORE...
WELL...
THE ONES IN THERE...? THERE WAS A PREGNANT WOMAN...
...AND I FIGURED SHE WOULD COME AT ME LIKE ALL THE OTHERS...
...SO I SHOT HER IN THE HEAD TO STOP HER.

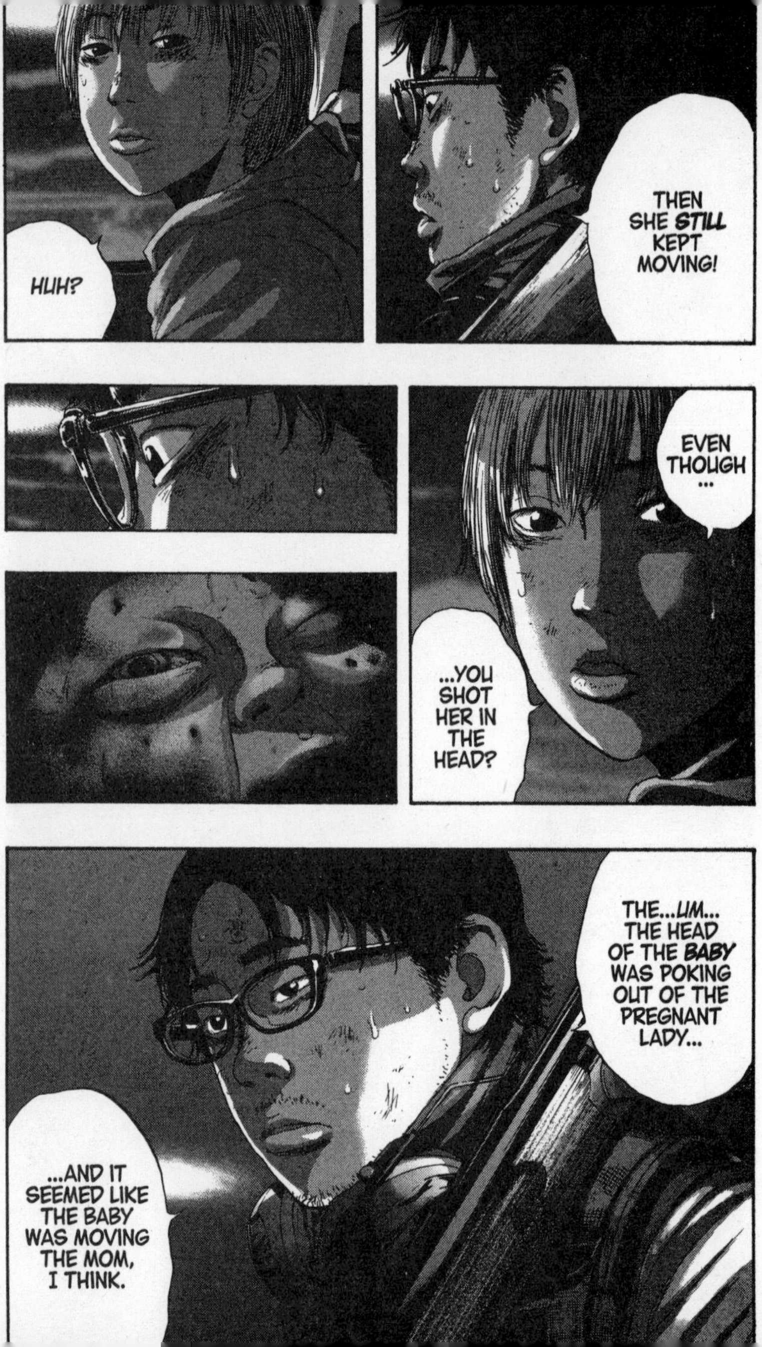
THEN SHE STILL KEPT MOVING!
HUH?
EVEN THOUGH ...
...YOU SHOT HER IN THE HEAD?
THE...UM... THE HEAD OF THE BABY WAS POKING OUT OF THE PREGNANT LADY...
...AND IT SEEMED LIKE THE BABY WAS MOVING THE MOM, I THINK.

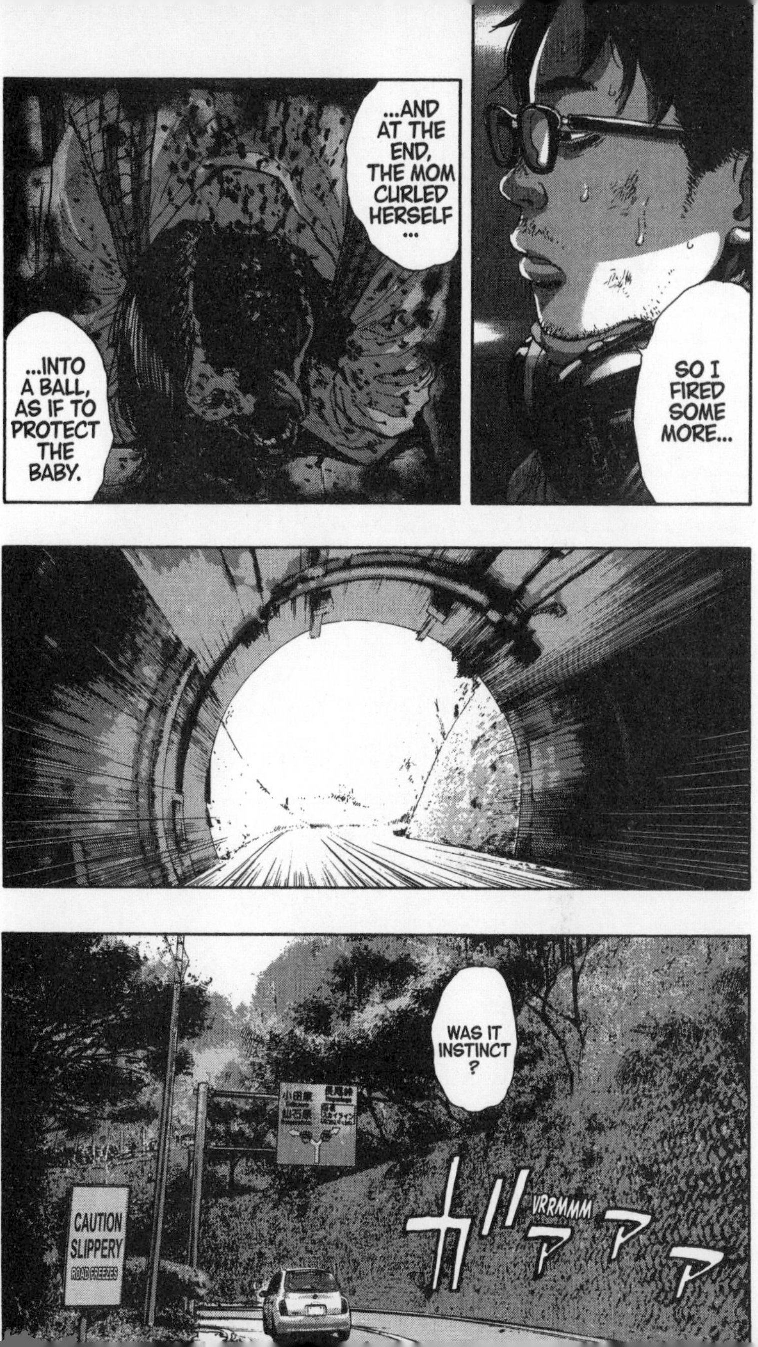
SO I FIRED SOME MORE...
...AND AT THE END, THE MOM CURLED HERSELF ...
...INTO A BALL, AS IF TO PROTECT THE BABY.
WAS IT INSTINCT?
VRRMMM
CAUTION SLIPPERY
ROAD FREEZES

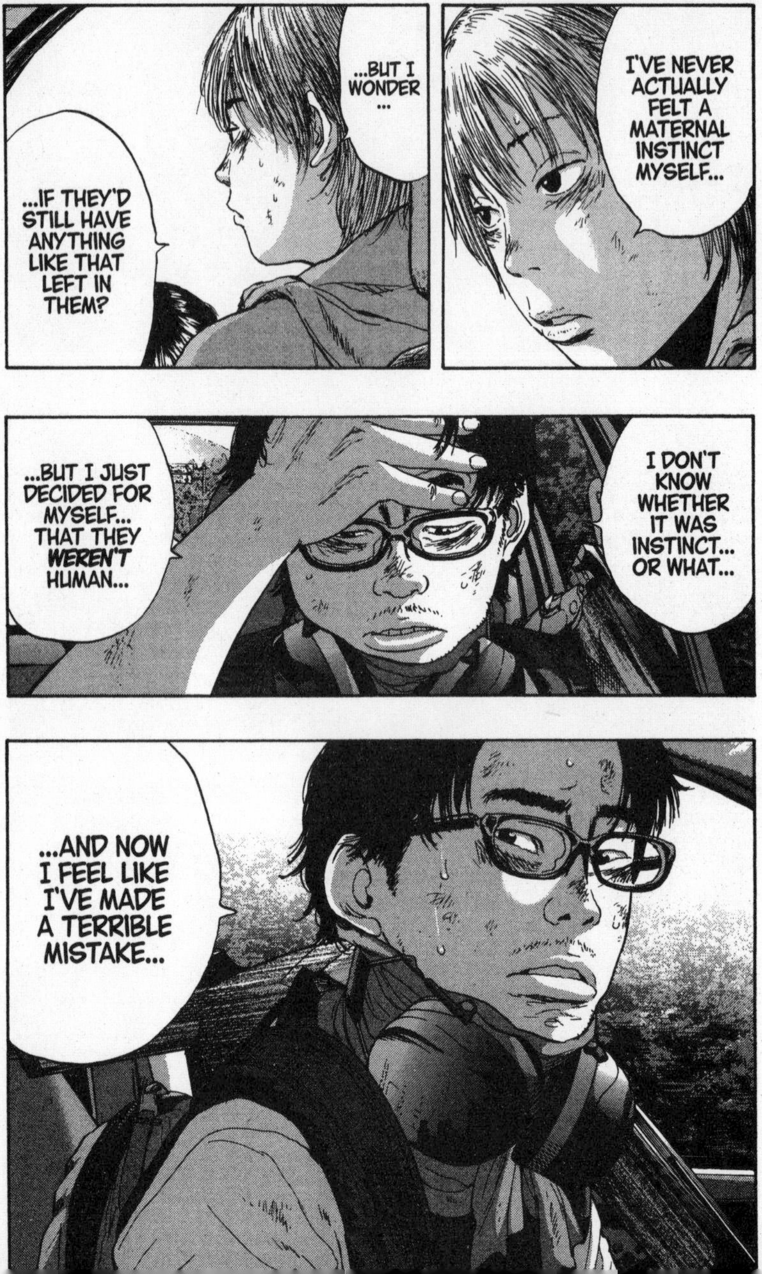
I'VE NEVER ACTUALLY FELT A MATERNAL INSTINCT MYSELF...
...BUT I WONDER ...
...IF THEY'D STILL HAVE ANYTHING LIKE THAT LEFT IN THEM?
I DON'T KNOW WHETHER IT WAS INSTINCT... OR WHAT...
...BUT I JUST DECIDED FOR MYSELF... THAT THEY *WEREN'T* HUMAN...
...AND NOW I FEEL LIKE I'VE MADE A TERRIBLE MISTAKE...

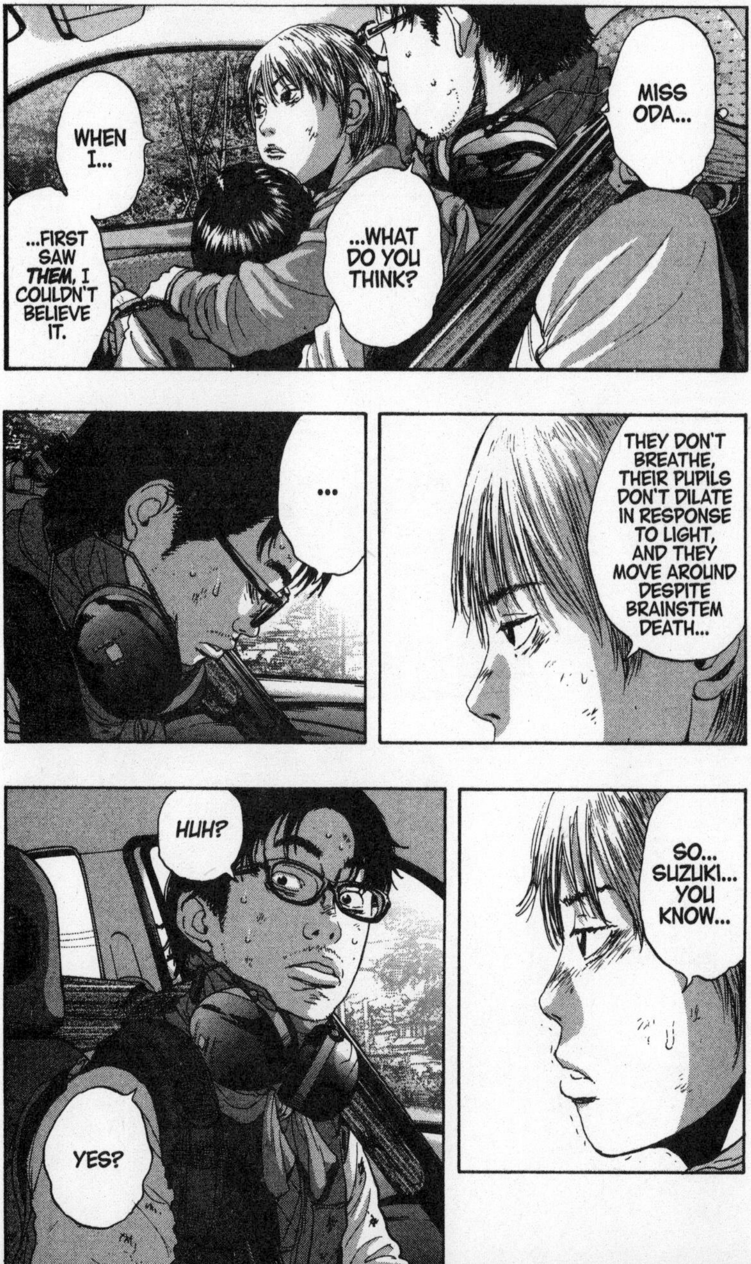
MISS ODA...
...WHAT DO YOU THINK?
WHEN I...
...FIRST SAW *THEM*, I COULDN'T BELIEVE IT.
THEY DON'T BREATHE, THEIR PUPILS DON'T DILATE IN RESPONSE TO LIGHT, AND THEY MOVE AROUND DESPITE BRAINSTEM DEATH...
...
SO... SUZUKI... YOU KNOW...
HUH?
YES?

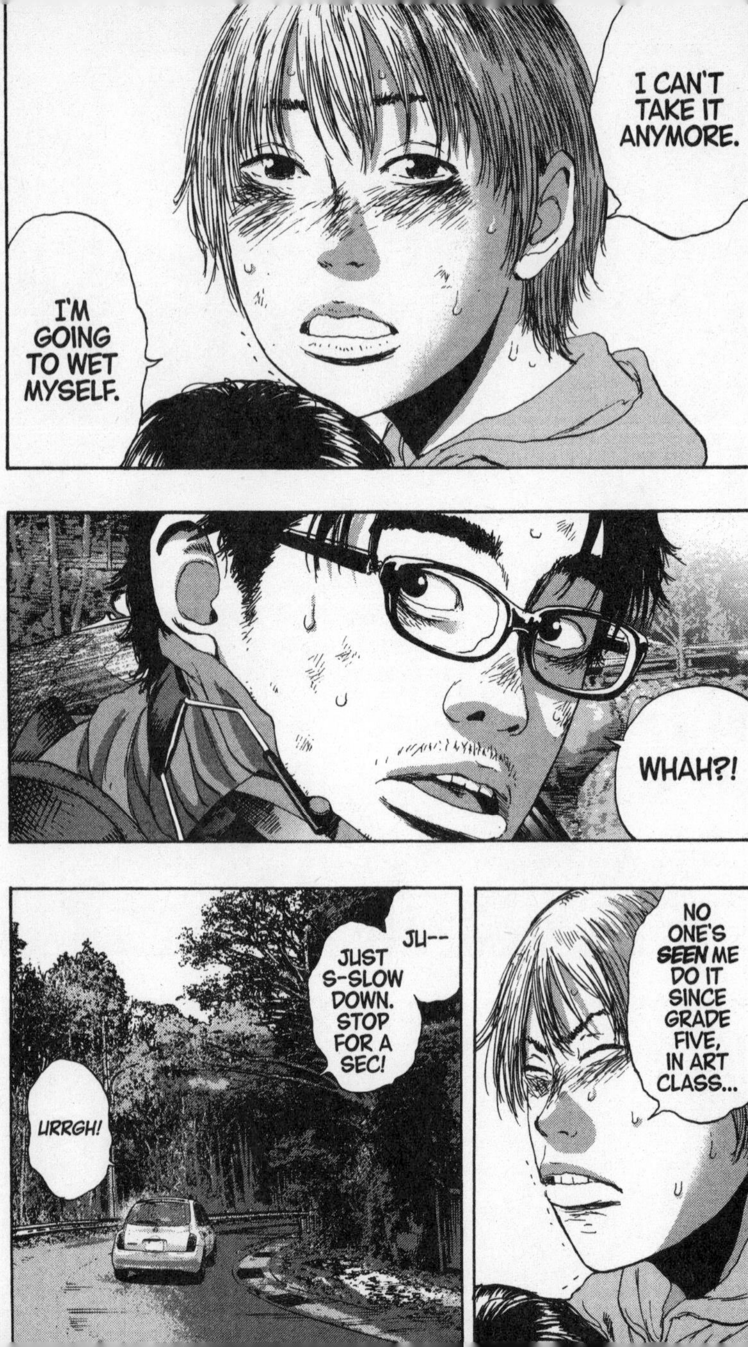
I CAN'T TAKE IT ANYMORE.
I'M GOING TO WET MYSELF.
WHAH?!
NO ONE'S **SEEN** ME DO IT SINCE GRADE FIVE, IN ART CLASS...
JU--
JUST S-SLOW DOWN. STOP FOR A SEC!
URRGH!

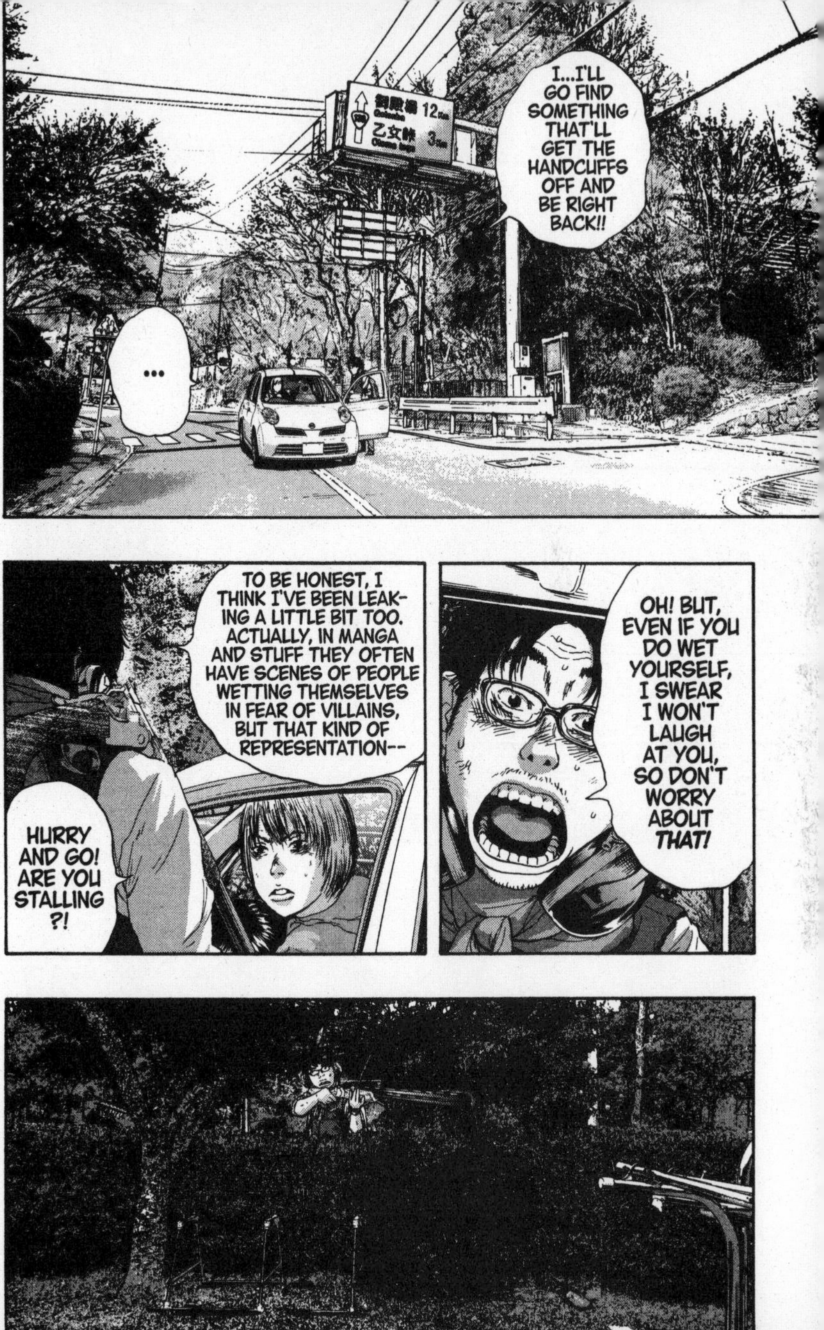
I...I'LL GO FIND SOMETHING THAT'LL GET THE HANDCUFFS OFF AND BE RIGHT BACK!!
御殿場 12km
乙女峠 3km
...
OH! BUT, EVEN IF YOU DO WET YOURSELF, I SWEAR I WON'T LAUGH AT YOU, SO DON'T WORRY ABOUT THAT!
TO BE HONEST, I THINK I'VE BEEN LEAK-ING A LITTLE BIT TOO. ACTUALLY, IN MANGA AND STUFF THEY OFTEN HAVE SCENES OF PEOPLE WETTING THEMSELVES IN FEAR OF VILLAINS, BUT THAT KIND OF REPRESENTATION--
HURRY AND GO! ARE YOU STALLING ?!

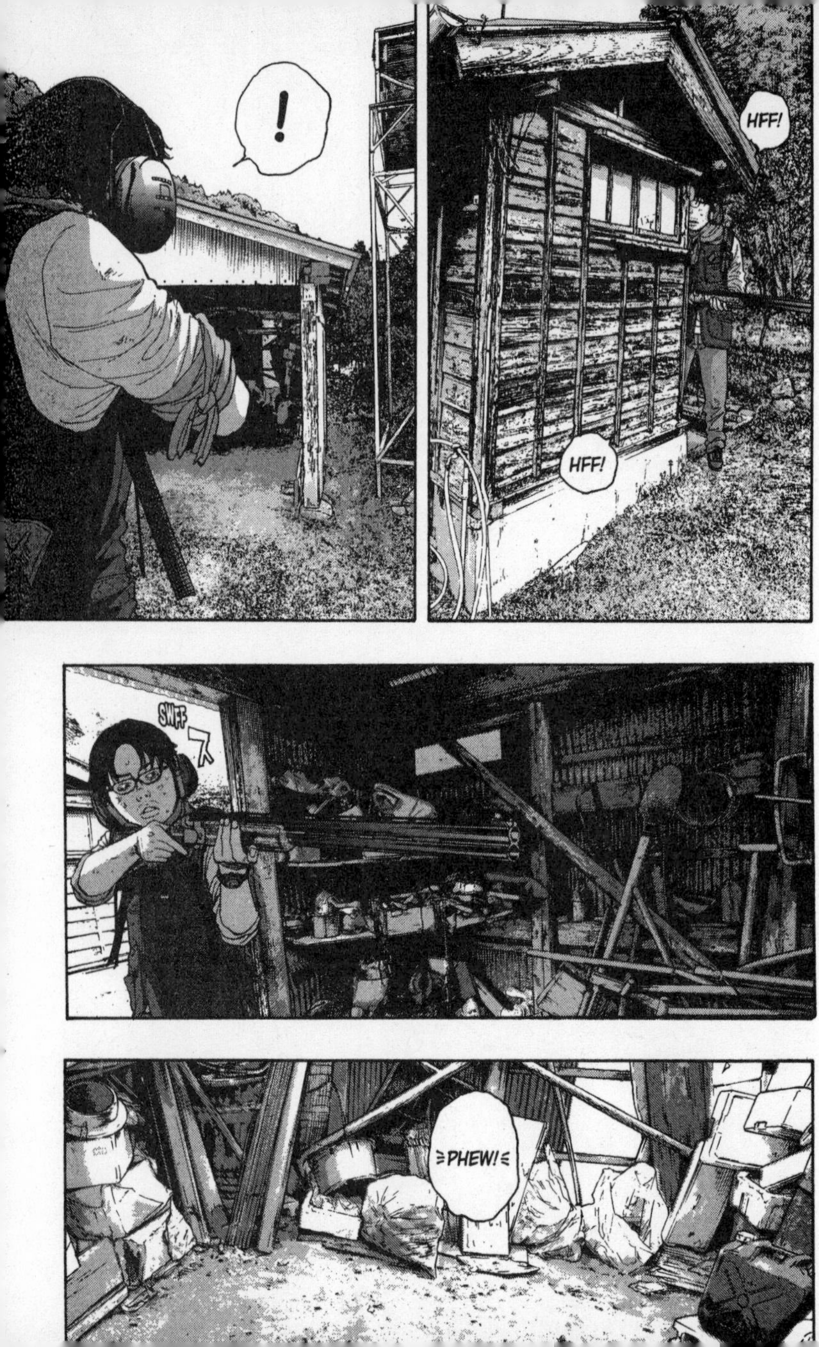
HFF!
HFF!
!
SWFF
PHEW!

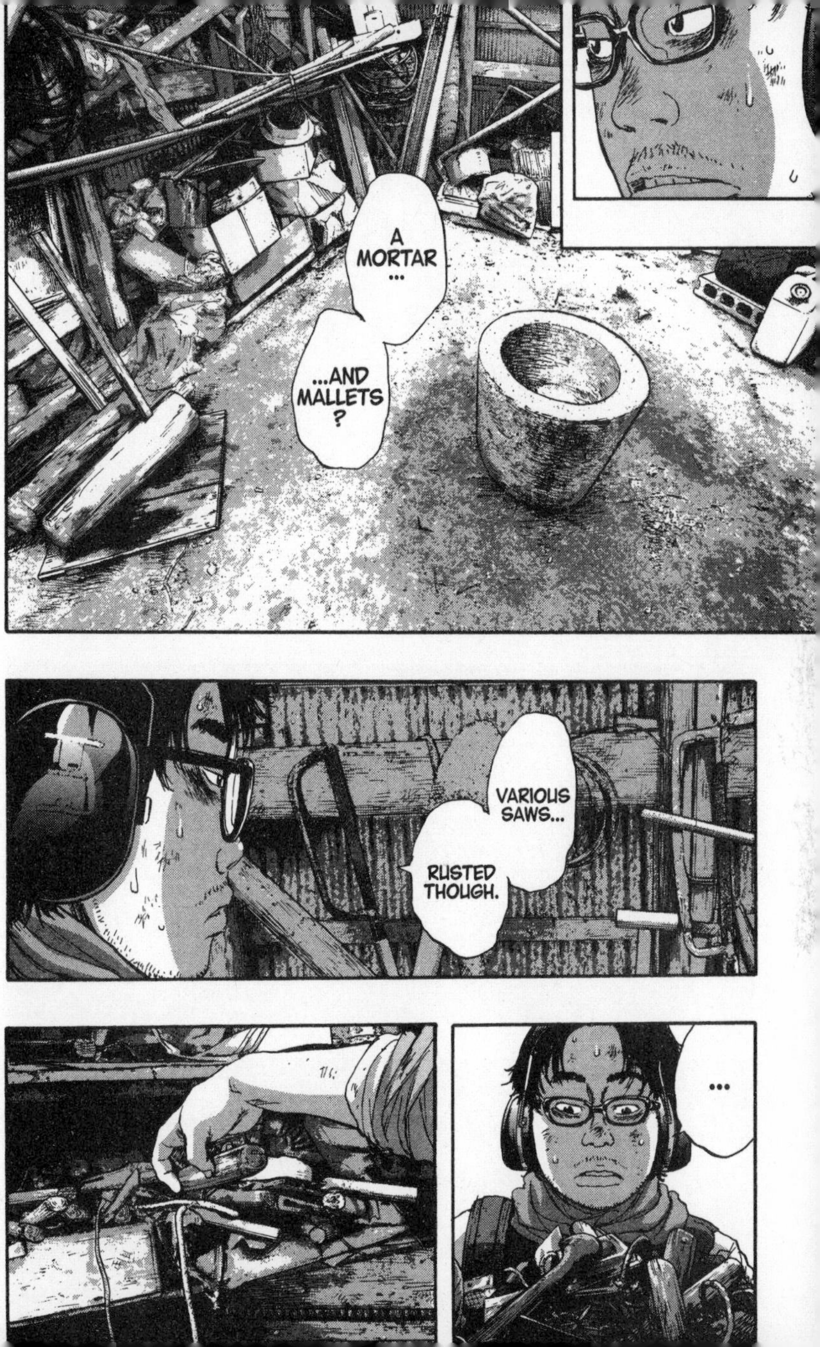
A MORTAR ...
...AND MALLETS ?
VARIOUS SAWS...
RUSTED THOUGH.
...

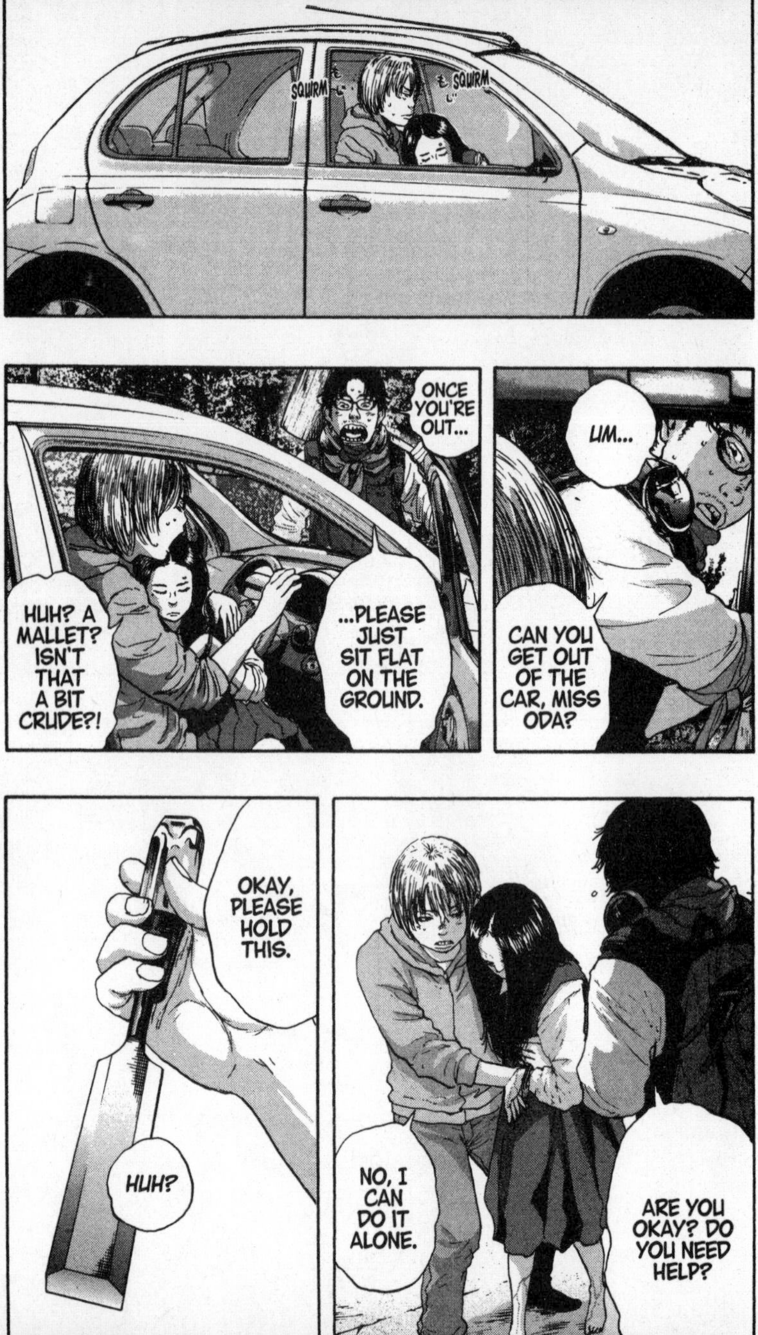
SQUIRM
SQUIRM
UM...
CAN YOU GET OUT OF THE CAR, MISS ODA?
ONCE YOU'RE OUT...
...PLEASE JUST SIT FLAT ON THE GROUND.
HUH? A MALLET? ISN'T THAT A BIT CRUDE?!
ARE YOU OKAY? DO YOU NEED HELP?
NO, I CAN DO IT ALONE.
OKAY, PLEASE HOLD THIS.
HUH?

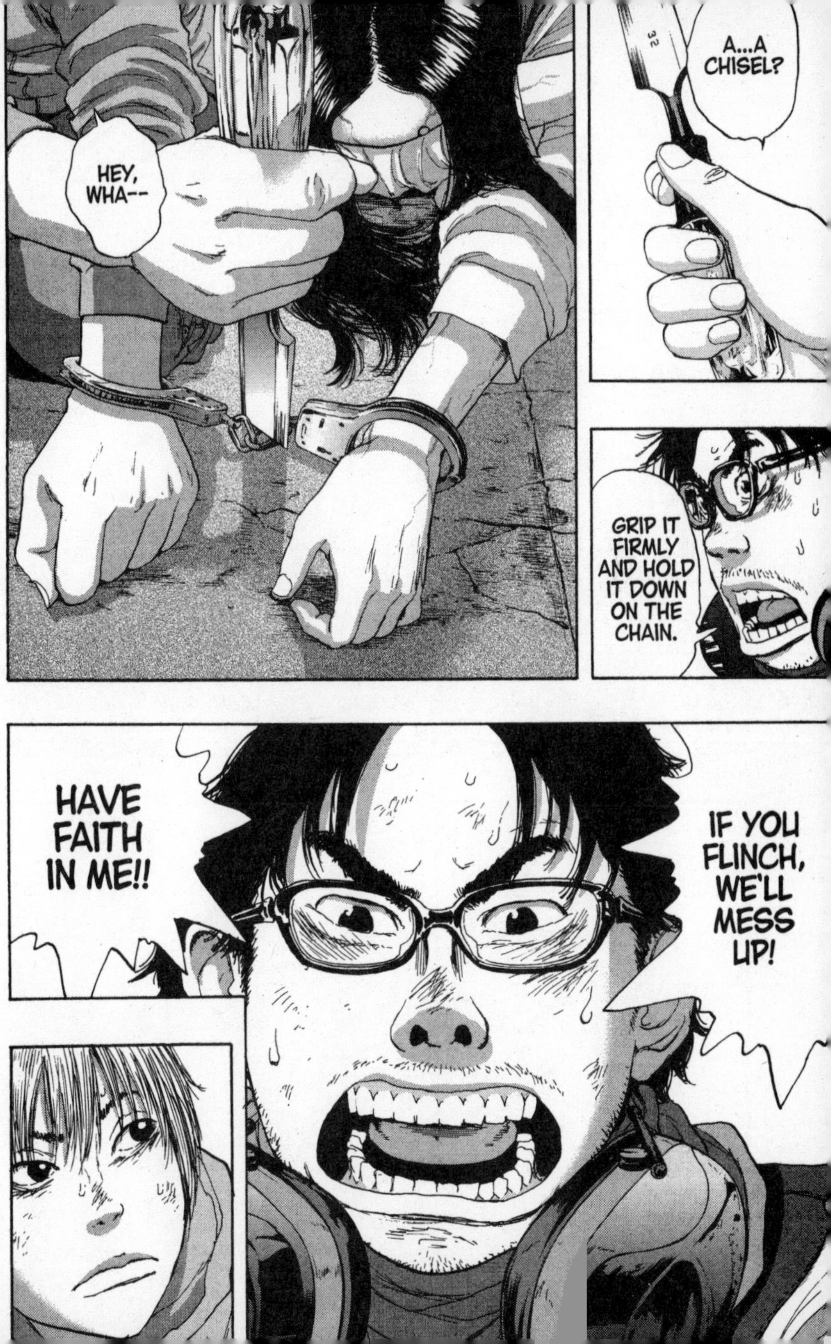
A...A CHISEL?
GRIP IT FIRMLY AND HOLD IT DOWN ON THE CHAIN.
HEY, WHA--
IF YOU FLINCH, WE'LL MESS UP!
HAVE FAITH IN ME!!

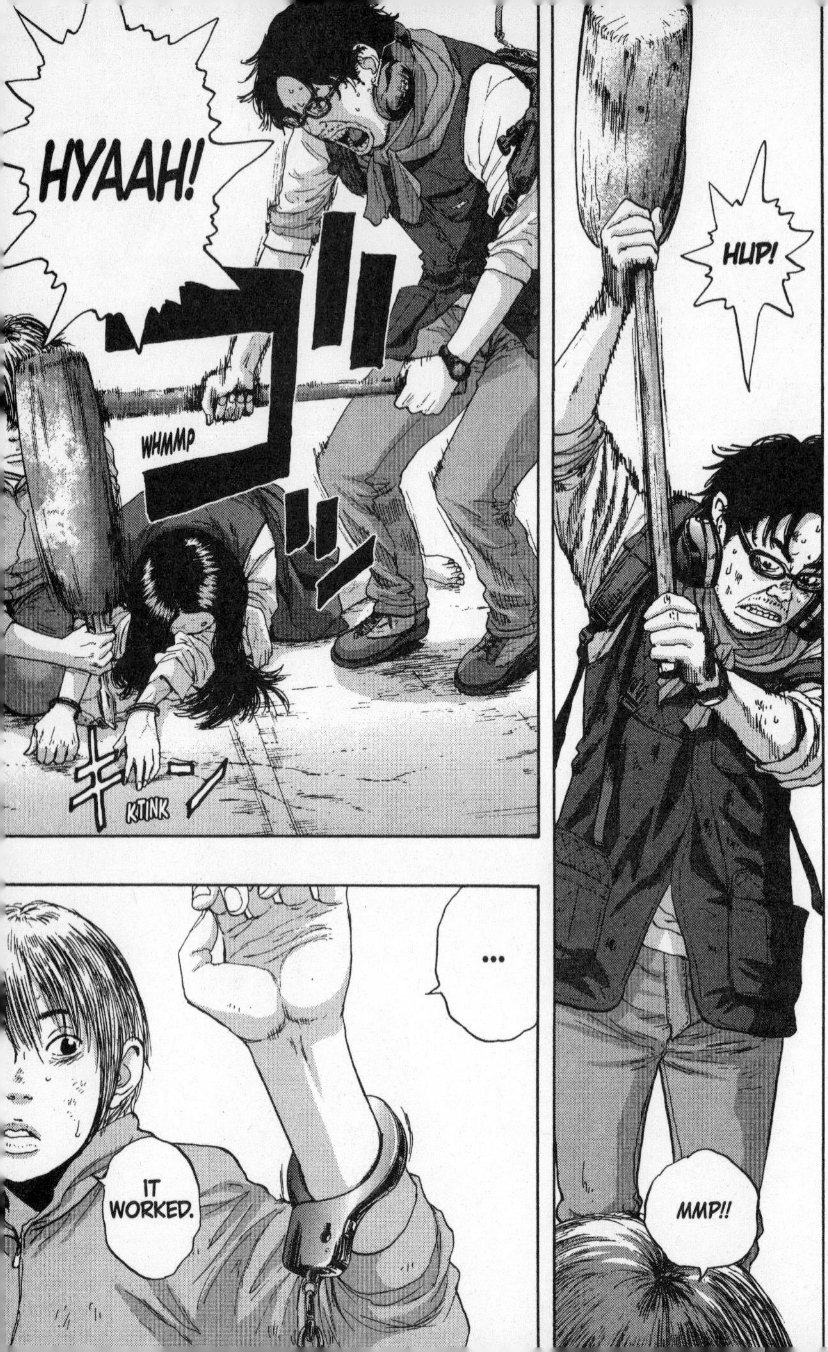
HUP!
MMP!!
HYAAH!
WHMMP
KTINK
...
IT WORKED.

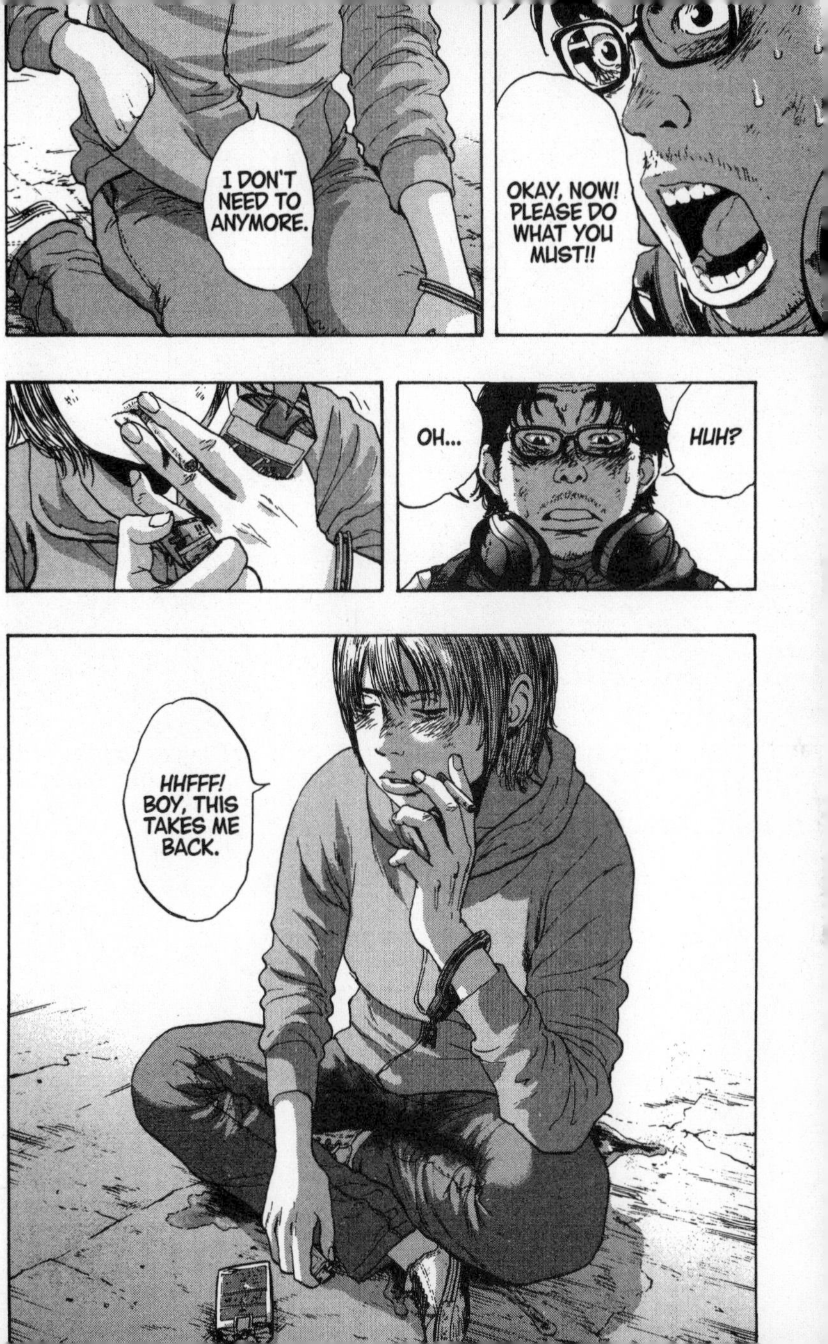
OKAY, NOW! PLEASE DO WHAT YOU MUST!!
I DON'T NEED TO ANYMORE.
HUH?
OH...
HHFFF! BOY, THIS TAKES ME BACK.

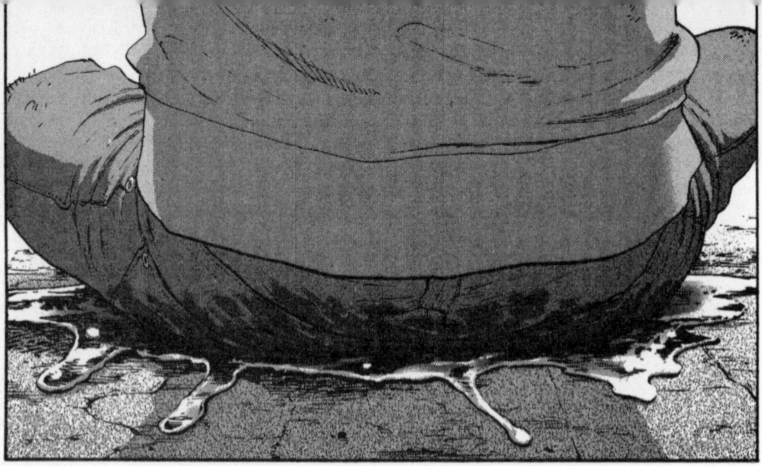

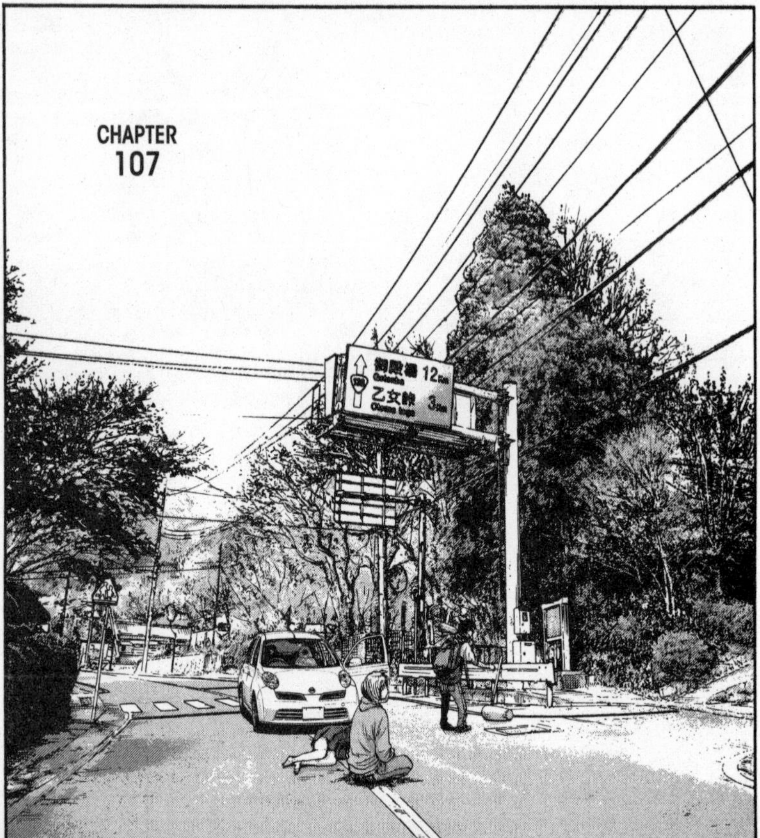
CHAPTER
107

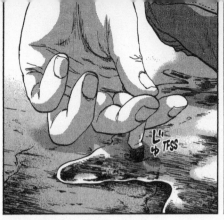

TFSS

LAST TIME I WET MYSELF WAS, *UH*, IN KINDERGARTEN.

I WAS IN SECOND OR THIRD YEAR CLASS, AND WE HAD AN "OVERNIGHT NURSERY"...

ER... UH...

AH!

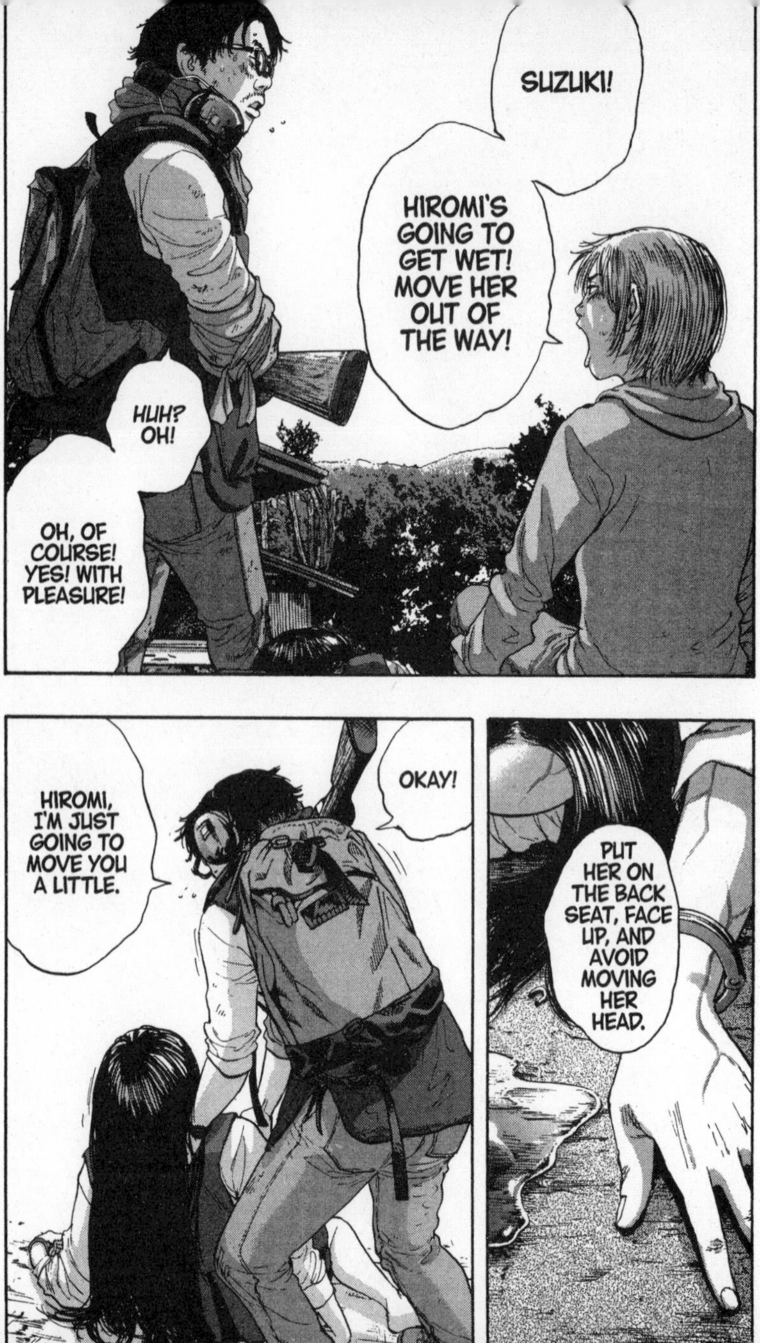
SUZUKI!
HIROMI'S GOING TO GET WET! MOVE HER OUT OF THE WAY!
HUH? OH!
OH, OF COURSE! YES! WITH PLEASURE!
PUT HER ON THE BACK SEAT, FACE UP, AND AVOID MOVING HER HEAD.
OKAY!
HIROMI, I'M JUST GOING TO MOVE YOU A LITTLE.

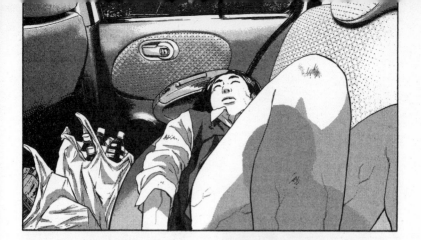

SORRY...

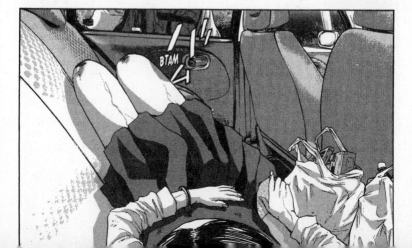

BTAM

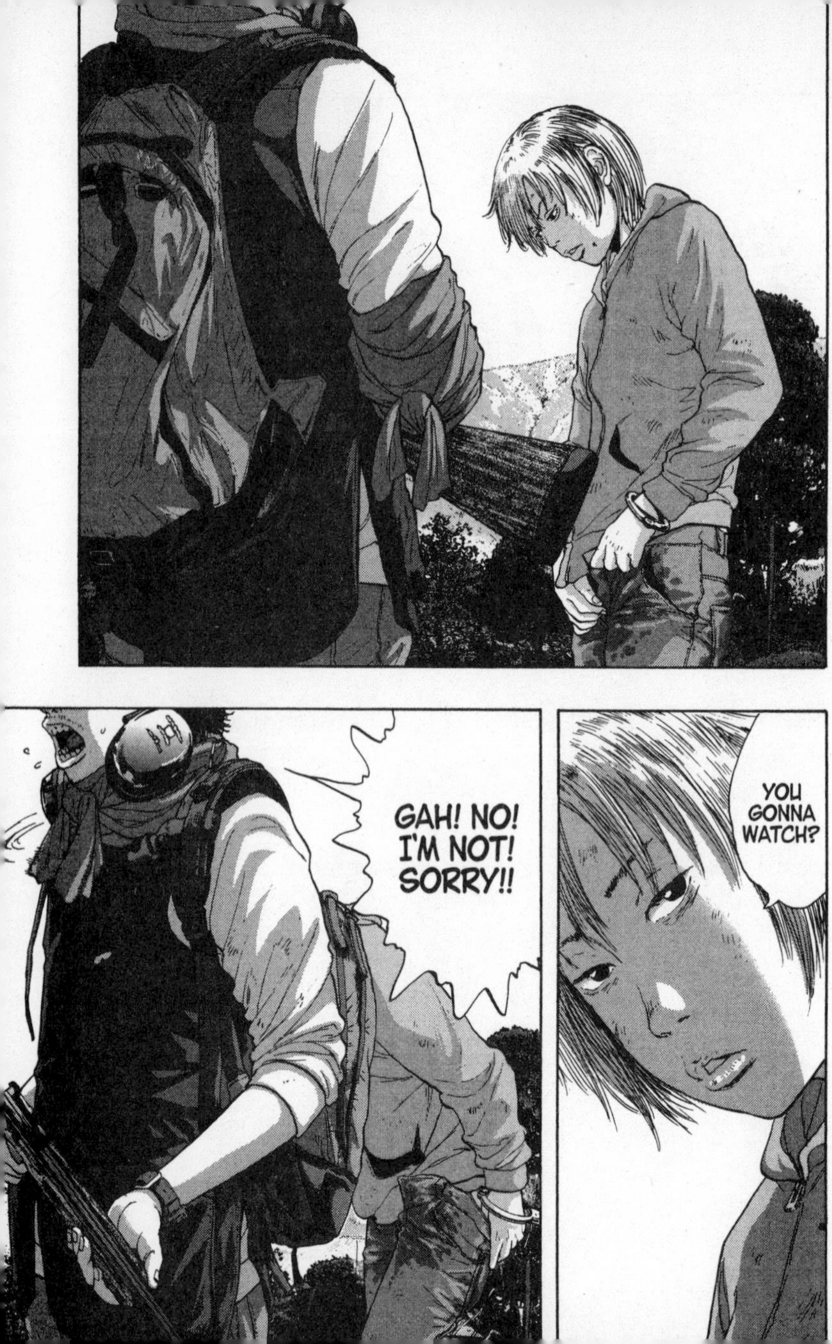
YOU GONNA WATCH?
GAH! NO! I'M NOT! SORRY!!

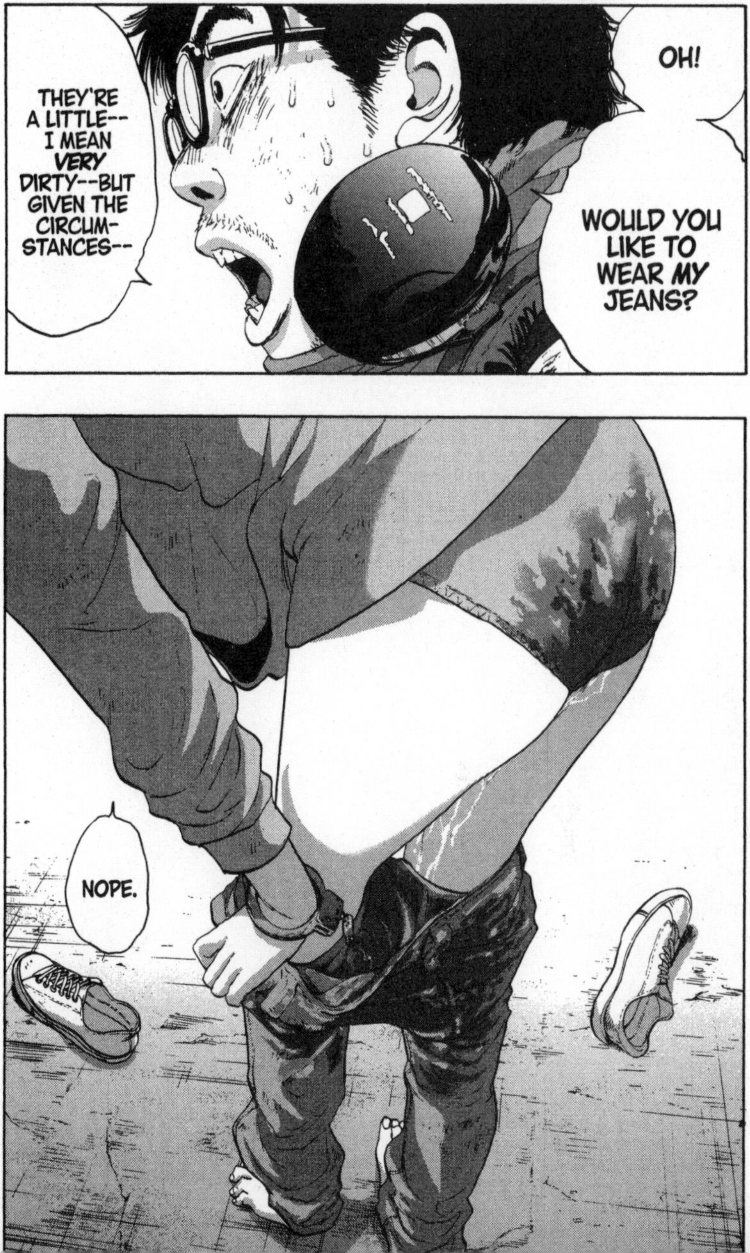
OH!
WOULD YOU LIKE TO WEAR *MY* JEANS?
THEY'RE A LITTLE-- I MEAN *VERY* DIRTY--BUT GIVEN THE CIRCUM-STANCES--
NOPE.

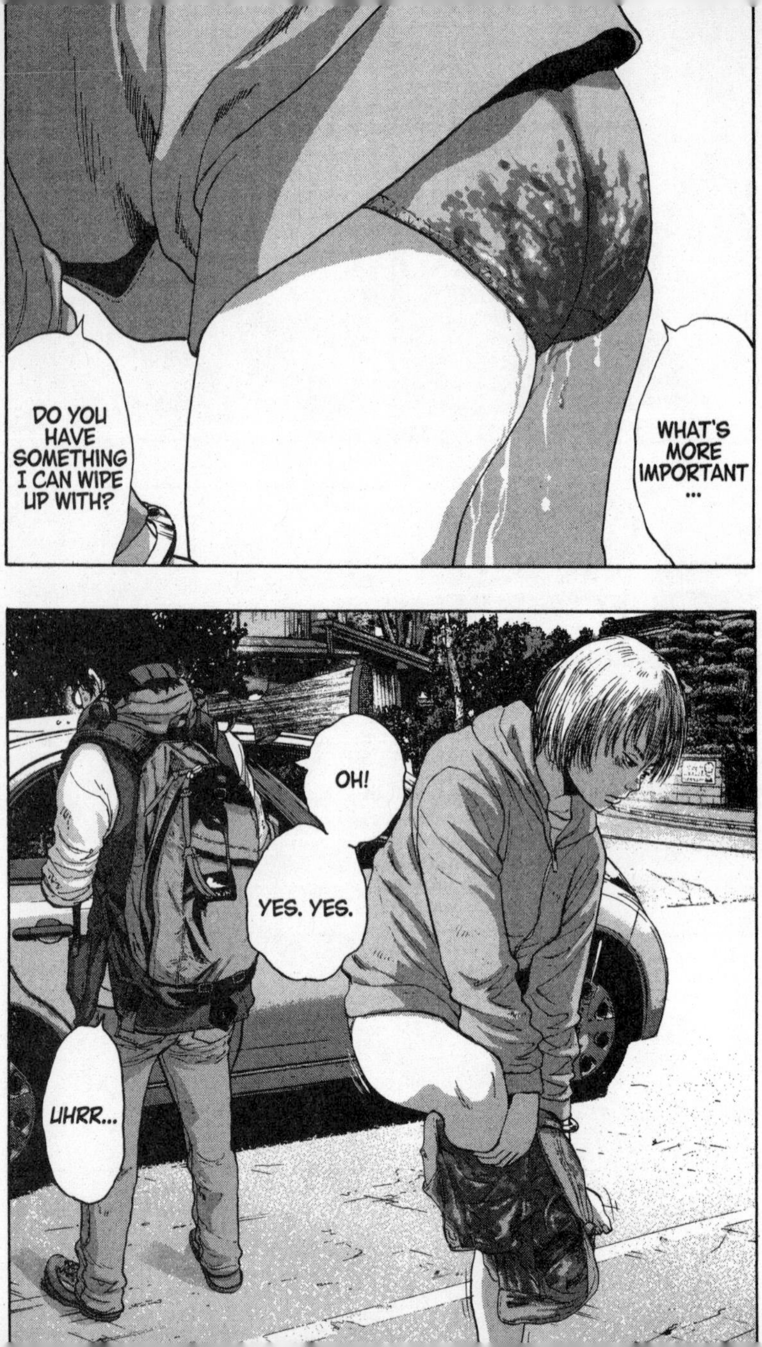
WHAT'S MORE IMPORTANT ...
DO YOU HAVE SOMETHING I CAN WIPE UP WITH?
OH!
YES. YES.
UHRR...

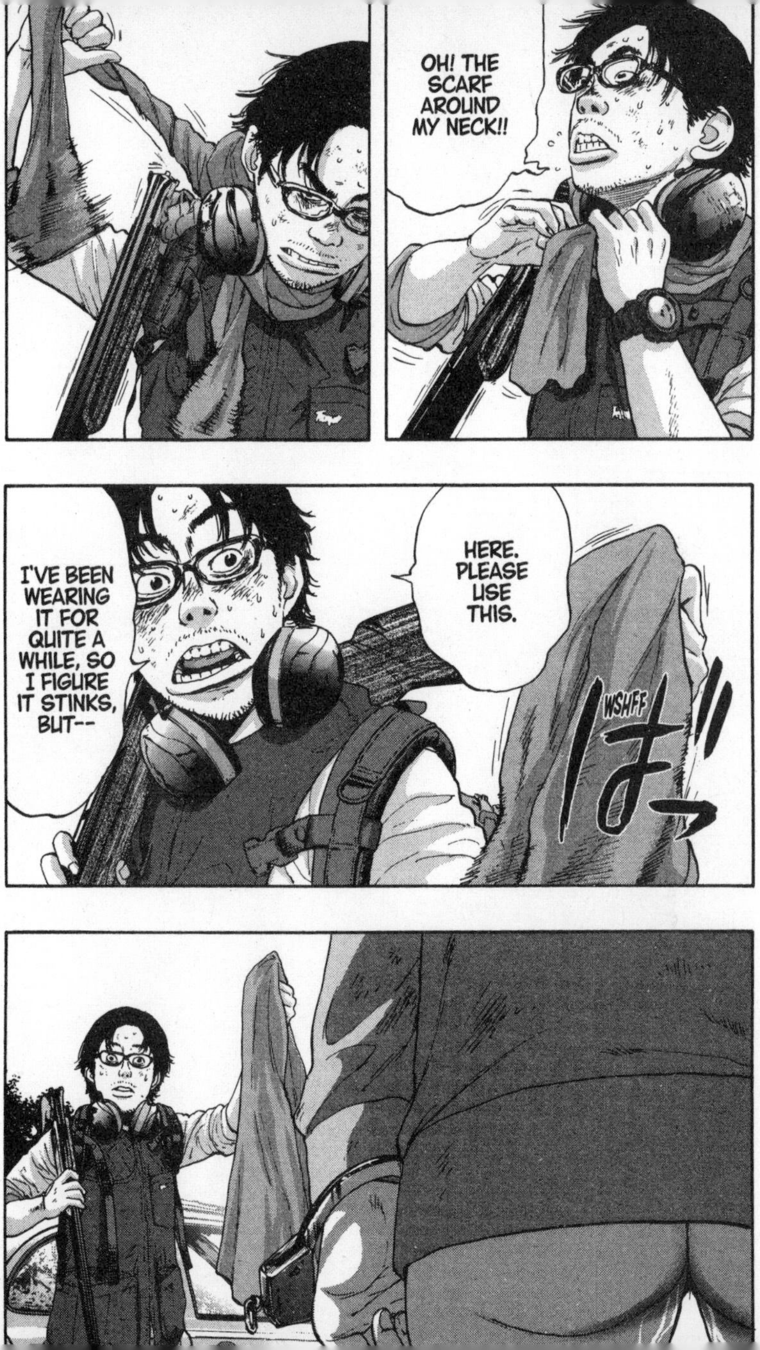
OH! THE SCARF AROUND MY NECK!!
HERE. PLEASE USE THIS.
I'VE BEEN WEARING IT FOR QUITE A WHILE, SO I FIGURE IT STINKS, BUT--
WSHFF

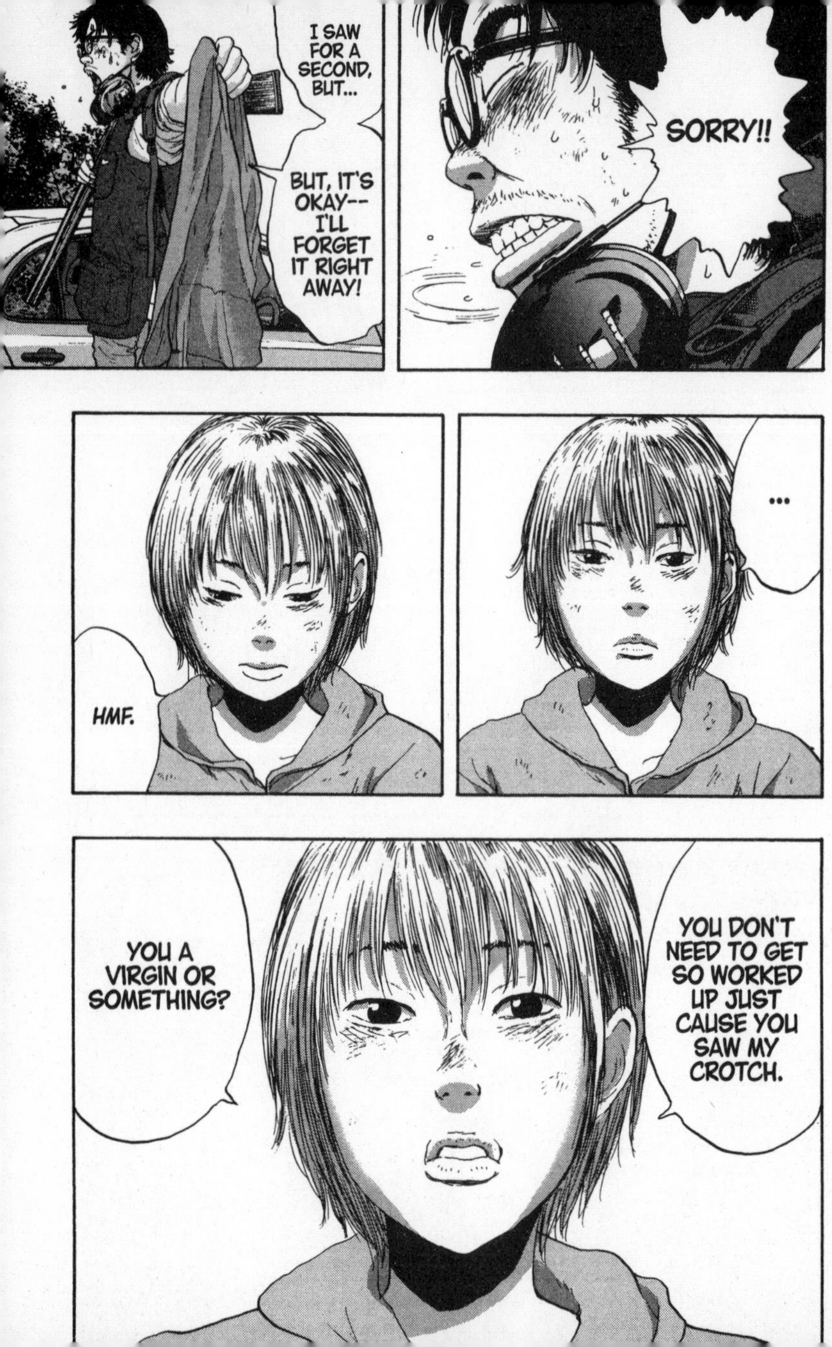
SORRY!!
I SAW FOR A SECOND, BUT...
BUT, IT'S OKAY-- I'LL FORGET IT RIGHT AWAY!
...
HMF.
YOU DON'T NEED TO GET SO WORKED UP JUST CAUSE YOU SAW MY CROTCH.
YOU A VIRGIN OR SOMETHING?

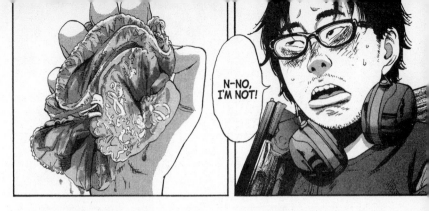

N-NO, I'M NOT!

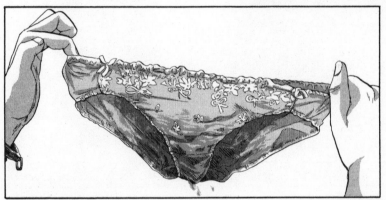

...WANNA SEE?

EEYUCK! GROSS!

NO.

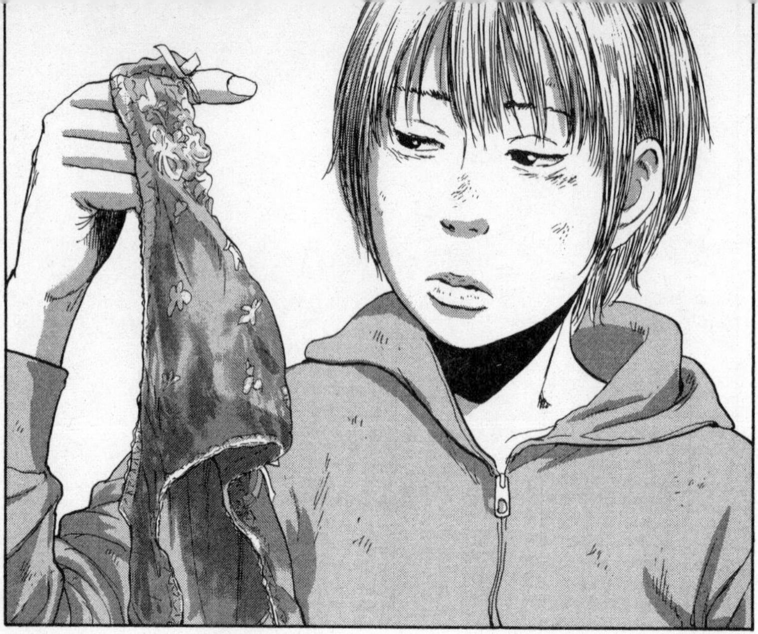
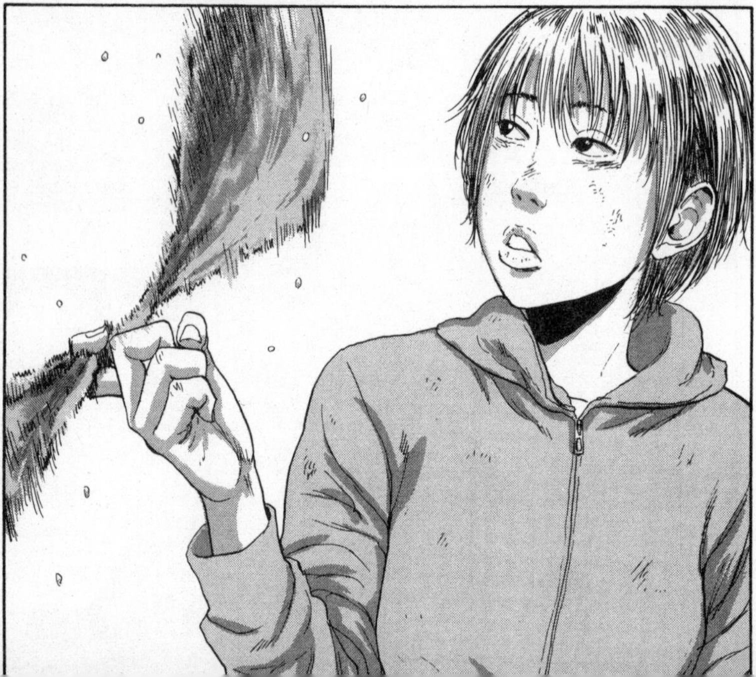

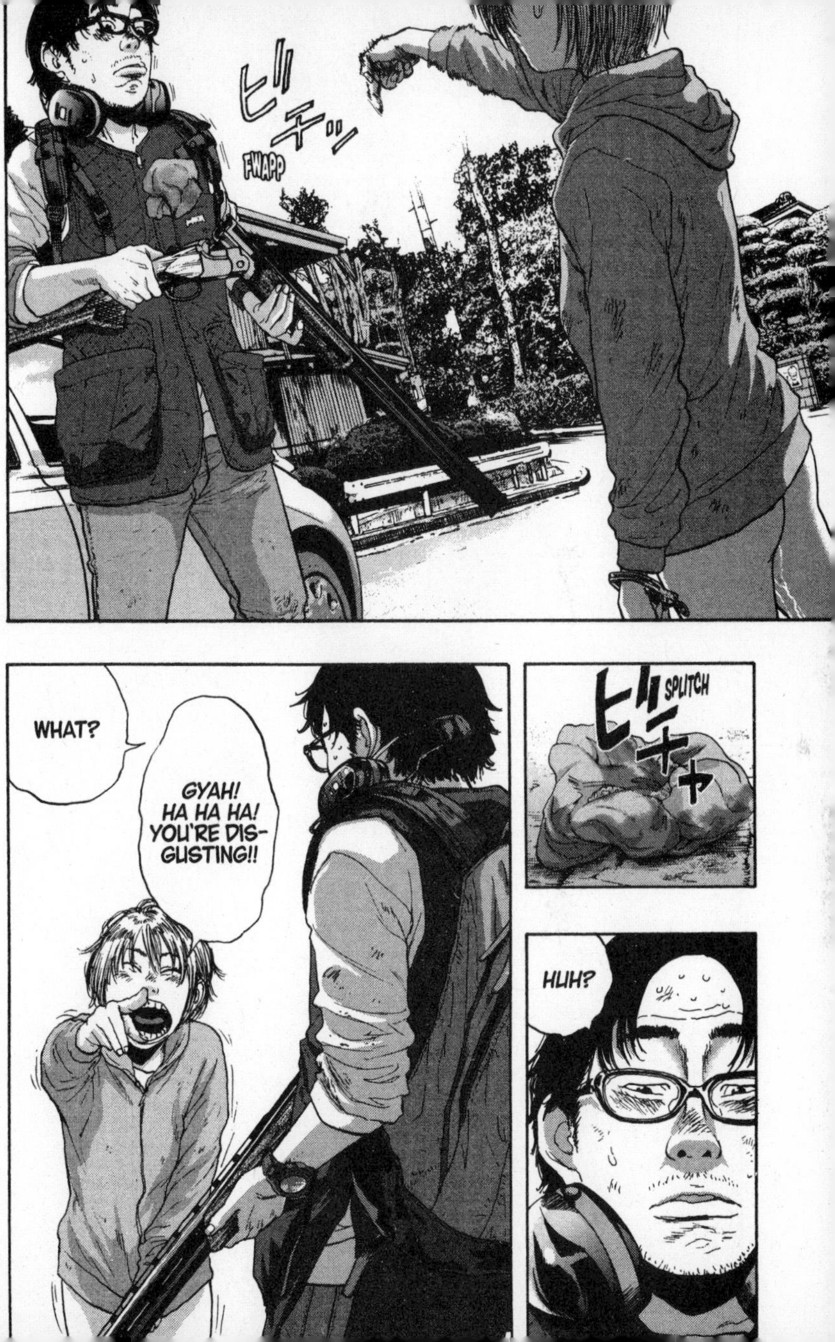

ビリチッ
FWAPP
SPLUTCH
HUH?
GYAH! HA HA HA! YOU'RE DIS-GUSTING!!
WHAT?

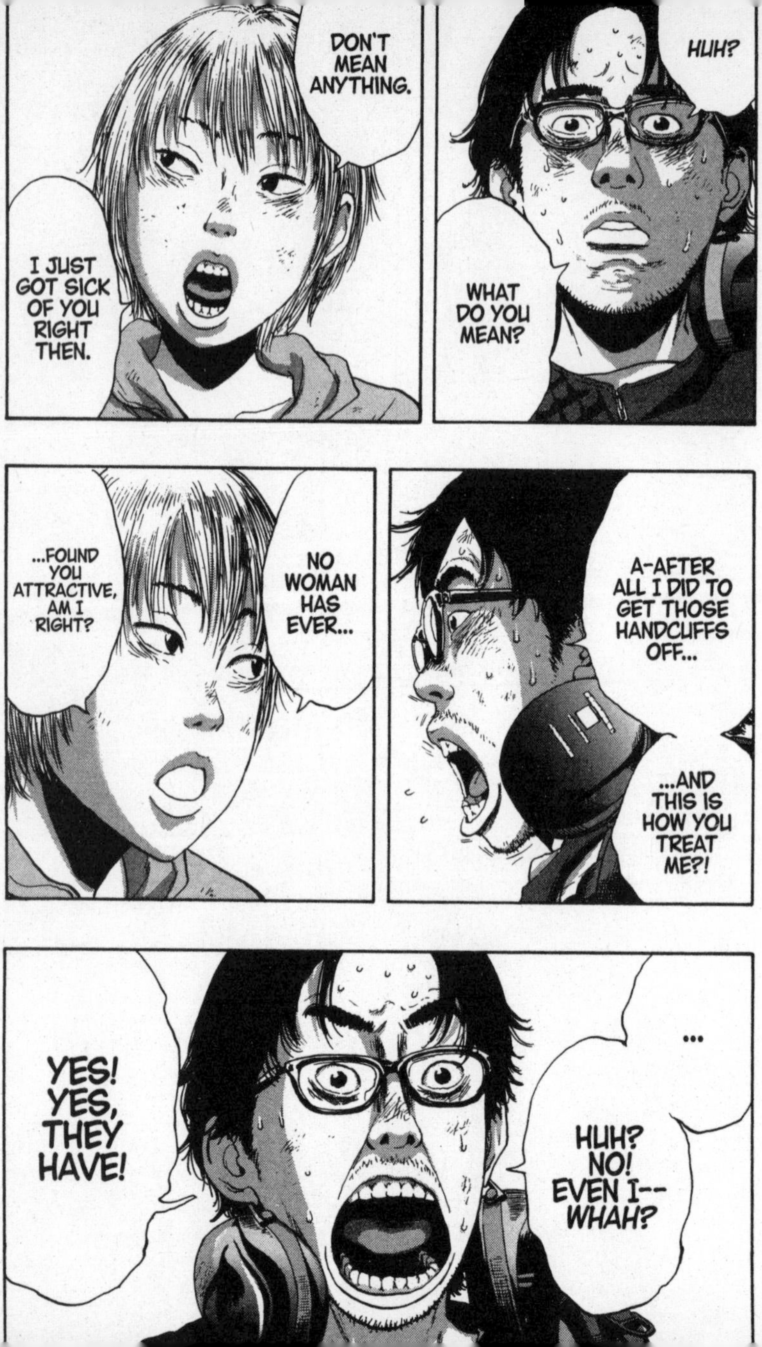
HUH?
WHAT DO YOU MEAN?
DON'T MEAN ANYTHING.
I JUST GOT SICK OF YOU RIGHT THEN.
A-AFTER ALL I DID TO GET THOSE HANDCUFFS OFF...
...AND THIS IS HOW YOU TREAT ME?!
NO WOMAN HAS EVER...
...FOUND YOU ATTRACTIVE, AM I RIGHT?
...
HUH? NO! EVEN I-- WHAH?
YES! YES, THEY HAVE!

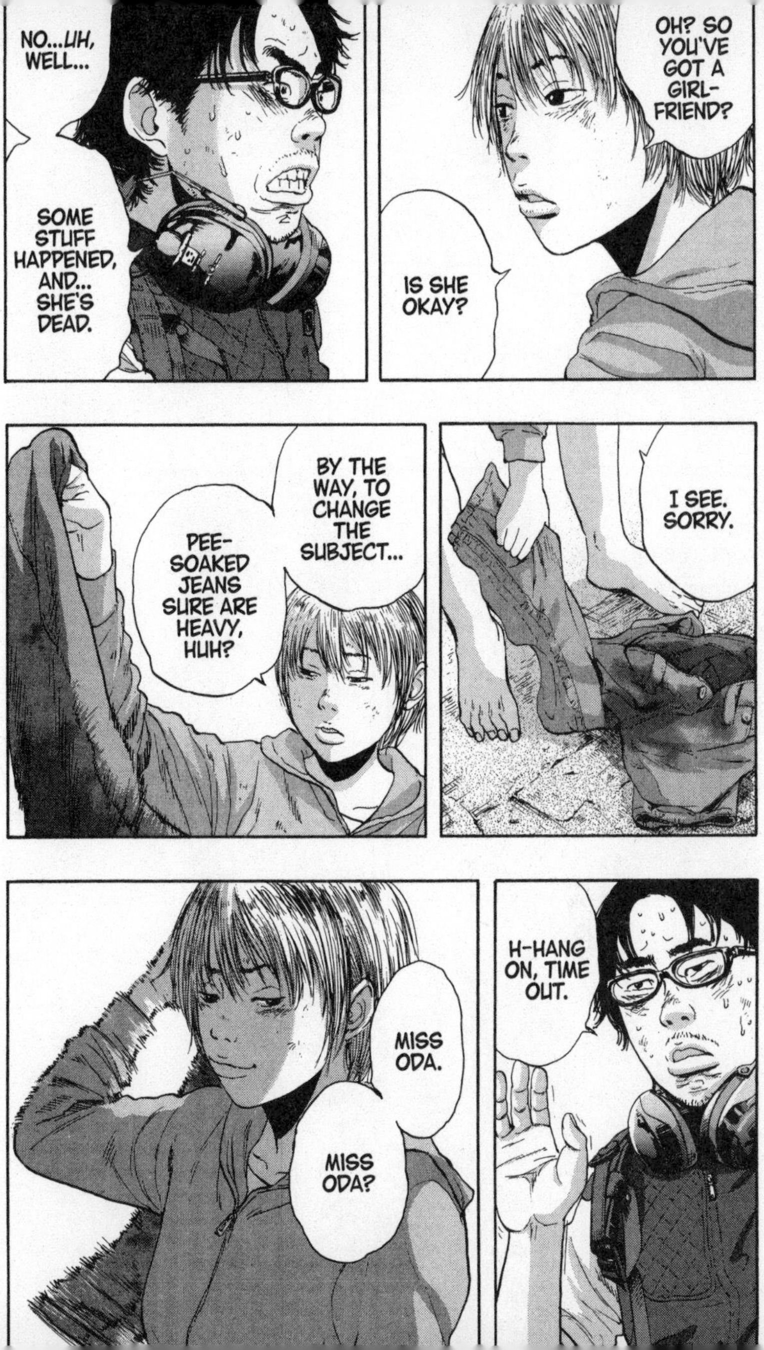
OH? SO YOU'VE GOT A GIRL-FRIEND?
IS SHE OKAY?
NO...UH, WELL...
SOME STUFF HAPPENED, AND... SHE'S DEAD.
I SEE. SORRY.
BY THE WAY, TO CHANGE THE SUBJECT...
PEE-SOAKED JEANS SURE ARE HEAVY, HUH?
H-HANG ON, TIME OUT.
MISS ODA.
MISS ODA?

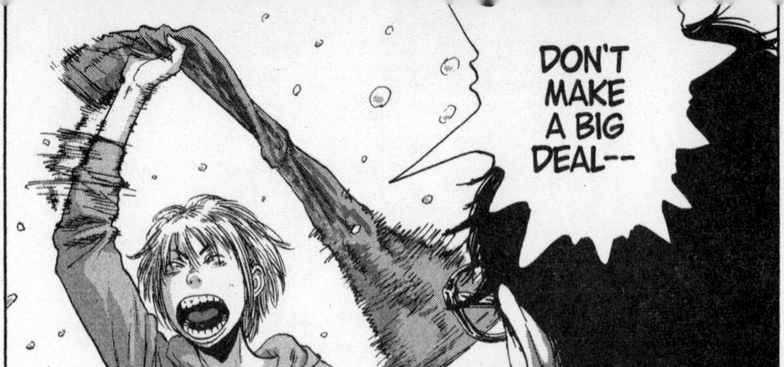
DON'T MAKE A BIG DEAL--
--ABOUT A LITTLE PISS, HIDEO!!
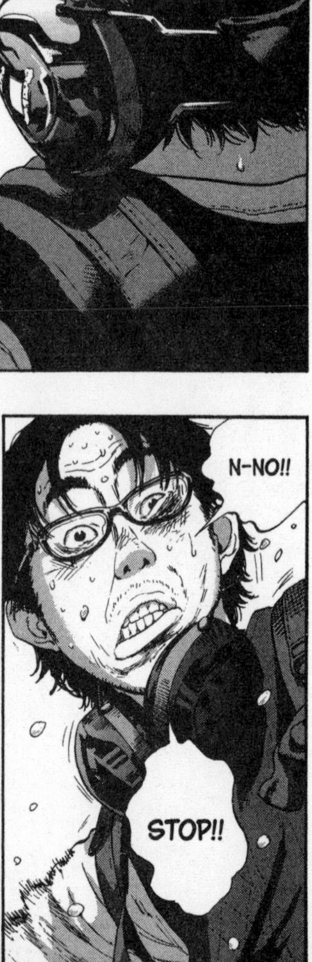
N-NO!!
STOP!!
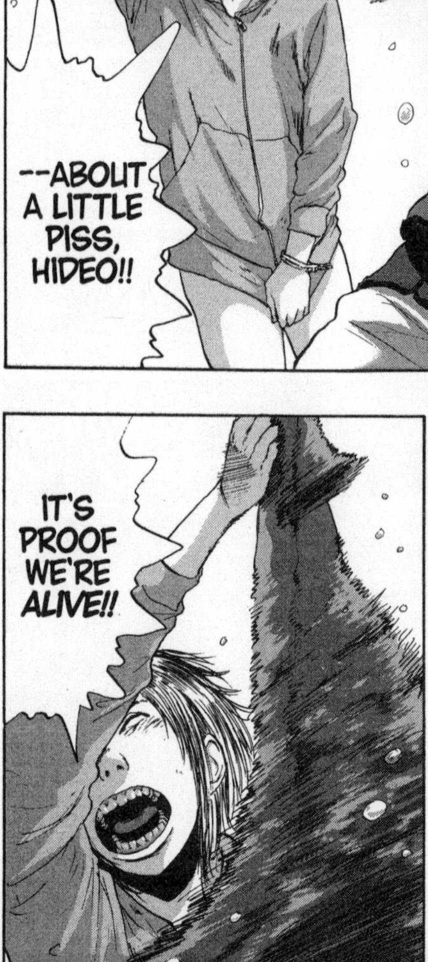
IT'S PROOF WE'RE ALIVE!!

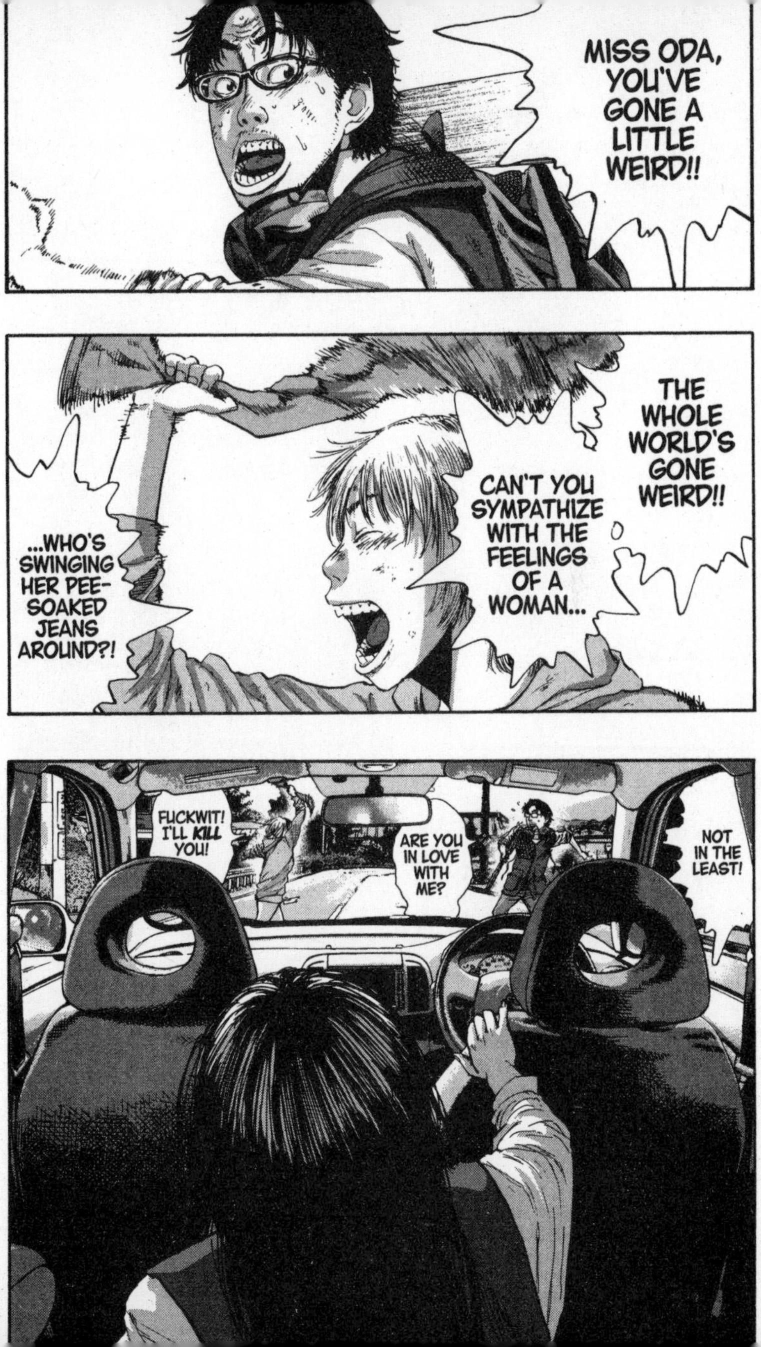
MISS ODA, YOU'VE GONE A LITTLE WEIRD!!
THE WHOLE WORLD'S GONE WEIRD!!
CAN'T YOU SYMPATHIZE WITH THE FEELINGS OF A WOMAN...
...WHO'S SWINGING HER PEE-SOAKED JEANS AROUND?!
NOT IN THE LEAST!
ARE YOU IN LOVE WITH ME?
FUCKWIT! I'LL KILL YOU!

CHAPTER 108

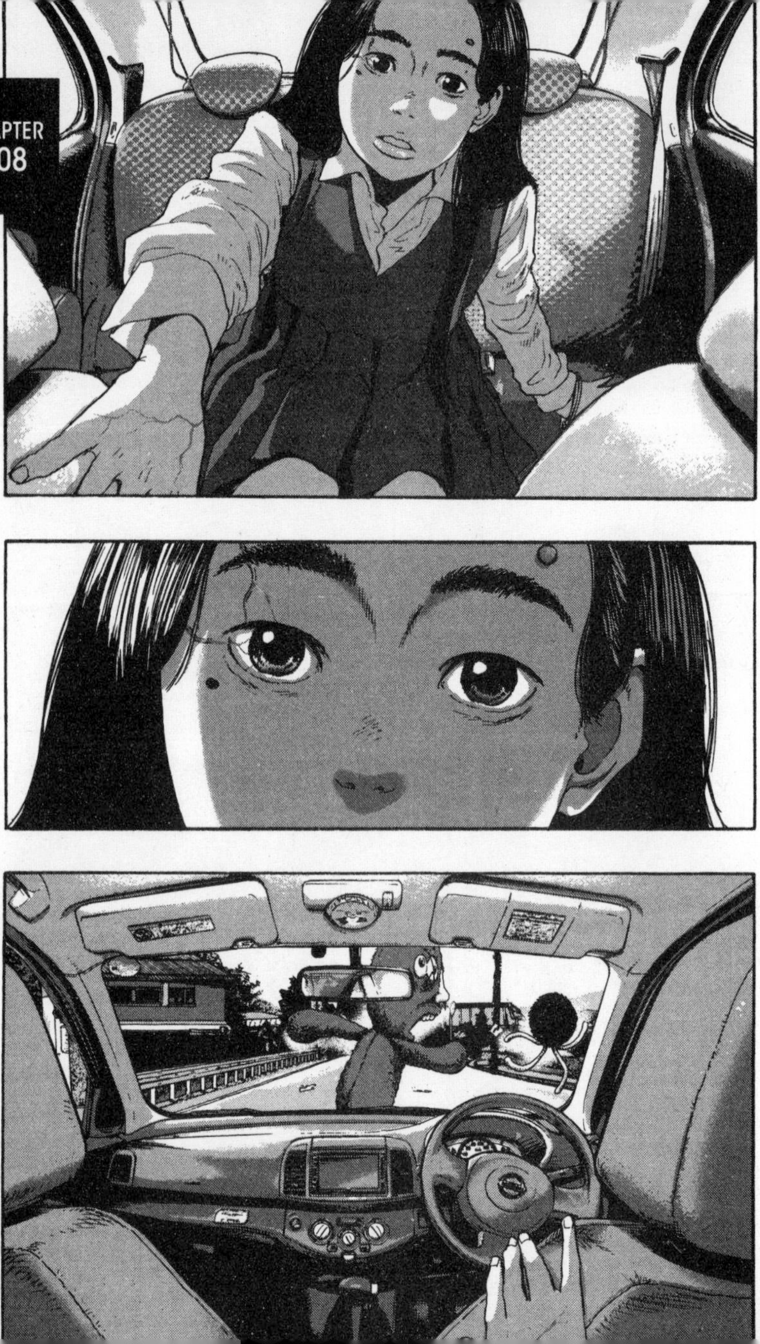

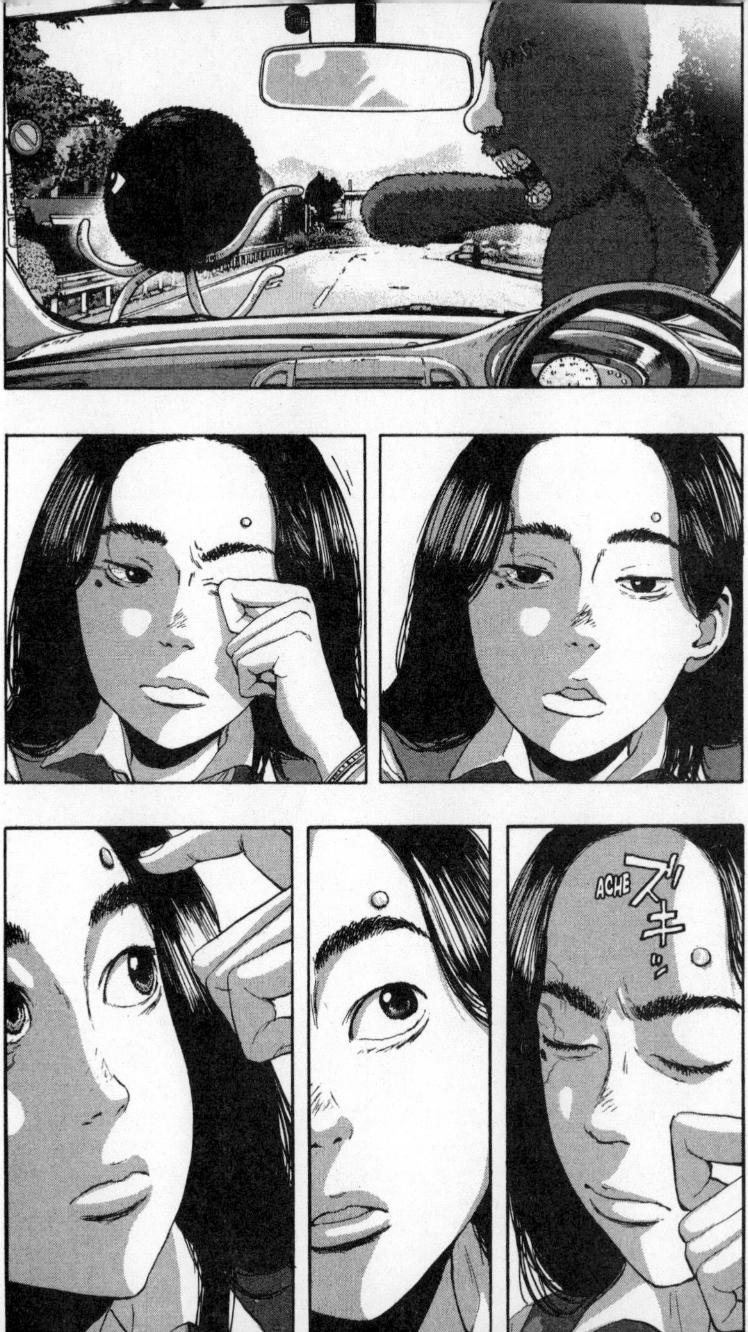
ズキッ
ACHE

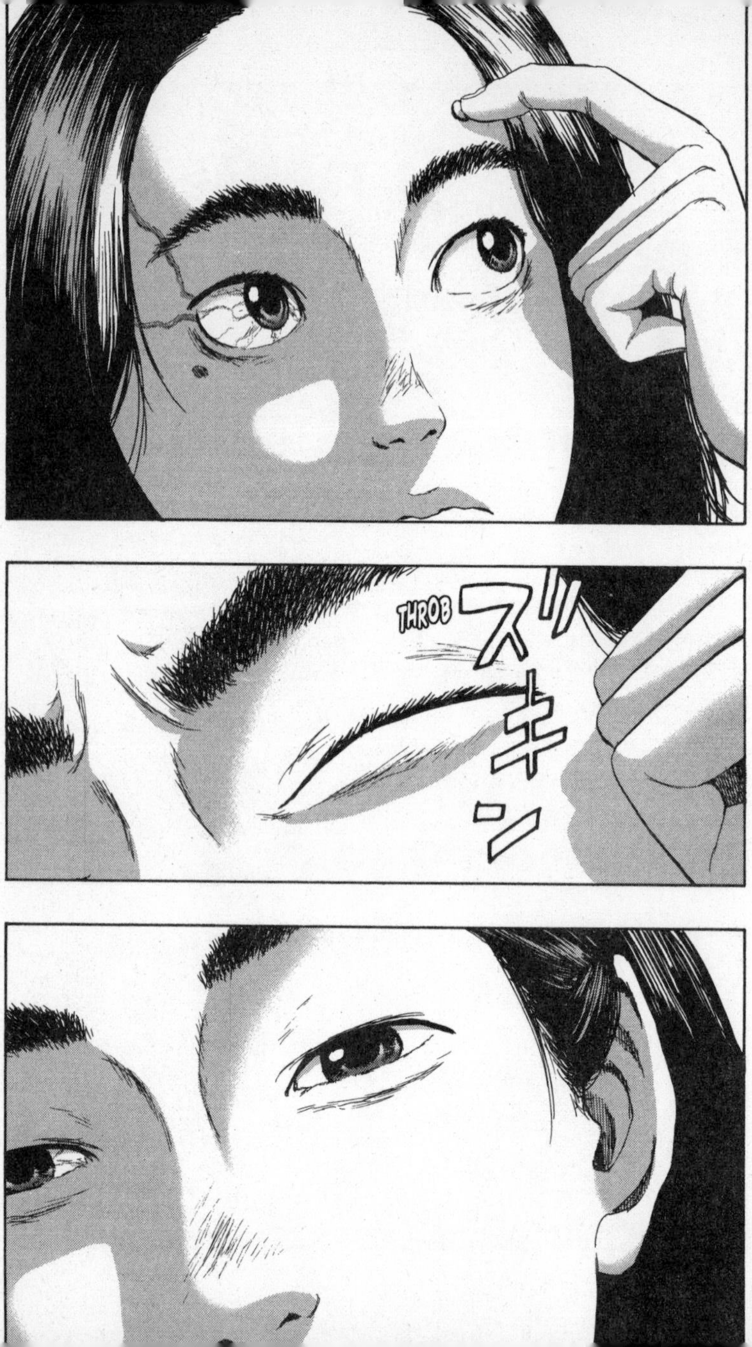
THROB
ズキン

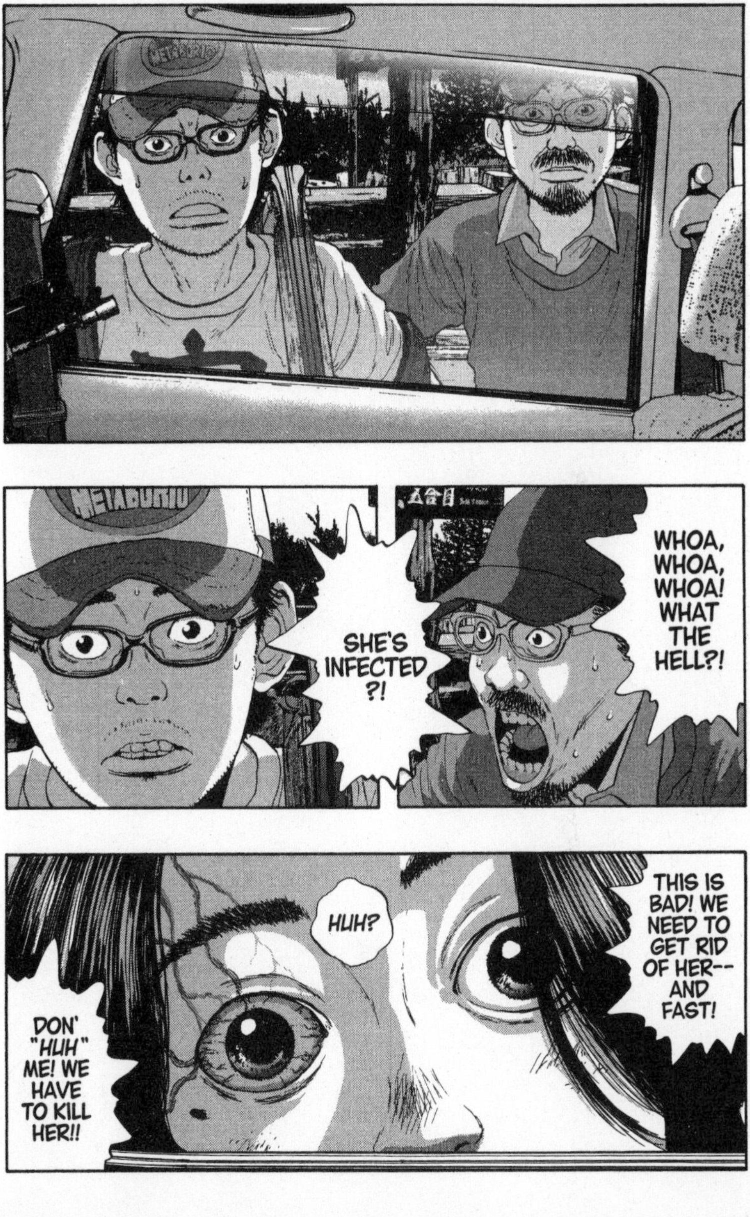

WHOA, WHOA, WHOA! WHAT THE HELL?!
SHE'S INFECTED?!
THIS IS BAD! WE NEED TO GET RID OF HER-- AND FAST!
HUH?
DON' "HUH" ME! WE HAVE TO KILL HER!!

THROB
ズキ

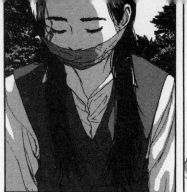

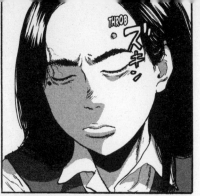

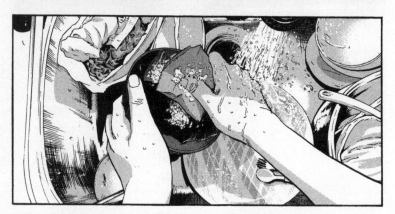

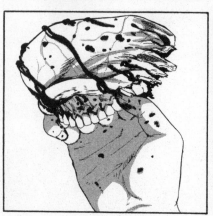

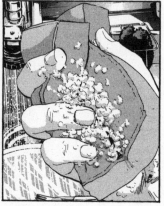

FLINCH
ブン
WHP
ブン
WHP
THROB
ズキッ
ズキ
THROB
DAN-DRUFF.
DAN-DRUFF.
DANDRUFF. DANDRUFF.
DANDRUFF.

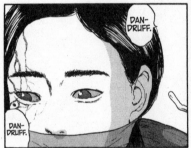

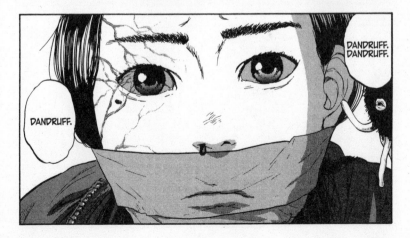

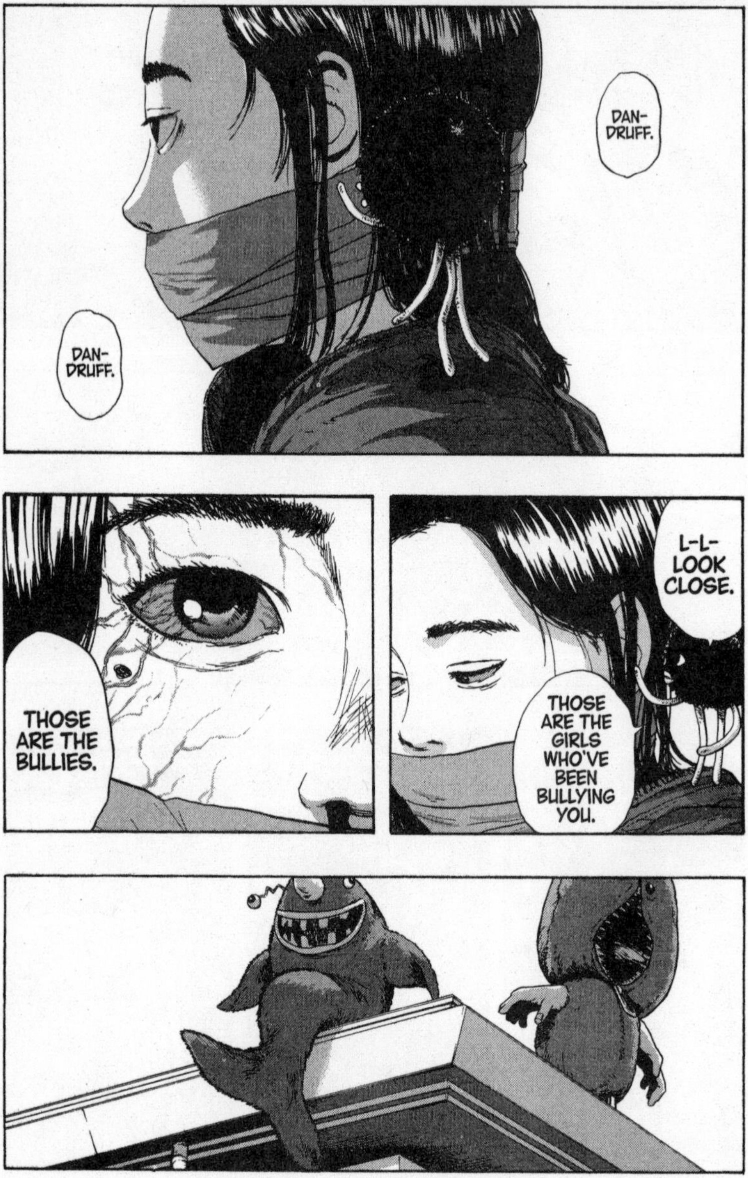
DAN-DRUFF.
DAN-DRUFF.
L-L-LOOK CLOSE.
THOSE ARE THE GIRLS WHO'VE BEEN BULLYING YOU.
THOSE ARE THE BULLIES.

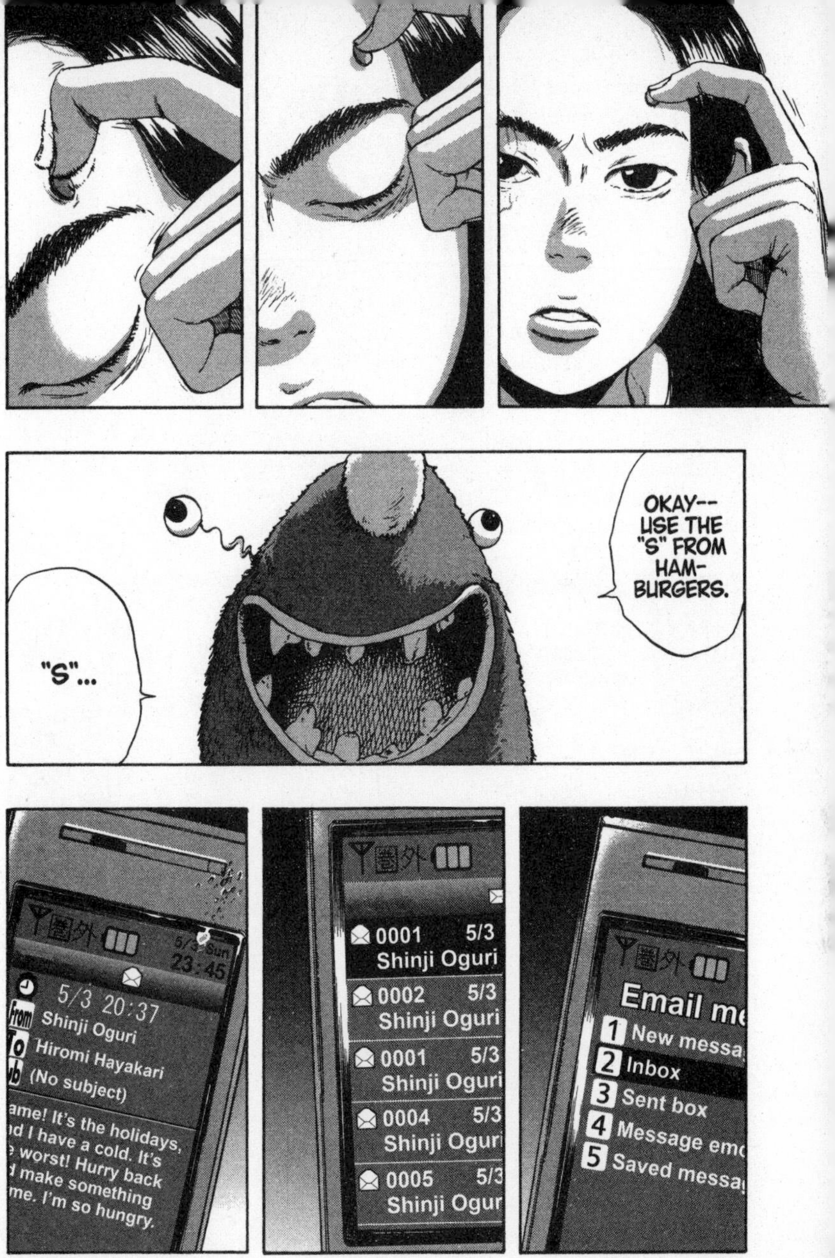
OKAY-- USE THE "S" FROM HAM-BURGERS.
"S"...
圏外
Email me
1 New messa
2 Inbox
3 Sent box
4 Message emo
5 Saved messa
圏外
0001 5/3 Shinji Oguri
0002 5/3 Shinji Oguri
0001 5/3 Shinji Oguri
0004 5/3 Shinji Oguri
0005 5/3 Shinji Ogur
圏外
5/3 Sun 23:45
5/3 20:37
From Shinji Oguri
To Hiromi Hayakari
(No subject)
ame! It's the holidays,
nd I have a cold. It's
e worst! Hurry back
d make something
me. I'm so hungry.

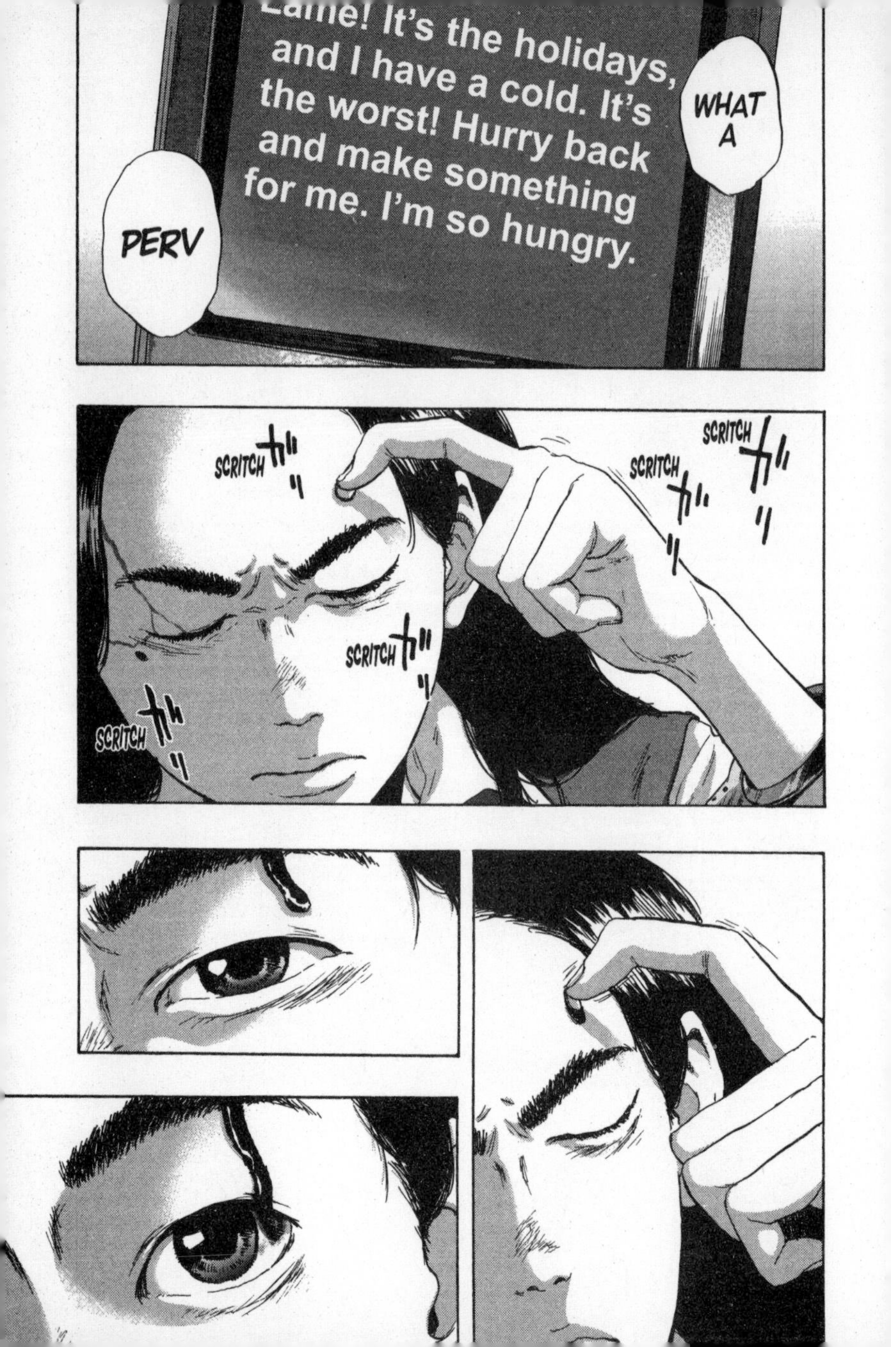
It's the holidays, and I have a cold. It's the worst! Hurry back and make something for me. I'm so hungry.
WHAT A
PERV
SCRITCH
SCRITCH
SCRITCH
SCRITCH
SCRITCH

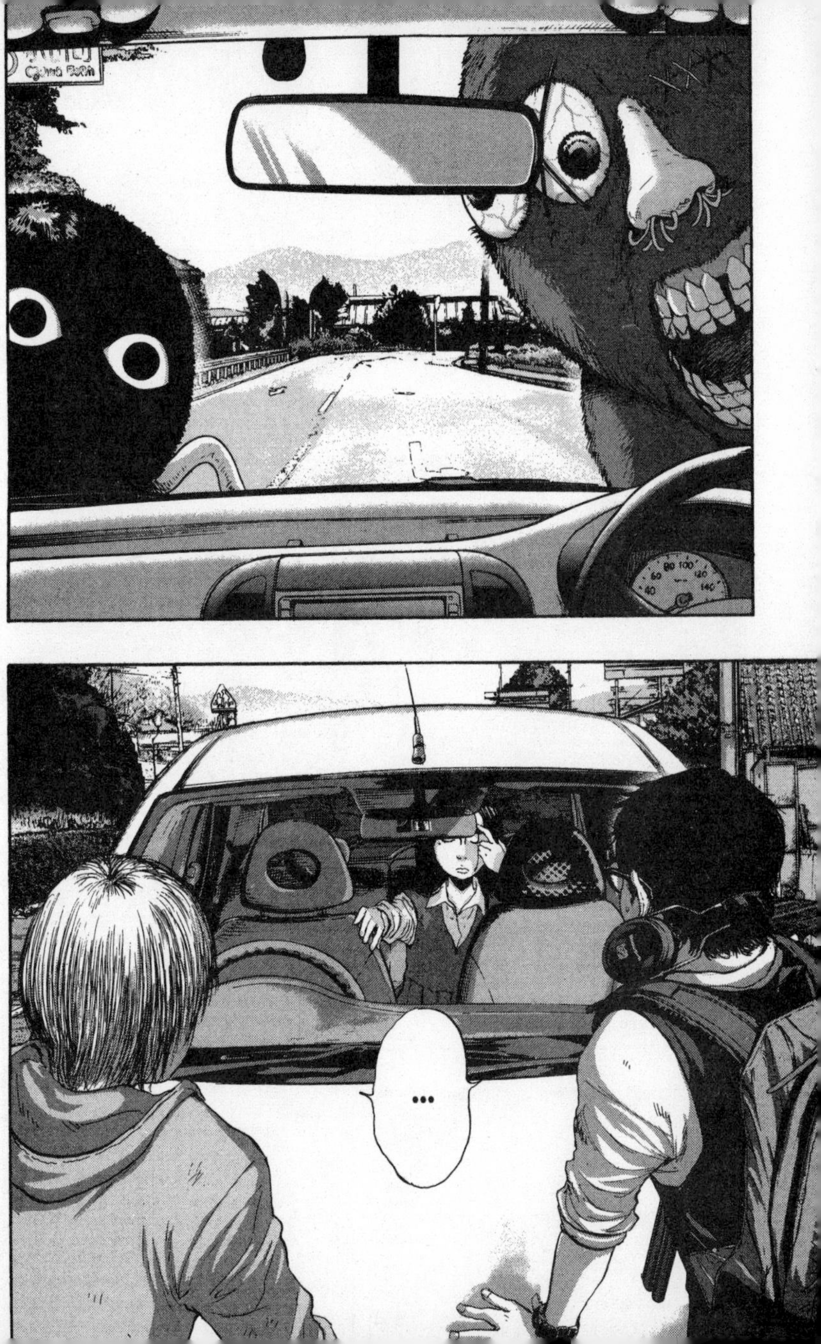
...

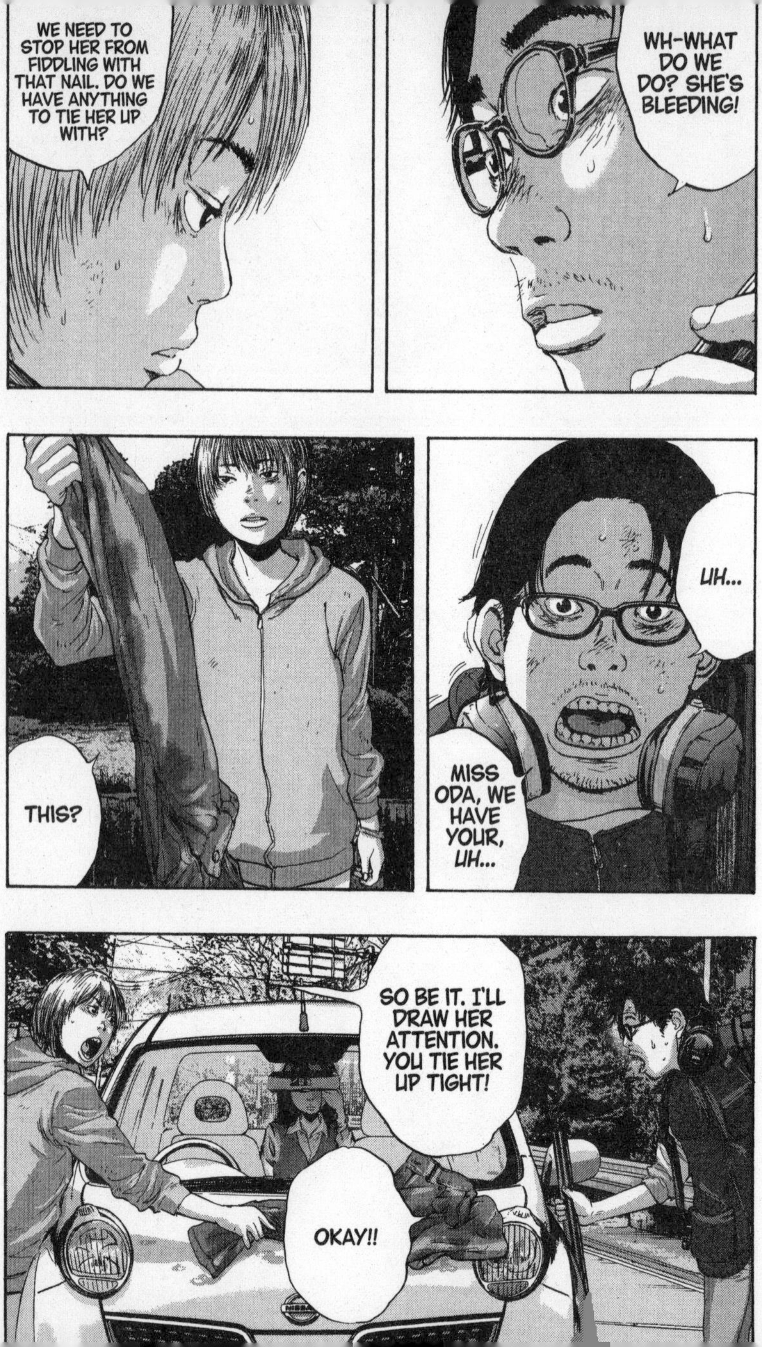
WH-WHAT DO WE DO? SHE'S BLEEDING!
WE NEED TO STOP HER FROM FIDDLING WITH THAT NAIL. DO WE HAVE ANYTHING TO TIE HER UP WITH?
UH...
MISS ODA, WE HAVE YOUR, UH...
THIS?
SO BE IT. I'LL DRAW HER ATTENTION. YOU TIE HER UP TIGHT!
OKAY!!

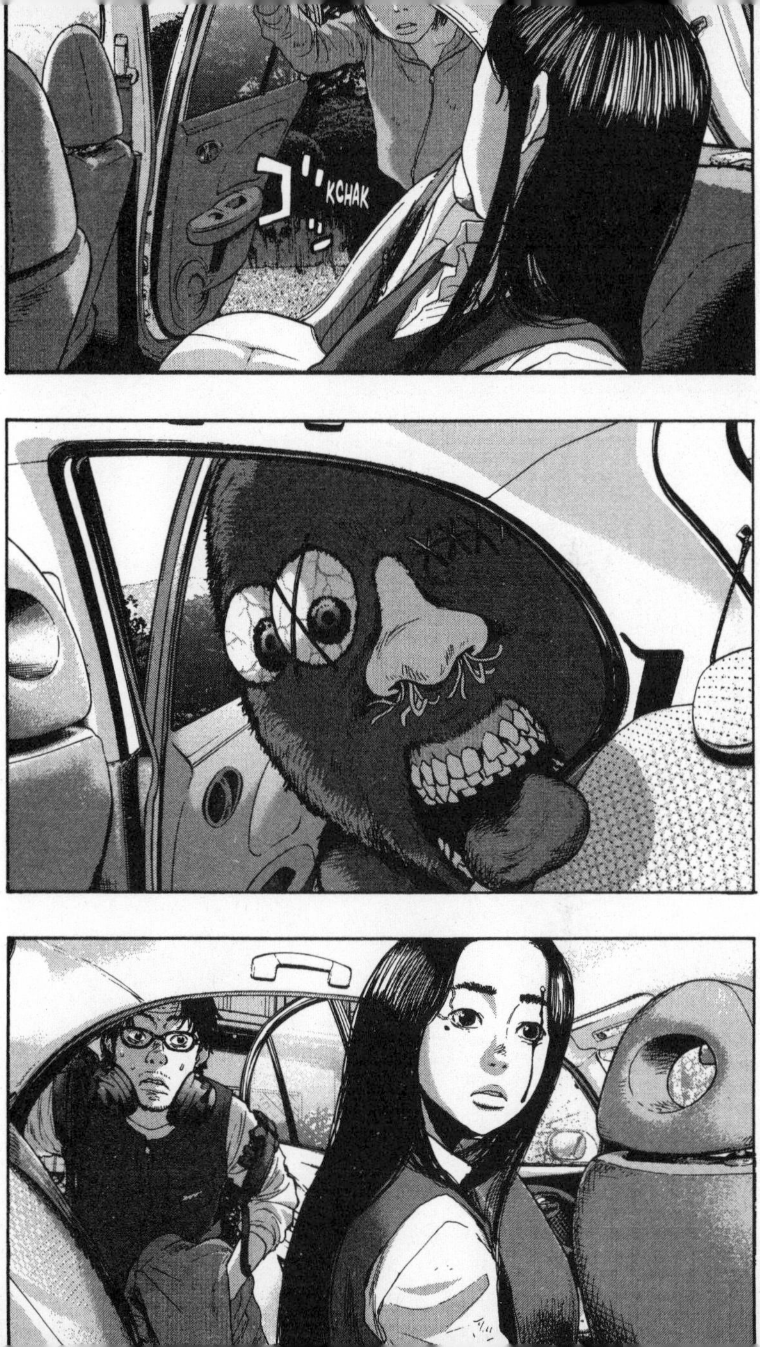
KCHAK

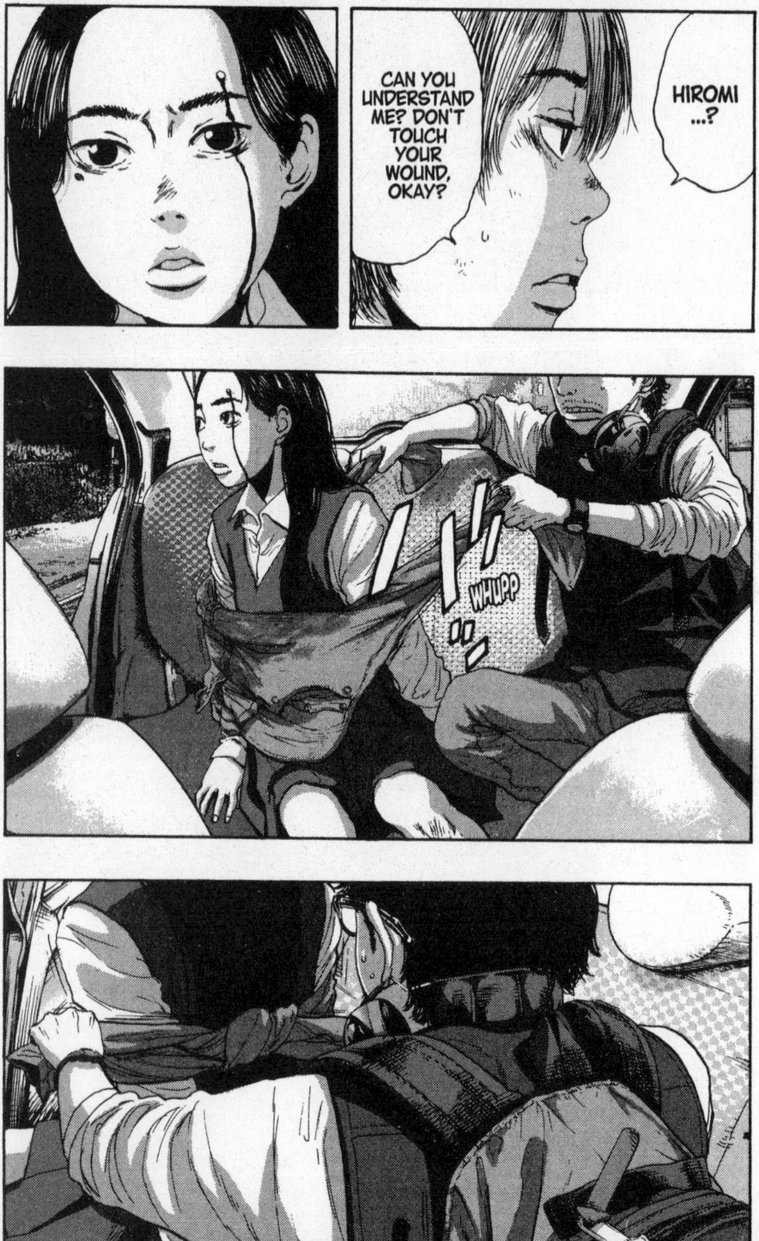
HIROMI ...?
CAN YOU UNDERSTAND ME? DON'T TOUCH YOUR WOUND, OKAY?
WHUPP

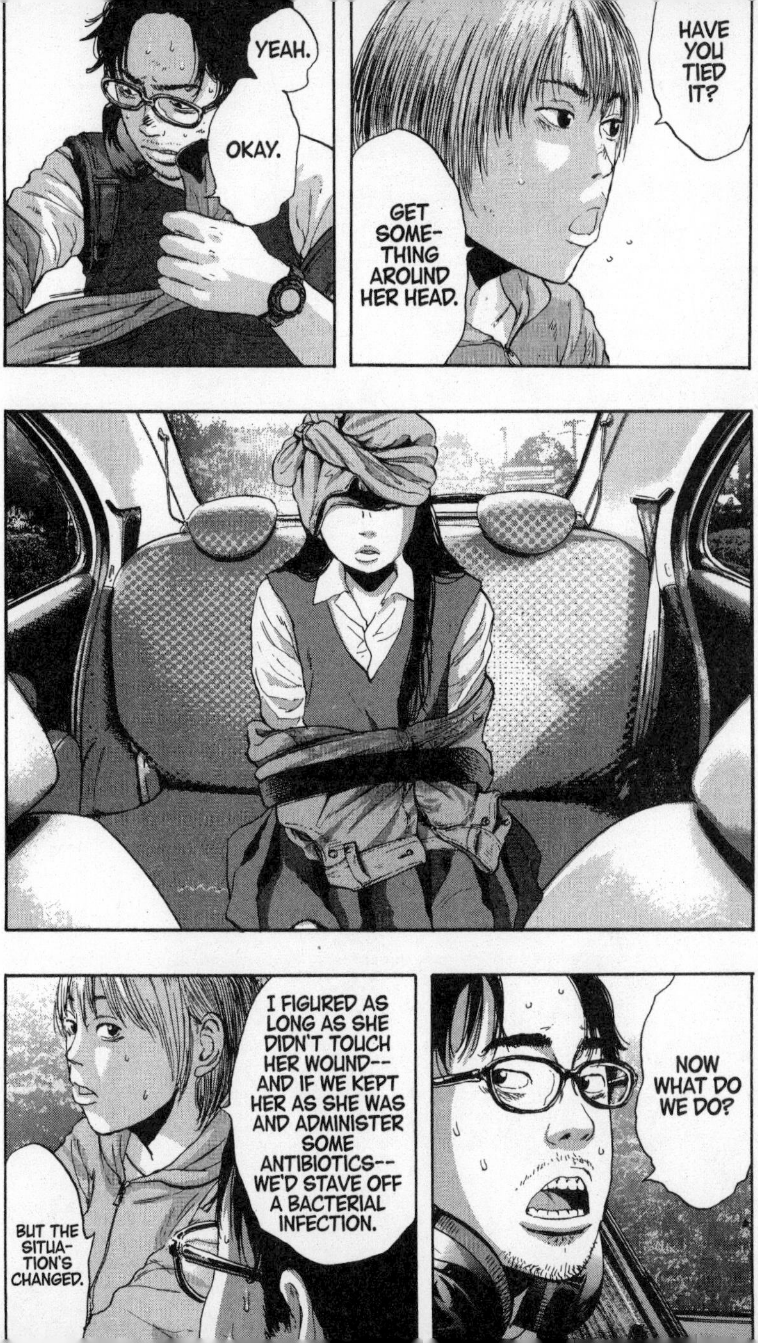
HAVE YOU TIED IT?
GET SOME-THING AROUND HER HEAD.
YEAH.
OKAY.
NOW WHAT DO WE DO?
I FIGURED AS LONG AS SHE DIDN'T TOUCH HER WOUND-- AND IF WE KEPT HER AS SHE WAS AND ADMINISTER SOME ANTIBIOTICS-- WE'D STAVE OFF A BACTERIAL INFECTION.
BUT THE SITUA-TION'S CHANGED.

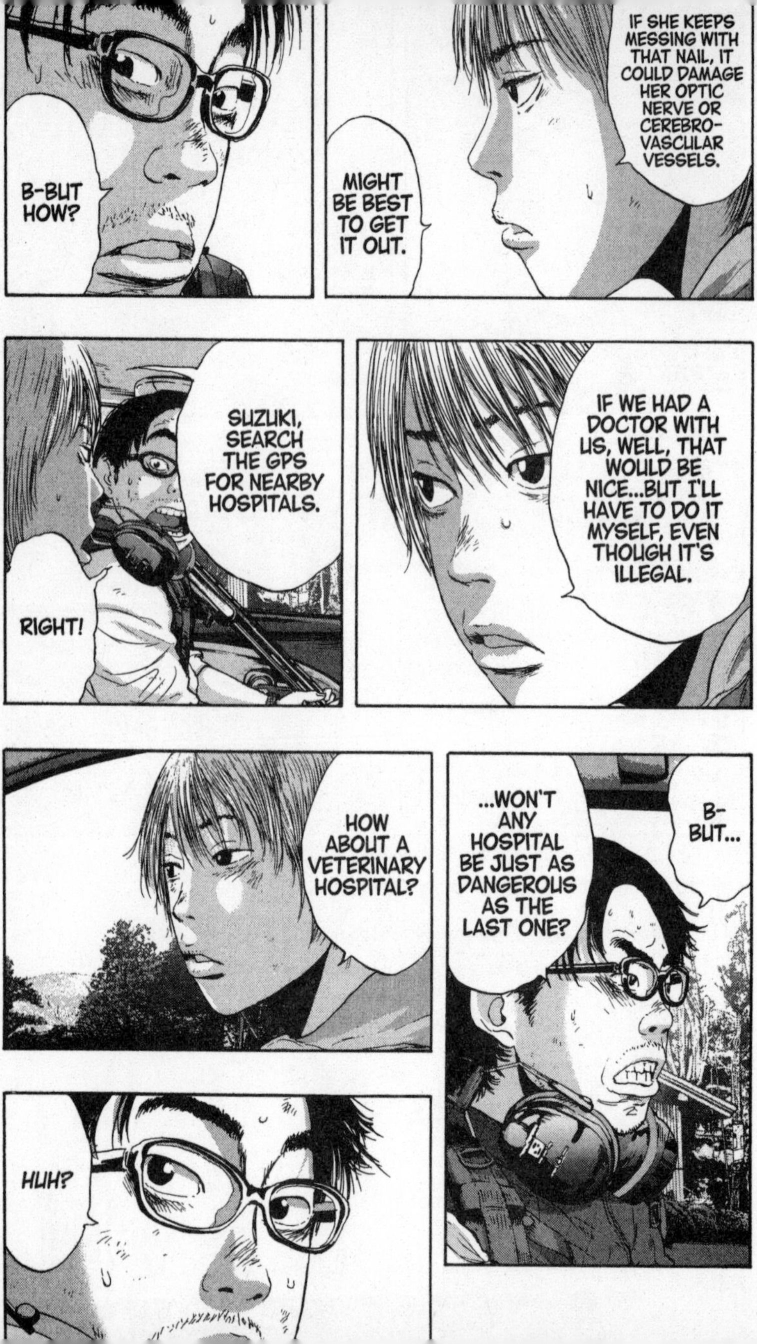
IF SHE KEEPS MESSING WITH THAT NAIL, IT COULD DAMAGE HER OPTIC NERVE OR CEREBRO-VASCULAR VESSELS.
MIGHT BE BEST TO GET IT OUT.
B-BUT HOW?
IF WE HAD A DOCTOR WITH US, WELL, THAT WOULD BE NICE...BUT I'LL HAVE TO DO IT MYSELF, EVEN THOUGH IT'S ILLEGAL.
SUZUKI, SEARCH THE GPS FOR NEARBY HOSPITALS.
RIGHT!
B-BUT...
...WON'T ANY HOSPITAL BE JUST AS DANGEROUS AS THE LAST ONE?
HOW ABOUT A VETERINARY HOSPITAL?
HUH?

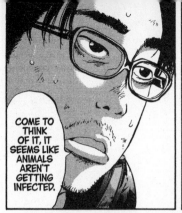

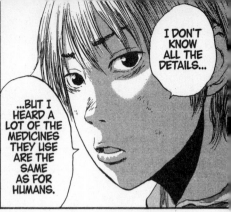

I DON'T KNOW ALL THE DETAILS...
...BUT I HEARD A LOT OF THE MEDICINES THEY USE ARE THE SAME AS FOR HUMANS.
COME TO THINK OF IT, IT SEEMS LIKE ANIMALS AREN'T GETTING INFECTED.
UM...
HOSPITALS
EAR, NOSE & THROAT
PEDIATRICS
GENERAL HOSPITALS
VETS, ANIMAL HOSPITALS
INTERNAL MEDICINE
DERMATOLOGY
VETS! THERE!
HOSPITALS > VETERINARY HOSPITALS, ANIMAL DOCTORS
LAKE ASHINOKO PET CLINIC
KANAGAWA PREFECTURE
KANAGAWA PREFECTURE
OOO! HERE WE GO!
THREE KILOMETERS FROM HERE!!
ASHINOKO PET CLINIC
HAKONE FOREST
LAKE ASHINOKO
HAKONE STATION
IT'S NEAR LAKE ASHINOKO!!

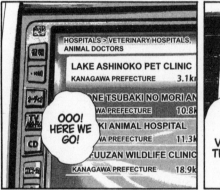

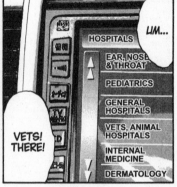

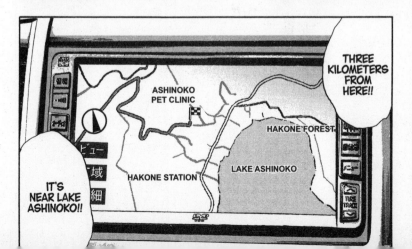

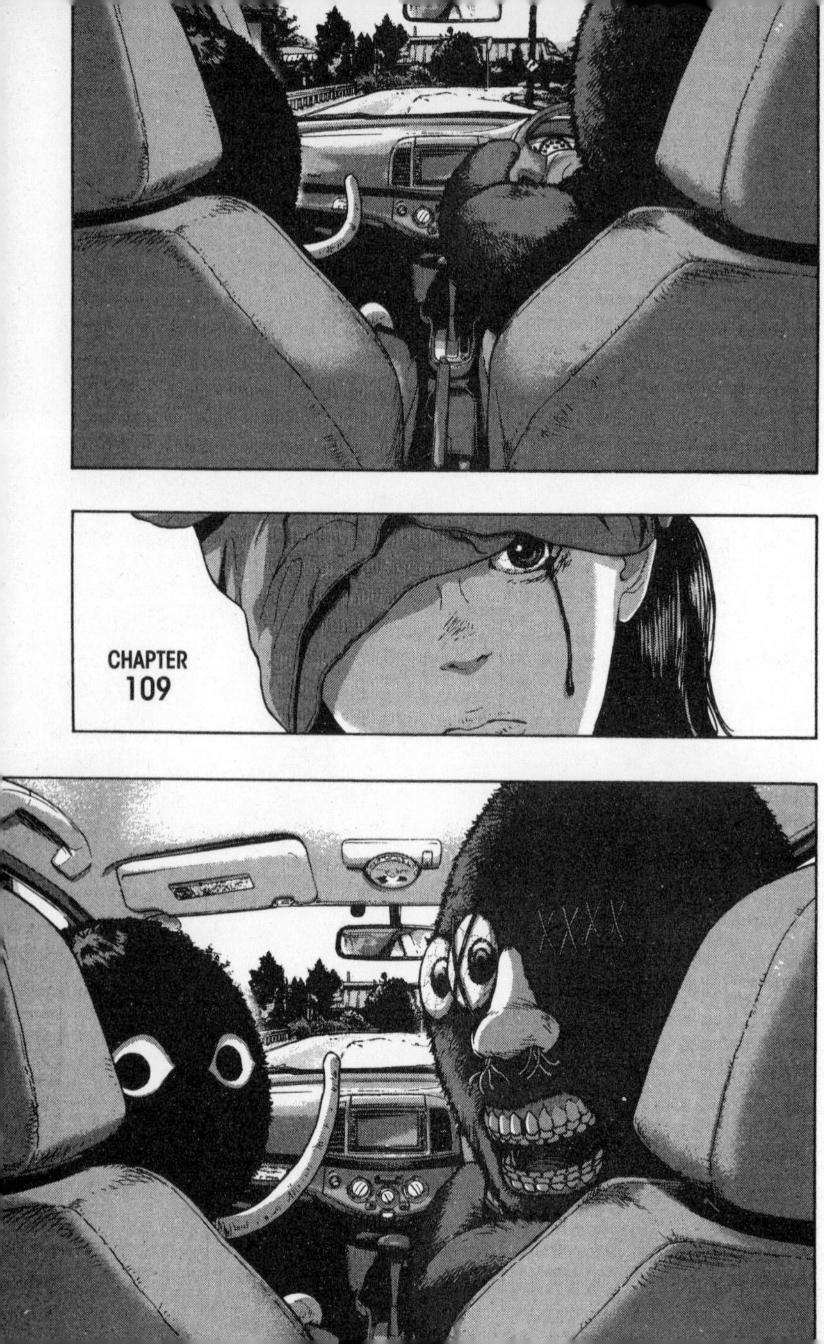
CHAPTER
109

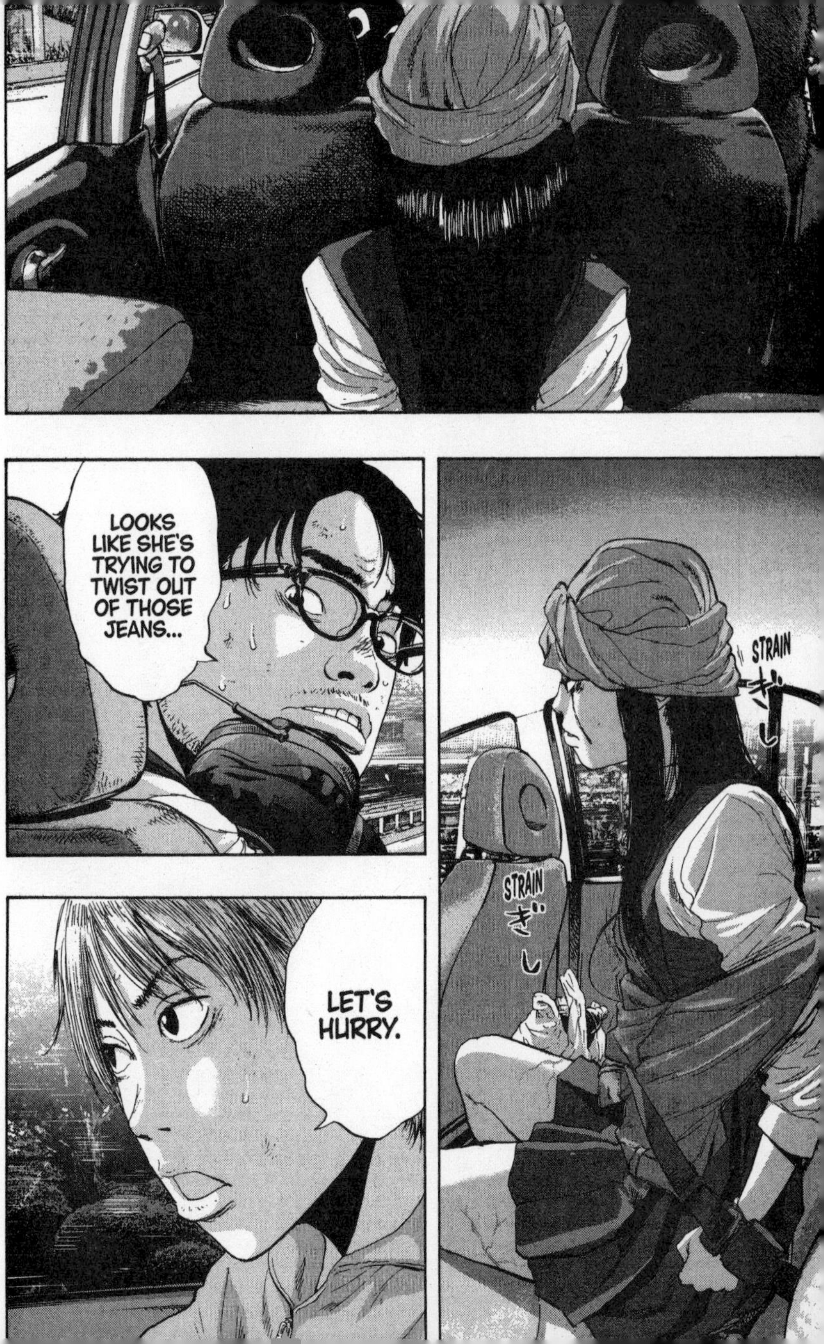
STRAIN ぎし
STRAIN ぎし
LOOKS LIKE SHE'S TRYING TO TWIST OUT OF THOSE JEANS...
LET'S HURRY.

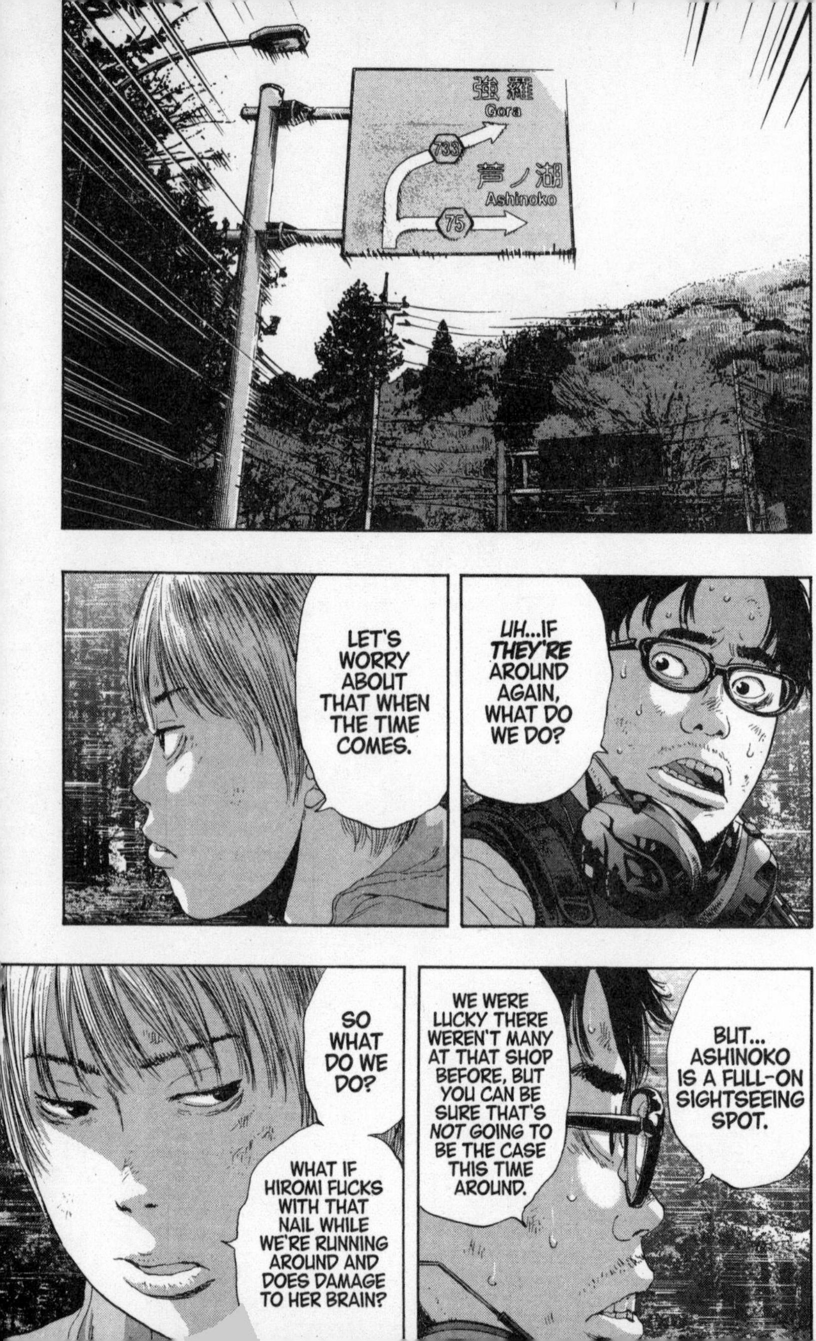
強羅
Gora
733
芦ノ湖
Ashinoko
75
UH...IF *THEY'RE* AROUND AGAIN, WHAT DO WE DO?
LET'S WORRY ABOUT THAT WHEN THE TIME COMES.
BUT... ASHINOKO IS A FULL-ON SIGHTSEEING SPOT.
WE WERE LUCKY THERE WEREN'T MANY AT THAT SHOP BEFORE, BUT YOU CAN BE SURE THAT'S *NOT* GOING TO BE THE CASE THIS TIME AROUND.
SO WHAT DO WE DO?
WHAT IF HIROMI FUCKS WITH THAT NAIL WHILE WE'RE RUNNING AROUND AND DOES DAMAGE TO HER BRAIN?

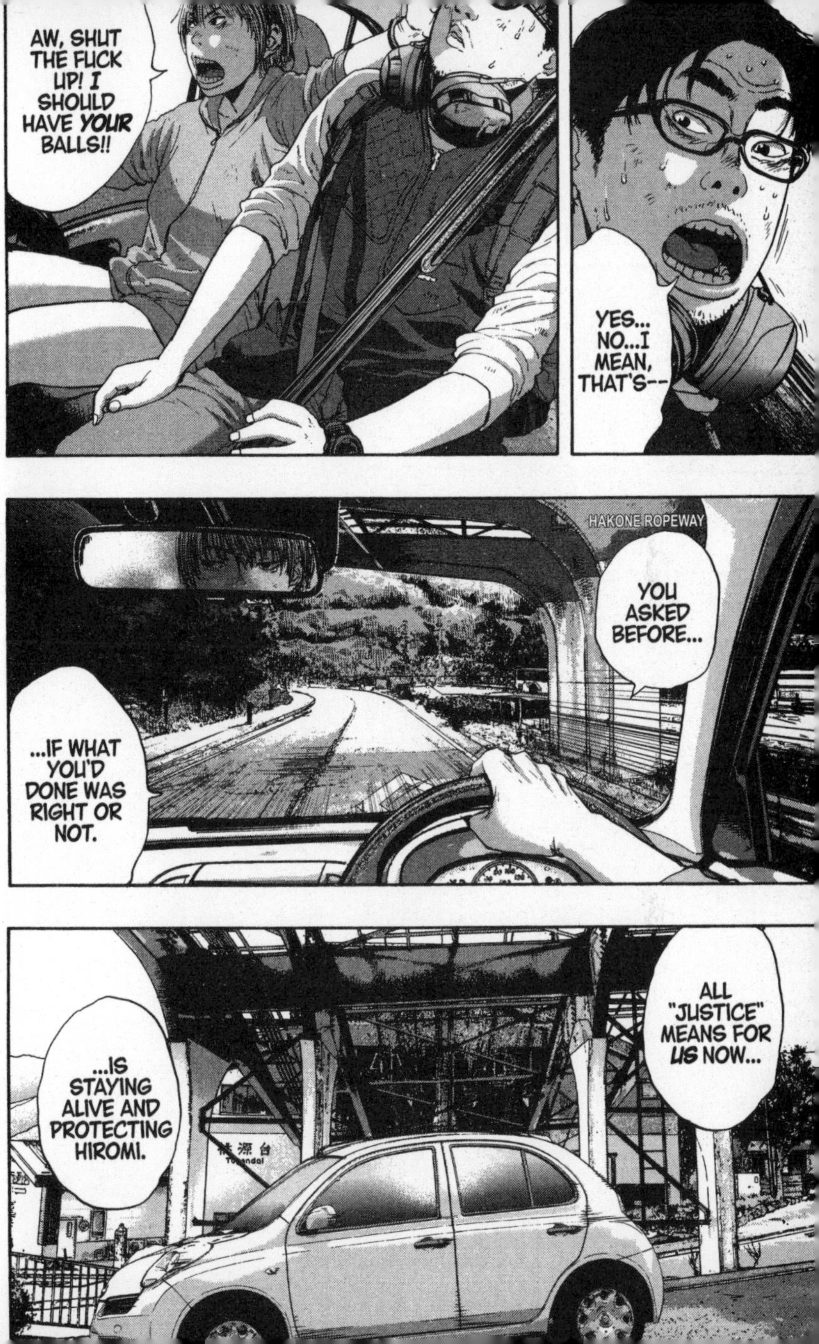
YES... NO...I MEAN, THAT'S--
AW, SHUT THE FUCK UP! I SHOULD HAVE *YOUR* BALLS!!
HAKONE ROPEWAY
YOU ASKED BEFORE...
...IF WHAT YOU'D DONE WAS RIGHT OR NOT.
ALL "JUSTICE" MEANS FOR *US* NOW...
...IS STAYING ALIVE AND PROTECTING HIROMI.

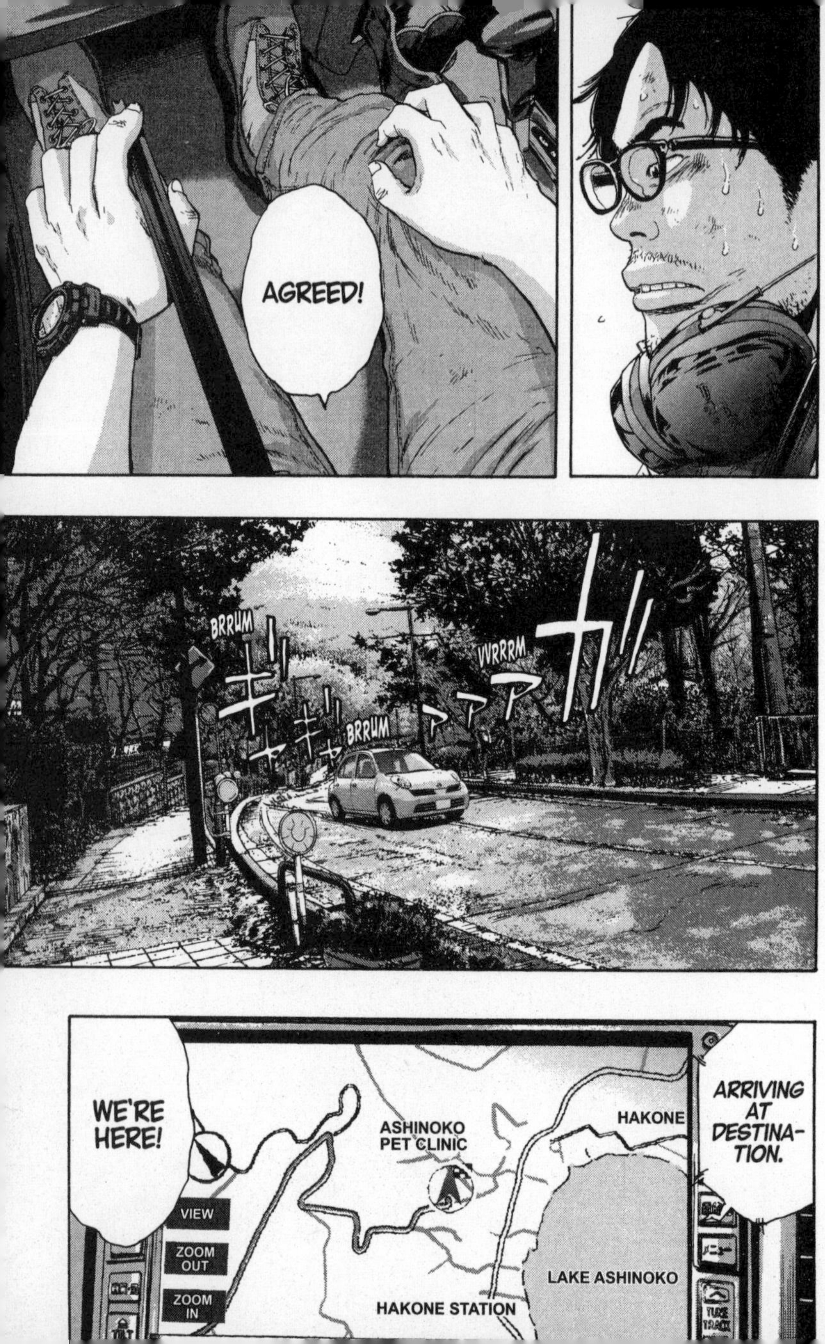
AGREED!
VVRRRM
BRRUM
BRRUM
ARRIVING AT DESTINATION.
HAKONE
ASHINOKO PET CLINIC
LAKE ASHINOKO
HAKONE STATION
VIEW
ZOOM OUT
ZOOM IN
WE'RE HERE!

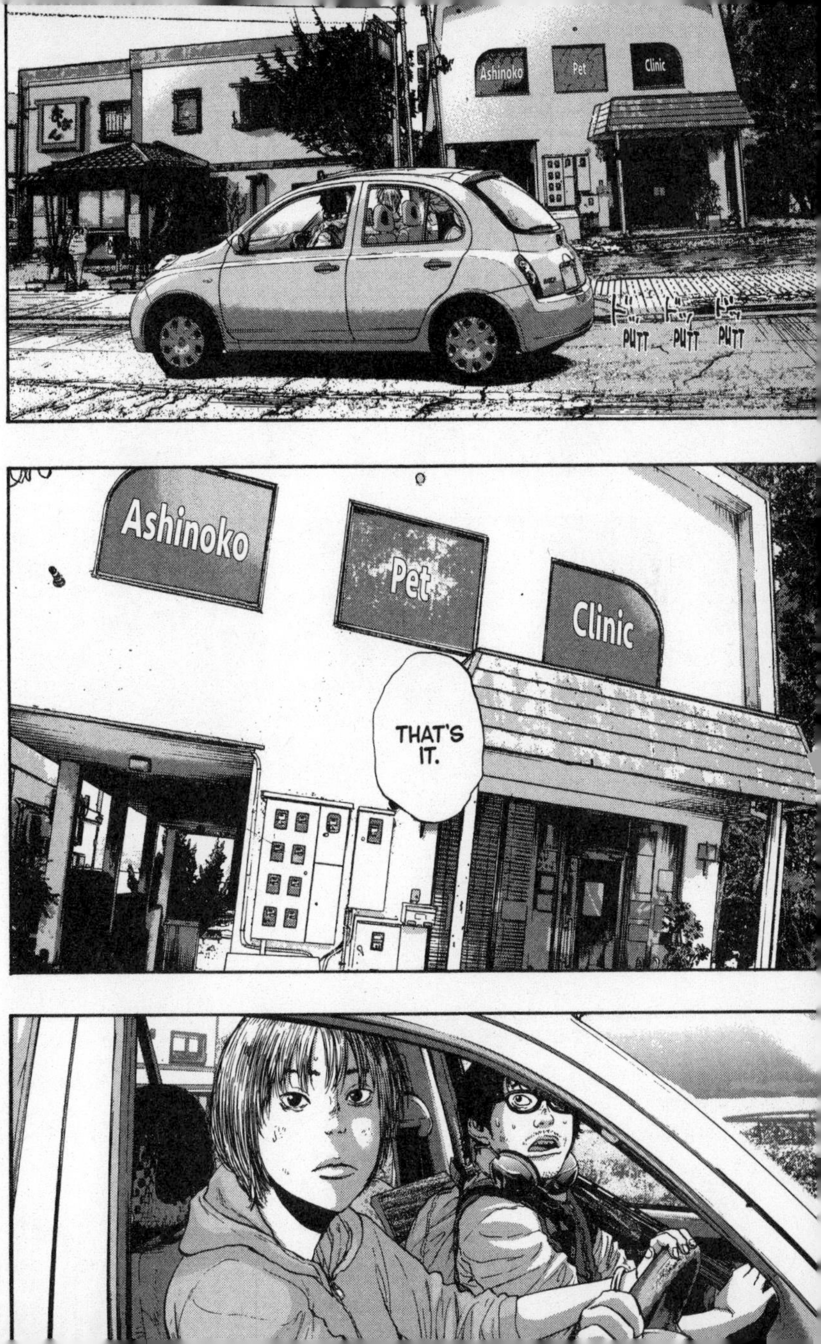
Ashinoko
Pet
Clinic
ドッ ドッ ドッ
PUTT PUTT PUTT
Ashinoko
Pet
Clinic
THAT'S IT.

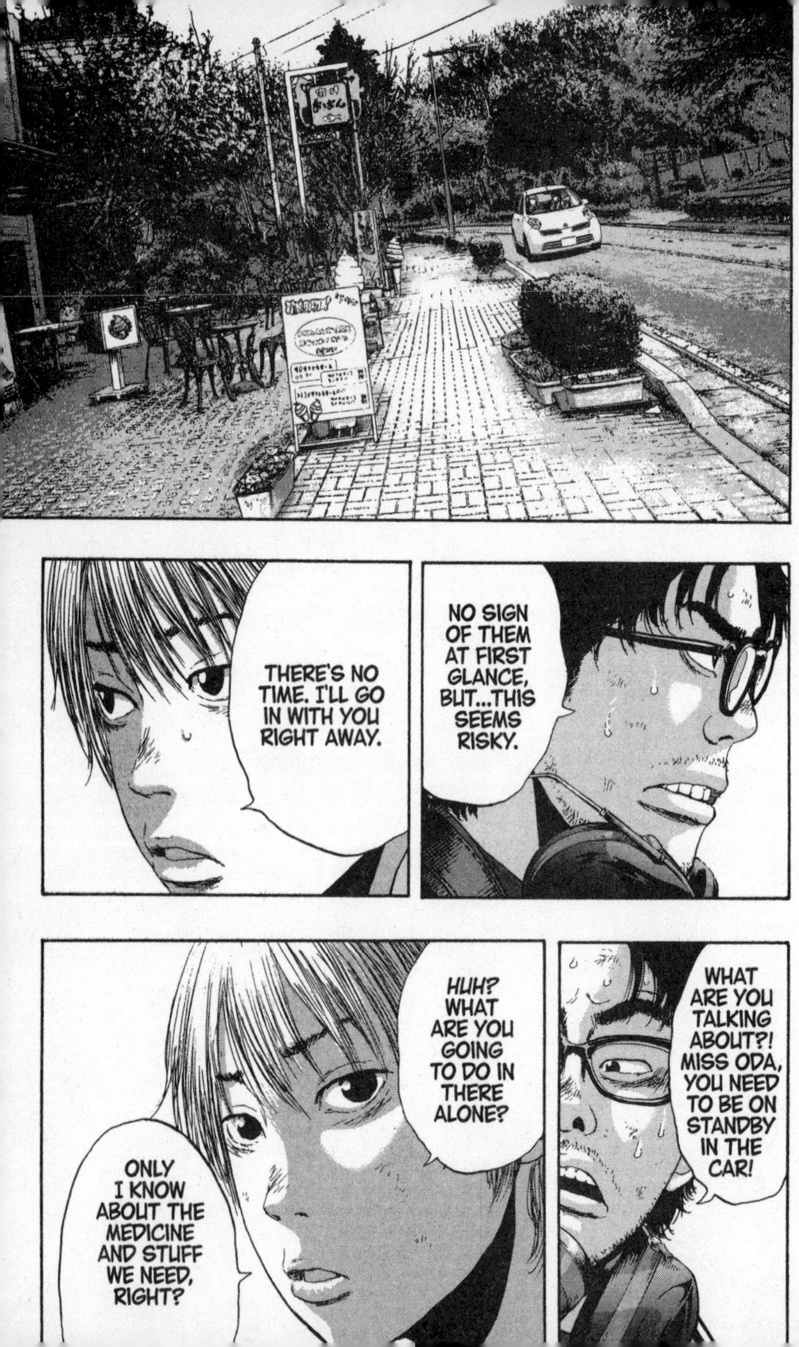

NO SIGN OF THEM AT FIRST GLANCE, BUT...THIS SEEMS RISKY.
THERE'S NO TIME. I'LL GO IN WITH YOU RIGHT AWAY.
WHAT ARE YOU TALKING ABOUT?! MISS ODA, YOU NEED TO BE ON STANDBY IN THE CAR!
HUH? WHAT ARE YOU GOING TO DO IN THERE ALONE?
ONLY I KNOW ABOUT THE MEDICINE AND STUFF WE NEED, RIGHT?

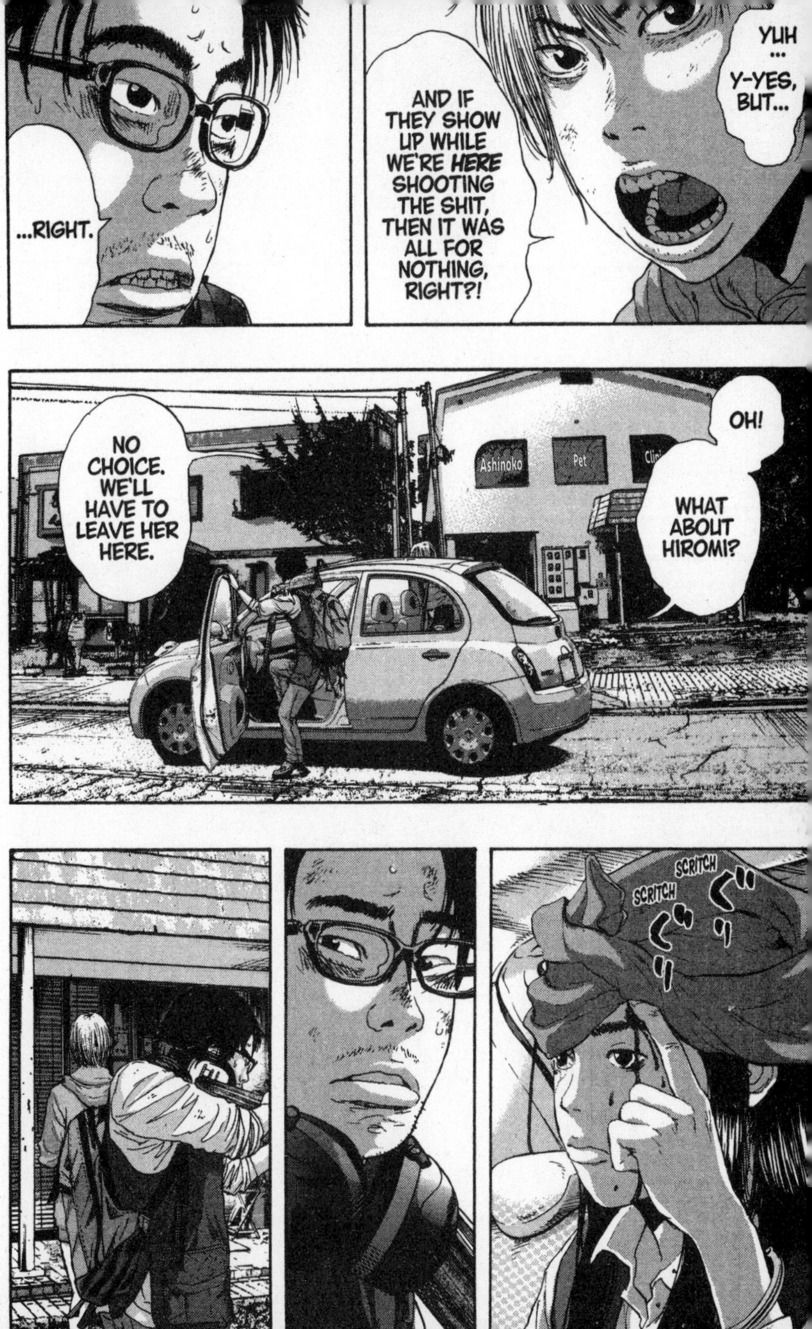
YUH ... Y-YES, BUT...
AND IF THEY SHOW UP WHILE WE'RE *HERE* SHOOTING THE SHIT, THEN IT WAS ALL FOR NOTHING, RIGHT?!
...RIGHT.
OH!
WHAT ABOUT HIROMI?
Ashinoko
Pet
NO CHOICE. WE'LL HAVE TO LEAVE HER HERE.
SCRITCH
SCRITCH

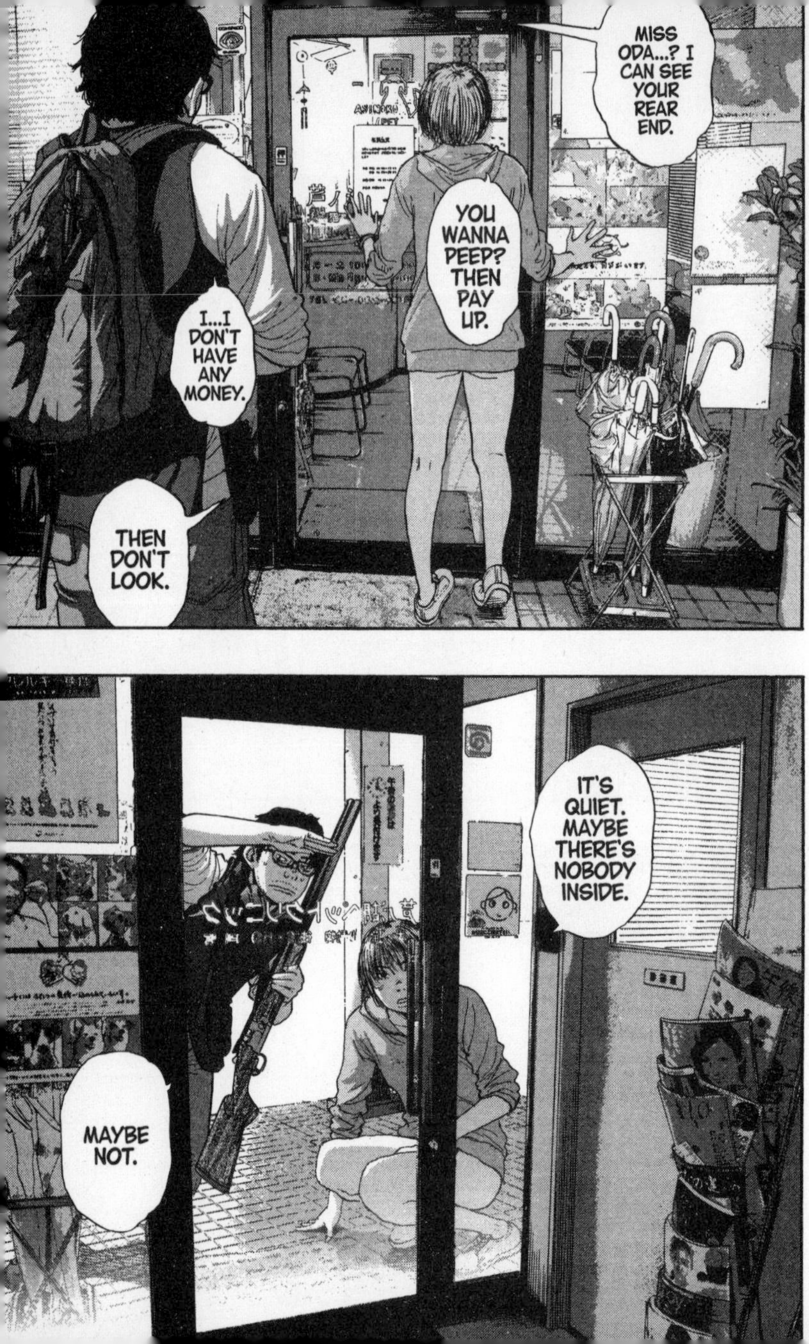
MISS ODA...? I CAN SEE YOUR REAR END.
YOU WANNA PEEP? THEN PAY UP.
I...I DON'T HAVE ANY MONEY.
THEN DON'T LOOK.
IT'S QUIET. MAYBE THERE'S NOBODY INSIDE.
MAYBE NOT.

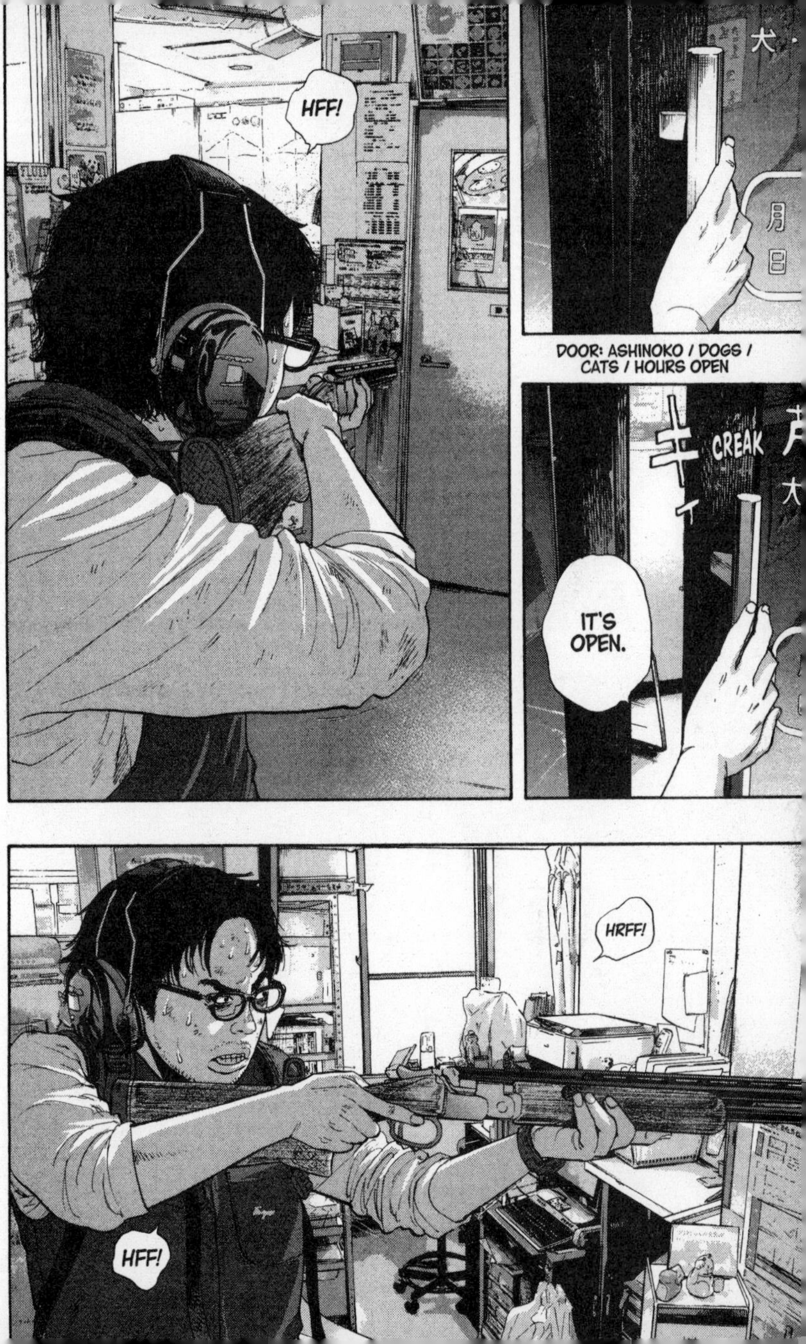
DOOR: ASHINOKO / DOGS / CATS / HOURS OPEN
CREAK
IT'S OPEN.
HFF!
HRFF!
HFF!

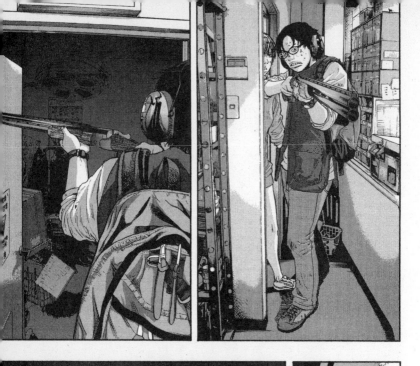

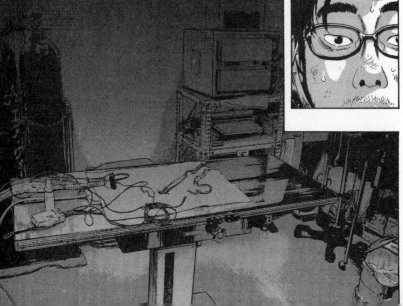

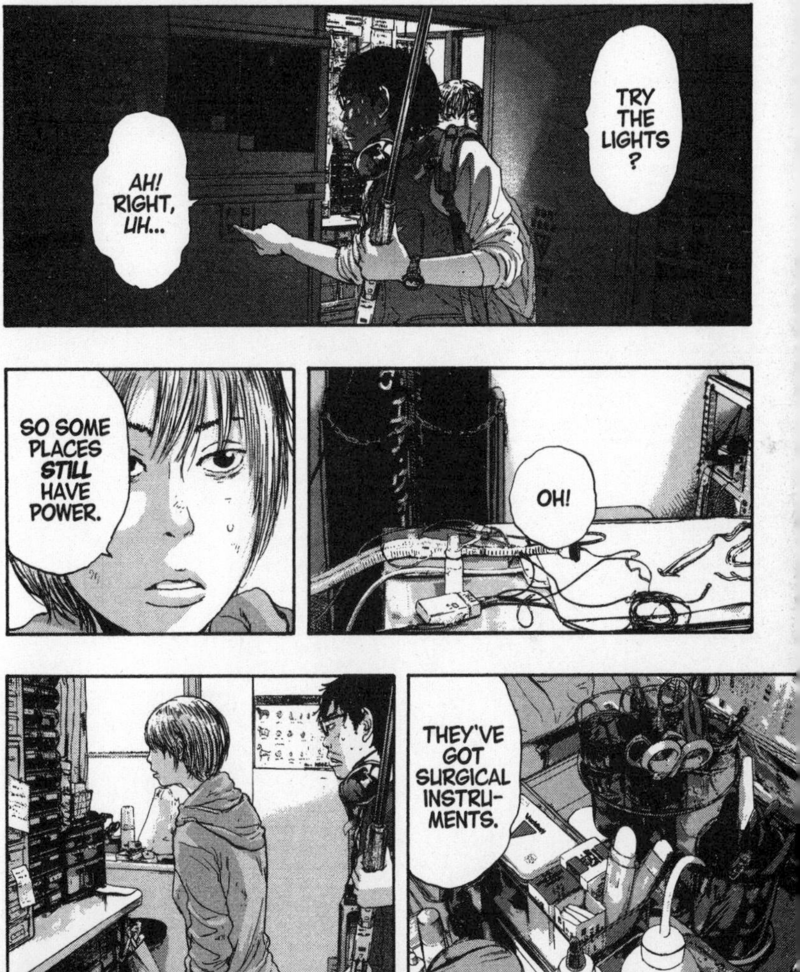
TRY THE LIGHTS?
AH! RIGHT, UH...
OH!
SO SOME PLACES STILL HAVE POWER.
THEY'VE GOT SURGICAL INSTRU-MENTS.

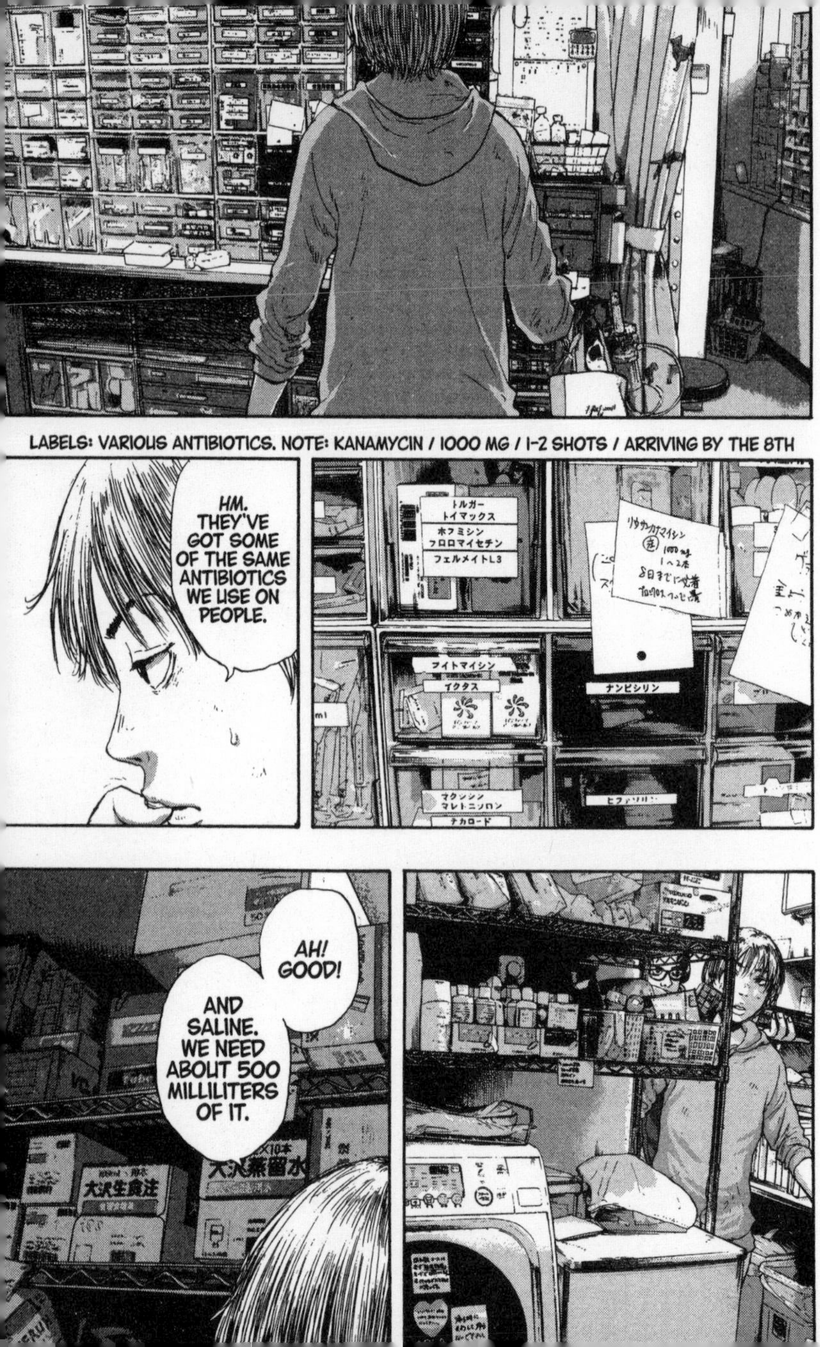
HM. THEY'VE GOT SOME OF THE SAME ANTIBIOTICS WE USE ON PEOPLE.
AH! GOOD!
AND SALINE. WE NEED ABOUT 500 MILLILITERS OF IT.
LABELS: VARIOUS ANTIBIOTICS. NOTE: KANAMYCIN / 1000 MG / 1-2 SHOTS / ARRIVING BY THE 8TH

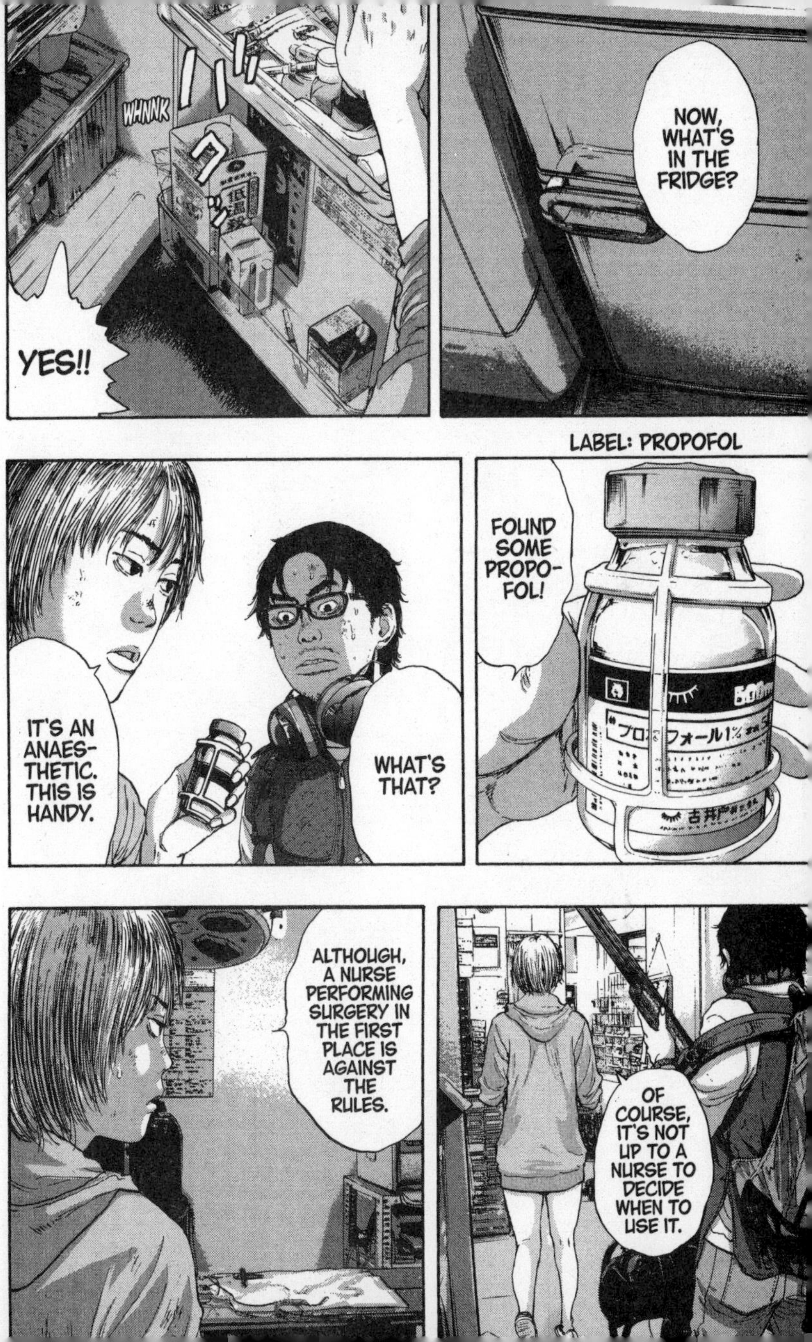
NOW, WHAT'S IN THE FRIDGE?
WHNNK
YES!!
LABEL: PROPOFOL
FOUND SOME PROPO-FOL!
WHAT'S THAT?
IT'S AN ANAES-THETIC. THIS IS HANDY.
OF COURSE, IT'S NOT UP TO A NURSE TO DECIDE WHEN TO USE IT.
ALTHOUGH, A NURSE PERFORMING SURGERY IN THE FIRST PLACE IS AGAINST THE RULES.

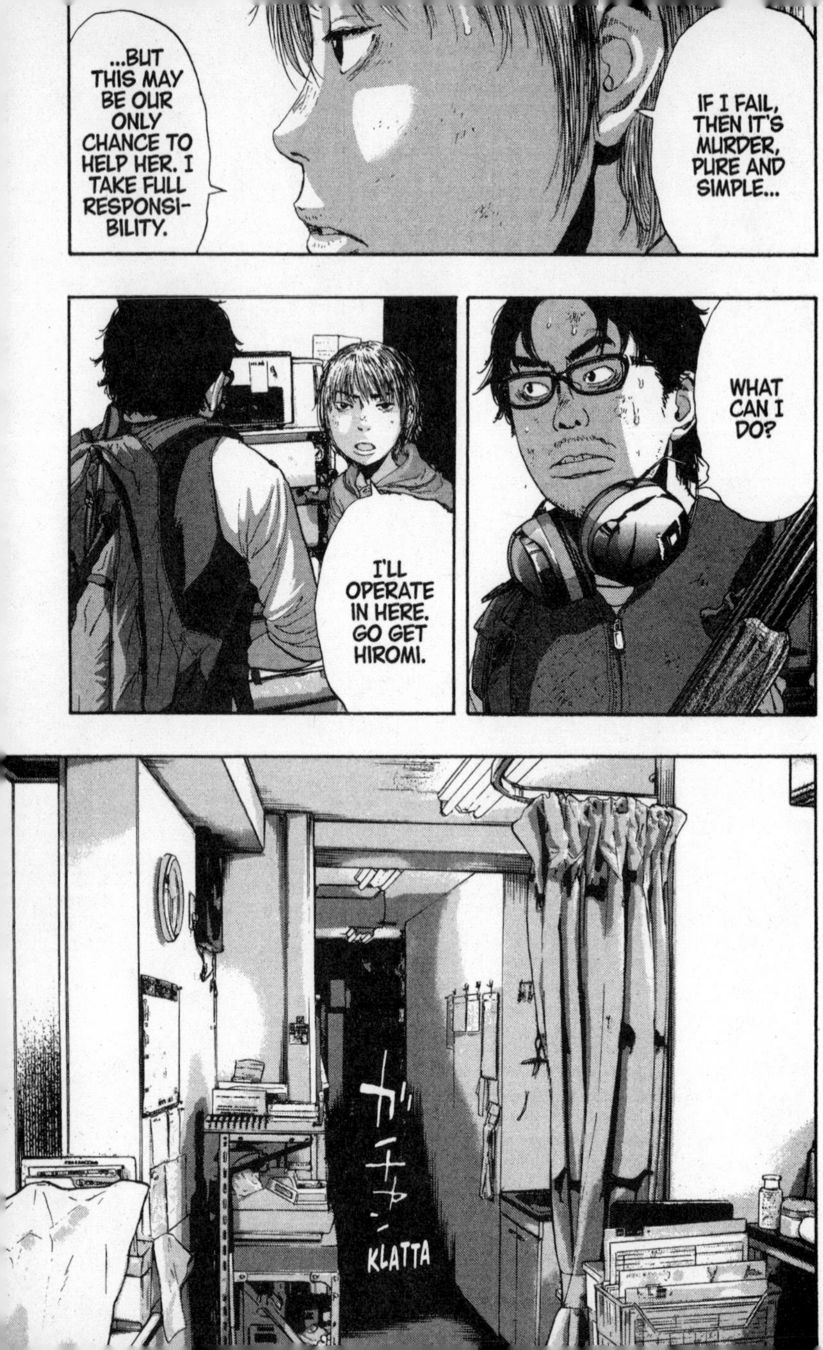
IF I FAIL, THEN IT'S MURDER, PURE AND SIMPLE...
...BUT THIS MAY BE OUR ONLY CHANCE TO HELP HER. I TAKE FULL RESPONSIBILITY.
WHAT CAN I DO?
I'LL OPERATE IN HERE. GO GET HIROMI.
KLATTA

SHHH!

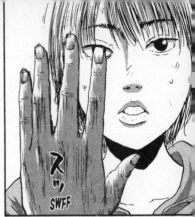

ス
ッ
SWFF

WHAT IS IT?

I HEARD... A SOUND. FROM A BACK ROOM...?

CHAPTER
110

MISS ODA, COULDN'T WE TAKE THE INSTRUMENTS YOU NEED AND RELOCATE SOMEWHERE ELSE?

IF I'M REALLY GOING TO OPERATE, THIS IS THE PLACE TO DO IT!

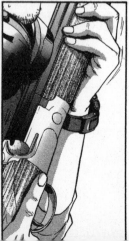

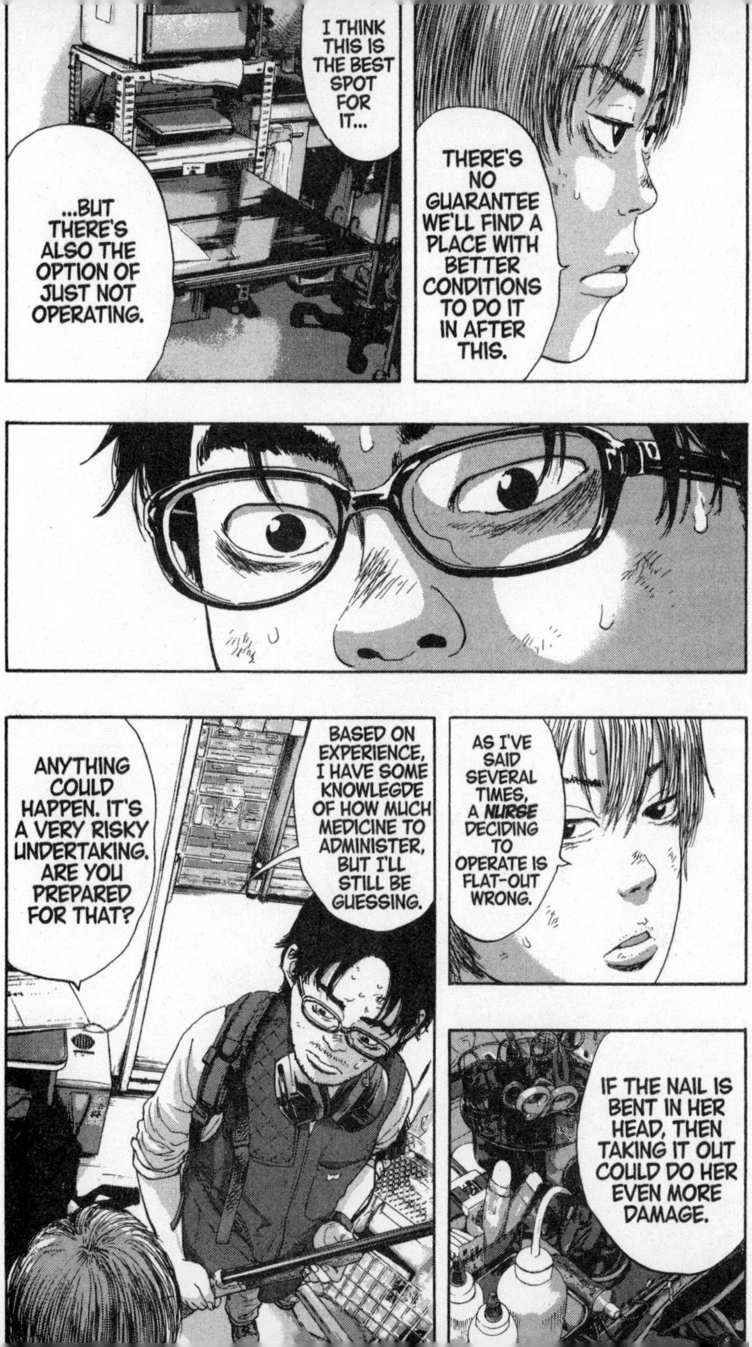
THERE'S NO GUARANTEE WE'LL FIND A PLACE WITH BETTER CONDITIONS TO DO IT IN AFTER THIS.
I THINK THIS IS THE BEST SPOT FOR IT...
...BUT THERE'S ALSO THE OPTION OF JUST NOT OPERATING.
AS I'VE SAID SEVERAL TIMES, A NURSE DECIDING TO OPERATE IS FLAT-OUT WRONG.
IF THE NAIL IS BENT IN HER HEAD, THEN TAKING IT OUT COULD DO HER EVEN MORE DAMAGE.
BASED ON EXPERIENCE, I HAVE SOME KNOWLEGDE OF HOW MUCH MEDICINE TO ADMINISTER, BUT I'LL STILL BE GUESSING.
ANYTHING COULD HAPPEN. IT'S A VERY RISKY UNDERTAKING. ARE YOU PREPARED FOR THAT?

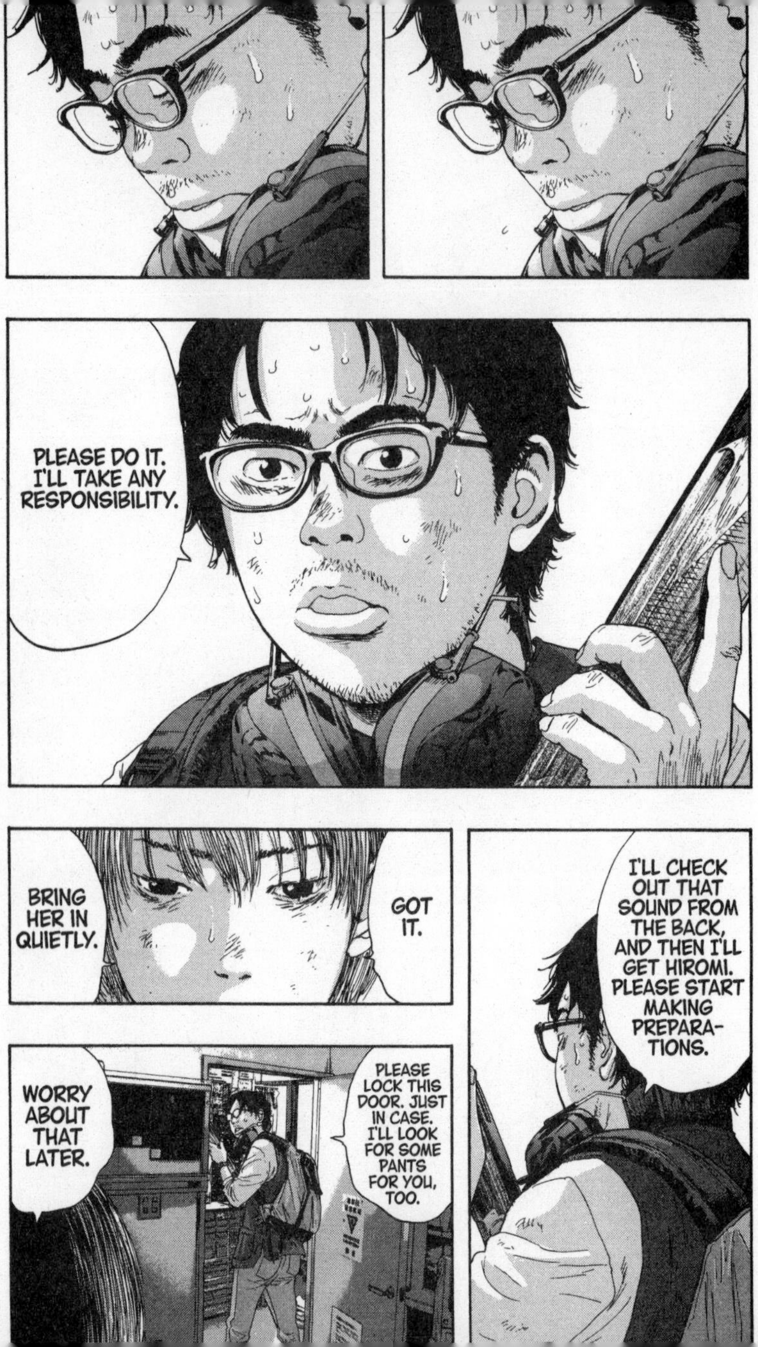
PLEASE DO IT. I'LL TAKE ANY RESPONSIBILITY.
I'LL CHECK OUT THAT SOUND FROM THE BACK, AND THEN I'LL GET HIROMI. PLEASE START MAKING PREPARA-TIONS.
GOT IT.
BRING HER IN QUIETLY.
PLEASE LOCK THIS DOOR. JUST IN CASE. I'LL LOOK FOR SOME PANTS FOR YOU, TOO.
WORRY ABOUT THAT LATER.

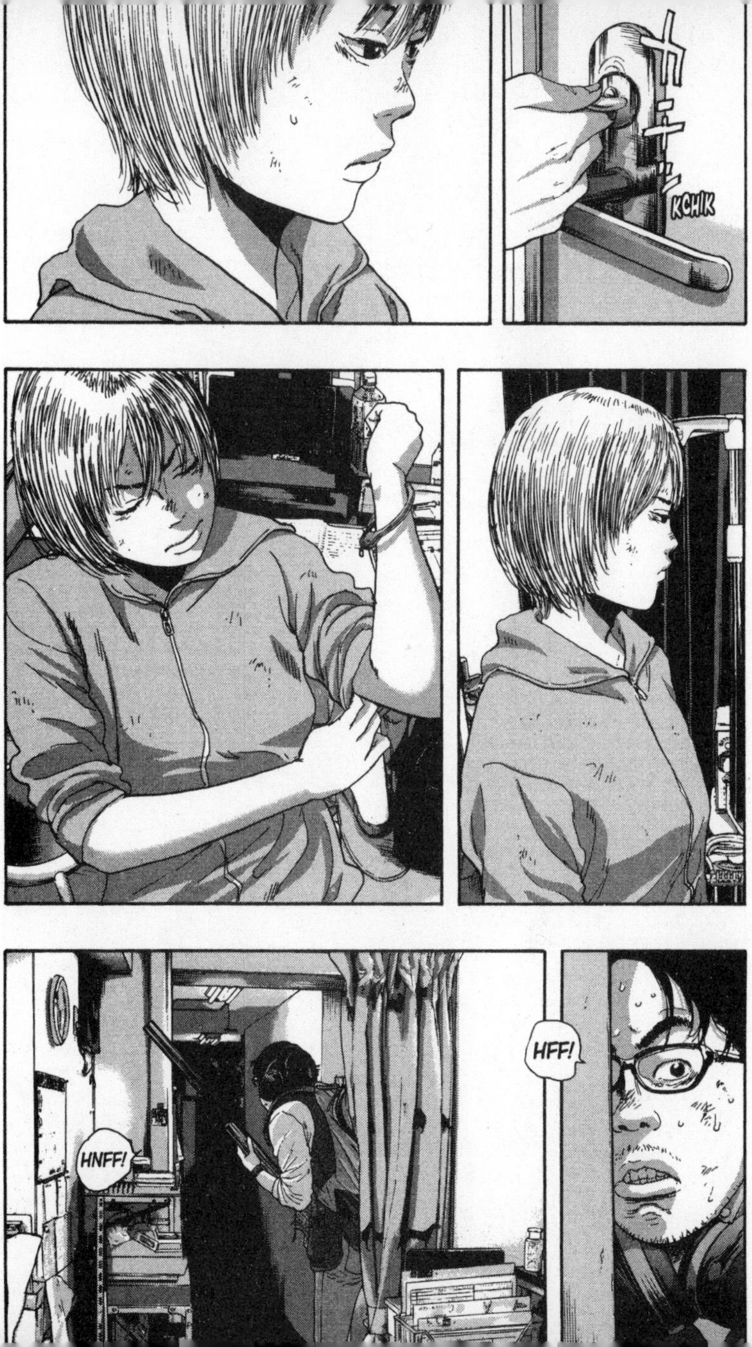
KCHIK
HFF!
HNFF!

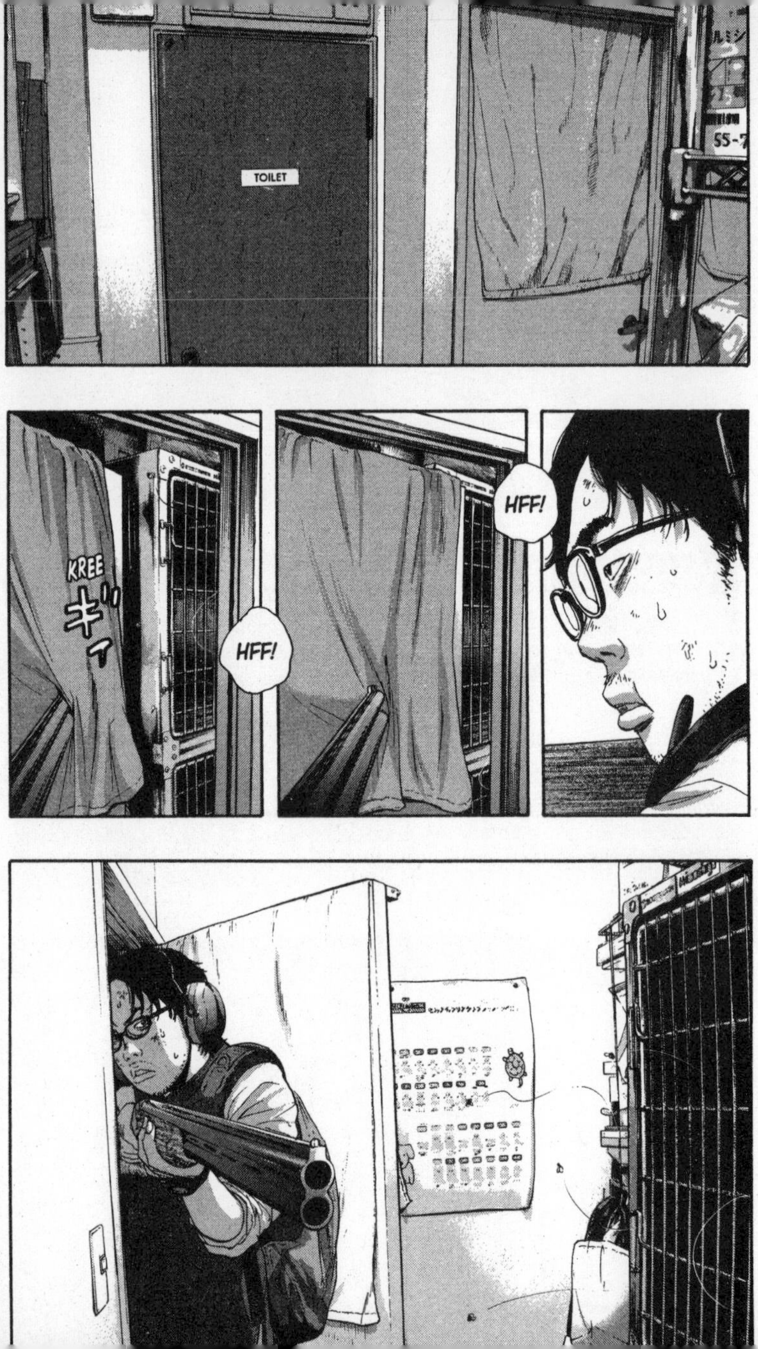
TOILET
HFF!
HFF!
KREE
キィ

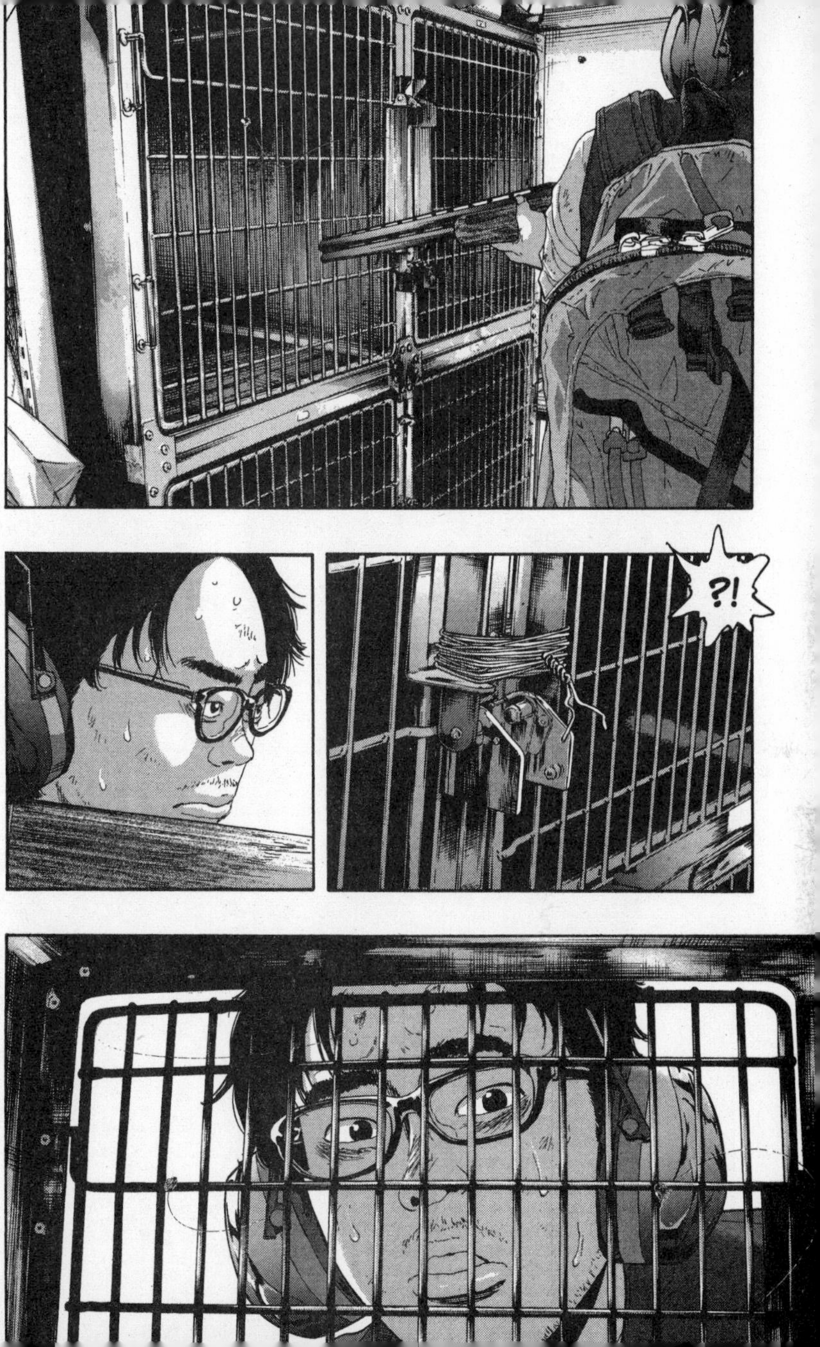
?!

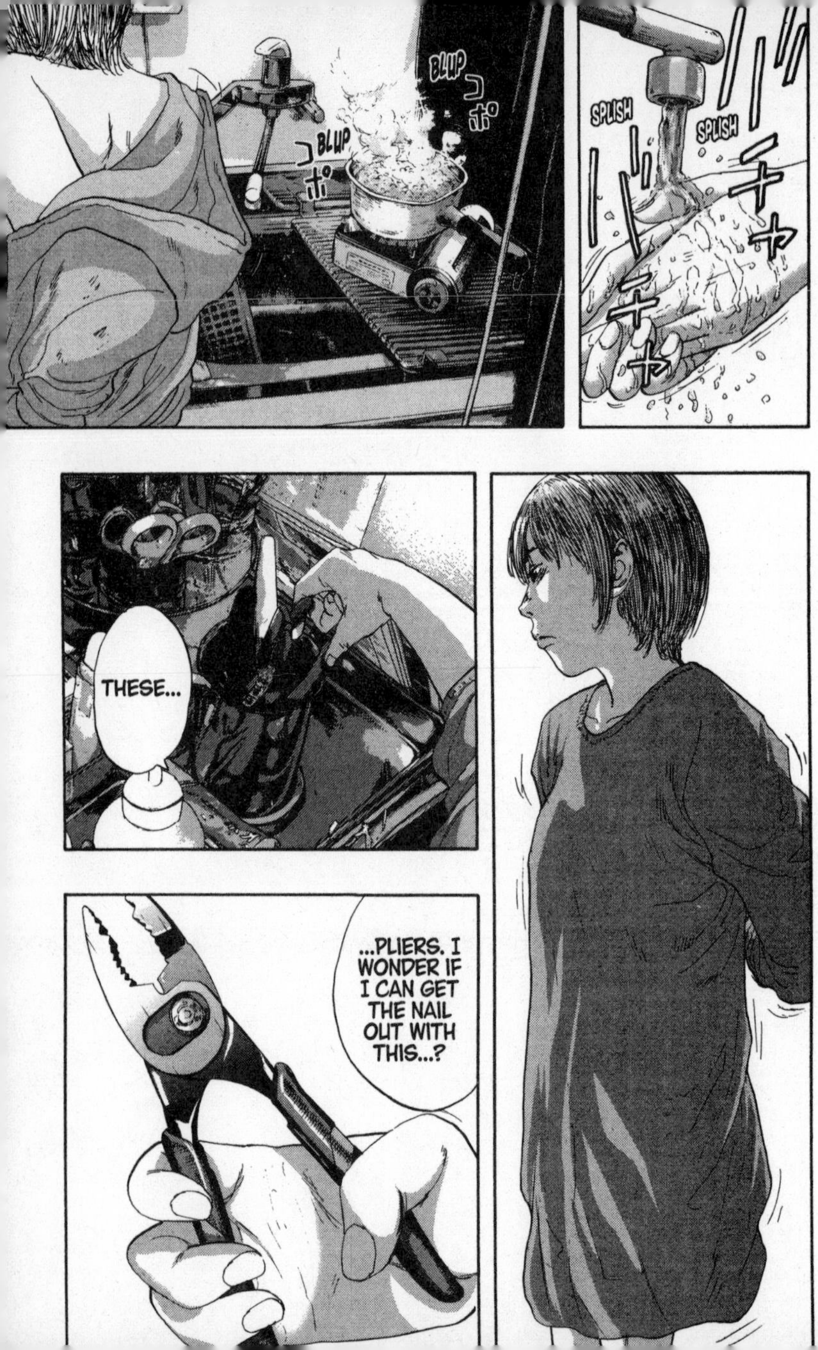
SPLISH
SPLISH
チャ
チャ
BLUP
コポ
BLUP
コポ
THESE...
...PLIERS. I WONDER IF I CAN GET THE NAIL OUT WITH THIS...?

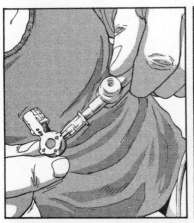

LABEL: PROPOFOL

LABEL: DEXTROSE / INTRAVENOUS INFUSION

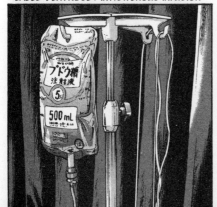

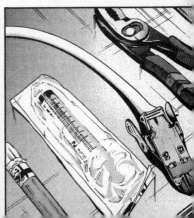

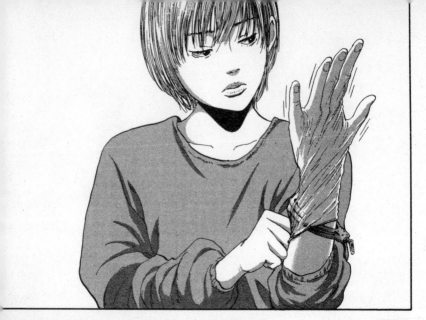

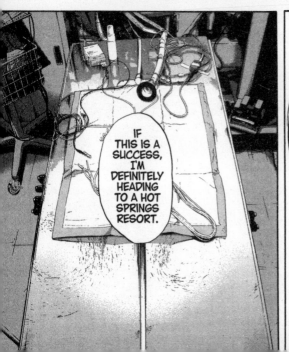

IF THIS IS A SUCCESS, I'M DEFINITELY HEADING TO A HOT SPRINGS RESORT.

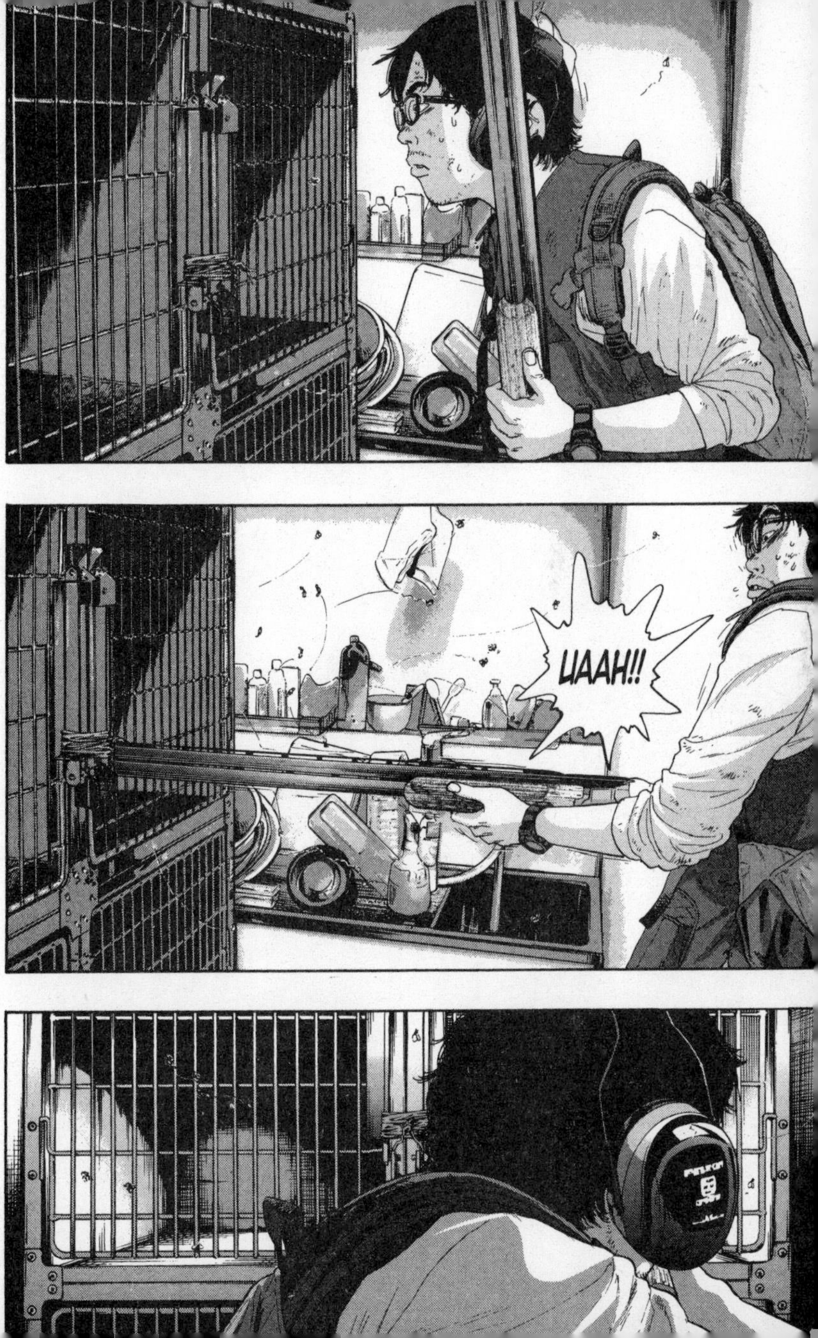
UAAH!!

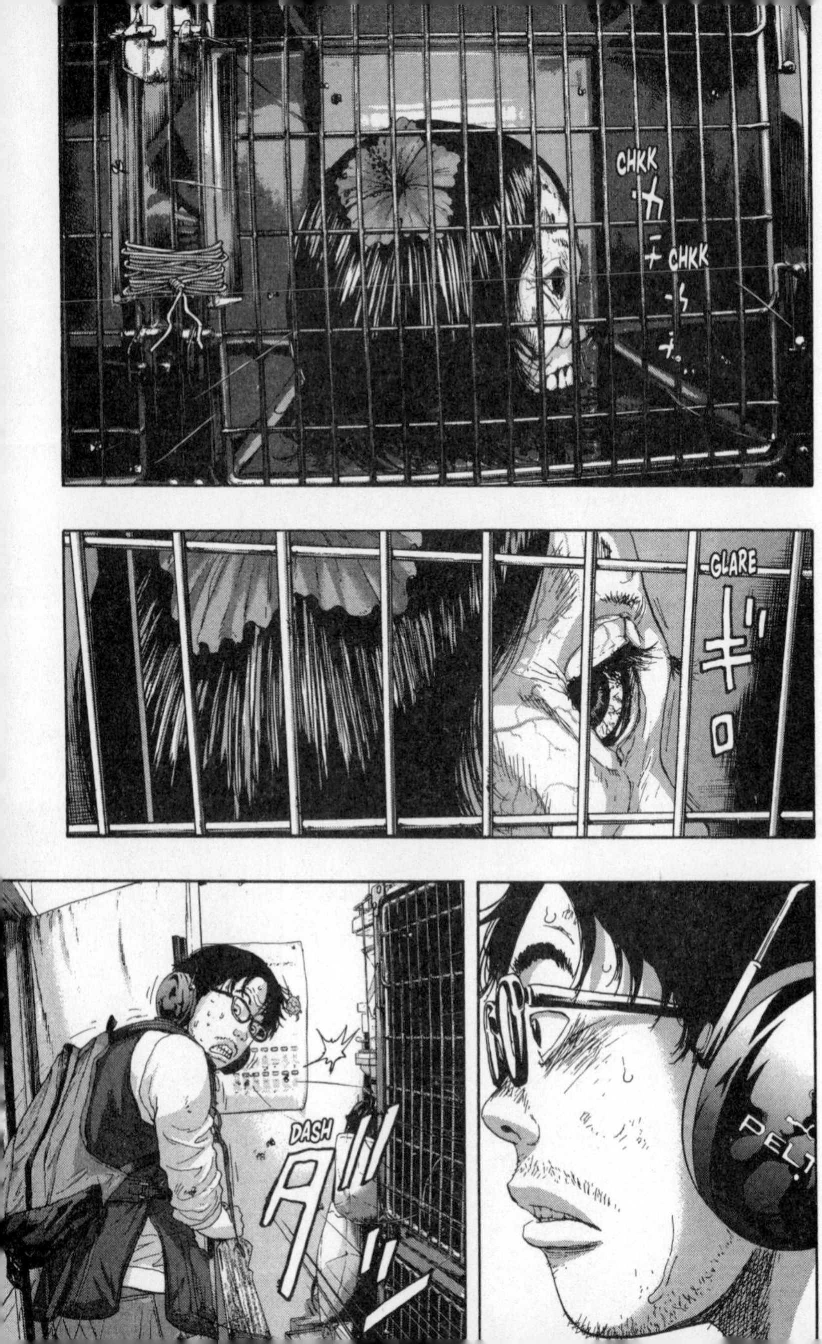
CHKK
CHKK
GLARE
ギロ
PELT
DASH
タッ

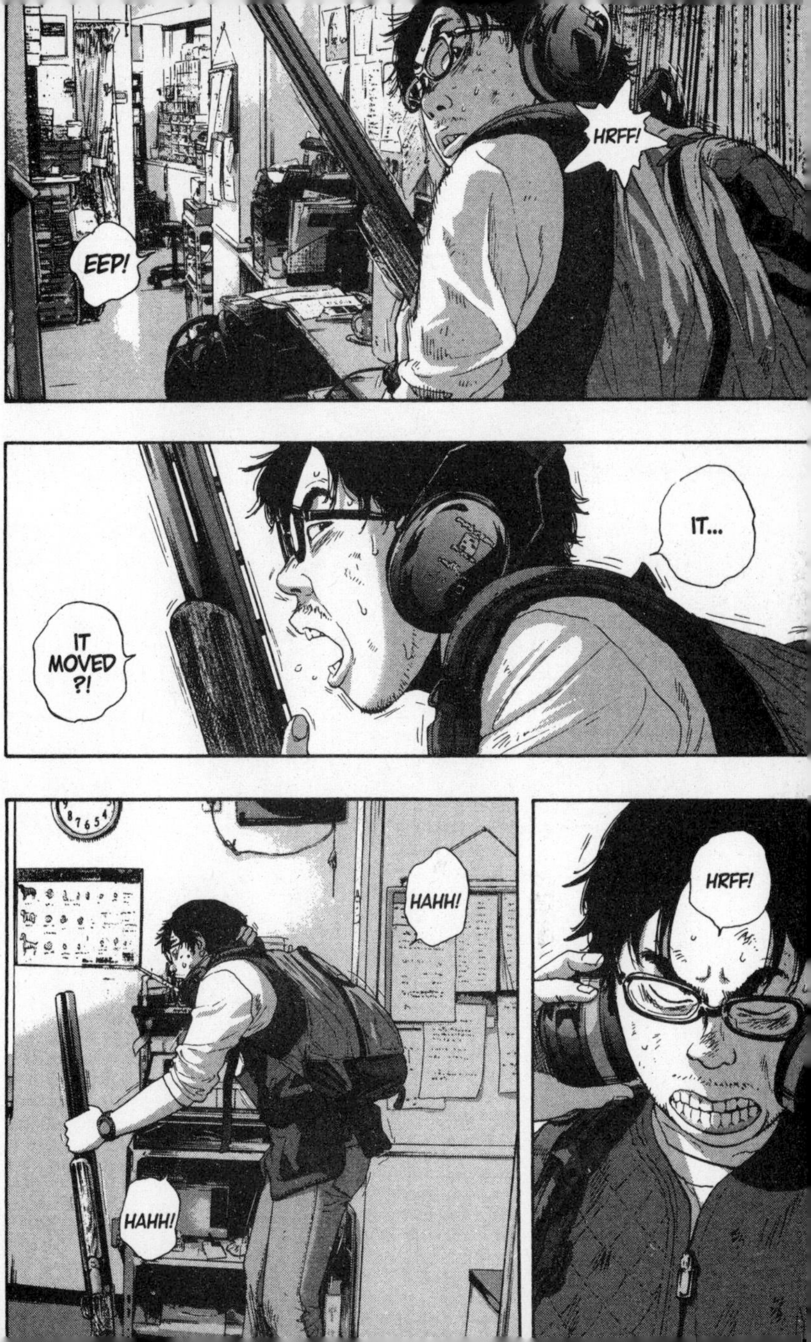
HRFF!
EEP!
IT...
IT MOVED ?!
HRFF!
HAHH!
HAHH!

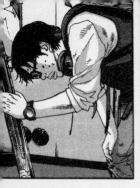

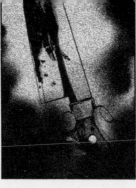

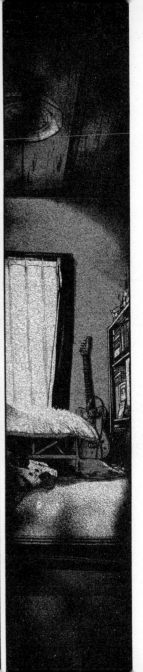

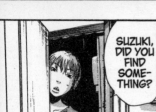

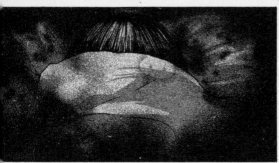

WHAT IF TEKKO IS--
SUZUKI, DID YOU FIND SOME-THING?
UH, YES. NO. WELL... THERE WAS A HEAD IN ONE OF THE PET CAGES...AND IT MOVED...

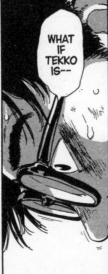

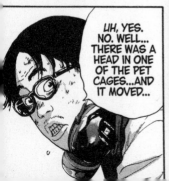

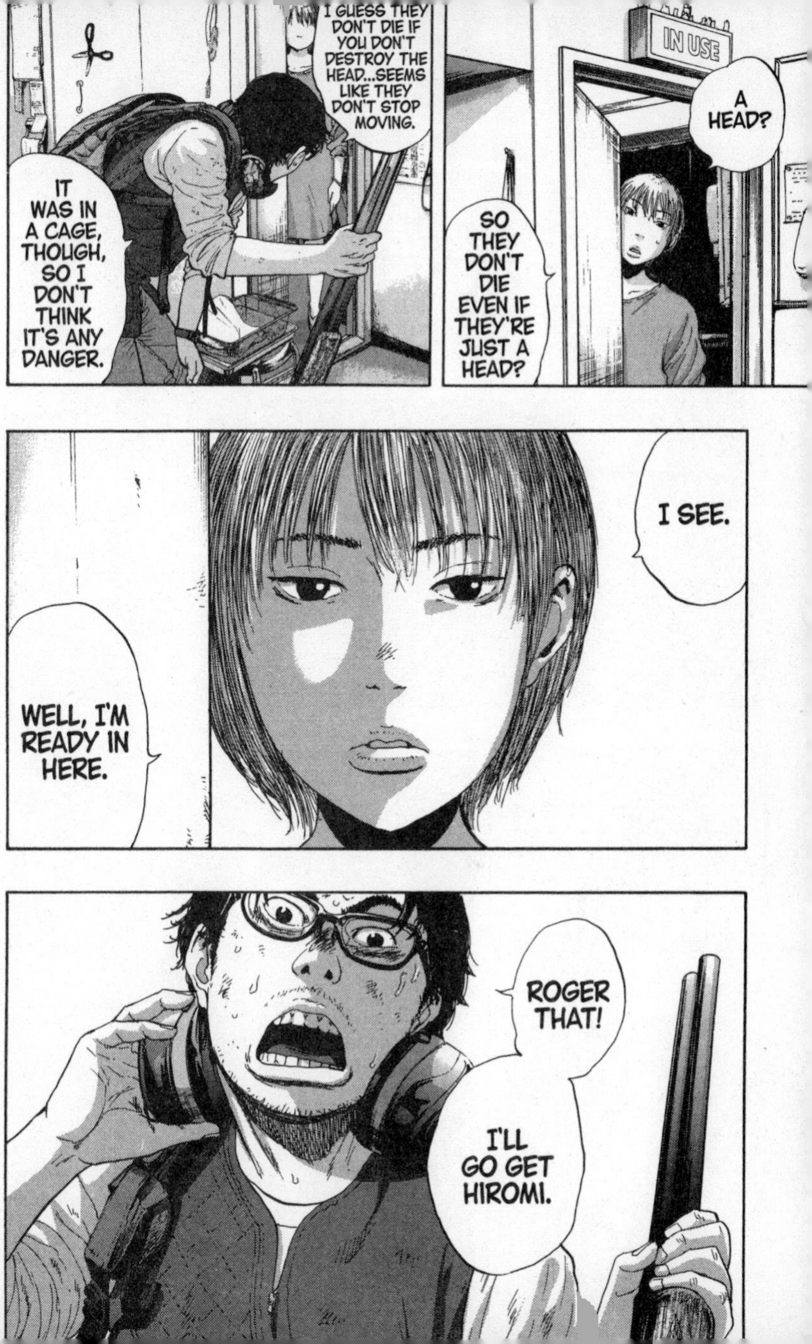
A HEAD?
SO THEY DON'T DIE EVEN IF THEY'RE JUST A HEAD?
I GUESS THEY DON'T DIE IF YOU DON'T DESTROY THE HEAD...SEEMS LIKE THEY DON'T STOP MOVING.
IT WAS IN A CAGE, THOUGH, SO I DON'T THINK IT'S ANY DANGER.
I SEE.
WELL, I'M READY IN HERE.
ROGER THAT!
I'LL GO GET HIROMI.

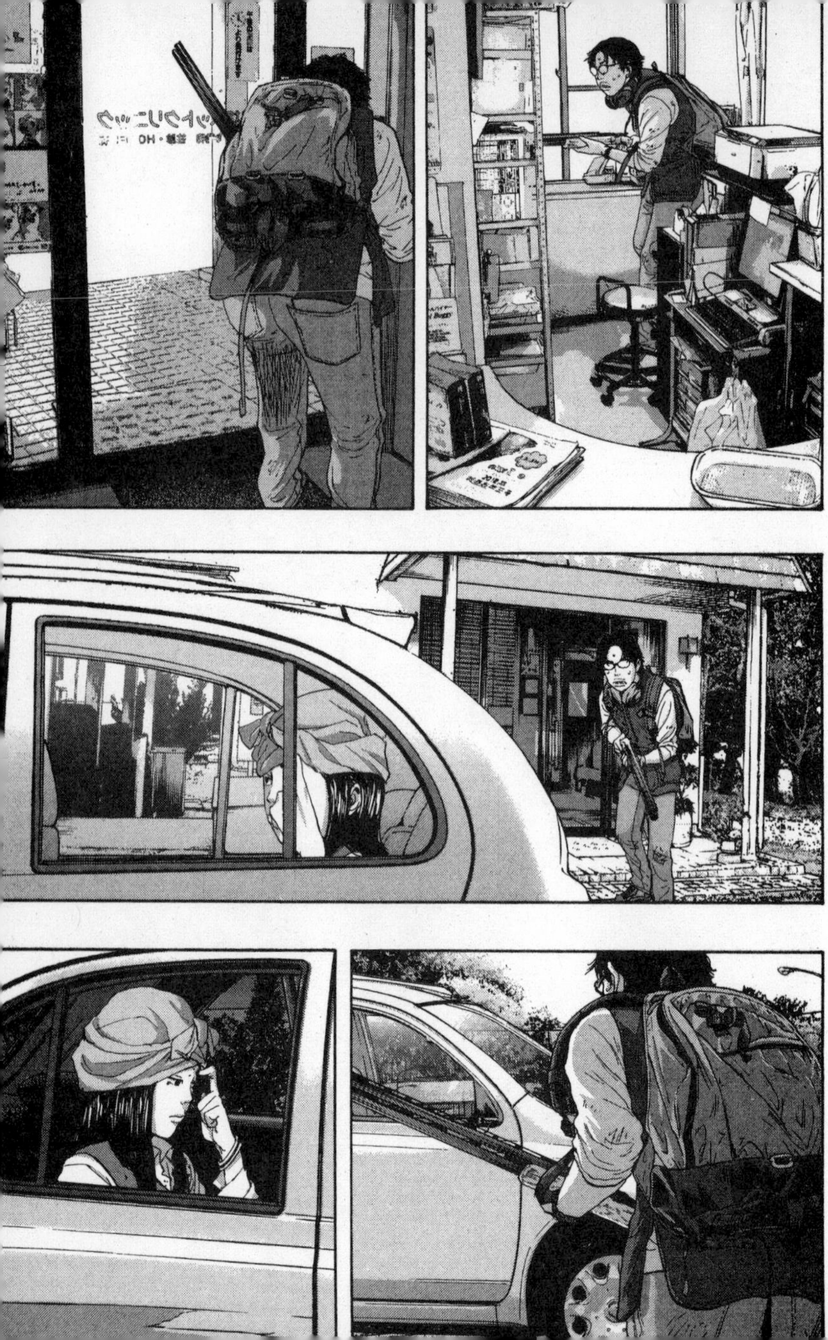

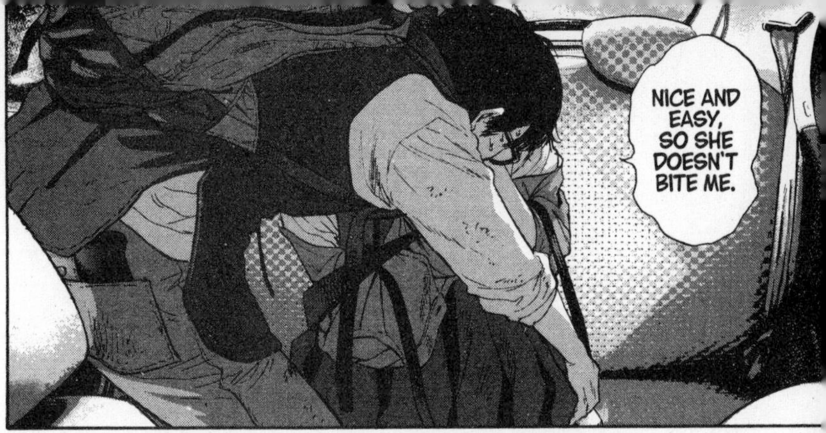
NICE AND EASY, SO SHE DOESN'T BITE ME.
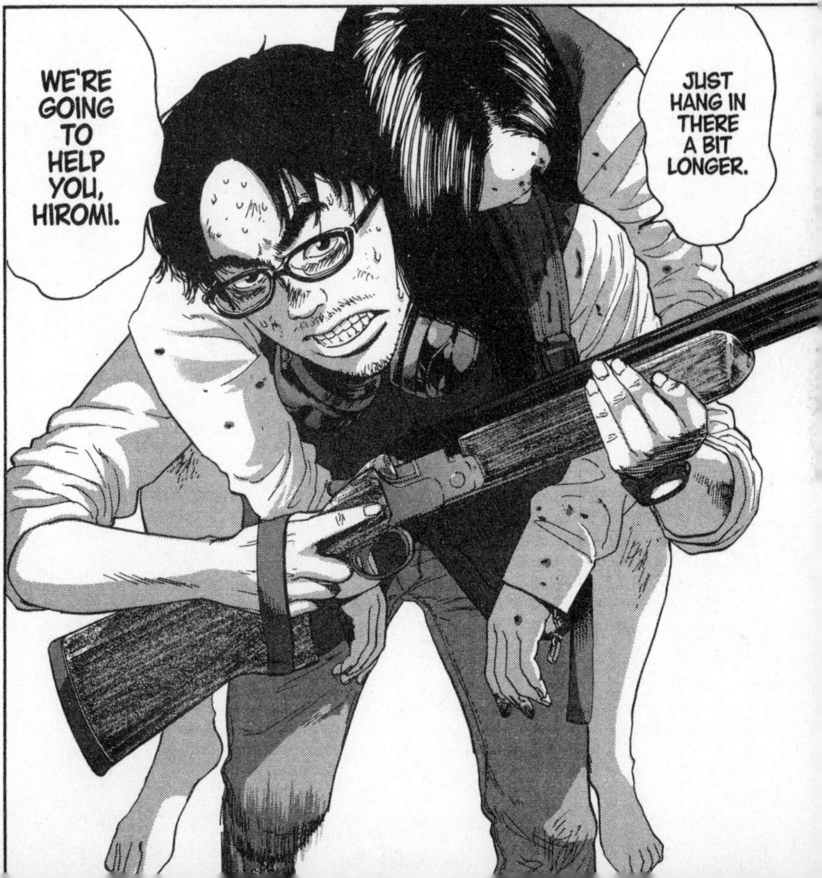
JUST HANG IN THERE A BIT LONGER.
WE'RE GOING TO HELP YOU, HIROMI.

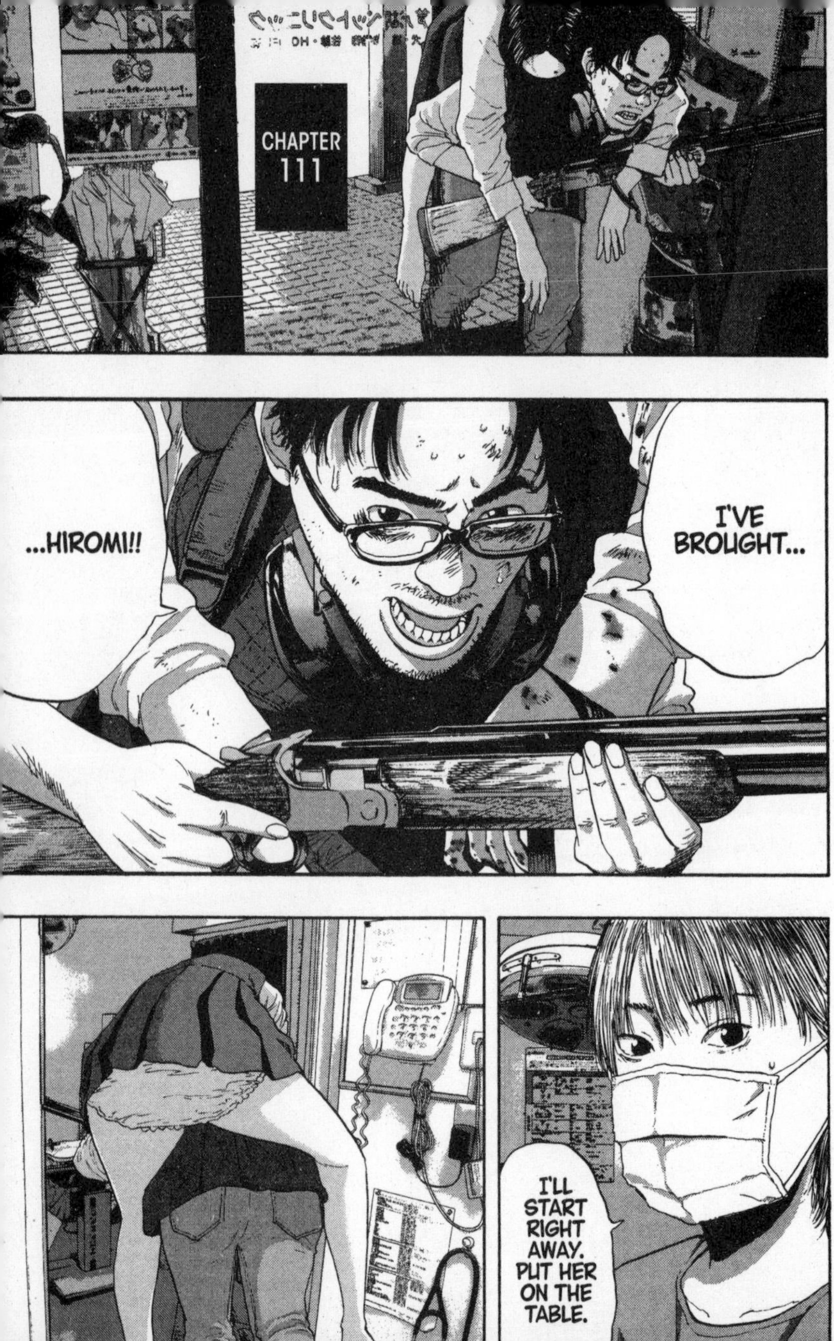
CHAPTER 111
I'VE BROUGHT...
...HIROMI!!
I'LL START RIGHT AWAY. PUT HER ON THE TABLE.

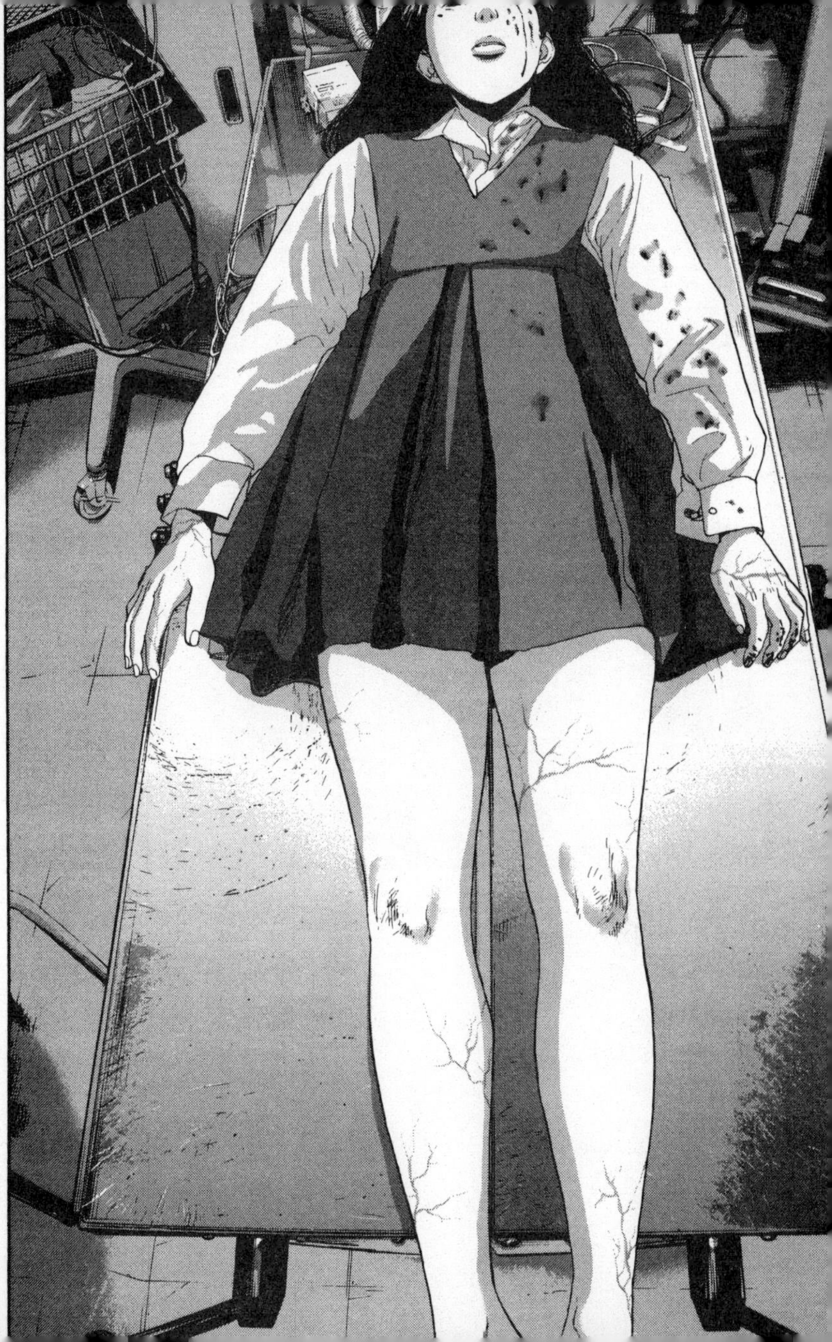

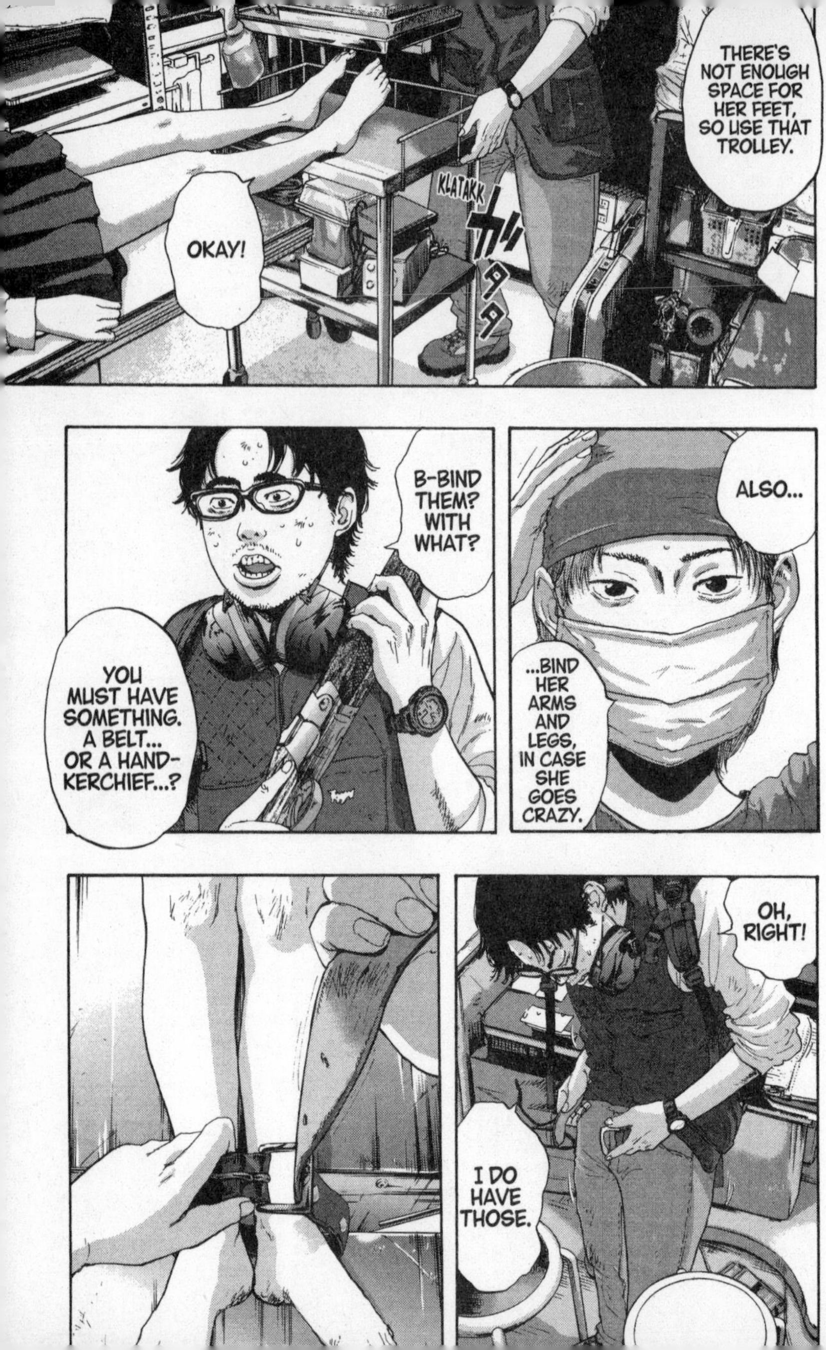
THERE'S NOT ENOUGH SPACE FOR HER FEET, SO USE THAT TROLLEY.
KLATAKK
OKAY!
ALSO...
...BIND HER ARMS AND LEGS, IN CASE SHE GOES CRAZY.
B-BIND THEM? WITH WHAT?
YOU MUST HAVE SOMETHING. A BELT... OR A HAND-KERCHIEF...?
OH, RIGHT!
I DO HAVE THOSE.

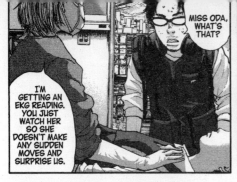

MISS ODA, WHAT'S THAT?
I'M GETTING AN EKG READING. YOU JUST WATCH HER SO SHE DOESN'T MAKE ANY SUDDEN MOVES AND SURPRISE US.
CAN DO!
I WAS A PRETTY BAD NURSE, BUT I WAS STRICTLY TAUGHT...
...NOT TO DO ANY PROCEDURES WITHOUT A DOCTOR'S INSTRUC-TIONS.

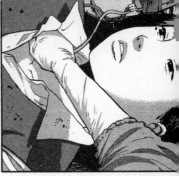

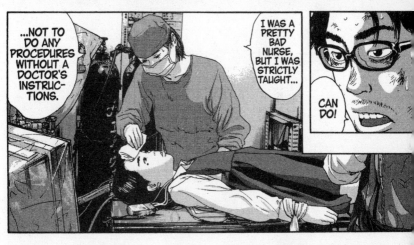

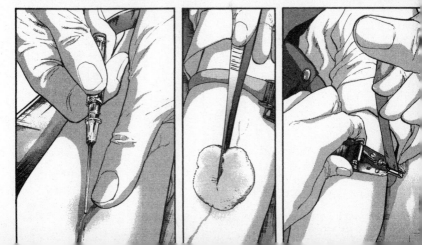

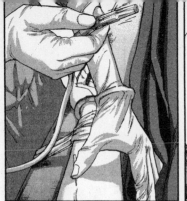

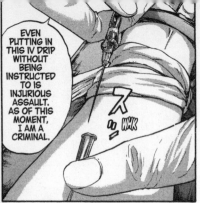

EVEN PUTTING IN THIS IV DRIP WITHOUT BEING INSTRUCTED TO IS INJURIOUS ASSAULT. AS OF THIS MOMENT, I AM A CRIMINAL.
WHK
TIKK
PLIP
PLIP
PROPOFOL'S ALL SET.
ブドウ糖
注射液
500 mL
THE ANAESTHETIC WILL BE EFFECTIVE FOR ABOUT THIRTY MINUTES.

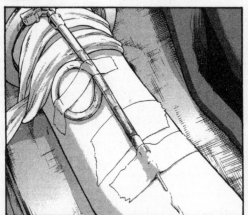

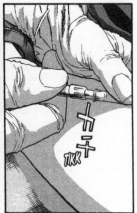

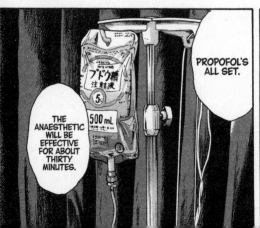

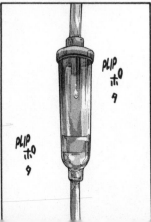

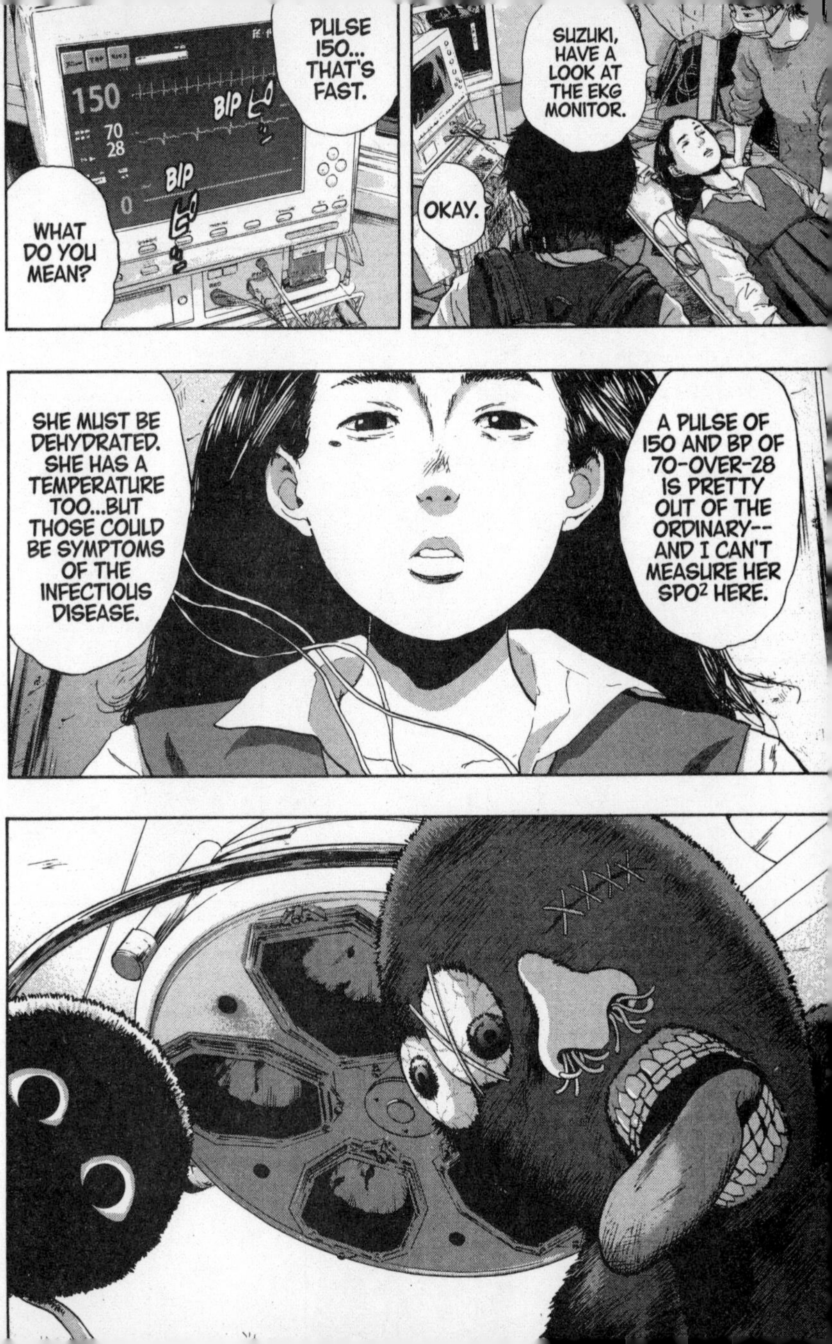
SUZUKI, HAVE A LOOK AT THE EKG MONITOR.
OKAY.
PULSE 150... THAT'S FAST.
150
70
28
0
BIP
BIP
WHAT DO YOU MEAN?
A PULSE OF 150 AND BP OF 70-OVER-28 IS PRETTY OUT OF THE ORDINARY-- AND I CAN'T MEASURE HER SPO2 HERE.
SHE MUST BE DEHYDRATED. SHE HAS A TEMPERATURE TOO...BUT THOSE COULD BE SYMPTOMS OF THE INFECTIOUS DISEASE.

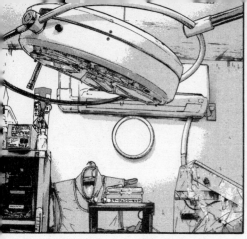

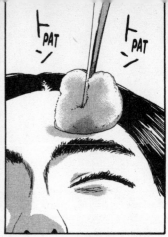

トン PAT   トン PAT

GOOD.

THE ANES-THETIC'S PROBABLY KICKED IN...

ぎゅうっ

SQUEEZE

PINCH

ぐいっ

I'LL DOUBLE CHECK, JUST IN CASE.

NOW I'LL BEGIN PRO-CEDURES TO REMOVE THE NAIL.

GOOD.

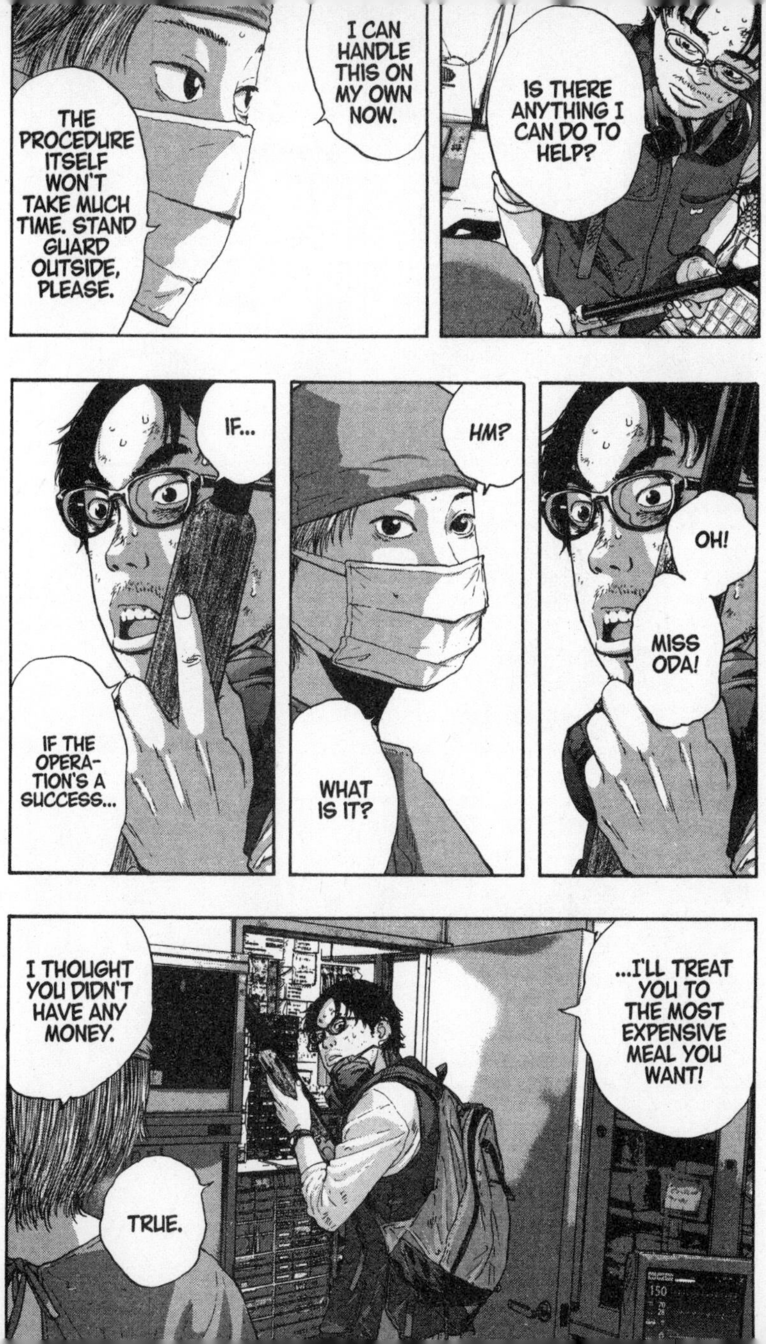
IS THERE ANYTHING I CAN DO TO HELP?
I CAN HANDLE THIS ON MY OWN NOW.
THE PROCEDURE ITSELF WON'T TAKE MUCH TIME. STAND GUARD OUTSIDE, PLEASE.
OH!
MISS ODA!
HM?
WHAT IS IT?
IF...
IF THE OPERA-TION'S A SUCCESS...
...I'LL TREAT YOU TO THE MOST EXPENSIVE MEAL YOU WANT!
I THOUGHT YOU DIDN'T HAVE ANY MONEY.
TRUE.

K-CHAK

BEST OF LUCK TO BOTH OF YOU.

GOOD. THE ISODINE...

...HAS DRIED.

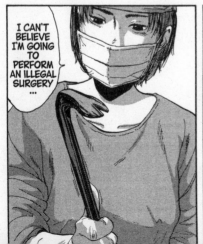

I CAN'T BELIEVE I'M GOING TO PERFORM AN ILLEGAL SURGERY...

HFOO!

KTAK

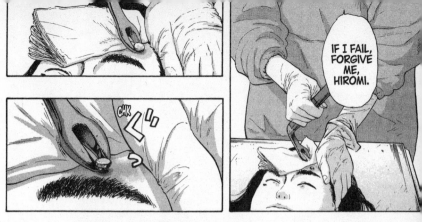

IF I FAIL, FORGIVE ME, HIROMI.

CHK ピ

CHK ピ

CHK ピ

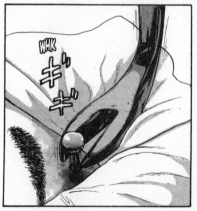

WHK ギ ギ

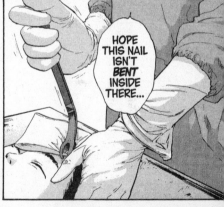

HOPE THIS NAIL ISN'T *BENT* INSIDE THERE...

WHK ギ

WHK ギ

WHK ギ

WHK ギ

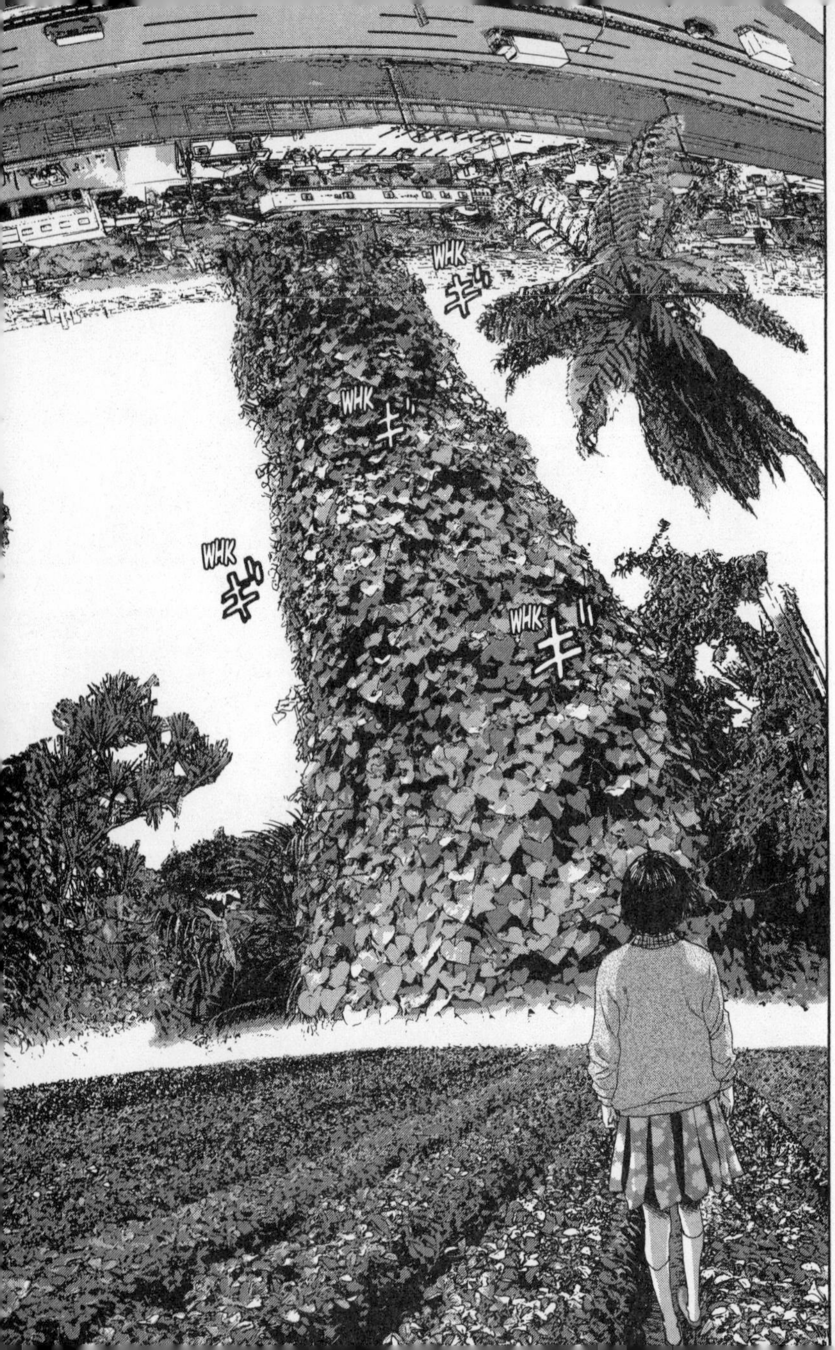
WHK
WHK
WHK
WHK

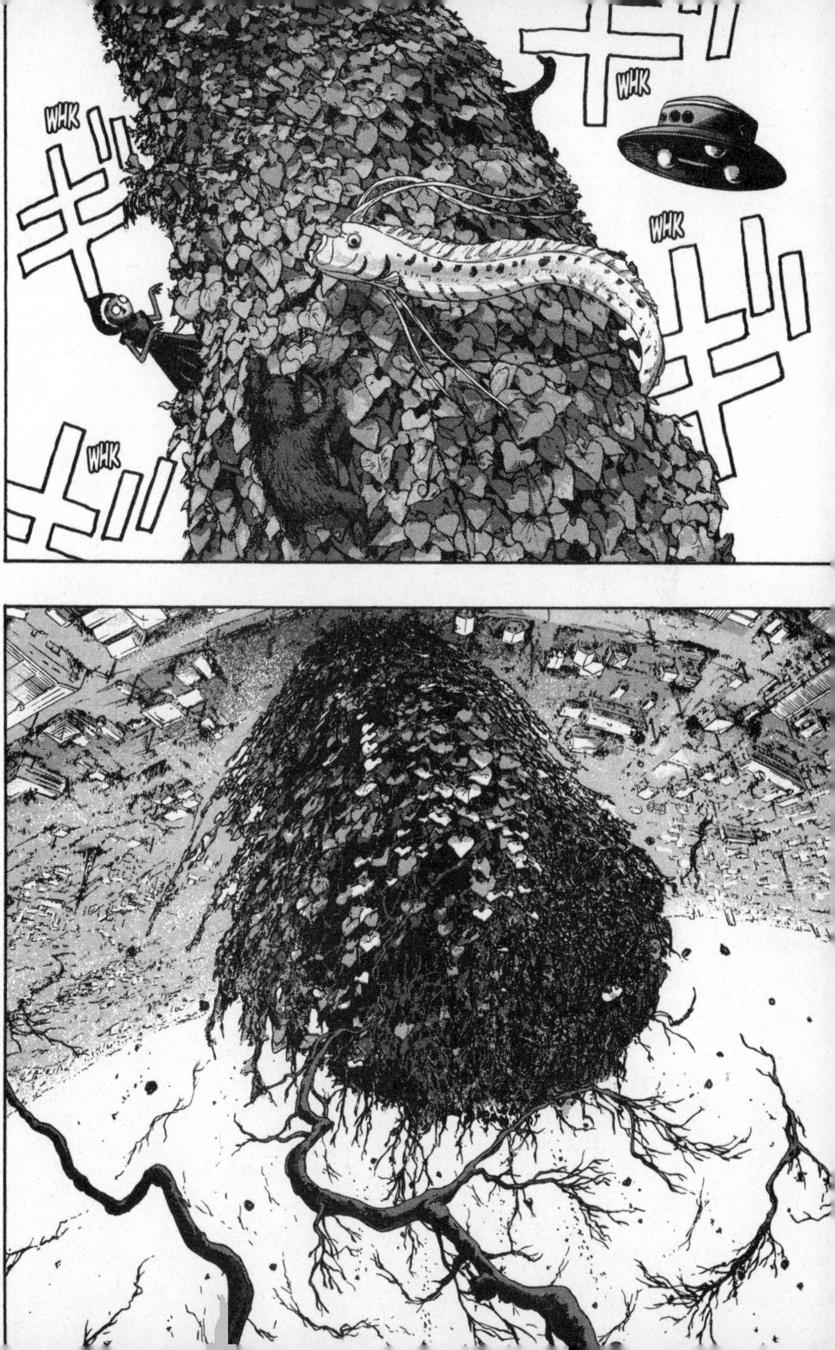
WHK
WHK
WHK
WHK

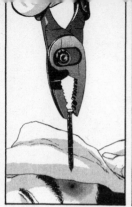

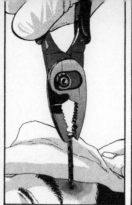

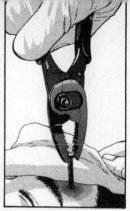

HFF!

HFF!

FOO!

GOT
IT
OUT.

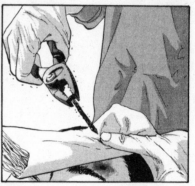

TIKK

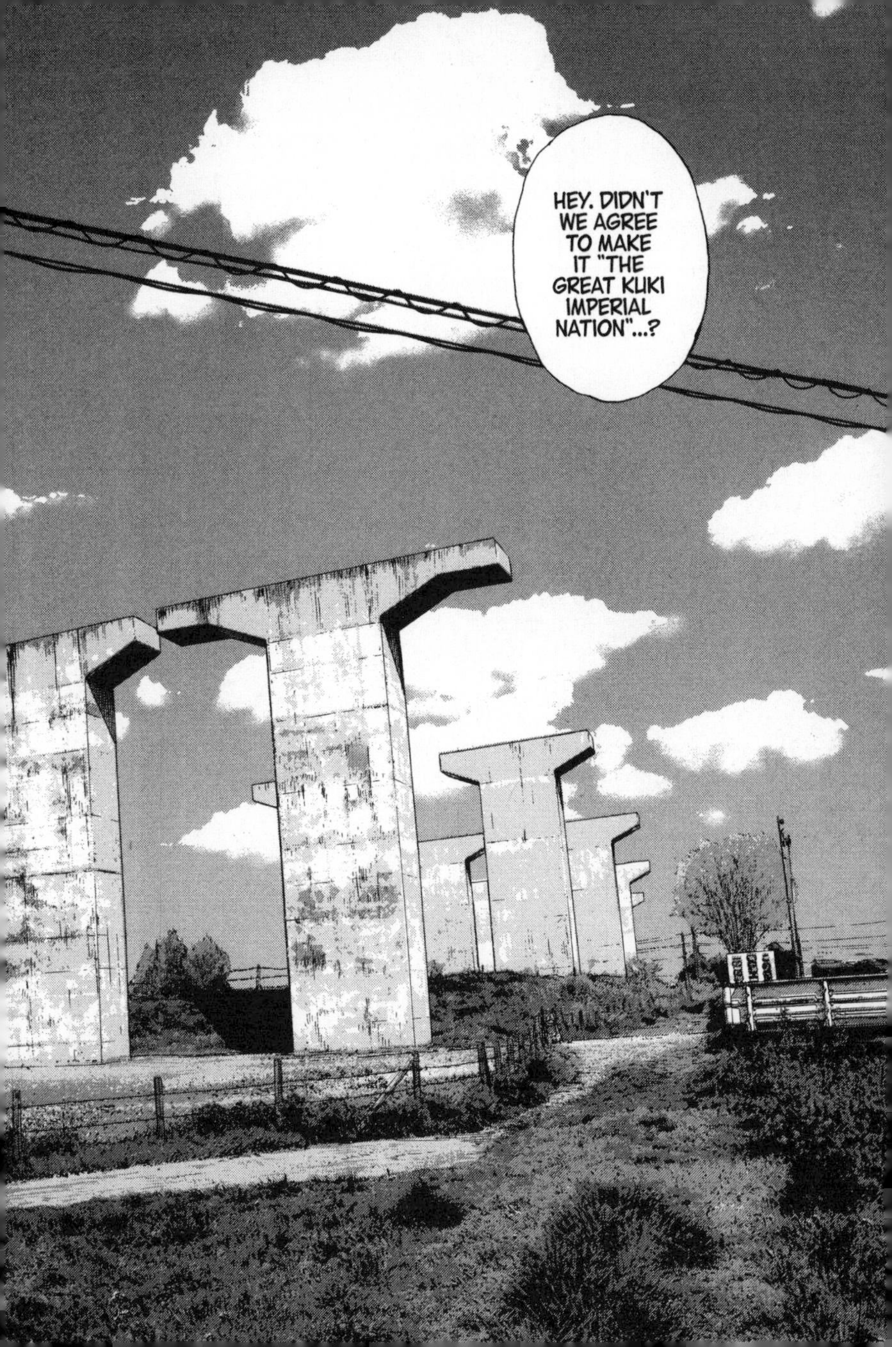
HEY. DIDN'T WE AGREE TO MAKE IT "THE GREAT KUKI IMPERIAL NATION"...?

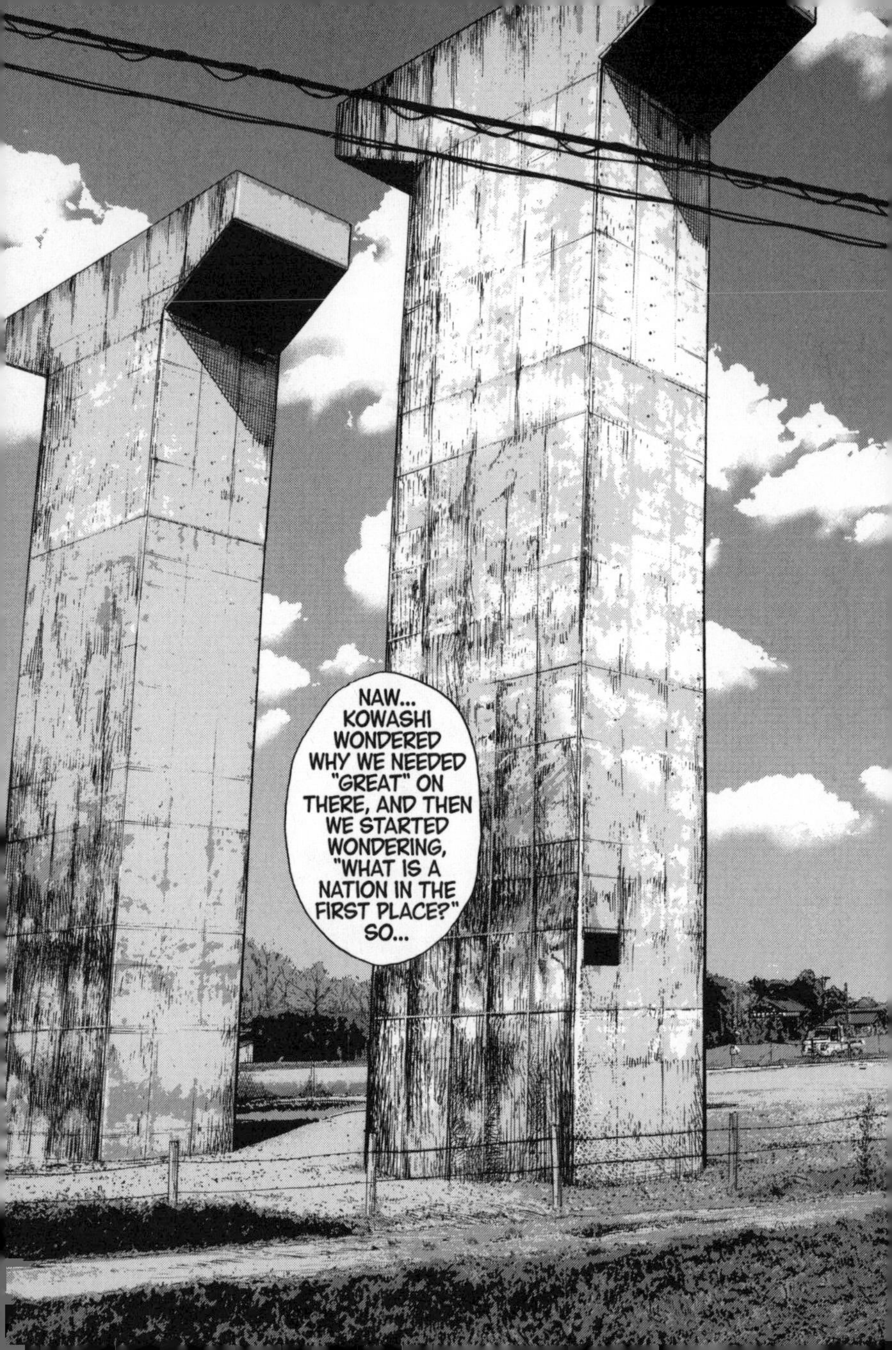
NAW... KOWASHI WONDERED WHY WE NEEDED "GREAT" ON THERE, AND THEN WE STARTED WONDERING, "WHAT IS A NATION IN THE FIRST PLACE?" SO...

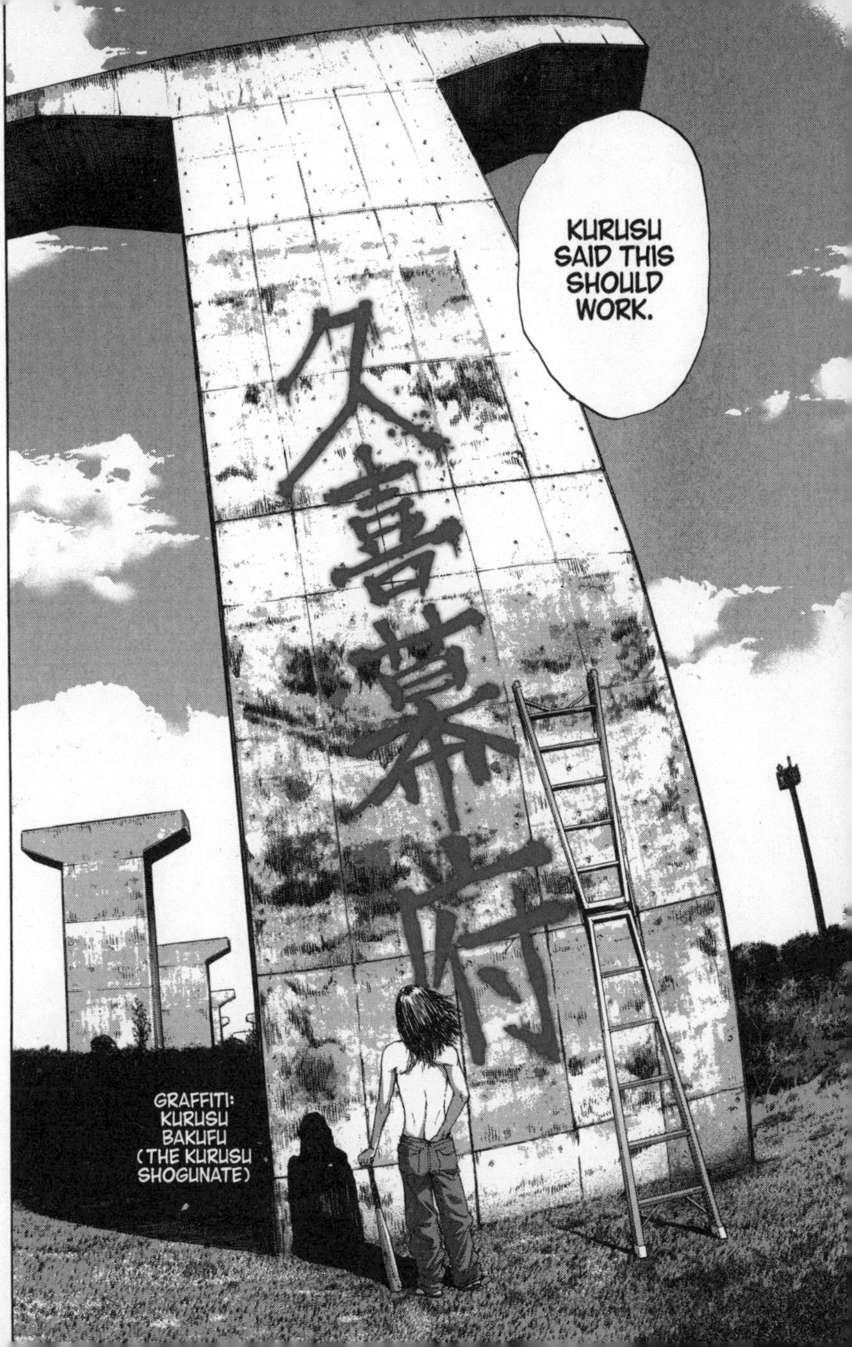
KURUSU SAID THIS SHOULD WORK.
GRAFFITI: KURUSU BAKUFU (THE KURUSU SHOGUNATE)

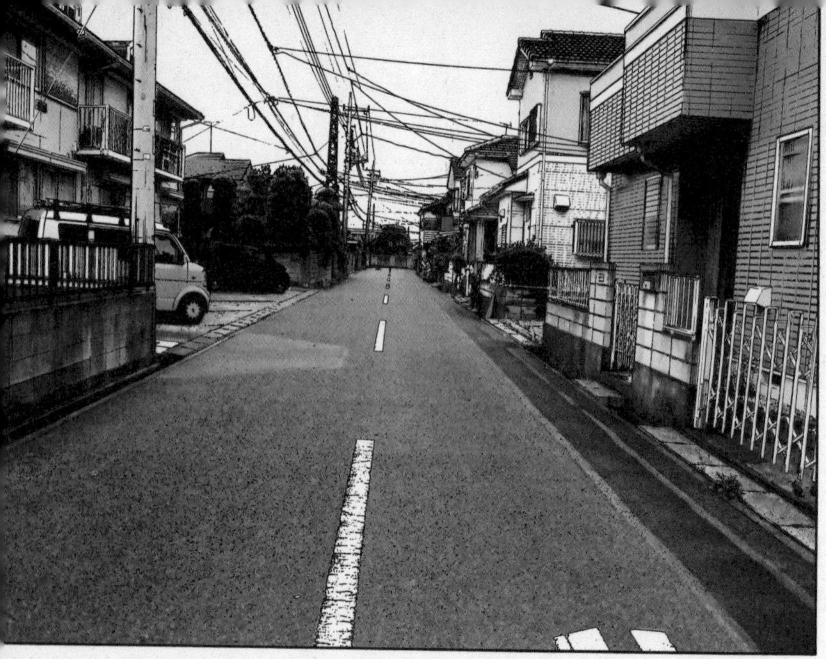

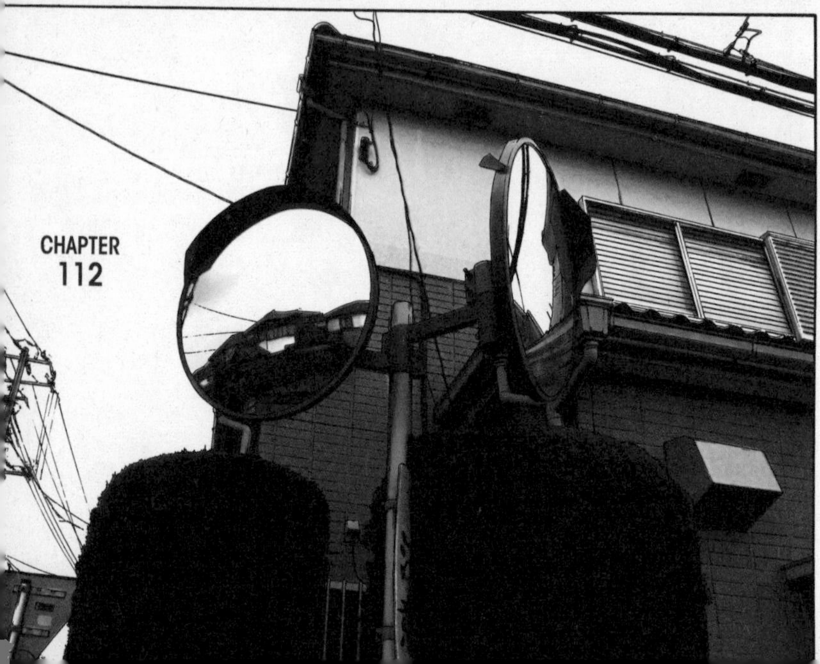
CHAPTER
112

532: **Doctor Toro:** 2009/05/11 (Mon) 13:18:49 ID:Eia8siS
This is just a hypothesis, but I've been thinking the cause of this series of incidents could be a prion. It could be a new type of transmissible spongiform encephalopathy (TSE), a well-known form of which is Mad Cow Disease.

533: **Anonymous Hero:** 2009/05/11 (Mon) 13:19:38 ID:jfi
Hmm, yes, I was just about to say the same thing myself, but do tell.

534: **Anonymous Hero:** 2009/05/11 (Mon) 13:23:13 ID:U
Does the "Toro" in "Doctor Toro" mean "toro" as in "futile?" I've got a bad feeling about this...

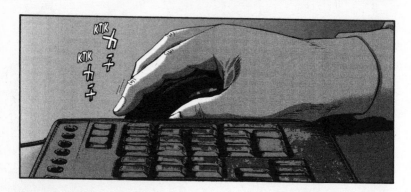

541: **Doctor Toro:** 2009/05/11 (Mon) 13:43:08 ID:Eia8siS
I believe this is a heretofore completely unknown distorted protein--thus prion--infection spreading through humans. Unfortunately, the employees at the research facility I was working at became infected one after the other in the first stages of the panic. It was forced to close before we could make any detailed study, but after examining some patients, we observed that their brains had become spongiform.

542: **Anonymous Hero:** 2009/05/11 (Mon) 13:48:11 ID:xei55p2
Doctor Toro, you da man, dawg! So how do you stop it?

543: **Anonymous Hero:** 2009/05/11 (Mon) 13:49:23 ID:vi4s4iS
Our savior! ———{-{-{{((= ､ (°∀°)ﾉ=)}}}-}-}———!!!!

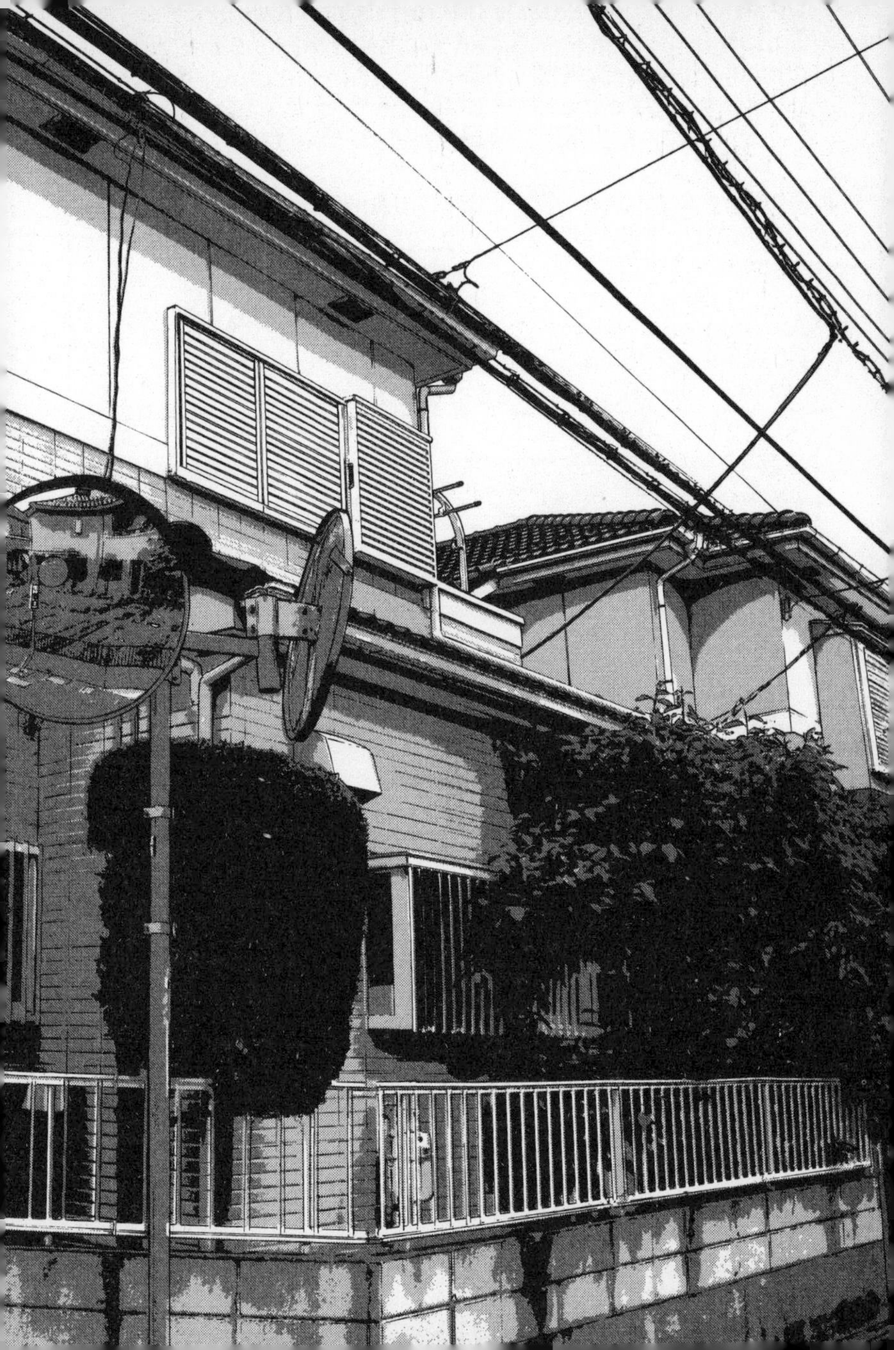

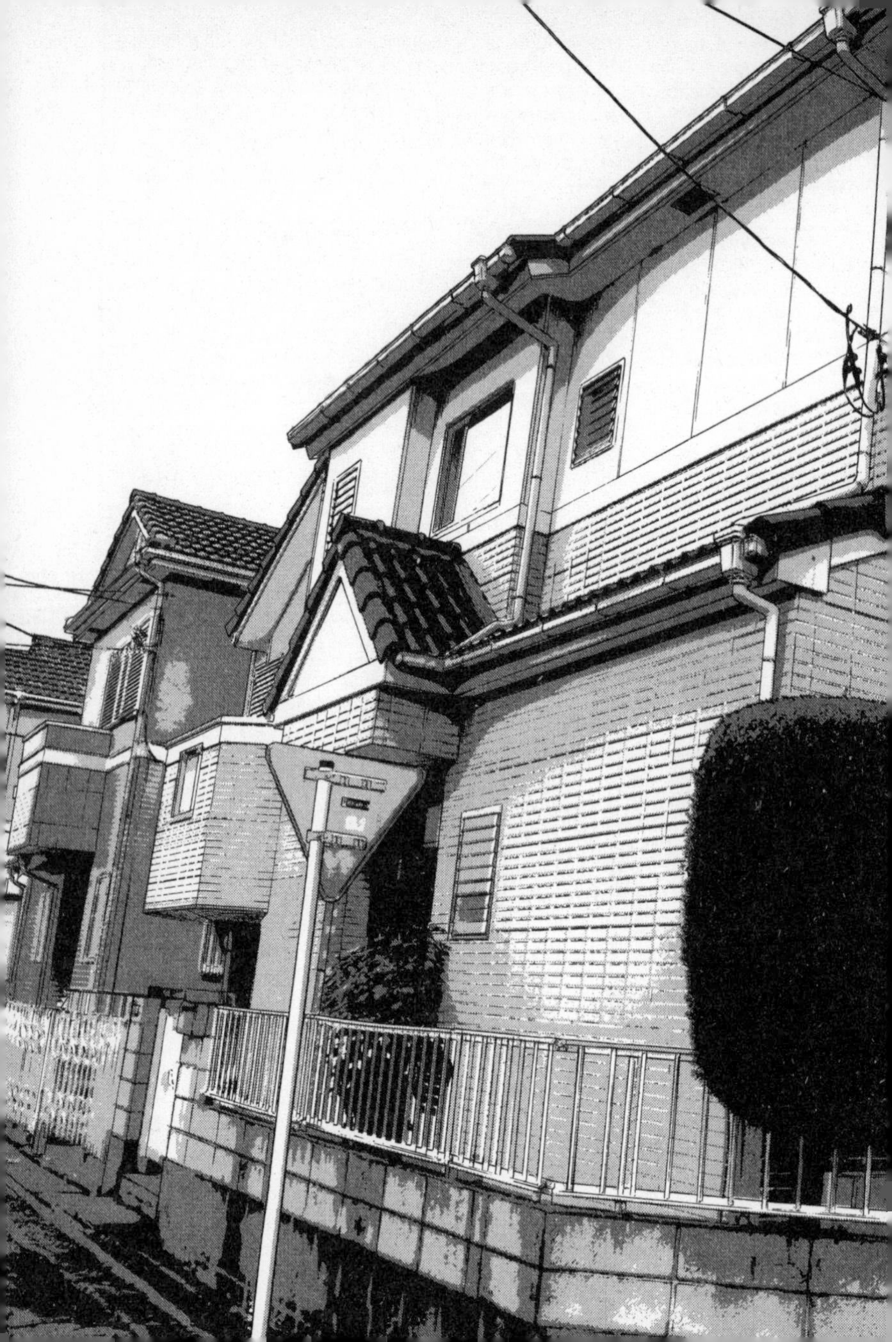

555: Doctor Toro: 2009/05/11 (Mon) 13:52:11 ID:Eia8siS
However, in terms of symptoms of those infected by such a prion, there
should be ambulation impairment from the initial phases of the disease,
but in this case they are unusually active. Furthermore, they are selecting
previously non-infected persons, biting them, and through such activities
spreading the infection. I cannot understand it in the least.
I still can't believe it. I'm truly surprised.

571: Anonymous Hero: 2009/05/11 (Mon) 13:57:01 ID:hdgp6ju
Didn't they say mad cow disease came from them feeding meat and bone
meals to the cows? In other words it was cannibalism. Maybe that's what's
causing the flesh eating this time too?

572: Anonymous Hero: 2009/05/11 (Mon) 13:57:14 ID:pos25yn
dunno bout that. u mean like the zqns first appeared because there was
cannibalism?

573: Anonymous Hero: 2009/05/11 (Mon) 13:58:27 ID:UW8d93v
Could it be Kuru Disease or something? Symptoms are completely diff
though.

574: Anonymous Hero: 2009/05/11 (Mon) 13:59:35 ID:RyoMo12

HEH
HEH!

601: Anonymous Hero: 2009/05/11 (Mon) 14:07:49 ID:Hgfc
Maybe it's a mutation. Totally extreme, though!

602: Anonymous Hero: 2009/05/11 (Mon) 14:10:15 ID:Lgf2
If I'm gonna get eaten I want it to be by a girl in grade 8

603: Anonymous Hero: 2009/05/11 (Mon) 14:10:40 ID:fhj5
Only 8th graders? I kinda get u

...Psych! As if! Fuck off!!

604: Anonymous Hero: 2009/05/11 (Mon) 14:15:54 ID:L2h
I'm 15 and hoping for an older girl

605: Anonymous Hero: 2009/05/11 (Mon) 14:16:01 ID:Mai
I'll eat you! ｛・∀・｝ heehee

610: Anonymous Hero: 2009/05/11 (Mon) 14:24:02 ID:Y4785jh
The biggest problem is that the ZQNs keep walking around even
though they're dead. I stabbed my wife over and over, but she still
won't stay down!

611: Anonymous Hero: 2009/05/11 (Mon) 14:27:18 ID:urhblp8
Calling the cops! Couldn't get through though...

612: Doctor Toro: 2009/05/11 (Mon) 14:30:00 ID:Eia8siS
I myself have already been infected, and my condition is worsening.

Anonymous Hero: 2009/05/11 (Mon)
Whoa! Yer infected?! lulz

670: **Doctor Toro:** 2009/05/11 (Mon) 15:10:11 ID:Eia8siS
I am unable to hide my surprise that the infection has spread so quickly.

671: **Anonymous Hero:** 2009/05/11 (Mon) 15:10:11 ID:iluf4l2
You are never anything but surprised, aren't you sir?! (•_•)σ

683: **Anonymous Hero:** 2009/05/11 (Mon) 15:11:24 ID:rtmEp1s
Forget about just being surprised all the time and come up with a new drug or countermeasure or something...

684: **Anonymous Hero:** 2009/05/11 (Mon) 15:11:43 ID:n0icAn7
As if! lol! A new drug will take years roflmao

685: **Anonymous Hero:** 2009/05/11 (Mon) 15:11:47 ID:oq66zro
I'm the one that's surprised! Doctor, I'm so hungry. Please help!

686: **Anonymous Hero:** 2009/05/11 (Mon) 15:12:49 ID:efjia14
Seriously, what do we do? (· □·)

99: **Anonymous Hero:** 2009/05/11 (Mon) 15:30:16 ID:ea8avi3
I'm out of food. This is seriously bad... ZQNs are swarming around outside. I never imagined my life would end like this... 3 days ago I fought with my mom and there was okonomiyaki left over. I wish I could eat now.

00: **Anonymous Hero:** 2009/05/11 (Mon) 15:30:23 ID:ae4jifr
Waaahh!!!! ----- °(|□`)° ------ Who gives a shit?!?

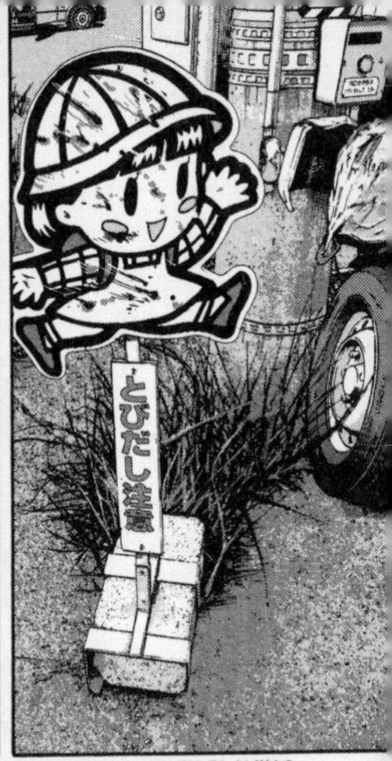
とびだし注意

SIGN: CAREFUL WHEN PLAYING

705: **Patriotic Fire Brigade Member:** 2009/
I live in a fishing village in Mie Prefectur
It's a tiny place with a reduced populatio
but there were some infected people am

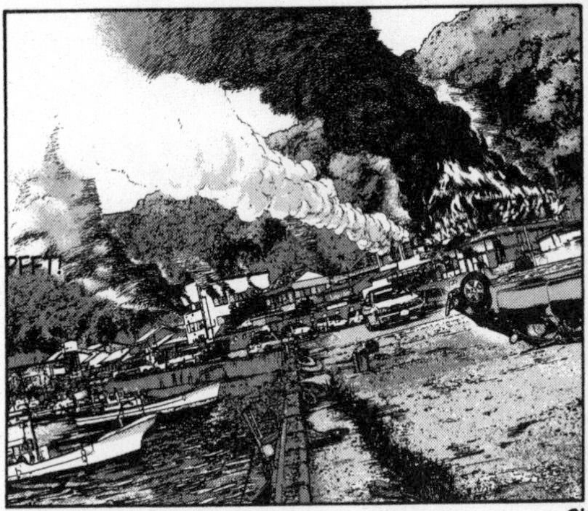

705: **Patriotic Fire Brigade Member:** 2009/05/11 (Mon) 15:35:14 ID:Mjuv59h
I live in a fishing village in Mie Prefecture. It's a tiny place with a reduced population, but there were some infected people among those who were evacuated here. The village folk caught the disease and now the village is in ruins.
It seems some of the villagers escaped in boats, but most of my fellow fire brigade members were killed. We're about to begin the final resistance. As a fire brigade member, it is wrong for me to do such a thing, but there is no other way. I will take them down into the hellfire with me.

706: **Anonymous Hero:** 2009/05/11 (Mon) 15:35:32 ID:pot5fs9
>>705
Fight the good fight!!

707: **Anonymous Hero:** 2009/05/11 (Mon) 15:35:35 ID:job11fa

711: **Anonymous Hero:** 2009/05/11 (Mon) 15:37:29 ID:kshf58l
>>705
Good luck in your battle.

712: **Anonymous Hero:** 2009/05/11 (Mon) 15:37:48 ID:A4649jh
>>705
You're a hero. I'd love to die like that, but there's nobody around.

713: **Anonymous Hero:** 2009/05/11 (Mon) 15:38:15 ID:dl8u5mn
>>712
Well, that's because we're shut-ins.

716: **Unrequited Love for Sister:** 2009/05/11 (Mon) 15:47:04 I
I just got kicked by my sister and bitten in the back...
Ate a lot of one arm off too...
Doesn't hurt too bad...

717: **Anonymous Hero:** 2
WTF?!
You're still alive?!?!

PFFT!

718: **Anonymous Hero:** 2009/05/11 (Mon) 15:47:47
>>716
Are you still alive?!!

719: **Anonymous Hero:** 2009/05/11 (Mon) 15:47:53
>>716
bah ha ha lolololololol

720: **Anonymous Hero:** 2009/05/11 (Mon) 15:48:20
>>716
it's been 6 days since you were last on here

721: **Anonymous Hero:** 2009/05/11 (Mon) 15:49:06
Fuck off! How the fuck are you typing then?!
I thought you had no arms!

722: **Anonymous Hero:** 2009/05/11 (Mon) 15:49:09
haha! lol! made me spill my last meal!!

723: **Anonymous Hero:** 2009/05/11 (Mon) 15:49:52
You must be infected now Unrequited...

724: **Anonymous Hero:** 2009/05/11 (Mon) 15:50:36
Too funny lol

725: **Anonymous Hero:** 2009/05/11 (Mon) 15:52:06
I haven't laughed this much since the panic
started lol Mercy buckets to you "Unrequited"!
Well, I'm off to my death, then...

726: **Anonymous Hero:** 2009/05/11 (Mon) 15:53:10
Well done! See you in the afterworld! (^_^)/

727: **Anonymous Hero:** 2009/05/11 (Mon) 15:53:13
Seeyuz Later

728: **Anonymous Hero:** 2009/05/11 (Mon) 15:55:01 ID:TY12gfw
I will deign to have sex with you if you help me! SRSLY!

729: **Anonymous Hero:** 2009/05/11 (Mon) 15:55:38 ID:ocyhsAj
>>728
"Deign"? Who the hell are you? How old are you, grandma?

730: **Anonymous Hero:** 2009/05/11 (Mon) 15:56:11 ID:TY12gfw
>>729
18 yr old girl. And I wasn't talking to you! Somebody save me!

731: **Anonymous Hero:** 2009/05/11 (Mon) 15:56:57 ID:O4kshie
>>728
Even if you beg us to save you, princess, we need to know your address. Also, when asking people for favors, you should use the appropriate language.

33: **Anonymous Hero:** 2009/05/11 (Mon) 15:57:49
The infected are moving according to a specific principle.

734: **Anonymous Hero:** 2009/05/11 (Mon) 15:58:05 ID:i58l2dg
>>733
Details please.

WOULD ANYONE...

735: **Anonymous Hero:** 2009/05/11 (Mon) 15:58:12 ID:TY12gfw
>>731
As if I'd write my address!! If you're a man, save me!!

736: **Anonymous Hero:** 2009/05/11 (Mon) 15:58:22 ID:8jxftAK
What should we do about her?

737: **Anonymous Hero:** 2009/05/11 (Mon) 15:58:37 ID:g975syt
Jeez. Fuck that. lol

738: **Anonymous Hero:** 2009/05/11 (Mon) 15:58:52 ID:sifbeu3
So how the fuck are we supposed to help you? lol

...SAVE A GIRL LIKE THAT?

740: **Anonymous Hero:** 2009/05/11 (Mon) 16:06:05 ID:O4kshie
>>728
Ya know, everyone on this BBS is basically a shut-in, or not employed, OR in school, so we only escaped the crisis by chance, and we barely have the ability to survive in the first place. It seems you think there's value in being an 18 year old girl, but we're in different times now.
Everyone's doing everything they can to survive.

741: **Want SEX:** 2009/05/11 (Mon) 16:06:35 ID:hsgyy7u
>>728
Give us your address and a pic of your face for now anyway.
Then we'll talk. (´・ω・`)

742: **Anonymous Hero:** 2009/05/11 (Mon) 16:06:58 ID:yaf7986

The people who called us creeps are turning to US for help now...

751: **Anonymous Hero:** 2009/05/11 (Mon) 16:14:56 ID:x3fe9eR
>>750
Don't lump me in with you! lol! I'm different. If you're near Chikusa Ward, Nagoya City, I'll help you. Come to Higashiyama Sky Tower. ヾ^_^/

752: **Anonymous Hero:** 2009/05/11 (Mon) 16:15:22 ID:oq66zro
If this were a manga, a pack of super-trained tough guys would show up to help, but all we've got is a bunch of twisted slacker parasites! lololol

760: **Anonymous Hero:** 2009/05/11 (Mon) 16:16:01 ID:vn489rD
I've been a shut-in since grade 11, and it's because of false charges of putting a hidden camera in the girls' bathroom by condescending bitches like this one.
I hope you die afraid!

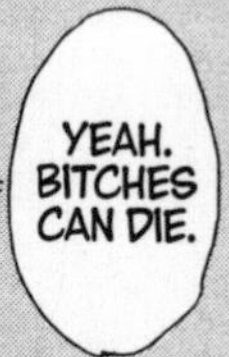
YEAH. BITCHES CAN DIE.

761: **Anonymous Hero:** 2009/05/11 (Mon) 16:16:11 ID:iluf
>>760
That's got nothing to do with this lol

762: **Anonymous Hero:** 2009/05/11 (Mon) 16:16:34 ID:8G3lswp
>>760
I've got no reason for being a shut-in... Just sorta happened...

777: **Anonymous Hero:** 2009/05/11 (Mon) 16:20:13 ID:bB4i8
So what's gonna happen now?
Even if we survive we can't maintain a civilization of this level.

Hey, I got lucky sevens! lol

778: **Anonymous Hero:** 2009/05/11 (Mon) 16:21:05 ID:63nSi
I guess we'll go back to the Stone Age.
But since we have no life skills, we'll probably go extinct! lol

779: **Anonymous Hero:** 2009/05/11 (Mon) 16:21:11 ID:bB4i8
>>778
True dat lol

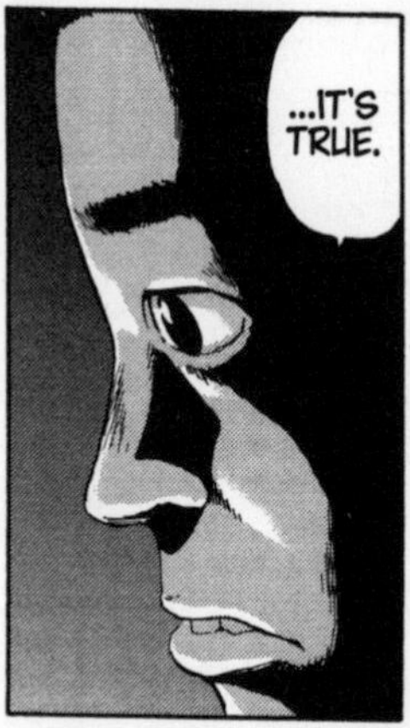
...IT'S TRUE.

790: **Anonymous Hero:** 2009/05/11 (Mon) 16:47:04 ID:ae4jifr
What's happening overseas?

791: **Anonymous Hero:** 2009/05/11 (Mon) 16:47:52 ID:3drqysT
The situation was similar in South Korea and Taiwan. Is it only in Asia?

792: **Anonymous Hero:** 2009/05/11 (Mon) 16:48:24 ID:efjiE5s
No, it seems to be worldwide. Time to throw in the towel! lols

I don't want to die! (´；ω；`)

800: **Anonymous Hero:** 2009/05/11 (Mon) 16:53:58 ID:ksJg553
Mankind will go extinct.
I thought we would last forever, but the end is coming.

801: **Anonymous Hero:** 2009/05/11 (Mon) 16:54:17 ID:sj583HJ
It's a cliché, but maybe it's retribution against humanity.
It's easy to look at humans eating each other as divine punishment for
destroying nature... And other awful stuff.

802: **Anonymous Hero:** 2009/05/11 (Mon) 16:54:49 ID:VBHpas2
There are ZQNs in my garden... It's time I faced the music.
I don't think they'll read this, but I have a message for my wife and child.

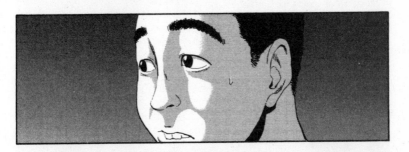

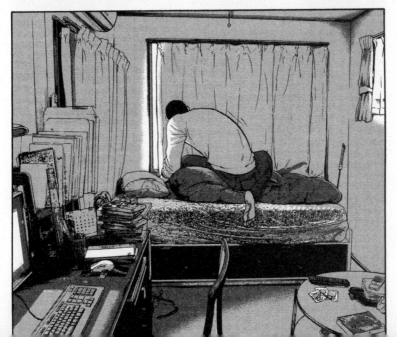

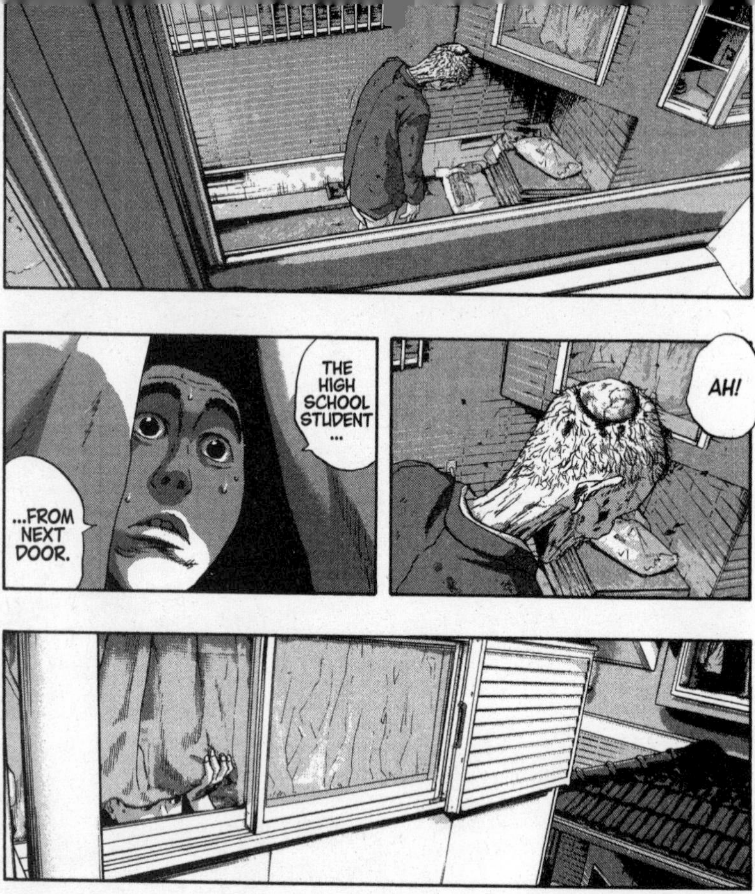
AH!
THE HIGH SCHOOL STUDENT...
...FROM NEXT DOOR.

810: **Anonymous Hero:** 2009/05/11 (Mon) 17:11:44 ID:Puygv
Come to think of it, what's the deal in Okinawa?
Isn't the all-powerful American army there to protect it?!

811: **Anonymous Hero:** 2009/05/11 (Mon) 17:12:02 ID:N8j5c
No hope. They wouldn't protect anything more than their own base anyway.

812: **Anonymous Hero:** 2009/05/11 (Mon) 17:14:43 ID:Lnfcu
Yeah, I live in Ginowan City, Okinawa, and it's fucked.
It's like civil war here.

813: **Anonymous Hero:** 2009/05/11 (Mon) 17:15:00 ID:j1312

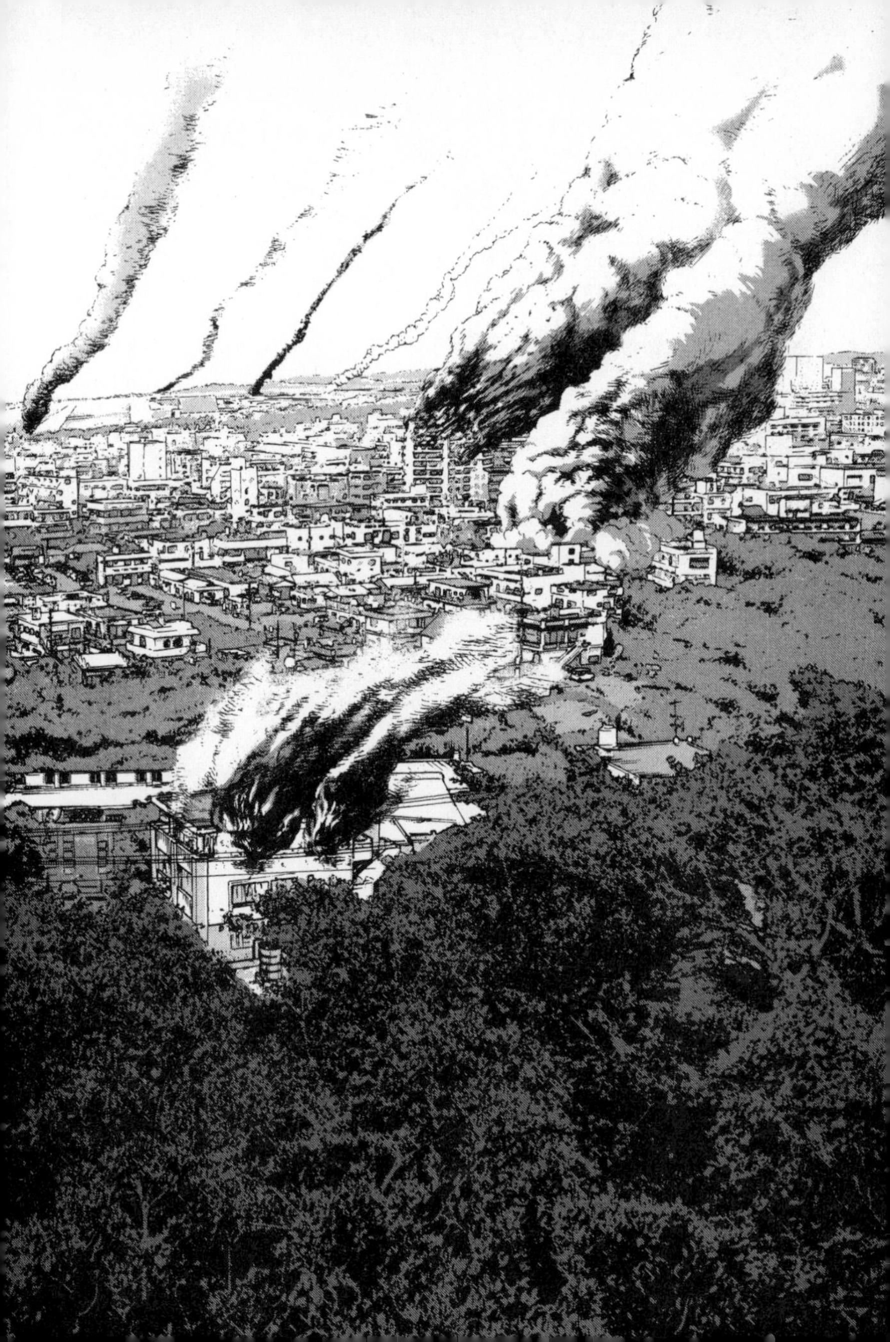

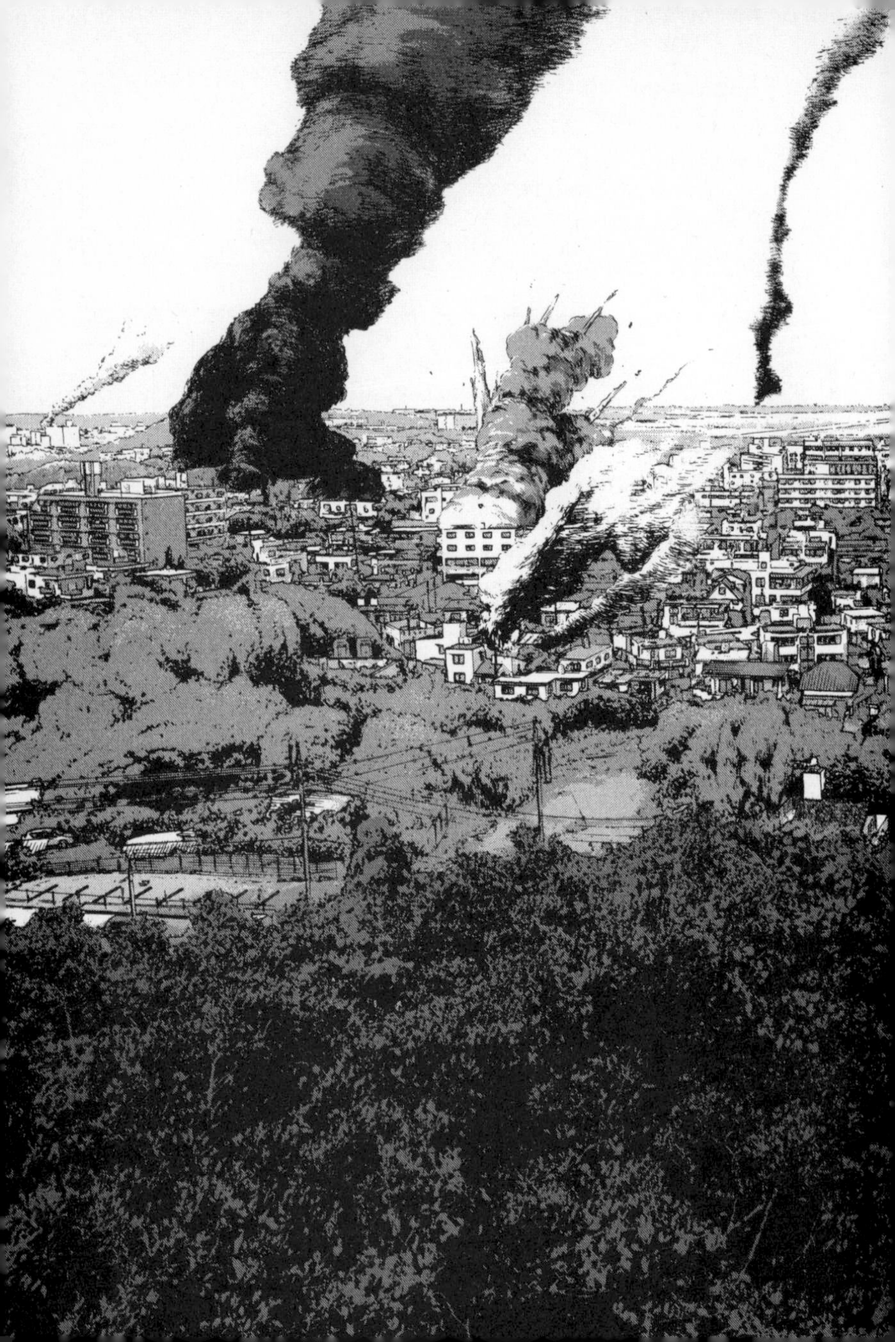

815: **Anonymous Hero:**
So Okinawa's fucked too...

816: **Anonymous Hero:** 2009/05/11 (Mon) 17:17:41 ID:Ksjdcv2
How about isolated islands?

817: **Anonymous Hero:** 2009/05/11 (Mon) 17:22:02 ID:8s2a7dT
If a single infected person got there, game over.
Fuck, I'd love some sushi. Goya chanpuru would be awesome too. Shit, I can't take this anymore!!

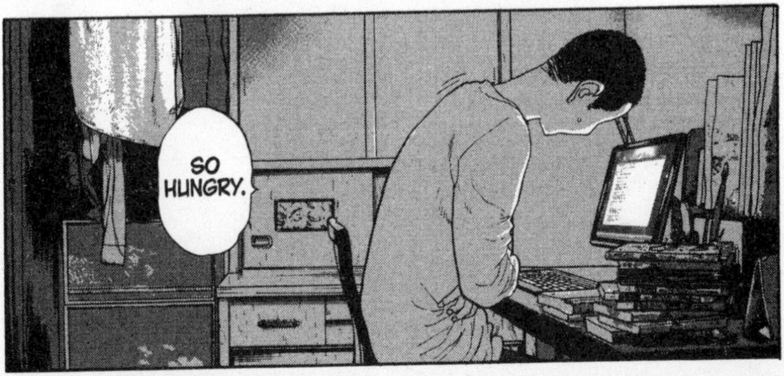
SO HUNGRY.

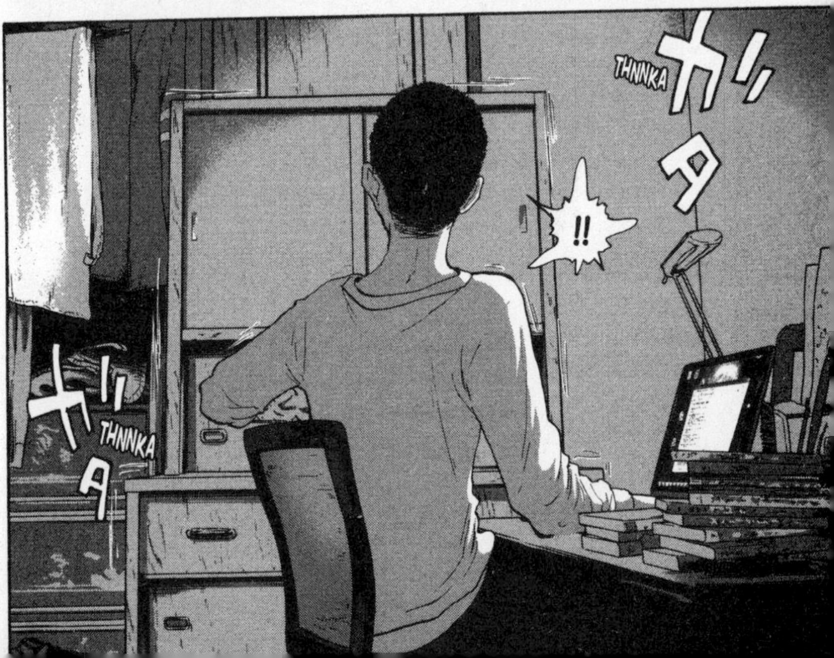
THNNKA
!!
THNNKA

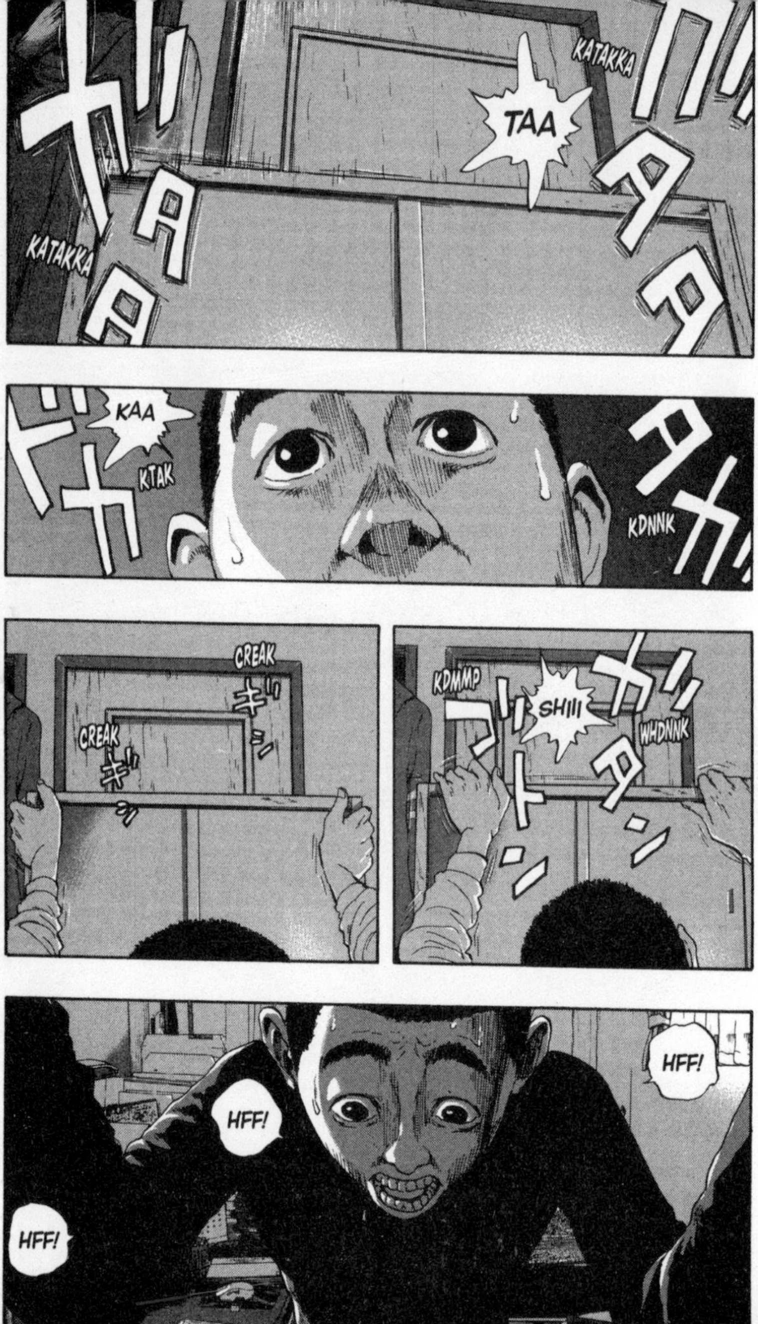
KATAKKA
TAA
KATAKKA
KDNNK
KAA
KTAK
WHDNNK
SHIII
KDMMP
CREAK
CREAK
HFF!
HFF!
HFF!

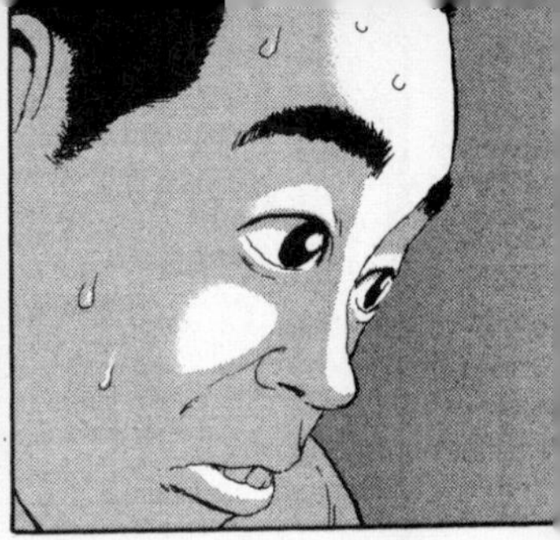

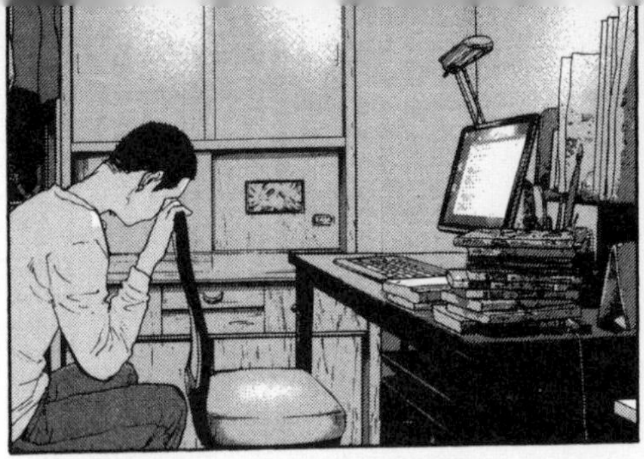

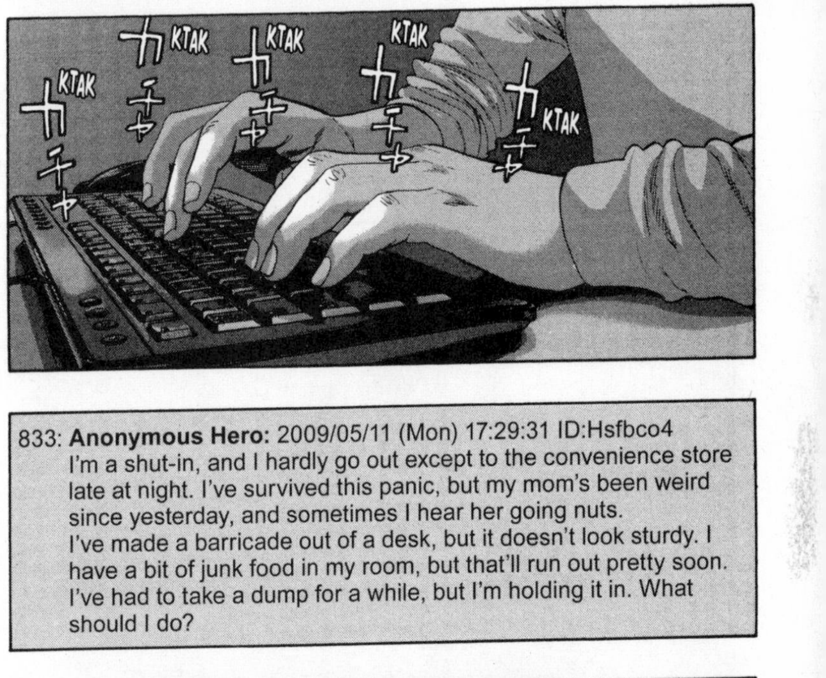
カチャ
KTAK
カチャ
KTAK
カチャ
KTAK
カチャ
KTAK
カチャ
KTAK

833: **Anonymous Hero:** 2009/05/11 (Mon) 17:29:31 ID:Hsfbco4
I'm a shut-in, and I hardly go out except to the convenience store late at night. I've survived this panic, but my mom's been weird since yesterday, and sometimes I hear her going nuts.
I've made a barricade out of a desk, but it doesn't look sturdy. I have a bit of junk food in my room, but that'll run out pretty soon. I've had to take a dump for a while, but I'm holding it in. What should I do?

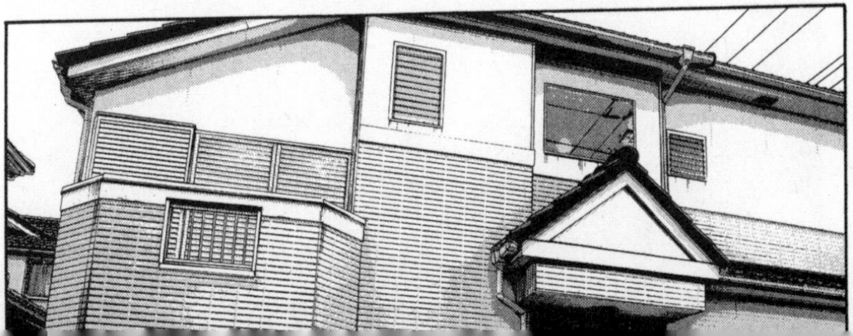

So what? I haven't eaten in 3 days, and my room's full of shit.
You've got it easy.
Right now, I'm mulling over a final decision about my pet hamster.
If I don't eat it, I'll die.

836: **Anonymous Hero:** 2009/05/11 (Mon) 17:32:14 ID:PUhhyf7

840: **Anonymous Hero:** 2009/05/11 (Mon) 17:35:22 ID:Olyebnh
>>835
Just let the hamster go, and YOU can die!

841: **Anonymous Hero:** 2009/05/11 (Mon) 17:39:10 ID:9kh573f
>>833
It's harder for some of us than others, but we're similar to a degree. Finish yourself off with dignity. Keep your humanity intact.

5: **Kurusu Rep Kowashi:** 2009/05/11 (Mon) 17:44:16 ID: Rs
Anyone who wants to join us in the fight, state your address, name, and age

THEY'RE HERE?!

856: **Anonymous Hero:** 2009/05/11 (Mon) 17:45:19
Aomori Prefecture, Aomori City, Satomi X-XX
Mizoyu Asou, age 38 Save me!

857: **Anonymous Hero:** 2009/05/11 (Mon) 17 23
Hiroshima Prefecture, Shimochi ty
Toreta Katadama, age 27

>>856
Scared? Lost a testicle?

858: **Anonymous Hero:** 2009/05/11 (Mon) 17:45:24
Hyogo Prefecture, Nishinomiya City,
Matsuyamacho X-XX
Honyuurui Saki, age 25
I'm really gonna die! Save me!

859: **Anonymous Hero:** 2009/05/11 (Mon) 17:45:28
Ishikawa Prefecture, Hakusan City,
Kashiwamachi X-X
Reo Yoshii, 32

1: **Anonymous Hero:** 2009/05/11 (Mon) 17:47:17 ID:TY12gfw
Ibaraki Prefecture, Ishioka City, Takahama XXXX
Manko Kusai, age 18

Save me and I'll have sex with you! SEX

2: **Anonymous Hero:** 2009/05/11 (Mon) 17:47 ID: kavyq
Kagoshima Prefecture, Akune City, Omarucho XX
Minami Koseki, age 43 Please save my children!

3: **Anonymous Hero:** 2009/05/11 (Mon) 17:47:19
Mie Prefecture, Nabari City, Hirao XXXX
Naomi Suga, age secret.
In hiding with my elderly mom and dad. We can pay money.

4: **Anonymous Hero:** 2009/05/11 (Mon) 17:47
Shimane Prefecture, Yasugi City, Kiyoichi X
Takao Doi, age 63 Tomiichi, wife, age 61
We'll pay however much money you ask.
How much do you want?

5: **Anonymous Hero:** 2009/05/11 (Mon) 17:47:21 BHG8AW
Kanagawa Prefecture Yokosuka City, Yasuuracho X-X
Sachi Hamada

We're Sachi & Mami. We're both 17, boys!☆ Happy to do threesomes!☆ Save us, huh, babes?! ･ﾟ･(ノД`)･ﾟ･

6: **Anonymous Hero:** 2009/05/11 (Mon) 17:47:22 ID:paj7r2b
Chiba Prefecture, Noda City, Goki XXX

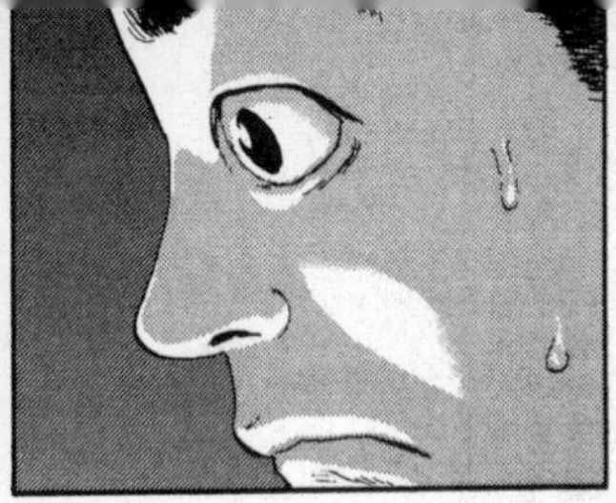

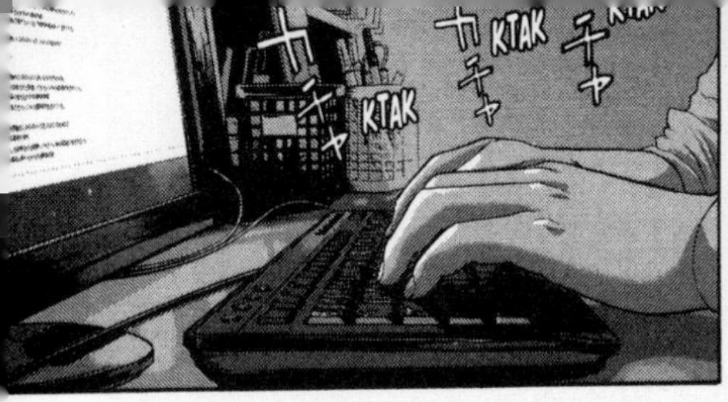
KTAK
KTAK

953: **Anonymous Hero:** 2009/05/11 (Mon) 17:56:21 ID:Hsfbco4
>>855
Saitama Prefecture, Kuki City, Yoshiba X-X-X
Takashi Ezaki Age 21
I will fight by your side.

954: **Anonymous Hero:** 2009/05/11 (Mon) 17:56:48 ID:iyuys66

Save me, Lord Kurusu!!

999: **Kurusu Rep Kowashi:** 2009/05/11 (Mon) 18:01:53 ID:Rs9hs2b
>>953
Understood.

1000: **Anonymous Hero:** 2009/05/11 18:02:00 ID:FHdm8t6
1000

1001: 1001: Over 1000 Thread
This thread has reached 1000 posts.
The limit has been reached, so a new thread must be started

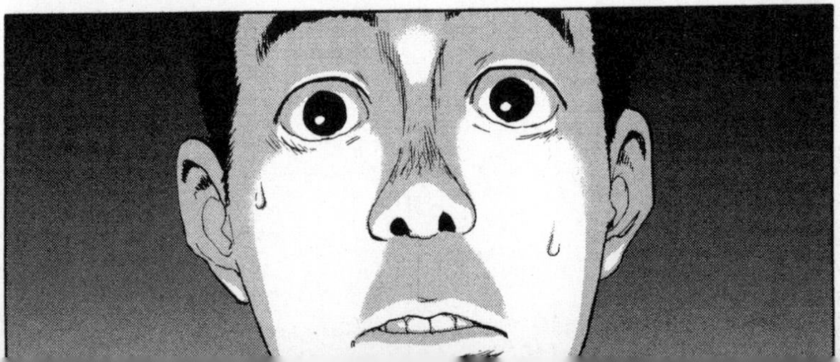

CHAPTER 113

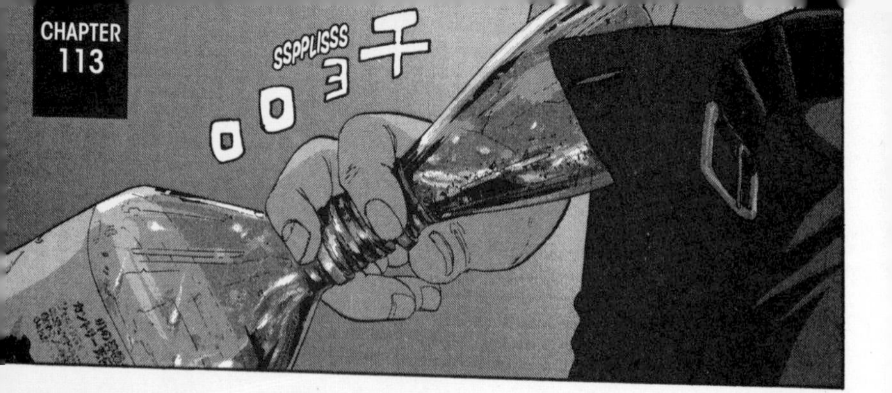
SSPPLISSS
チョロロ

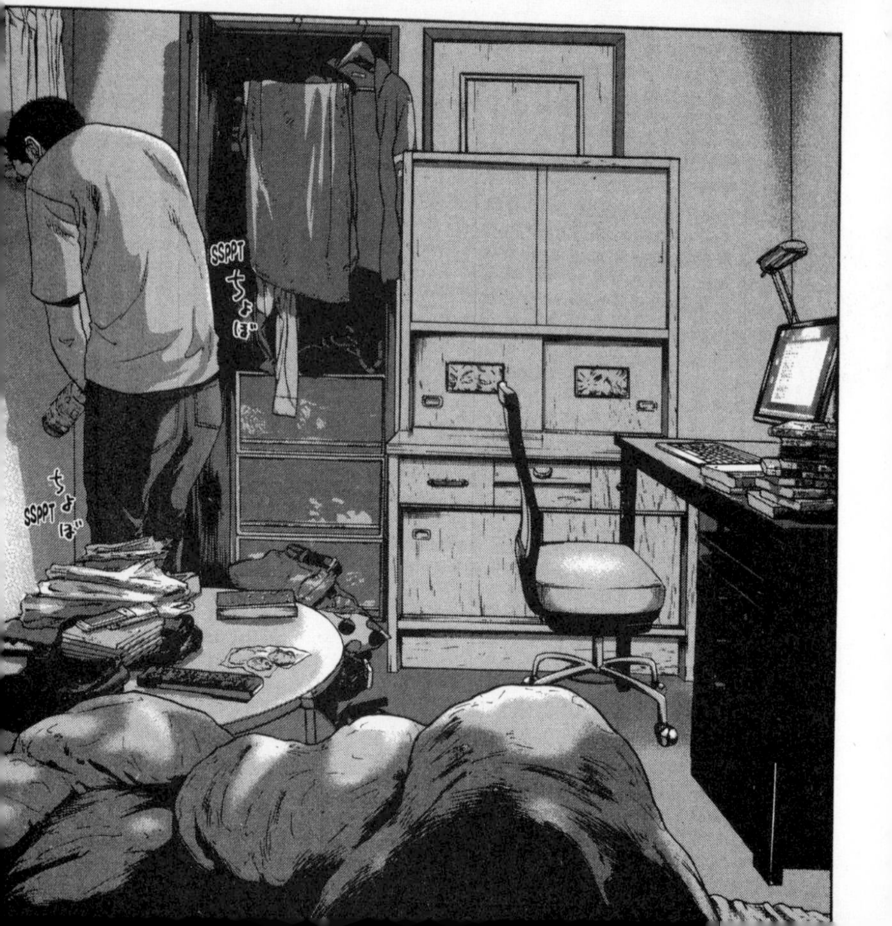
SSPPT
ちょぼ
SSPPT
ちょぼ

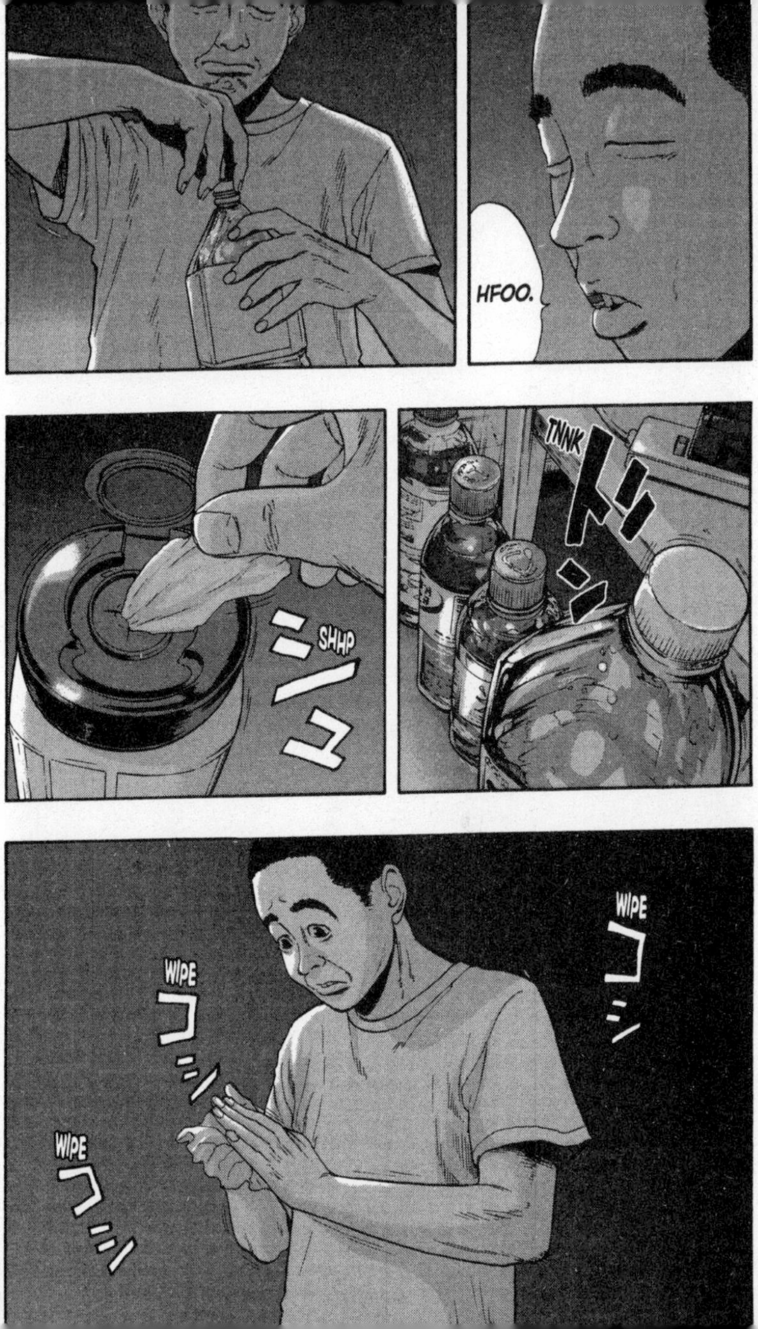
HFOO.
TNNK
ドッ
SHHP
シュ
WIPE
コシ
WIPE
コシ
WIPE
コシ

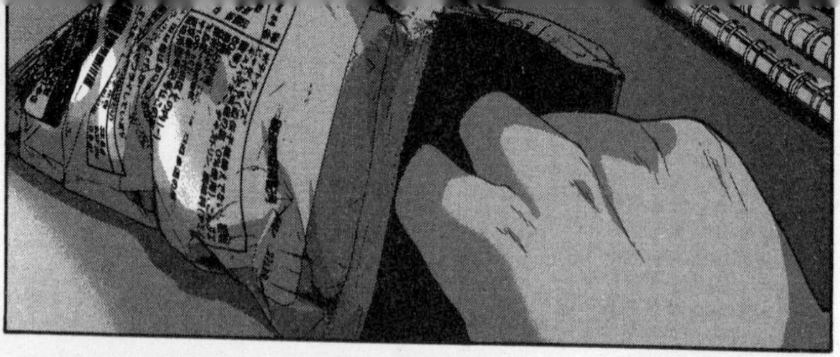

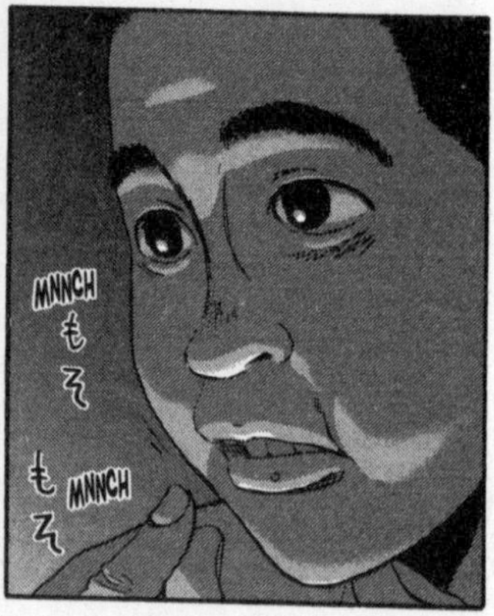
MNNCH
MNNCH

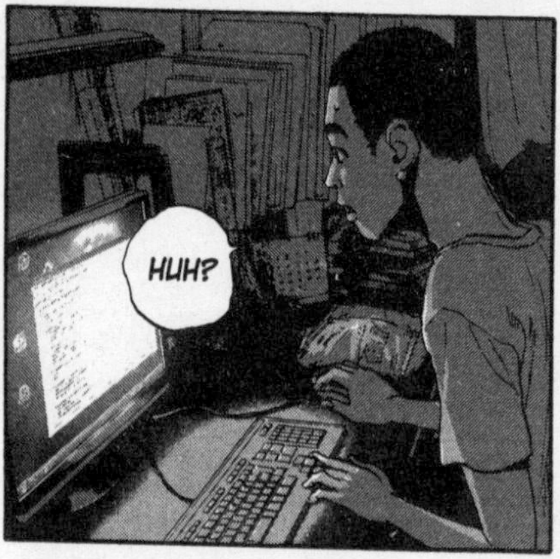
HUH?

253: **Anonymous Hero:** 2009/05/11 (Mon) 19:35:21 ID:47o
How to escape from your house.
The ZQNs act according to ingrained habits they had when they were alive.
In other words, they might repeat the actions of getting up in the morning, going to an office, and returning to bed at night. If you work out the details of the ZQNs patterns, a way to escape will inevitably become self-evident.

254: **Anonymous Hero:** 2009/05/11 (Mon) 19:38:41 ID:kdap
>>253
My brother said the same thing and tried to escape.
Then my mom ate him right at the front door!

255: **Anonymous Hero:** 2009/05/11 (Mon) 19:38:52 ID:k789
rofl

257: **Anonymous**
>>253
are you stupid? lol! once you escape, then what?
is there some safe place out there once you leave?!

258: **Anonymous Hero:** 2009/05/11 (Mon) 19:47:52 ID:58gtsoi
I'm fucking starving. I'm not a ZQN, but I'd eat another person. Somebody help me get well again!

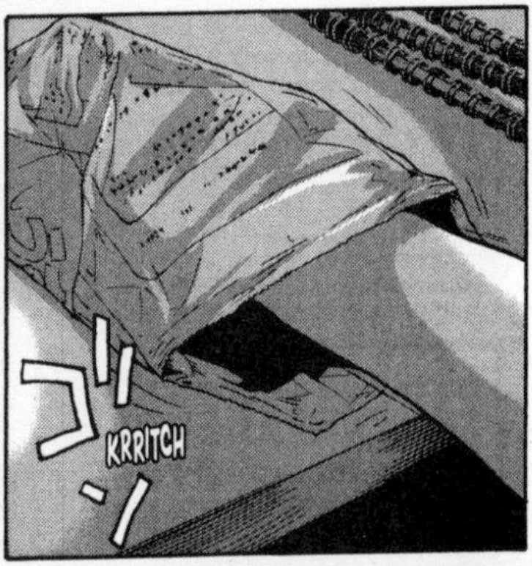
KRRITCH

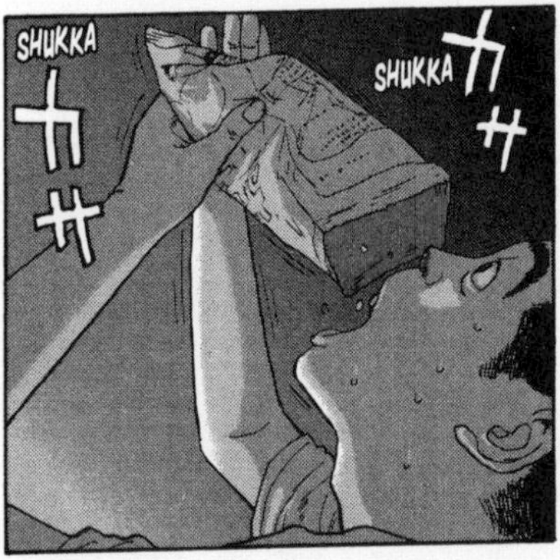
SHUKKA
SHUKKA

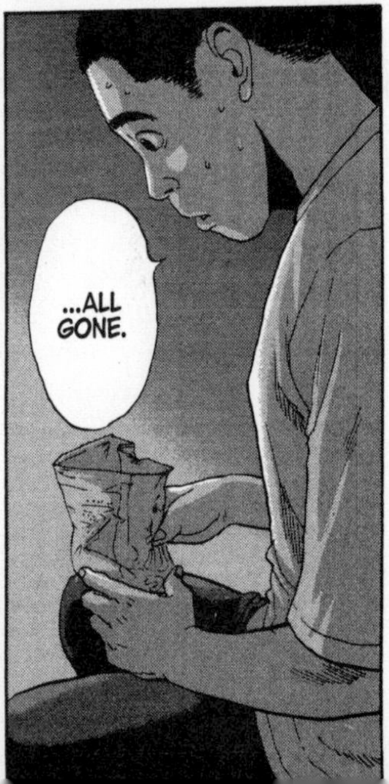
...ALL GONE.

260: **Anonymous Hero:** 2009/05/11 (Mon) 19:4
There should still be food in the kitchen, but my mom (who's full ZQN) is in there, so I can't get close. Our condo is on the seventh floor, so I can't escape. I'm a goner.

261: **Anonymous Hero:** 2009/05/11 (Mon) 19:5
It sucks being this hungry. Vision's getting blurry.

262: Anonymous Hero: 2009/05/11 (Mon) 19:5

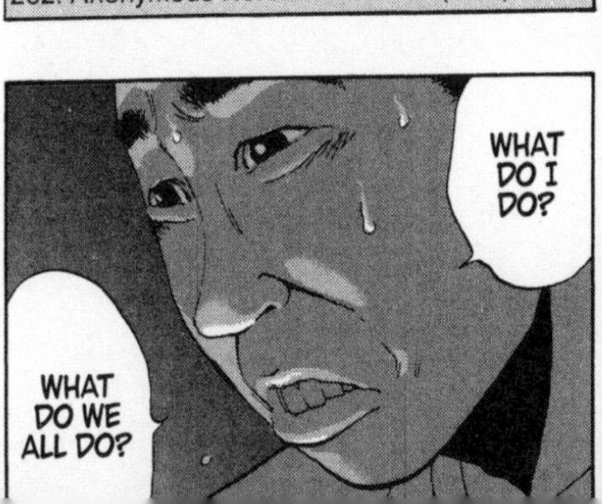
WHAT DO I DO?
WHAT DO WE ALL DO?

Looks like there's nothing left except to die...
Well, it's not like I had any future or hopes to begin with, but I'm kinda like... whoa

274: **Anonymous Hero:** 2009/05/11 (Mon) 20:02:23 ID:b
Us shut-ins were committing slow suicide anyway, and this is just making our deaths a little sooner.
That's all.

275: **Anonymous Hero:** 2009/05/11 (Mon) 20:04:56 ID:

300: **Anonymous Hero:** 2009/05/11 (Mon) 20:56:12 ID:VBnVZkC
Maybe so.
We may be lucky that we can still make decisions for ourselves, unlike those people who have become ZQNs and are wandering around.

301: **Anonymous Hero:** 2009/05/11 (Mon) 20:57:11 ID:mdvfi89
Well.
I don't know if ZQNs have any sort of consciousness, but I don't want to end up like that.

305: **Anonymous Hero:** 2009
Although, if we became ZQNs, we wouldn't end up wandering around, we'd just stay shut inside.

306: **Anonymous Hero:** 2009
Totally! Lols

307: **Anonymous Hero:** 2009
>>305
Sad but true.

308: **Anonymous Hero:** 2009
Can't we evacuate to some safe spot?

309: **Anonymous Hero:** 2009
If you did, you'd never tell anyone about it.
Or nobody's done it.
Which is it?

310: **Anonymous Hero:** 2009

HA HA HA!
IF I BECAME A ZQN, I GUESS I'D JUST STARE AT MY COMPUTER.

312: **Anonymous Hero:** 2009/05/11 (Mon) 2
So, shall we all die simultaneously?

313: **Anonymous Hero:** 2009/05/11 (Mon) 2
>>312
Communal internet suicide?

314: **Anonymous Hero:** 2009/05/11 (Mon) 2

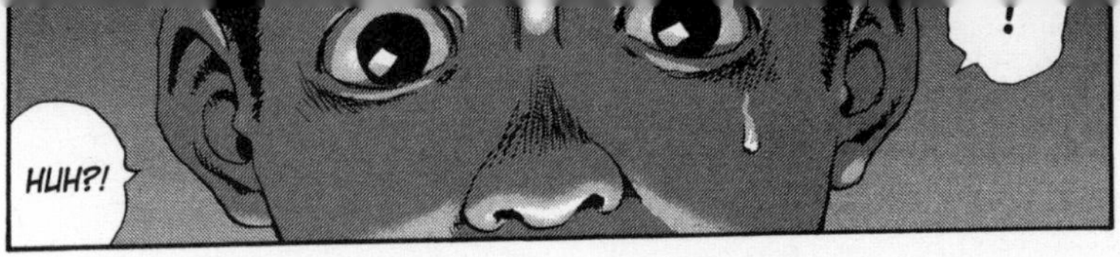
!
HUH?!

317: **Anonymous Hero:** 2009/05/11 (Mon) 21:09:52 ID:POhgq58
>>312
Maybe not a bad idea
If it's between infection or being eaten, suicide's better lol

318: **Anonymous Hero:** 2009/05/11 (Mon) 21:10:13 ID:13rawec
>>312
I'm in.
I'm sick of being alive.

319: **Anonymous Hero:** 2009/05/11 (Mon) 21:14:34 ID:lahsvxt
This is Doi who wrote that message before. Mr. Kowashi, the Kurusu rep, I haven't heard from you yet. We have money. Please contact me.

320: **Anonymous Hero:** 2009/05/11 (Mon) 21:14:44 ID:vgt5m6z
↑ stfu

325: **Anonymous Hero:** 2009/05
So how do we do it?
Hang ourselves?

326: **Anonymous Hero:** 2009/05
I don't have any beams or rope to do it with in my room

327: **Anonymous Hero:** 2009/05
me neither

328: **Anonymous Hero:** 2009/05
How about slitting our wrists? We should all have box cutters or something?

329: **Anonymous Hero:** 2009/05
oh, ya I do

330: **Anonymous Hero:** 2009/0

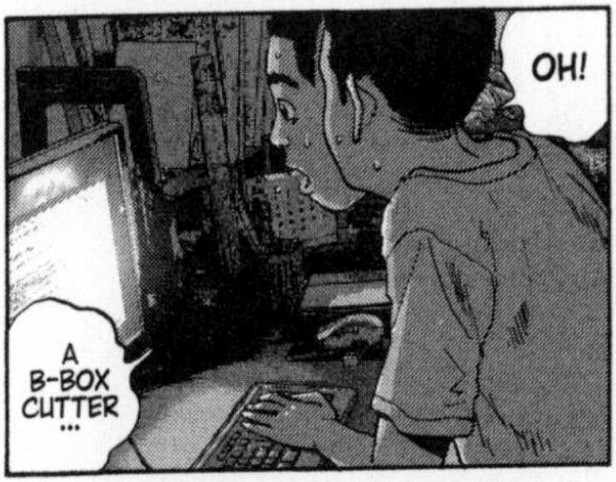
OH!
A B-BOX CUTTER ...

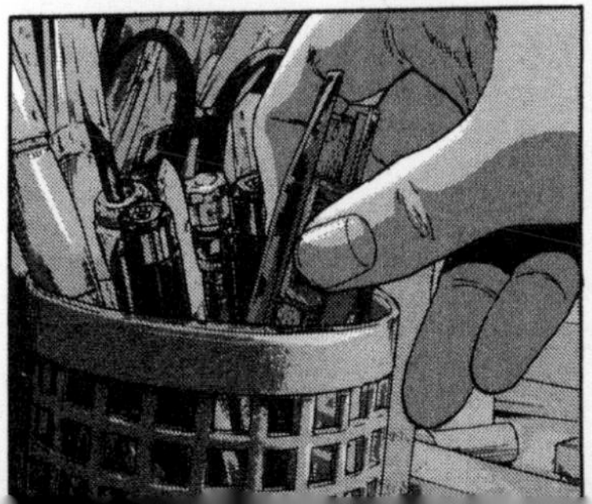

Suicide by slashing your wrists is pretty hard, man. Don't bother. You have to slash the artery. And cutting the sinews and nerves in your wrists is super painful.

336: **Internet Group Suicide Club:** 2009/05/11 (Mon) 21:18:03 ID:9kh573f
If you cut along the line of your arm, it'll kill you. There'll be a lot of blood, so don't be surprised

337: **Anonymous Hero:** 2009/05/11 (Mon) 21:18:33 ID:p854mn3
↑you can stfu

338: **Anonymous Hero:** 2009/05/11 (Mon) 21:20:50 ID:redfhkm
Is everybody ready? Counting down now! Lol

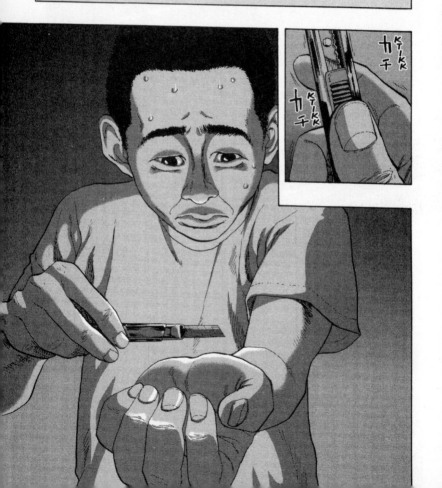

340: **Anonymous Hero:** 2009/05/11 (Mon) 21:22:21 ID:xxxxxxy
Ready!

341: **Anonymous Hero:** 2009/05/11 (Mon) 21:22:22 ID:bya8965
Set!!

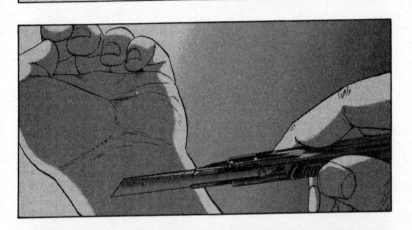

352: Anonymous Hero: 2009/05/11 (Mon) 21:24:31 ID:Loaqivc
Well? Everyone dead?
353: Anonymous Hero: 2009/05/11 (Mon) 21:25:48 ID:cvbzxmn
Just another second... just kidding lol
354: Anonymous Hero: 2009/05/11 (Mon) 21:26:15 ID:Vg741hg
No way. Too much of a headache.
I hate pain.
355: Anonymous Hero in Heaven: 2009/05/11 (Mon) 21:27:37 ID:258bhuy
This is a nice place! lols
356: Anonymous Hero: 2009/05/11 (Mon) 21:27:57 ID:Qhy7956
...!
YIKES!
...
HFF!
KTAK
KTAK
KTAK
KTAK
KTAK
KTAK

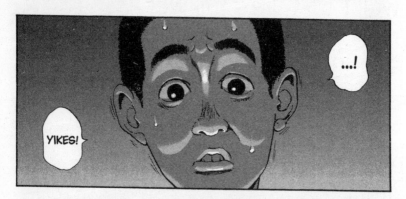

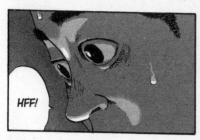

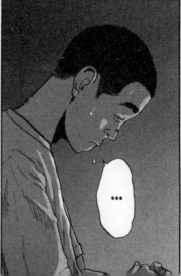

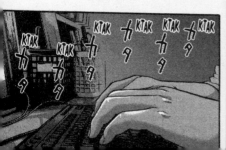

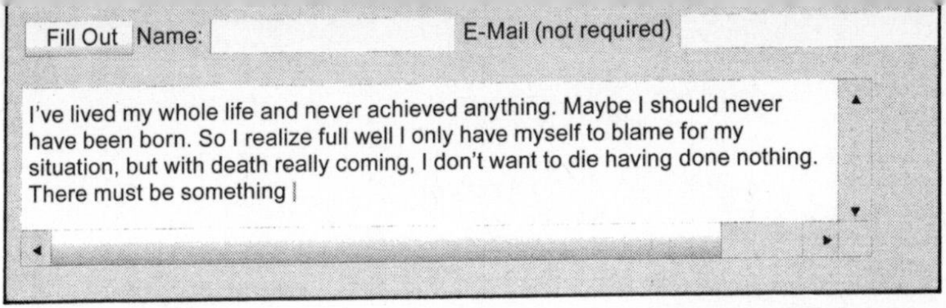
Fill Out Name:
E-Mail (not required)
I've lived my whole life and never achieved anything. Maybe I should never have been born. So I realize full well I only have myself to blame for my situation, but with death really coming, I don't want to die having done nothing. There must be something

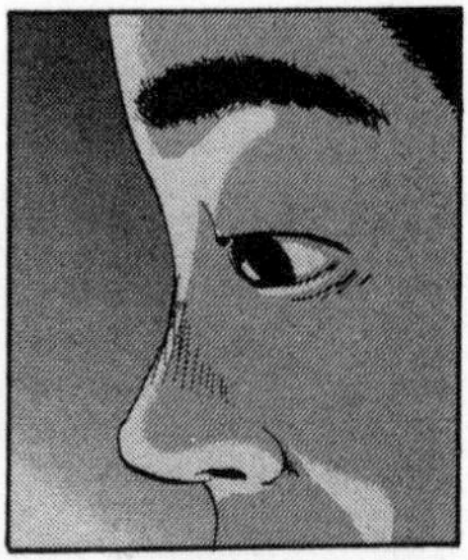

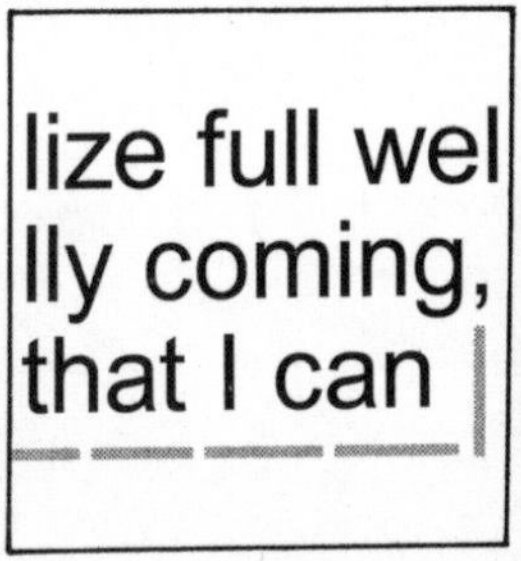
lize full wel
lly coming,
that I can

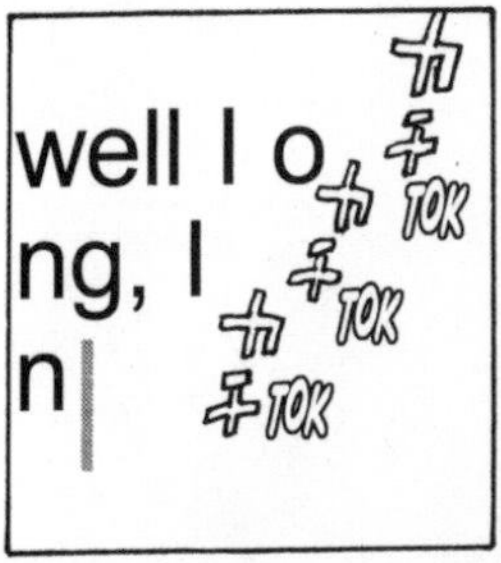
well I o
ng, I
n
TOK
TOK
TOK

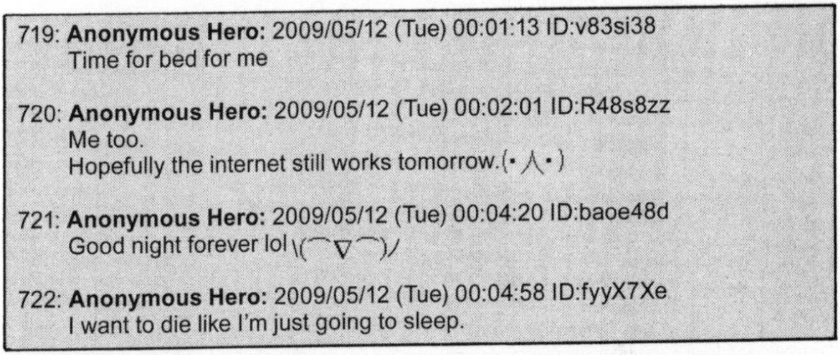
719: Anonymous Hero: 2009/05/12 (Tue) 00:01:13 ID:v83si38
Time for bed for me
720: Anonymous Hero: 2009/05/12 (Tue) 00:02:01 ID:R48s8zz
Me too.
Hopefully the internet still works tomorrow.(・人・)
721: Anonymous Hero: 2009/05/12 (Tue) 00:04:20 ID:baoe48d
Good night forever lol \(￣▽￣)/
722: Anonymous Hero: 2009/05/12 (Tue) 00:04:58 ID:fyyX7Xe
I want to die like I'm just going to sleep.

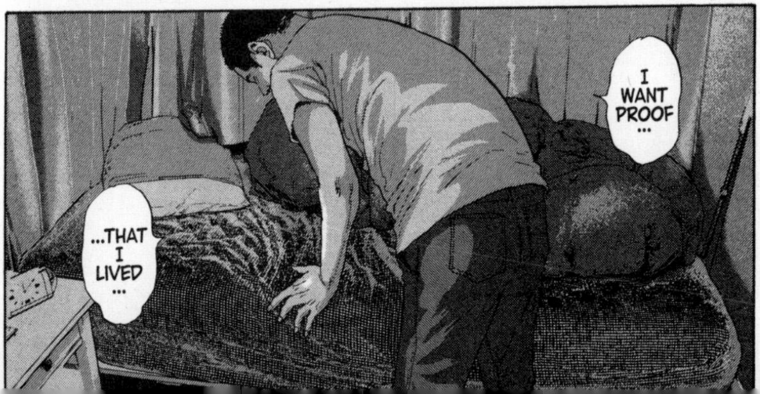
I WANT PROOF...
...THAT I LIVED...

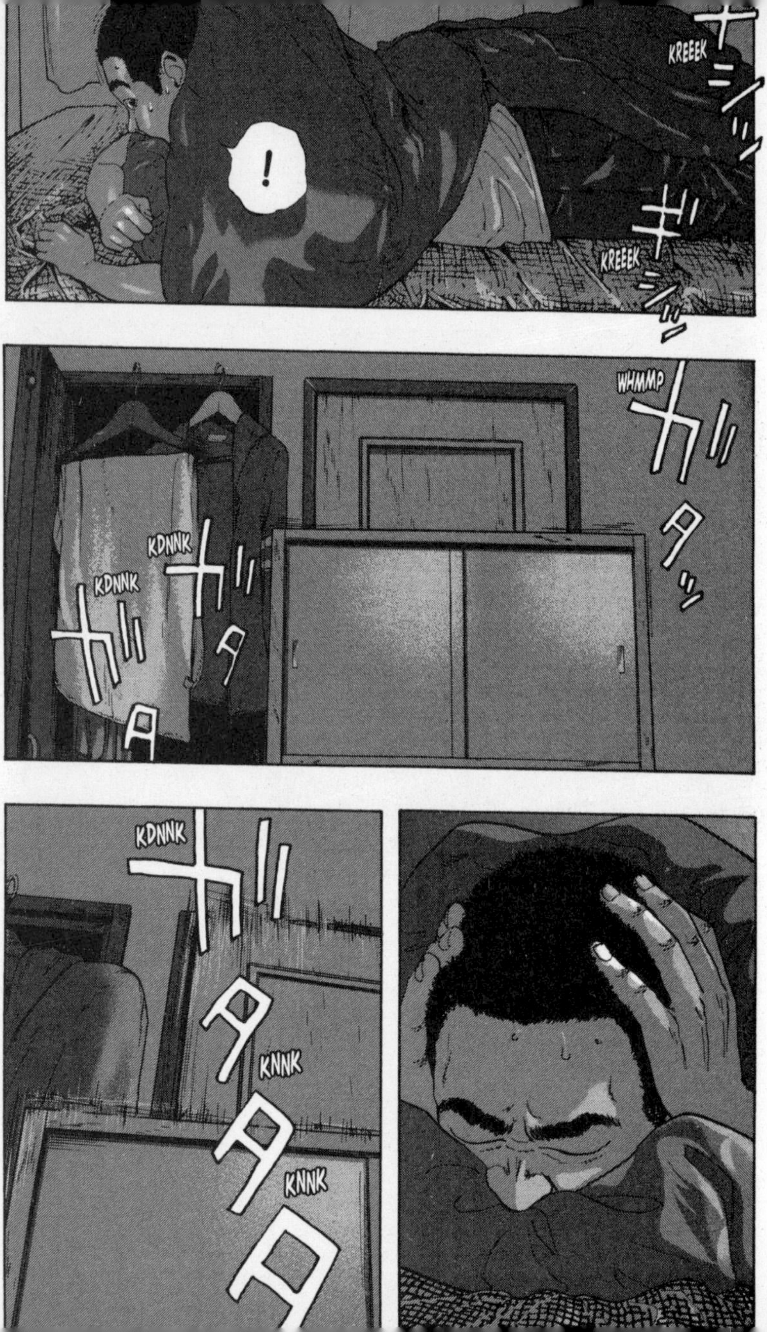

KREEEK
!
KREEEK
WHMMP
KDNNK
KDNNK
KDNNK
KNNK
KNNK

KREEEK
TAA
KREEEK
KAA
KREEEK
KREEEK
!

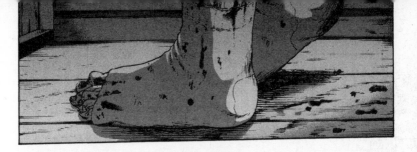

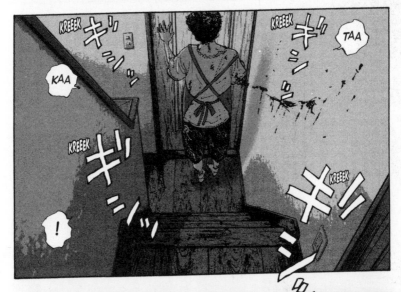

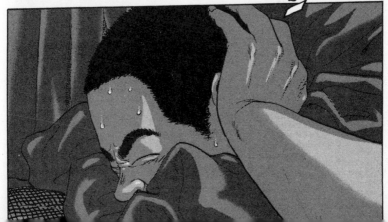

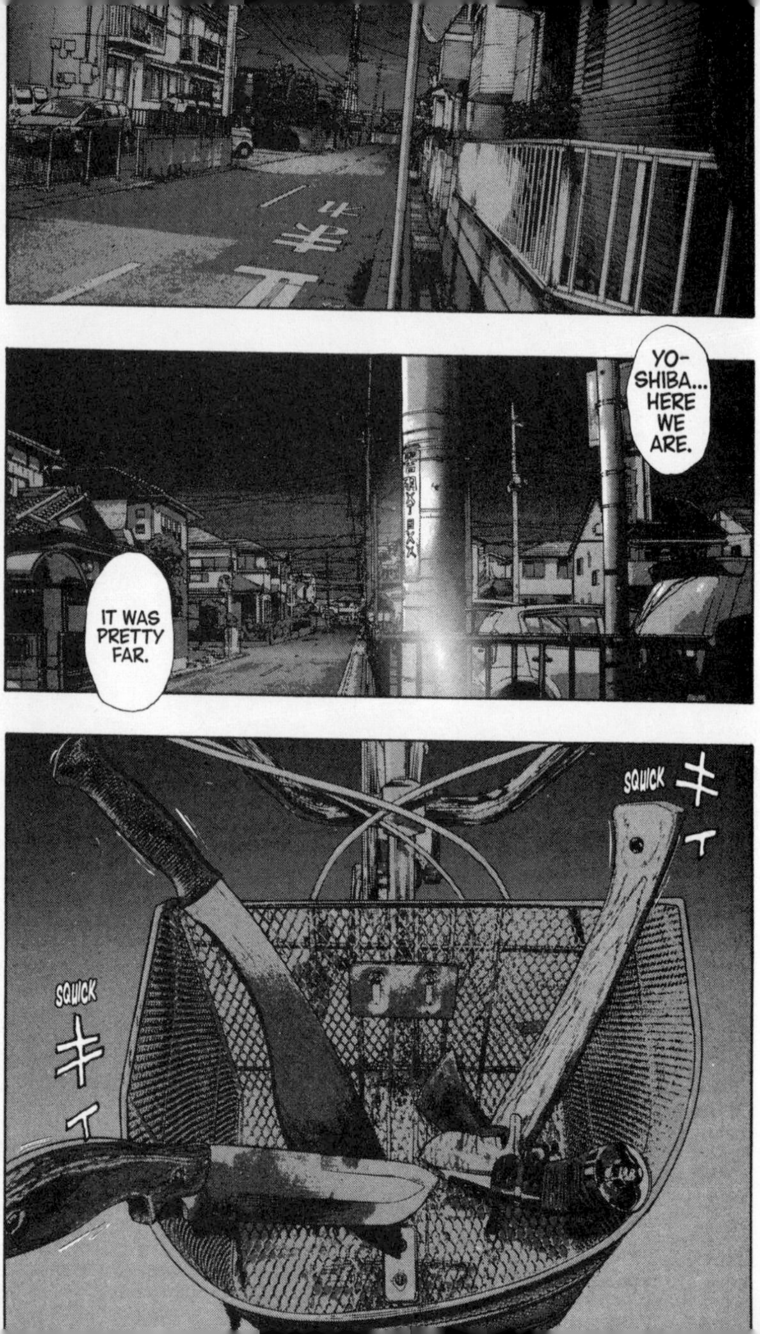
YO-SHIBA... HERE WE ARE.
IT WAS PRETTY FAR.
SQUICK
キイ
SQUICK
キイ

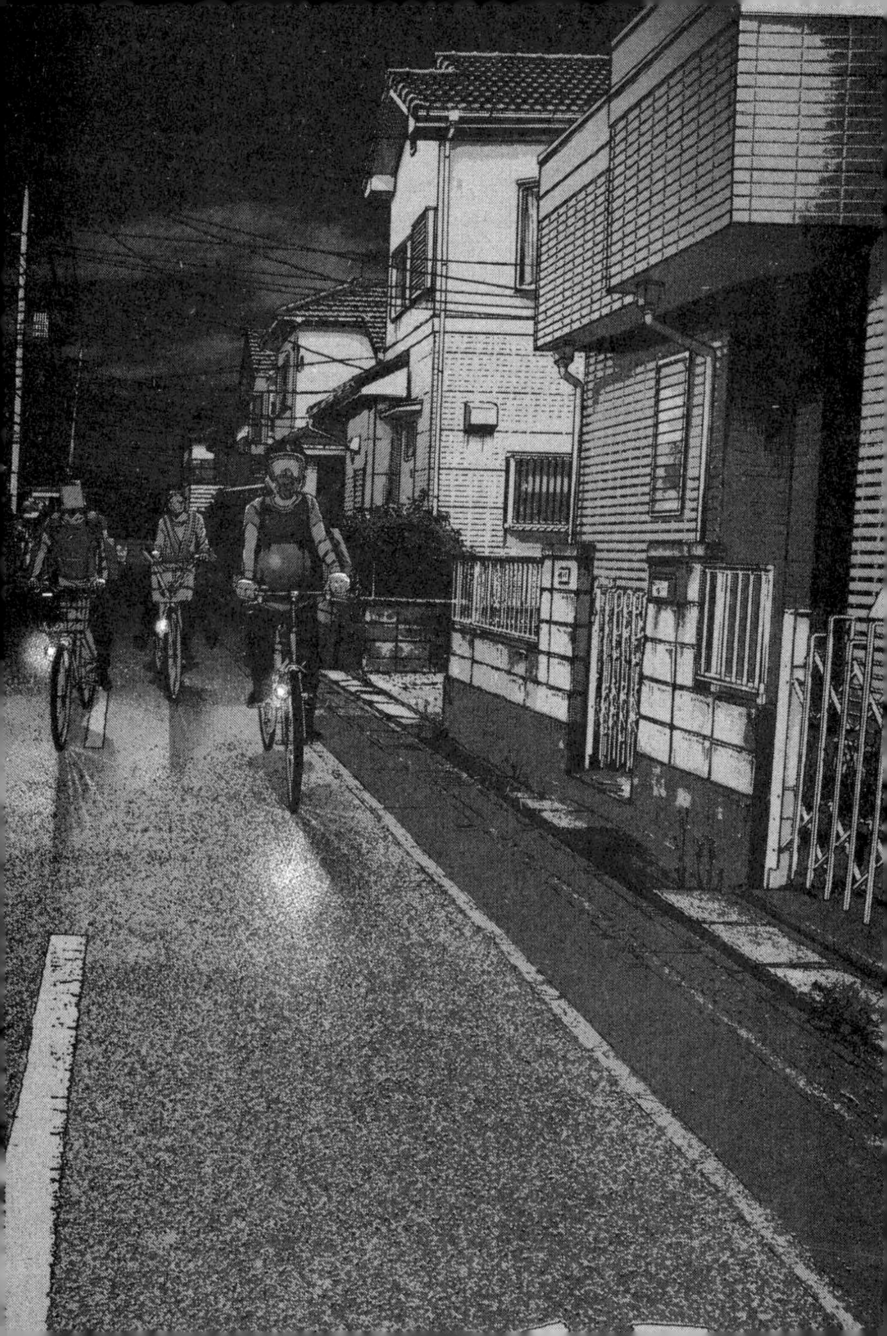

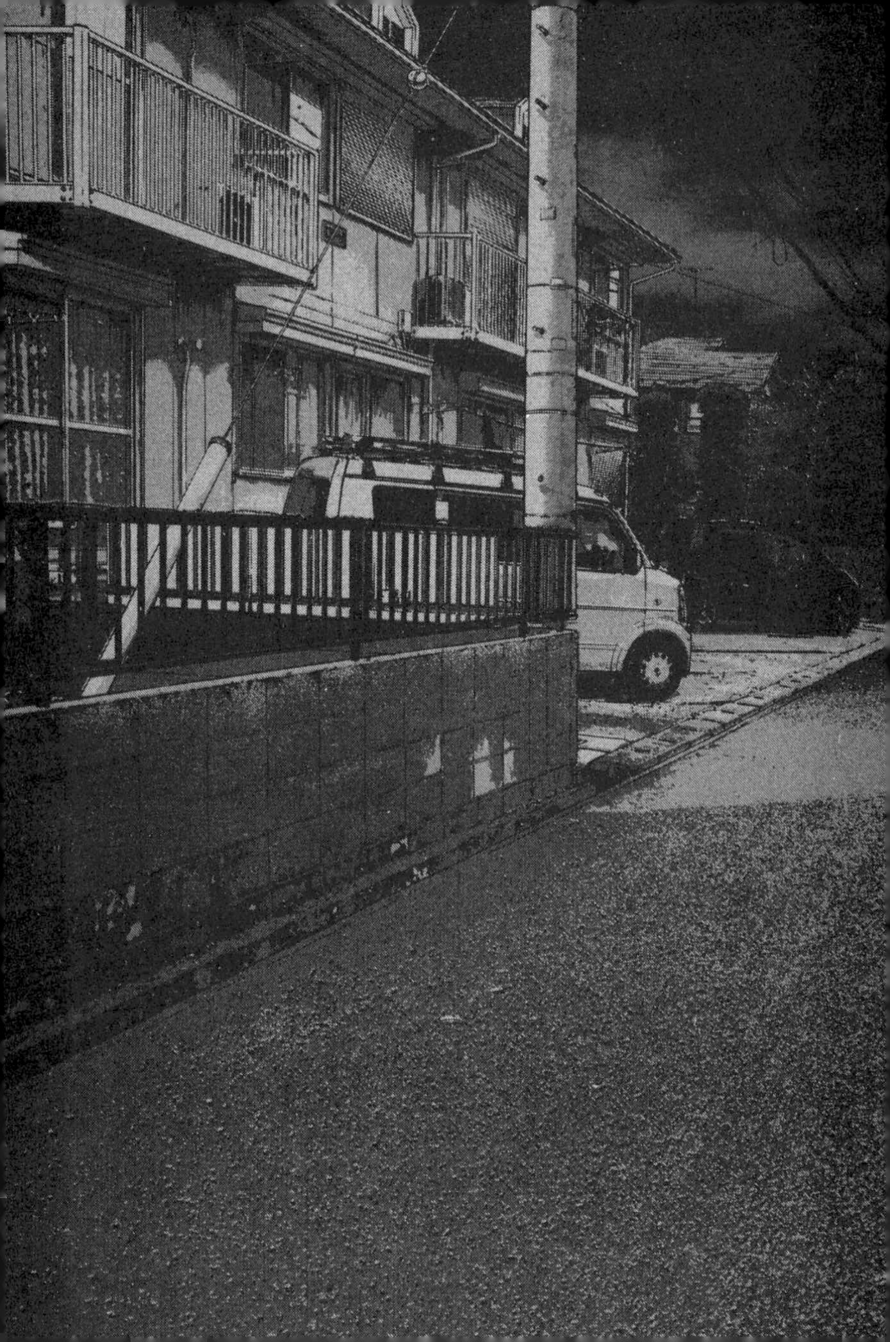

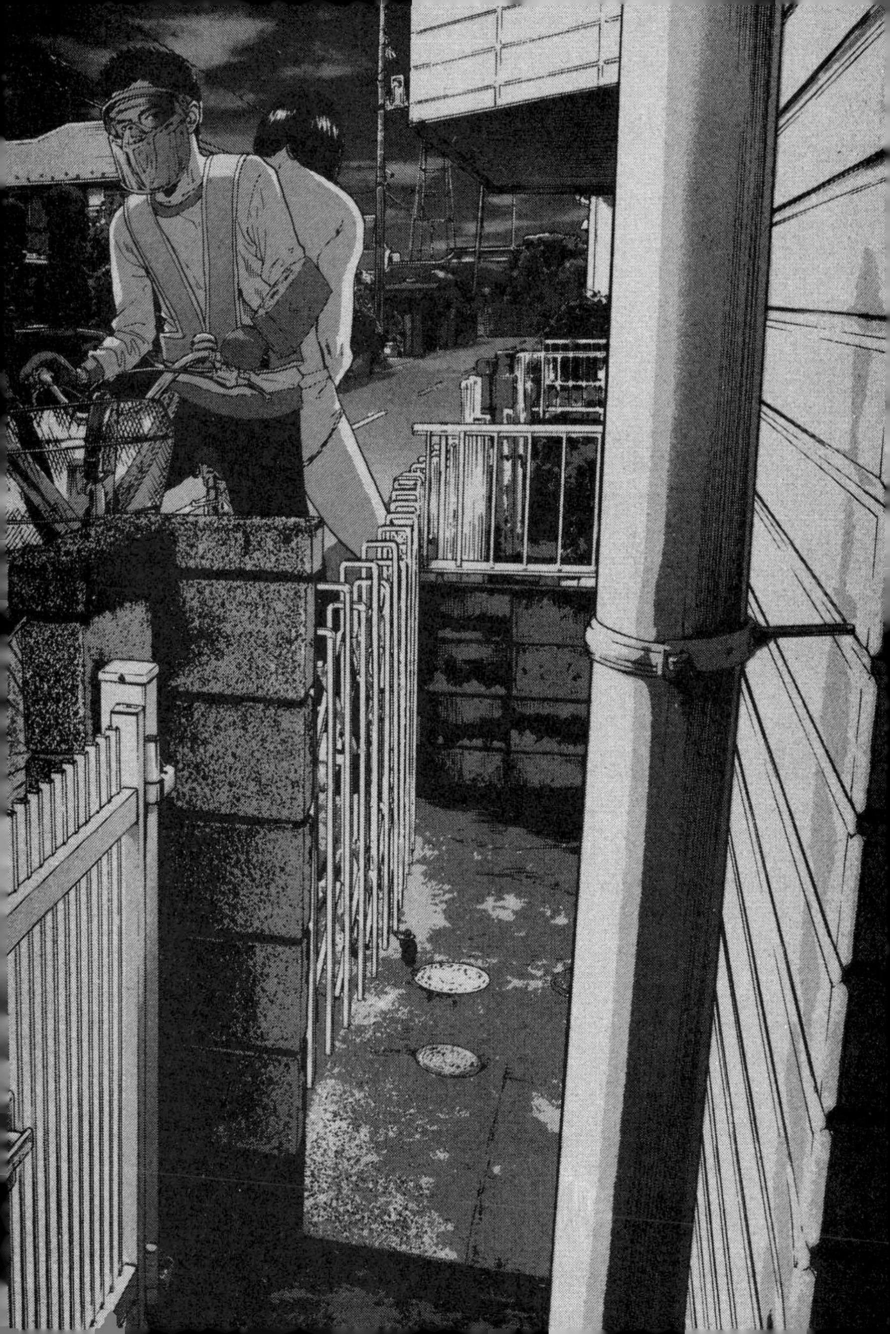

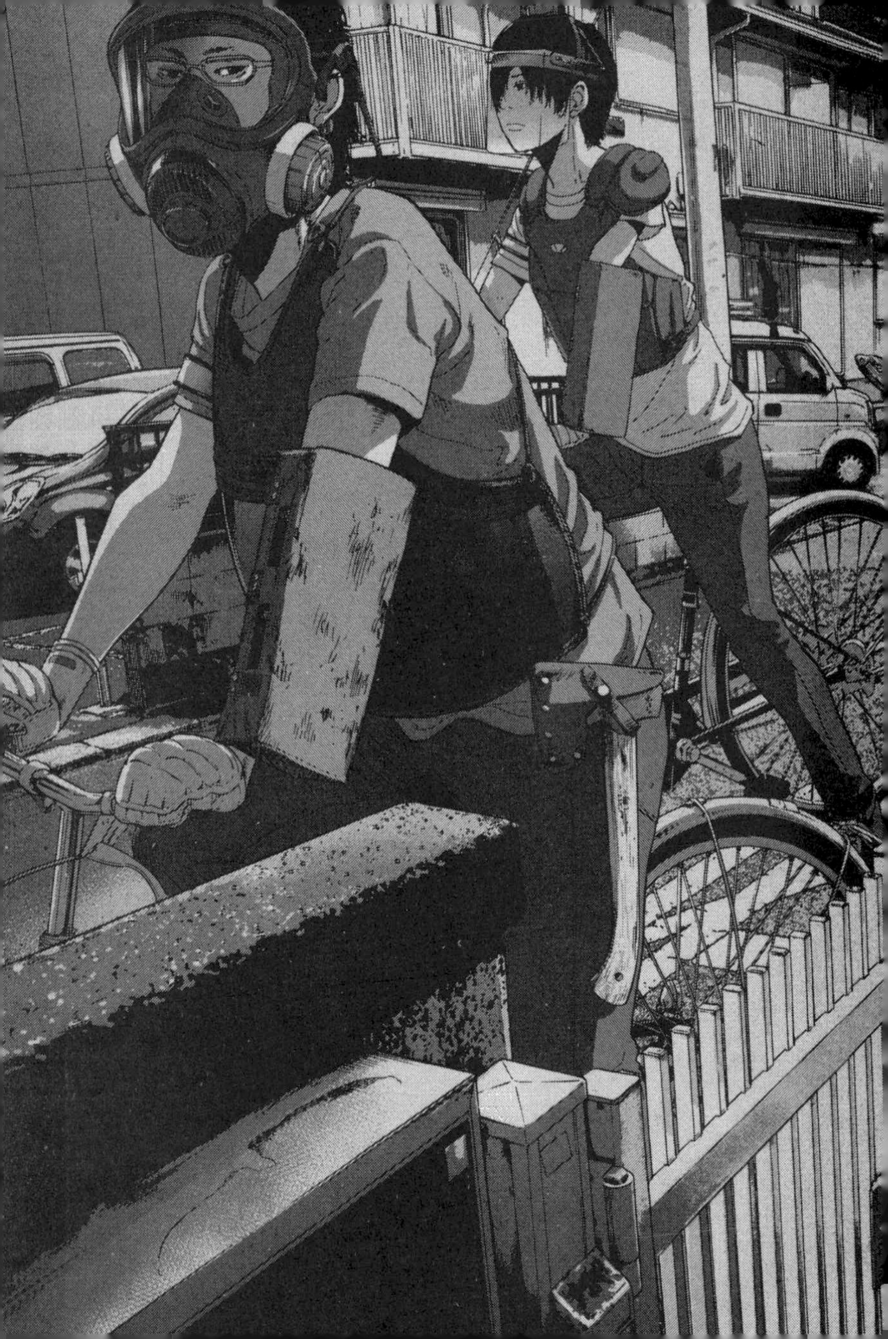

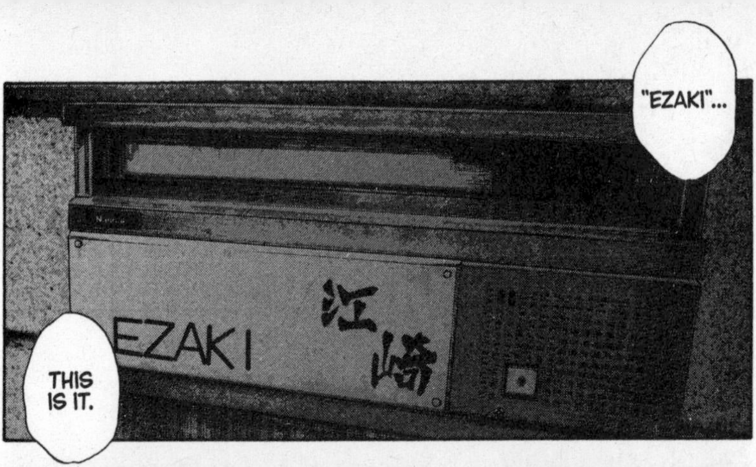
"EZAKI"...
江崎
EZAKI
THIS IS IT.

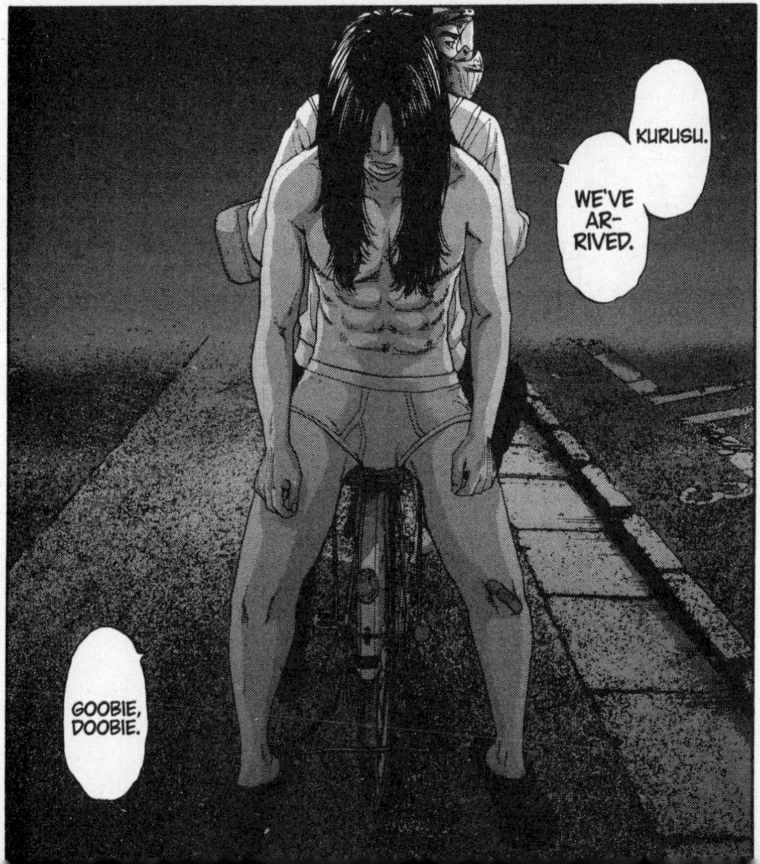
KURUSU.
WE'VE AR-RIVED.
GOOBIE, DOOBIE.

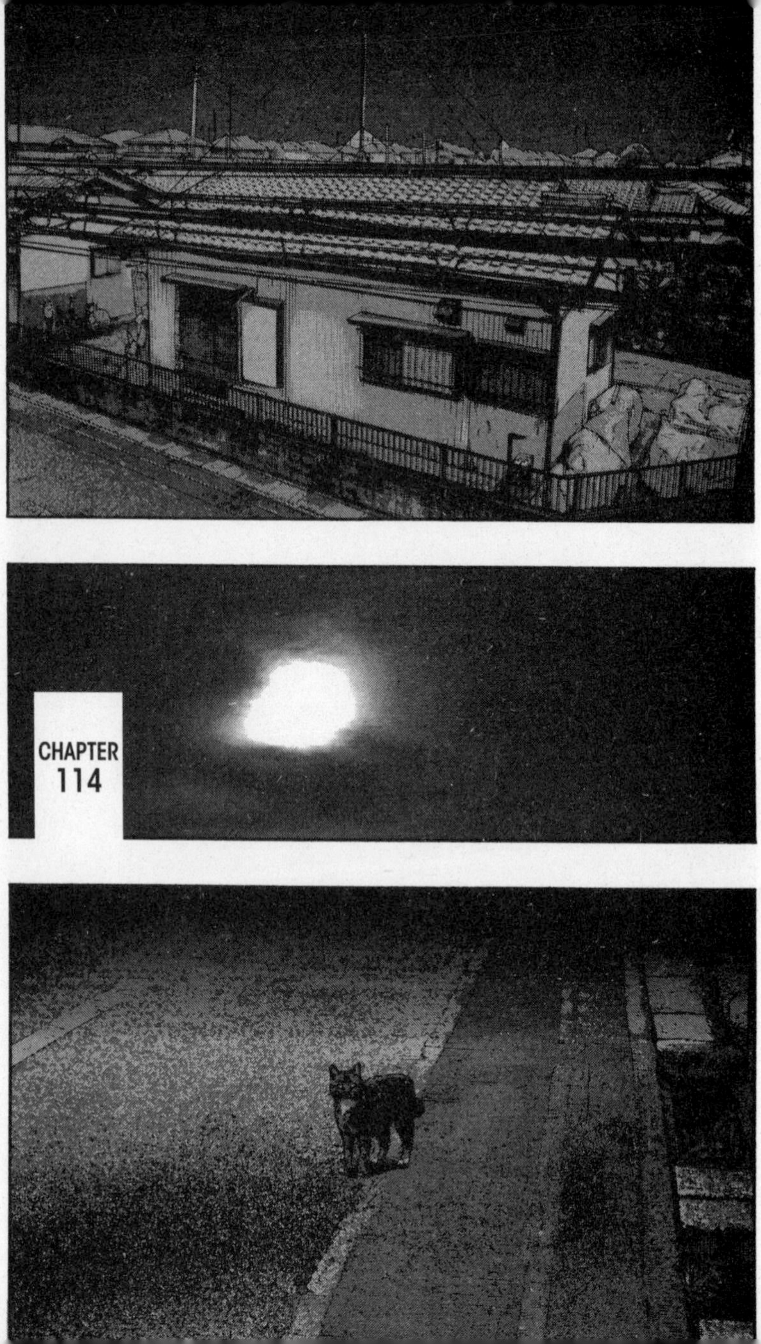
CHAPTER
114

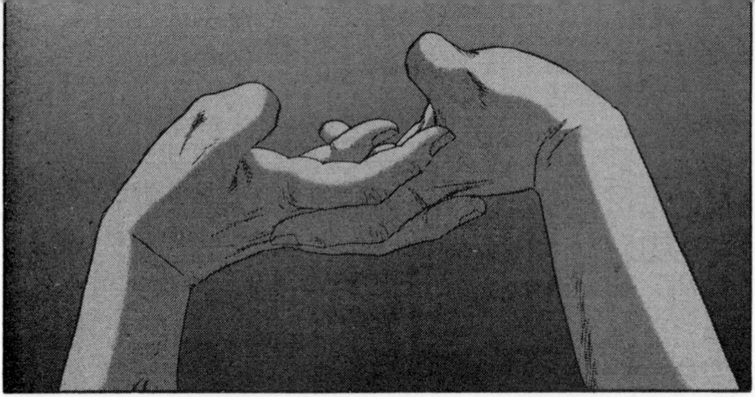
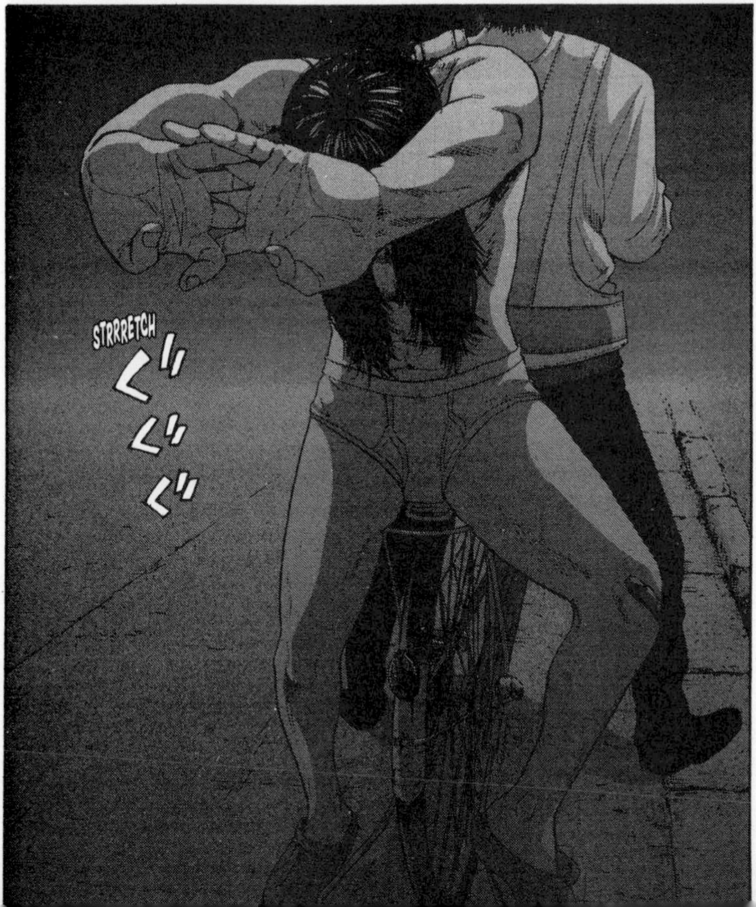
STRRRETCH

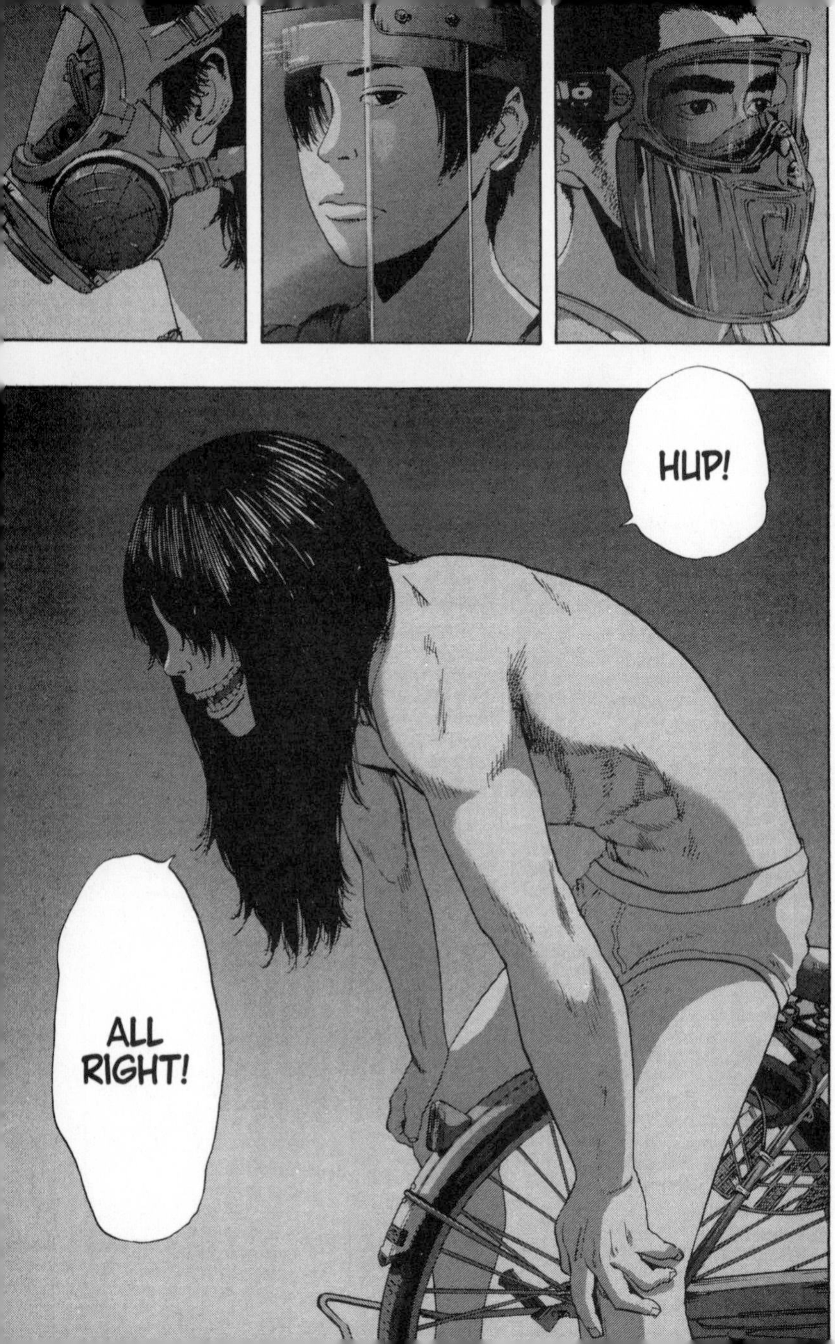
HUP!
ALL RIGHT!

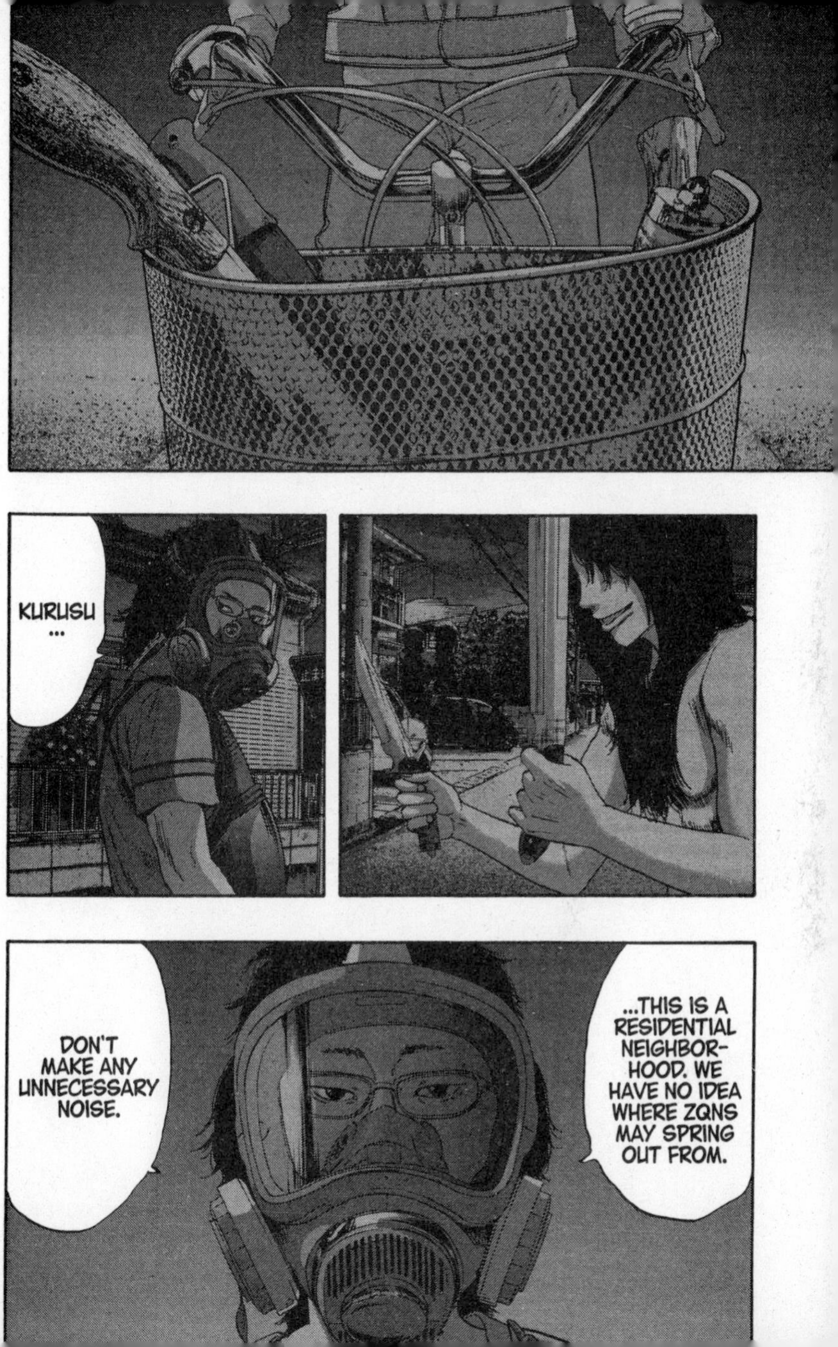
KURUSU ...
...THIS IS A RESIDENTIAL NEIGHBOR-HOOD. WE HAVE NO IDEA WHERE ZQNS MAY SPRING OUT FROM.
DON'T MAKE ANY UNNECESSARY NOISE.

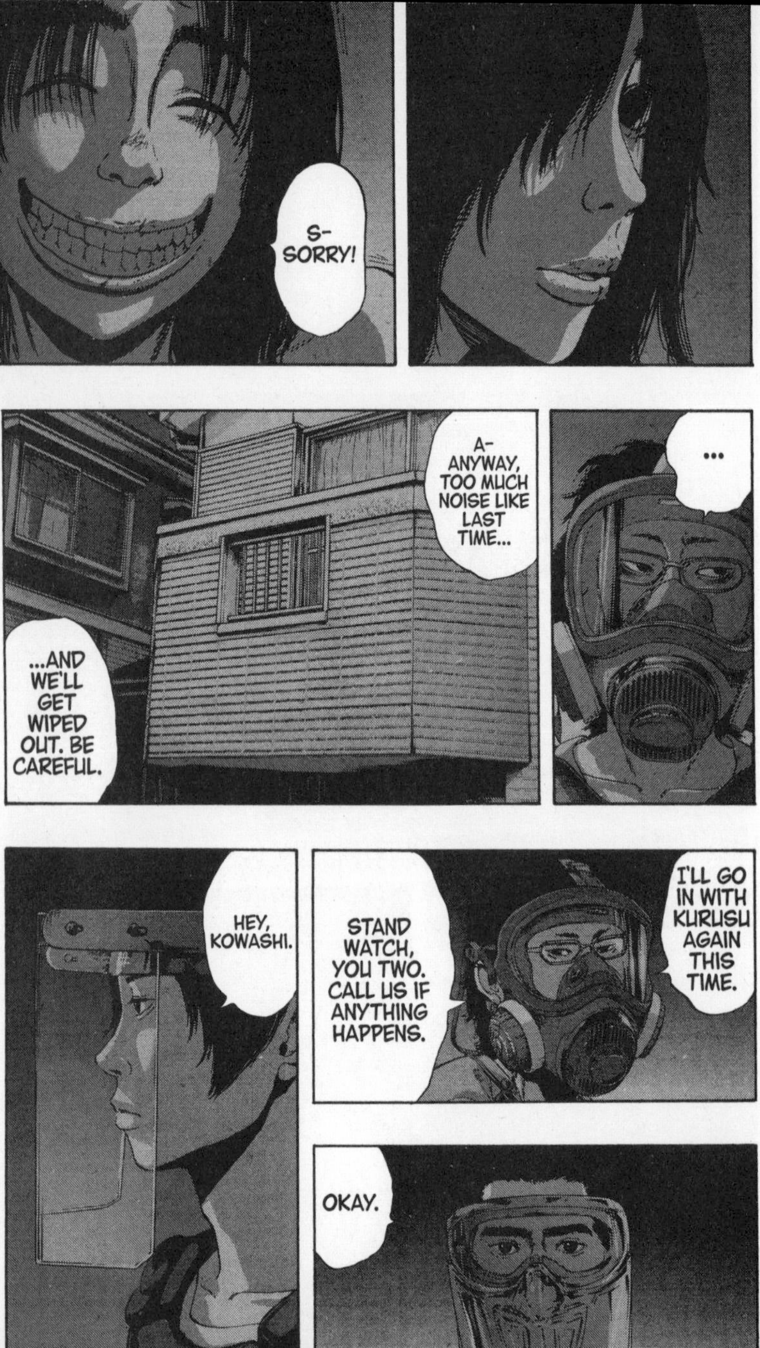
S- SORRY!
...
A- ANYWAY, TOO MUCH NOISE LIKE LAST TIME...
...AND WE'LL GET WIPED OUT. BE CAREFUL.
I'LL GO IN WITH KURUSU AGAIN THIS TIME.
STAND WATCH, YOU TWO. CALL US IF ANYTHING HAPPENS.
OKAY.
HEY, KOWASHI.

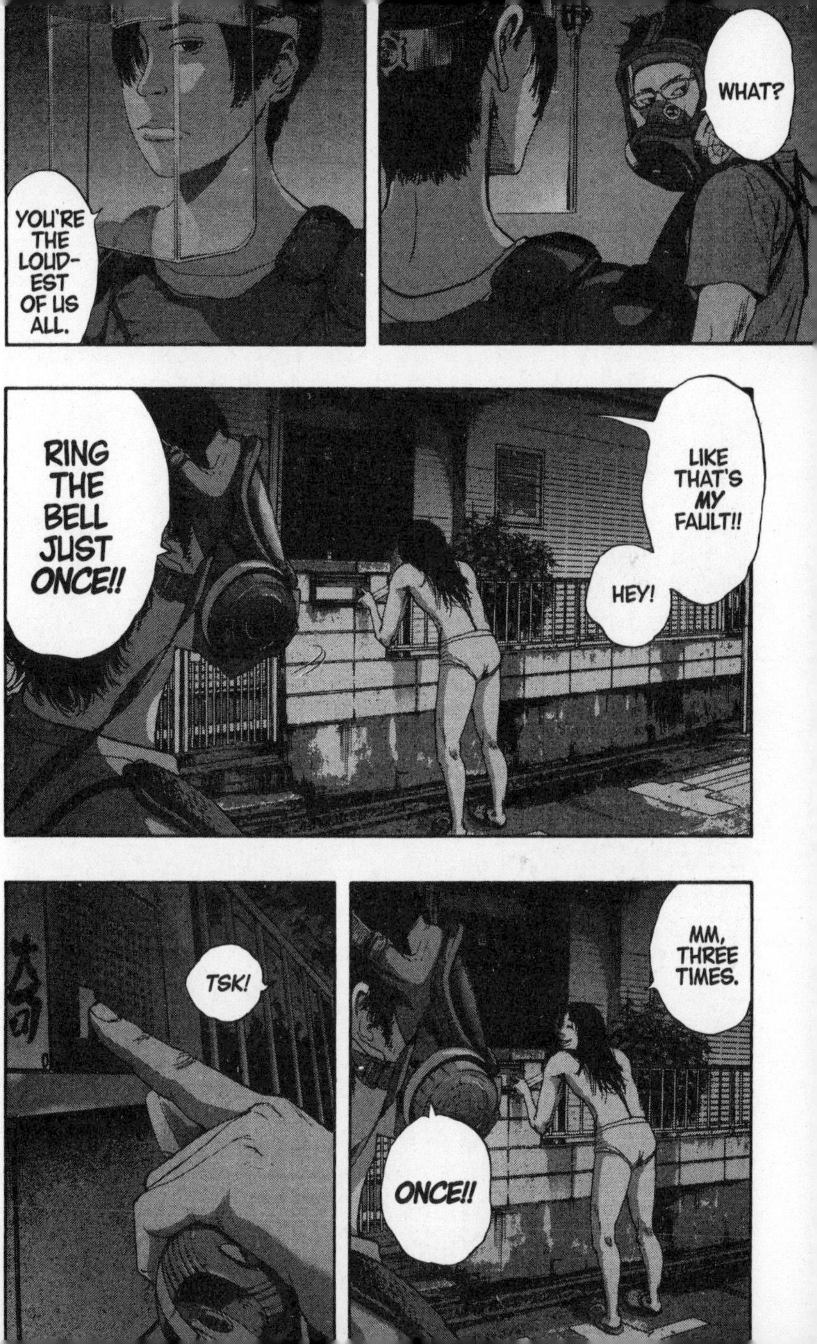
WHAT?
YOU'RE THE LOUD-EST OF US ALL.
LIKE THAT'S *MY* FAULT!!
HEY!
RING THE BELL JUST ONCE!!
MM, THREE TIMES.
ONCE!!
TSK!

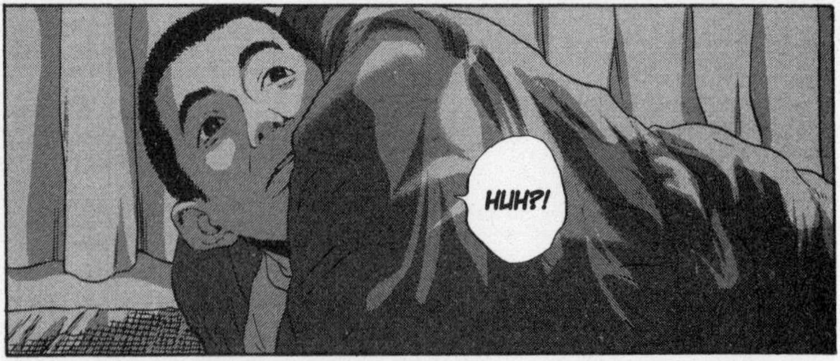
HUH?!
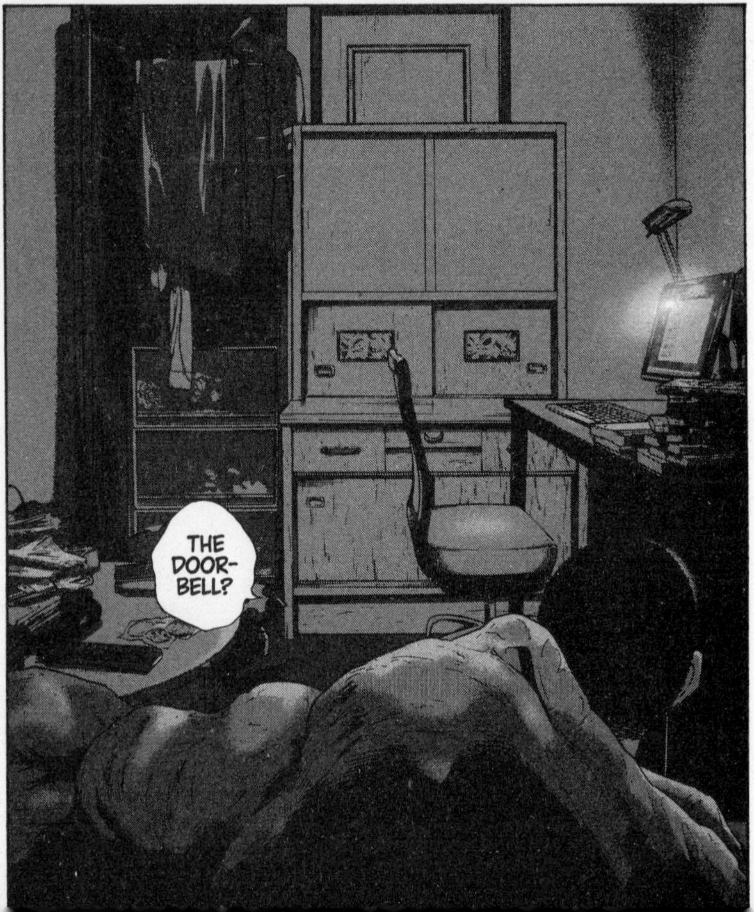
THE DOOR-BELL?

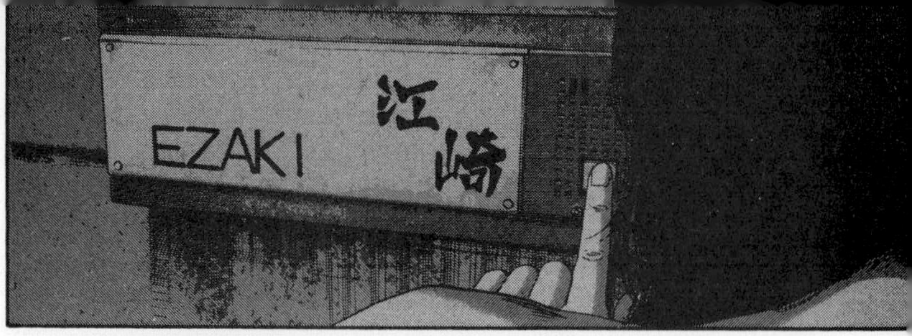
EZAKI
江崎

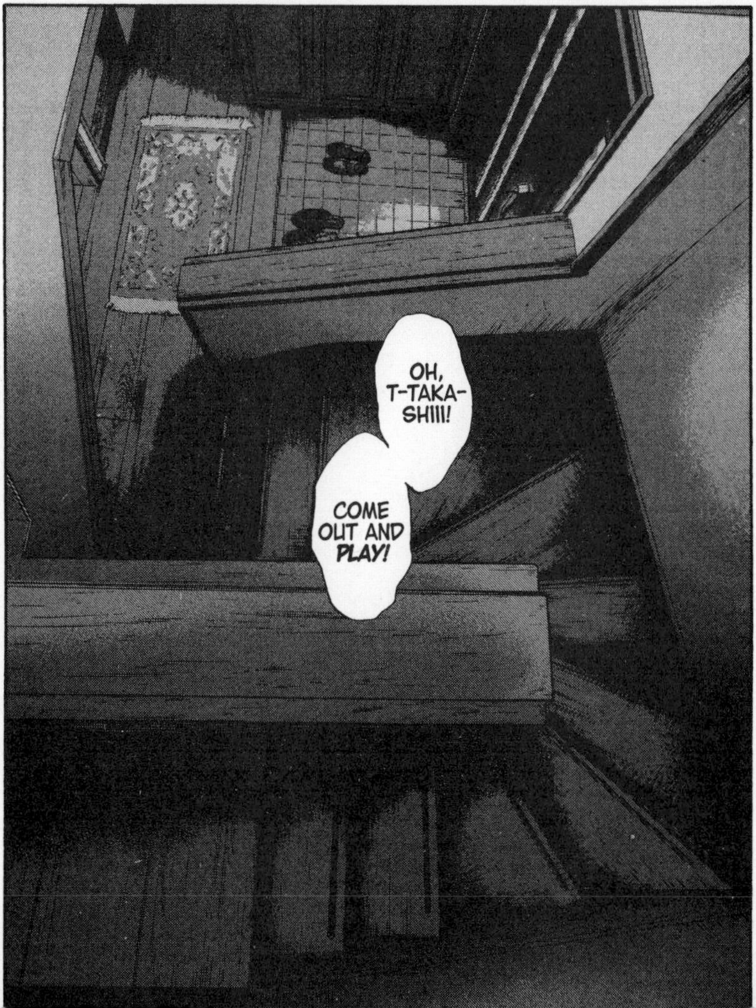
OH, T-TAKA-SHIIII!
COME OUT AND PLAY!

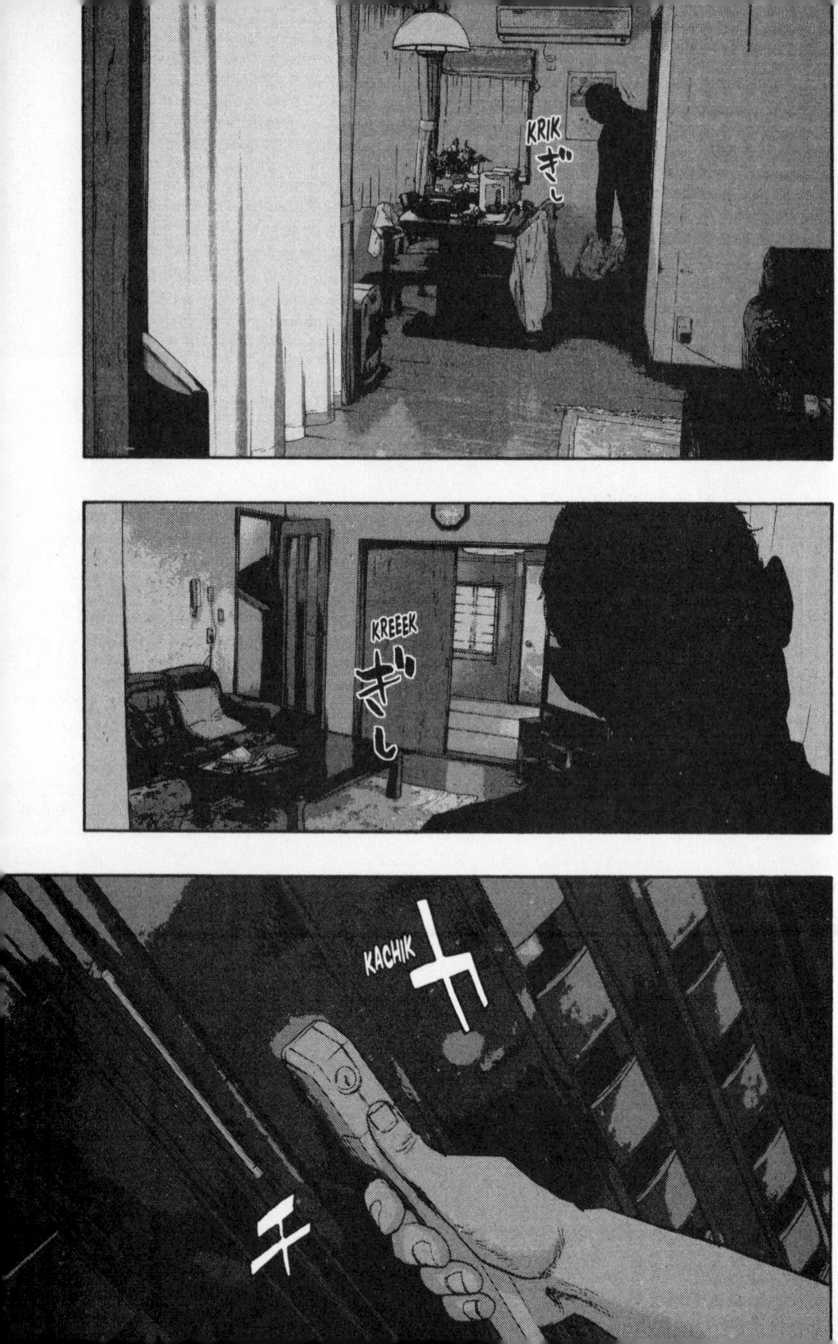
KRIK
ぎし
KREEEK
ぎし
KACHIK

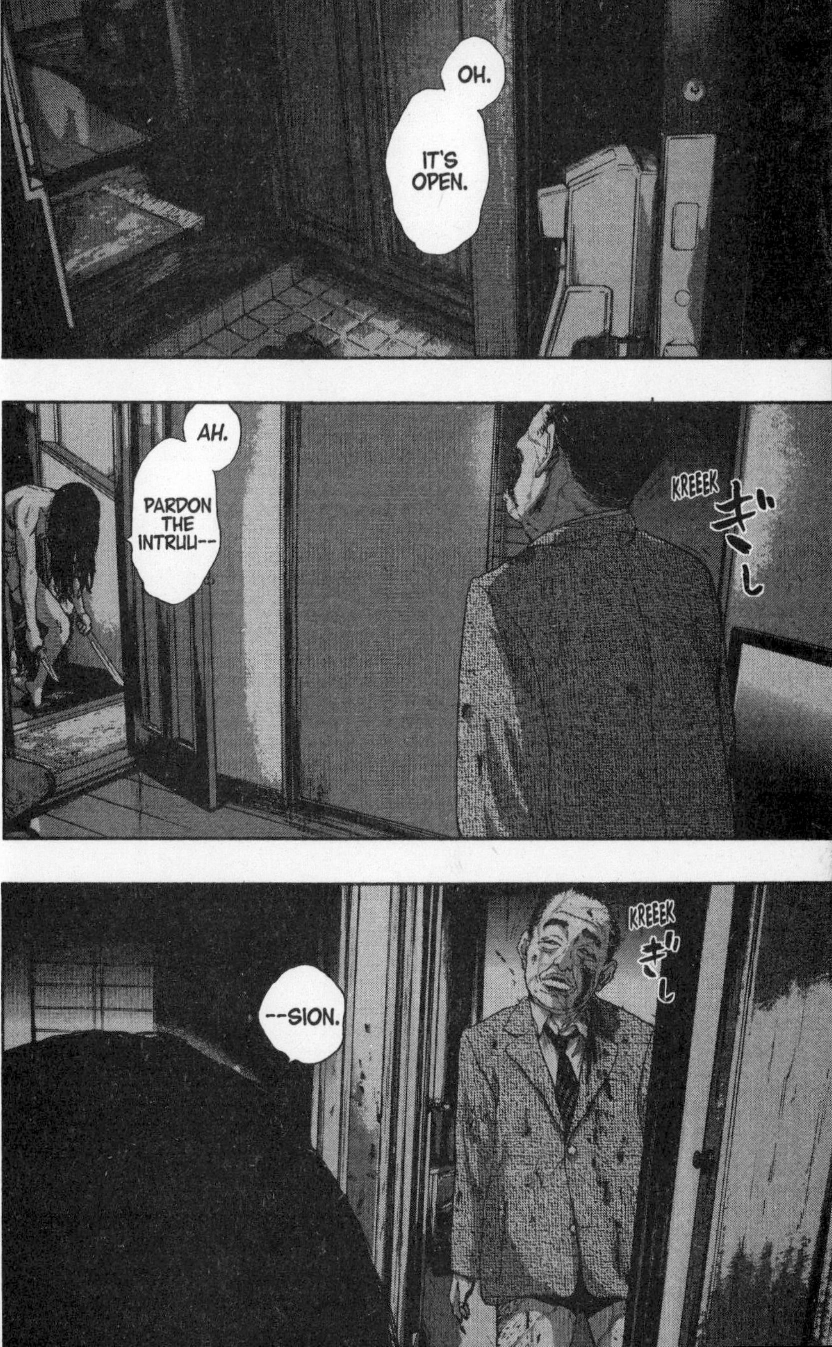
OH.
IT'S OPEN.
KREEEK
ぎし
AH.
PARDON THE INTRUU--
KREEEK
ぎし
--SION.

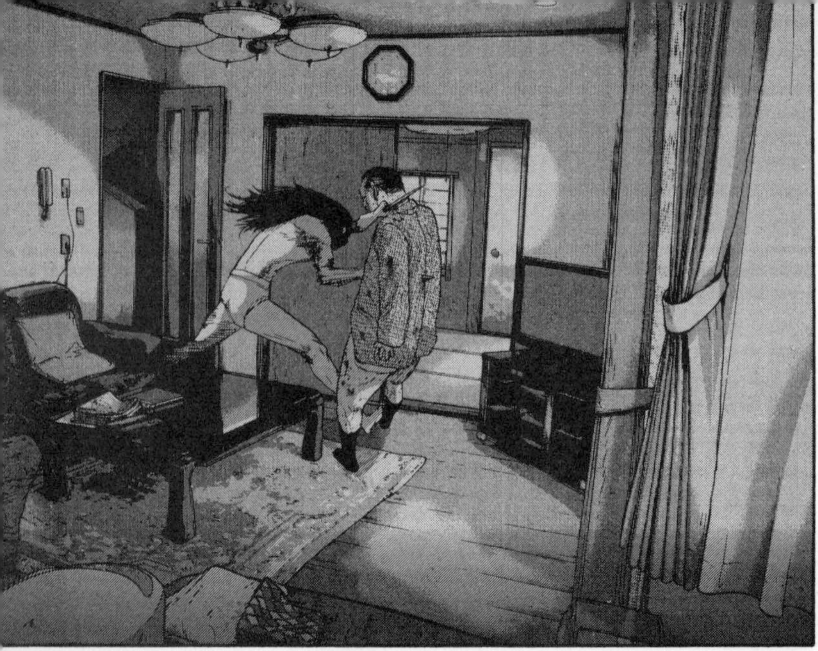
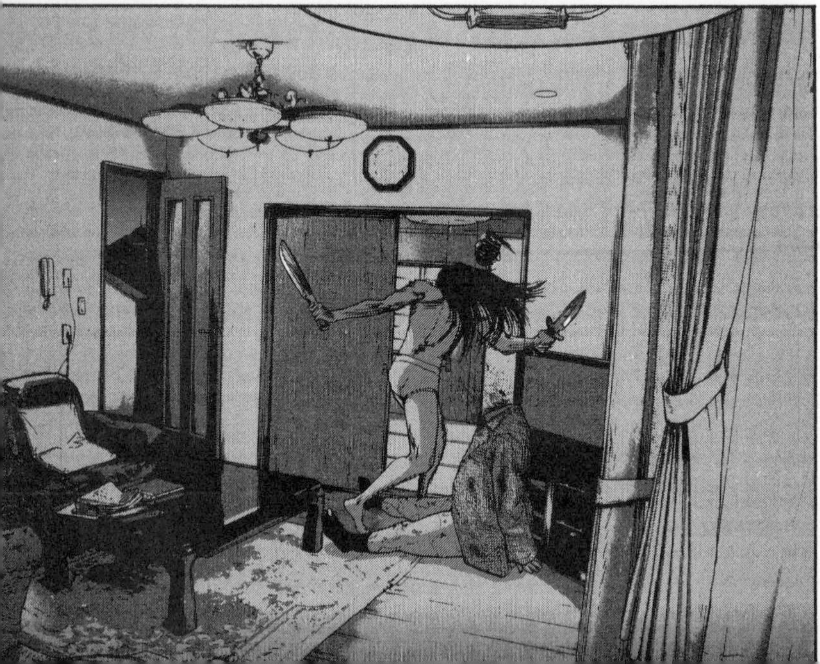

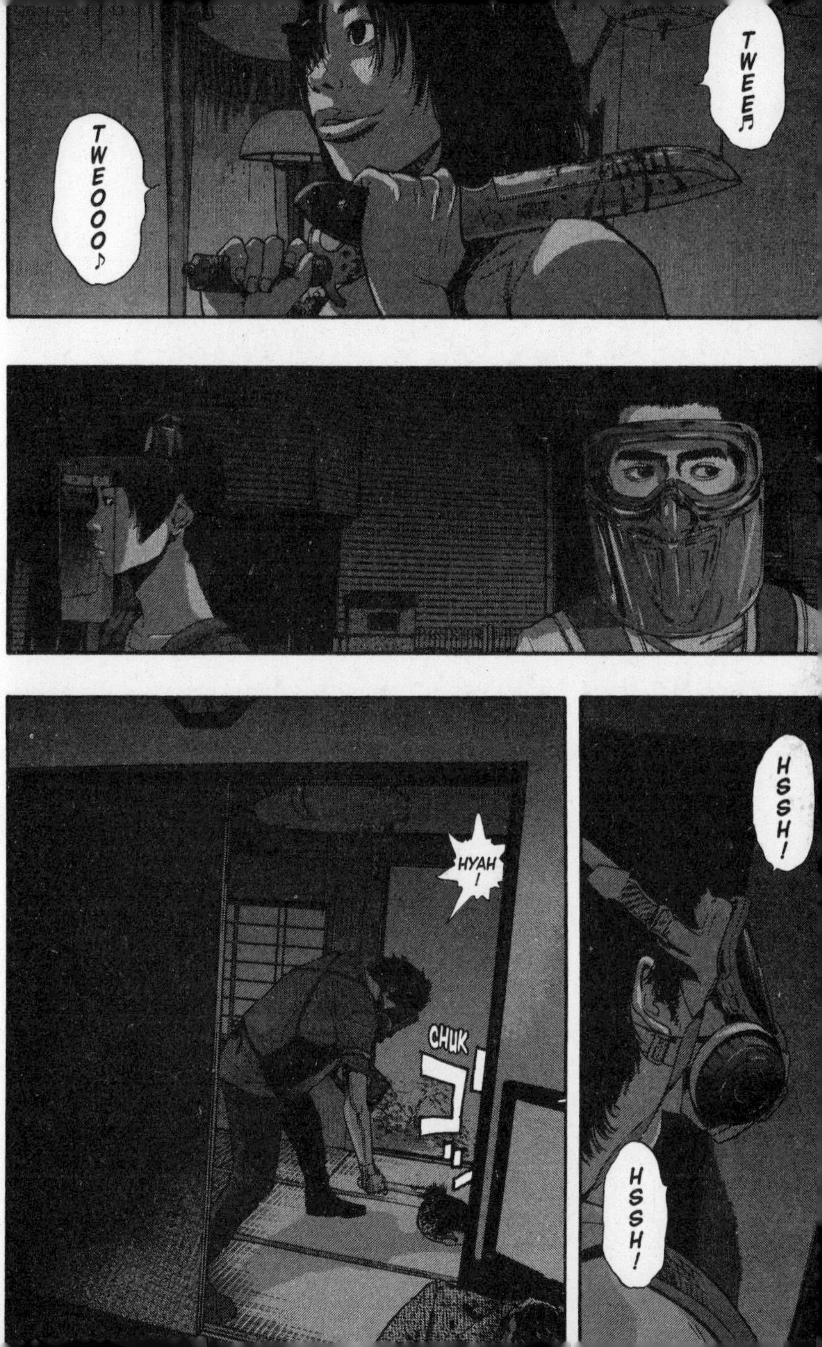
TWEE♬
TWEOOO♪
HSSH!
HSSH!
HYAH!
CHUK

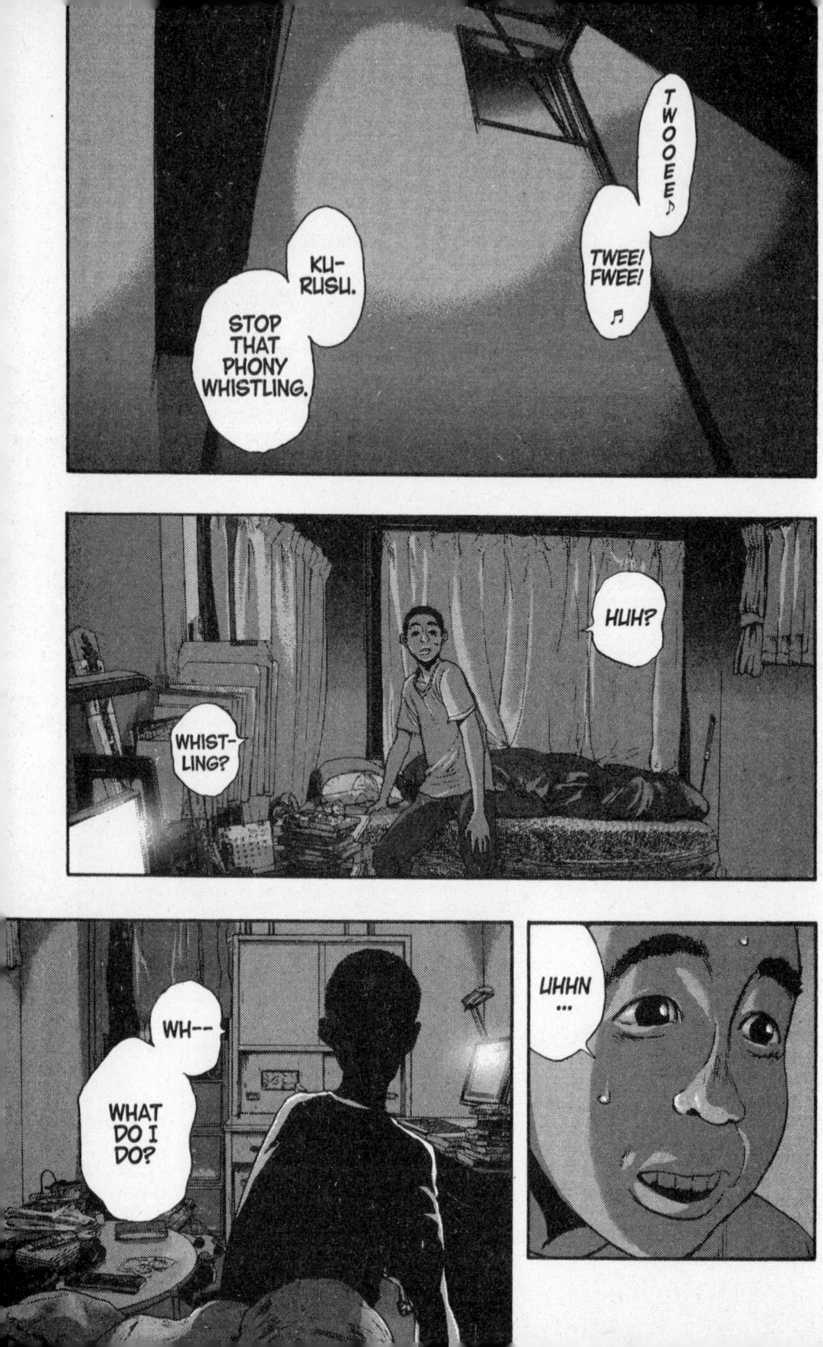
TWOOEE♪
TWEE! FWEE! ♬
KU-RUSU.
STOP THAT PHONY WHISTLING.
HUH?
WHIST-LING?
UHHN...
WH--
WHAT DO I DO?

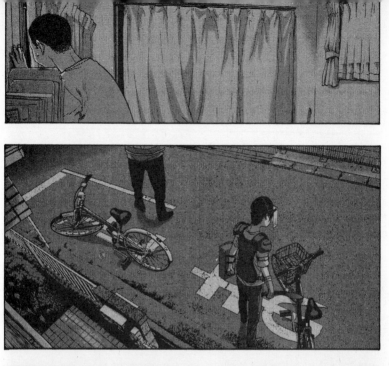

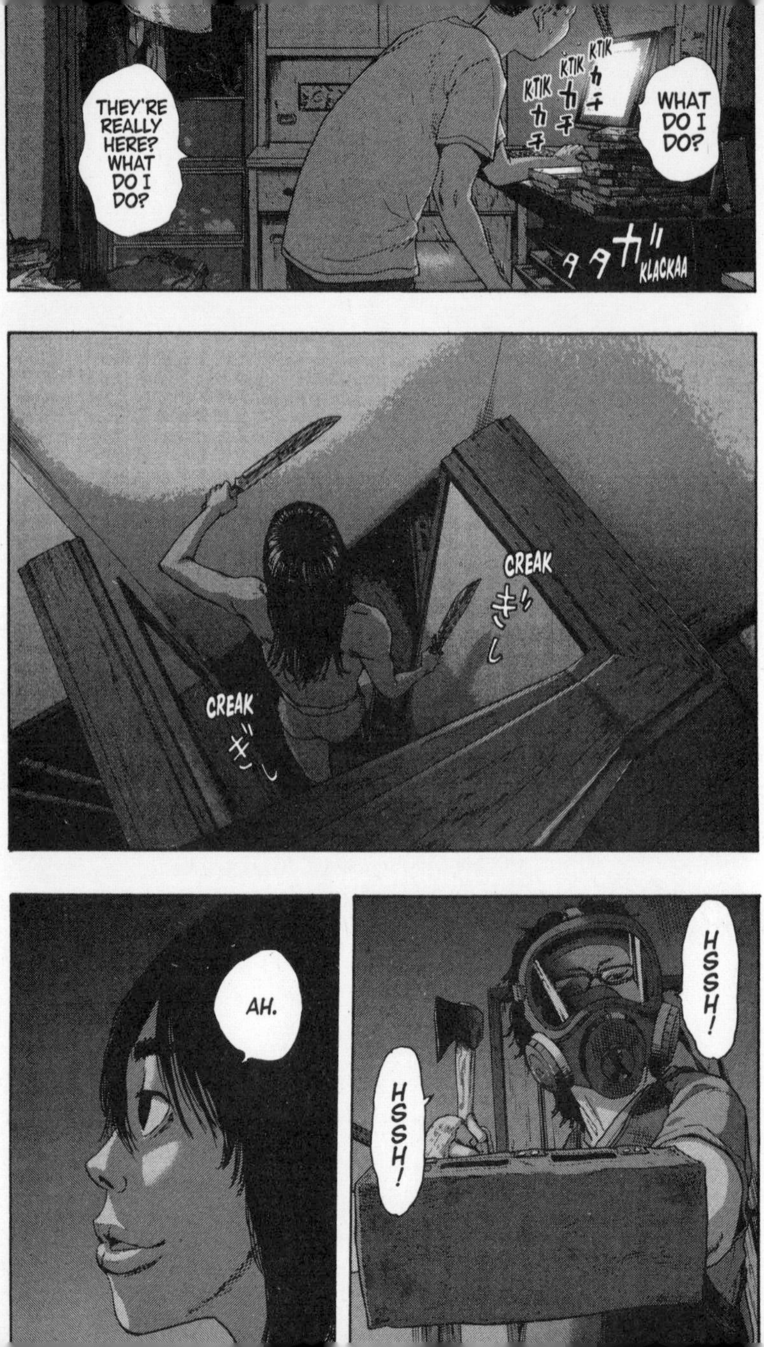
WHAT DO I DO?
KTIK カチ
KTIK カチ
KTIK カチ
THEY'RE REALLY HERE? WHAT DO I DO?
タタカ" KLACKAA
CREAK ぎし
CREAK ぎし
HSSH!
HSSH!
AH.

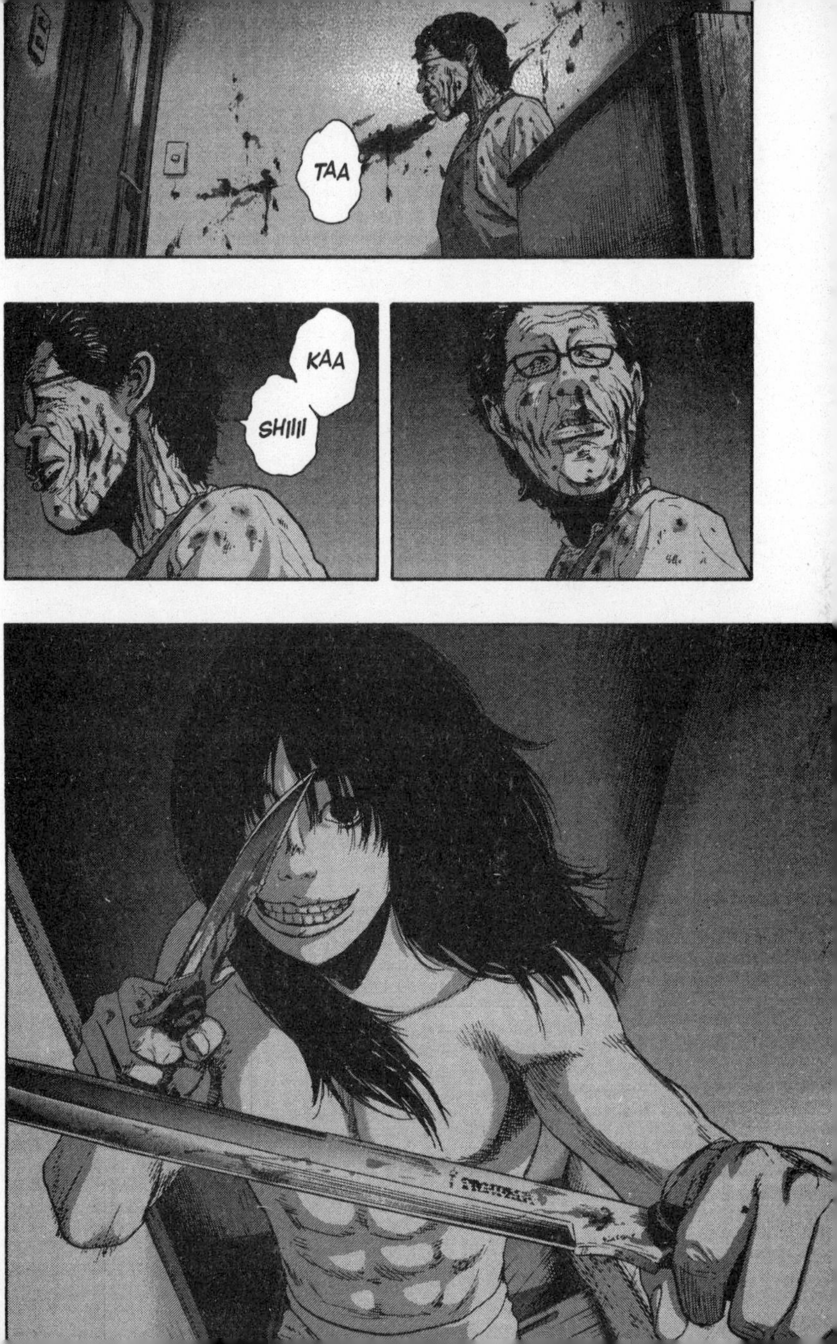
TAA
KAA
SHIIII

スリスリスリ
SHFFSHFFSH

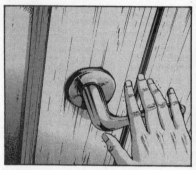

KCHAK

ド
THOKK

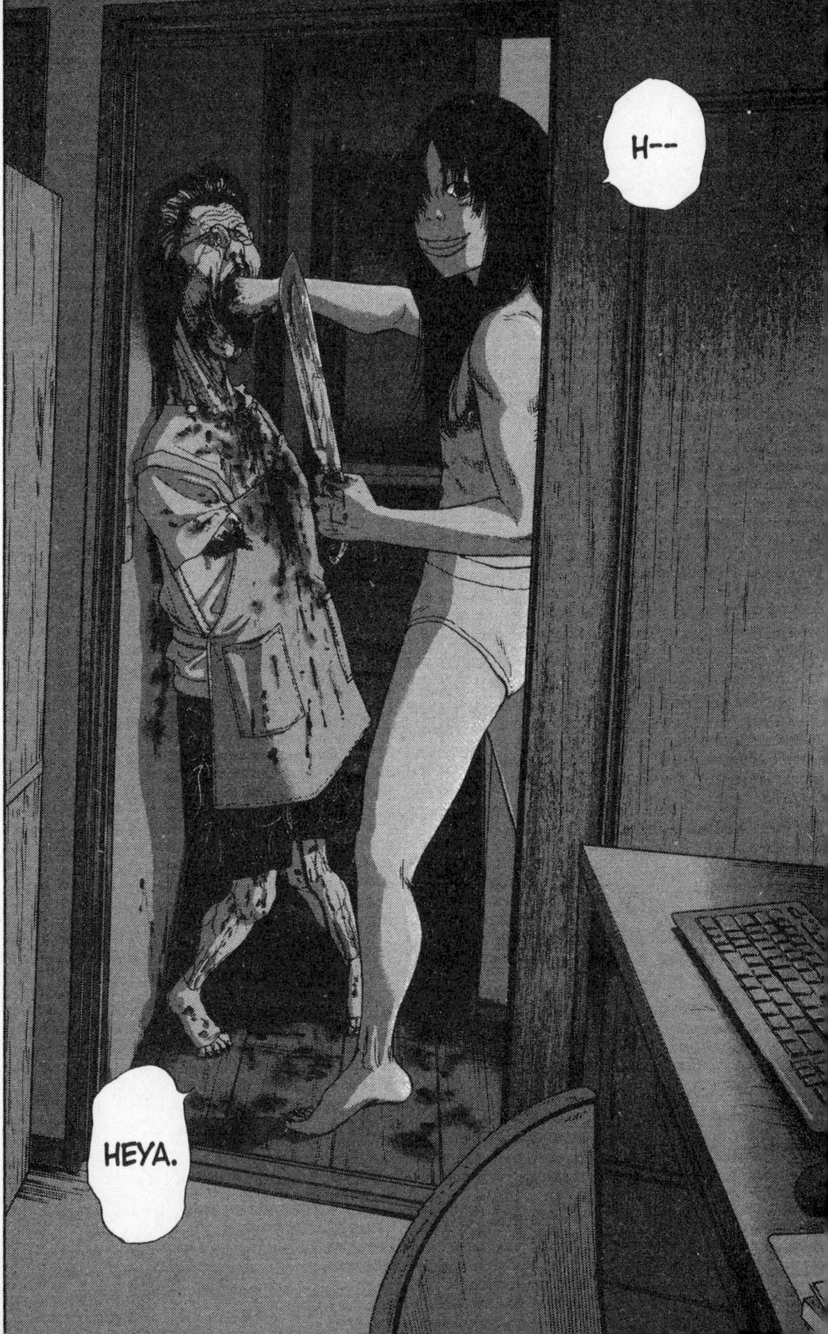
H--
HEYA.

CHAPTER 115

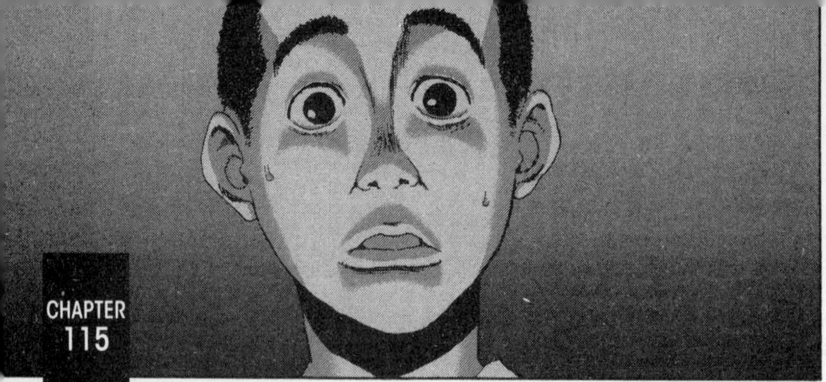

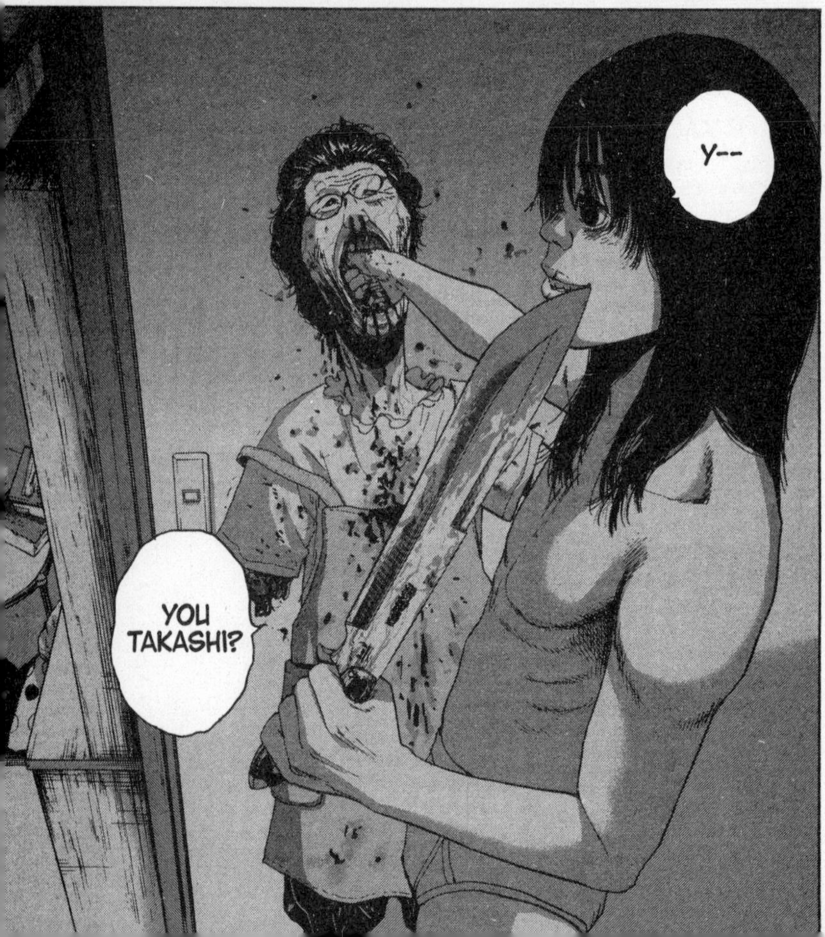
Y--
YOU TAKASHI?

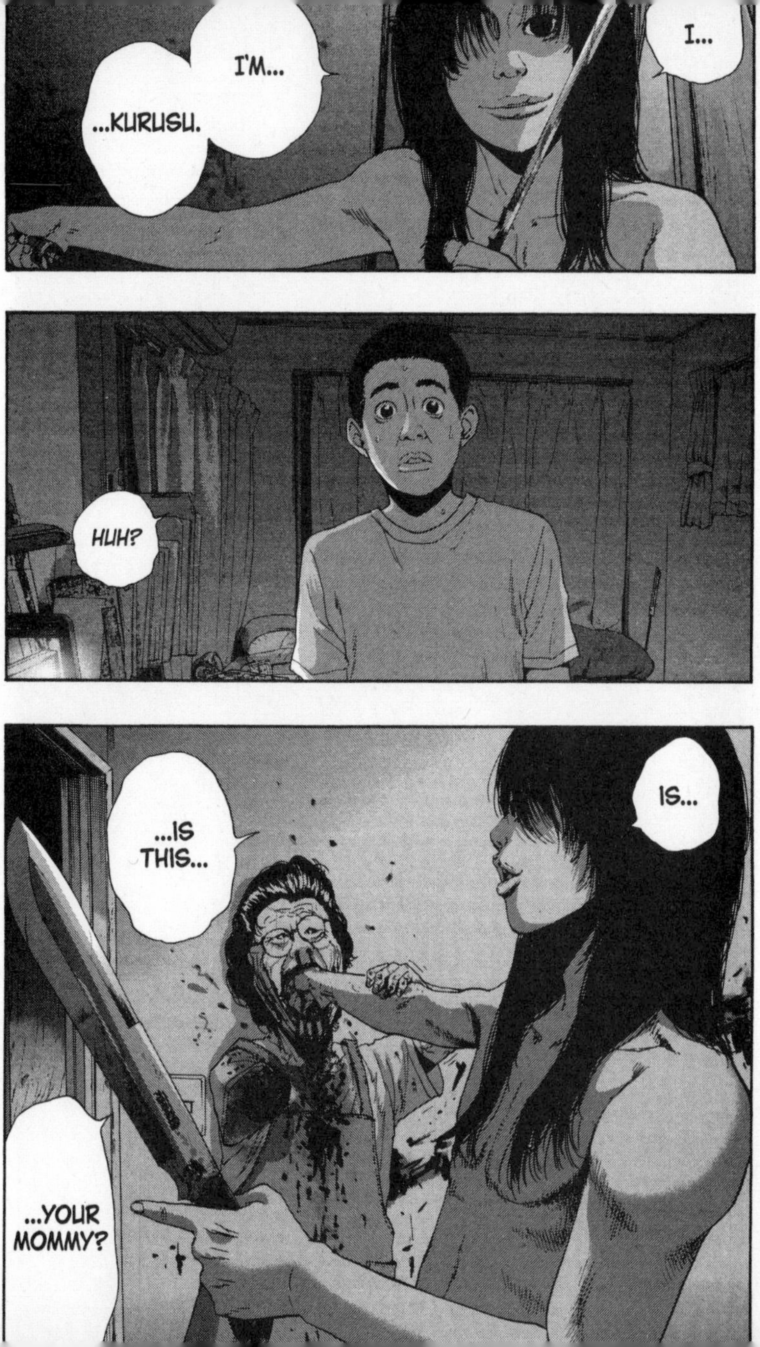
I...
I'M...
...KURUSU.
HUH?
IS...
...IS THIS...
...YOUR MOMMY?

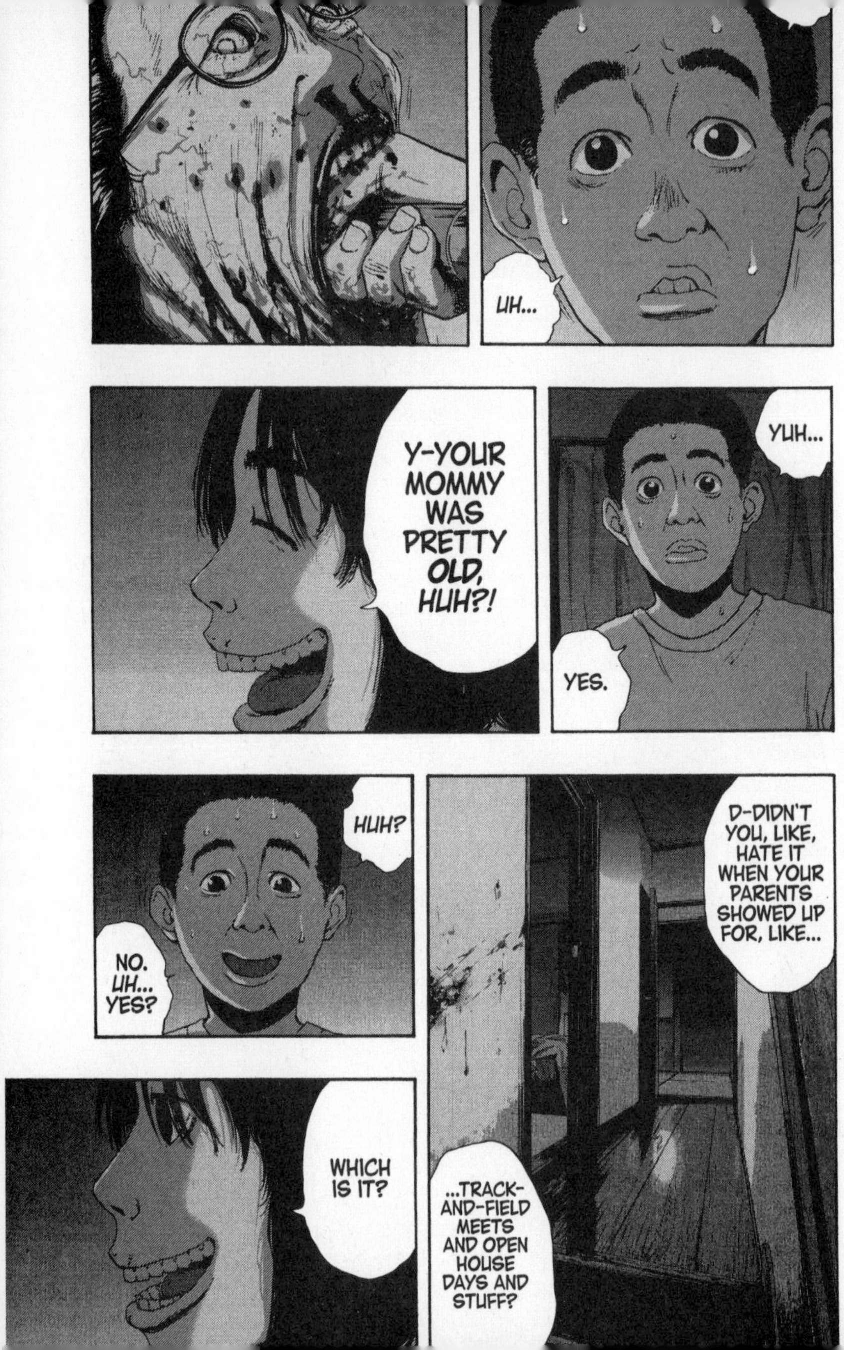
UH...
YUH...
YES.
Y-YOUR MOMMY WAS PRETTY OLD, HUH?!
D-DIDN'T YOU, LIKE, HATE IT WHEN YOUR PARENTS SHOWED UP FOR, LIKE...
...TRACK-AND-FIELD MEETS AND OPEN HOUSE DAYS AND STUFF?
HUH?
NO. UH... YES?
WHICH IS IT?

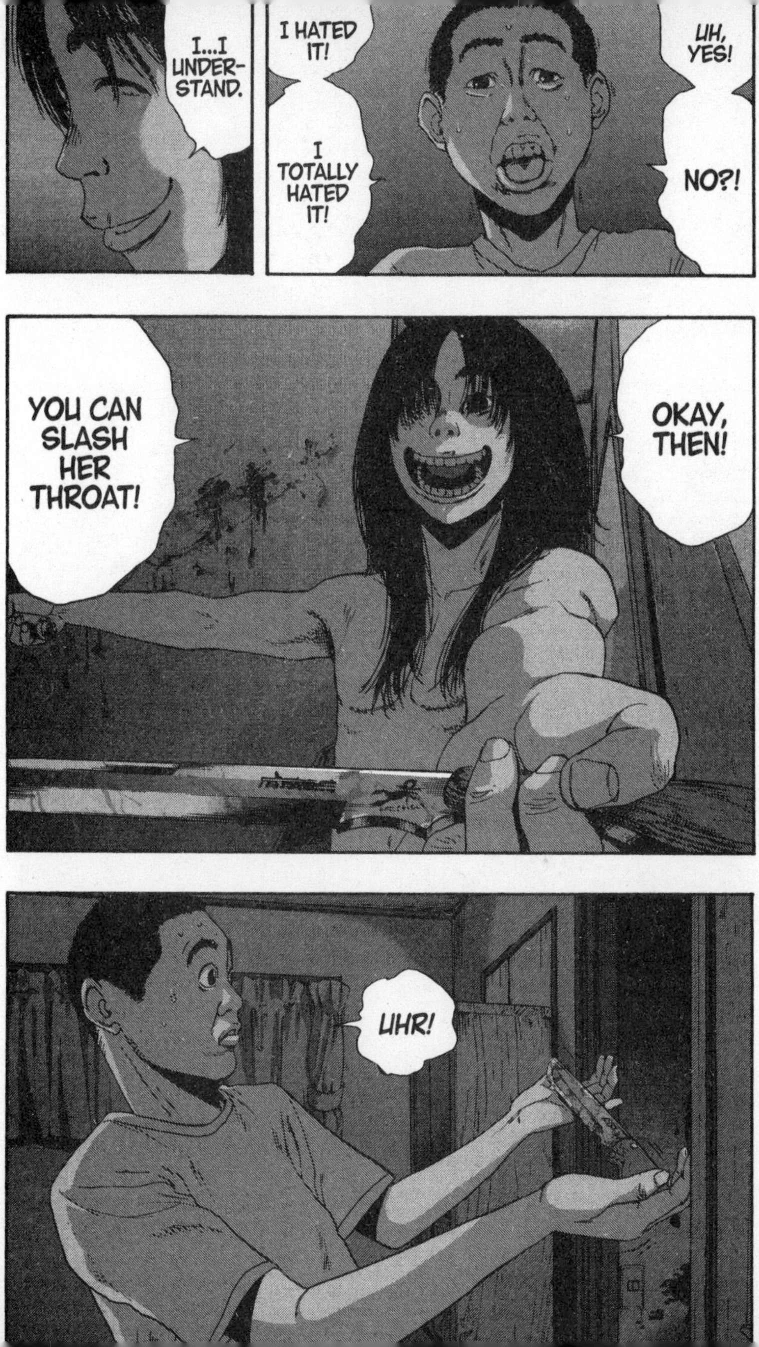
UH, YES!
NO?!
I HATED IT!
I TOTALLY HATED IT!
I...I UNDERSTAND.
OKAY, THEN!
YOU CAN SLASH HER THROAT!
UHR!

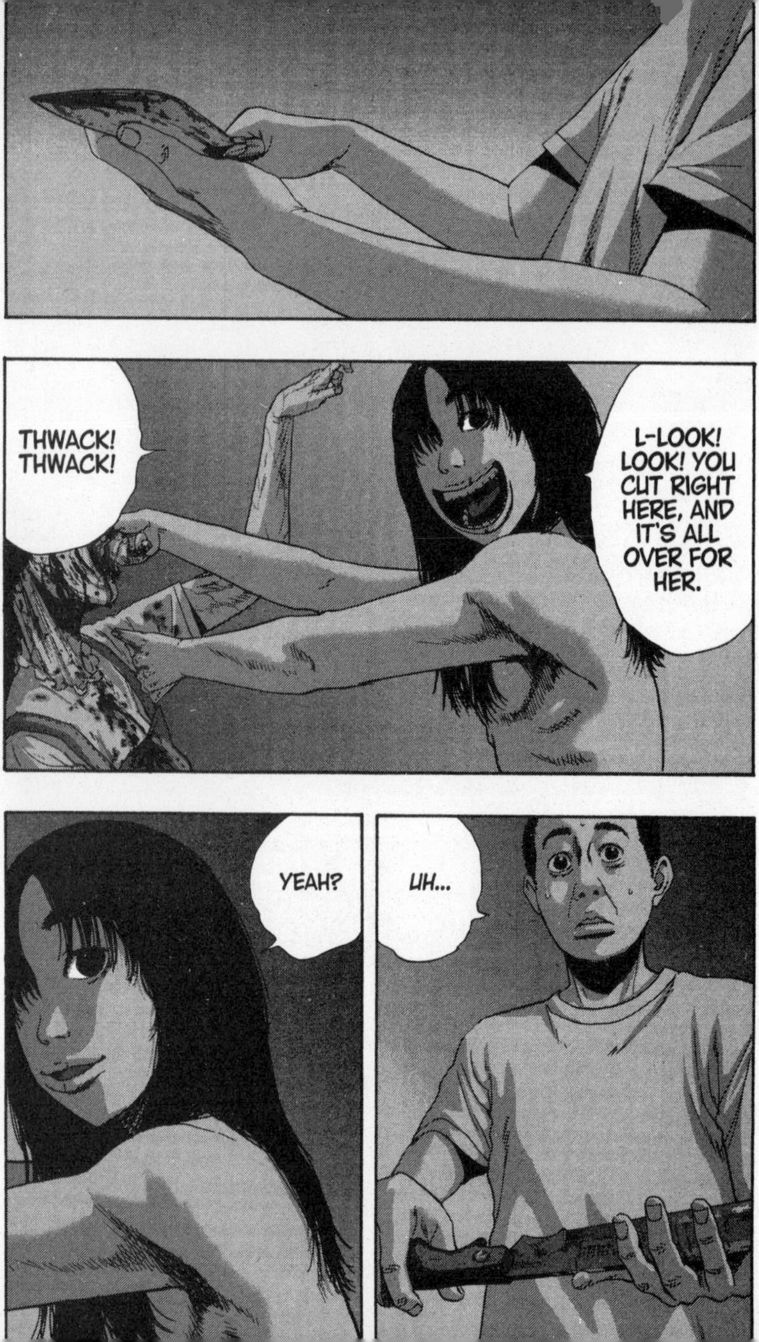
L-LOOK! LOOK! YOU CUT RIGHT HERE, AND IT'S ALL OVER FOR HER.
THWACK! THWACK!
UH...
YEAH?

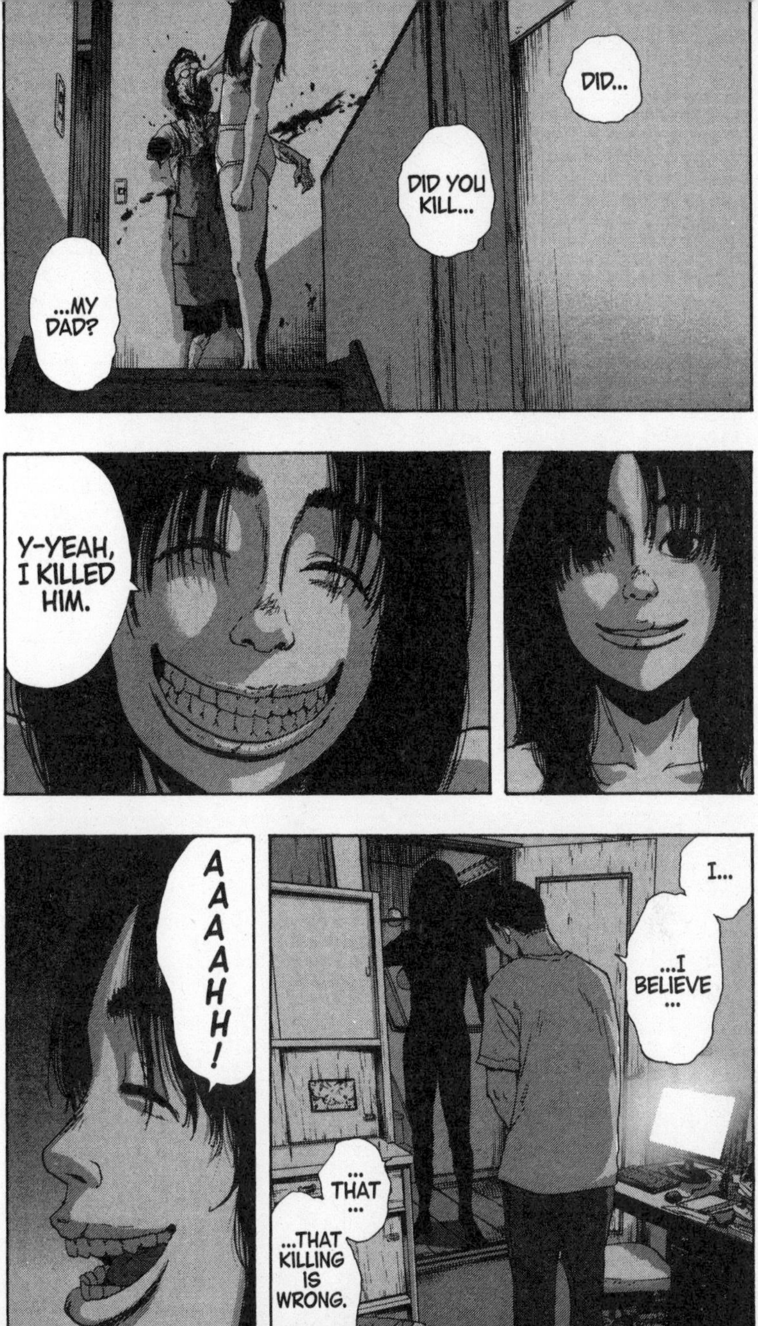
DID...
DID YOU KILL...
...MY DAD?
Y-YEAH, I KILLED HIM.
I...
...I BELIEVE ...
... THAT ...
...THAT KILLING IS WRONG.
AAAAHH!

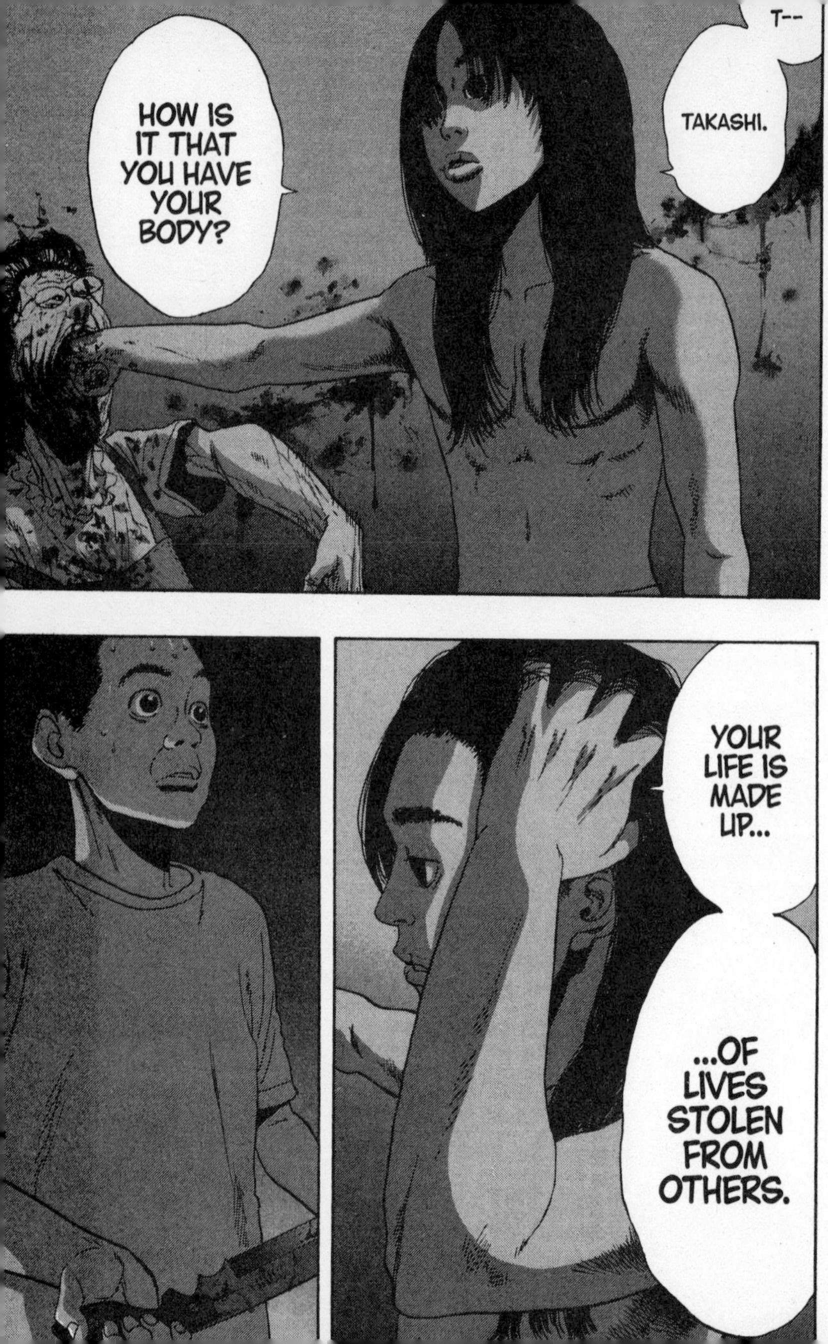
T--
TAKASHI.
HOW IS IT THAT YOU HAVE YOUR BODY?
YOUR LIFE IS MADE UP...
...OF LIVES STOLEN FROM OTHERS.

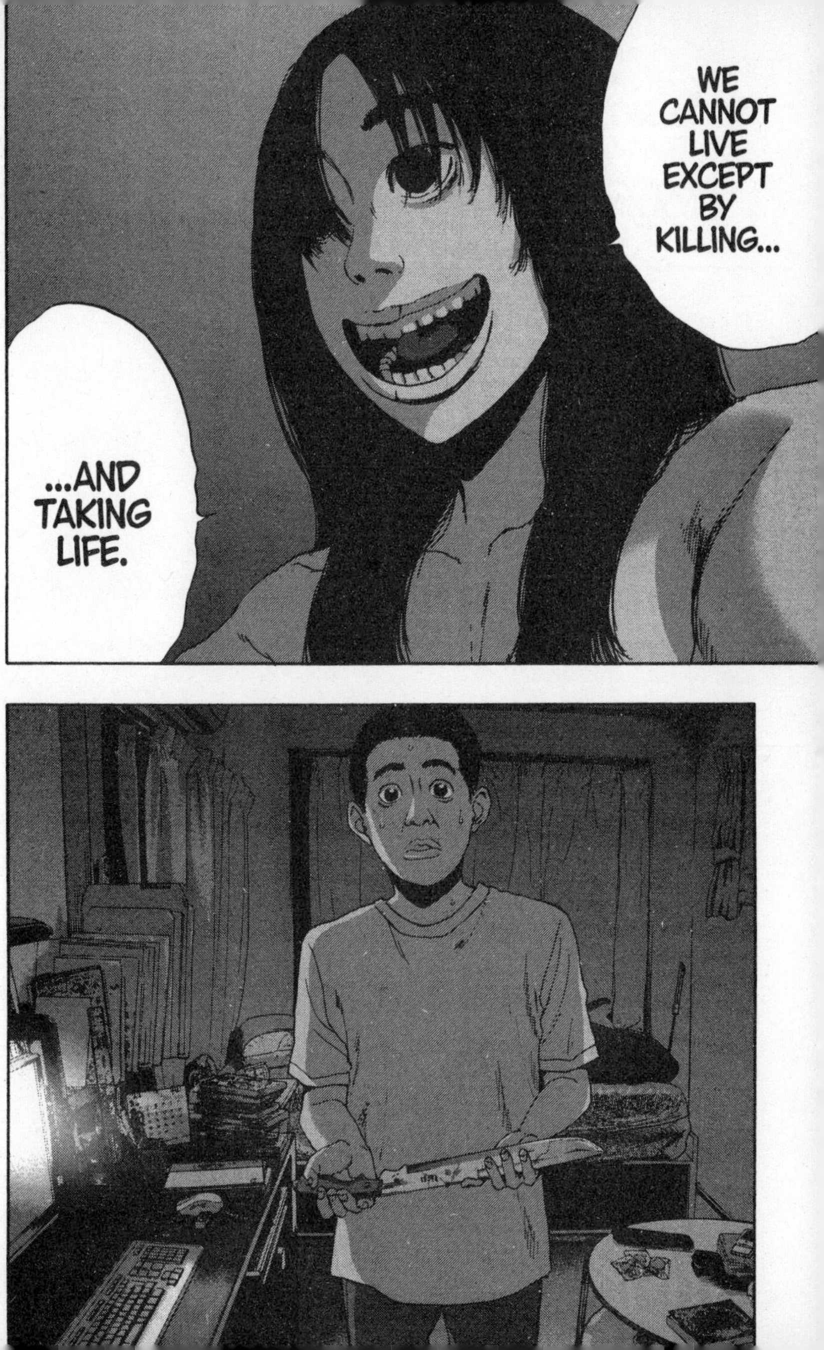
WE CANNOT LIVE EXCEPT BY KILLING...
...AND TAKING LIFE.

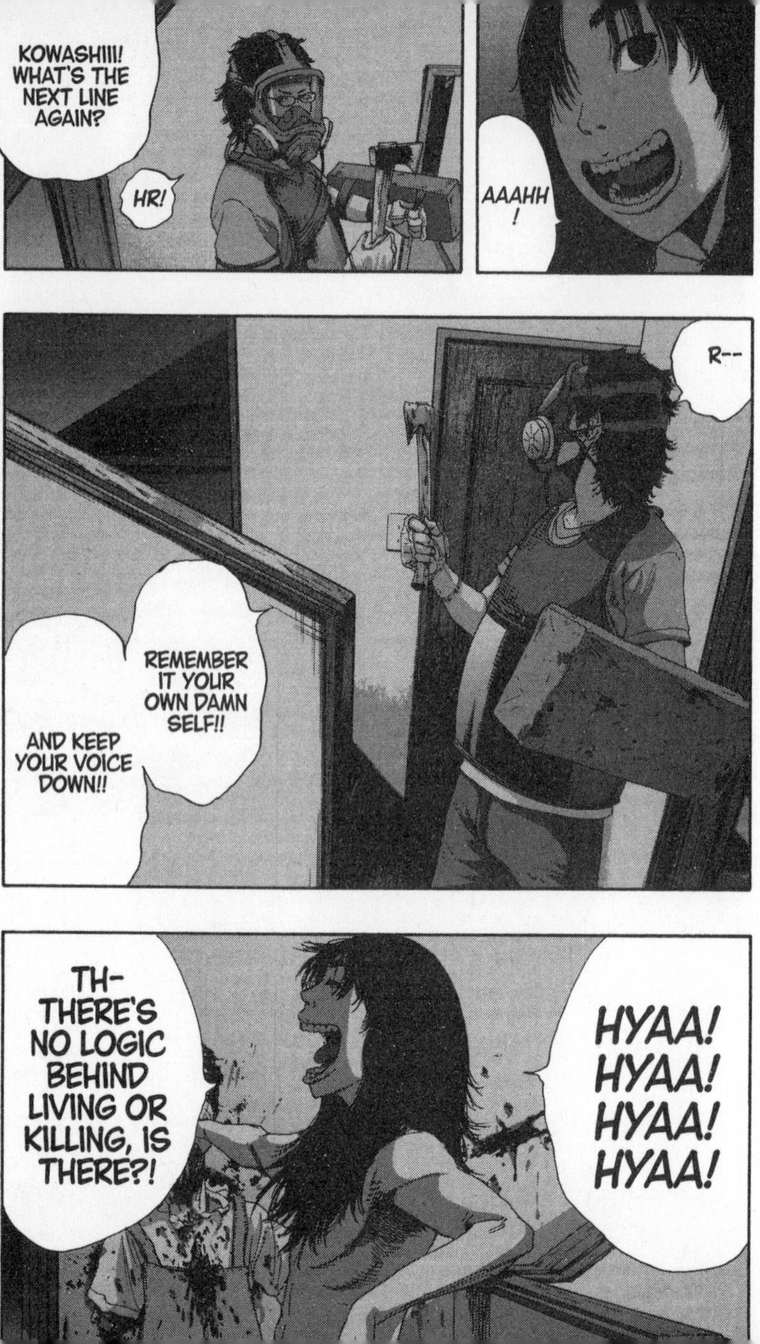
AAAHH!
KOWASHIII! WHAT'S THE NEXT LINE AGAIN?
HR!
R--
REMEMBER IT YOUR OWN DAMN SELF!!
AND KEEP YOUR VOICE DOWN!!
HYAA! HYAA! HYAA! HYAA!
TH- THERE'S NO LOGIC BEHIND LIVING OR KILLING, IS THERE?!

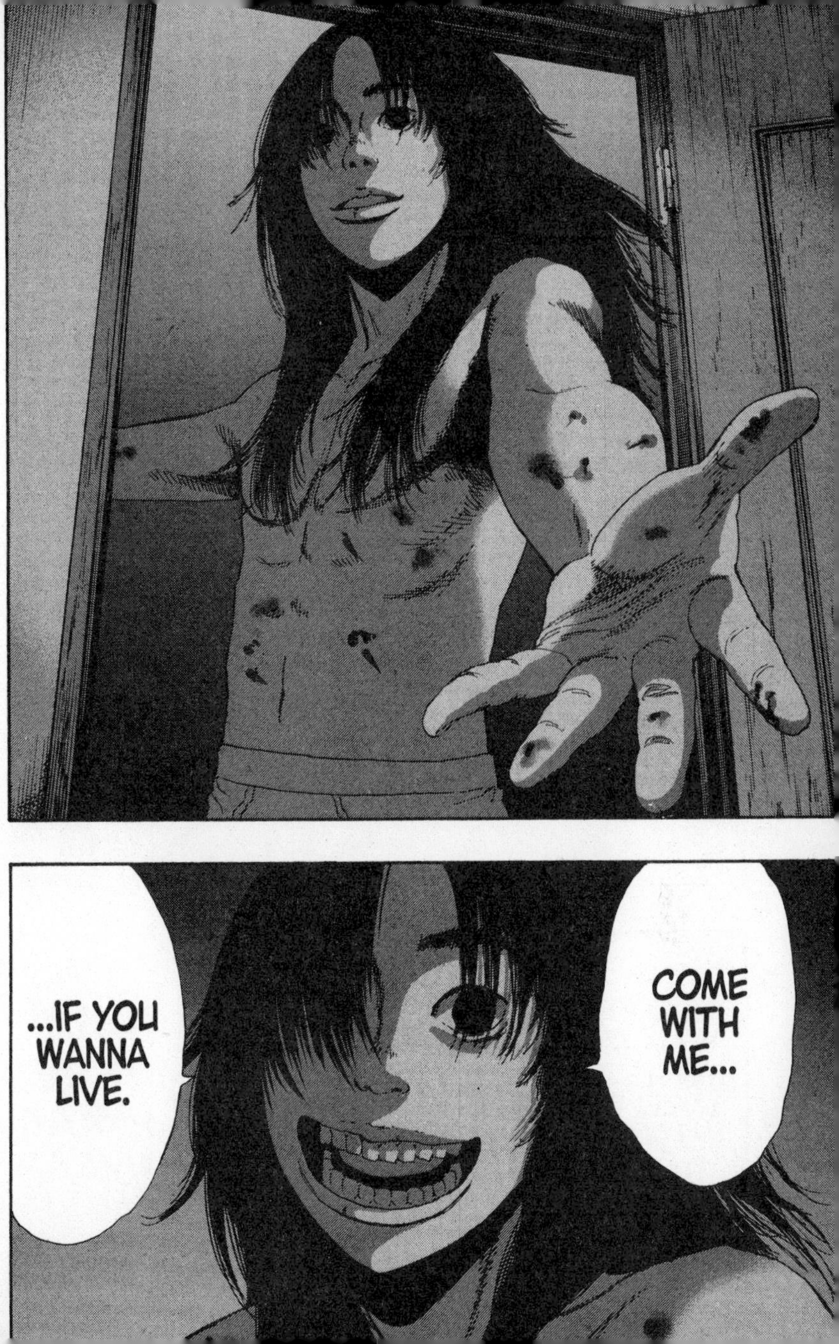
COME WITH ME...
...IF YOU WANNA LIVE.

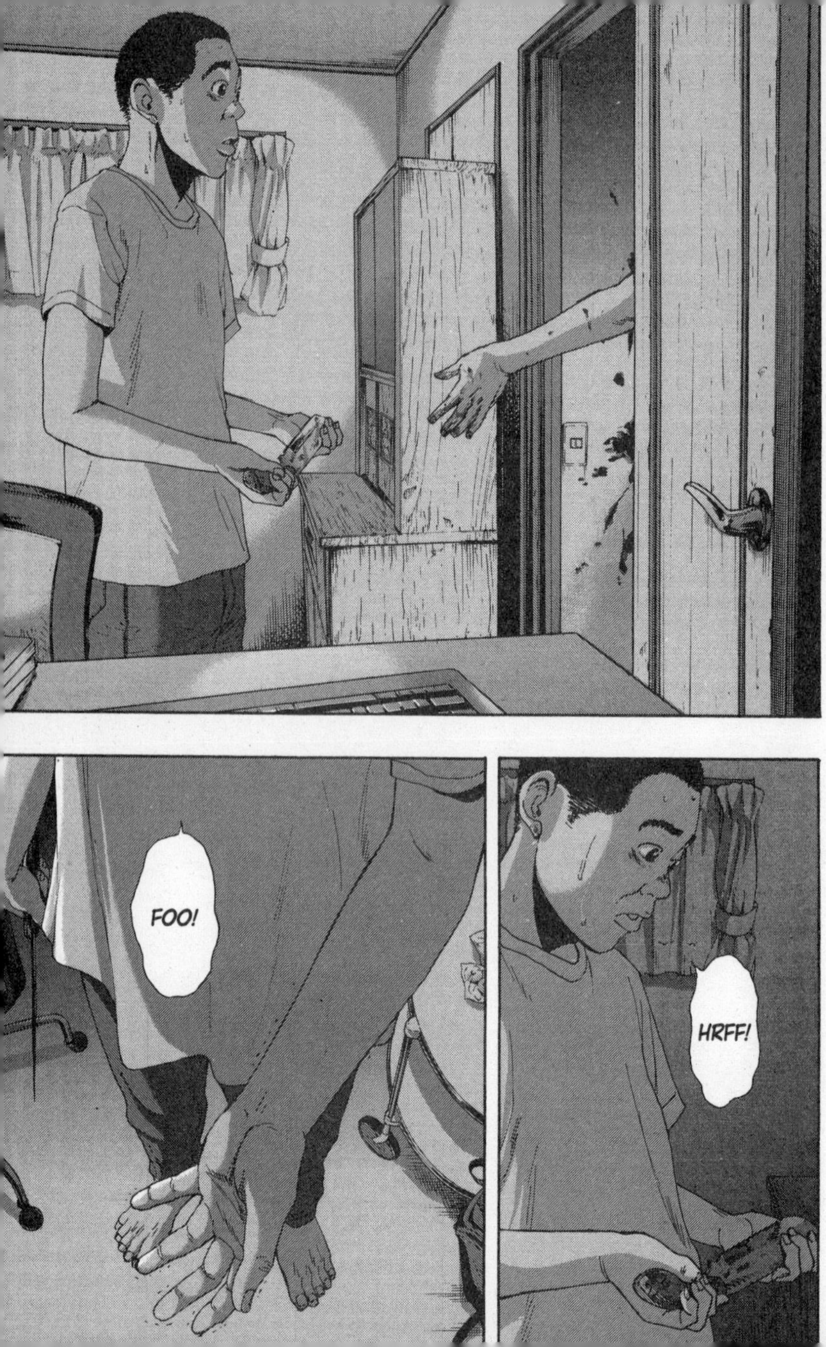
HRFF!
FOO!

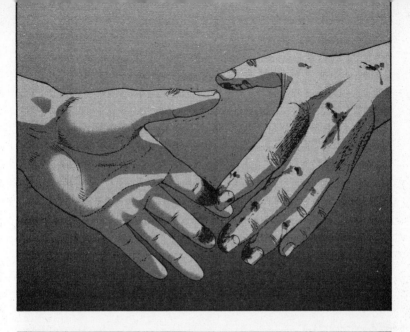

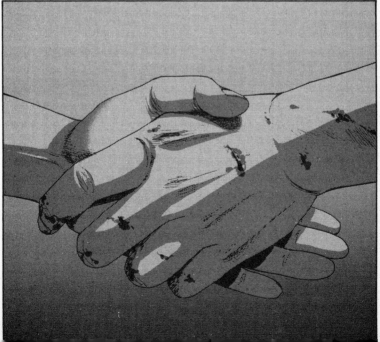

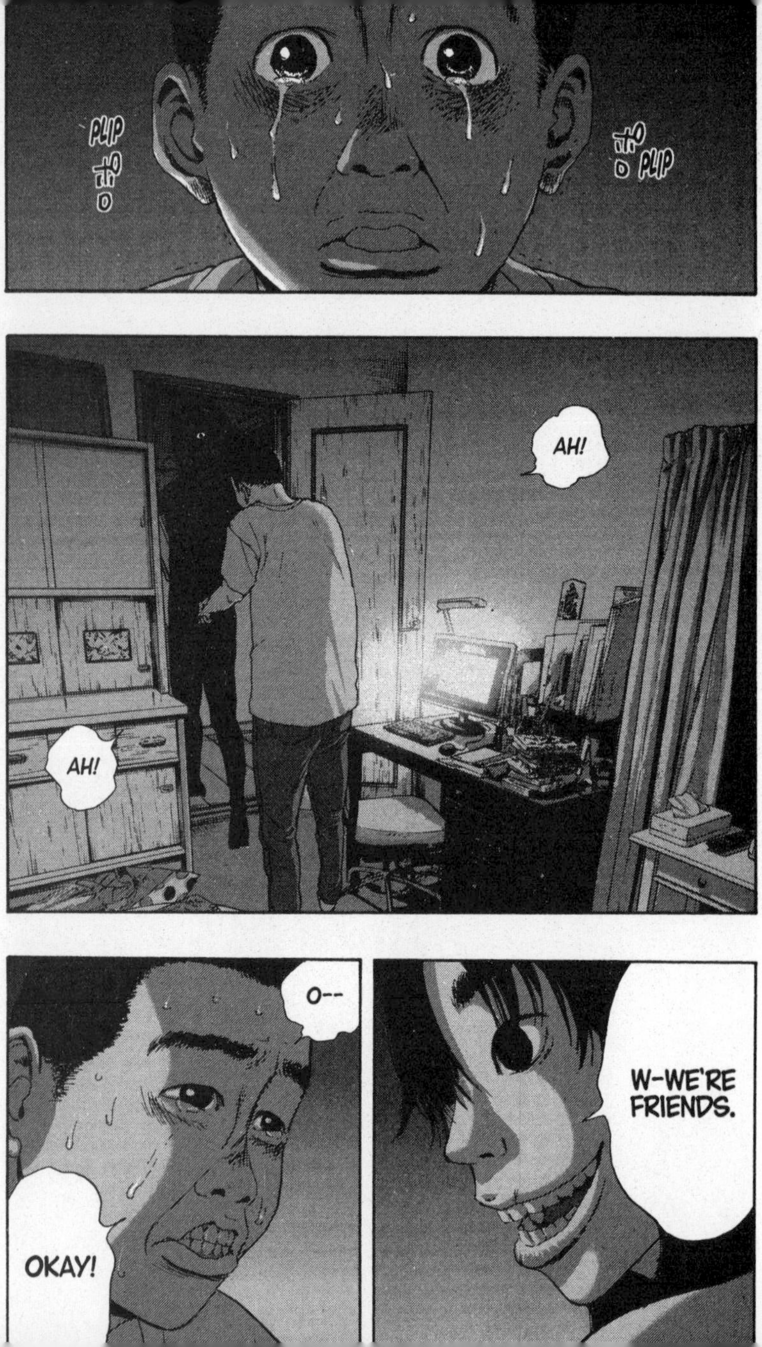
PLOP PLIP
PLIP PLOP
AH!
AH!
W-WE'RE FRIENDS.
O--
OKAY!

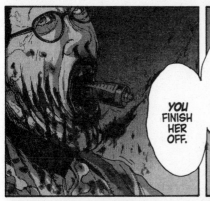

BUT SHE'S *YOUR* MOMMY.

YOU FINISH HER OFF.

NGH!

FOO!

HRNN!

HOHH!

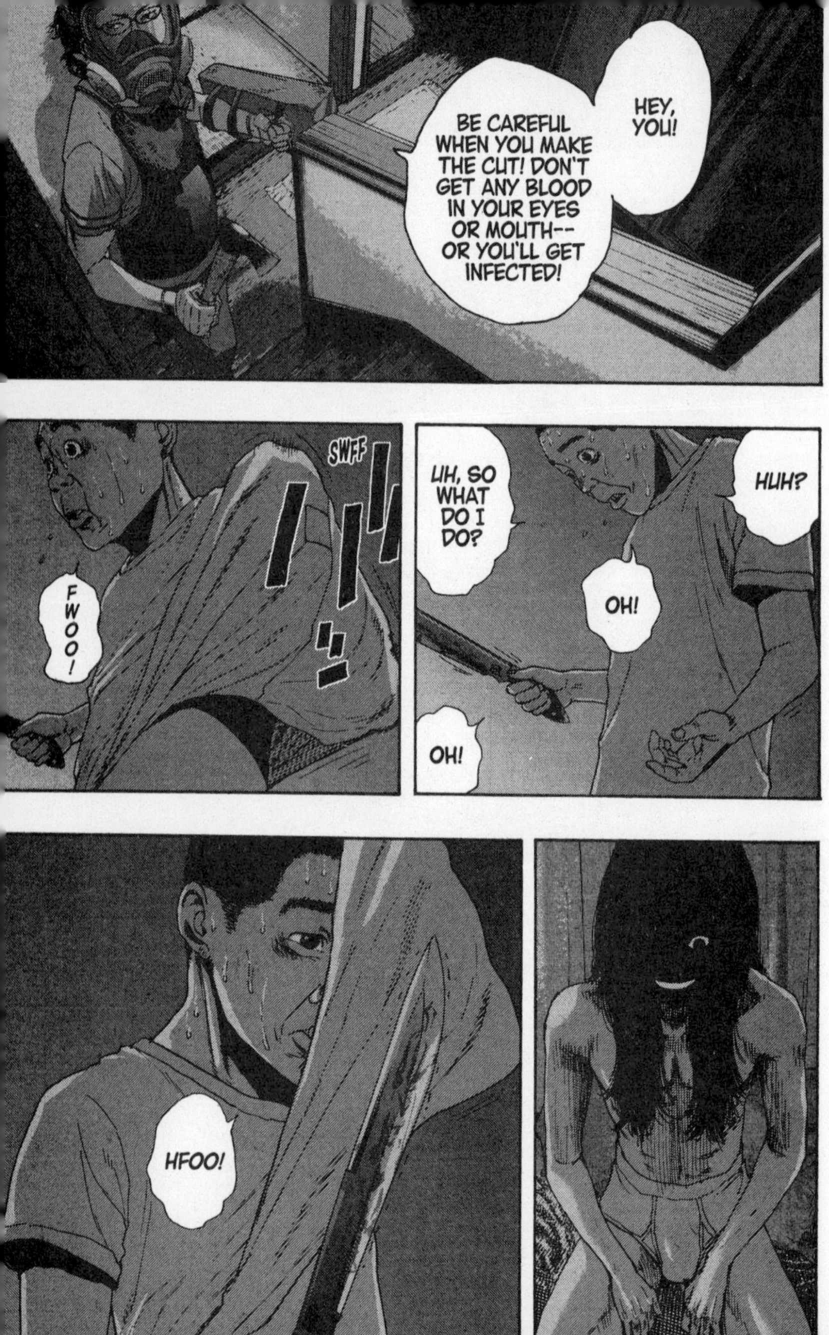
HEY, YOU!
BE CAREFUL WHEN YOU MAKE THE CUT! DON'T GET ANY BLOOD IN YOUR EYES OR MOUTH-- OR YOU'LL GET INFECTED!
HUH?
UH, SO WHAT DO I DO?
OH!
OH!
SWFF
FWOO!
HFOO!

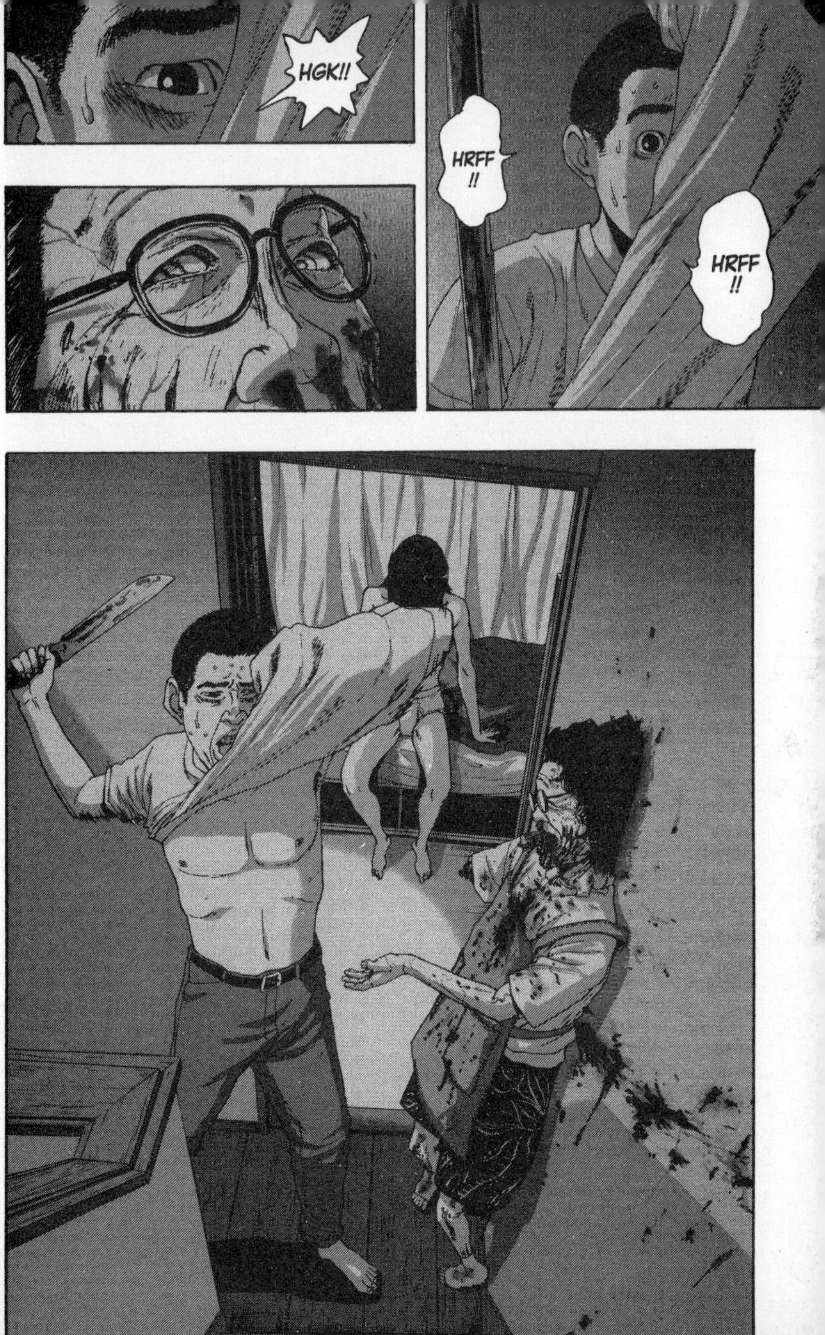
HRFF !!
HRFF !!
HGK!!

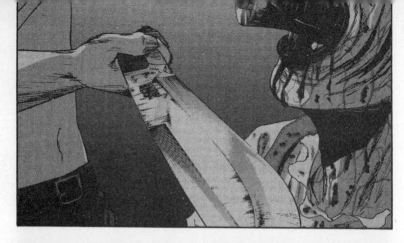

...THAT
SOUND
?

KSSHRAKK

?!

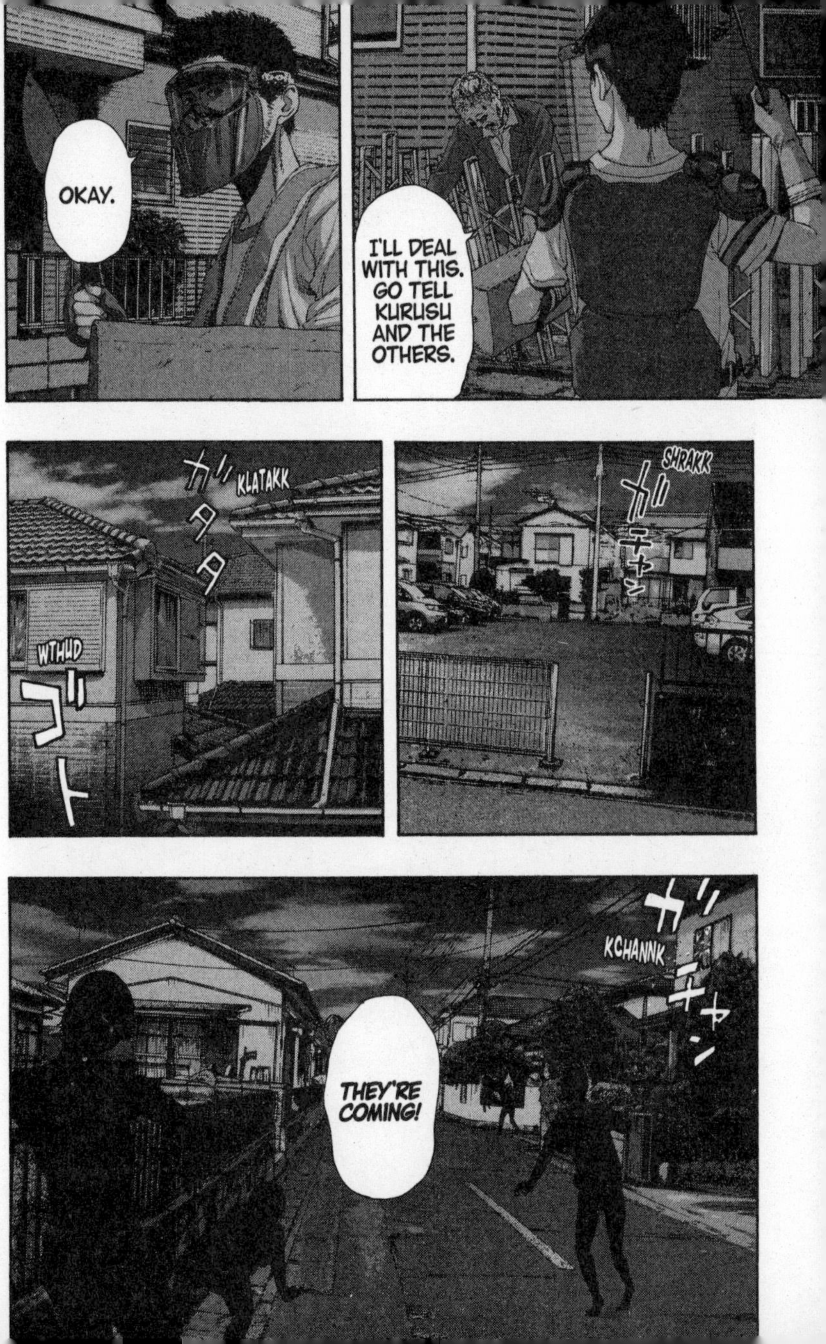
I'LL DEAL WITH THIS. GO TELL KURUSU AND THE OTHERS.
OKAY.
SHRAKK
KLATAKK
WTHUD
KCHANNK
THEY'RE COMING!

CHAPTER 116

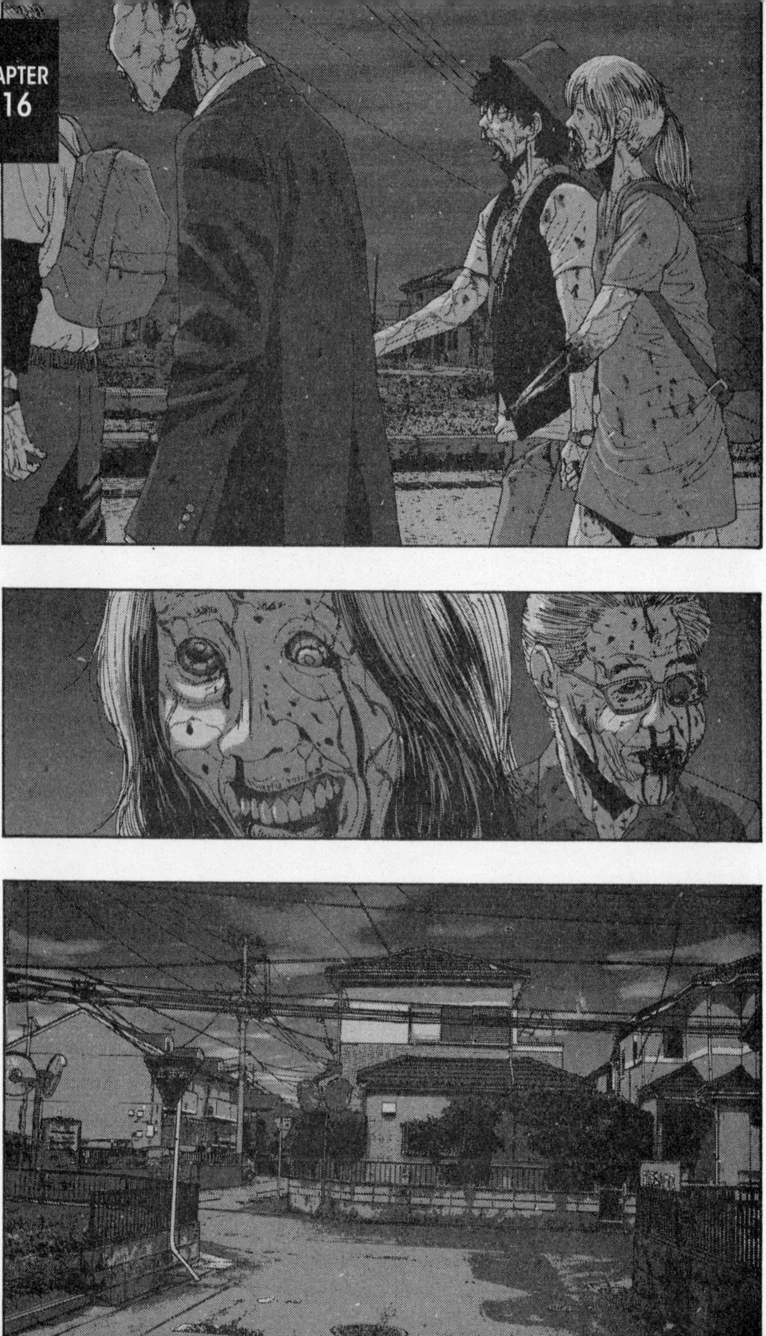

I AM
A HERO

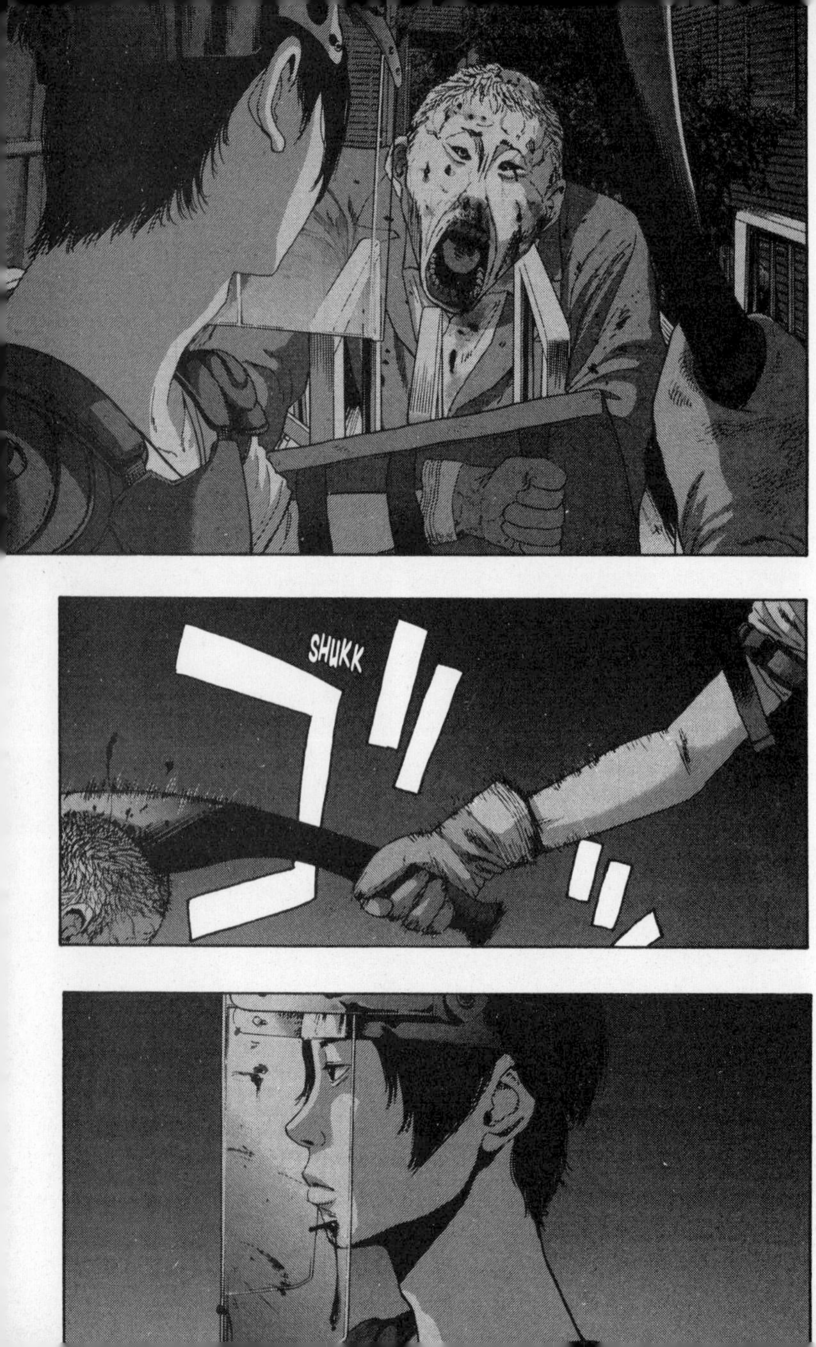
SHUKK

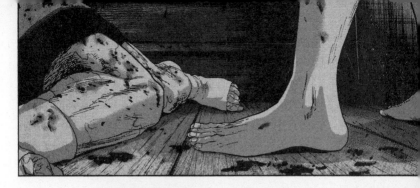

O-OKAY. SHALL WE GO?

GRAB

SHLUTTCH

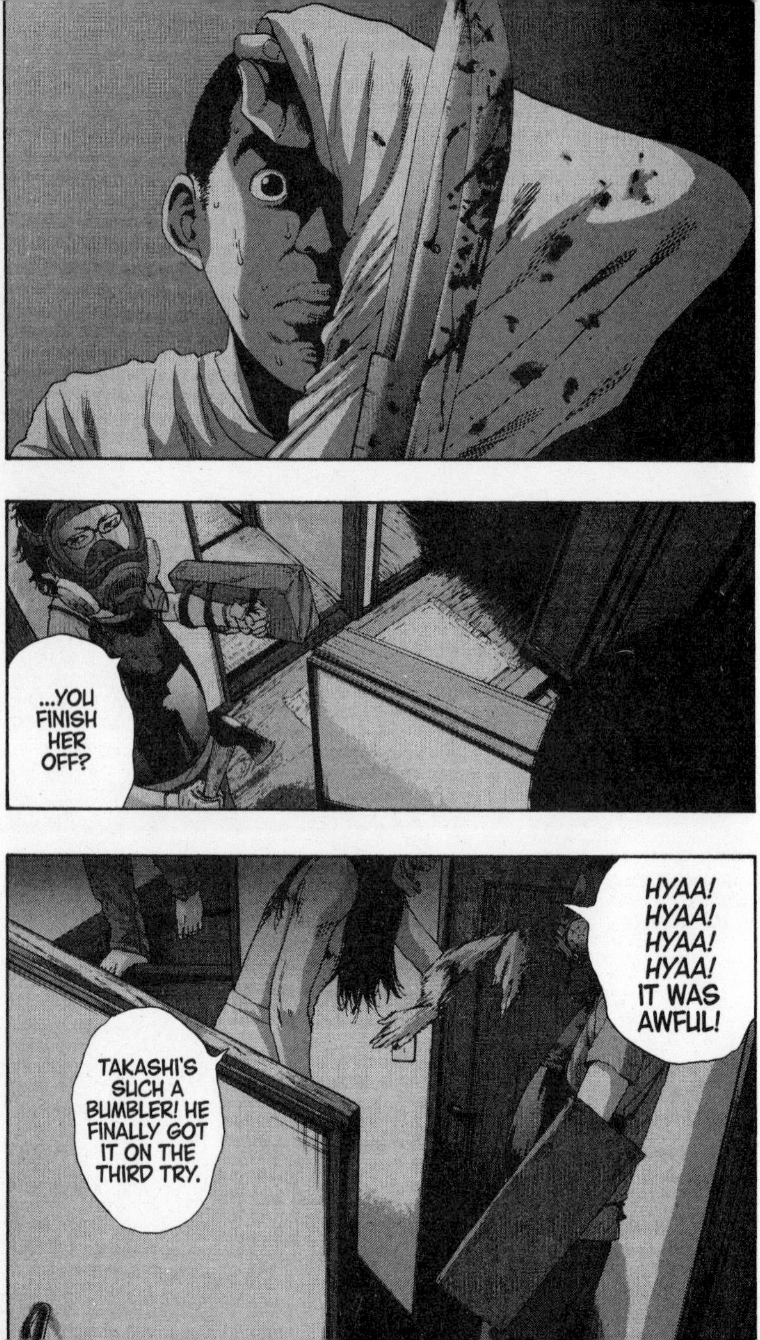
...YOU FINISH HER OFF?
HYAA! HYAA! HYAA! HYAA! IT WAS AWFUL!
TAKASHI'S SUCH A BUMBLER! HE FINALLY GOT IT ON THE THIRD TRY.

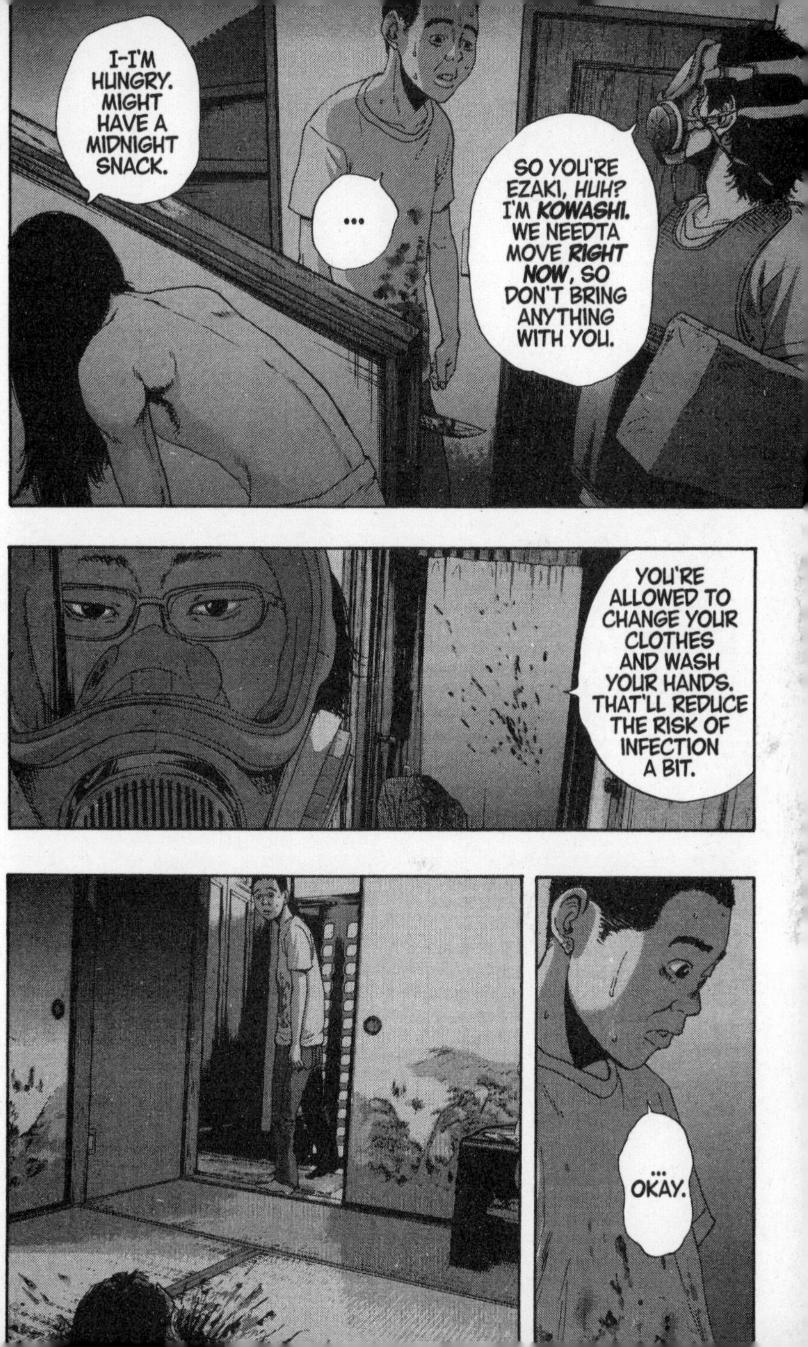
SO YOU'RE EZAKI, HUH? I'M **KOWASHI.** WE NEEDTA MOVE **RIGHT NOW**, SO DON'T BRING ANYTHING WITH YOU.
...
I-I'M HUNGRY. MIGHT HAVE A MIDNIGHT SNACK.
YOU'RE ALLOWED TO CHANGE YOUR CLOTHES AND WASH YOUR HANDS. THAT'LL REDUCE THE RISK OF INFECTION A BIT.
...OKAY.

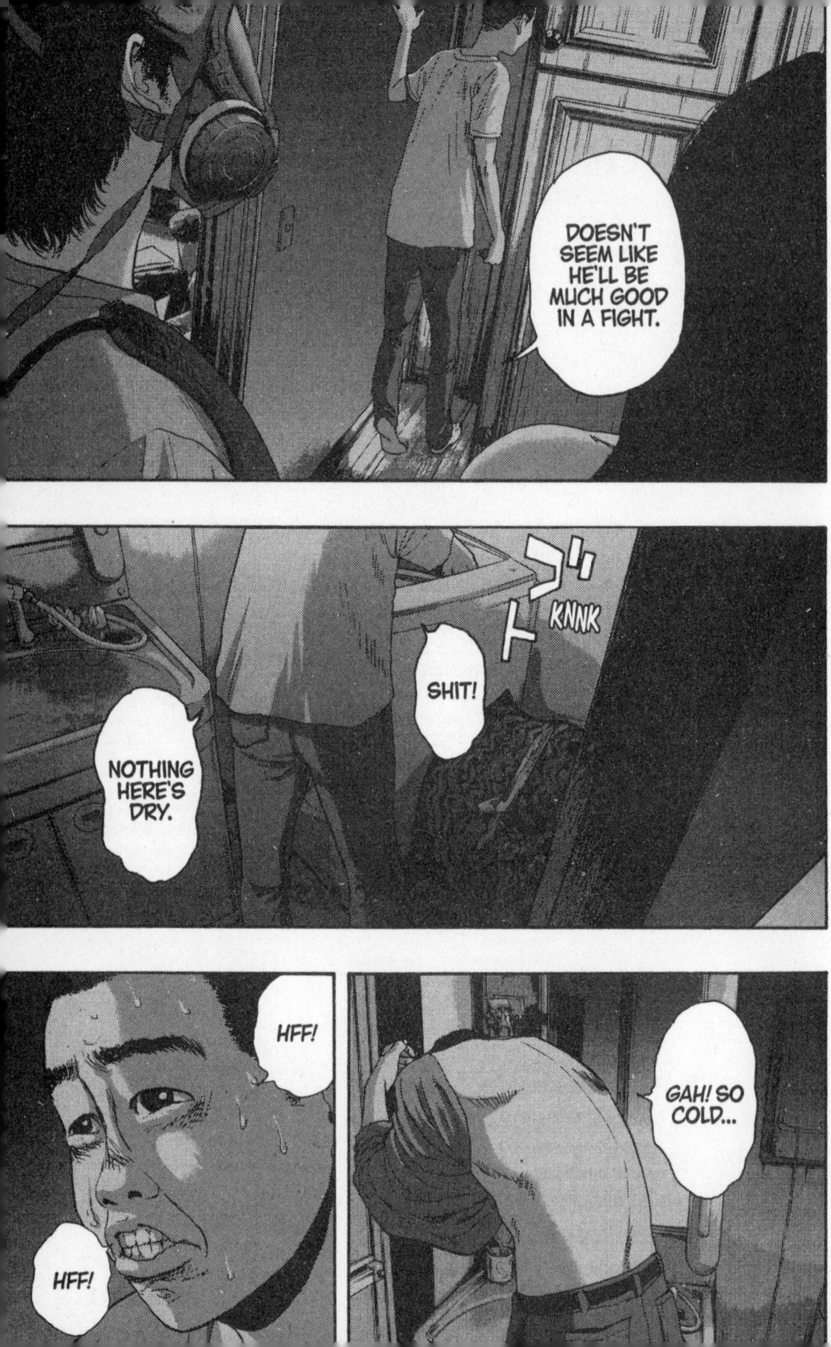
DOESN'T SEEM LIKE HE'LL BE MUCH GOOD IN A FIGHT.
ゴット
KNNK
SHIT!
NOTHING HERE'S DRY.
GAH! SO COLD...
HFF!
HFF!

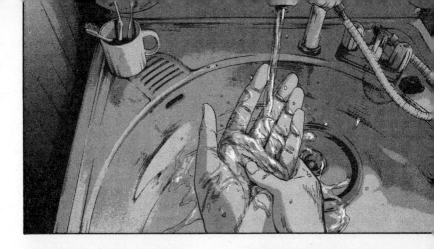

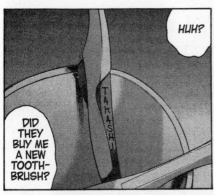

HUH?

DID THEY BUY ME A NEW TOOTH-BRUSH?

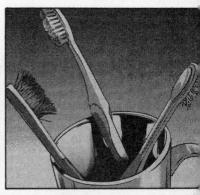

HEY!

I...I NEVER NOTICED.

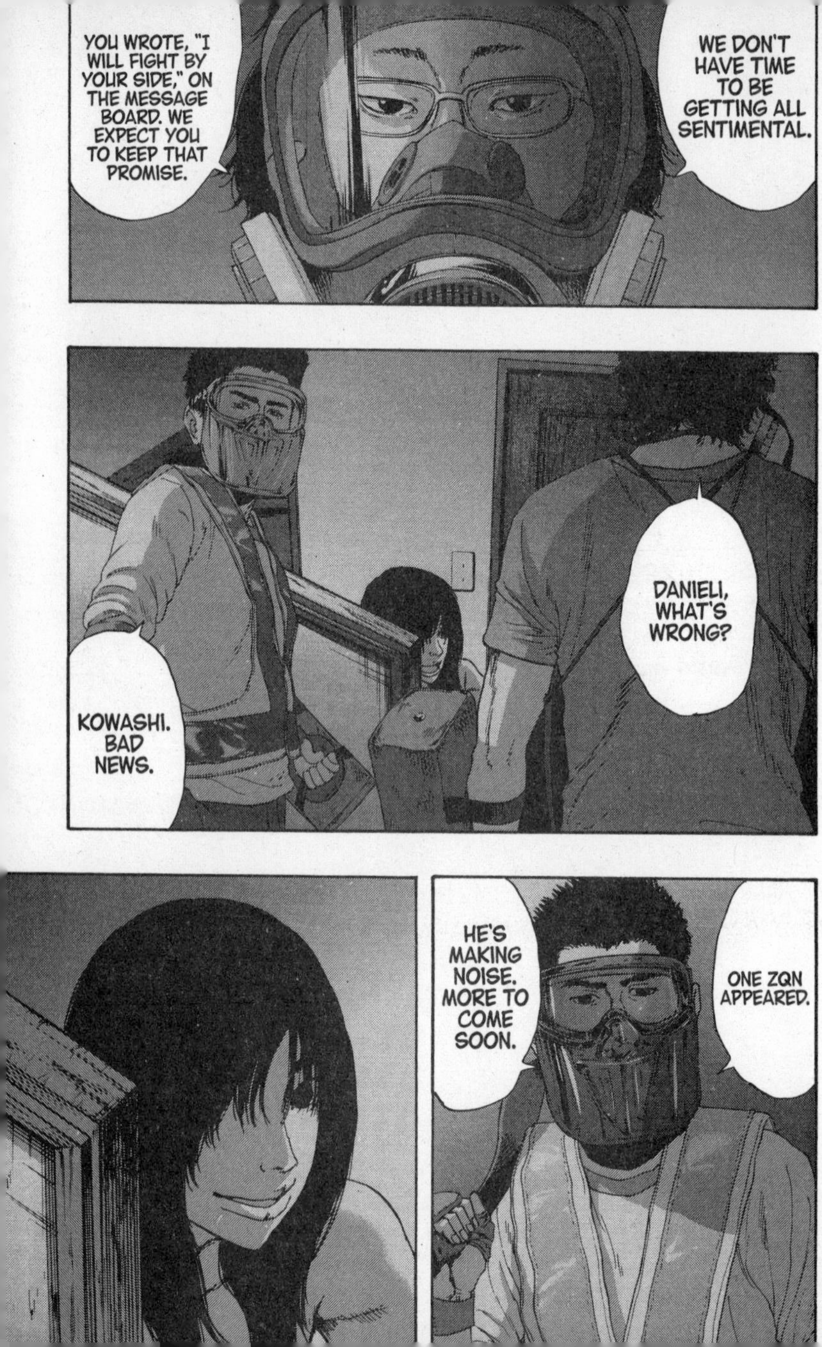
WE DON'T HAVE TIME TO BE GETTING ALL SENTIMENTAL.
YOU WROTE, "I WILL FIGHT BY YOUR SIDE," ON THE MESSAGE BOARD. WE EXPECT YOU TO KEEP THAT PROMISE.
DANIELI, WHAT'S WRONG?
KOWASHI. BAD NEWS.
ONE ZQN APPEARED.
HE'S MAKING NOISE. MORE TO COME SOON.

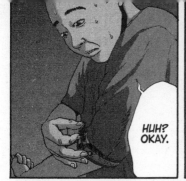

PUT THIS REFLECTIVE TAPE AROUND YOUR ARM.
HUH? OKAY.
IF WE DON'T TAKE OFF FAST, LOTS MORE ZQNS WILL SHOW UP.
IF WE ARE SURROUNDED LIKE BEFORE, WE'RE DONE FOR.
I KNOW.

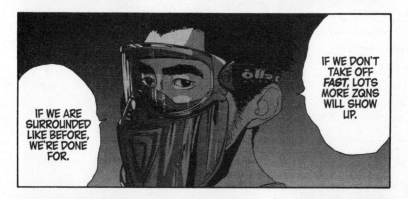

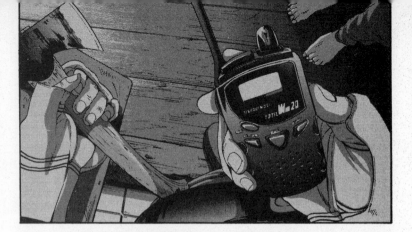

CHFF ZZT

KSSSH

WE'RE MAKING OUR GETAWAY. COVER US.

GETAWAY TIME.

ROGER THAT!

...

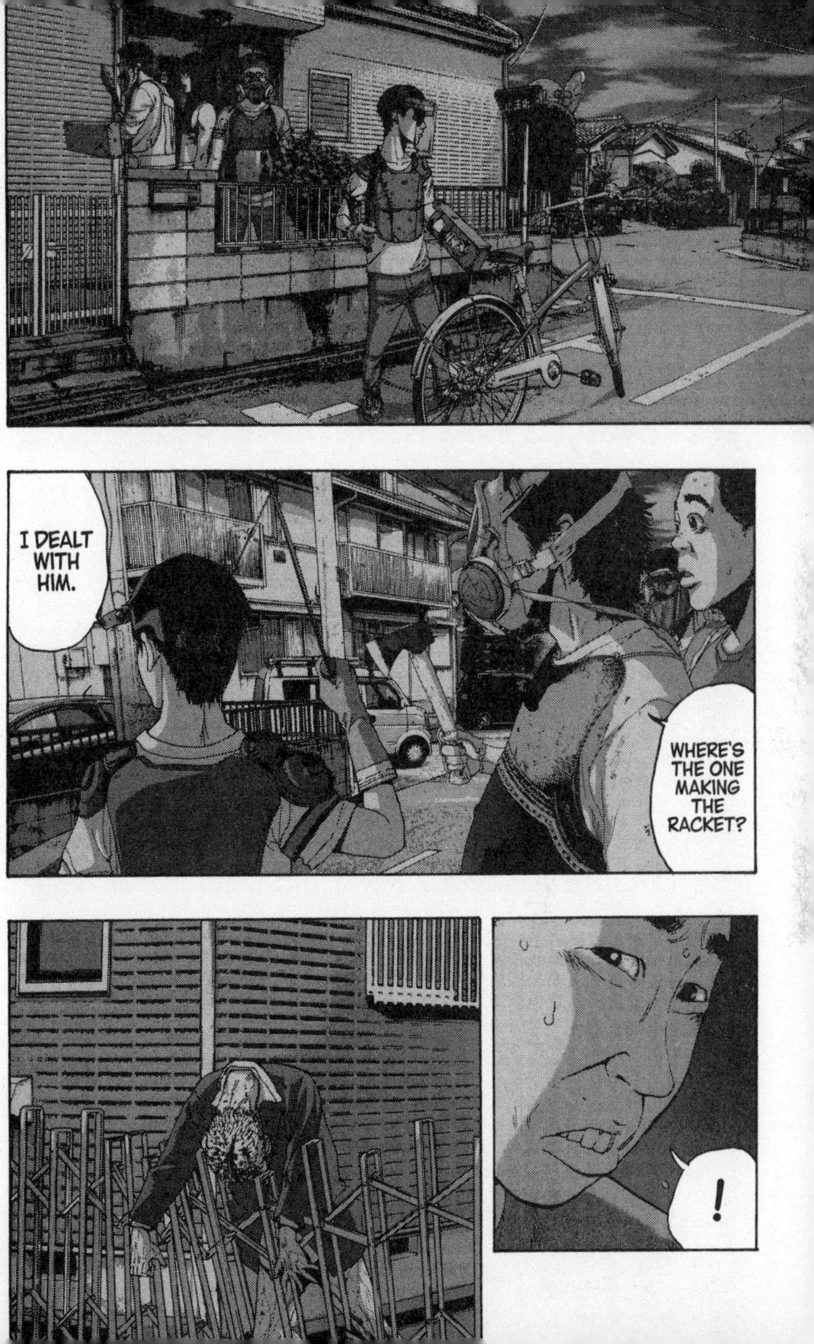
WHERE'S THE ONE MAKING THE RACKET?
I DEALT WITH HIM.
!

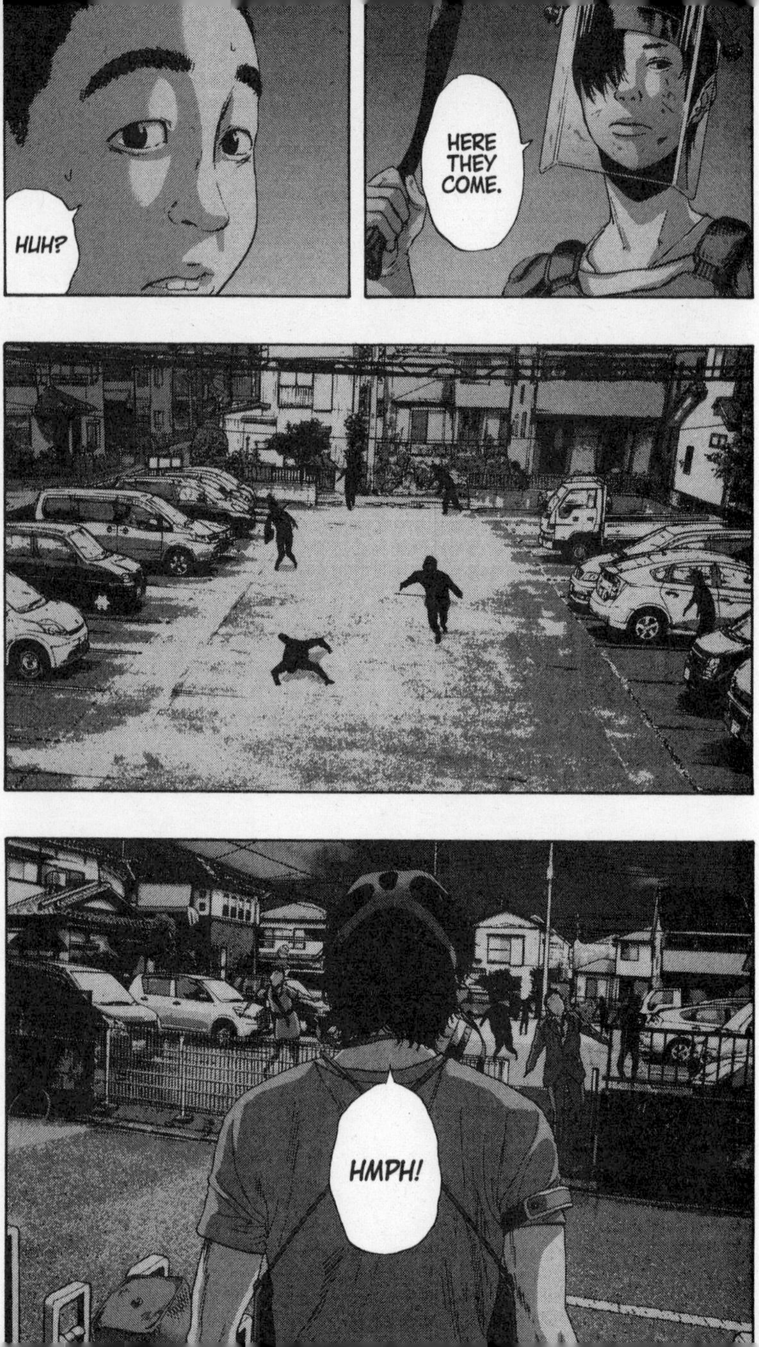
HERE THEY COME.
HUH?
HMPH!

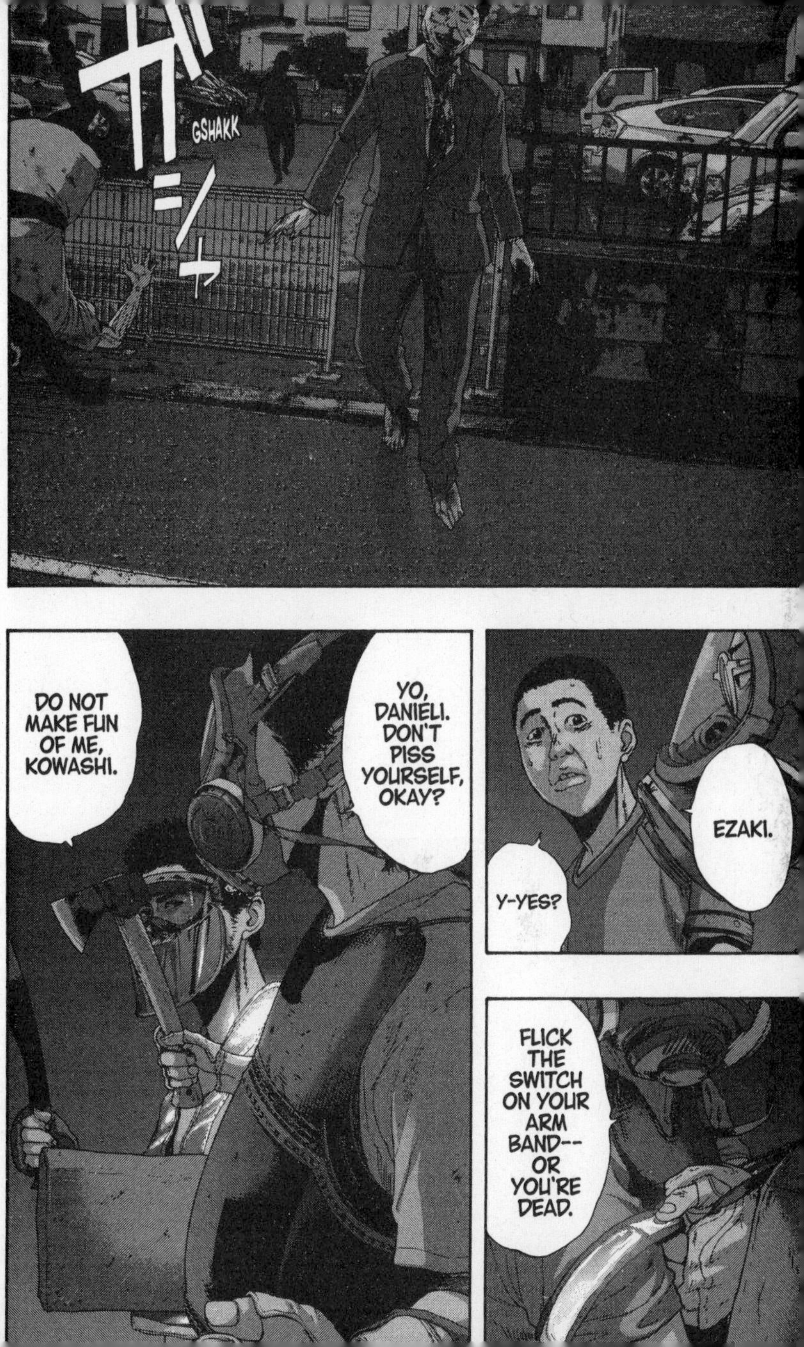
GSHAKK
EZAKI.
Y-YES?
FLICK THE SWITCH ON YOUR ARM BAND-- OR YOU'RE DEAD.
YO, DANIELI. DON'T PISS YOURSELF, OKAY?
DO NOT MAKE FUN OF ME, KOWASHI.

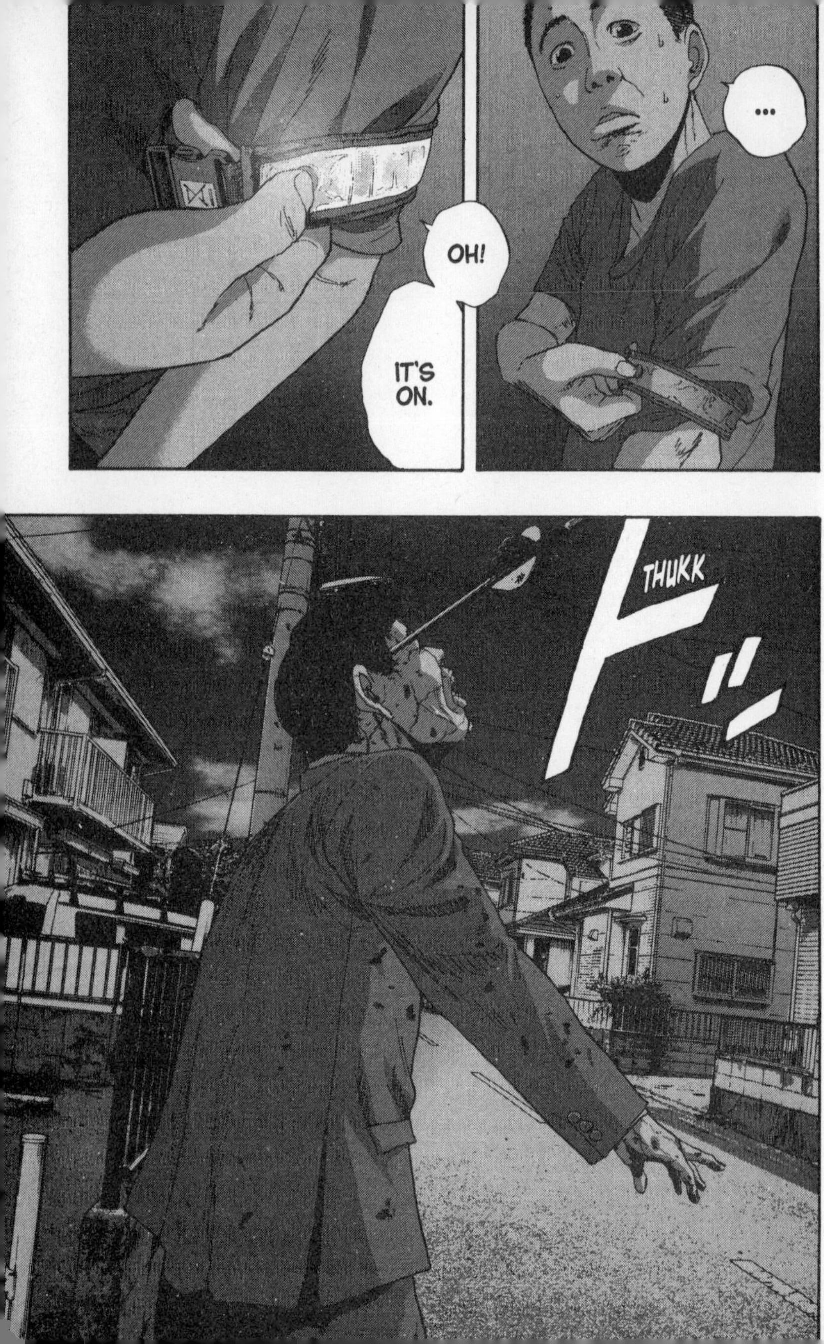
...
OH!
IT'S ON.
THUKK

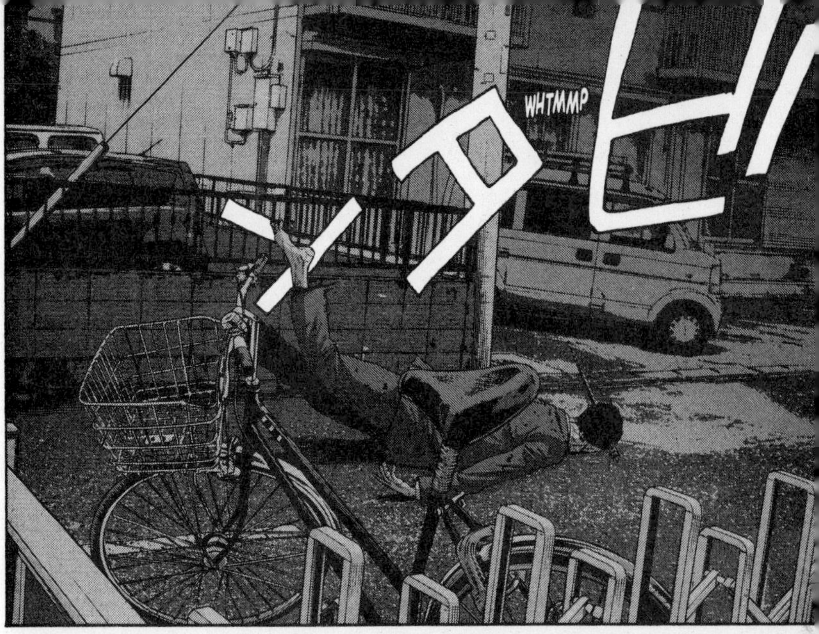
WHTMMP
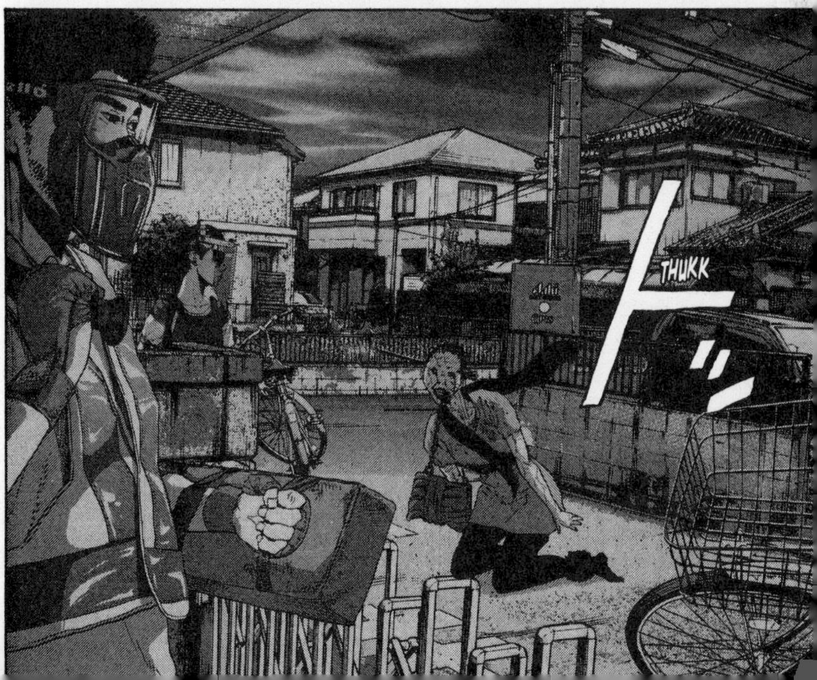
THUKK

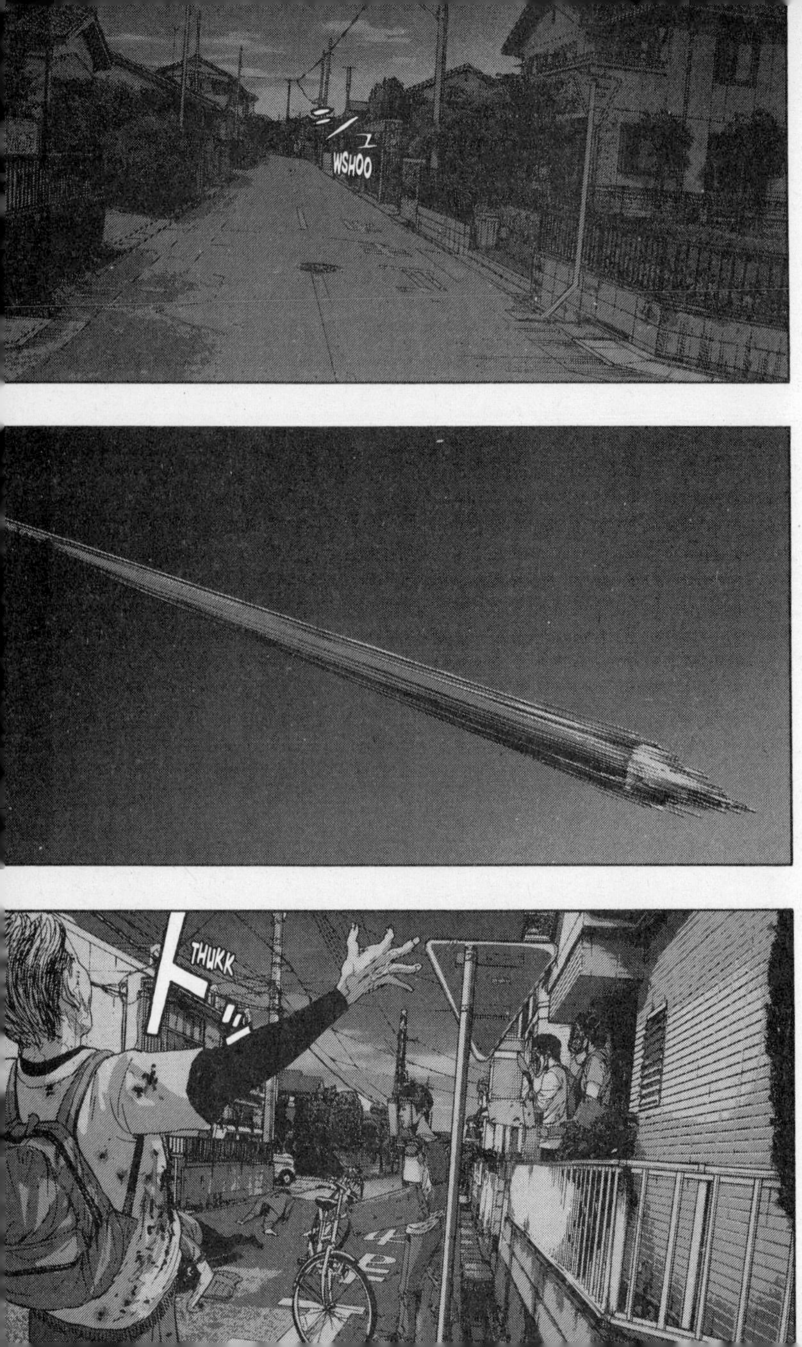
WSHOO
THUKK

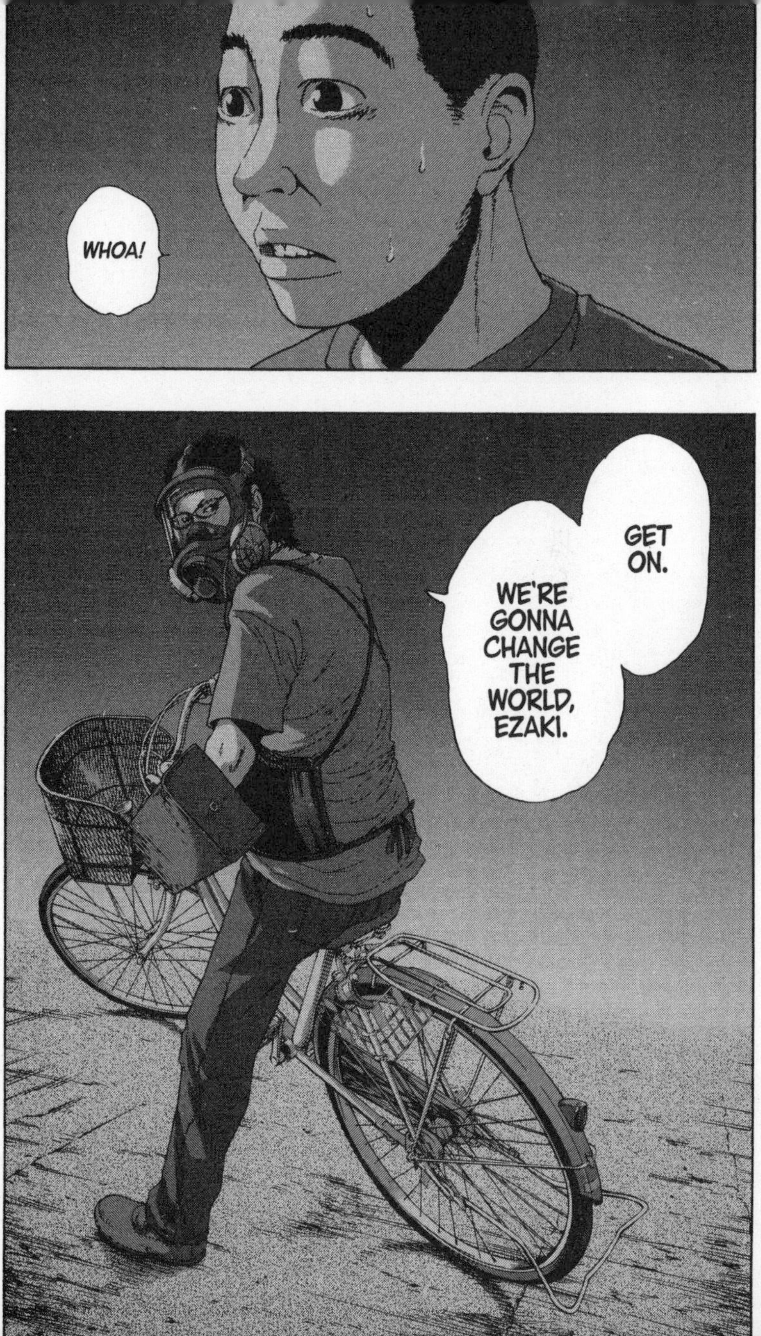
WHOA!
GET ON.
WE'RE GONNA CHANGE THE WORLD, EZAKI.

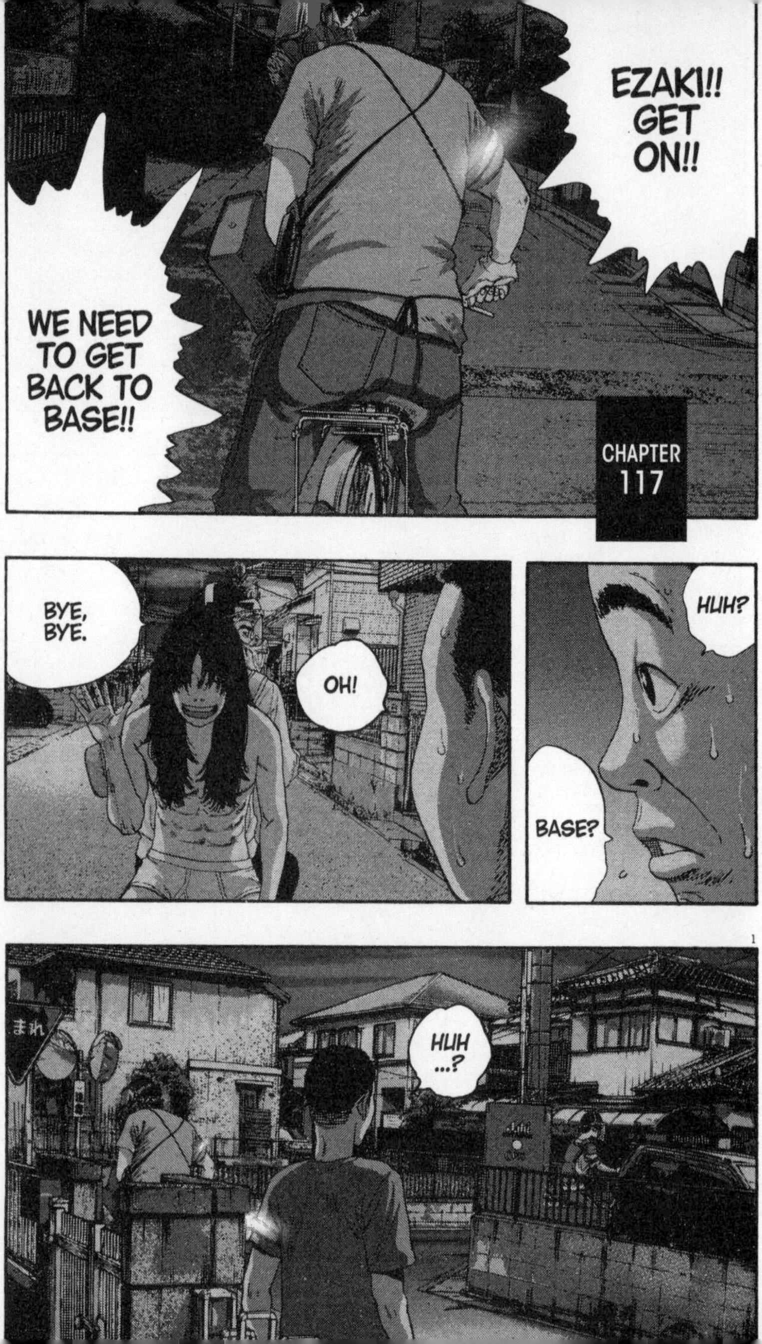
EZAKI!! GET ON!!
WE NEED TO GET BACK TO BASE!!
CHAPTER 117
HUH?
BASE?
OH!
BYE, BYE.
HUH ...?

1

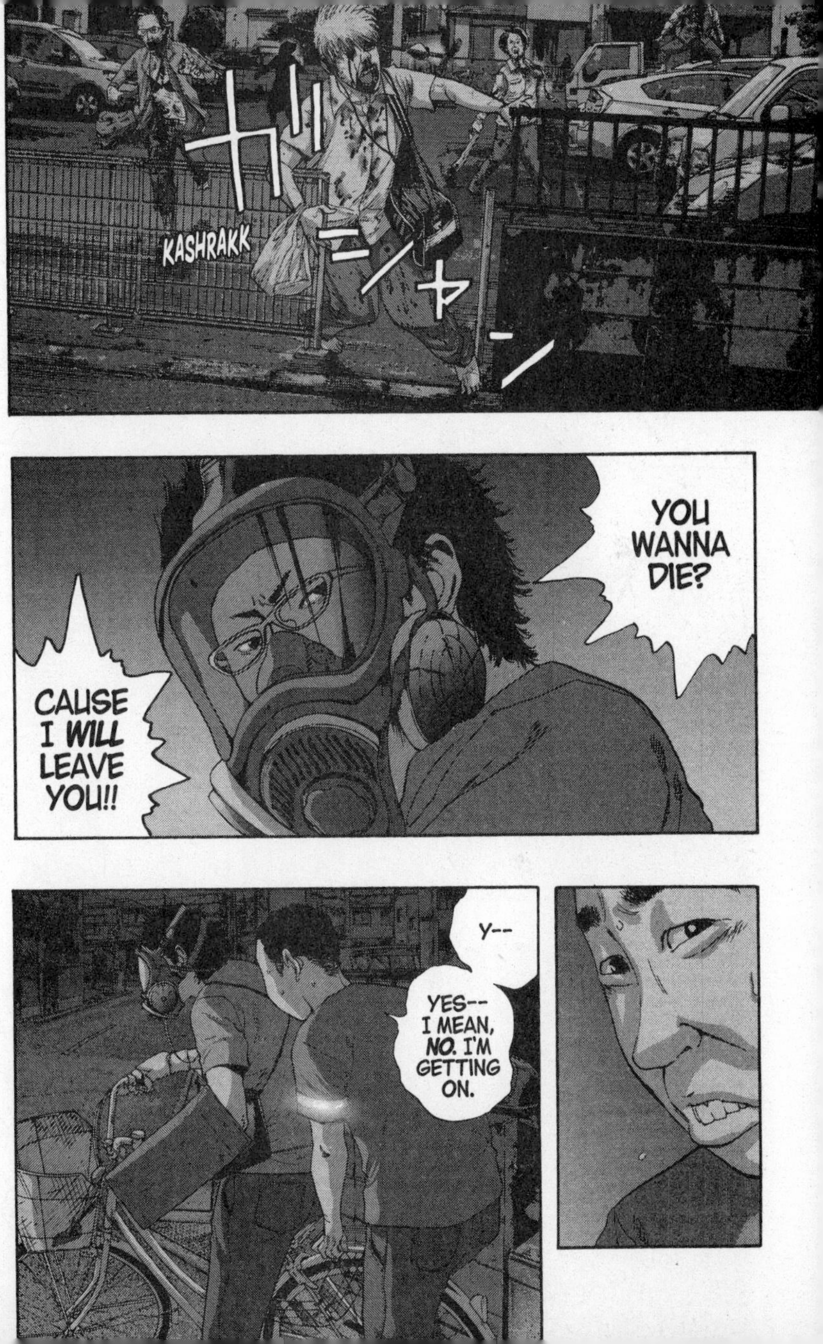
KASHRAKK
YOU WANNA DIE?
CAUSE I WILL LEAVE YOU!!
Y--
YES-- I MEAN, NO. I'M GETTING ON.

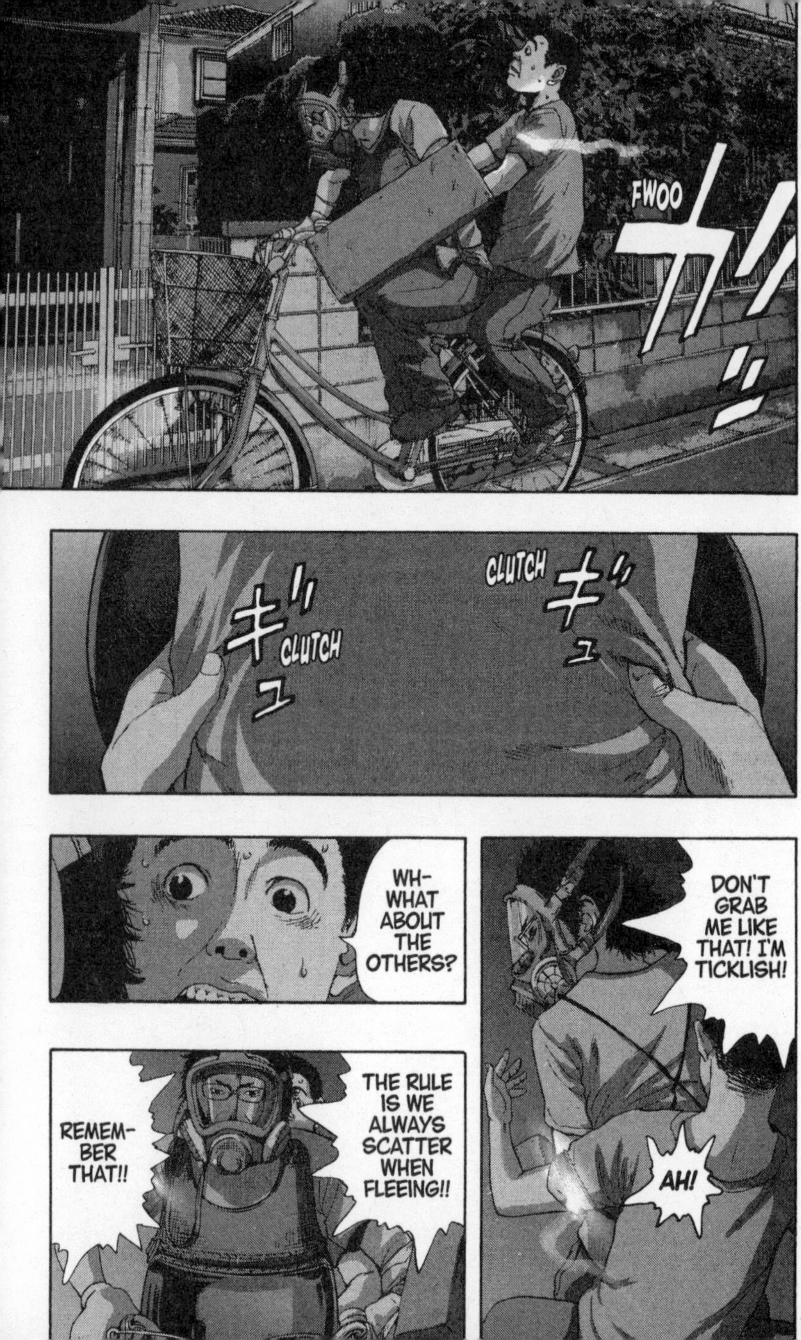
FWOO
CLUTCH
ギュ
CLUTCH
ギュ
DON'T GRAB ME LIKE THAT! I'M TICKLISH!
AH!
WH-WHAT ABOUT THE OTHERS?
THE RULE IS WE ALWAYS SCATTER WHEN FLEEING!!
REMEMBER THAT!!

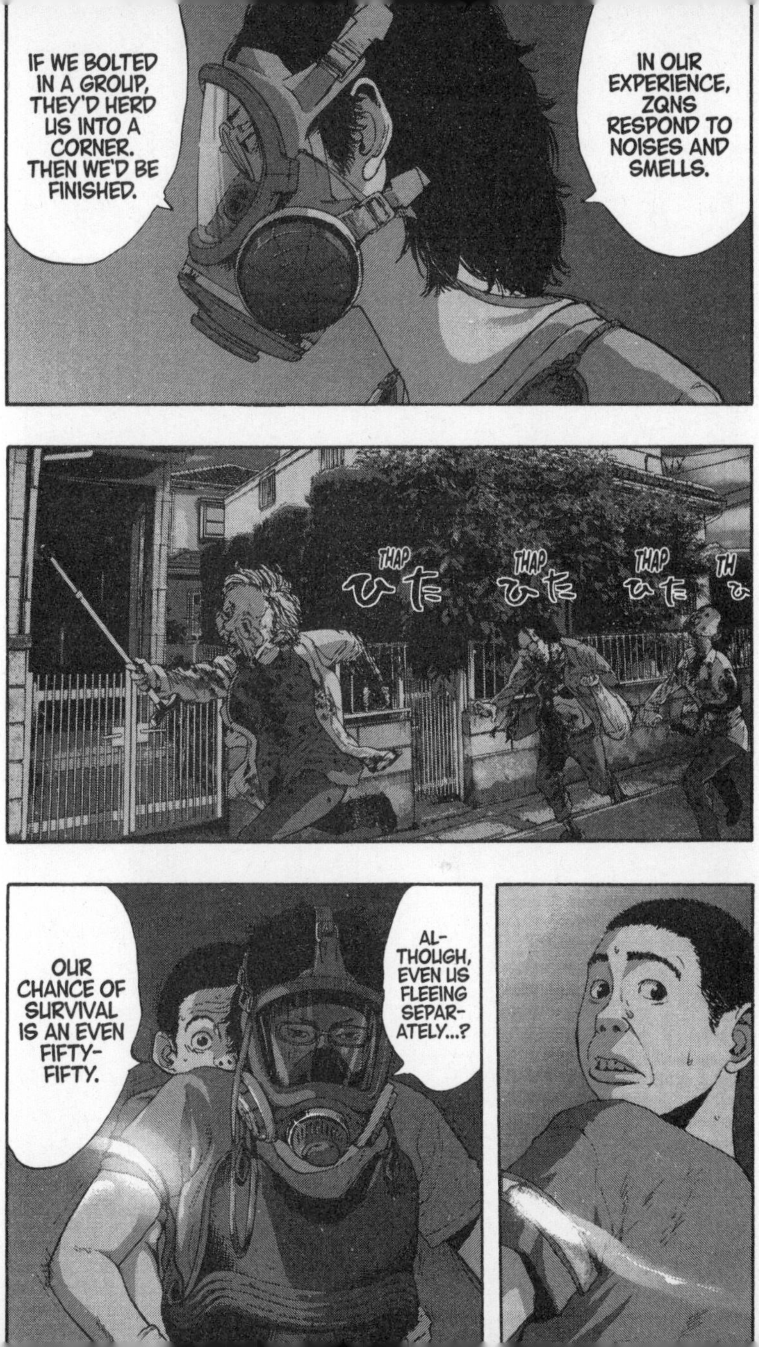
IN OUR EXPERIENCE, ZQNS RESPOND TO NOISES AND SMELLS.
IF WE BOLTED IN A GROUP, THEY'D HERD US INTO A CORNER. THEN WE'D BE FINISHED.
TH ひ
THAP ひた
THAP ひた
THAP ひた
AL-THOUGH, EVEN US FLEEING SEPAR-ATELY...?
OUR CHANCE OF SURVIVAL IS AN EVEN FIFTY-FIFTY.

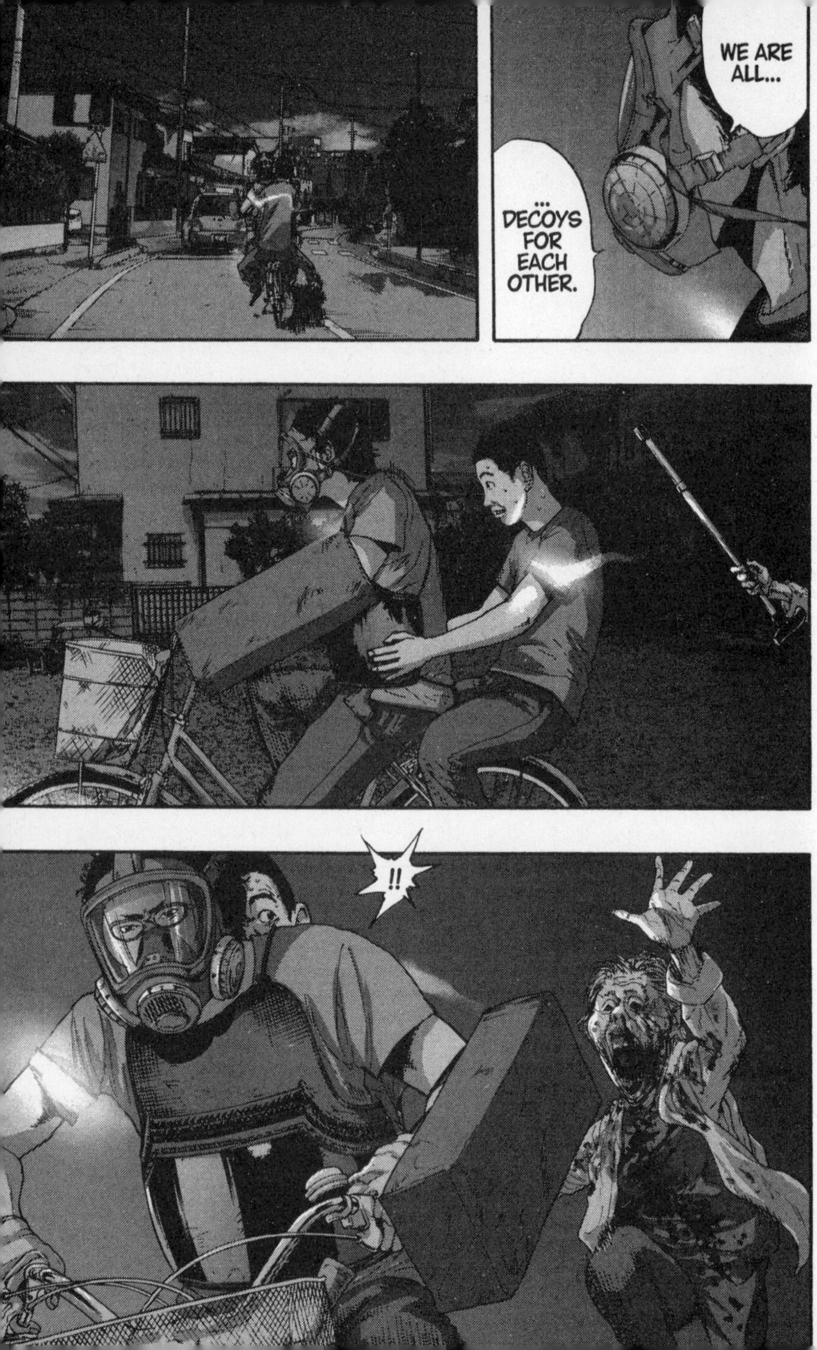
WE ARE ALL...
... DECOYS FOR EACH OTHER.
!!

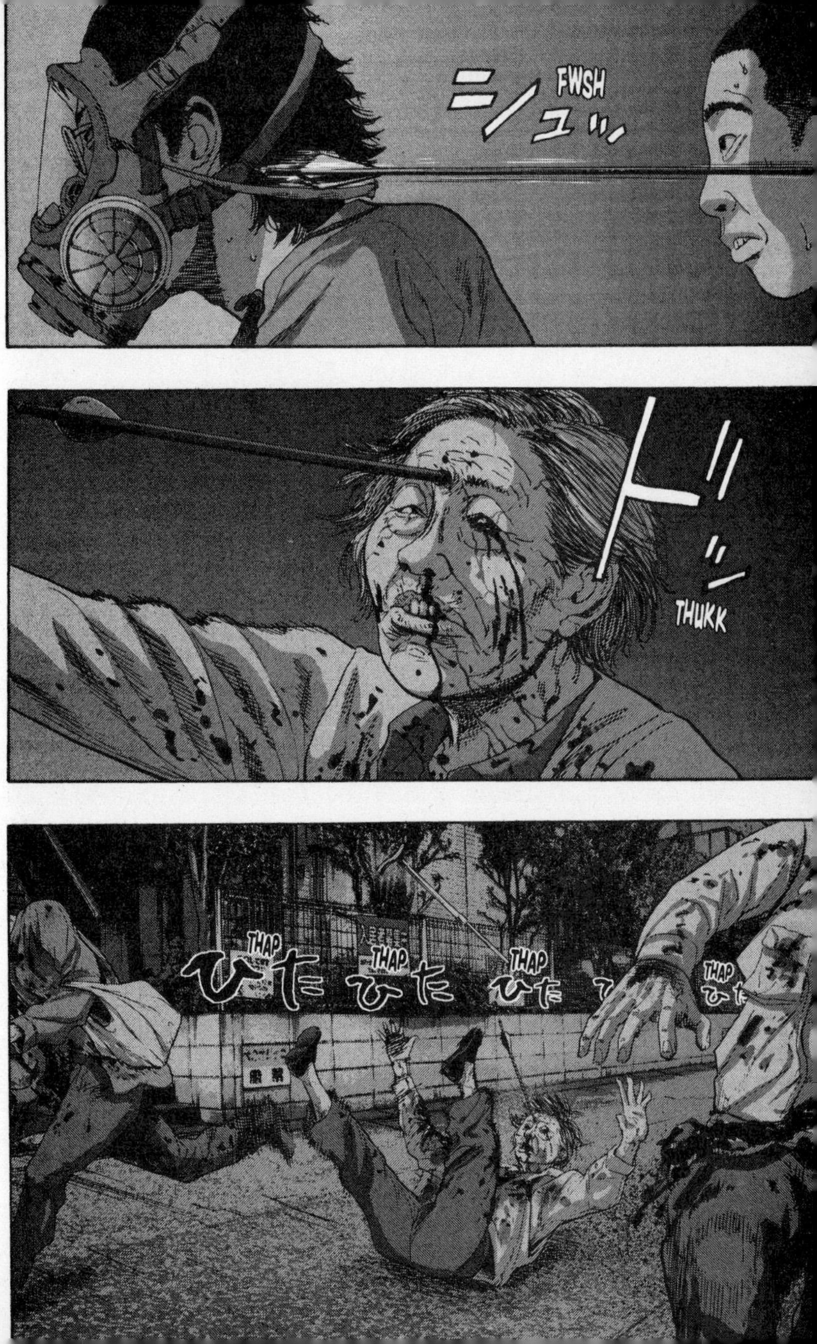
FWSH
THUKK
THAP
THAP
THAP
THAP

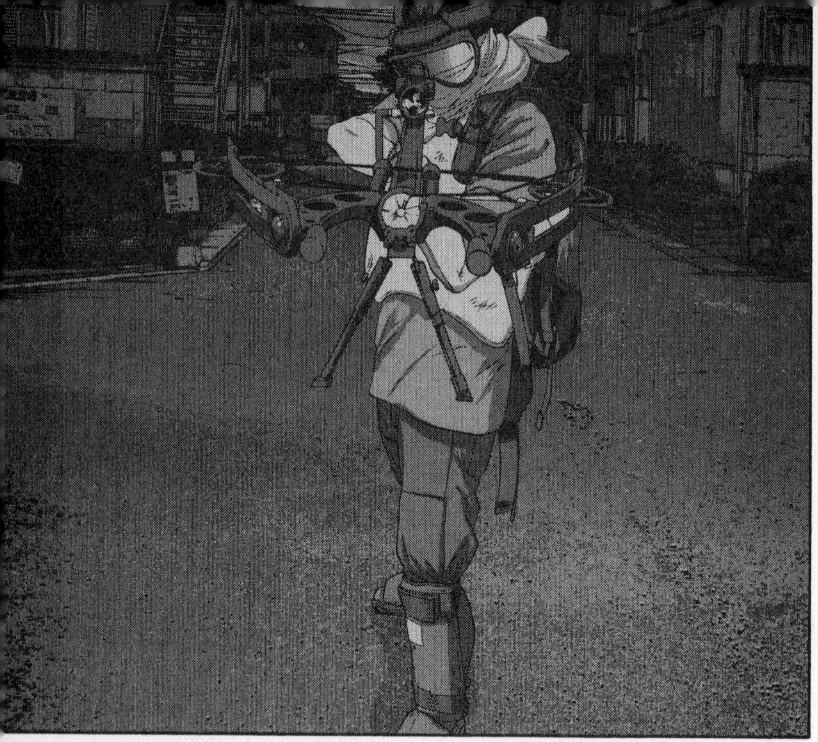

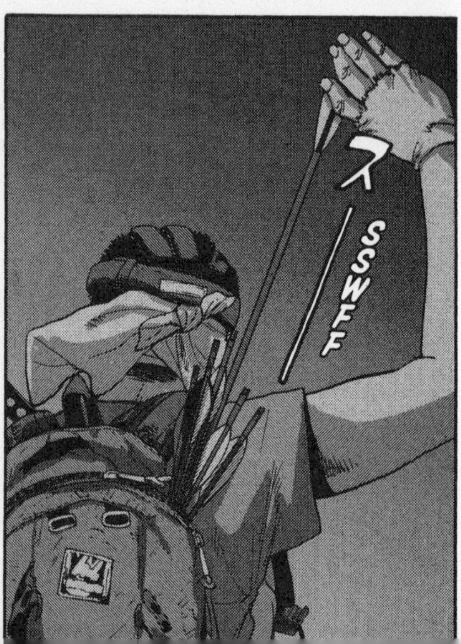
ス
SSWFF

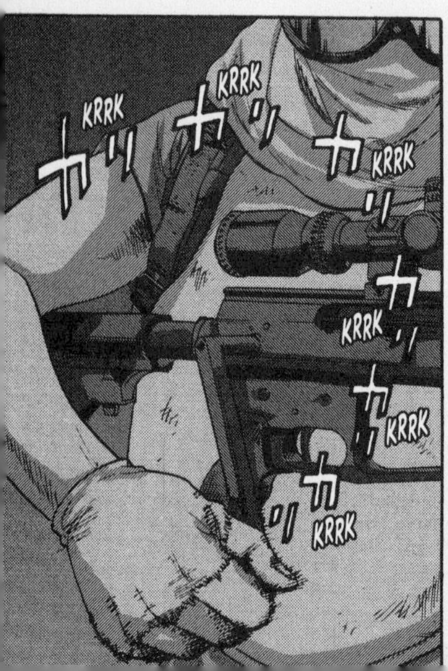
カッ
KRRK
カッ
KRRK
カッ
KRRK
カッ
KRRK
カッ
KRRK
カッ
KRRK
カッ
KRRK

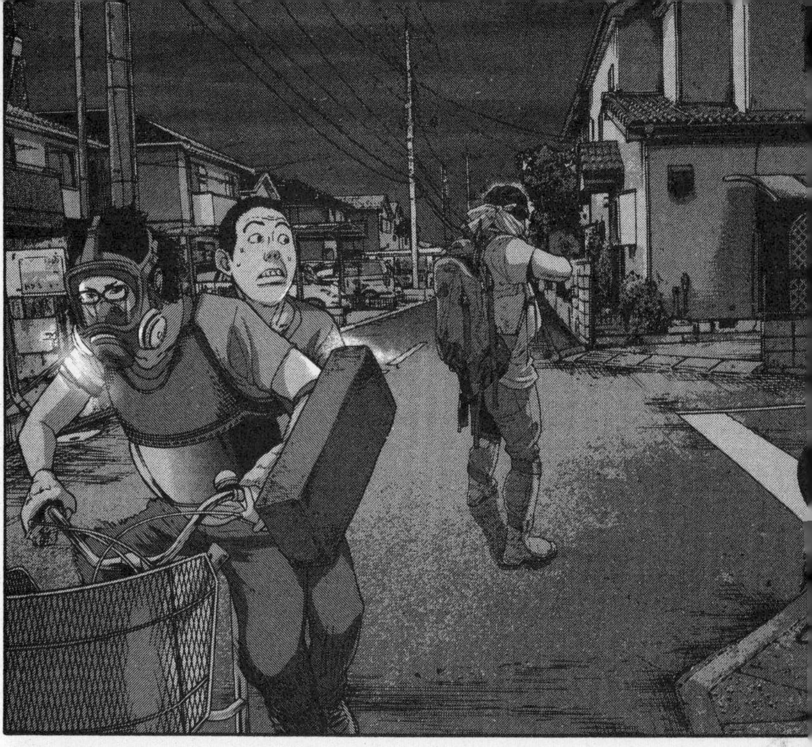

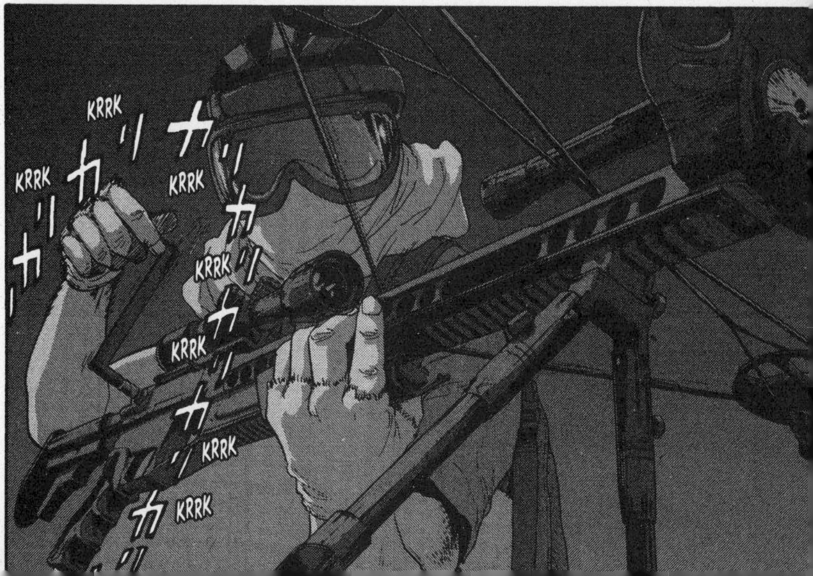
KRRK
KRRK
KRRK
KRRK
KRRK
KRRK

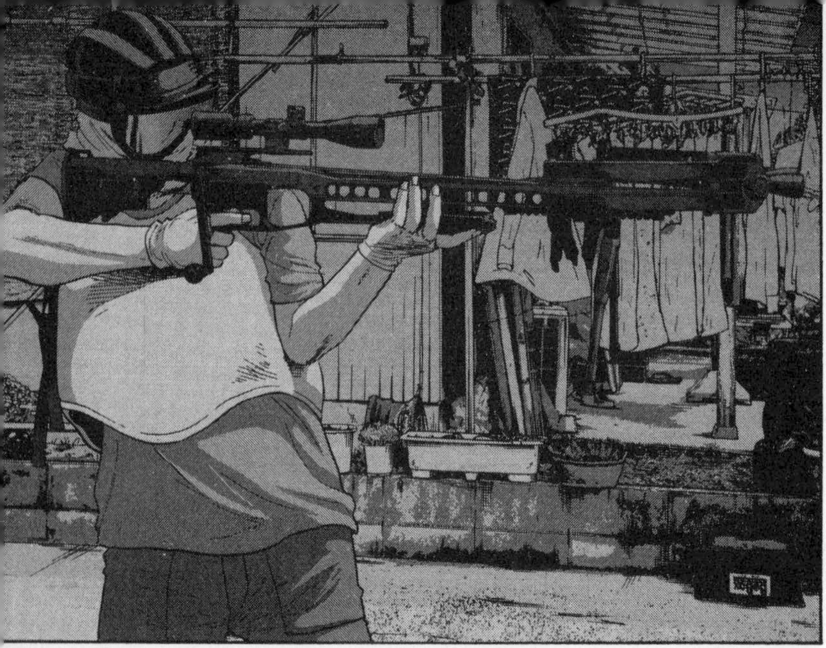

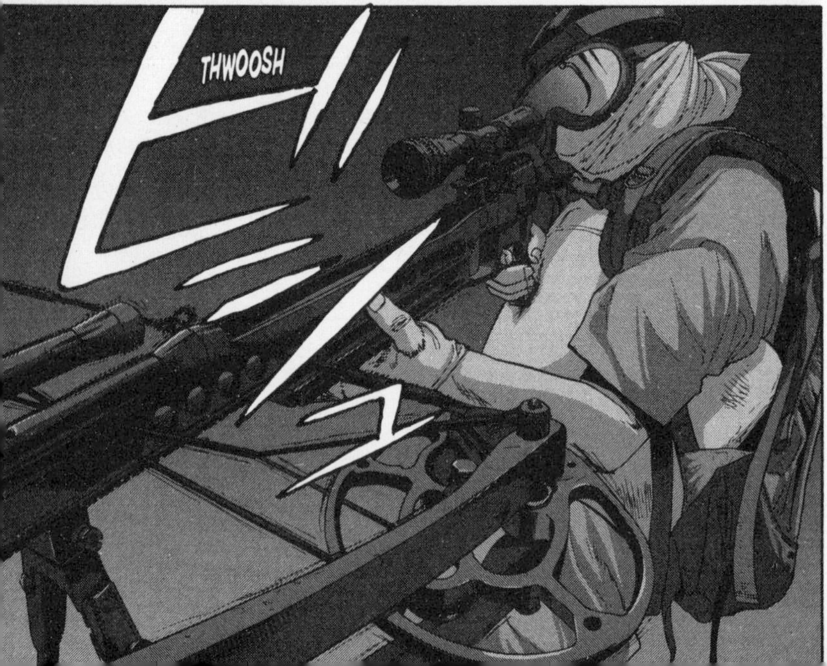
THWOOSH

THUKK

FWSH

KTAK

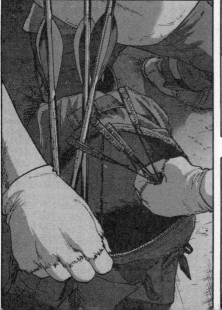

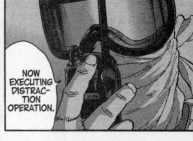

NOW
EXECUTING
DISTRAC-
TION
OPERATION.

WHMFF

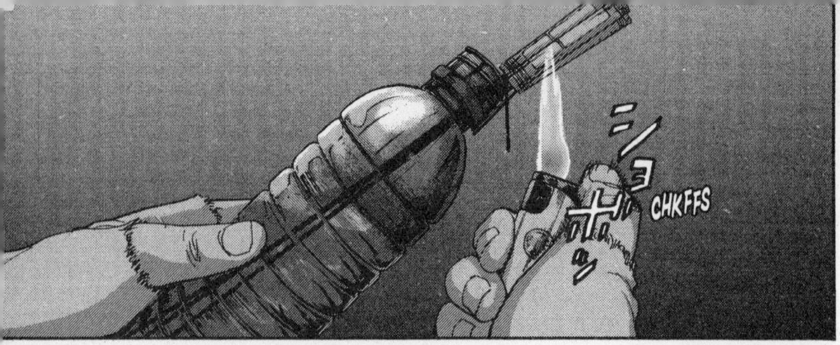
CHKFFS
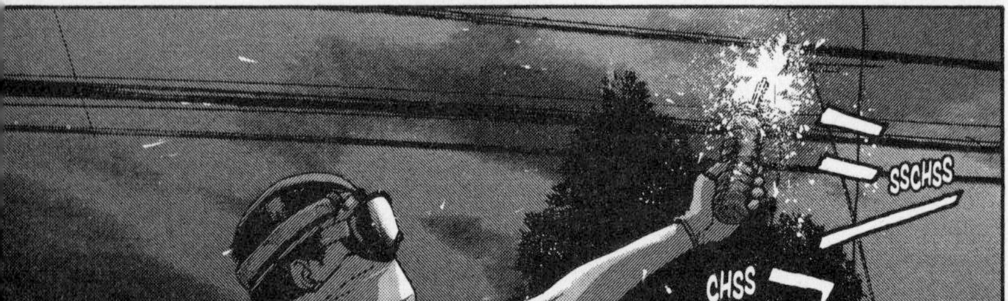
SSCHSS
CHSS
POP
POP
POP
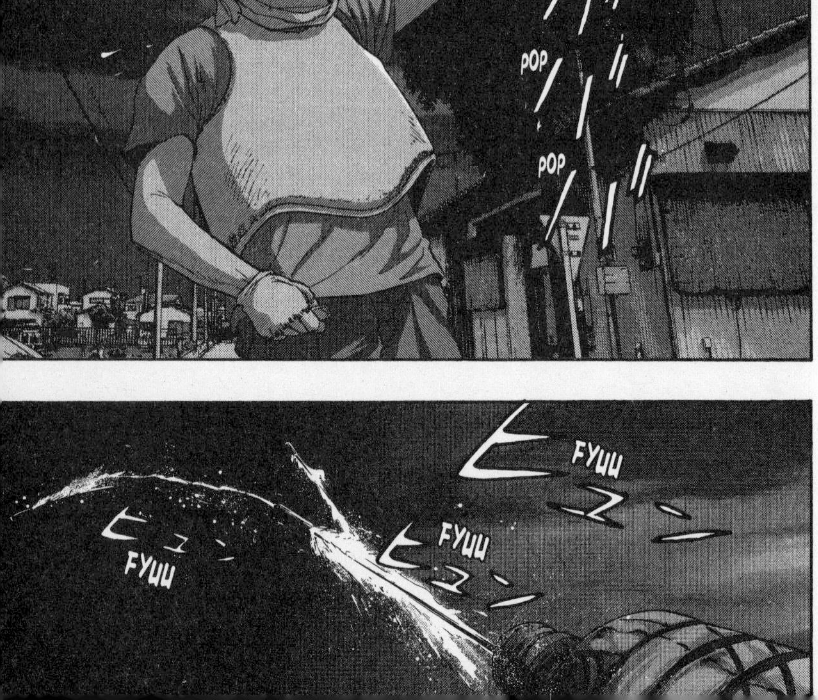
FYUU
FYUU
FYUU

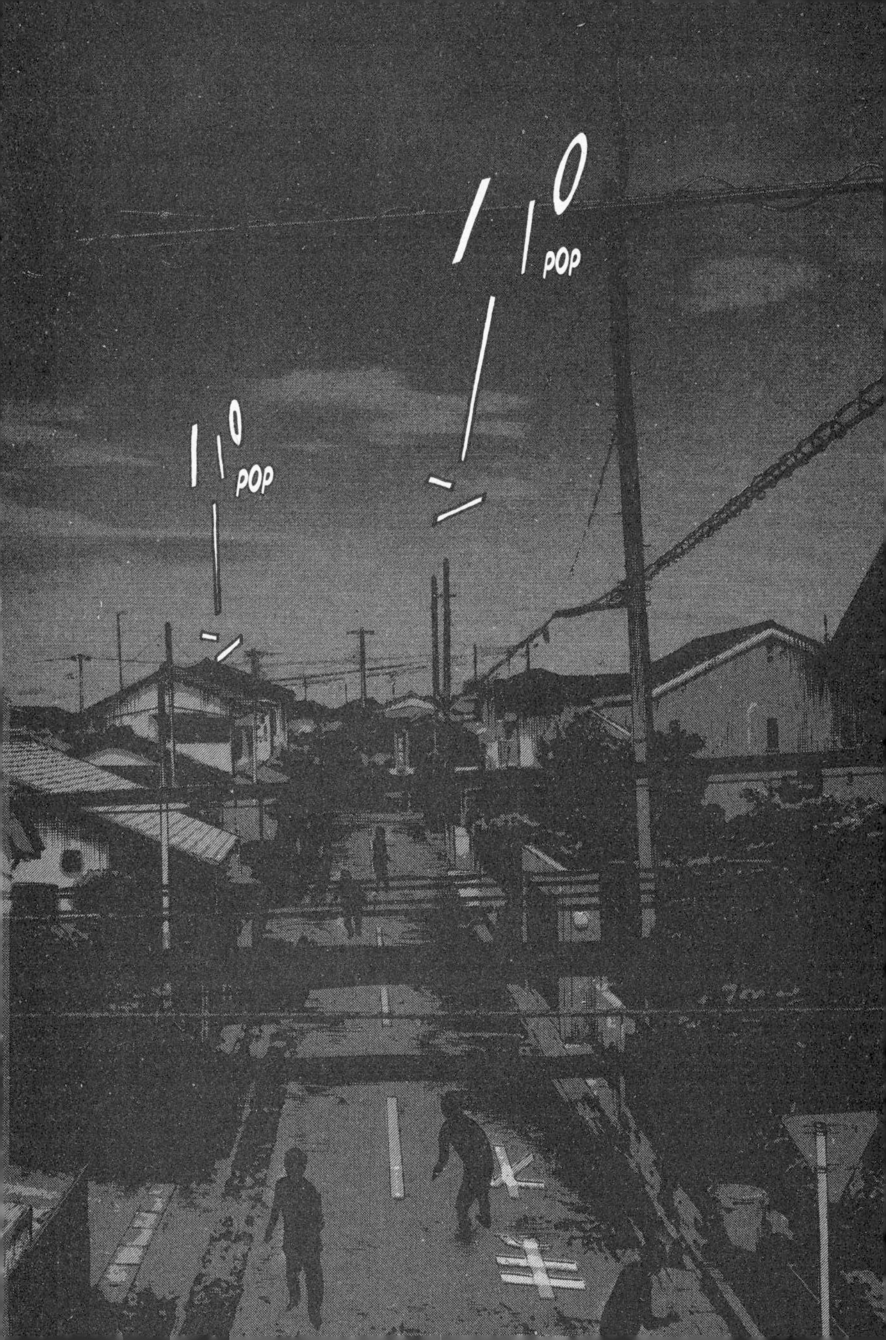
POP
POP

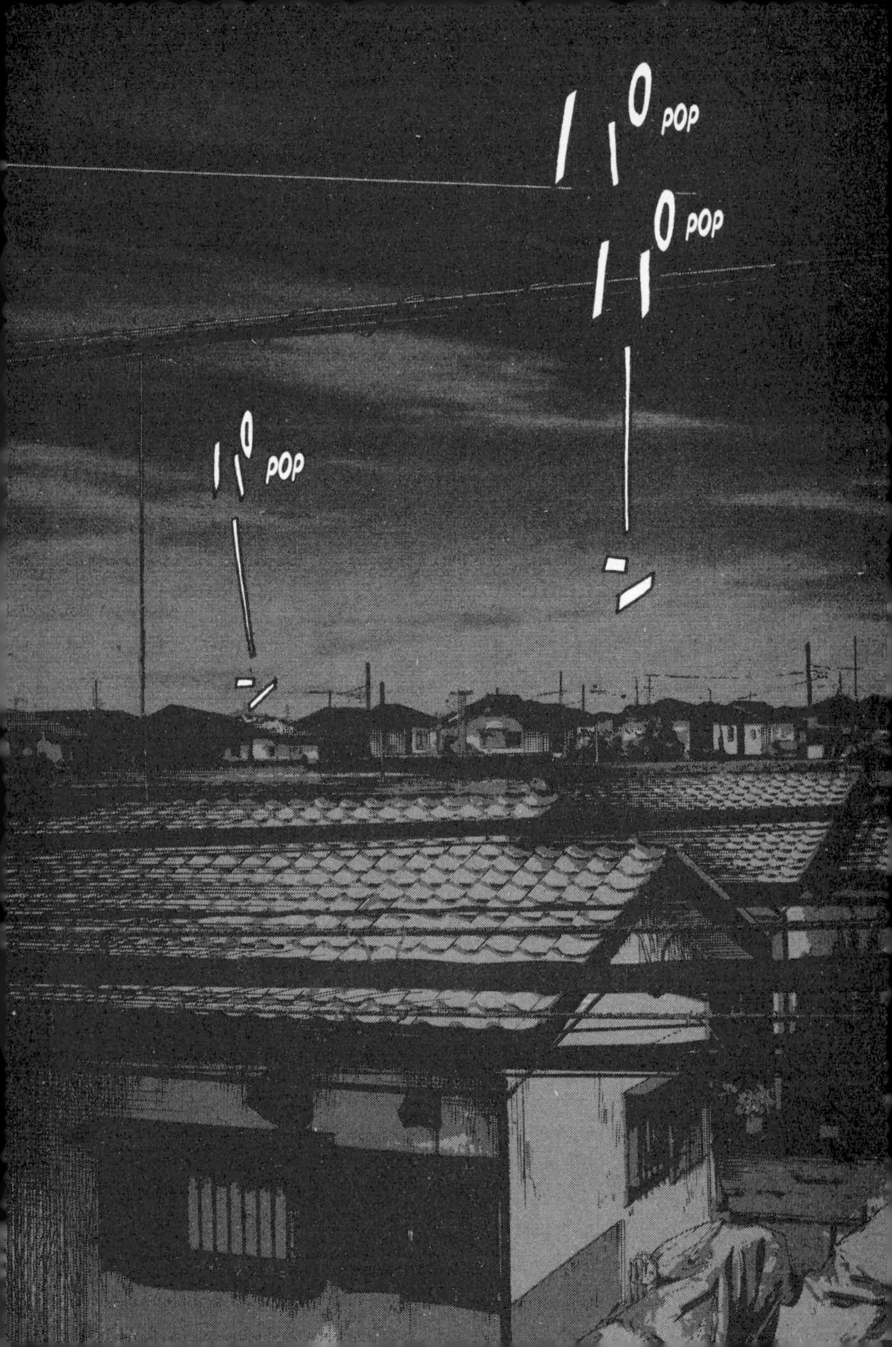
POP
POP
POP

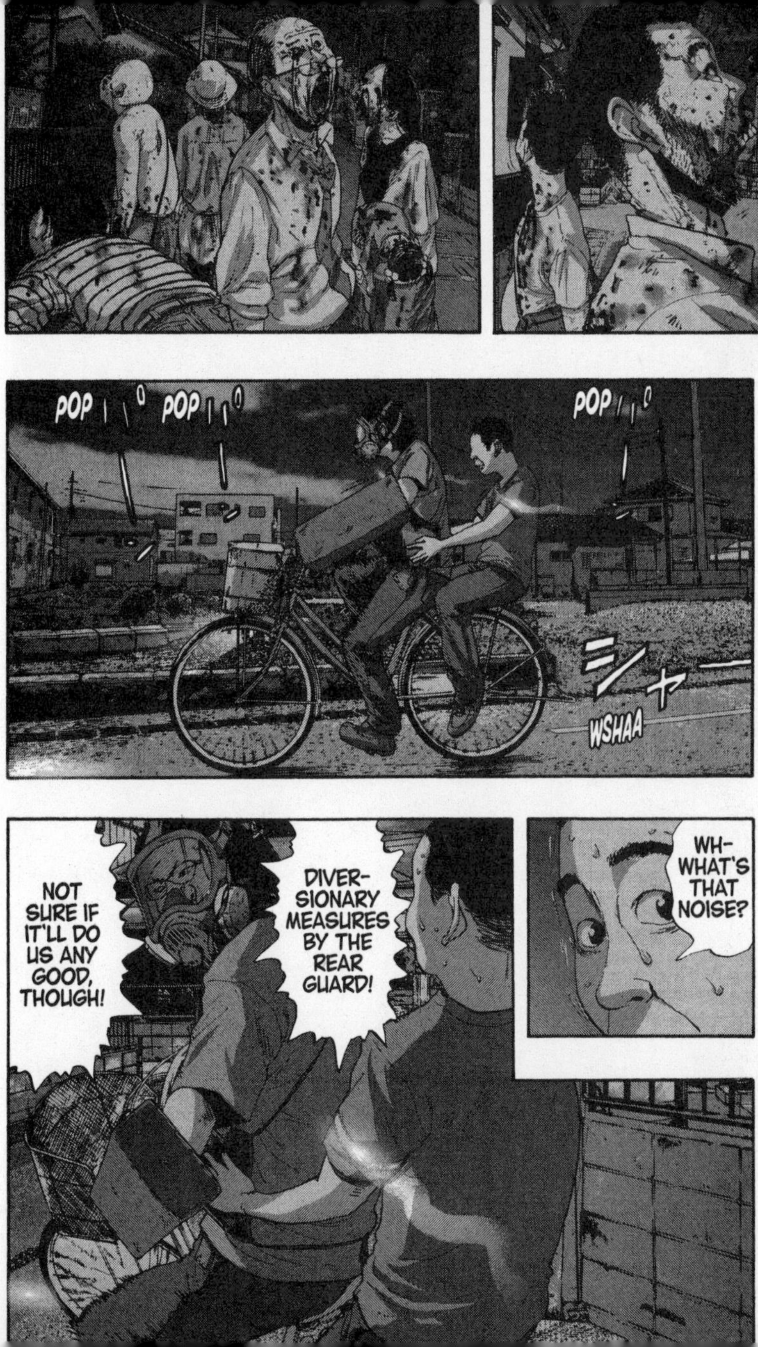
POP
POP
POP
シャー
WSHAA
WH-WHAT'S THAT NOISE?
DIVERSIONARY MEASURES BY THE REAR GUARD!
NOT SURE IF IT'LL DO US ANY GOOD, THOUGH!

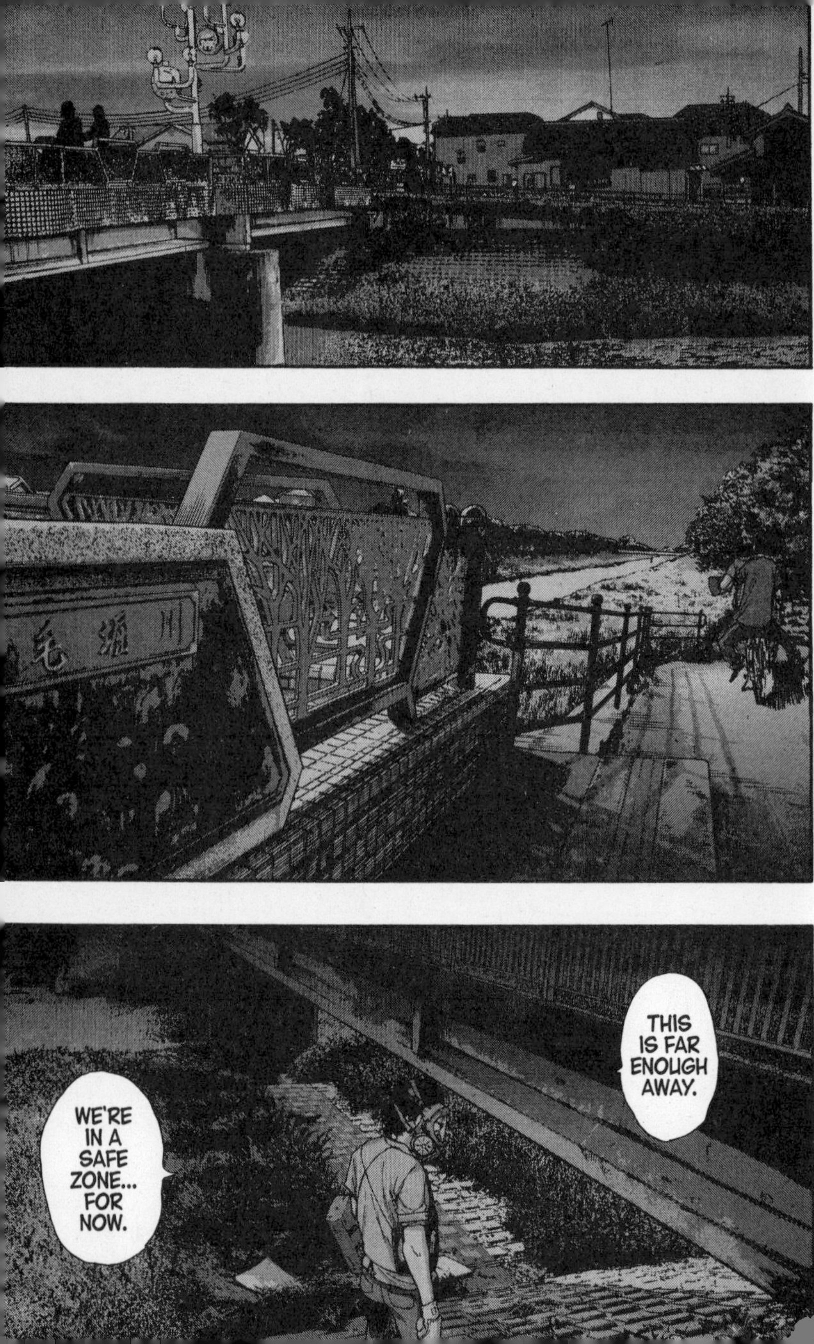
THIS IS FAR ENOUGH AWAY.
WE'RE IN A SAFE ZONE... FOR NOW.

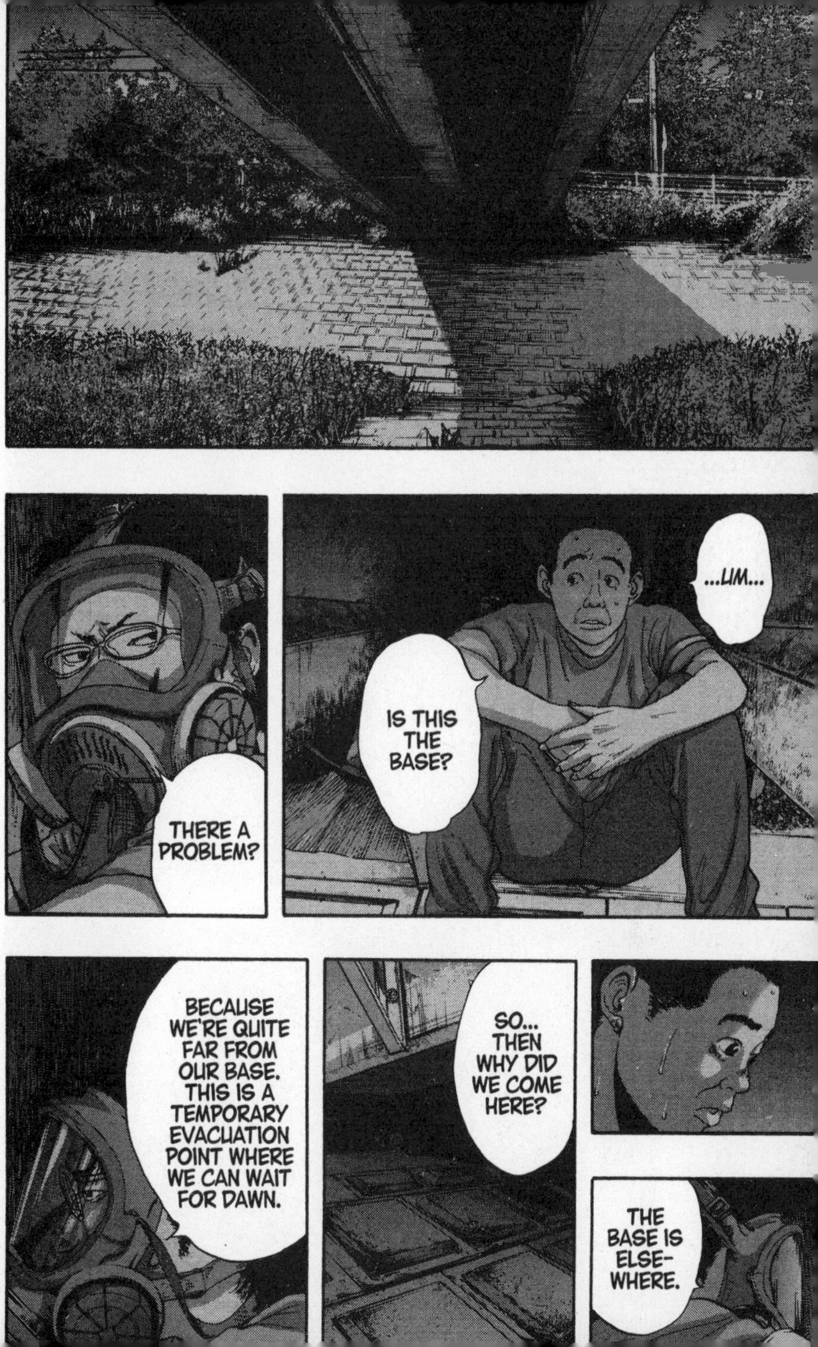
...UM...
IS THIS THE BASE?
THERE A PROBLEM?
THE BASE IS ELSE-WHERE.
SO... THEN WHY DID WE COME HERE?
BECAUSE WE'RE QUITE FAR FROM OUR BASE. THIS IS A TEMPORARY EVACUATION POINT WHERE WE CAN WAIT FOR DAWN.

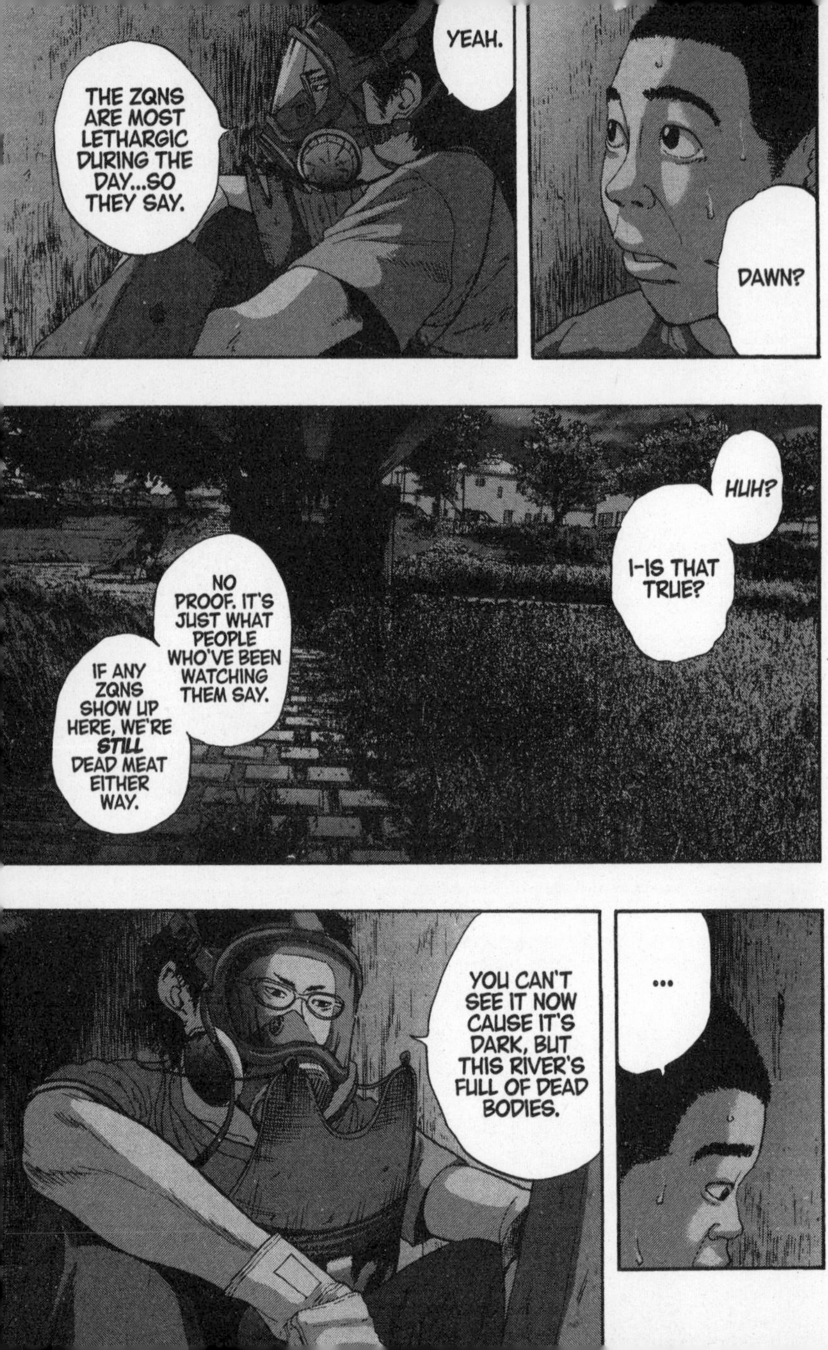
DAWN?
YEAH.
THE ZQNS ARE MOST LETHARGIC DURING THE DAY...SO THEY SAY.
HUH?
I-IS THAT TRUE?
NO PROOF. IT'S JUST WHAT PEOPLE WHO'VE BEEN WATCHING THEM SAY.
IF ANY ZQNS SHOW UP HERE, WE'RE STILL DEAD MEAT EITHER WAY.
...
YOU CAN'T SEE IT NOW CAUSE IT'S DARK, BUT THIS RIVER'S FULL OF DEAD BODIES.

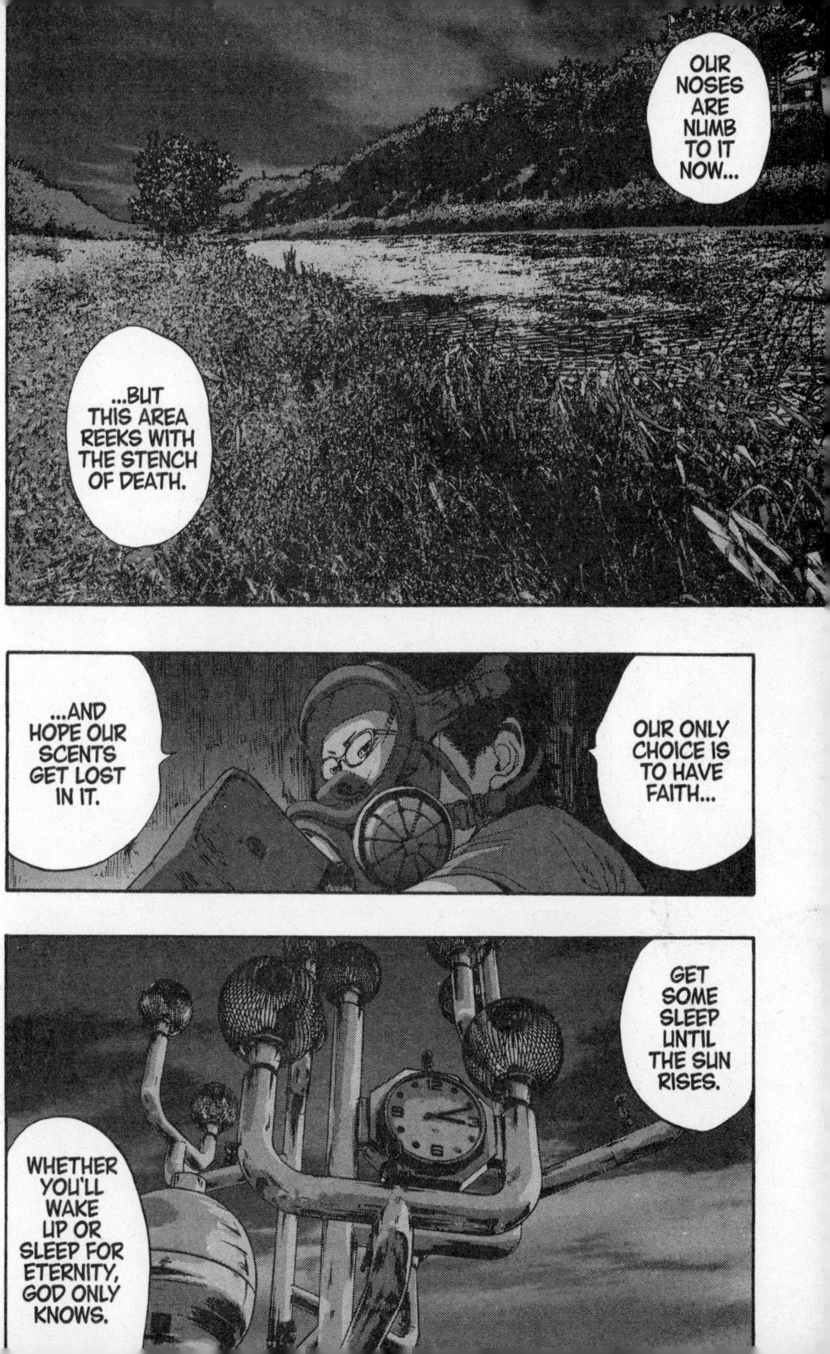
OUR NOSES ARE NUMB TO IT NOW...
...BUT THIS AREA REEKS WITH THE STENCH OF DEATH.
OUR ONLY CHOICE IS TO HAVE FAITH...
...AND HOPE OUR SCENTS GET LOST IN IT.
GET SOME SLEEP UNTIL THE SUN RISES.
WHETHER YOU'LL WAKE UP OR SLEEP FOR ETERNITY, GOD ONLY KNOWS.

I AM
A HERO

I AM A HERO

TRANSLATION NOTES

CHAPTER 94

As Kazuya and Kaori walk the streets of Taiwan, some bystanders are talking about food. One says, "Let's get a small sausage in a large sausage," which is indeed a popular meal in modern Taiwan. The meal is also called Da Chang Bao Xiao Chang (literally, "a small intestine wrapped inside a large intestine").

CHAPTERS 94 TO 97, KAZUYA'S NOTEBOOK TEXT BITS THROUGHOUT THIS SECTION:

May 5, 11 pm
(it's 12 am back in Japan)
or is it 10 am?
The streets are quiet at the moment
I could hear sporadic gunshots until well into the night, but now the night stays still.
It's been six days since we came here now.
The end is near
so hungry.
Does the quiet mean that the army or the police have quelled the violence?
Want to drink water so bad.
Peking duck
What the hell is happening?
I still have no idea
The TV was broadcasting erratically since a few days ago, but since yesterday there's been nothing at all.
I can't get any Japanese shows, and I don't know any Chinese. No idea what's going on.
Is Japan in the same state as Taiwan? Is it worldwide?
I saw on YouTube that things are going crazy in South Korea, too. Unbelievable. Impossible. Maybe it's all CG...?
It's bad. Saw footage of a Japanese plane crashing
Is it the world? Only Asia?

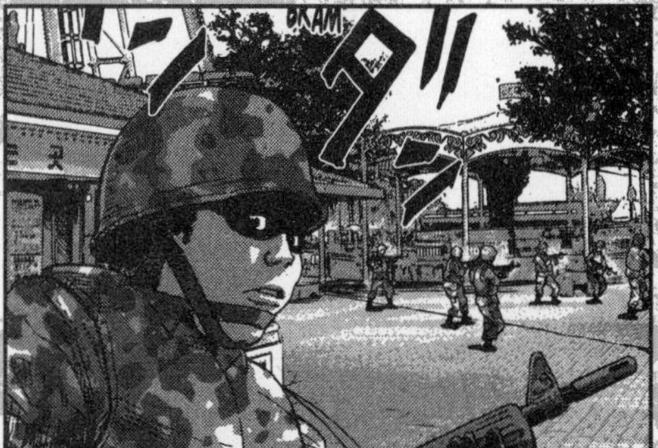
BRAM

So hungry.
Goddamn it.
What do I do?
To get back to Japan alive
Matsuyama Airport
Airplanes aren't flying
Can't get back to Japan.
Can't get in touch either.
We became separated, and I don't know where she is.
I need to find her quick.
For now, I'll write down everything that's happened so far.
At 10 am on May 1 (Fri), we landed in Taiwan. We left first thing in the morning, so we arrived before noon.

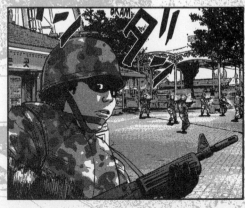

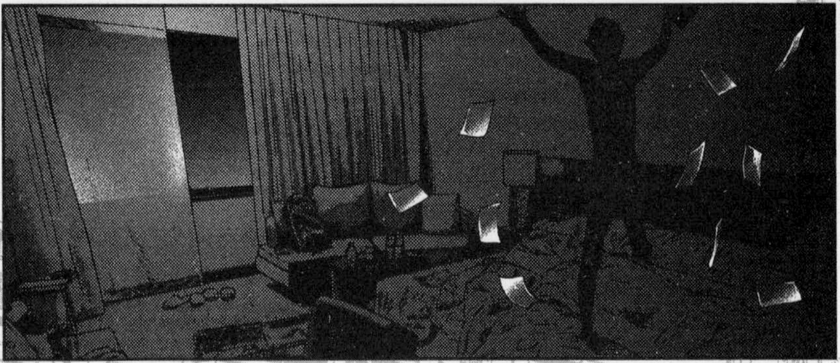

Mr. Toda and Mr. Yamamura from editorial became sick, so I hurriedly took reference photos for the manga by
While strolling in the Shilin District that night, my cell phone was stolen. Sound of guns again.
That night, after we got back to the hotel, I saw the news about Korea.
I was tired so I went straight to sleep.

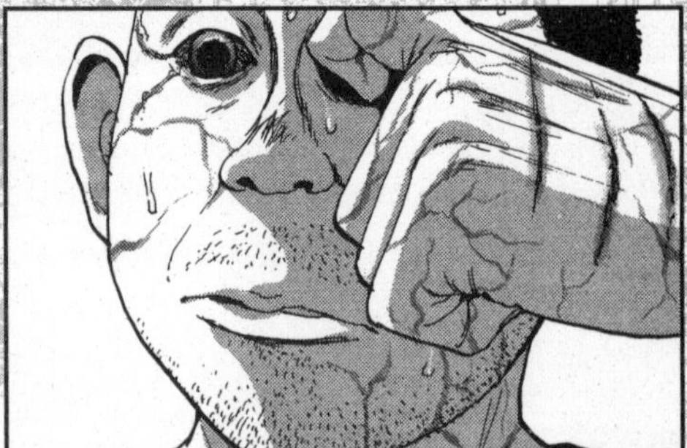

May 2 (Sat), I got up at 9:30 am.
We'd planned to go to Jiufen to take pictures today. For some reason, I had a sense of foreboding.
I was worried about the Korean news, too, so I thought about calling it off.
But she had come along to take pictures, so
It was a mistake to bring her here.
Forgive me forgive me forgive me forgive me forgive me forgive me forgive me
begin serialization of Suzuki's manga
unnatural death
have to go to Jiufen.

CHAPTER 96, THE MANIC TAXI DRIVER'S "DIARY" ENTRIES:

In Taiwan, Jan. 5, 2007
When I got to the station, this guy kinda forced me to go with him, and when I got to his taxi, it was a real hunk of junk. It was dented all over the place, and I wondered if I would be okay. I was right to be worried! He speeds like mad and drives all over the lines, and he almost crashed into another car! The other driver got pissed and chased us with this demonic look on his face! He looked like a yakuza, so I was scared to death wondering if I'd end up murdered. But this driver pretended like he didn't see any of it!

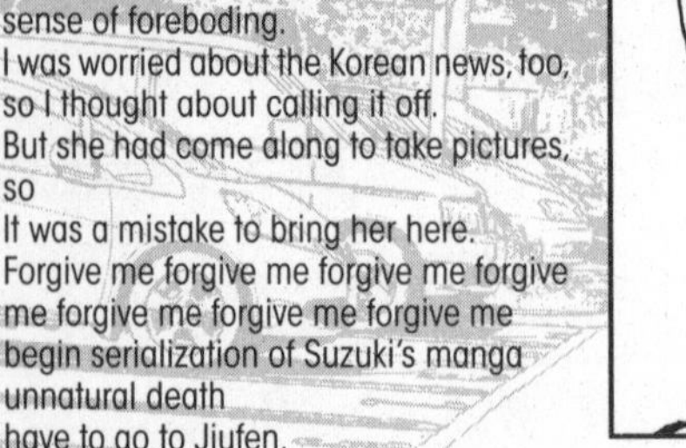

May 5
Thought I was gonna die. How is this "okay"? Look at the road when you're driving!
Do not take this taxi!!
You will die!!!

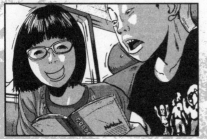

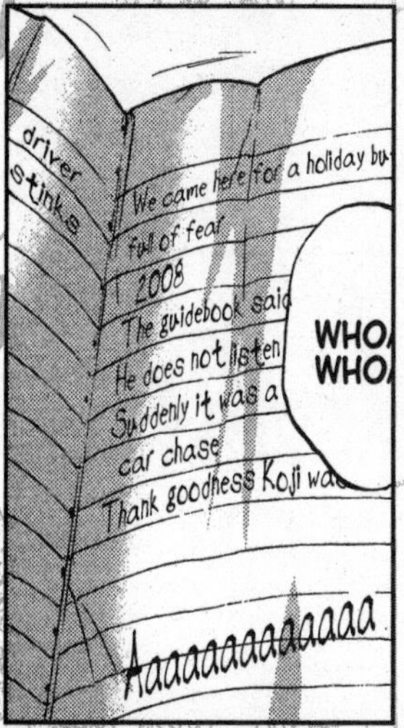
driver stinks
We came here for a holiday bu
full of fear
2008
The guidebook sai
He does not listen
Suddenly it was a
car chase
Thank goodness Koji wa
Aaaaaaaaaaaa

I thought we were going to die!!
Thank god we made it out alive!!
2008, Feb. 14
He talks on his phone while driving! And don't drive with your head turned backwards,
dumbass! Are you trying to kill us?!
2008, Aug 7.
Save me, Buddha!
Guy can't take no for an answer!
I will never take this again! But if you wanna die, go for it!
Demon car!!
It was like a car chase!
I'm so scared I'm so scared I'm so scared!!! —Ryoko
driver stinks
We came here for a holiday but full of fear
2008
The guidebook said
He does not listen
Suddenly it was a car chase
Thank goodness Koji was here
Aaaaaaaaaaaa

CHAPTER 100
On Yuba's digital car map, we see "Pagella Gotemba," which is called Pavilla Gotemba in the real world, and "Saotome Hayaship Park," which is actually the Otome Shinrin Park.

Hideo mentions that he is from Nerima, which is a ward of Tokyo that is sometimes called Nerima City.

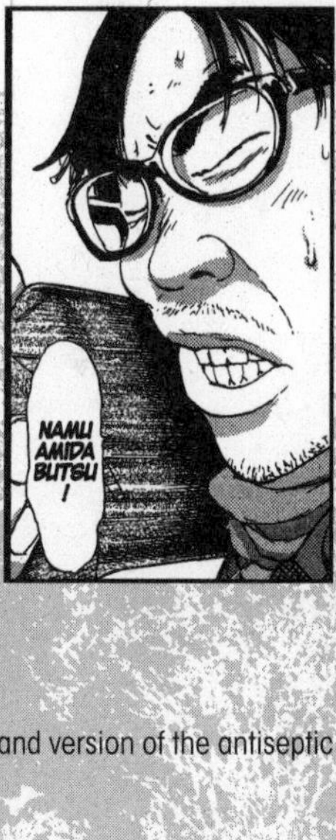
NAMU AMIDA BUTSU!

CHAPTER 102
As seen in previous volumes, when anxious and severely stressed, Hideo sometimes tries to meditate using the *namu amida butsu* and *namu myoho renge kyo* Buddhist prayer chants—but they never seem to help him focus.

CHAPTER 106
Hideo marvels as he luckily stumbles upon a "Mortar . . . and mallets?" Actually, he's found an *usu* and a *kine*—a large, Japanese-style stamp mill and pestle for pounding rice or millet.

CHAPTER 109
As Hideo enters this room in the Ashinoko Pet Clinic, he passes under a sign saying "in use," which would be lit up if anyone had the operating room door closed and was performing surgery in there.

CHAPTER 111
Yuba mentions that "The Isodine has dried." This is a Japanese-brand version of the antiseptic povidone-iodine.

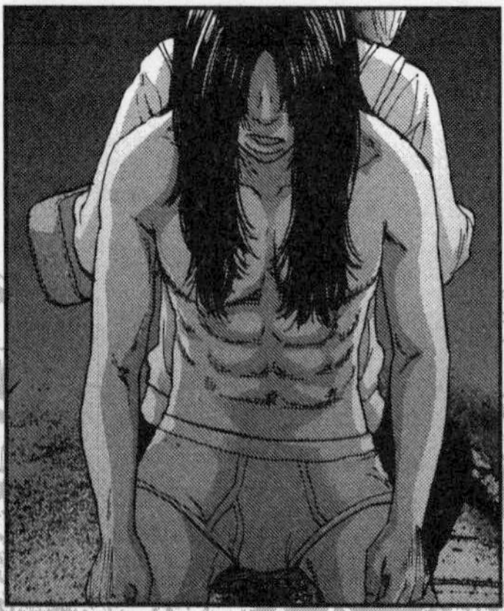

Kuki is a city in Saitama Prefecture.

The graffiti seen on the pylon at the end of this chapter declares, in red, that this is "Kurusu Bakufu" or "Kurusu Shogunate" territory. This refers to the older Japanese feudal military governments. The Tokugawa Shogunate (also known as the Edo-era Bakufu) was Japan's last, ending the system in 1868.

CHAPTER 112

In this long scene, we see Takashi trapped in his bedroom. After a while his mother, now a ZQN, moans his name: "Taa . . . Kaa . . . Shiii . . ."

CHAPTER 113

"Goobie, doobie," is just some nonsense that Kurusu spouts.

CHAPTER 116

The use of crossbows for hunting or any other activity is illegal in Japan, except on target ranges—like the ones Hideo used to use for his shotgun.

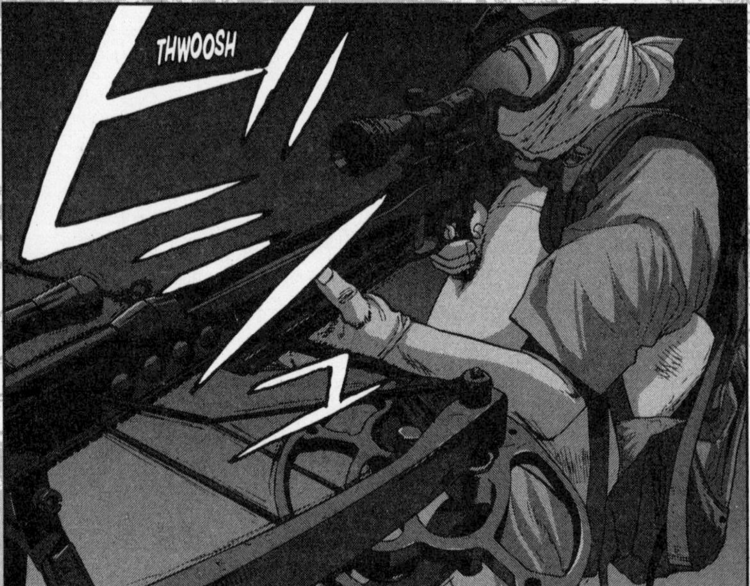
THWOOSH

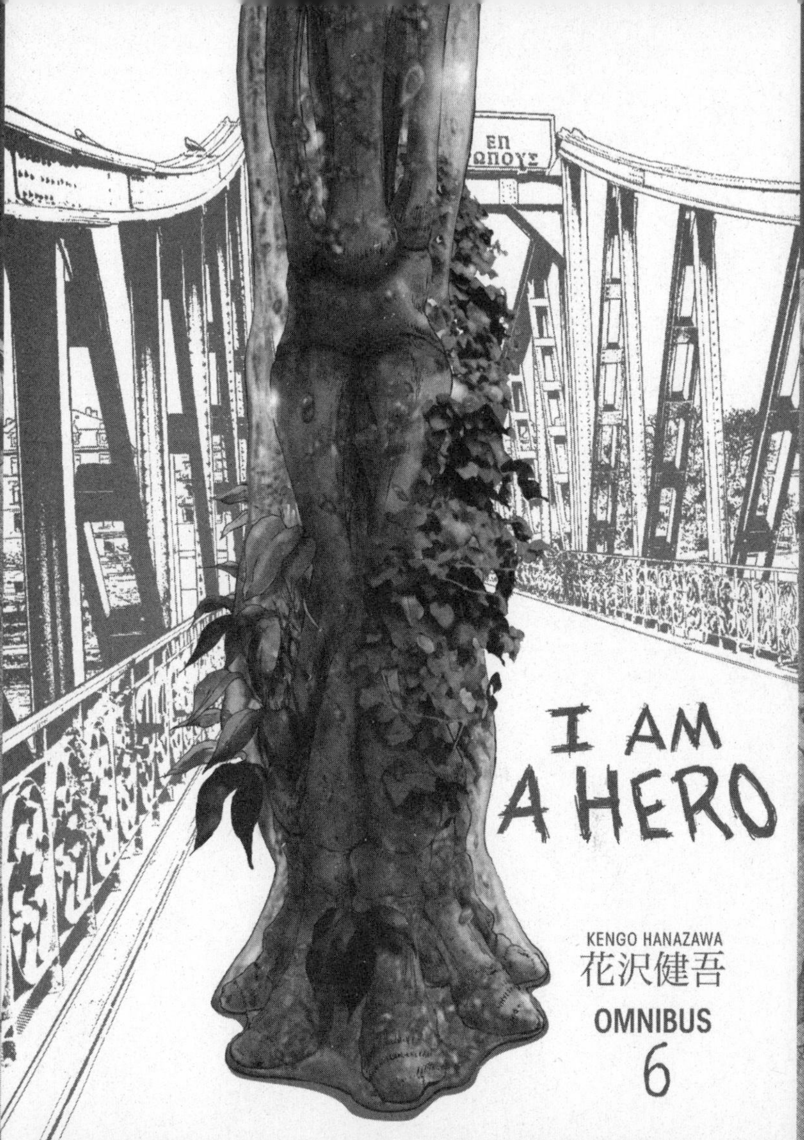

I AM A HERO

KENGO HANAZAWA
花沢健吾

OMNIBUS
6

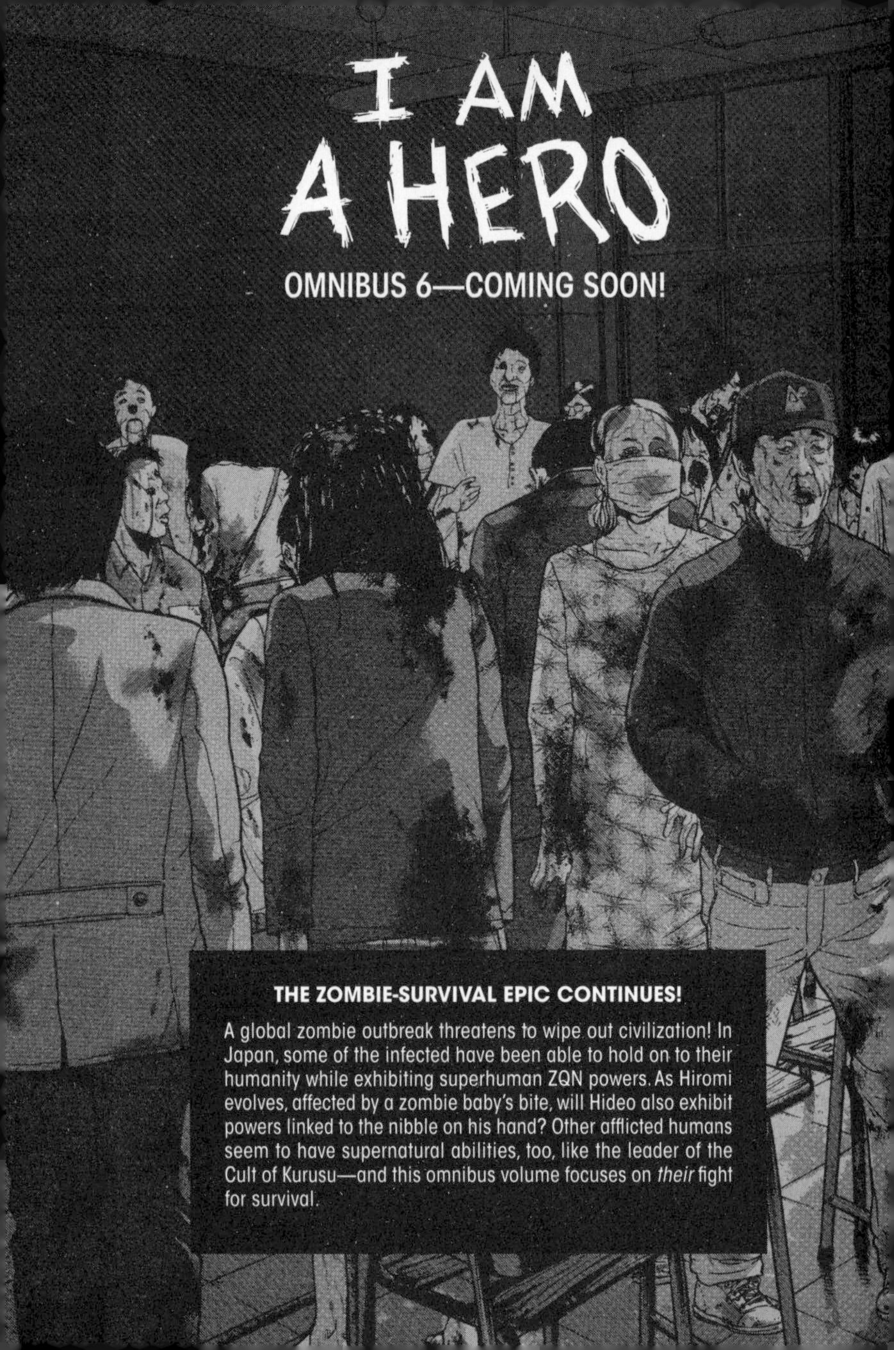
I AM A HERO
OMNIBUS 6—COMING SOON!
THE ZOMBIE-SURVIVAL EPIC CONTINUES!
A global zombie outbreak threatens to wipe out civilization! In Japan, some of the infected have been able to hold on to their humanity while exhibiting superhuman ZQN powers. As Hiromi evolves, affected by a zombie baby's bite, will Hideo also exhibit powers linked to the nibble on his hand? Other afflicted humans seem to have supernatural abilities, too, like the leader of the Cult of Kurusu—and this omnibus volume focuses on *their* fight for survival.

Created by Kentaro Miura, *Berserk* is manga mayhem to the extreme—violent, horrifying, and mercilessly funny—and the wellspring for the internationally popular anime series. Not for the squeamish or the easily offended, *Berserk* asks for no quarter—and offers none!

Presented uncensored in the original Japanese format!

$14.99 each!

DARK HORSE MANGA

DarkHorse.com

AVAILABLE AT YOUR LOCAL COMICS SHOP OR BOOKSTORE
To find a comics shop near your area, call 1-888-266-4226. For more information or to order direct:
•On the web: darkhorse.com •E-mail: mailorder@darkhorse.com •Phone: 1-800-862-0052 Mon.–Fri.
9 AM to 5 PM Pacific Time.

GANTZ
HIROYA OKU Works.

The last thing Kei and Masaru remember was being struck dead by a subway train while saving the life of a drunken bum. What a waste! And yet somehow they're still alive. Or semi-alive? Maybe reanimated . . . by some kind of mysterious orb! And this orb called "Gantz" intends to make them play games of death, hunting all kinds of odd aliens, along with a bunch of other ordinary citizens who've recently met a tragic semi-end. The missions they embark upon are often dangerous. Many die—and die again. This dark and action-packed manga deals with the moral conflicts of violence, teenage sexual confusion and angst, and our fascination with death.

Dark Horse is proud to deliver one of the most requested manga ever to be released. Hang on to your gear and keep playing the game, whatever you do; _Gantz_ is unrelenting!

FLCL

STORY BY GAINAX
ART BY HAJIME UEDA

OMNIBUS

The complete *FLCL* manga adaptation–
now with bonus color illustrations and
remastered story pages!

"This show will change your life."
—Adult Swim

ISBN 978-1-59582-868-2
$19.99

FROM THE STUDIO THAT BROUGHT YOU *EVANGELION!*

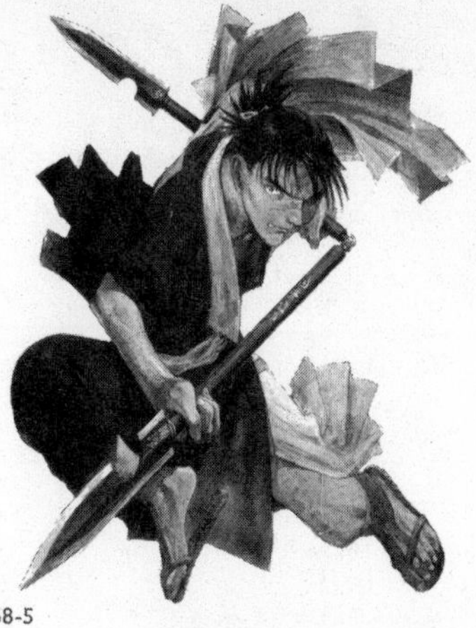

publisher
MIKE RICHARDSON

editor
PHILIP R. SIMON

assistant editor
MEGAN WALKER

collection designer
LIN HUANG

digital art technician
CHRISTINA McKENZIE

Special thanks to Michael Gombos and Carl Gustav Horn for editorial assistance and advice. Special thanks to Chitoku Teshima and Velan Sivasubramanian for translation assistance.

Art staff, original volume 9: Jurii Okamoto, Hiroki Tomizawa, Yukihiro Kamiya, and Masaki Ando. Art staff, original volume 10: Jurii Okamoto, Hiroki Tomizawa, Yukihiro Kamiya, Junki Nabekura, and Yuu Ouchi.

Original Cover Design: Norito INOUE Design Office

This omnibus volume collects the original *I Am a Hero* volumes 9 and 10, published in Japan.

Dark Horse Manga | A division of Dark Horse Comics, Inc.
10956 SE Main Street, Milwaukie, OR 97222

DarkHorse.com

To find a comics shop in your area, visit the Comic Shop Locator Service at comicshoplocator.com

First edition: January 2018 | ISBN 978-1-50670-350-3

Printed in the United States of America | 10 9 8 7 6 5 4 3 2 1

STOP

This is the back of the book!

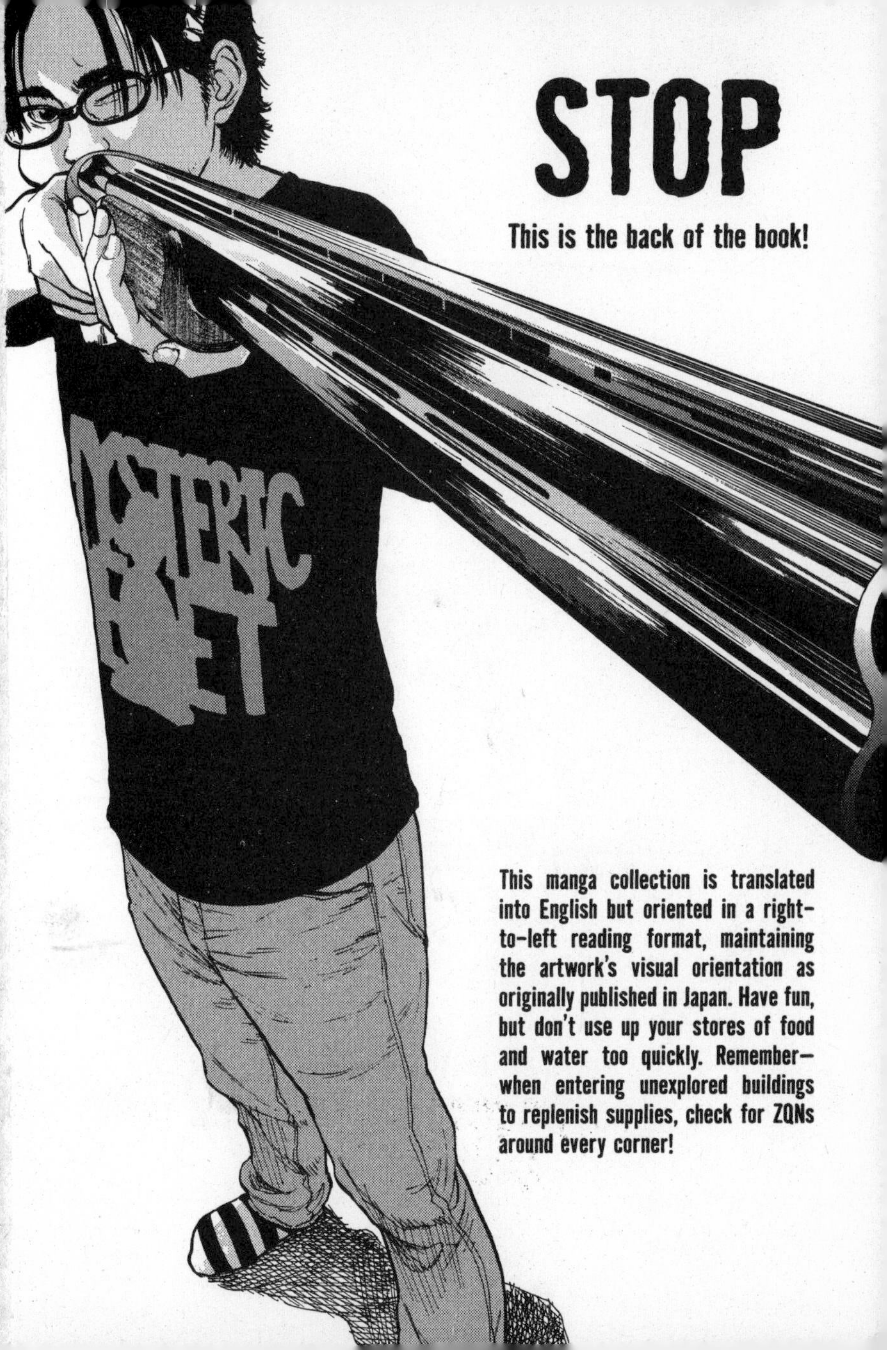

This manga collection is translated into English but oriented in a right-to-left reading format, maintaining the artwork's visual orientation as originally published in Japan. Have fun, but don't use up your stores of food and water too quickly. Remember—when entering unexplored buildings to replenish supplies, check for ZQNs around every corner!

Art and story
KENGO HANAZAWA
花沢健吾

This Dark Horse Manga omnibus
collects *I Am a Hero* chapters 94
to 117, first appearing in Japan
as *I Am a Hero* Volumes 9 and 10.

Translation
KUMAR SIVASUBRAMANIAN

English adaptation
PHILIP R. SIMON

Lettering
STEVE DUTRO

OMNIBUS 5

I AM
A HERO